THE FOUR GOSPELS

A STUDY OF ORIGINS

THE FOUR GOSPELS

A STUDY OF ORIGINS

TREATING OF

THE MANUSCRIPT TRADITION,
SOURCES, AUTHORSHIP, & DATES

BY

BURNETT HILLMAN STREETER

WIPF & STOCK · Eugene, Oregon

Wipf and Stock Publishers
199 W 8th Ave, Suite 3
Eugene, OR 97401

The Four Gospels
A Study of Origins treating of The Manuscript Tradition, Sources,
Authorship, & Dates
By Streeter, Burnett Hillman
ISBN 13: 978-1-55635-797-8
ISBN 10: 1-55635-797-4
Publication date 1/9/2008
Previously published by Macmillan & Co., 1924

In Memoriam

GULIELMI SANDAY, S.T.P.

INSIGNISSIMI APUD OXONIENSES

HORUM STUDIORUM FAUTORIS

The inquiry of truth, which is the love-making or wooing of it; the knowledge of truth, which is the presence of it; and the belief in truth, which is the enjoying of it—is the sovereign good of human nature.

BACON.

Quis nescit primam esse historiae legem ne quid falsi dicere audeat, deinde ne quid veri non audeat.

CICERO.

Men disparage not Antiquity, who prudently exalt new Enquiries.

Sir THOMAS BROWNE.

found in the Latin, Syriac and Armenian, must go back to the oldest form of the " Western " text, which has been in places corrected by a Greek MS. belonging to another family. Evidently, the words found only in these MSS. are the original " Western " reading ; the ordinary reading was written in the margin of an ancestor of these MSS. by a corrector ; but the correction, instead of being substituted for the text by the next copyist, was added to it. Now comes the point. The New Gospel quotes the phrase in Greek, but as it appears in these MSS., and not as it appears in the ordinary Greek MSS. ; he must therefore have used a Greek MS. with a " Western " text.

(3) In the same year, a little later, Mr. C. H. Roberts identified and published a papyrus fragment [1] containing most of John xviii. 31-33 and 37-38. This papyrus is believed by expert papyrologists to be earlier than A.D. 150—and therefore to be the oldest known document containing any portion of the New Testament.

(4) Another find (less recent) is a fragment of a handsome fourth-century codex containing Luke xxii. 44-56, 61-63, which has an almost pure " Western " text. This codex is notable for its support of the Old Latin MSS. a, b, e, ff_2, i, l^*, r in omitting Lk. xxii. 66—the retention of which in the text (see below, p. 323) creates a difficulty for the generally accepted solution of the Synoptic Problem.

. (5) Another important papyrus, probably to be dated early in the fourth century, is the Michigan papyrus 1571, containing most of Acts xviii. 27-xix. 6 and xix. 12-16.[2] This papyrus again quite definitely represents the " Western " text.

Evidence is thus increasing that texts of very different types, including " Western " and " Caesarean," were in circulation in Egypt. This fact much simplifies the hypothesis suggested on p. 600 of this book to account for the curious mixture of texts

---

[1] *An Unpublished Fragment of the Fourth Gospel*, Manchester University Press, 1935.

[2] Published by H. A. Sanders, *Harvard Theol. Review*, xx. 1, 1927.

in W—a MS. also discovered in Egypt ; for the stages of revision that this hypothesis demands could have taken place without assuming an owner of the MS. who moved from place to place. Indeed, since there is a specially close contact between W and the Chester Beatty variety of the " Caesarean " text in Mark, the exact type of replacement of lost leaves which I suggest would more easily have been effected in Egypt than in Caesarea. Further, this new evidence of textual variety in Egypt strengthens the case for the view I had very tentatively adopted (cf. p. 124 f.) that Hort's " Neutral Text," *i.e.* that of the Codex Vaticanus B and its supporters, represents a recension made by the Alexandrian scholar Hesychius about A.D. 300. From Jerome's preface to the Vulgate it is clear that the main reason which prompted Pope Damasus to authorise him to produce a revised version was the practical inconvenience of the great diversity that existed between different MSS. of the Old Latin version. The new evidence that there was a similar diversity between Greek MSS. current in Egypt shows that there would be a motive for an official Alexandrian recension. Greek scholarship in Alexandria, beginning on the poems of Homer, had worked out principles of textual criticism ; in particular the importance of procuring the most ancient MSS. was recognised. Hesychius doubtless sought out such MSS. and based his recension upon them. He was a third-century Hort ; and, perhaps unfortunately, shared Hort's disdain of the " Western " text.

In the first impression of this book I pointed out (p. 70 ff.) that the then recently discovered *Epistula Apostolorum* (±A.D. 160) used the " Western " text. Accepting the view of its editor, C. Schmidt, that the document emanated from Ephesus, I used it as evidence for the early text of that city. If, however, as scholars now incline to think, it belongs to Egypt, it affords additional evidence for the " Western " in that country.

To turn from textual to historical criticism : In a footnote on p. xxi I adduce some analogies to the " we " sections in Acts.

Yet another has been communicated to me by Mr. G. F. Bridge
—taken from Clarendon's *History of the Great Rebellion*, IX, 149
(Macray's ed., IV, p. 140). In an account of a debate whether
Prince Charles should go to Jersey or to Scilly, there is a long
sentence stating that " the public resolution was for Scilly."
The historian then goes on : " And so the resolution being im-
parted to no more that night than was of absolute necessity (for
we apprehended clamour from the army, from the country, and
from that garrison in whose power the prince was) the next
morning. . . ."

In conclusion I may mention the discovery in 1933 of a small
fragment of the *Diatessaron* of Tatian *in Greek* (cf. p. 9 f.).[1]
This was found in an embankment known to have been made
between A.D. 254 and 257 to strengthen against a siege the city
wall of Dura-Europus on the Euphrates ; and is therefore not
later than that date. The discovery is an awkward one for those
scholars who maintained that the *Diatessaron* was written in some
other tongue than Greek.

[1] *A Greek Fragment of Tatian's Diatessaron*, by C. H. Kraeling (London,
Christophers, 1935) ; cf. also F. C. Burkitt, *Journal of Theological Studies*,
July 1935, p. 255 ff.

8th May 1936.

PREFACE TO FOURTH IMPRESSION

FRESH discoveries, and the kindness of friends in pointing out errors, have necessitated numerous alterations—so numerous that, had not many of them been already made in the second and third impressions, this might not improperly have been styled a Revised Edition. The alterations, however, are all concerned with points of detail; on no large question do I wish to withdraw from, or substantially qualify, any position taken up when the book was first published in 1924. On the contrary, subsequent research has in important respects tended to substantiate the views then put forward.

In the field of textual criticism the basis of evidence for the importance and antiquity of the text underlying the Koridethi MS. Θ and its allies has been notably widened; and my identification of it as the text current in the third century at Caesarea has been confirmed. (1) In 1926 I myself discovered, in time to add an Appendix to the second impression of this work, that for Mark v. 31-xvi. 8 the Washington MS. W (approximately dated A.D. 400) belongs to this family of MSS. (2) The provisional hypothesis (cf. p. 90 f.) that the Old Georgian version was based on a Greek text of this type has since been verified by the joint labours of K. Lake, R. P. Blake and S. New, published in an enlarged number of the *Harvard Theological Review*, Oct. 1928. They also make out a strong case for the view that this same text lay behind the oldest Armenian version. (3) Finally, the researches of these scholars not only confirm my discovery that Origen used this text—shortly, though not immediately, after he reached Caesarea in A.D. 231—but have also proved that it was the text of Eusebius, the historian bishop of that Church.

Recent German scholarship has been concerned to investigate the history of separate incidents and sayings in the Gospels *before* they were brought together into the written documents Mark and Q. It is the fundamental assumption of this *Formgeschichtliche* school [1] that each incident (and most sayings) had its own history—having at one time circulated *by itself* in oral tradition. This school marks an extreme reaction from the position of men like Oscar Holtzman thirty years ago, who believed that in the Gospel of Mark there can be traced a definite evolution not only in the historical situation but also in the mind of Christ Himself. In protest against the Holtzman attitude I wrote, in 1910, in the *Oxford Studies in the Synoptic Problem,* " Mark is a collection of vignettes—scenes from the life of the Master. . . . The traces of a development which have been noticed . . . show that the author has some knowledge of the correct order of events, but far too much has been made of this. In the last resort Mark is a series of roughly-arranged sketches or reminiscences exactly as Papias describes it." In this matter the pendulum of German scholarship has by now, I venture to think, swung too far—in the direction towards which I was myself at that time looking. To the extent, however, that scholars of the *Formgeschichtliche* school have substantiated their contention that stories and sayings must have circulated separately in oral tradition, and also that the exigences of practical teaching must have early created a demand for accounts of the Passion and Resurrection, they have considerably strengthened the case for the views put forward in this volume in the chapters entitled " A Four-Document Hypothesis " and " Proto-Luke." When stories or sayings circulate in oral tradition, it is inevitable that they should be current in more than one version. Where, therefore, Matthew and Luke give *widely divergent* versions of the same item—*e.g.* of the Beatitudes,

[1] Important work along this line has also been done in the United States, *e.g.* by H. S. Cadbury, *The Making of Luke-Acts* (Macmillan, 1927), and B. S. Easton, *The Gospel before the Gospels* (Scribner, 1928).

the Lord's Prayer, the Parable of the Lost Sheep—it is unscientific to explain this divergence on the theory of manipulation by the respective editors of the common written source Q ; it is far more likely to be due to the currency of divergent traditions. The same thing applies whenever the account of an incident given by Luke exhibits really striking differences from the version found in Mark, as for example in the Call of Peter, the Rejection at Nazareth, the Anointing, and the Passion narrative.

I take the opportunity of this reprint to call attention to certain phenomena, of which the significance had previously escaped me, but which I now see constitute an additional argument for the theory of a Proto-Luke.[1]

In oral tradition it is very easy for details which properly belong to one story to get connected with another. In the passages I am about to quote, it will be noticed that the Lucan account combines details from events which in Mark are quite separate in a way most naturally explicable on this hypothesis. They are not equally explicable as arbitrary recombinations by Luke of material in Mark ; for there is no obvious motive for the rearrangement, as there is for the bringing together by Matthew (and to a less extent by Luke) of sayings of Christ which deal with the same topics.

[1] My attention has been called to the fact that a hypothesis very similar to what I have called " Proto-Luke " was put forward as long ago as 1912 by Mr. E. R. Buckley in his *Introduction to the Synoptic Problem* (Arnold). I recollect reading the book at the time and saying in my lecture that I thought it an excellent book but mistaken on this point. When several years later a re-reading of one of Sir John Hawkins' Essays set me thinking out the problem afresh, I quite forgot Mr. Buckley's theory. It may well be that an unconscious recollection of his theory contributed something to the direction of the investigations I then began ; had the recollection been conscious, I should have been proud to acknowledge my debt to such an acute and original student of the subject. The theory has by now met with considerable acceptance from scholars and has been notably defended by Dr. Vincent Taylor in his *Behind the Third Gospel* (Clarendon Press, 1926). I may mention here that the " Four-Document Hypothesis " has been applied in further detail to the Sermon on the Mount by Prof. A. Pinchere of Rome in *Ricerche Religiose*, March 1926. My suggestion (p. 525 f.) as to the date of the acceptance at Rome of the Gospel of Matthew is supported by Prof. B. W. Bacon in *Harvard Theological Review*, April 1929.

b

(1) Luke's account of the Call of Peter (v. 1 ff., cf. Mk. i. 16 ff.) embodies the incident of Christ teaching from a boat, which in Mark (iv. 1) is the occasion of the Parable of the Sower, and which Luke omits when he reproduces that parable at the same point as in Mark's narrative. It also includes an account of a miraculous draught of fishes, similar to that in John xxi., along with a protest by Peter, " Depart from me, for I am a sinful man." This protest would gain much in force if we suppose that the story in which it occurs was originally told as an event subsequent to Peter's denial of his Master, and is, in fact, another version of the " second call of Peter " appropriately connected in John xxi. with a post-Resurrection Appearance. I argue below (cf. p. 355 f.) that John xxi. is based on a tradition substantially identical with that embodied in the lost endings of the Gospel of Mark and of the Apocryphal Gospel of Peter.

(2) In Luke's version of the Anointing (vii. 36 ff., cf. Mk. xiv. 3 ff.) there is included a pronouncement by our Lord of forgiveness, which evokes from His opponents the protest, " Who is this that forgives sins ? " which Mark connects with the healing of the paralytic (Mk. ii. 5 ff.). There is also included—though this is less significant—the saying which occurs elsewhere in Mark : " Thy faith hath saved thee, go in peace " (in Mk. v. 34 addressed to the woman with an issue of blood)—though the Greek word used for " go " is not the same. The words, " Go, thy faith hath saved," occur also (addressed to Bartimaeus), Mk. x. 52.

(3) Luke's account of the Great Commandment (x. 25 ff.) would seem to be derived from a tradition independent of Mark xii. 28 ff., in that the formulation of the summary, " Thou shalt love the Lord thy God . . . and thy neighbour as thyself," is made by the lawyer and approved by Christ, not *vice versa*. The point, however, to which I would call attention is that it is introduced not, as in Mark, by the question, " What commandment is the first of all ? " but by the question, " What shall I do to inherit eternal life ? " which occurs in Mark, but in connection with a different incident (cf. Mk. x. 17).

(4) Luke's account of the Last Supper—if, with WH, we accept the shorter text in Lk. xxii. 19-20—reflects a tradition (found also in the *Didache*) which reverses the order of the Bread and the Cup. The saying in Lk. xxii. 15-16 implies that the Last Supper was not the Passover, in which case it derives from a tradition which supports John against Mark in regard to the date of the Passion. Obviously, then, Luke got this incident (wholly, or in part) from a source other than Mark. Luke also appends to his account of the Last Supper a saying (about the Kings of the Gentiles and the greater acting as servant) which in substance corresponds to the reply given by Christ in Mark's story of the ambitious request of James and John (x. 42 ff.)—an incident which Luke omits. Where actual sayings of Christ are concerned, Luke usually reproduces fairly closely the wording of Mark ; hence, the verbal differences being here very great, it is more probable that his version in this case comes from another source than that it is a rewriting of that in Mark.

In each of the four passages discussed above the combination of fragments from different incidents is of a kind more likely to have originated in oral tradition rather than in editorial ingenuity on the part of Luke—the more so because Luke in general avoids conflation even when it is the obvious thing to do. Thus, whenever Mark and Q give parallel versions of the same item, Matthew conflates the versions ; Luke hardly ever does so (cf. p. 186 f.). In the first three passages discussed above Luke gives the story in a context far removed from that of the parallel in Mark (the fourth, the Last Supper, could only stand at one point in the story) ; he does the same thing with the three other considerable items of which he gives a version notably different from that of Mark, viz. the Rejection at Nazareth, the Beelzebub Controversy and the Parable of the Mustard-seed. As regards the last two we have positive evidence that the version which Luke gives is *not* obtained by a free editing of Mark ; for comparison with the parallels in Matthew (cf. p. 246 f.) enables us to see that what he gives is the version which stood in Q. This evidence creates a

presumption that in other cases, where Luke's version differs
strikingly from Mark's and also occurs in a context remote from
Mark's, he is not rewriting Mark but drawing from another
source. Moreover, the most reasonable explanation of his desertion of Mark's order (to which elsewhere he closely adheres) is
that he reproduces these items in the order and context in which
they stood in the source in which he found them.

This preference of the non-Marcan to the Marcan context is
found both where the item is traceable to Q and where it is
peculiar to himself ; again, this preference would be unnatural
unless the source from which he drew was a substantial document
comparable to Mark in scale and importance. Thus it would
seem probable that the Q material and the material peculiar to
Luke (or most of it) lay before the author of the Gospel already
combined into a single document.

Luke gives an account of the Resurrection which places the
Appearances in Jerusalem, and therefore cannot have been derived from the lost end of Mark, which seems to have placed them
in Galilee ; we have already seen that he had an account of the
Last Supper other and different from that in Mark. The presumption is strong, then, that the deviation from Mark in his
account of the intervening events—which include no less than
twelve changes of order [1]—is due to the influence of an account
of the Passion in the same source as that used for the Last Supper
and the Resurrection. In this part of his Gospel Marcan and
non-Marcan elements are inextricably blended, and the departures from the Marcan order would be explained if he were conflating a non-Marcan account with that of Mark ; usually he
avoids conflation, but in this case it would have been impossible
to keep the two strands apart. Of course, Luke may have found
the account of the Last Supper, Passion and Resurrection in one
source, and the bulk of his other non-Marcan material in another ;
no one can deny this possibility. Nevertheless, Luke's general
preference of his non-Marcan source, both as regards context and

[1] Cf. *Oxford Studies in the Synoptic Problem*, p. 81 ff.

version, as well as the considerable omissions which he makes
from Mark, are more readily explicable if all (or practically all)
of his non-Marcan material stood in a single work, which in that
case would be so substantial that he would naturally regard it as
an authority of equal or greater value than Mark.

It has been objected by certain scholars that Proto-Luke
would be an " amorphous " document, not sufficiently like what
we call a " Gospel " to be conceivable as a work having an independent existence. The objection overlooks the fact that the
Jews were not in the habit of writing the biographies of Prophets
or Rabbis ; they preserved sayings and parables, interspersed
with a few incidents, with the smallest attempt at systematic
arrangement. " Amorphous " would be a most appropriate
adjective to describe the book of Jeremiah (the Prophet about
whom we have most information) or the traditions about the
Jewish Rabbis which were written down some little time after
the Christian Era. Again, the document Q—the oldest written
account of our Lord that criticism can isolate—seems, so far as
we can reconstruct it, to have been quite amorphous. The
Formgeschichtliche school point to the evidence in 1 Corinthians
(xi. 23 ff., xv. 3 ff.) that, at least in Gentile churches, primitive
Christian teaching included a summary account of the events
from the Lord's Supper to the Resurrection Appearances ; and
they argue that the exigencies of missionary teaching must soon
have called into existence more detailed stories of this series of
events. We should expect, then, that the first addition made to Q
would have been an account of the Passion. That this expansion
of Q would have been accompanied by the addition of other sayings and parables, interspersed with a few interesting stories from
floating tradition, is antecedently probable. Such a document is
the Proto-Luke which remains if we deduct from our third Gospel
the Infancy narratives and the material derived from Mark.
What the historian has to explain, in a community of Jewish
origin, is not the existence of amorphous collections—which was
the normal thing—but the emergence of a non-amorphous bio-

graphy like Mark. This, I suggest (p. 496), was due to the demand of the Gentile world, especially at Rome with its interest in biography. The document Proto-Luke is not yet a Gospel in the biographical sense ; but being, as it is, a kind of half-way house between Q and Mark, it is the natural intermediate stage in the evolution of the biographical type of Gospel ; it represents a groping after, and is the next step towards, the satisfaction of this Gentile demand which was more clearly perceived and first adequately met by Mark.

Luke gets the greater part of his narrative material from Mark and he is writing a biography more or less according to Greco-Roman models ; he is, therefore, bound to some extent to adopt the Marcan framework of events ; but he does this in a way which suggests that Proto-Luke was *the document with which he started*, and which he preferred to Mark where they differed. For that reason I have styled Proto-Luke his " primary," Mark his " secondary " source. Luke's preference was, I imagine, mainly due to the relative poverty of Mark, and the incomparable richness of Proto-Luke, in regard to the teaching of our Lord. In the early church the biographical interest is subordinated to the didactic. This clearly holds good of Matthew, and is the natural explanation of his complete disregard of the order of events for the first half of Mark ; his drastic rearrangement of events is evidently determined by the desire to reach as soon as he possibly can the great block of teaching collected in the Sermon on the Mount. This desertion of Mark's order suggests that even the editor of our first Gospel regarded as in a sense " primary " his non-Marcan material (most of it perhaps being already combined into a single document) ; and if, as is probable, the name of Matthew was attached to this, so did the Christian community which named the Gospel after this source.

The only weighty objection to the Proto-Luke theory that I have come across arises from the fact that, where Mark and Luke give widely divergent accounts of the same item, the Marcan version usually looks decidedly the more primitive. The fact I

oncede ; but not the inference that the Lucan version is a
iterary manipulation of the Marcan, nor yet that it is later in
late. If the Gospels were (as I have argued) written by the
)ersons to whom tradition assigns them, Mark had more oppor-
unities of hearing the story first-hand than had Luke.[1] Mark's
nother resided in Jerusalem (Acts xii. 12) ; Luke had been there
∋ss than a fortnight (Acts xxi. 17-xxiii. 31). Mark had a special
onnection with Peter ; there is no reason to believe that Luke
ιad ever met him. Mark's account, then, of an event like the
)all of Peter ought to be superior to Luke's, even if Luke had
vritten his down long before Mark conceived the idea of composing
, Gospel. Stories which pass from mouth to mouth rapidly
hange their form ; but the change is due, not to the lapse of
ime as such, but to the number of intermediaries through whom
he tale has been transmitted. The superiority of Mark's version
ຣ to be attributed, not to the date at which he wrote—which was
nore than thirty years after the event—but to the fact that
o much of his story comes from persons who had first-hand
:nowledge of the facts.

B. H. STREETER

Feb. 14, 1930.
THE QUEEN'S COLLEGE,
OXFORD.

[1] For some new arguments for the Lucan authorship of the Acts cf. *New
'olutions of New-Testament Problems*, E. J. Goodspeed (Chicago, 1927). There
re mediaeval analogies to the " we " sections in the Acts (pointed out to mε
y Mr. A. S. L. Farquharson) in *Gesta Henrici Quinti*, 1416, and the *Record oj
Ʌluemantle Pursuivant*, 1471-2. Cf. *English Historical Literature*, by C. L.
∷ingsford, p. 47 f. and p. 381. In both cases the author drops naturally into
he first person in describing events of which he himself was an eye-witness.

CONTENTS

CHAPTER XV

CHAPTER XVI

PART IV.—SYNOPTIC ORIGINS

CHAPTER XVII

CHAPTER XVIII

APPENDICES

INDICES

INTRODUCTION

THE obscurity, commonly supposed to veil the origin of the
Gospels, is due not so much to the scantiness of the evidence
available as to the difficulty of focussing on this one point
the fresh evidence which has been accumulated during the
last half-century. Students in various specialised branches of
research, such as textual criticism, source-analysis, the cultural
background of the early Church, and the psychology of Mysticism, have worked at these subjects more or less in isolation ;
and without intensive specialisation the advance made would
have been impossible. But the time is now ripe for an attempt
to co-ordinate the results reached—so far as they bear on the
origin of the Gospels—and see them in their true relation in
a single organic process of historical evolution. In this volume
I have set out some researches of my own in two of these fields
of study, which, I believe, throw new light on certain aspects
of the problem ; but my main aim has been that co-ordination
of the results achieved along different lines of investigation
which, by using these to illuminate and consolidate one another,
provides a basis for further conclusions.

In the writing of the book I have had in view readers of
three quite different kinds. (1) There is the educated layman
who is sufficiently interested in the origin of the Gospels, the
manuscript authority for their text, the sources of information
possessed by their authors, and in the relation of the mystical
to the historical elements in the Fourth Gospel, to undertake a
piece of rather solid reading—provided that the book can be

understood without any previous technical knowledge. (2) I have had in mind the divinity student or minister of religion who desires an introduction to Textual Criticism, to the Synoptic Problem, and the Johannine question, but who does not know of any book which takes cognisance of the MS. discoveries, and light from other directions, which have become available in the last few years. (3) I desire to submit to the judgement of expert scholars the results of my own original research.

Accordingly I have endeavoured, wherever possible, to arrange the material in such a way that the argument and the nature of the evidence shall be clear to a reader who is unacquainted with Greek ; and I have relegated to footnotes matter with which the general reader (or the divinity student on a first reading) can afford to dispense ; I have also been at considerable pains to present a clear outline of the argument in the Synopsis at the head of each chapter, and in the Diagrams at the beginning of Parts I. and II. The reader to whom the whole subject is quite new would perhaps do well, at the first reading, to omit Ch. III.–VI., VIII.–XII. and XIV.

The expert will, I believe, find in every chapter suggestions which, whatever their value, have not previously been put forward ; but the most original conclusion, and perhaps the most important, is the identification of the text found in the new Koridethi MS. Θ, and its allies, with the text in use at Caesarea about A.D. 230. This identification supplies, as it were, the coping stone of the arch in that reconstruction of the various local texts of the Gospels current in the early Church at which scholars have been working for a generation ; it also leads on to a new conception of the history of the text during the first three centuries—differing as much from that held by Westcott and Hort as from the more recent view put forward by von Soden. The result is materially to broaden the basis of early evidence for the recovery of an authentic text.

The Synoptic Problem is another large issue in regard to which I have attempted to break new ground. While accepting, and indeed further consolidating, the received theory that Mark was one of the sources made use of by Matthew and Luke, I adventure a new approach towards the question of their other sources. Here, from the nature of the case, evidence of a demonstrative character is not forthcoming. Nevertheless, partly by bringing to bear on this problem results gained in the field of textual criticism, partly by considering anew the nature of parallelism in oral tradition and the probable connection of our Gospels, and also of their sources, with definite localities, I reach conclusions which seem to be sufficiently probable to justify my submitting them—under the conceptions of " Proto-Luke " and " A Four Document Hypothesis "—to the serious consideration of students. If correct, these conclusions are important, as enhancing our estimate of the historical value of much of the material which is preserved by Matthew or Luke only. I have also, I hope—by a new use of the MS. evidence available—finally disposed of the troublesome phantom of an " Ur-Marcus " (or earlier version of Mark) which has for too long haunted the minds of scholars.

The problem of the Fourth Gospel must, I am convinced, be approached from two sides. The results of historical and source criticism must be supplemented and interpreted in the light of a study of the psychology of the mystic mind. This done, the question of its authorship can be profitably discussed. My conclusions in regard to this Gospel are avowedly of a tentative character, and it is as a personal impression only that I put forward Part III. of this book. I feel sure, however, that, even if the conclusions reached are in some points erroneous, the method of approach is sound.

The questions treated of in Parts II. and III. cannot be considered entirely in isolation and apart from some considera-tion of the evidence as to the early circulation of the Gospels and their collection into a Canon of inspired writings ; accord-ingly I begin with a chapter, "The Selected Four," summarising as briefly as possible the main facts bearing on this point. And

I conclude in Part IV.—on the basis of the results reached in the previous sections of the book—with an endeavour to determine more exactly the dates and place of writing of the first three Gospels, and also to dispose of the difficulties still felt by some scholars in accepting the Lucan authorship of the Third Gospel and the Acts.

I should perhaps add that I have refrained from discussing recent attempts to reach by critical analysis the sources used by Mark; brilliant as some of these are, for reasons of the kind indicated p. 378 ff., they leave me unconvinced. I have also ventured to ignore many interesting theories, even though put forward by eminent scholars, which seem to me to have been adequately refuted by other writers. Very few dead hypotheses deserve the honour of a monument.

The Bibliographies in Moffatt's *Introduction to the N.T.* and —for textual criticism—in Gregory's *Textkritik* are so excellent and so well known that I early abandoned the idea of compiling one of my own, thinking it would be of more practical utility to supplement these by references in the notes to the best, or the most accessible, authority on each particular point as it arose.

I have to acknowledge gratefully assistance received from various friends—in particular from Dr. R. P. Blake of Harvard, Prof. Burkitt of Cambridge, Prof. Dodd of Mansfield College, Oxford, Miss Earp of Cumnor, and Archdeacon Lilley of Hereford, in careful reading of the proofs; to all of these I owe valuable suggestions. I have to thank Mrs. V. J. Brook of Oxford, for very great help in working out points of textual evidence, verifying references, and compiling Tables; the Rev. J. S. Bezzant, Vice-Principal of Ripon Hall, Oxford, and the Rev. R. D. Richardson, for the compilation of the Indices, and Mr. Norman Ault for drawing the Diagrams and Map.

B. H. STREETER.

OXFORD, *Sept.* 1924.

THE SELECTED FOUR

SYNOPSIS

THE IDEA OF A NEW TESTAMENT

The circulation of Gnostic Gospel and Acts and the still more dangerous competition of a compact New Testament put out by the semi-Gnostic Marcion forced the Church in self-defence to assign an exclusive canonical authority—not inferior to that heretofore ascribed to the Old Testament—to those older lives of Christ which it regarded as specially authentic. Thus *c.* A.D. 180 we find the Four Gospel Canon firmly established.

LOCAL GOSPELS

But a variety of considerations suggest that originally the Gospels were local Gospels circulated separately, and authoritative only in certain areas. The tradition which assigns Mark to Rome and John to Ephesus may safely be accepted. That connecting Luke with Achaea (*i.e.* Greece) and Matthew with Palestine is perhaps no more than conjecture ; Matthew may with greater probability be connected with Antioch.

The destruction of Jerusalem A.D. 70 deprived the Church of its natural centre. The capitals of the larger provinces of the Roman Empire succeeded to the place left vacant ; and among these the tradition of Apostolic foundation gave special prestige to Antioch, Ephesus, and Rome. The result was a period of about ninety years of more or less independent development, in doctrinal emphasis, in church organisation, and in the production of religious literature. Hence the history of the three succeeding centuries of Catholic Christianity is largely the story of a progressive standardisation of a diversity which had its roots in this period. The delimitation of the Four Gospel Canon was the first step in this process.

B

The Twilight Period

The dearth of early Christian literature outside the New Testament makes the ninety years after A.D. 64 the most obscure in the whole history of the Church. Hence the importance of supplementing the scanty evidence as to the existence and circulation of the Gospels during this period by the results of that critical comparison of the Gospels themselves which leads up to the identification of the sources used by their authors. Not infrequently, by bringing the external literary evidence into relation with the results of source-criticism, an unexpected degree of precision and definiteness can be reached. This point illustrated by examples bearing upon the evidence as to the early circulation of each of the four Gospels—a new interpretation being suggested of the evidence of Papias in regard to Matthew.

Source and Textual Criticism

Why these are important to the historian. The study of them can be made interesting, if approached from the right standpoint. Analogy between the method of these investigations and that of the science of Geology.

CHAPTER I

THE SELECTED FOUR

The Idea of a New Testament

THE primitive Church had all the advantages, without any of the disadvantages, of an authoritative collection of sacred books. Some temperaments are attracted by the idea of novelty, others by the appeal of an immemorial antiquity. The early Church could provide for both. Only yesterday, it taught, under Pontius Pilate, God had sent His Son to die for man ; but this recent event was but the culminating point of an eternal purpose revealed to man by a line of Prophets in a sacred literature of prodigious age. On the one hand the Gospel was preached as a new salvation ; on the other—the point is elaborated in all the early defences of Christianity [1]—its truth was demonstrated by the exact conformity of events in the life of Christ to what had been foretold by writers of an antiquity immensely greater than the poets, philosophers and historians of the Greeks. Yet, though the Church had the advantage of resting on a basis of ancient revelation, its free development was not, as has so often happened in religious history, fettered by its past. For with the coming of the Messiah the Law of Moses, to the Jews the most inspired portion of the whole Old Testament, was abrogated to a large extent—though exactly to what extent was a matter of much controversy—and while the Church of Christ was

---

[1] Cf. Theophilus (A.D. 180), *Ad Autolycum*, iii. 20, " The Hebrews . . . from whom we have those sacred books which are older than all authors."

understood to be in a sense identical with the " Church in the wilderness,"[1] it was no less clearly understood to have been, as it were, refounded ; it had received a further revelation and had made a fresh start.

But, since, for practical purposes, no revelation is complete unless there is an authentic record of it, there was logically implicit from the first, in the idea of a " further revelation," the conception of a New Testament to supplement the Old. The Church was intellectually in a weak position until and unless it could support its specific doctrines by the appeal to a collection of sacred books which could be regarded as no less authoritative and inspired than the ancient Jewish Bible. But, although a canonised New Testament was necessary, the need for it was only slowly realised. Nor, had the need been felt, could it have been satisfied all at once. A community can only invest with canonical authority literature which is already ancient, and which has already, by its own intrinsic merit, attained to a high degree of authority and repute. Official canonisation cannot create scripture ; it can only recognise as inspired books which already enjoy considerable prestige. The Epistle traditionally attributed to Clement of Rome[2] is in this respect particularly illuminating. The writer's theology is largely taken over from the Epistle to the Hebrews, while Romans and 1 Corinthians are quoted in a way which implies that they are classics ; but, quite clearly, the Old Testament alone is regarded as inspired Scripture.

The formation of an authoritative Canon of the New Testament would in any case have been a natural and obvious development. It was enormously accelerated owing to the wide prevalence of various schools of fantastic theosophy, classed together under the general name of Gnosticism, which seem to have had an extraordinary fascination for the half-educated mind

[1] Acts vii. 38.

[2] Usually dated A.D. 96 ; cf. add. note to Ch. XVII. below. As I hold that it is indubitably quoted by Polycarp c. 115, I cannot accept the late date recently proposed by E. T. Merrill, *Essays in Early Church History* (Macmillan, 1924), p. 217 ff.

in the second century. In points of detail the systems of the various Gnostic leaders differed immensely. But common to them all is the idea that matter is essentially evil, and that therefore the material universe cannot be the creation of the Supreme Good God, but of some inferior Power from whose grip Christ, the emissary of the Good God, came to deliver man. Gospels, Acts, and other writings claiming to be by Apostles were circulated everywhere, in which Christ was represented as a Divine Being not having a real body of flesh and blood, and as having therefore suffered only in semblance on the cross ; or in which, alternatively, it was recorded that the Divine Christ came down upon the man Jesus at the baptism, and was taken up again to heaven at the Crucifixion. " My Power, My Power, why hast thou forsaken me ? " says Jesus in the Apocryphal Gospel of Peter ; and, adds the author, " immediately he (i.e. the Divine Christ) was taken up." It was because this kind of thing, grotesque as it appears to us, had a wide appeal in that age, that the Church was compelled, sooner than might otherwise have been the case, to draw a line between books which might, and books which might not, be " read," that is, accepted as authorities for true and Apostolic doctrine.

The necessity for an official list of accepted books was more especially brought home to the Church by the extraordinary success of the semi-Gnostic Marcion. Marcion came to Rome from Pontus on the Black Sea in A.D. 139, and lived there for about four years in communion with the Church. Being unable to convert the Roman Church to his peculiar views, he proceeded to found a new church, of which a fundamental tenet was the existence of two Gods. The Old Testament he rejected, as being the revelation of the inferior of these two deities who was the Creator of this evil world. The Good God, the deliverer of mankind, was first revealed in Christ ; but the original Apostles had unfortunately misunderstood Christ, and supposed the God whom He revealed to be the Creator, the inferior deity who inspired the Old Testament. Christ's new revelation was therefore repeated to Paul. Hence his Epistles and the Gospel of Luke—with all passages conflicting with Marcion's views carefully expurgated as Jewish-Christian interpolations—constituted the sole authentic record of the new revelation made by Christ. Thus Marcion for the first time emphatically presented, both to the Jewish and to the Christian world, the conception of a fixed and definite collection of Christian literature conceived of as having canonical authority *over against and in distinction from the Old Testament*. Marcion combined the dualistic explanation of the problem of evil, which was the main attraction of all types of Gnosticism, with the simplicity and fervour of the specifically Pauline type of Christianity. He himself united intense religious conviction with great organising capacity ; and within his own lifetime he had founded a compactly organised church extending throughout the Roman Empire. Its members, in the asceticism of their lives and their readiness for martyrdom, equalled and claimed to excel those of the Catholic Church. Earlier Gnostics had maintained that their particular tenets had been originally a mystic revelation, too precious to be committed to the vulgar, and had been handed down to them by a secret tradition from some one or other of the Apostles. Marcion made a new point when he averred that the Twelve Apostles themselves had been in error. To the Gnostics in general the answer of the Church was to appeal to the unbroken tradition of the great sees founded by Apostles and to the Gospels, Acts, and Epistles recognised by those Churches ; against Marcion in particular the tradition of the Church of Rome gained special importance from its claim to represent the united tradition of both Peter and Paul—whom Marcion's theory set at variance with one another.

Marcion was the most formidable, precisely because he was the most Christian, of all the Gnostics. The existence of his canon forced the Church explicitly to canonise the books which it accepted ; for his position could not effectively be opposed if the Church ascribed to its own Gospels, and to its own version of the Epistles, a degree of plenary inspiration less than that attributed by Marcion to the books in his collection. But when the Church had taken this step it found its position unexpectedly strong. After all, *four* Gospels does sound more imposing than one ; and a collection of books which included the Acts, and works attributed to Matthew, John, Peter, and Paul could colourably be regarded as representative of the concurrence of *all* the Apostles. Once this collection was definitely regarded as scripture, as a *New* Testament on the same level of inspiration as the *Old*, the apologetic of the Church was provided with a far broader foundation than the one Gospel and single Apostle to which Marcion appealed. Incidentally the possession of a New Testament made it possible to reply more effectively than heretofore to the more damaging arguments of Jewish opponents ; for the difference between Jew and Christian was no longer a matter of the correct interpretation of the prophecies of the ancient scriptures, but of the recognition of the new. Whether the explicit recognition of the New Testament writings as inspired scripture was the result of some official pronouncement agreed upon by the authorities of the Great Churches we do not know. What we do know is that by about the year A.D. 180 the Four Gospels had attained this recognition in Antioch, Ephesus, and Rome.

For Antioch our evidence is the statement of Jerome that Theophilus, bishop of that church *c.* 180, wrote a commentary on the Four Gospels, coupled with the fact that, in his one surviving treatise, Theophilus quotes the Fourth Gospel as " inspired scripture," and by the name of John.[1] For Ephesus and Rome combined our authority is Irenaeus, bishop of Lyons. He had listened to Polycarp in Smyrna as a boy, had resided and lectured in Rome in 177, and played the mediator between Ephesus and

---

[1] *Ad Autolycum*, ii. 22. Jerome's language in his Epistle to Algarsia (Vallarsi, i. 858) may imply that Theophilus made a Harmony of the Gospels before commenting on them. Some think he may actually have used Tatian's Diatessaron ; but, even so, the fact that this was a harmony of " the Four," along with the ascription of scriptural authority to John, justifies the inference that the Four were regarded by him as the inspired Four.

Rome in 191, when Victor of Rome had excommunicated the churches of Asia—" Asia " is the Roman name for one province of Asia Minor—over a difference as to the manner and time of keeping Easter. The main argument in Irenaeus' comprehensive *Refutation of the Knowledge falsely so called* (usually cited as *Adversus Haereses*) is the appeal, against the Gnostic claim to possess *secret* Apostolic traditions, to the uninterrupted *public* tradition of the bishops of the Apostolic sees of Rome and Asia. Accordingly we may be certain that what he says about the Gospels represents the official view at Rome and Ephesus at the time he wrote (c. 185). What that view was the following extracts will sufficiently indicate.

" Matthew published his written Gospel among the Hebrews in their own language, while Peter and Paul were preaching and founding the church in Rome. After their decease Mark, the disciple and interpreter of Peter, also transmitted to us in writing those things which Peter had preached ; and Luke, the attendant of Paul, recorded in a book the Gospel which Paul had declared. Afterwards John, the disciple of the Lord, who also reclined on his bosom, published the Gospel, while residing at Ephesus in Asia." [1]

" It is impossible that the Gospels should be in number either more or fewer than these. For since there are four regions of the world wherein we are, and four principal winds, and the Church is as seed sown in the whole earth, and the Gospel is the Church's pillar and ground, and the breath of life : it is natural that it should have four pillars, from all quarters breathing incorruption, and kindling men into life. Whereby it is evident, that the Artificer of all things, the Word, who sitteth upon the Cherubim, and keepeth all together, when He was made manifest unto men, gave us His Gospel in four forms, kept together by one Spirit. . . . For indeed the Cherubim had four faces, and their faces are images of the dispensation of the Son of God. . . . For the Living Creatures are quadriform, and the Gospel also is quadriform." [2]

[1] Iren. *Adv. Haer.* iii. 1. 1.   [2] *Ibid.* iii. 11. 8.

To the modern reader, language like this seems fantastic ; but it is supremely interesting for what it implies. No one, even in that age, could have used it except about books whose sacrosanctity was already affirmed by a long tradition.

LOCAL GOSPELS

The existence of four Gospels is so familiar that we are apt to take it as a matter of course ; to us, as to Irenaeus (though for different reasons), it seems almost part of the nature of things. But once we begin to reflect upon it, the acceptance by the Church of four different official Lives of Christ is a fact which cries out for an explanation. To begin with, the practical inconvenience of having so many Lives is very great, especially as these alternately agree and differ from one another in a way which makes it extremely hard to get a consistent view of the story as a whole. The inconvenience has been felt by every one who has tried to give practical religious instruction. Again, already in the second century heretics were making capital out of the discrepancies between the Gospels.[1] So far as we can judge from the solutions produced by later writers, it would appear that criticism was principally directed to the divergence between the genealogies of our Lord in Matthew and Luke and between the chronology of the Fourth Gospel and that of the Synoptics. But there are other hardly less striking divergences which, then as since, must have given trouble to the apologist.

Tatian (who left Rome for Mesopotamia c. A.D. 172) tried to overcome these difficulties by combining the Gospels into a single connected narrative. And until about 430 his Diatessaron, or Harmony,[2] which carefully weaves the four Gospels into a

[1] Iren. *Adv. Haer.* iii. 2. 1. The Muratorian Canon (c. A.D. 200), *l* 16-25, seems to glance at the same debate. Julius Africanus, c. A.D. 230, reconciles the genealogies by a theory of Levirate marriages. Eusebius, perhaps following Hippolytus (cf. B. W. Bacon, *The Fourth Gospel in Research and Debate*, pp. 226 ff.), discusses the reconciliation of the Synoptic and Johannine chronology, *H.E.* iii. 24.
[2] The original of this is lost, but we have Arabic. Latin, and Old Dutch

continuous story, while preserving as far as possible their original wording, seems to have been the only form in which the Gospels were publicly read in the Churches (and even commented on by theologians) among the Syriac-speaking Christians. In that part of the world the " Separate Gospels " were very little used, while the Diatessaron was commonly spoken of simply as " the Gospel." Fortunately for the historian, though perhaps less so for the Sunday School teacher, the experiment of substituting a single official Life for the four separate Gospels did not commend itself to the Greek and Latin Churches, otherwise our Gospels might have survived only as conjectured " sources " of the Diatessaron.

Another thing that requires explanation is the inclusion of Mark among the selected Four. Modern scholars, it is true, are unanimous in accepting the view that Mark is the oldest of the Gospels, and was one of the main sources from which Matthew and Luke drew their information. And Mark preserves a number of small details, omitted or blurred in the other Gospels, which, to the historical instinct of the twentieth century, are of the utmost interest. But the very fact that these details were not reproduced in the later Gospels shows that they were uninteresting, or even positively distasteful, to the Church of that age. Again, Mark has no account of the Infancy, nor (in the text as given in the oldest MSS. and versions) of the Resurrection Appearances, and it contains comparatively little of the teaching of our Lord. Apart from the minor details already mentioned, it includes only two miracles and one parable not in Matthew or Luke, and most of its contents are to be found in *both* the other two. It is the Gospel least valued, least quoted, and most rarely commented on by the Fathers. Augustine can even venture to speak of Mark as " a sort of lackey and abridger of Matthew." [1]   And in the Western Church, till Jerome's Vulgate,

---

versions, besides an Armenian version of a commentary on it by Ephraem the Syrian (*c.* 360). The most recent discussion of the comparative value of these authorities is by F. C. Burkitt, *J.T.S.*, Jan. 1924.

[1] "Marcus eum (*sc.* Matthaeum) subsecutus tanquam pedisequus et breviator ejus videtur," Aug. *De cons. evan.* ii.

in spite of the fact that tradition averred that the Gospels were
written in the sequence Matthew, Mark, Luke, John, they were
officially arranged in the order Matthew, John, Luke, Mark,[1]
so as to put the least important Gospel last. They so stand in
many Old Latin MSS. and in the Greek MSS. D and W, which
give a definitely Western text. Why, then, was it thought
necessary to ascribe to it canonical authority at all ? Why did
not Mark, like the other ancient sources used by Matthew and
Luke, cease to be copied—being superseded by its incorporation
in these fuller and more popular works ?

The foregoing considerations prove that the inclusion of four
Gospels, and of these particular four, in the Canon, was not
determined by considerations of practical convenience ; and it
involved the Church in obvious apologetic difficulties. Thus it
can only be accounted for on the hypothesis that, at the time
when the Canon was definitely settled, each of the four had
acquired such a degree of prestige that no one of them could be
excluded, or could even have its text substantially altered in
order to bring it into harmony with the rest.

Certain of the divergences between the Gospels, in particular
those between Matthew and Luke, are of such a character that
it is difficult to believe that these books originated in the same
church, or even in the same neighbourhood. The contrast
between the Jewish atmosphere of Matthew and the even more
markedly Gentile proclivities of Luke is enhanced by a still more
notable contrast between the divergent cycles of tradition on
which they draw. The formal contradiction between the two genealogies is really less significant than the extraordinarily meagre
contacts between their two accounts of the Infancy and of the
Resurrection Appearances, for these were matters of much more

[1] This order is explained and stated to be official in the so-called
Monarchian Prologues : " Qui (*sc.* Johannes) etsi post omnes evangelium scrip-
sisse dicitur, tamen dispositione canonis ordinati post Matthaeum ponitur."
These Prologues to the Gospels, found in some Latin MSS., are printed in
Wordsworth and White's Vulgate ; also in convenient pamphlet form in
Kleine Texte. P. Corssen, in *Texte und Untersuchungen*, xv. 1, dates them as
third century ; others attribute them to Priscillian $\pm$ 380.

general interest. Churches in which the traditions current were
so completely independent in regard to points of such absorbing
interest as these must, one would suppose, have been geographically
remote from one another. Again, the survival of Mark would
be adequately explained if it had had time to become an
established classic in one or more important churches some time
before its popularity was threatened by competition with the
richer Gospels produced in other centres.

Thus we are led on to the view that the Gospels were written
in and for different churches, and that each of the Gospels must
have attained local recognition as a religious classic, if not yet
as inspired scripture, before the four were combined into a
collection recognised by the whole Church. The tradition, for
what it is worth, decidedly supports this view. Mark is assigned
to Rome, John to Ephesus, Luke to Achaea, and Matthew to
Palestine. The tradition connecting the Gospels of Mark and
John with Rome and Ephesus is so early and fits in so well with
other pieces of evidence that it may safely be accepted. In
particular, the view that Mark was the old Gospel of the all-
important Church of Rome would completely account for its
inclusion in the Canon. The tradition connecting Luke, the most
Hellenic of the Gospels, with old Greece cannot be traced earlier
than the (probably third century) Monarchian Prologues to the
Latin Gospels. It may be only a conjecture—if so, it is a
happy one. The evidence connecting Matthew with Palestine
must be largely discounted, insomuch as it is bound up with the
statement that it was written in Hebrew, which does not seem
to hold good of our present Gospel. I shall shortly return to this
question ; but, at any rate, the tradition constitutes *prima facie*
evidence that the Gospel originated in the East—probably at
Antioch.[1]

All four Gospels were certainly known in Rome by A.D. 155,
if not before. Justin Martyr, who was writing in Rome,

---

[1] See below, p. 500 ff. So also Foakes-Jackson and Lake, *Beginnings of
Christianity*, i. p. 329 f. (Macmillan, 1920.)

150 years—he himself says—after the birth of Christ, speaks of " Memoirs which are called Gospels," [1] and again of " Memoirs composed by the Apostles and their followers." These he says were read at the weekly service of the Church. And in his writings are to be found something like a hundred quotations or reminiscences of Matthew and Luke, and some of Mark and John. There is so very little in Mark which does not also occur in Matthew or Luke that we should expect the allusions to matter peculiar to Mark to be few. But the paucity of his quotations from John is a little strange when set side by side with the central position in his apologetic system of the Johannine doctrine of the Logos. From this, some scholars have inferred that, while Justin himself—who had been converted to Christianity in Ephesus—accepted the Ephesian Gospel, the Roman public for which he wrote did not put it on quite the same level as the other three. Moreover, it is possible, though not I think probable, that he made occasional use of other Lives of Christ besides the four we have. If so, he used them only as subordinate authorities. But although Justin's evidence shows that by A.D. 155 all four Gospels have reached Rome, once the idea that the Gospels were originally local Gospels is presented to us, we realise that each of the Gospels must have an earlier history, which requires to be separately investigated and must go back a considerable period before the date when the collection of Four was made. But the separate histories of the Gospels cannot be properly appreciated if considered apart from the histories of the several churches in which they were produced. In this connection I would stress a consideration to which scholars in general have, I think, given too little attention.

The original capital of Christianity was the mother Church of Jerusalem. But Jerusalem was destroyed by the Romans in

---

[1] Justin, *Apol.* i. 66; *Dial.* 103. Convenient tables illustrating Justin's use of the Gospels are given by W. Sanday, *The Gospels in the Second Century*, pp. 91 ff., 113 ff.

A.D. 70, after a long and peculiarly horrible siege. By that time most, if not all, of the original Apostles had died. Naturally, therefore, Christians in the smaller cities of the Roman Empire tended more and more to look for guidance and direction to those other ancient capitals upon which in secular affairs they and their ancestors had been most directly dependent. Rome, the political centre of the civilised world, was in a more special sense the capital of the West. In the East the old capitals of conquered states were still the headquarters of provincial administration, the most important being Alexandria and Antioch on the Orontes, the capitals respectively of the old Egyptian Empire of the Ptolemies and of the old Seleucid Empire of Syria. Of the lesser kingdoms which had been incorporated into the Roman Empire, one of the most prosperous was that province of Asia Minor known by the Romans and in the New Testament as "Asia," of which Pergamum was the official capital but Ephesus the most notable city. Two other provinces which for special reasons are important in the history of the early Church were Achaea and Palestine, of which the administrative capitals were Corinth and Caesarea. The Church in all these cities could claim special association with, if not actual foundation by, Apostles. Hence during the second century, when Gnosticism seriously menaced the essential character of Christianity, and when it seemed that it could only effectively be resisted by the appeal to Apostolic tradition, their Apostolic connection gave these churches—and especially the three most important of them—Antioch, Ephesus, and Rome—a prestige which made their influence for the time being determinant in the development of Christianity. It is notable that it was not until after A.D. 190, by which time the Four Gospel Canon seems to have been universally accepted, that Alexandria began to exercise any considerable influence on the Church at large.

During the century or more after the death of the original Apostles and the fall of Jerusalem there was no unifying authority, no world-wide organisation, however informal, to check the

independent development of the various local churches each on
its own lines. Inevitably this independence resulted in local
diversity—in regard to doctrinal emphasis, Church organisation,
the religious literature most valued, and also, as we shall see,
in regard to the manuscript tradition of such books as they had
in common. Thus the history of Catholic Christianity during
the first five centuries is very largely the history of a progressive
standardisation of a diversity the roots of which were planted in
the sub-Apostolic age. It was during the earlier part of this
period of maximum independence that the Gospels were written ;
and the delimitation of the Four Gospel Canon was the first step
in the process of standardising.

The Twilight Period

The story of the Acts of the Apostles leaves Paul in Rome a
couple of years or so before the persecution under Nero (A.D. 64),
in or shortly after which probably Paul, and possibly Peter,
fell. Owing to the extreme paucity of early Christian literature
(apart from the New Testament) the ninety years which separate
this event from the writings of Justin is the most obscure in
the history of the Church. It was during this period that the
Gospels were written, and during the earlier part of it each must
have had a separate history. In the last three chapters of this
book I attempt to trace something of this history. By a scrutiny
of the evidence sufficiently minute, more especially by the piecing
together of results gained along different lines of research, it is, I
believe, possible to do this, and to determine the dates, authorship, and place of origin of the several Gospels with a greater
degree of assurance than is commonly supposed. But for the
moment the point I desire to emphasise is that among the most
important of the facts on which these larger historical conclusions must be based are the results attained by a critical study of
the mutual relations of the Gospels to one another and the light
which this throws on the sources which their authors used.

In order to illustrate this point, and at the same time to make
an opportunity of setting down certain facts to which I may have
occasion to refer back later on, I will cite four pieces of evidence
bearing on the origin and dates of the Gospels—indicating the
way in which they are amplified or reinforced by the result of
the critical studies upon which the reader of this volume is about
to embark.

(1) Ignatius, bishop of Antioch, on his way to martyrdom
in the Colosseum at Rome, c. A.D. 115, wrote seven short letters.
In these we find a dozen or more reminiscences of material
found in the Synoptic Gospels. But, if these allusions are
critically examined by a student of the Synoptic Problem, he
will note that while all of them *may*, some of them *must*, be
regarded as reminiscences of Matthew ; for in certain cases the
language of Ignatius implies a knowledge of passages which such
a student recognises as attributable to the editor of that Gospel
and not his sources.[1] Matthew, then, was a standard work at
Antioch before 115. This would fit in with the tradition of
Palestinian origin ; but, for reasons I shall develop later, I
think it more probable that, though it may incorporate a
Palestinian source, the Gospel itself is really the local Gospel of
the important Church of Antioch. At any rate, its use by
Ignatius fixes a point in the history of the Gospels.

(2) I have already mentioned how, after a four years' member-
ship of the Roman Church, Marcion founded the most vigorous
of all the early sects, and how, rejecting the Old Testament, he
elevated to the rank of inspired Scripture the Epistles of Paul
(the only Apostle who had really understood Christ) and the
Gospel of Luke—all heavily bowdlerised to accord with his own
views. Now even so forcible a person as Marcion could hardly
have induced his followers to attribute plenary inspiration to an
existing document unless it was one which enjoyed considerable

---

[1] *E.g.* Ignatius clearly alludes to Mt. iii. 14-15 (*Smyrn.* i. 1) and to Mt. viii.
17 (*Polyc.* i. 2-3). In Ch. XVII. below I comment on the more striking allusions in Ignatius to passages in the Gospel.

prestige ; hence we may infer that, at any rate in Rome, the Gospel of Luke was, by A.D. 140, already a Church classic of some years' standing. If, however, we wish to trace the history of the Gospel further back, we find that, though possible reminiscences of it (and its sequel, the Acts) may be found in the scanty literature of the period, they fall short of certainty. At once the importance is seen of the question whether or no Luke was known to the author of the Fourth Gospel, since (if the view maintained in Ch. XV. be correct) this cannot be later than A.D. 100 and may quite possibly be as early as 90. Thus the problem of the sources of the Fourth Gospel bears also on the history of the Third.

(3) Eusebius, the father of Church History, *c.* 325, had a fortunate habit of quoting his authorities verbatim ; and, as we can check his accuracy by those which still survive, we can trust it in regard to those which do not. Among these are two passages from Papias, bishop of Hierapolis, ten miles from Laodicea, of the "seven churches of Asia." As to the date at which Papias wrote his *Exposition of the Oracles of the Lord*, from which Eusebius quotes, there has been much dispute ; but the limits on either side would seem to be 135 and 165. It runs as follows :

"And the Elder said this also : Mark, having become the interpreter of Peter, wrote down accurately everything that he remembered, without however recording in order [1] what was either said or done by Christ. For neither did he hear the Lord, nor did he follow Him, but afterwards as I said (attended) Peter who adapted his instructions to the need (of his hearers) but had no design of giving a connected account of the Lord's oracles. So then Mark made no mistake while he thus wrote down some things as he remembered them ; for he made it his one care not to omit anything that he heard or to set down any false statement therein " (Eus. *H.E.* iii. 39).

---

[1] I dissent from F. H. Colson (*J.T.S.*, xiv. 62 f.) that rhetorical, rather than chronological, τάξις is meant.

From the context in Eusebius it would appear that the Elder
spoken of was the Elder John. His identity must be inferred
from another quotation by Eusebius, this time from the Preface
of Papias' work.

" And again, on any occasion when a person came in my way
who had been a follower of the Elders, I would enquire about
the discourses of the Elders—what was said by Andrew, or by
Peter, or by Philip, or by Thomas or James, or by John or
Matthew, or any other of the Lord's disciples, and what Aristion
and the Elder John, the disciples of the Lord, say."

Aristion and the Elder John, it appears from this, were
in the unique position of being " disciples of the Lord " who
ranked after the Apostles themselves as depositories of authentic
tradition. Presumably they must at least have seen the Lord in
the flesh. Irenaeus [1] tells us how in his youth he heard Polycarp
speak of " John and the others who had seen the Lord," and it
is not impossible that Polycarp was alluding to John the Elder,
though Irenaeus seems to have understood him to mean the
Apostle John. Some critics wish to emend the Greek in the
quotation from Papias so as to make Aristion and the Elder
disciples, not of the Lord, but of the Apostles. In my own view
the emendation is arbitrary and improbable. But, even so,
Aristion and the Elder John are left as immediate followers of the
Apostles—like Mark or Luke. That is to say, on any view, the
statement of the Elder John as to the origin of Mark is the
evidence of a contemporary.

Contemporary evidence as to the origin of the oldest of our
Gospels is of the utmost historical importance. But the question
has been raised, Was the Gospel of Mark of which the Elder spoke
the Gospel we possess or some earlier edition ? The answer to
this question is bound up with the answer to the other question,
whether the extant Gospel of Mark, or some earlier edition
of it, was known to, and used by, the authors of Matthew and
Luke. Further, it will appear (in Chap. XI.) that this last point

_____
[1] In his letter to Florinus, quoted p. 443 below.

cannot satisfactorily be decided without a correct estimate of
the comparative value of the several lines in the manuscript
tradition of the text of the Gospels. That is to say, the question
as to the original Mark can only be settled on the basis of the
combined results of both Synoptic and Textual criticism.

(4) To the quotation from Papias about Mark, Eusebius adds
one about Matthew : " So then Matthew composed the oracles
(τὰ λόγια) in the Hebrew language, and each one interpreted
them as he could." Volumes have been written on this enigmatic
fragment. In this place all I can do is to state in a seemingly
dogmatic way an hypothesis, which I believe to be original, and
which I shall attempt to justify at greater length in the sequel.

(a) Irenaeus is known to have read Papias ; we infer that his
statement about the Hebrew original of Matthew, and all the
similar statements by later Fathers, are probably derived from
Papias. Since, then, the credibility of any statement depends
on its origin, not on the number of persons who repeat it, the
statements of the later authors can be ignored, if only we can
find what exactly is the meaning and authority of this passage
in Papias.

(b) Whoever was the author of the Fourth Gospel, there can
be no reasonable doubt that it was written in Ephesus. And at
the date at which Papias wrote—and the later we make this
date, the stronger the argument—it must have been officially
recognised in Papias' own province of Asia. Further, as Lightfoot pointed out, in the list of Apostles mentioned in the previously
quoted fragment of Papias, the order and selection of names is
that of their occurrence in the Fourth Gospel, not of the
Synoptic lists. We are bound, then, to consider the curiously
disparaging tone of Papias' remarks about Matthew and Mark in
the light of this presumption that Papias knew the Fourth Gospel.

Of Mark, Papias, or rather the Elder his informant, says in
effect " the facts are correct—that follows from Mark's connection
with Peter—but, as Mark had only his memory to rely upon, he
has got them in the wrong order." In regard to Matthew he

says that " the original of the discourses (τὰ λόγια) was in Hebrew and there is *no authorised translation*." Now this depreciation of Gospels used in the Church is quite unaccountable unless it seemed necessary in order to defend the superior accuracy of some other Gospel which was in conflict with them in regard to certain points.

Now obviously the Fourth Gospel is in violent conflict with Mark in regard to the order of events. But it has not, I think, hitherto been realised, in this particular connection, that the Fourth Gospel is equally in conflict with Matthew in regard to the " prophetic utterances "—that is the strict meaning of τὰ λόγια—of our Lord. Matthew is the Gospel which lays most emphasis on the idea of an early visible Second Coming ; John is the Gospel which all but substitutes for this visible return of Christ the coming of the Paraclete. Papias himself was a Millenarian ; but it is probable—Eusebius is ambiguous here—that the passage about Matthew, like that about Mark, is quoted from the Elder John. In that case the two fragments of Papias represent what Asian tradition recollected of John the Elder's reply to critics who impugned the accuracy of the Fourth Gospel on the ground of its divergence from Matthew and Mark.

Heretofore scholars have taken it for granted that τὰ λόγια was the title of a book—differing only in their view as to whether the book referred to was our Gospel of Matthew, a lost collection of sayings of the Lord, or a collection of proof-texts. I submit that if—in the lost context of the fragment—Papias was talking, not about books, but their subject-matter, τὰ λόγια would be the natural phrase to use in speaking of the sayings of Christ which form so conspicuous an element in the existing Gospel of Matthew. The Elder—thinking, partly of the Judaistic, but mainly of the Apocalyptic, sayings in Matthew—says that the *discourses* in this Greek Gospel cannot always be relied on as accurately representing the original Hebrew (cf. p. 416).

If this explanation is correct, the Elder may have known of the existence of a Hebrew (prob. = Aramaic) collection of

sayings of Christ by Matthew (though he need not actually have
seen it), and he does not wish to deny that this had been used
by the author of the Greek Gospel. But he declines to regard
as a wholly apostolic, and therefore in all points authoritative,
work the Greek Gospel which, at the time when he was speaking,
was in all probability a new arrival in Ephesus and not yet
generally accepted in that church. But, supposing the fragment
represents a protest on behalf of the local Ephesian Gospel
against the superior claims made by certain persons in favour
of a Gospel recently introduced from outside, we are not entitled
to infer from the expression " each one translated them as he
could " that the Elder knew of any other Greek versions of
Matthew's Hebrew work. More probably his language is a
slightly contemptuous exaggeration intended to assert that the
particular Greek version (i.e. our Gospel of Matthew), to the
authority of which the critics of the Fourth Gospel were appealing,
was an anonymous version having no claim to direct apostolic
authority. What he is anxious to assert is that the Greek
Gospel of Matthew, like that of Mark, is only deutero-apostolic,
and that, therefore, its authority cannot be quoted as final where
it conflicts with the Fourth Gospel. This does not necessarily
imply that he attributed the Fourth Gospel to an Apostle.
On the contrary, supposing that the Elder knew that this Gospel
was by an unknown disciple of John, or supposing that he were
himself (as I shall argue) the author, it would only be the more
necessary to point out that Gospels like Matthew and Mark,
which were at times in conflict with it, were no more directly
apostolic than itself.

In the interpretation of the meaning of a fragment, torn from
its original context, there must always be an element of doubt.
But the above interpretation has two great merits. First, it
explains the extraordinary fact that the earliest allusion in
Christian literature to the Gospels is an endeavour to minimise
their accuracy and Apostolic authority. Secondly, the view
that the Elder John meant to affirm that the Greek Matthew

was *not* the work of an Apostle, though embodying a work
originally written in Hebrew by the Apostle Matthew, fits in
admirably with the result of a critical comparison of the Synoptic
Gospels, which suggests that the author of our First Gospel used
Mark and at least one other source mainly consisting of discourse. There is not, however, I may incidentally remark, any
reason to suppose that the Hebrew work of Matthew was ever
known by the title " Logia."

SOURCE AND TEXTUAL CRITICISM

These examples will suffice to show how the critical study
of the internal relations of the Gospels to one another may
illuminate the external evidence as to their authorship, date,
or locality of origin. But, if we are to pass on from the history
of the Gospels themselves to a consideration of their value as
historical authorities for the life of Christ, the analysis of sources
is still more important. For our estimate of the historical value
of the Gospels depends in the last resort upon the opinion we
frame as to the sources of information upon which the several
authors relied, and of the degree of accuracy with which they
reproduced them.

The historian, moreover, must go on to ask the question, How
far does the text of the Gospels that has come down to us
represent what the authors wrote ? The earliest MSS. we possess,
apart from a few papyrus fragments, are separated by a matter
of two and a half centuries from the authors' original. Since
absolute accuracy is an ideal not attainable by mortal man,
every time a MS. is copied some errors will get into the text.
But the errors which will arise and be propagated along one line
of transmission will not be the same as those along another.
Thus by a comparison of MSS. representing different textual
traditions the errors of one can be corrected from another.
But if this is to be done, it is vital to ascertain the number and
character of these different traditions and how far they are

independent of one another. I have already indicated how in
certain ways the study of textual criticism, in the light of recent
MS. discoveries, throws unexpected light on some of the obscurer
aspects of the Synoptic Problem ; incidentally it provides further
evidence of the necessity of studying the history of the Gospels in
each of the Great Churches separately.

Many of those who recognise that both textual criticism and
the analysis of sources are an essential preliminary to a truly
historical investigation are nevertheless inclined to recoil from
the study of these problems, fearing lest they may become choked
by the dust of multifarious detail. To such I would venture
to suggest that whether a particular investigation is instinct
with interest or fraught with tedium depends very much on the
spirit in which it is approached. The problems discussed in the
present volume have, if one cares to look at it in that light,
much the same kind of intellectual appeal as the quest for the
solution of a difficult acrostic or of a problem in chess. An even
better analogy would be the science of Geology ; for that is
recognised as truly a science, though a science which, from the
nature of the case, is compelled to dispense with the method of
experiment and relies solely on observation. Geology attempts
to reconstruct the history of the past by a highly scientific
application of the method of observation. Facts, over as wide
a range as possible, are collected, sifted, and compared, in order
that hypotheses may be framed which will satisfactorily account
for the observed phenomena. The critical investigations pursued
in this volume are of a precisely similar character. And the
student who enters upon these problems in the same spirit of
scientific inquiry as he would if they were problems of Geology
will find the method not without interest and the results well
worth the trouble.

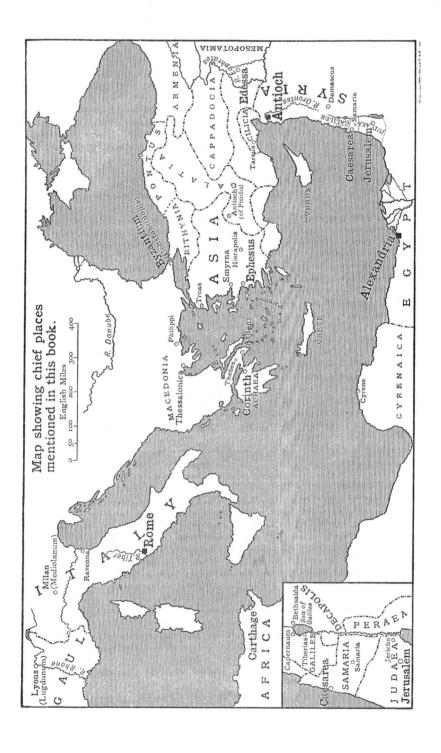

Map showing chief places mentioned in this book.

English Miles

0   50   100   200   300   400

PART I

THE MANUSCRIPT TRADITION

(I) THE THEORY OF "LOCAL TEXTS"

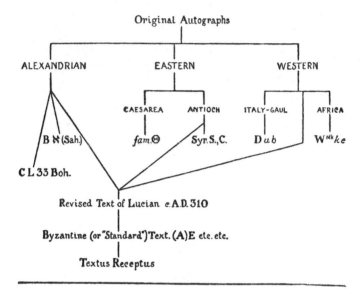

Original Autographs

ALEXANDRIAN   EASTERN   WESTERN

CAESAREA   ANTIOCH   ITALY-GAUL   AFRICA

B ℵ (Sah.)   *fam.*Θ   Syr.S.,C.   D *a b*   W *ᴺᵏ k e*

C L 33 Boh.

Revised Text of Lucian *c.* A.D. 310

Byzantine (or "Standard")Text. (A)E etc. etc.

Textus Receptus

(II) WESTCOTT & HORT'S THEORY

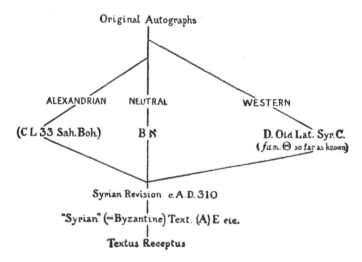

Original Autographs

ALEXANDRIAN   NEUTRAL   WESTERN

(C L 33 Sah.Boh.)   B ℵ   D. Old Lat. Syr.C.
                                                (*fam.* Θ so far as known)

Syrian Revision *c.* A.D. 310

"Syrian" (=Byzantine) Text. (A) E etc.

Textus Receptus

II

LOCAL AND STANDARD TEXTS

SYNOPSIS

A Bird's Eye View

The Received Text represents approximately the Byzantine text found in the majority of MSS. But the earliest MSS. and Versions afford evidence of the existence at an early date of a number of local texts, differing considerably from one another, which in the course of time were gradually submerged by the Byzantine standard text. Recent discovery and investigation necessitates considerable modifications of the theories put forward by Westcott and Hort.

(1) The two oldest MSS., B ℵ (on which W.H. mainly based their edition of the Greek Testament), represent the local text of Alexandria.

(2) What is called the " Western " text is really not a single text, but a group of distinct local texts within which an Eastern type (with two sub-varieties current in Antioch and Caesarea respectively) must be clearly distinguished from the Western type (used with some slight differences in Africa and Italy).

The materials for the textual criticism of the Gospels contrasted with those available for classical authors. Note on von Soden's edition.

Local Texts

Brief survey of the conditions of copying and correcting MSS. which led to the development of local texts. The maximum of divergence between local texts probably reached c. A.D. 200. This is reflected in the oldest Latin, Syriac and Egyptian Versions.

The great majority of various readings are, in regard to points of grammar, order of words, etc., so small as to make no essential difference to the sense ; but for the identification of the various local texts, the concurrence in a group of MSS. of a large number of these minute variants is of chief significance. Large omissions or interpolations, though more striking, are for this purpose less important, since in the period when the churches were comparing different texts and correcting one by another, the more conspicuous variants would be the first

27

to attract attention, and would thus be adopted from one text into another.

STANDARDISATION

As Constantinople came more and more to dominate the Greek-speaking Church, MSS. representing the old local texts were gradually by a series of corrections brought into conformity with the Byzantine standard text. An analogy from the history of ancient liturgies. Similarly MSS. of the Old Latin version were corrected into conformity with the revised version produced by Jerome at the command of Pope Damasus in 381. The result of this standardising process was the production of " mixed " texts, *i.e.* of MSS. in which one set of readings survive from ancestors representing an old local text, while others agree with the standard text. In mixed MSS. the only readings that need be noticed are those which differ from the standard text.

THE FATHERS AND THE STANDARD TEXT

Since later scribes who copied the works of the Fathers were themselves familiar with the standard text of the Gospels, there was an inevitable tendency for them to correct quotations from the Gospels occurring in an early Father so as to make them conform to the standard text. Two striking illustrations of this process. It follows that when in the printed editions of an early Father (few Fathers have been critically edited from the best MSS.) a quotation from the Gospels is found to agree with the Byzantine text against the local text which that Father elsewhere seems to use, there is a presumption against that particular reading being what that Father originally wrote ; it is more likely to be the result of a scribal correction in the MS. of the Father.

AN ILLUSION ABOUT MSS.

The distinction between MSS. written in uncial (*i.e.* capital) letters, or in a cursive (*i.e.* small running) hand, in no way corresponds to a difference in their value to the textual critic. Many cursives are quite as important as any uncials after the first five, אBLDΘ ; the practice of citing uncials by a capital letter, cursives by a number, makes the difference between them appear far greater than it really is. After A.D. 600 MSS. with a substantial mixture of the old local texts were rarely copied except in out-of-the-way places or by some accident, and this might occur at quite a late date ; also a late cursive may be a direct copy of an early uncial. Of special interest are 33, 579 (allies of B א) ; also 1, 28, 565, 700, and the " Ferrar Group " (13 &c.), which, together with Θ, form a family (*fam.* Θ) preserving the text of Caesarea.

CHAPTER II

LOCAL AND STANDARD TEXTS

A BIRD'S EYE VIEW

To those who read the Gospels in order to obtain a general
idea of the life and teaching of Christ, or who value them mainly
for devotional purposes, it makes very little difference whether
they use the Authorised or the Revised Version. All they want
the textual critic to tell them is within what limits of error the
text of either version represents what the authors wrote. Any one,
however, who wishes to study the subtler shades of meaning in
particular passages, or who is interested in the evidence for every
detail of the life and teaching of our Lord, will be more exact-
ing, and will demand the most accurate text that a scientific
study of the MSS. can produce ; while to the student of the
Synoptic Problem, endeavouring by a microscopic comparison of
the Gospels to determine the sources which their authors used, the
minutest variant may be of the utmost significance. Indeed, as
will appear in a later chapter, it is precisely because most writers
on the Synoptic Problem have been content to use without
question *Synopses* of the Gospels in Greek, based either on the
text of Tischendorf or on that of Westcott and Hort, that a
completely satisfactory explanation of the relation of Matthew
and Luke to Mark has not sooner been attained.

The facts which constitute the main difficulty in our quest
for the original text may be summed up in a paragraph.

There are over twelve hundred manuscripts of the Gospels in

Greek, beginning with the eighth century MS. commonly cited as
E, which present a text of a remarkably uniform character. This
text was named by Griesbach the " Byzantine text "—a name
preferable to that of " Syrian " given it by Hort, since, whatever
its origin, it was indubitably the standard text of the Byzantine
Empire all through the Middle Ages. In sharp contrast to the
general uniformity of the Byzantine text is the extent of variation exhibited by the half-dozen Greek MSS. that survive from
the fourth and fifth centuries, and by the Greek texts underlying the Old Latin, the Old Syriac and the older Egyptian,
Versions, of which we possess MSS. of an equally early date.
Of the six oldest Greek MSS. only one, A, has a text that in all four
Gospels approximates to the Byzantine standard. The other five,
ℵ B C D W,[1] and the three ancient Versions just mentioned have
texts which differ to a remarkable extent both from one another
and from the Byzantine text. What is even more significant—
the quotations from the Gospels made by all Christian writers up
to about A.D. 360 almost invariably agree with one or other of
these older MSS. or Versions rather than with the Byzantine text.

Thus there is forced upon our notice evidence that in the
earlier period there was great diversity between the texts of the
New Testament current in the Church—a diversity which was
succeeded later on by a high degree of uniformity. We notice
at once an analogy between the history of the text and that of
the settlement of the canon and the formulation of doctrine.
Here, as elsewhere, the final result, it would seem, is a standardisation of an earlier variety.

The problems which the textual critic has to solve are three.
(1) He must account for the great divergence between the types
of text current in the second, third and fourth centuries.
(2) He must explain the origin of the Byzantine standard text
and the process by which it replaced the other types. (3) Finally,
in the light of the conclusions reached on these two points, he

---

[1] I accept the date (fifth century) assigned to D, the Codex Bezae, by
F. C. Burkitt and E. A. Loew. Cf. *J.T.S.*, July 1902 and April 1913.

must endeavour to determine which of these types of text, or
what kind of combination of them, will represent most nearly
the text of the Gospels as they left the hands of their several
authors. The third problem is of course much the most important; but he cannot hope to solve it rightly unless he has
first found a reasonably satisfactory solution to the other two.
The relation of our printed Greek Testaments and of the
English versions to the types of text found in the MSS. may be
summarily stated in a very few words. Erasmus was the first
to produce an edition of the Greek Testament in print; a
subsequent revision of his edition by the Paris printer Stephanus,
1550, became the standard printed text or Textus Receptus.
Readings of this text are commonly cited by the abbreviation
T.R. or the Greek letter ς (= st). Since both Erasmus and
Stephanus used (all but exclusively) late Byzantine MSS., the
English Authorised Version, which was translated from the Textus
Receptus, represents a late stage of the Byzantine text. On the
other hand, in the great critical editions of Westcott and Hort
and Tischendorf the Byzantine tradition is entirely abandoned
and the text is based almost entirely on the two oldest MSS. of
all, B (Vaticanus) and ℵ (Sinaiticus)—of which the first probably, the second possibly, dates from the reign of Constantine
(d. A.D. 337). Where these two MSS. differ, Westcott and Hort
usually follow B; Tischendorf more often prefers ℵ (Aleph), his
own discovery. The "Revisers' text," from which the Revised
Version was translated, and which is published by the Oxford
University Press, represents a compromise, on the whole a very
reasonable one, between the views of Hort, who championed a
text based on B, and those of the more conservative members
of the Committee who defended the Byzantine text.

At that time neither party was concerned to put in a plea
for any readings (except a few omissions) supported only by D
(Codex Bezae), by the then known MSS. of the Old Latin and
Old Syriac version, or by certain late Greek MSS. exhibiting texts
of an unusual type. These authorities were all lumped together

under the general name of the "Western text," and their readings were treated as interesting eccentricities. But investigations by more recent scholars and fresh discoveries—of which the Sinaitic Syriac (Syr. S.), the Koridethi MS. Θ, the Freer MS. W, and 700 are the most notable—have changed this. (1) It is now generally realised that B ℵ represent, not, as Hort held, some almost impeccable "Neutral" text connected with no particular locality, but the text of Alexandria in its purest form. (2) The question has been raised whether, under the misleading name "Western," Griesbach and Hort did not group together what in reality are several distinct local texts.

In Chapters III. and IV. I shall submit an outline of the evidence which compels us to recognise in what they called the "Western" text two distinct types, an Eastern and a strictly (in a geographical sense) Western text. Each of these types can be further divided into at least two distinct local texts. Indeed it can, I think, be shown that recently discovered MSS., if properly used, enable us to get a fairly clear idea of the different types of text current about A.D. 230, not only in Alexandria, but in Caesarea and Antioch in the East, and in Italy and Carthage in the West.

If this is established, obviously the basis of evidence on which the text of the Gospels rests is greatly widened. Of these five early local texts that of Alexandria (B ℵ) is, as we should expect from the tradition of textual scholarship native to the place, undoubtedly the best; but no MS. and no line of textual tradition is infallible, and it will not infrequently appear that the true reading of a particular passage, lost at Alexandria, has been preserved in one or other of the rival texts.

It is, however, quite impossible for the student to interpret rightly the evidence by which the identification of local texts is achieved unless he has previously considered (a) the conditions which originally gave rise to the existence of these local texts, and (b) the exact nature of that process of progressive correction into conformity with the Byzantine standard text to which many of our most important authorities have been subjected. The present chapter, therefore, will be mainly devoted to a discussion of these two points.

In the field of classical literature the main difficulty of the textual critic, except in the case of a few extremely popular authors like Homer or Virgil, is the paucity and late date of MSS. No portion of Tacitus, for example, survived the Dark Ages in more than one ; and the number of famous works of which, apart from Renaissance reproductions, there are less than half a dozen MSS. is very large. Again, apart from fragments, there are no MSS. of the Greek classics earlier than the ninth century, and very few older than the twelfth. The student of the text of the Gospels is confronted with a difficulty of an opposite character. There are more than 1400 Greek MSS., about forty of which are more than a thousand years old ; there are over 1300 Lectionaries which contain the greater part of the text of the Gospels arranged as lessons for the year ; there are fifteen Versions in ancient languages, which are evidence of the Greek text used by their translators. In addition, there are innumerable quotations by early Fathers, which are, in effect, fragments of other early MSS. now lost. The mass of material to be considered is crushing. The consequences of this are twofold. On the one hand the degree of security that, in its broad outlines, the text has been handed down to us in a reliable form is *prima facie* very high. On the other, the problem of sorting the material in order to determine those minuter points which interest the critical student is proportionately complex—how complex is only known to those who have given considerable attention to the study. Nevertheless so much has been accomplished in this way by the labours of generations of scholars, that it is now possible—if we disregard minor issues and accept as provisionally established certain conclusions to which a minority of experts might demur—to present " a bird's eye view " of the history of the text, which will be both intelligible to the plain man and at the same time in principle scientific. Such a view will be in one

D

sense a further development of, in another an attempt to supersede, the theory put forward by Westcott and Hort in the
Introduction to their famous edition of the Greek Testament.
Thus it will frequently be necessary to criticise certain of the
views of Hort—by whom that Introduction was written. I
wish, therefore, once and for all to affirm that this implies no
undervaluing of the truly epoch-making character of the work of
that great scholar. There is no greater name in the history of
Textual Criticism. But for Hort, no such thing as what I am
here attempting would be possible ; and such modification of
his views as seems to be necessary is mainly due to discoveries
made since the time he wrote.[1]

[1] Of the views of H. von Soden it is impossible to speak in such terms as
I should wish, retaining, as I do, pleasant recollections of a personal interview
with him a few years before his tragic death. Soden had at his disposal a large
sum of money given to enable him to employ numerous assistants, in order to
scour the libraries of the East for MSS. hitherto either unknown or not carefully
examined ; but unfortunately not much of the first importance was discovered.
The Byzantine text he styles **K** (= κοινή), the Alexandrian **H** (= Hesychian);
all other authorities, whether Eastern or Western, are assigned to an **I**
(= Jerusalem) text. In Chapter IV. I shall attempt to discriminate between
the almost equally balanced elements of truth and falsehood in his conception
of an **I** text.

In his colossal Introduction he has succeeded in illuminating the grouping of
late MSS. and the history of the Byzantine text. But his theories of the influence
of Tatian and of a II[cent.] I—H—K text are, if I may borrow a phrase once
used by Dr. Sanday, "not only wrong but wrong-headed." I am informed
by one of the leading scholars in Germany that Soden's theories, in so far
as they are original, are universally rejected in that country, and that his
grouping of the MSS. is considered arbitrary. Of his cumbrously conceived
attempt to introduce an entirely new naming and numbering of the MSS. I
need say nothing, as the vast majority of scholars in Europe and America
have agreed that they will not accept it, but will henceforth use Gregory's
revision of the old notation. Advanced students, however, must have some
acquaintance with his views, for without that the Apparatus Criticus of his
edition cannot be deciphered, much less understood. They should, however,
be warned that it is very inaccurate. (On this point there is some damaging
evidence in the Introduction to the "New Collation of Codex 22" by Prof. H. A.
Sanders, *Journal of Biblical Studies*, xxxiii. p. 91 ff.) Such students I would refer
to an invaluable pamphlet by Prof. K. Lake, *Prof. H. von Soden's Treatment
of the Text of the Gospels* (Otto Schultze, Edin. ; a reprint of articles in
Review of Theology and Philosophy, Oct.-Nov. 1908). This paper gives an
extremely clear account of Soden's grouping of the MSS. and a sympathetic
exposition of his very complicated views, followed by a very courteous but, in
effect, annihilating criticism of them.

LOCAL TEXTS

The invention of printing made it possible that every copy of a book should be exactly the same. This was a new thing in the history of literature. So long as books were copied by hand, no two copies could be *exactly* the same; every copy included certain scribal errors. In the scriptoria of the great libraries it was customary in antiquity for a corrector, διορθωτής, to go over a MS., sometimes with the original from which it was copied, more often, apparently, with another copy. The most obvious mistakes, including accidental omissions, would thus to a large extent be rectified. But this is unlikely to have been done in the earliest MSS. of the Gospels, which would be cheap copies and often made by amateur scribes. In that case an error which made nonsense or spoilt the grammar of a sentence would be subsequently corrected by the owner of the book—probably, from lack of another copy, by conjecture. If, however, the error was one which left a reading which still made sense, it would be likely to escape notice altogether. In either case the new reading would be reproduced by all subsequent scribes who used this copy as an exemplar. Now as soon as there were numerous copies of a book in circulation in the same area, one copy would constantly be corrected by another, and thus within that area a general standard of text would be preserved. But what we have to consider is that it is unlikely that the errors in the first copy of the Gospel of John, for example, which reached Rome would be the same as those in the first copy which came to Alexandria; and as each of these would become the parent of most other copies used in those respective cities, there would, from the very beginning, be some difference between the local texts of Rome and Alexandria.

Once the Gospels were regarded as inspired, they were copied with scrupulous accuracy and by the most skilful scribes available. But during the first and most of the second century they would be, for the most part, copied by amateurs—for Christians were a poor community and a secret society under the ban of the police. It was during this period that all the really important various readings arose. Both insertion and omission would be more possible then than at a later date. For, on the one hand, it was a time when incidents or sayings not included in the original Gospels would still survive in oral tradition, and when their inclusion in a text not yet regarded as sacred would be least resented. On the other hand, accidental omissions—the commonest of all errors in copying, whether in ancient or modern times—would most easily become permanent ; for at a period when the churches were relatively isolated, a passage once omitted from the earliest copy which reached a particular church would not for a long while, if ever, be replaced. This is the explanation of what is the most conspicuous difference between one text and another, that caused by the presence in some MSS. of sentences or paragraphs not found in others. Of these variants the so-called Pericope Adulterae, *i.e.* the story of the woman taken in adultery (Jn. vii. 53 ff.), and the last twelve verses of Mark are much the most considerable ; but there are quite a number of other interesting passages, from half a verse to a couple of verses in extent, which are found in some MSS., but omitted in others. The textual critic is called upon to decide in each particular case whether the reading is the result of accidental omission in the texts which lack, or of interpolation in the texts which contain, these passages. The principles on which such decisions can be made will be discussed later.

But variants of this kind, though the most conspicuous, are not the most important to the critic who is seeking to identify early local texts, for the simple reason that they are so conspicuous that they would be the first passages to strike the eye of later scribes or editors who wished to correct or supplement their own text by that of another church. A convincing proof that a group of MSS. represents the text of a particular locality is only forthcoming if they are found to concur in a large number of minor variants which are either not found at all or found but rarely in other MSS.

For a discussion, with illustrative examples, of the causes and exact character of these minor variants I refer the reader to Appendix I., "The Origin of Variants." In this place I need only say that the number of such variants is immense. Between the Textus Receptus and Westcott and Hort, that is, practically between the Byzantine text and that of B, there are, in the Gospels alone, about 4000 differences.[1] And the number of differences between the text of B and that of D would, I imagine, be quite twice as many. But no less remarkable is the infinitesimal character of the vast majority of these differences. For the most part they consist in variations in the relative order of words in a sentence, in the use of different prepositions, conjunctions and particles, in differences in the preposition with which verbs are compounded, or in slight modifications of a grammatical nature.[2] Indeed the great majority of them cannot be represented in an English translation.

The main influences which operate to produce differences of text are illustrated by the passages discussed in Appendix I. These are all influences which would operate in every locality. Where a change would effect an obvious grammatical improvement or tend to assimilate the text of one Gospel to another, the same alteration might easily be made independently in two different neighbourhoods. But only rarely would any of the other causes of corruption result in a coincident alteration of exactly the same kind along two different lines of textual transmission. On the contrary, corruption as a rule causes texts to become in the course of time more and more different. In this way local texts would inevitably develop, not only in the greater,

[1] Any one who would like to study these may find a collation of the two texts in W. Sanday, *Appendices ad Novum Testamentum*, Oxford, 1889.

[2] Such phenomena are by no means confined to the text of the New Testament. They are a conspicuous feature of the texts of the Fathers; they are found, though to a much less extent, in the texts of some classical writers. See the remarks about MSS. of Augustine quoted by F. G. Kenyon, *The Textual Criticism of the New Testament* (Macmillan, 1912), p. 355 note.

but also in the smaller centres of Christianity. But, along with a growing veneration for the text as that of inspired Scripture, there would come a tendency, whenever a new copy of the Gospels for official use in the public services was wanted, to lay more and more stress on the importance of having an accurate text. This would naturally result in the smaller churches obtaining new copies from the greater metropolitan sees, since these would be thought likely to possess a pure text. From these any copies in private hands in the smaller churches would be corrected. Thus the local texts of smaller churches would tend to become assimilated to those of the greater centres in their immediate neighbourhood. The next stage would be for the great churches to compare their texts and endeavour to reach a standard text which would be universally accepted.

To this process the history of the text of Homer, obscure though it is in certain ways, presents some analogies. The quotations of ancient authors and the earliest papyrus fragments attest readings not found in the κοινή, or standard text, which has come down to us ; and grammarians often cite readings of other texts which are described as κατὰ πόλεις, that is, apparently, local texts once current in certain famous cities.

In the light of these antecedent probabilities we should expect to find the maximum of diversity between local texts of the Gospels in the early part of the third century. After that date, with the increasing possibilities of communication between churches and the rapid spread of Christianity among the more educated classes, there would gradually arise a demand for a standard text. All the evidence points in this direction. The oldest Greek MSS., the oldest versions, the quotations of the oldest Fathers, all attest diversity. Scholars like Rendel Harris, Chase and Hoskier have made ingenious attempts to discount the evidence of the ancient Versions and to discredit, as due to retranslation, the text of the Greek MSS. like D or B which are most closely allied to them. Such attempts are inspired by the assumption, only half conscious but wholly fallacious, that

at the beginning of the third century there was anything
approaching a uniform Greek text in use throughout the Church.
On the contrary, antecedent probability and the evidence of
Patristic quotations alike point to the period ± A.D. 200, when
the older Versions were produced, as that of maximum local
diversity. And it is precisely because they preserve this diversity
that these versions are of primary importance to the critic as
evidence for the older local texts.

The ultimate aim of textual criticism is to get back behind
the diverse local texts to a single text, viz. to that which the
authors originally wrote. But the high road to that conclusion
is first to recover the local texts of the great churches, and then
to work back to a common original that will explain them all.

STANDARDISATION

The Byzantine text, we shall see later, most probably originated in a revision based on older local texts made by Lucian of
Antioch about A.D. 300. The fact of such revision, and still more
the precise relation of it to the older texts, is a matter on which
opinions may differ. What is not open to question is that this
type of text, whatever its origin and whatever its value, did
gradually oust all other types and become the standard text
in the Greek-speaking Church. It is therefore important to
recognise the difference which the invention of printing has made
in the mechanism, so to speak, of the process by which a standard
text can be introduced where it was not previously in use. If
the proper authorities in the Church of England should decide
that henceforth the Lessons be read from the Revised Version
instead of from the Authorised, the change would for the most
part be made in three months. A certain number of clergy
might resist it ; in that case, some churches would henceforth
be using the one version, and some the other. But by no
possibility could a *mixed version* be anywhere used. In antiquity
it was just the reverse. From the end of the third century the

relatively cheap papyrus roll was replaced by the magnificent "codex" (*i.e.* MS. in book form) written on parchment. It was not practicable, except in the largest cities, to discard the Bibles already in use and obtain new ones. No doubt this would be done in the great cathedrals and in the larger monasteries. Elsewhere existing MSS. would be corrected more or less carefully from some copy of the standard text—much as an incumbent is still legally bound to correct the copies of the Prayer Book belonging to the parish, when the names in the prayers for the King and Royal Family require to be changed on the accession of a new monarch. This is no mere conjecture. In some of our oldest MSS. we can see the process actually at work. ℵ, for example, has been corrected by several hands at different dates, and (apart from corrections by the διορθωτής and an all but contemporary scribe) the great majority of corrections are into conformity with the standard text; the same thing holds good of the corrections in W.[1]

Doubtless the wealthier and more important churches or monasteries would get from Antioch or Constantinople completely new copies of the approved text. Bishops and priests in smaller towns would bring their old MSS. with them next time they had occasion to visit the provincial capitals and take the opportunity of making the necessary corrections. Let us suppose that the text of the Gospels in a particular city or monastery was of the B type, and that the Bishop or Archimandrite, on a visit to Constantinople, wished to correct it to the standard text. He would bring his own copy with him and tell off one of his attendant priests or monks to collate it with the model. Two-thirds of the 4000 or more differences which the microscopic eye of a Tischendorf, trained by a lifetime of such comparison, would detect, this man would never notice. Of the

---

[1] This can be conveniently verified in Scrivener's *A Full Collation of the Codex Sinaiticus* (Cambridge, 1864), *passim*, and in H. A. Sanders, *The N.T MSS. in the Freer Collection* (Macmillan Co., New York, 1912), pp. 31, 36.

rest, at least half would seem to him too unimportant to record, since they make no real difference to the sense.   If the corrector were more than usually careful, and had plenty of leisure for the work, he might make 500 corrections ; if careless or pressed for time, perhaps only 50.   The copy thus corrected would be taken back ; and from it other local copies would be made, *embodying these corrections in the text.*   What then would be the character of the resultant text ?   It would be a *mixed text*, some of its readings being Alexandrian, others Byzantine.   Some actual examples of mixed texts of this type are discussed below (p. 61 ff.) and in Ch. IV.

This sort of thing would be going on everywhere ; but the results would differ in every case.   For instance, a priest from another town might also bring a B text to be corrected ; but the list of differences which he happened to notice, or to think worth correcting, would be quite a different one.   This time the resultant text, although equally a mixture of B and the standard text, would be a *different* mixture.   Again, from other centres the MSS. brought for correction might be of one of the types of text commonly called " Western."   Descendants of these MSS., as corrected, would show a mixture of " Western " and Byzantine readings.   And now suppose that, a century or so later, some conscientious bishop or monk arose who again compared his partially corrected local text by the Byzantine standard.   The same process would be repeated ; but it would result in a still further diminution of the Alexandrian or " Western " elements in the text current in that locality.   Since this process of successive standardisation was going on for centuries, the remains of the pre-Byzantine texts would gradually get revised away.

In the later period of classical antiquity a text more or less pure of the great authors was preserved by the tradition of scrupulous accuracy and careful correction maintained in the great libraries—especially that of Alexandria.   And, as every one who wanted a good text resorted to these centres, a standard text gradually supplanted that of cheap popular copies.   In the

Middle Ages the library tradition passed to some of the greater monasteries, and doubtless this had a similar effect in fixing and propagating the standard text. Thus after the eighth century it was only here and there, in small monasteries in remote districts, that MSS. would be copied which still contained a substantial proportion of readings characteristic of the older texts.

According to Hort there are (not counting fragments) only three MSS., B, ℵ and D, which have altogether escaped some measure of correction to the Byzantine standard; and it is significant that two of them are a century older than any others. It is also noticeable that D was written by an ill-educated scribe, and that the same thing applies to other important MSS. with a large non-Byzantine element, e.g. L, Δ, 28 and, still more conspicuously, Θ. This suggests that they were written in out-of-the-way places, where the Byzantine text had not yet penetrated or had only recently done so. Zoology presents us with an analogy; the last survivors of species, once widely prevalent but now on the way to extinction, are found in remote and isolated spots.

The slow and haphazard working of this process of standardisation explains the comparative failure of any standard revision of the Old Testament to oust the older texts. In the first place, anxiety to correct and recorrect, in the endeavour to attain what was regarded as the purest text, would be much less acute for the Old Testament than the Gospels.[1] Secondly, the Old Testament being so much longer, and therefore so much more expensive to copy, than the New, many even of the cathedrals and larger monasteries would prefer to correct old, rather than to purchase new, copies. Thirdly, only selections of the Old Testament were

---

[1] The reputation of Origen's *Hexapla*, a work we shall speak of later (p. 111 f.), which was preserved at Caesarea till the city was sacked by the Saracens, made that, as the scholia prove, an alternative to the revision of Lucian of Antioch as a standard of correction. The majority of MSS. of the LXX give a mixed text; though it is believed that in B we have an early Alexandrian, in a few other MSS. a text derived from the *Hexapla*, in rather more the text of Lucian, and in some few a text which is thought to represent the revision by Hesychius alluded to by Jerome.

LOCAL AND STANDARD TEXTS

read in the Church services, and for this purpose Lectionaries were used. The complete Old Testament was a work of reference for theologians, copies of it not being subject to the wear and tear of daily use lasted a long while. Indeed this is the probable explanation of the fact that, although MSS. containing the whole New Testament are comparatively rare and MSS. containing the whole of the Old Testament rarer still, of our five oldest MSS., four, B ℵ A C, originally contained the whole Bible. There must always have been an overwhelming proportion of MSS. containing the four Gospels only ; but, while most early copies of the Gospels were worn out by constant use, the four great Bibles survived because they were kept in libraries as works of reference.

To this standardisation of the text of the New Testament there is an illuminating parallel in the history of the Greek liturgies during the same period. In the sixth centuries the Patriarchates of Antioch and Alexandria had each its own liturgy, known respectively by the names of St. James and St. Mark ; and there were various other local rites in use. But gradually the later Byzantine rite superseded all others within the remains of the old empire. Then the churches of Syria and Egypt, which survived under Mohammedan rule, gradually assimilated the Liturgies of St. James and St. Mark to the Byzantine standard. Thus all the surviving Greek texts of these liturgies have been, to a large extent, standardised. But the original form can be recovered by means of the vernacular liturgies of the Syriac and Coptic churches.[1] It is an interesting reflexion that, had no Greek MSS. earlier than the tenth century survived, we should in the same way be dependent on Latin, Syriac, and Coptic translations for our knowledge of the older forms of the text of the Greek Testament.

Precisely the same process of standardisation can be traced in the Latin church. In 381 Jerome was commissioned by Pope Damasus to produce a revised translation of the New Testament

---

[1] Cf. F. E. Brightman, *The English Rite*, i. p. xx ff. (Rivington, 1915).

in order to remedy the confusion arising from the great diversity in the text and renderings of the Old Latin version at that time current. Two years later his translation of the Gospels was formally presented to the Pope as a first instalment. Revised versions are rarely popular at first, and for some little time copies of the old version continued to be reproduced. Indeed, Pope Gregory, writing in 595, lays down [1] that both versions are recognised by the Catholic Church. Gradually, however, the text of Jerome's translation, which we know as " the Vulgate," prevailed. But its influence spread quite as much through the correction of old copies by the new standard as by the substitution of new text for old. The result is that we have a number of MSS. the text of which is a mixture, in varying proportions, of Old Latin and of Vulgate elements. Indeed, just as the Greek Textus Receptus includes certain readings (e.g. the Pericope in John) which, though found in some pre-Byzantine MSS., are absent from the earliest MSS. of the Byzantine text, so in the " received " text of the Vulgate certain Old Latin readings are found which Jerome had discarded. Fortunately, however, our MSS. of the Vulgate are so numerous and ancient that the text of the version as it left Jerome's hands can be recovered with approximate certainty. This has been done in the magnificent edition of Wordsworth and White. With a copy of this edition in his hands, the student can readily distinguish in any mixed MS. the readings characteristic of the Old Latin.

We may now formulate a canon of criticism of the first importance. *Of MSS., whether Greek or Latin, later than the fifth century, only those readings need be noted which differ from the standard text.* That does not mean that readings of the Byzantine Greek or the Vulgate Latin are necessarily wrong ; most of them are to be found in one or other of the earlier texts. It means that, since the authorities for any reading

---

[1] " Sedes apostolica, cui auctore Deo praesideo, utraque utitur (v.l. utrique nititur)," *Moralia in Job*, Pref. Ep. *ad fin.*   It is possible, however, that Gregory's remark only applies to the Old Testament.

adopted in the standard text number in Greek twelve hundred, in Latin five thousand, a few hundred more or less makes no difference. But, as will shortly appear, our knowledge of the earlier types of text current in the East, not counting Egypt, depends mainly on the fragments of older MSS. which survive in mixed texts, and these fragments can only be identified by noting those readings which differ from the standard text.

The Fathers and the Standard Text

The standard text has also influenced the textual tradition of quotations from the New Testament in the works of the Greek and Latin Fathers. As a general rule it may be laid down that in late and inferior MSS. of the Fathers the Biblical quotations accord much more closely with the Byzantine text or the Latin Vulgate, as the case may be, than in good or early MSS. That is to say, that same process of assimilating earlier texts to the later standard, which we find in our MSS. of the Gospels, can also be traced in the quotations from the Gospels found in the works of the Fathers. Seeing that quotations by early Fathers are the principal means by which we identify and localise the type of texts found in pre-Byzantine or pre-Vulgate MSS., this consideration is of great importance. It may be illustrated by a concrete example. Hort had detected a connection between the text of the Old Latin Codex Bobiensis, known as *k*, and the text of Cyprian. Dr. Sanday pressed the investigation a stage further. Working from the printed texts of Cyprian he found that, in general, the quotations of Cyprian agreed with *k* ; but, especially in the work entitled *Testimonia*, they frequently agreed with the Vulgate against *k*. He noticed, however, that in a number of cases when a quotation in the *Testimonia* agreed with the Vulgate, the same quotation occurred in other works of Cyprian in a form which agreed with *k*. Pursuing the subject further he studied the MSS. of the works in question, and made the illuminating discovery that the quotations as given in one group of MSS.

accorded with the text of *k*. The MS. which had been followed in Hartel's edition of Cyprian had suffered some correction from the standard text.[1] A precisely similar thing happened in regard to the recently recovered *Expositions of XIII. Epistles of St. Paul* by Pelagius. The first MS. identified gave an almost pure Vulgate text, which led one famous scholar to conjecture that the Vulgate revision of the Epistles was the work of Pelagius, not of Jerome. Subsequently the Balliol MS. of the commentary was discovered, in which the text commented on by Pelagius is clearly not the Vulgate, but the Old Latin.[2]

For a very large number of the Fathers the only printed texts available are the Benedictine editions or the reprint by Migne. These are frequently based on late MSS. Hence confidence can be placed in their texts of the quotations from the Gospels in the earlier Fathers only where these give a reading which differs from the standard text. I give an illustration of this from Origen's *Commentary on Matthew*—a work I shall have occasion to refer to again. Origen quotes Mt. xxvi. 3-5 and then proceeds to comment on the passage. In his quotation according to the Benedictine edition the words "and the scribes" occur, as in the Byzantine text; but his comment makes it clear that these words were absent from the MS. he was using, as they are from B ℵ 1 &c., 13 &c., and many other extant MSS.

The Ante-Nicene Fathers survive in so few MSS. that caution must be exercised even in regard to the texts of those Fathers of whom modern critical editions are available. For example, all our authorities for Origen's *Commentary on John*[3] go back to a single X[cent.] MS. This, on the whole, is a reason-

---

[1] *Old Latin Biblical Texts: No. II.* (Oxford, 1886), p. xliii ff., p. lxii ff., and p. 123 ff.

[2] A. Souter, *Texts and Studies*, ix. 1, p. 157 (Cambridge, 1922).

[3] Of this there are two excellent critical editions, that of A. E. Brooke (Cambridge, 1896), and that of E. Preuschen (Berlin Corpus, 1903). There is no critical text of the equally important *Commentary on Matthew*, the Berlin Corpus not yet having reached this work.

ably good MS., and in this work of his we very rarely find quotations of the Gospels by Origen agreeing with the Byzantine against one or other of the pre-Byzantine texts. This shows that the quotations have suffered very little from scribal assimilation to the standard text ; but it does not constitute even an antecedent presumption that they have not suffered at all. Here and there Origen quotes a verse with a reading characteristic of the Byzantine text. But it is quite unsafe for the critic to build upon these exceptional cases. A tenth-century scribe, presumably a monk, must have known the Gospels—at any rate, Matthew, Luke, and John, from which the Church lessons were mostly taken—almost by heart, and that according to the Byzantine text. However faithfully he tried to copy the text before him, there is always an interval between reading and writing in which, in moments of inadvertence, the human memory has time enough to substitute a familiar for an unfamiliar phrase. Hort was well alive to the danger of taking for granted the texts of the Fathers, but it seems necessary to reiterate the caution since, for all practical purposes, it has been ignored by von Soden, with disastrous consequences to his evaluation of patristic evidence for the pre-Byzantine texts.

AN ILLUSION ABOUT MSS.

The student who desires detailed information about the dates, history, and paleography of individual MSS., I must refer to the standard text-books.[1] But it will be well to begin the discussion of the whole subject by clearing out of the way a misapprehension which has affected the practice, if not the conscious theory, of even distinguished scholars. Before the

---

[1] *E.g.* Sir F. G. Kenyon's *Handbook to the Textual Criticism of the N.T.* (Macmillan, 1912); C. R. Gregory, *Textkritik des N.T.* (Leipzig, 1909); *Eb. Nestles Einführung*—rewritten and brought up to date by E. von Dobschütz (Göttingen, 1923)—is excellent on a smaller scale. A bare list of select MSS., with dates and with von Soden's enumeration, is to be found in the Introduction to A. Souter's edition of the Revisers' Greek Testament, which also has a selected Apparatus Criticus (Oxford, 1910). See also *Index of MSS.*, p. 601 ff.

year A.D. 800 Greek books were written in capital letters or
" uncials," but shortly after that date a " minuscule " or " cursive " hand—previously only used for informal writing—began
to come into use for books also. The modern printed Greek
characters, it may be remarked, bear much the same relation to
this cursive script as printed italics do to ordinary handwriting.
But it took a couple of centuries before the cursive finally supplanted the uncial style, and an actual majority of the uncials
of the Gospels which survive in at all a complete state belong to
this transitional period. Now Greek uncial MSS. are commonly
cited by the capital letters of the English or Greek alphabet,
except the Codex Sinaiticus, to which is assigned the Hebrew א
(aleph). Cursives, on the other hand, are cited by a number.
Now, it is much easier for most people to individualise a MS.
which is cited by a letter. But, through the overlapping of the
English and Greek alphabets, there are only about forty letters
available ; and some of these have been traditionally assigned
to MSS. of the Gospels which are mere fragments. Thus over
1000 MSS. remain to be cited by a number. But, while a letter
has something of the quality of a proper name, a number is a
" mere number." Hence an illusion of the superior importance
of uncial testimony is created, which subtly infects the judgement
and the practice even of commentators and others who should
know better. The illusion is fostered by the practice, which
on principle I discard, of referring to uncials as MSS., but
to cursives as *mss.* The leading MSS. are B א D ; next in
importance come L and the newly discovered Θ. These five
are all uncials. Again the three V$^{\text{cent.}}$ uncials, A C W, have
from their antiquity claim to special consideration. But there
are several cursives which are quite as important as these
three, and which are of decidedly greater value than any uncial
after the first eight.

A cursive is not necessarily later than an uncial. There is a
curious ninth-century MS. of which the first part (cited as **566**),
containing Matthew and Mark, is written in a cursive hand,

while the second half (cited as Λ) is uncial. To the same century belong 33, "the queen of cursives," one of the main supporters of the B ℵ text; and 565, the gold and purple "Empress Theodora's Codex," the most important ally of Θ, so far as Mark is concerned. These two are actually earlier in date than some, and they contain a more important text than any, of those fifteen uncials which, being designated by the capital letters E F, etc., look so much more impressive in an Apparatus Criticus. Of course the mass of cursives are considerably later than the mass of uncials ; but a notable fact about the authorities for the text of the New Testament is that, once we get past the year 600, the value of a MS. for determining the text is very little affected by the date at which it was written. The explanation of this is that the Byzantine text, except perhaps in Egypt, became more and more the universally accepted standard, and, as we have already pointed out, only in out-of-the-way places, or by some oversight, could a MS. which did not (as regards the bulk of its readings) conform to this type be copied without drastic corrections being first made.[1] And when such a MS. did get copied, it was an accident which might occur at practically any date. Thus, to take an extreme instance, the readings of the XV[cent.] Leicester cursive 69—one of the best representatives of the so-called "Ferrar Group" (13 &c.)—are of the greatest interest to critics. It seems to have been copied from an ancient uncial surviving in a monastery in S. Italy which had long lost

---

[1] An apparent exception is the specially fine illuminated XII[cent.] MS. 157. The text of this, regarded by Hort as the cursive next in importance to 33, cannot be due to an oversight, since it was written for the reigning Emperor. It is to be explained, I believe, by the colophons at the end of all four Gospels stating that it was "copied and corrected from ancient exemplars from Jerusalem preserved on the Holy Mountain." As the same colophons are found also in the much older MS. Λ-566, they must have been in the ancestor from which 157 was copied. I suggest that a mediaeval Emperor seeing or hearing of a MS. purporting to represent the old text of Jerusalem might well wish to possess a copy, although aware that it differed from the standard text. The "Jerusalem colophon" occurs also in 565, another "imperial" MS., but only after Mark; here, too, it may explain the preservation in that Gospel of an older text. New collation of 157 by Hoskier, *J.T.S.*, xiv. p. 78 ff.

E

contact with the main stream of Greek Christianity. Again, it has been shown [1] that the XIII[cent.] Paris cursive 579 was (in Mk., Lk., Jn.) almost certainly copied directly from a VI[cent.] uncial having a text akin to B ℵ (cf. p. 62). Hence for all practical purposes these late cursives must be treated as if they were among our older uncials. The same thing applies to the XI-XII[cent.] cursives numbered 1, 28 and 700. These, as we shall see later, are—along with Θ 565 and the Ferrar Group— the most important members of the family of MSS. (*fam.* Θ) in which is preserved the ancient text of Caesarea. *The precedence of MSS. depends, not on their age, but on their pedigree.*

[1] **A.** Schmidtke, *Die Evangelien eines alten Unzialcodex* (Leipzig, 1903).

III

THE TEXTS OF THE GREAT SEES

SYNOPSIS

THE VERSIONS AS A CLUE

The antecedent probability that the oldest forms of the Coptic, Latin and Syriac versions were derived respectively from the Greek texts current in Alexandria, Rome and Antioch is confirmed in the first two cases by quotations of early Fathers, in the third by less cogent evidence.

THE TEXT OF ALEXANDRIA

Summary of evidence that B ℵ represent, not what Hort called a " Neutral " text, but the purest type of Alexandrian text.

The text found in Clement, which is largely Western, probably not really Alexandrian. The B ℵ text used in Origen's *Commentary on John* begun at Alexandria before A.D. 230.

Doubt whether the " partially degenerate form of the B text " (found especially in C L and the Bohairic), to which Hort gave the name " Alexandrian," ever existed as a definite recension.

The distinction between degeneration of a text caused (*a*) by scribal blunders or stylistic emendation, which are necessarily wrong readings, (*b*) through infiltration of occasional readings from other ancient local texts, which, in certain cases, may preserve a true reading.

CORRECTED ALEXANDRIAN TEXTS

The survival of B ℵ side by side with certain MSS. which represent the Alexandrian text partially corrected to the Byzantine standard, enables us to study the actual process of standardisation. It appears (*a*) that the revision was often very irregular, (*b*) that the text of Mark has frequently escaped with much less revision than that of the other Gospels. Hence emerges the canon of criticism—

"research into the pedigree of a MS. should begin with the study of its text of Mark."

THE WESTERN TEXT

The Old Latin version survives in some few MSS. in a very pure form, in others with a greater or less amount of correction to the standard of Jerome's Vulgate. There are two main families : (1) the African, best preserved in *k* (shown by Hort and Sanday to preserve the text used by Cyprian of Carthage, *c.* 250) ; (2) the European, of which *b* is the type MS. It is possible that *a* may represent a third local type. The probability is that the African Latin (*k* supported by *e*) was translated from a very old form of the Roman text. The Codex Bezae D for all four Gospels, and the recently discovered W for Mark i.-v. 30, give, roughly speaking, the Greek equivalent of the type of text found in the Old Latin, and in the quotations of Irenaeus of Lyons, *c.* 185.

THE TEXT OF EPHESUS

Our evidence far too scanty to justify a definite conclusion ; but, such as it is, it suggests that the old text of Ephesus may have been allied to that of D.

THE TEXT OF ANTIOCH

The new evidence discovered since Hort wrote makes it possible to make a clear distinction between an Eastern and a Western text. The Old Syriac and the mixed cursives can no longer be treated as authorities for the " Western " text.

Summary of reasons for supposing that the Old Syriac represents approximately the ancient text of Antioch. Relation of this to the later Syriac and to the Armenian versions.

CHAPTER III

THE TEXTS OF THE GREAT SEES

The Versions as a Clue

OUR jumping-off point, so to speak, for a scientific study of the text of the New Testament is the consideration that the churches of Rome, Alexandria and Antioch were the frontier stations of Greek-speaking Christianity. After the fall of Jerusalem, these naturally became the " home base " of missions to the peoples whose native speech was Latin, Coptic or Syriac. This fact facilitates our quest for the early local texts of the Gospels ; for there is obviously a presumption that the Latin, Egyptian and Syriac versions were derived from the Greek texts current respectively in Rome, Alexandria and Antioch. In the case of Rome and Alexandria this is more than a presumption. Marcion *c.* 140, Justin *c.* 150, and Hippolytus *c.* 190–236 wrote in Rome, and Tatian about A.D. 172 compiled the Harmony of the Four Gospels, known as the Diatessaron, either at, or immediately after leaving, Rome. All these wrote theological works in Greek and so presumably read the Gospels in Greek, especially as this was the language of the liturgy of the Roman Church. But their quotations show that the text they used was similar to that which appears in the surviving MSS. of the Old Latin. A similar inference may be drawn from the general coincidence between quotations of the Gospels by Origen, Athanasius and Cyril of Alexandria with the type of text found in the Coptic (*i.e.* Egyptian) versions.

53

Unfortunately we cannot test the early text of Antioch in the same way. Theophilus, A.D. 180, is said to have composed a commentary on the Four Gospels, but in his one surviving work his quotations of them are too rare to be of use to the textual critic ; and the next writer of this church is Chrysostom, 360. Nevertheless reasons, less than demonstrative but still cogent, can be produced in support of the view, in itself antecedently probable, that the Old Syriac approximately represents an early text of Antioch. The identification of the old text of Caesarea, which is the main contribution which I personally have to make to the subject, will be discussed in the following chapter. But in the course of this chapter I venture in regard to the text of Ephesus to put forward a suggestion which avowedly is no more than mere conjecture.

THE TEXT OF ALEXANDRIA

Our first step is to scrutinise the Greek MSS., especially those of early date, to see if the text of any of them exhibits any close connection with that of one or other of the three types which the early versions attest. At once our search is rewarded by the discovery that the text of the two oldest MSS. B ℵ and their VIII[cent.] ally, L, is closely connected with that of the Coptic version —which exists complete in two dialects, the Sahidic and Bohairic —and to that implied in quotations of the New Testament by Origen and Cyril of Alexandria. Moreover, a text identical with that found in ℵ B L is found in the fifth century fragments of Luke and John, known as T. T is bilingual, Graeco-Sahidic, so that this alone would, as it were, anchor this type of text in Egypt. Besides this, papyrus fragments of the third and fourth centuries have been found at Oxyrhynchus agreeing closely with B ℵ,[1] while the text found in later papyri is predominantly,

---

[1] Cf. esp. the fragments of John in *Oxyrhynchus Papyri* 208 and 1781, probable date A.D. 250–300. Though printed in different volumes (ii. and xv.) these are part of the same MS. This is the oldest known MS. of any part of the Gospels and is in book (not roll) form

though not exclusively, of this type.   Additional evidence
may be found in the fact that readings found in the B ℵ text
are sometimes spoken of as "Alexandrian" in the scholia in
certain MSS.[1] Lastly, the readings specially characteristic of
this text are not found in the quotations of any early Fathers
outside Egypt.

Bousset has compiled a series of half a dozen tables of
various readings to illustrate the relation between the text of
ℵ B L and the various Graeco-Sahidic fragments T.   As these
tables also serve to illustrate the relations of ℵ L to one another
and to B, I reproduce the first of them,[2] in which he analyses the
104 variants occurring in the fragment containing Lk. xxii. 20-
xxiii. 20.   The left-hand column shows the number of variants
supported by each of the four MSS.; the others show the
number of times that T is supported by B, ℵ and L respectively.

		B.	ℵ.	L.
B ℵ L T	64	64	64	64
B ℵ T	7	7	7	..
B L T	11	11	..	11
B T	15	15	..	..
ℵ T	4	..	4	..
ℵ L T	1	..	1	1
T	2	..	..	..
Total	104	B T 97	ℵ T 76	L T 76

This table is fairly typical of the series, and it shows not only
the close relation of this group of MSS., but the central position
occupied by B.   When we find that in 97 out of 104 variants the
reading of B has the support of one or more of the other MSS.,

---

[1] *E.g.* in *c*, to Mt. xxv. 1, there is the note, "sponsa non in omnibus
exemplariis invenitur, nominatim in Alexandrino"; to Lk. xxii. 43-44, in
Syr. Hier^mg, "This section is not found in the Gospels among the Alex-
andrians." Cf. Tischendorf, *ad loc.*

[2] W. Bousset, *Textkritische Studien zum Neuen Testament* (Leipzig, 1894),
p. 77.

while there are only five cases in which the others combine against B, the inference that in at least 90 % of its readings B preserves the text of the common ancestor of the group can hardly be resisted.

In 1923 a IV[cent.] MS. of John, representing an older form of the Sahidic, was found in Egypt. Sir Herbert Thompson in his noble facsimile edition (Quaritch, 1924, p. xxvi) shows that this text also is very closely allied to that of B.

The Sahidic, the older of the two complete Egyptian versions, has only recently been made known to the world [1] in a reliable form in the magnificent edition of Dr. Horner, along with the fullest Apparatus Criticus of the Greek text at present available in English. The Sahidic, it is now clear, goes in the main with the B ℵ text; but in an important minority of readings it goes over to the side of the text represented by D and the Old Latin version especially in its African form. From the figures given in Dr. Horner's analysis of readings it would appear (op. cit. iii. p. 387) that for all four Gospels the Sahidic has 505 readings characteristic of D (with or without Latin support) and 157 distinctively Old Latin. The meaning of this " Western" element in the Sahidic cannot be appreciated if considered in isolation. It must be studied in connection with the appearance of Western readings in ℵ, in L, and in the other MSS. which have a text akin to B. Of these the most important are C 33, and, for Mark, Δ Ψ.[2] Again, Dionysius, bishop of Alexandria c. 260, seems also to have used a form of the B text which had an

---

[1] *The Coptic Version of the New Testament in the Southern Dialect, otherwise called Sahidic and Thebaic* (no name), Oxford, Clarendon Press, 1921.

[2] Actually the closest supporters of ℵ B L T are the two fragments Z Ξ, which contain respectively about one-third of the Gospels of Matthew and Luke, Z being nearer akin to ℵ and Ξ to L. C and 33 have a considerable mixture of other texts. With a very much greater amount of mixture the Alexandrian text is preserved in the three cursives, 579, 892 (esp. in Mk.), and 1241 (=Sod. ε 371). A few notable readings of the later Alexandrian type are found in X. Soden, rightly I incline to think, classes 157 with supporters of the " I text." He does the same (here I have not checked him) with the uncial fragments P Q R, except that for John he regards Q as Alexandrian. For 157 see pp. 49 and 76 note. 892 was collated by J. Rendel Harris, *Journal of Biblical Literature*, 1890.

infusion of Western readings. The notable fact, however, is that whenever one or more of these authorities desert B to give a Western reading, almost always there are others of them found ranged in support of B. The natural conclusion to draw from this is that B represents approximately the oldest text of Alexandria, but that at a very early date MSS. with a Western text were in circulation in Egypt. Considering the close connection between Alexandria and Rome, which was mainly dependent on Egypt for its corn supply, there must frequently have been Christians from Rome coming to Egypt on business and bringing with them copies of their Gospels. Odd variants from these would naturally be entered on the margin of local MSS., and would thus creep into the text. But, since this happened in a haphazard way, one set of Western readings would get into one Egyptian MS., a quite different set into another.

To the view that B represents, not merely an Alexandrian text but also the earliest form of such, an objection, at first serious, arises from the Gospel quotations of Clement of Alexandria, 190–200, since these are found to have a specially large infusion of Western readings.[1] It ought not, however, to be taken for granted that these quotations represent an average Alexandrian text of that date. (1) It is thought by some that his extant writings were composed after he had left Alexandria. (2) Clement was not a native of Alexandria, but came there fairly late in life. He had lived for many years in S. Italy. Is it likely that, when he migrated from thence, he left his copy of the Gospels behind ? Clement usually quoted from memory ; now in regard to the vagaries of the human memory an appeal to personal experience is valid. I am myself in the habit of reading the New Testament in the Revised Version, but I was " brought up " on the Authorised, and it is still the version commonly read publicly in the Church of England. As a result of this I find, when revising MS. for the press, that, when I have quoted from memory, the resultant is nearly always a

---

[1] P. M. Barnard in *Texts and Studies*, v. 5 (Cambridge, 1899).

mixture of the old and the new versions. Now, if Clement's own copy of the Gospels represented an early form of Western text but he commonly heard them read in church from a text akin to B, it would be inevitable—seeing that he was apparently not interested in textual criticism—that his quotations would represent now one, now the other, type of text. I would go further and suggest that, as Clement was head of the catechetical school, his pupils would be likely to note on the margins of their own copies notable variants from the master's ; and as these pupils subsequently became leaders of the Church, the readings from their copies would tend to get into the texts used in some of the principal churches. In that case the text of Clement, so far from representing the earliest text of Alexandria, would be a main source of its decline.

But the determining piece of evidence (cf. p. 93 ff.) that the B text represents the early text of Alexandria is its use by Origen in the *earlier* books (the limitation is intentional) of the series of homiletical lectures known as his *Commentary on John*. Of course the MS. used by Origen was not absolutely identical in text with B. No two MSS. are exactly identical. Sometimes Origen agrees with ℵ against B ; more rarely he agrees with one of the other manuscripts belonging to the same family; occasionally he has a reading characteristic of D. The few readings in which he appears to support the Byzantine text may be suspected as probably the result of corruption in the text of our only MS. of this work of his. But, all said and done, it would be safe to say that the manuscript used by Origen for the first ten books of his *Commentary on John* differed from B less than B and ℵ differ from one another. This evidence is highly important for three reasons.

(1) The Fathers, including Origen himself, frequently quote from memory ; but in this work, which contains a long series of quotations from John with a running commentary upon them, we have absolute security that, in regard at any rate to the longer quotations, Origen is not quoting from memory but reproducing a written MS.

(2) Textual criticism belonged to the tradition of Alexandrian scholarship and it was a subject in which Origen himself was supremely interested. He had already spent some years on his famous *Hexapla*—a critical edition of the Greek Old Testament. There is no reason to suppose that at this time he contemplated a critical edition of the New Testament. But it would be incredible that he should not have provided himself with the best text of the Gospels available, before starting his Commentary on them. To an Alexandrian critic the best text meant one based on the oldest MS. procurable. But the oldest MS. which Origen could procure would have gone behind the time of Clement, his immediate predecessor in the Catechetical School. Indeed, its date may well have been nearer the middle than the end of the second century.

(3) We can exactly date the evidence. Origen himself tells us that the first five books of the *Commentary on John* were written before he left Alexandria for good and migrated to Caesarea. This took place in the year 231. We have therefore a fixed point for the textual criticism of the Gospels. The text of the Gospels preserved in B ℵ (practically, that is, the text printed by Westcott and Hort) is to all intents and purposes the text on which Origen lectured in Alexandria in the year 230.

In the quotations of the Alexandrian fathers, especially in Cyril (d. 444), and in the Bohairic version—which on the whole is even closer to B than is the Sahidic—occur a number of readings which look like attempts at grammatical and stylistic improvements of the B text. Readings of this class crop up in all the Alexandrian MSS., except B. Some are found even in ℵ ; but they occur most thickly in L, and next to that in C 33 Ξ Δ$^{Mk.}$ Ψ$^{Mk.}$. An importance greater than either their number or their character deserves was attributed to them by Hort. Hort declined to recognise any connection of B ℵ with Alexandria ; the B ℵ text he named the "Neutral text," and assigned it to no definite locality. And he gave the name "Alexandrian" to a text conceived of as the B text modified by the minor stylistic improvements found in the readings of C L **33**, etc., wherever these differ from both B and the " Western " texts in any readings not also found in the " Syrian " (=Byzantine) text. This so-called " Alexandrian " text he described as " a partially degenerate form of the B text." While admitting that no single MS. preserved this text entire, he ranged it alongside the " Neutral " and " Western " as one of three great families of pre-Byzantine, or, to use his own title, " pre-Syrian," texts. It is generally recognised that this was a mistake. MSS. in which readings of this type are found may well be described in Hort's words as exhibiting " a partially degenerate form of the B text." But all of them include a number of Western readings; and there is no evidence that any MS. ever existed which con tained what Hort calls the " Alexandrian " readings but did *not* also include many Western readings. Nor is it certain that the whole number of the " Alexandrian " readings ever coexisted in any single MS. It is quite as likely that " Alexandrian " stylistic correction and infiltration of Western readings were two concurrent processes gradual in character acting upon individual MSS. in the natural course of textual corruption, and thus affecting different MSS. in different degrees.

If, however, we use a word like " corruption " or " degeneration " in this connection, we must be on our guard against an easy fallacy. Any departures in these MSS. from the B type, which are of the nature of grammatical and stylistic correction, are " corruptions " in the strictest sense of the term ; that is to say, they are alterations, intentional or accidental, of what the original authors wrote. But departures from the B text which consist in the substitution of a reading found in ancient authorities belonging to the Western family are corruptions in a quite different sense. In so far as they are departures from the oldest form of the Egyptian text they are a degeneration *of that particular textual tradition.* But the Western authorities represent a textual tradition of great antiquity belonging to a different locality, and it may well happen that they sometimes preserve a true reading which has been lost in the B text. This is a point on which clear thinking is extremely necessary. To say that the text of B is a purer representative of its type than ℵ is by no means the same thing as saying that it is a purer representative of the original text of the Gospels as the authors wrote it. That is quite a different question. For example, the incident of the Bloody Sweat (Lk. xxii. 43 f.) was, I am inclined to think, in the original copy of Luke's Gospel. If so, ℵ, which contains the passage, preserves the true text; B, which omits it, does not. But a comparison of the MSS. and Versions which contain or reject the passage shows that its absence is characteristic of the particular line of textual transmission which ℵ B on the whole represent. If so, its presence in ℵ is due to "contamination" with a MS. of the "Western" type. But what follows? Whenever ℵ has a "Western" reading, it ceases to be an authority for the Alexandrian text; but it becomes for the time being the oldest Greek MS. with a "Western" text. To put it metaphorically, B is a thoroughbred; ℵ is a cross, but a cross between two thoroughbreds of different stocks. Hence, as evidence for what the authors wrote, the "Western" readings of ℵ are a most valuable authority; but, if we mistake them for evidence of the primitive text of Alexandria, we fall into hopeless confusion. The reader may ejaculate that he is not interested in the primitive text of Alexandria, but only in what the original authors wrote. In textual criticism there are no short cuts; and, since local texts of the Gospels came into existence in the second century, it will not be till we have got back to these in their most primitive form that we have all the materials on which to base our judgement as to what the original authors wrote.

CORRECTED ALEXANDRIAN TEXTS

The fortunate preservation of representatives of the Alexandrian text so ancient and relatively pure as B ℵ presents us with an exceptionally favourable opportunity of studying the phenomenon of correction of MSS. of an ancient local text to the Byzantine standard. It will be instructive to consider some examples of this.

The first point to notice is that correction was often extremely "patchy" and unsystematic. Thus the corrector of א, whom Tischendorf styles א[b], corrected the earlier chapters of Matthew with scrupulous care; but his interest in the work seems to have flagged, and he makes few corrections in the latter part and hardly any in the other Gospels. This actual instance of a corrector's work explains at once a peculiarity of L, an ancestor of which must have suffered a similar fate; for the text of L is almost the Byzantine in Mt. i.-xvii., but it has only a thin sprinkling of Byzantine readings in the latter part of Matthew and in the other Gospels.[1] The V or VI[cent.] correctors of א, however, whom Tischendorf calls א[c] and א[cb], were more systematic than א[b]. Indeed, if א had been copied after these various correctors had finished, the result would have been a mixed text of components and general character very like C, which has a large proportion of Byzantine (and a few miscellaneous) readings in all four Gospels, but more so in Matthew and Luke than in Mark and John.

The XIII[cent.] cursive 579 (cf. p. 50) has in Matthew an ordinary Byzantine text. In the other Gospels, especially in Luke, it has a considerable number of Alexandrian readings. In the Introduction to his edition of this MS., Schmidtke gives a list of readings in which it differs from the Byzantine text in order to support one or other member of the Alexandrian group. On the basis of these lists I have compiled the following figures : agreements with B א, 31 ; with B against א, 132 ; with א against B, 111 ; with one or other of the group C L 33 Δ Ψ 892 against both B and א, 134. We must, however, recollect that the Byzantine text is much more closely allied to the Alexandrian than to the Western. Hence the great majority of the agree-

---

[1] Interesting figures as to Byzantine correction in L, C and Δ may be found in E. A. Hutton, *An Atlas of Textual Criticism*, p. 13 (Cambridge, 1911).

ments of 579 with ℵ B C L 33 are necessarily excluded from a list
of readings which purports to include only differences between
579 and the Byzantine text. Again, many of the readings in
which B ℵ agree against that text are of a conspicuous nature,
and therefore would be particularly likely to attract the notice
of the corrector. Bearing this in mind, the interest of the above
figures is the demonstrative proof they afford that, although the
majority of readings in 579 are in agreement with the Byzantine
text, an ancestor must have been a MS. the text of which stood
right in the middle of the Egyptian group of MSS. The value
of a MS. of this kind appears where it supports a reading of
B, ℵ or L, which otherwise is unsupported. Every MS. has a
larger or smaller number of errors due to mistakes by the scribe
who wrote it or one of its immediate ancestors. Such errors in
no sense constitute readings characteristic of the local text
which the MS. as a whole represents. If, however, a " singular "
reading of any MS. is supported by another MS., which on other
grounds we can connect with the same family, we have sufficient
proof that the reading in question is not an accident or
idiosyncrasy of the particular MS. in which it occurs. If that
MS. happens to be B or ℵ, such support for " singular " readings
is of special interest.

Another point about mixed texts is illustrated from the
Egyptian group. Except in Mark, Δ and Ψ have the ordinary
Byzantine text with a few scattered readings of the later
Alexandrian type ; but in Mark this state of things is exactly
reversed. The fundamental text is the later Alexandrian with
a few scattered Byzantine readings—the proportion of Alexandrian readings in the other Gospels being rather larger
in Ψ than in Δ. If these two MSS. stood alone we should
infer that Mark was copied from an exemplar belonging to a
different family from that used for the other Gospels. But
these two MSS. are only an extreme example of a regularly
recurrent phenomenon. A study of mixed texts belonging to
other families than the Alexandrian shows that it is not the

exception but the rule for the Gospel of Mark to have a much smaller proportion of Byzantine readings than the other Gospels. Nearly every one of the MSS. of which the text is discussed in our next chapter exhibits this—more especially the Codex Theodorae 565. The phenomenon must, therefore, be explained on the hypothesis that these MSS. were copied from exemplars in which the text in all four Gospels had originally been pre-Byzantine, but which had been more thoroughly corrected to the standard text in the first three Gospels than in Mark. Mark provided very few lessons for the selection read in the public services of the Church. It was much less used and much less commented on than the other Gospels ; of this an interesting illustration is the X^{cent.} MS. X, which has a marginal commentary on the three longer Gospels, but merely gives the bare text of Mark. Hence the comparative carelessness shown in correcting Mark to the fashionable type of text is easily accounted for.

There emerges a principle of some importance, but one which heretofore has been insufficiently emphasised. Seeing that the Gospel of Mark has escaped Byzantine revision in more copies and to a greater extent than the other Gospels, it follows that our materials for reconstructing the old local texts are far more abundant and more trustworthy in this Gospel. From this we deduce the following canon of textual criticism. *Research into the pedigree of a MS. should begin with a study of its text of Mark.*

THE WESTERN TEXT

Jerome's Vulgate, as has been already indicated, played in the Latin Church the same part as the Byzantine text in the Greek. The process of haphazard correction of older MSS. to the standard text resulted in the production of a number of copies having a mixed text, partly Vulgate, partly Old Latin. Fortunately, besides these, a few MSS. with a text entirely Old Latin, or with only a small admixture of Vulgate readings, still survive. These differ from one another very considerably ; and they differ even more in the Latin words chosen to represent the Greek than in the underlying Greek text they presuppose. Hence many scholars think there must have originally been two independent translations from the Greek, which subsequently have become somewhat confused by mixture with one another as a result of sporadic correction of MSS. of the one translation by MSS. of the other. However this may be, it is the fact that the Old Latin MSS.—which it is customary to cite by small italic letters—sort themselves roughly into two main groups, of which the most typical representatives are *k* (Bobiensis) and *b* (Veronensis).

One of the most important contributions to the criticism of the Gospels made in recent years was the demonstration by Dr. Sanday that the text of *k* is to all intents and purposes identical with that used by Cyprian of Carthage *c.* 250. This gives us another fixed point towards the determination of early local texts. Accordingly the type of text found in *k* is commonly spoken of as the " African Latin." Unfortunately *k* is only extant for Mk. viii.-xvi. and Matt. i.-xv. But another MS. *e* (Palatinus), also incomplete, while overlapping with *k* to some small extent, contains those parts of the Four Gospels which in *k* are missing. In *e* we have a somewhat later form of the same text as *k*, with a slight mixture of European Latin readings. In fact the type of text in *e* has much the same relation to that of *k* as L bears to B. The African text, so far as Mark and Luke are concerned, is also supported by *c*, a twelfth-century MS. which has a text, roughly speaking, half Vulgate and half Old Latin, though in the other Gospels the Old Latin approximates nearer to the type of *b*.[1] The *Speculum*, a collection of proof-texts, cited as *m*, perhaps of Spanish origin, helps to eke out our scanty authorities for this African Latin text.

Tertullian, the predecessor of Cyprian at Carthage, speaks of the Apostolic Sees, with special reference to Rome, as the " wombs

---

[1] Cf. F. C. Burkitt, *J.T.S.*, Jan. 1908, p. 307 ff. *The Old Latin and the Itala* (*Texts and Studies*, iv. 3, 1896) by the same author must be read by all students of the Latin versions.

F

of the Catholic Church." [1] From this and from the general
probabilities of the case we may tentatively infer that African
Christianity came from Rome, and that the African Latin was
ultimately derived from an early form of Roman text. Further
evidence, slight but pointing in the same direction, may be seen
in the noticeable points of contact between the African Latin
MSS. and Fathers and what little we know of the text of Marcion,
who was in Rome 140–144. The African Latin, it is important
to notice, in many of its readings agrees with B ℵ against the type
of Old Latin of which I will now proceed to speak.

The other type of the Old Latin is called by some scholars the
" European," by others the " Italic." The MS. that occupies the
same sort of central position among the European Latin MSS. as
B does among the Alexandrian is, curiously enough, denoted by
the letter b (Veronensis). As the Dean of Christ Church puts it,
" b indeed seems to be almost a typical European MS. ; as the
other MSS. of European and of Italian origin, such as $a f h i q r$,
all resemble b more closely than they resemble each other." [2] The
most constant supporter of b is ff^2 (Corbiensis II.). Of the MSS.
mentioned above the oldest [3] is a (Vercellensis) IV[cent.]. This MS.,
supported by the fragment n, stands a little apart from the others.
The difference between a and b is at its maximum in Mark, so that
the critical canon just enunciated justifies the suspicion that it
may possibly represent a third local type, intermediate between
b and k, which in the other Gospels has been partially conformed
to the b text.[4]

[1] *De Praescr. Haer.* 21.

[2] H. J. White, *Old Latin Biblical Texts*, iii. p. xxii., Oxford, 1888. This
vol. contains an edition of q, the Introduction to which is invaluable to the
student of Old Latin texts.

[3] Burkitt argues that k also is IV[cent.] (*J.T.S.*, Oct. 1903, p. 107); b and e
are uniformly dated V[cent.], ff^2 V or VI[cent.].

[4] The VI[cent.] MS. f (Brixianus) has a large number of readings which
occur in the Byzantine text but not in other Old Latin MSS. ; many of these
occur in the Vulgate. There is a difference of opinion among experts as to
whether this MS. represents an attempt earlier than Jerome's to revise the
Latin by comparison with the Greek, or whether it is a Vulgate MS. corrupted
by the influence of the text of the Gothic version, as it seems to have been

Of the European Latin as a whole it may be said that it represents a type of text at the furthest remove from that of B.   And even the African Latin, which in small points frequently deserts the European to support B, is conspicuous for the number of striking additions—"interpolations" Hort calls them—to the B text. The Roman theologians, up to and including Hippolytus, d. 236, wrote in Greek ; and the liturgy of the Roman Church was in Greek possibly till an even later date.   The number of quotations in the fragments of Marcion or in the writings of Justin and Hippolytus sufficiently definite to be used for critical purposes is not very large, but such as they are they imply the use of a Greek text, roughly speaking, corresponding to the Old Latin.   We know also that the Diatessaron or Harmony of the Four Gospels compiled by Tatian was produced about 170, either during, or immediately after, his long residence in Rome ; and this had a text of the same character.   But the use of the Greek language slowly died out in the West.   Hence it is not surprising that we have few MSS. which preserve the type of Greek text used in the West during the period when Greek was still spoken there.   For the Epistles of St. Paul four such survive ; but for the Gospels until recently there was only one, the Codex Bezae D.

Being practically the sole representative of the Greek text used in the West towards the end of the second century, D has a quite unique importance, and a large literature has come into existence about it.   Its text stands fairly well in the middle of the various MSS. of the Old Latin.   Where these differ from one another, D sometimes supports one type, sometimes another ; but on the whole it is nearer to the European than to the African type.   In a certain number of readings it supports B against the Old Latin ; in a much larger number it agrees with B against the Byzantine text.   Its date, according to the latest authority, is fifth century.

copied from the Latin side of a bilingual Gothic-Latin MS.   Cf. Wordsworth and White, *Nov. Test. . . . Hieronymi*, p. 656, and F. C. Burkitt, *J.T.S.*, Oct. 1899.

D is a bilingual MS., having the Greek on the left, the Latin on the right-hand page.[1] Theodore Beza, who presented the MS. to the University of Cambridge, states that it was found in the monastery of St. Irenaeus at Lyons; and Dr. E. A. Lowe [2] produces good reasons for the belief that it was already in Lyons in the ninth century. Where it was originally written is a question on which there is at present no agreement among experts. Southern Italy, Sardinia, or the Rhone valley are the favourite guesses. In favour of the last-mentioned locality is the close relation of the text of D to that used by Irenaeus, Bishop of Lyons c. 177–195. This relation was noted long ago, but is re-affirmed with further confirmation in Sanday and Turner's recent edition of the New Testament Text of Irenaeus.[3] We may, however, infer that it was written in some rather out-of-the-way church or monastery, for two reasons. First, the corruptions in the text imply an ignorant scribe. Secondly, the story of the man working on the Sabbath inserted by D after Lk. vi. 4, and the attempt to assimilate the genealogy of our Lord in Luke to that found in Matthew, are readings so remarkable that they almost demand comment. Yet, to the best of my knowledge, no allusion is made to either by any ecclesiastical writer. This is easily explicable if these readings were current only in some out-of-the-way church.

The solitary position of D as the Greek representative of the Old Latin text has been partially relieved, so far as the Gospel of Mark is concerned, by the discovery in 1906 of W (the Freer MS. V[cent.]), the possession of which gives the library of Washington the distinction of containing one of the six most ancient copies of the Gospels. The text of W presents a unique problem. Its editor, Prof. H. A. Sanders,[4] thinks it is descended from an ancestor

---

[1] It is customary to cite the Latin half of D, which not infrequently differs from the Greek, as d. Similarly the (far less important) interlinear Latin of Δ is cited as δ.

[2] J.T.S., April 1924, p. 270 ff.

[3] Novum Testamentum S. Irenaei (Oxford, 1923).

[4] Cf. the elaborate introduction to his collation of W, The New Testament MSS. in the Freer Collection, Part I. (The Macmillan Co., New York, 1912).

made up of fragments from different rolls of the Gospels pieced together after the attempt of Diocletian to crush Christianity by destroying the sacred books.   (For another and, I think, more probable explanation see Appendix V.)   Some portions seem to have been drastically revised to conform to the B ℵ, others to the Byzantine, text.   In the whole of Matthew and in Lk. viii. 13 to the end it presents a text mainly Byzantine ; since most of Matthew is wanting in A (the only other MS. as early as the fifth century which gives a text closely allied to the Byzantine) we have in W a welcome accession to the early evidence for this type of text.   For the first seven chapters of Luke and in John (v. 12 to the end) [1] the text of W is mainly of the Alexandrian type.   But the most notable feature of W is its text of Mark.

For Mk. i.-v. 30 the text of W is almost word for word the Greek equivalent of the old Latin version in what seems to be its oldest form ; [2] it has special points of contact with the " African " Latin MSS. e and c (k is not here extant).   So far, then, as this part of Mark is concerned we have in W a valuable addition to the evidence afforded by D for the ancient Greek text current in the West—to which text alone the title " Western " will in these chapters be applied.   For Mk. v. 31-xvi. 8, however, W—for evidence see Appendix V—is much the most ancient authority for the type of " Eastern " text discussed in Chap. IV.

THE TEXT OF EPHESUS

Constantinople, as we shall see shortly, appears to have adopted its text as well as its theology from Antioch.   It was inevitable, therefore, that at Ephesus, situated as it was between these two dominant patriarchates, the old local text should succumb at an early date to the standard text used by both these Sees.   There is reason to believe that some time in the fourth century Ephesus was compelled to surrender its ancient liturgy in favour of the Byzantine. [3]   But there is a certain

---

[1] Jn. i. 1-v. 11 is by a different scribe and on different parchment, and seems to have been added to replace a lost quire.

[2] Cf. H. A. Sanders, *op. cit.* p. 67.   [3] W. Palmer, *Origines Liturgicae,* i. 106.

amount of evidence that in the second century the text used at Ephesus was akin to that found in D and the European Latin.

The recently discovered second-century document known as the *Epistula Apostolorum* is supposed by its editor Carl Schmidt [1] to be of Ephesian origin. The evidence adduced is not conclusive ; and other scholars assign it to Alexandria. The author of this work is clearly familiar with all four Gospels. But for our present purpose the most interesting point is that he seems to have read them in a text like that we call Western in the strictest geographical sense.

(*a*) In ch. 2 he has a very remarkable list of the apostles in which the name of John stands first ; and one of the names is Judas Zelotes. It might have been imagined that this was due to a conjectural combination, made by the author himself, between the names of the two apostles mentioned in Lk. vi. 16, Judas of James and Simon Zelotes ; but this same combination, Judas Zelotes, occurs (Mt. x. 3), as a *substitute* for the ordinary Thaddaeus = Lebbaeus, in the Old Latin *a b h q* etc. It also occurs in the fifth-century mosaics in the Baptistry of the Orthodox at Ravenna, which are in another respect connected with the Western text, in so much as they arrange the evangelists in the order Matthew, John, Luke, Mark, found in D, W, several Old Latin MSS., and in the Monarchian Prologues (p. 11).

(*b*) In ch. 3 *ad fin.* we read " He is the word made flesh, born in the sacred Virgin's womb, conceived by the Holy Ghost, not by carnal lust, but by the will of God." This seems to imply the famous Western reading of Jn. i. 13, which substitutes ὅς . . . ἐγενήθη for οἳ . . . ἐγενήθησαν and thereby makes the fourth Gospel also assert the Virgin Birth of Christ. This reading is found in *b*, in three quotations of Irenaeus, two of Tertullian, and was also known to Ambrose, Augustine, and probably to Justin Martyr.

(*c*) Possibly his text also included the Longer Conclusion

---

[1] In *Texte und Untersuchungen*, 1919.

[2] Cf. C. Schmidt, *op. cit.* pp. 219, 224, also below, p. 348.

CH. III THE TEXTS OF THE GREAT SEES 71

of Mark.[2] This is a characteristic Gallic and Italian reading. It is absent from the African Latin, from the oldest Alexandrian MSS., from the majority and the oldest MSS. known to Eusebius of Caesarea, from Syr. S., which seems to represent the old text of Antioch, and from the Eastern authorities mentioned p. 88. But it is found in D, in all Old Latin MSS. except k, and in the text used by Irenaeus and Tatian.

These striking agreements between the text quoted in a document of the second century, probably Ephesian, and the text used in Italy and Gaul, tempt me to review the nature of the patristic evidence for the Western text. We notice at once a special connection between most of our earliest authorities for the Western text and the Roman province of Asia of which Ephesus was the capital.

(a) Justin Martyr was converted to Christianity in Ephesus ; and according to the evidence given by himself at his trial, though he had lived and taught in Rome, he had done so without any very close affiliation to the local Church.[1] The text of the Gospels he used is therefore more likely than not to have been the one he brought from Ephesus. Tatian was a pupil of Justin, and may well have used his master's text.

(b) Irenaeus as a boy sat at the feet of Polycarp of Smyrna, and never tires of emphasising the value of the apostolic tradition of the Churches of Asia and Rome. But the connection between Asia and the Church of Lyons, of which Irenaeus was a member and ultimately bishop, was in no sense personal to Irenaeus himself. Eusebius preserves the letter written by the Churches of Lyons and Vienne to the Church of Ephesus to tell them the story of the martyrdoms in the persecution of 177. This implies a special affiliation of these Gallic Churches to the Church of Asia. The Greek-speaking communities of the Rhone valley seem always to have kept up a connection, mainly no doubt for trade purposes, with the cities

---

[1] Cf. the Martyrdom of Justin and the discussion by K. Lake, *Landmarks of Early Christianity*, p. 127 (Macmillan, 1920).

of Ionia, of which they had originally been colonies.[1] It is, therefore, exceedingly probable that the Christianity of the Rhone
valley was derived from Ephesus. In that case the text of the
Gospels used there would naturally be the Ephesian text.

(c) Since Justin, Tatian, and Irenaeus all resided and taught
in Rome, some readings from the text they used would get into
the local text. The text of Irenaeus, we have seen, is closely
related to that of D and the Old Latin. This suggests the
possibility that the earliest Latin translation used in Gaul was
derived, not from the Greek text used in Rome, but from that
used in the Rhone valley. This translation might have spread
thence into Gallia Cisalpina, the consanguineous district of
N. Italy.

The evidence available is quite insufficient to justify any
definite conclusion, but it at least suggests the tentative
hypothesis that while regarding the African Latin as a descendant of the older Roman text, we should look on D and
the European Latin as representing a mixture, varying with
individual MSS., between the Roman and the Ephesian text.

The Old Text of Antioch

We pass on to consider a field of inquiry which more than
any other has been illuminated by recent discovery—the old
local texts of the Asiatic provinces of the Roman Empire. When
Hort wrote, the materials at the disposal of critics were insufficient
to justify any definite conclusion, and we are still hampered by
the lack of ecclesiastical writers from whose quotations of the
New Testament the type of text current in these provinces can
be ascertained. In fact the only early writer native to these
provinces of whom enough survives to be of any practical use for
this purpose is the historian, Eusebius of Caesarea, c. 325. It had

---

[1] Three inscriptions have been found in Lyons set up by persons described
as *natione Graeca*, and one by a lady, *natione Asiana*. Cf. Vasile Pârvan, *Die
Nationalität der Kaufleute im römischen Kaiserreiche*, pp. 90, 107 (Breslau,
1919).

long been recognised that Eusebius used a "Western" text, but
one of a peculiar kind, that is to say, a text which, although more
closely allied to D than to א B L, is markedly distinct from D.
But the only MS. giving a continuous text of early date which
could be certainly assigned to the Eastern provinces was the
fragmentary Cureton MS. of the Old Syriac version (Syr. C.), which
contains less than half the total contents of the Gospels, and of
Mark only four verses.   Hence Hort was justified in including the
Old Syriac and the sporadic non-Byzantine readings of a similar
character found in cursives like 565 or the Ferrar group under
the general designation of the "Western text"—a title which he
inherited from Griesbach,—although he quite recognised the geographical inappropriateness of this extended use of the adjective.

   Since Hort wrote, the situation has been completely changed
by a series of discoveries.   Of these the one which has opened up
the prospect of our obtaining at least a general idea of the ancient
text of Antioch was the discovery in 1892 of the Sinaitic Syriac
(which I shall cite as Syr. S.), a fourth-century palimpsest containing, with some lacunae, a fairly complete text of the Four
Gospels in the Old Syriac version.   The Syriac text of Syr. S. and
Syr. C., along with an English translation, purposely so literal that
even the order of words in the original can often be followed, was
published in 1904 by F. C. Burkitt under the title *Evangelion
Da-Mepharreshe* = " Gospel of the Separate," as distinguished
from the Diatessaron or " Gospel of the Mixed."   The Introduction and Notes to this edition form a contribution to textual
criticism the value of which to the advanced student cannot be
over-estimated.

   It appears that Syr. S. and Syr. C. represent fundamentally
the same version, but that one or the other must have been
revised partially from a Greek MS. having a slightly different
type of text.   Burkitt thinks that Syr. S. gives the version most
nearly in its original form, while Syr. C. has been revised here and
there by a Greek MS. more or less similar to the Codex Bezae.
However this may be, the fact remains that the version as a

whole is more closely allied to the Western text than to B,
although Syr. S., especially in the matter of omission, frequently
supports B against both Syr. C. and D. For instance, it omits
the last twelve verses of Mark and the two notable passages
Lk. xxii. 43 f. (the Bloody Sweat) and Lk. xxiii. 34 ("Father,
forgive them "). But, though on the whole it ranges itself on
the side of D and the Old Latin against B and its allies, the
Old Syriac has a sufficiently large number of distinctive readings
found neither in D nor B to justify our regarding it as a third
type of text.

Burkitt was, I believe, the first to work out in any detail the
suggestion that the Greek text underlying the version of the Old
Syriac preserved in Syr. S. was derived from the older text of
Antioch.[1] His argument, briefly, is as follows. Tatian, who
seems to have been the first effectively to plant Christianity in
Mesopotamia, introduced there, not the Four Gospels, but the
Syriac Diatessaron—which for centuries was spoken of as "the
Gospel." The Four Gospels, known by contrast to the Diatessaron as "the Gospel of the Separate," were a later introduction.
Syr. S. seems to be an earlier form than Syr. C. of the Syriac
version of the Separate Gospels. Its translator was familiar
with the Diatessaron, and its readings, as well as its renderings,
may sometimes have been affected by that fact; hence the
original Greek text from which Syr. S. was translated will have
differed from the Diatessaron even more than does the translation. Now the text of the Diatessaron is closely akin to D and
the Old Latin. This resemblance, coupled with the fact that
Tatian came from Rome about A.D. 172, makes it highly probable
that the text used for the Diatessaron was the Roman text.
Where, then, did the text of Syr. S. come from ? Geographically,
the province of which Antioch is capital marched with the
Syriac-speaking district. More than this, there is evidence that,
after the disorganisation caused by a period of persecution,
Serapion the Patriarch of Antioch, c. A.D. 200, re-established the

[1] *Evangelion Da-Mepharreshe*, ii. p. 254.

Syriac Church by consecrating Palût, the bishop from whom in after years that Church reckoned its episcopal succession. Thus the revived Syriac-speaking Church was in a special way a daughter church of Antioch, and would naturally obtain therefrom the text of the "separate" Gospels which hitherto it did not possess. The presumption, then, that the Old Syriac represents the second-century text of Antioch is decidedly high. Moreover, I would observe that, if any one prefers the view of certain scholars that the old Syriac version of the Gospels is earlier than the Diatessaron, the presumption that its text came from Antioch is considerably enhanced ; for the only reasonable ground for doubting the Antiochene origin of the Syriac text arises from the known connection of Tatian with Rome.

Burkitt points out that a number of readings of the Old Syriac, which are not found in any other Greek MS., occur in one or more of the cursives 1 &c., 13 &c., 28, 565, 700. Those MSS., I shall argue in the next chapter, preserve (with much Byzantine admixture) the old text of Caesarea. Seeing that Caesarea and Antioch were the capitals of adjoining provinces, the discovery that those MSS. represent the text of Caesarea cannot but add weight to the view that the cognate text implied in the Old Syriac has some special connection with the neighbouring Church of Antioch.

Any evidence is welcome which throws further light on the true text of a version which survives only in two MSS., both imperfect. For this purpose some use can be made of the Peshitta —the Syriac version used at the present day in all branches of the Syriac-speaking Church. Of this we have MSS. as early as the fifth century. Burkitt [1] has shown that the Peshitta represents a revision of the Old Syriac made by Rabbula, Bishop of Edessa, about 425. The MSS. used by Rabbula evidently represented the Byzantine text, and his revision was fairly thorough. Nevertheless the number of readings of the Old Syriac which

[1] "S. Ephraim's Quotations from the Gospels," in *Texts and Studies*, vii. 2 (Cambridge, 1901).

survive in the Peshitta is considerable, though the proportion which these bear to the whole is less than that borne by the Old Latin readings surviving in Jerome's Vulgate. Wherever, therefore, the reading implied in the Peshitta differs from that of the Byzantine text, there is a fair presumption that it represents the reading of an Old Syriac MS.

The other Syriac versions are of less value as evidence for the text of the Old Syriac. We have a number of MSS. of a revision made for the Jacobite sect by Thomas of Harkel in 616 ; but this revision went still further in the direction of assimilating the Syriac to the Byzantine Greek text. He noted in the margin the readings of three old Greek MSS. in the Gospels and of one in the Acts which differed from the Byzantine text. These readings (cited as Syr. Hcl$^{mg.}$) are of considerable interest ; but their importance lies in the evidence they afford for pre-Byzantine Greek texts, not for the light they throw on the Old Syriac.

Much the same may be said of the " Palestinian " or " Jerusalem " Syriac (cited as Syr. Hier.). Burkitt has shown that this was not a native Palestinian product.[1] It was produced in a monastery near Antioch as part of an effort of Justinian to combat Nestorianism in Palestine by providing orthodox literature in the vernacular. It is probable that the translators made some use of previous Syriac versions, but Syr. Hier. cannot be safely quoted as an authority for the Old Syriac—still less, as von Soden thought, for the Greek text used at Jerusalem.[2]

The Armenian version is held by Dean Armitage Robinson [3] to have been originally made, wholly or in part, from the Old Syriac. In that case it may be used as supplementary evidence for the original form of that version. This view, however, has lately been disputed (cf. p. 104) ; I shall venture later on (p. 104 f.) to put forward a suggestion of my own in regard to the most debateable point.

[1] *J.T.S.*, Jan. 1901, pp. 174 ff.
[2] Hoskier, *J.T.S.*, Jan. 1913, p. 242, notes points of contact between the text of this version and the mixed cursive 157.
[3] Cf. " Euthaliana " in *Texts and Studies*, iii. 3 (1895).

THE KORIDETHI MS. AND THE TEXT OF CAESAREA

SYNOPSIS

THE Θ FAMILY

The new Koridethi MS. Θ has been shown by K. Lake to be the most important member of a family of MSS. of which the next in importance are the cursives 1 &c., 13 &c., 28, 565, 700. Accordingly the whole group may appropriately be styled *fam.* Θ. Each member of this family has been partially corrected to the Byzantine standard ; but, since in each a different set of passages has been so corrected, we can, by the simple expedient of ignoring the Byzantine readings, approximately restore the text of the original ancestor. This illustrated by a Table. In an Appendix evidence is adduced for assigning to *fam.* Θ certain other less important MSS., in particular the group 1424 &c.

RELATION TO OTHER ANCIENT TEXTS

(1) The text of *fam.* Θ is slightly, but only slightly, nearer to the Western than to the Alexandrian type ; also it has a large and clearly defined set of readings peculiar to itself.

(2) In *fam.* Θ are found certain striking additions to the T.R. which the Syriac shares with D and the Old Latin, beside others found only in the Syriac or Armenian.

(3) As regards, however, the longer omissions from the T.R. found in B and Syr. S., *fam.* Θ nearly always supports the shorter text.

(4) *Fam.* Θ is nearer to the Old Syriac than is any other surviving Greek text, but it is by no means identical ; it is frequently supported by the Armenian against the Syriac. Most frequently of all it is supported by the oldest MSS. of the Georgian version.

Θ AND THE TEXT OF ORIGEN

Griesbach discovered that Origen used two different texts of Mark ; but, owing to the paucity of MS. evidence then available, he slightly misinterpreted the facts. These are as follows. In the surviving portions of the first ten books of his *Commentary on John*, Origen used the B ℵ text of Mark ; but in the later books of this work, in his *Commentary on Matthew* and his *Exhortation to Martyrdom*, he used a text practically identical with that of *fam*. Θ. The *Commentary on John* was begun in Alexandria but finished at Caesarea, and both the other works mentioned were written at Caesarea.

It further appears that the text of Matthew used by Origen in his Commentary on that Gospel was the *fam*. Θ text—a fact partly disguised in the printed editions in which the text of *fam*. Θ has been sporadically corrected to the Byzantine standard. Throughout the *Commentary on John*, Origen used an Alexandrian text of John, but in the later books he changed his text of Luke for one of the Θ type. These conclusions tested against tables drawn up by Preuschen. At a later date Origen seems to have used the Θ text for John also.

Reasons for believing that the *fam*. Θ text was already in possession at Caesarea when Origen arrived and was not a recension which he made himself.

The MSS. sent to Constantine

The possibility that the fifty copies supplied by Eusebius to Constantine in 331 represented the old text of Caesarea. By 380 Constantinople had adopted the revised text of Lucian. This would lead to the correction of the older MSS. to the Lucianic (*i.e.*, practically, to the Byzantine) standard. Some of these partially corrected copies would get into the provinces, and may be the parents of some existing MSS. of *fam*. Θ. Possibility that the Greek texts used by SS. Mesrop and Sahak to revise the Armenian were of this character.

Concluding Survey

Significant fact that the local texts identified above form a series corresponding to the geographical propinquity of the churches with which they are connected.

Practical bearing of these results. The textual critic, in weighing the amount of external evidence in favour of any reading, should consider primarily, not the number or age of the MSS. which support it, but the number and geographical distribution of the ancient local texts in which it can be traced.

It follows that MSS. should be cited, not in alphabetical or numerical order, but in groups corresponding to the local texts which they represent. When at least three of the leading representatives of any local text support a reading, very little is gained by citing the additional evidence of MSS. which normally support the *same* local text.

CHAPTER IV

THE KORIDETHI MS. AND THE TEXT OF CAESAREA

The Θ Family

THE uncial MS. to which the letter Θ is assigned was discovered in a remote valley in the Caucasus, where it had long been a kind of village fetish ; but at a much earlier date it belonged to a monastery at Koridethi—at the far end of the Black Sea just inside the old frontier between Russia and Turkey. Owing to a chapter of accidents—including a disappearance for thirty years—its complete text only became available to scholars in 1913.[1] Dr. R. P. Blake, in a joint article by himself and Prof. K. Lake in the *Harvard Theological Review* for July 1923, argues that the scribe was a Georgian, familiar with the Coptic script, but extremely ignorant of Greek. At any rate the ordinary tests by which the handwriting of MSS. can be dated are difficult to apply ; but it probably belongs to the eighth century.

The discovery is comparable in importance to that of ℵ or the Sinaitic Syriac—but for a different reason. The importance of ℵ and Syr. S. depends on their early date and the relative purity of the types of text they respectively preserve. Θ is neither so old nor so pure : it has suffered considerably from Byzantine revision. Its importance lies in the fact that it supplies a

---

[1] In the edition by G. Beerman and C. R. Gregory, Leipzig, 1913. The student should be warned that the Appendix which gives the MS. support of all variants in Θ is quite unreliable so far as its cursive supporters are concerned. As the MSS. most closely allied to Θ are all cursives, this is a serious defect. An edition of Θ, with Mark in reduced facsimile, was published by the Moscow Archeological Society, 1907 ; but this is not easily procured.

missing link and enables us to see the real connection between certain cursives, the exceptional character of which has long been an enigma to the critic. In the demonstration of the relation between Θ and this group of cursives, the first and most important step was made by Lake in the brilliant article referred to above in the *Harvard Theological Review*.

The cursives in question are the following : (*a*) Codex **1** and its allies, commonly cited as *fam.* **1**, or **1** &c. Of this family of MSS. the only one comparable in importance to **1** is **1582** (X^cent.) recently discovered in the Vatopedi Monastery on Mt. Athos. But the inferior members occasionally preserve original readings which have been revised out in the two better MSS.[1] (*b*) The " Ferrar group " (cited as *fam.* **13** or **13** &c.), extended by later discovery from the four MSS. **13—69—124—346**, edited by Ferrar and Abbott, to twelve, all of which are probably derived from a single lost uncial. Within this group **69, 124**, and **983** are specially important as often preserving readings not found in other members.[2] (*c*) The Paris MS. **28**. (*d*) The

---

[1] *Codex 1 of the Gospels and its Allies*, by K. Lake, *Texts and Studies*, vol. vii. (Cambridge, 1902), contains the full text of **1** collated with its inferior supporters **118—131—209**, along with a very valuable Introduction. No collation of **1582** has yet been published, but it is quoted by Soden (as ε 183). Soden also quotes from two others of much less importance, *i.e.* for Mark, Luke, John **2193** (Sod. ε 1131), for Mark only **872** (Sod. ε 203). Soden also includes **22** and **1278** in this family; the case of **22** is discussed by H. A. Sanders in " A New Collation of Codex 22 " (*Journal of Biblical Literature*, xxxiii., pt. 2) who in general agrees. As nearly all the readings of **22** not found in **1—118—131—209** occur in other members of *fam.* Θ, it matters little whether it is classed with *fam.* **1** or as an independent member of the larger family.

[2] A large literature has arisen round the Ferrar group (cf. *Further Researches into the History of the Ferrar Group*, pp. 1-8, by J. Rendel Harris, Cambridge Press, 1900). It would appear that most of the group **13—69—124—230—346—543—788—826—828—983—1689—1709** are descended from a MS. which in the twelfth century was preserved either in some monastery in Calabria in the "heel" of Italy, or in some allied monastery in Sicily. In the classical period, S. Italy was not Italian but Greek ; but by the end of the sixth century, apart from a few coast towns, it had become Latin. But in the eighth and following centuries there was an immense immigration of Greek-speaking monks—refugees from the Mohammedan invasions. In the twelfth century, under Norman rule, there was an intellectual revival in the Greek monasteries of S. Italy. There is excellent evidence (cf. K. Lake, *J.T.S.*, Jan. 1904, p. 189 ff.) that MSS. were collected at con-

" Empress Theodora's Codex " 565 (cited by Tischendorf as 2^{pe} and by Hort as 81).[1] For Mark this is the most, for the other Gospels the least, important of the MSS. here mentioned. (e) The very interesting British Museum MS. 700, acquired in 1882 but not fully made known to the world till 1890.[2]

Lake made the all-important discovery that Θ and these notable cursives, taken all together, form in reality a single family.   True Θ and the five other sets of authorities mentioned do not on the face of it exhibit a single type of text; but that is because each of them has been heavily corrected to the Byzantine standard, and in each case a *different* set of corrections has been made.   If, however, we eliminate from the text of all these manuscripts those variants which are found in the Byzantine text, we find that the residuary readings of the six different representatives of the family support one another to a quite remarkable extent.   Lake illustrates this by a table analysing the variants in the first chapter of Mark.

In order to indicate the nature of his argument and at the same time to test its validity in regard to Luke and John, I have compiled similar tables (p. 83 and App. II.), only with an additional column for the readings of *fam.* 1424.   On the left are printed the readings found in one or more MSS. of the family which differ from the Textus Receptus; on the right are the corresponding readings of the T.R.   The letter *f* stands wherever the MS. (or group) indicated at the head of the column supports the family reading, the symbol 𝄖 when it

---

siderable expense from different parts of Greece and from Constantinople to found, or refound, libraries. The magnificent purple Codex Σ, still preserved at Rossano, must have been written either in Constantinople or in Cappadocia. Accordingly, it is probable that the ancestor of the Ferrar group was brought to Italy from the East; there is no reason for connecting it with the primitive text of S. Italy, which in all probability was akin to D.

[1] Edited by J. Belsheim, Christiania, 1885 ; corrections by H. S. Cronin in an Appendix to his edition of N, *Texts and Studies*, vol. iv. p. 106 ff. Scrivener and Hoskier cite as **473**.

[2] Collation by H. C. Hoskier, as Codex **604** (Scrivener's number); with Appendix containing a collation of **1278**, which Soden reckons a weak member of *fam.* 1 (D. Nutt, 1890).

G

agrees with the T.R. If any MS. supports a third reading, this is indicated in the column appropriate to that MS. by the symbol "3rd." The readings of א B and D are also given in order to show how each of them alternately supports and deserts the *fam.* Θ text.

From Lake's table of variants in Mk. i. it appears that there are 76 instances in which at least two members of the family agree with one another in exhibiting readings not found in the Byzantine text ; while there are only 5 instances where a member of the family gives a non-Byzantine reading other than that supported by the family. The significance of these figures is made clearer when it is noted that in regard to this same set of 76 variants in Mk. i. א and B differ from one another no less than 12 times. It follows that the ancestors from which Θ and the five sets of allies were derived must have differed from one another in this chapter considerably less than א does from B. Clearly we are justified henceforth in referring to this group of MSS.[1] by the convenient title of *fam.* Θ. (For connection of W with *fam.* Θ, cf. Appendix V.)

In the article in the *Harvard Theological Review* the authors confined their discussion to the text of Mark—the Gospel in which, as we have seen before, the key to the history of the text of any particular MS. is usually to be found. But as I happened to have been exercising myself with the problem presented by the text of Θ, I could not rest until I had explored their solution a little further. The evidence that convinced me that Lake's conclusion holds good in regard to the other Gospels also is presented in Appendix II.

In the course of this investigation I came upon evidence that the family of which Θ is the head has numerous poor relations. That is to say, there are a large number of MSS. which appear to be ultimately descended from ancestors the

---

[1] When a reading is cited as occurring in *fam.* 13 or the like, this does not mean that it is found in *all* MSS. of that group, but that it occurs in at least two, and that practically all MSS. of the group which do not give it follow the Byzantine text instead.

TABLE ILLUSTRATING BYZANTINE CORRECTION IN *FAM. Θ*

	Readings of the Family	Θ	fam. 1	fam. 13	28	565	700	fam. 1424		Readings of ς
ℵD	Jn. vi. 66 +ουν (p. τουτου)	f	ς	f	(παρα)	f†	ς	ς	B	-ουν
B	+εκ (a. των)	ς	ς	f		f†	ς	ς	ℵD	-εκ
ℵBD	απηλθον (p. αυτου)	f	f	f	ς	ς	ς	f		απηλ. (a. των)
	67 +μαθηταις (p. δωδεκα)	f	ς	f	ς	ς	ς	ς	ℵBD	-μαθηταις
ℵB	68 -ουν (p. απεκριθη)	f	f	f	ς	f	ς	f	D	+ουν
	69 εγνωκ. ... πεπιστευκ.	ς	ς	ς	ς	ς	(ι)	f†	ℵBD	πεπιστ. ... εγνωκ.
	-συ (a. ει)	f	f	f	ς	f	f	ς	ℵBD	+συ
ℵBD	70 -του ζωντος	ς	ς	ς	ς	ς	ς	ς	ℵBD	+του ζωντος
	-ὁ Ις	f	f†	f	f	f†	f†	f	ℵBD	+ὁ Ις
	αυτω	ς	ς	ς	ς	ς	ς	ς	ℵBD	αυτους
	εξελεξαμην (a. υμας)	ς	ς	f	f*	f†	f	f	BD	εξελεξ. (p. δωδεκα)
	-και εξ υμων	ς	ς	ς	ς	ς	ς	ς	ℵBD	+και εξ υμων
ℵD	71 -τον (a. Ιουδαν)	ς	f	ς	ς	ς	ς	f	B	+τον
ℵB*	απο Καρυωτου	f	f*	ς	ς	f†	ς	ς		Ισκαριωτην (B 3rd)
ℵB	εμελλεν	f	i	f	f	f	f	ς	D	ημελλεν
BD	παραδιδοναι αυτον	f	f	f	f	f†	f†	ς	ℵℵ	αυτον παραδιδ.
BD	-ων	ς	f*	f*	ς	ς	ς	f		+ων
	-εκ	ς	ς	ς	ς	ς	ς	ς	ℵBD	+εκ
ℵD	vii. 1 -και	f	f	f	f	f	f	f	B	+και
ℵBD	μετα ταυτα (a. περεπατει)	f	i	i	ς	f†	ς	f		μετα ταυτα (p. Iς.)
	2 -εγγυς	ς	ς	f*	ς	ς	ς	ς	ℵBD	+εγγυς

* = in one (or two) MSS. only. † = Sod. but not in Belsheim or Hoskier. ‡ = some members have 3rd.

3rd = differing from both *fam.* and ς. a. = ante. p. = post.

same or similar to those of *fam.* Θ, but by lines of descent which have suffered far more correction to the Byzantine standard. For details I refer to Appendix II. Such MSS. are of interest in that they occasionally preserve apparently genuine readings of the family text which have been revised out of the (generally speaking) better representatives. Of these MSS. the most important is the group which von Soden styles I$^\Phi$, but which by parity of nomenclature I propose to cite as *fam.* 1424, since the X$^{cent.}$ Kosinitza MS. 1424 (Scrivener's ၊) is its oldest representative.

RELATION TO OTHER ANCIENT TEXTS

But before attempting to inquire further into the origin of the text represented in *fam.* Θ, we must clear up its relation to other ancient texts, especially to those of B, D and the Old Syriac. This is the more necessary as von Soden has misrepresented and confused the evidence, by putting D into the same sub-family as Θ, and by making the Old Syriac another witness to the same type of text.

My investigation of this question leads me to formulate four main conclusions :

(1) So far as minor variants are concerned—and these are much the most numerous, and are of course the most significant for the study of the relationship of different texts —the text of *fam.* Θ is almost equidistant from both the Alexandrian and the Western texts. The balance inclines slightly, but only slightly, to the Western side, while there are a very large proportion of readings found neither in D nor in the typical Alexandrian MSS. We have therefore in *fam.* Θ a clearly defined and distinctive text which may properly be ranked side by side with the three great texts, Alexandrian, Western and Byzantine (=Hort's " Neutral," " Western" and " Syrian ") hitherto recognised.

(2) In *fam.* Θ are found certain striking additions to the

T.R. which the Syriac shares with D and the Old Lat., besides others found only in the Syriac or the Armenian.

(3) On the other hand, as regards the longer omissions from the T.R. which are so conspicuous a feature of the conjunction of B with Syr. S., *fam.* Θ nearly always supports the shorter text.

(4) Though the text of *fam.* Θ is nearer than any other surviving Greek text to the Old Syriac, it is by no means its exact equivalent; and it frequently goes with the Armenian against the Syriac. Further, it would appear that it is supported most frequently of all by the oldest MSS. of the Georgian version.

I proceed to summarise the evidence on which these conclusions are based. But the reader who has not previously made a study of textual criticism is advised on a first reading to skip this and pass on to the next subsection, " Θ and the Text of Origen."

(1) Lake's table shows that in Mk. i., in cases where B and D differ, B supports *fam.* Θ against D 16 times, while D supports the family against B 15 times, also that in 9 cases *fam.* Θ is supported against B D combined by one or more of the later Alexandrian group א L Δ Ψ 33 579. That is to say, the text of *fam.* Θ, in this chapter of Mark, is somewhat more closely allied to that of Alexandria than it is to D and the Old Latin. But how far, we ask, is this proportion maintained throughout the four Gospels? To make a count of all the readings in all four Gospels is obviously impossible ; but in four different ways I have been able to compile statistics which give some indication of the proportion which prevails elsewhere between the number of Egyptian and D readings.

(a) Hoskier in his edition of 700 (p. ix) sets out all the agreements of that MS. with the great uncials against the Byzantine text. From these it appears that 700 is supported by B against D 63 times, by one or more members of the group א L C Δ against B D combined 34 times, while it joins D against B 111 times. (b) In the Introduction to Ferrar and Abbott's historic edition of 13—69—124—346 (p. xlviii) will be found an analysis of the variants in Mt. xix.-xx. and Mk. i.-ix. Only those variants are counted in which the four cursives agree against the T.R. Out of 25 variants in Mt. xix.-xx., 13 &c. agree 18 times with B, 17 with D. Out of 215 in Mk. i.-ix. they agree 88 times with B, 90 with D. Further, it appears that in a series of selected passages from all four Gospels *fam.* 13 *differs* 376 times from א, 367 from B, 496 from D. That is to say, while 700 is slightly nearer to D than to the Egyptian group, the Ferrar group is distinctly nearer to B א than to D. (c) The statistics given below (p. 90), compiled from the lists in Lake's *Codex 1 and its Allies,* show the numbers of agreements of *fam.* 1 with the principal authorities in turn, and show that *fam.* 1 is only a very little nearer to B א than it is to the Old Lat. and D. (d) For Θ there are no such statistics to refer to, but a study of the MS. support for variants in Mk. xiv. and xv. as set out in the Appendix of Gregory and Beerman's edition of Θ shows that for these two chapters the proportion of Alexandrian to Western readings is approximately as 3 to 4. All these several sets of statistics, it will be observed, come to much the same thing. It so happens that in *fam.* 1 and *fam.* 13 the Byzantine revisers have spared a slightly larger proportion of Alexandrian than Western readings, while in Θ and 700 the opposite has occurred ; but, considered as a whole, the text of *fam.* Θ is not very much nearer to D than it is to B. Thus the von Soden grouping, which puts D in the same group as Θ, 28, 565, 700, while excluding from that group *fam.* 1 and *fam.* 13, is a complete misapprehension of the evidence.

(2) More interesting, if not more important, is the relation of *fam.* Θ to the Syriac and the Armenian versions. This may be illustrated by selecting a few striking readings in which *fam.* Θ agrees with Syr. S., and usually Arm. also, *against* B.

Mt. i. 16. Ἰακὼβ δὲ ἐγέννησεν Ἰωσὴφ τὸν ἄνδρα Μαρίας, ἐξ ἧς ἐγεννήθη Ἰησοῦς is the ordinary reading. Instead of this

Ἰακὼβ δὲ ἐγέννησεν Ἰωσήφ, ᾧ μνηστευθεῖσα παρθένος Μαριὰμ ἐγέννησεν Ἰησοῦν τὸν λεγόμενον Χριστόν is found in Θ and the Ferrar MSS. 346—543—826—828 (hiat. 69), Old Lat. (incl. d. hiat. D^{Gk.}). Syr. C. agrees with this, approximately. The Armenian combines both readings—a sure sign that it is a mixed text—and reads " the husband of Mariam, to whom was betrothed Mariam the virgin, from whom was born Jesus." Syr. S. has a reading which would correspond to Ἰακὼβ δε ἐγέννησεν τὸν Ἰωσήφ· Ἰωσὴφ ᾧ μνηστευθεῖσα παρθένος Μαριὰμ ἐγέννησεν Ἰησοῦν κτλ. To me the reading of Syr. S. looks as if it was translated from a Greek MS. of the Θ 13 &c. type in which by accident the name Ἰωσήφ had been written twice. Dittography is a very common scribal error ; and seeing that every one of the preceding 39 names in the genealogy had been written twice, the repetition of this particular word would have been exceptionally easy. The reading of Syr. C. will then be explained as one among many other attempts to correct this MS. by a MS. of the D type.

Mt. xxvii. 16, 17. The name of Barabbas is Jesus Barabbas, Θ, 1 &c., Syr. S., Arm., Orig. in Mat.

Mt. xxviii. 18. After γῆς add καθὼς ἀπέστειλέν με ὁ πατήρ, κἀγὼ ἀποστέλλω ὑμᾶς Θ, 1604, Syr. Pesh. (hiant Syr. S. and C.), Arm. (hiat Orig.^{Mt.}).

Mk. x. 14. Before εἶπεν add ἐπιτιμήσας Θ, 1 &c., 13 &c., 28, 565, Syr. S., Arm.

Jn. xi. 39, om. ἡ ἀδελφὴ τοῦ τετελευκηκότος Θ, Syr. S. Arm. ; Old Lat.

Jn. xix. 13. For Γαββαθᾶ = pavement καπφαθᾶ = arch 1 &c., 565, Arm.^{codd.}. Syr. S. and C. are both lacking ; but Syr. Pesh. does not favour either Γαββαθᾶ or the reading of 1 &c. Θ has (χιφβαθα).

Jn. xx. 16. After διδάσκαλε add καὶ προσέδραμεν ἅψασθαι αὐτοῦ Θ, 13 &c., Syr. S. ; Old Lat.

Note, however, that fam. Θ gives no support to the Syriac in certain other conspicuous additions, e.g. in Lk. xxiii. 48, Jn.

iii. 6, Jn. xi. 39, Jn. xii. 12. Further we note that the Armenian also deserts the Syriac here.

(3) It would appear that *fam.* Θ agrees with Syr. S. in a number of notable *omissions wherein Syr. S. has the support of B.*

Mt. xvi. 2-3, " Signs of the times," om. **13** &c., Arm., Orig.^Mt.

Mt. xvii. 21, " This kind goeth not forth," &c., om. Θ, **1604** (Arm., Orig.^Mt. habent) ; *e.*

Mt. xviii. 11, " For the son of man came," &c., om. Θ, **1** &c., **13** &c., Orig.^Mt. (Arm. habet).

Mt. xxiii. 14, whole verse om. Θ, **1** &c., **23**, Arm., D *a e,* Orig.^Mt.

Mk. ix. 44, 46, " Where the worm dieth not " (1st and 2nd time), om. **1, 28, 565,** Arm. ; *k.*

Mk. ix. 49, " And every sacrifice shall be salted with salt," om. **1, 565, 700,** Arm. ; *k.*

Mk. xvi. 9-20. That this was originally absent from *fam.* Θ may be inferred from the scholion to ἐφοβοῦντο γάρ, Mk. xvi. 8, in certain members of the family. In the newly discovered Vatopedi MS. **1582**—the oldest MS. of *fam.* **1**—there is a concluding ornamentation after ἐφοβοῦντο γάρ, Mk. xvi. 8, followed by a scholion : [1] " In some copies the Gospel ends here, up to which point also Eusebius Pamphili made his canons, but in many (copies) there is also found this." Then follows xvi. 9-16. An identical scholion occurs in **1**, in the margin ; but Dr. Blake informs me that in **1582**, which he has photographed, this note is written right across the page in uncial letters *as a colophon.* In **22** the word τέλος is written after ἐφοβοῦντο γάρ and the same scholion, only with the allusion to Eusebius omitted, follows. In nine of the oldest Armenian MSS. the Gospel ends at this point. So also does the oldest (Adysh) MS. of the Georgian version.

Lk. ix. 55, " Ye know not of what spirit ye are," &c., om. **28, 1424** &c. (Arm. hab.).

Lk. xxii. 43-44. The angel and the Bloody Sweat, om. N

[1] Cf. Gregory, *Textkritik,* iii. p. 1160.

1071. In *fam.* **13** it is omitted here but inserted after Mt. xxvi. 39, where it occurs in Greek Lectionaries as a Good Friday Lesson. This is explicable only if it was originally absent from the text of the family in Luke, and was inserted in Matthew by a scribe who supposed the Lectionary to represent the true reading of that Gospel. Some MSS. of Arm. omit.

Lk. xxiii. 34, " Father, forgive them," om. Θ (Arm. hab.) ; D *a b.*

Jn. vii. 53-viii. 11. Pericope Adulterae, om. Θ, **22, 2193, 565, 1424** &c., Arm.; *a f q*; in **1** and **1582** at the end of the Gospel—with a note that it is found in some copies but not commented upon by the holy Fathers Chrysostom, Cyril Alex., and Theodore of Mopsuestia ; inserted by **13** &c. after Lk. xxi. 38. It is absent from all old Georgian MSS., having been introduced by George the Athonite in his revision, *c.* 1045.

In view of this concurrence between B, Syr. S. and *fam.* Θ, in the omission of conspicuous passages, three points require notice. (*a*) There is no evidence that *fam.* Θ omitted Lk. xxiii. 38, " in letters of Greek and Latin and Hebrew," with B, Syr. S. and C. (Arm. hab.); or Jn. v. 4 (the moving of the waters) with B, Syr. C. (hiat. Syr. S.), Arm.$^{codd.}$. Though, of course, the words may have been inserted in all MSS. of the family by Byzantine revisers. (*b*) *Fam.* Θ agrees with Syr. S. in certain conspicuous insertions, which are found also in D. By reference to any good Apparatus Criticus the student may verify this under the references Mt. v. 22, Mt. x. 23, Mt. xxv. 1, Mk. x. 24. (*c*) *Fam.* Θ seems to support B against both Syr. S. and D in omissions in Mt. iv. 10, Mt. xx. 16, Lk. xx. 34.

(4) It is clear that the Greek text from which the Old Syriac was translated is more closely related to that of *fam.* Θ than to any other extant Greek MSS. ; but it would be a great mistake to suppose that it is in any sense the same text. Indeed a notable feature of the *fam.* Θ text is the number of its agreements with B against the Syriac. It is also noteworthy that the *fam.* Θ is frequently supported by the Armenian against

the Old Syriac. The lists of readings in Lake's edition of Codex 1 provide materials on which a rough estimate may be based. From these lists I have compiled the following statistics:

Variants quoted in which *fam*. 1 differs from T.R. . . . 520
Of these, number peculiar to *fam*. 1 68

452

Readings of *fam*. 1 found in Syr. S. or C. but not in Arm.. . 57
,, ,, ,, Syr. S. or C. supported by Arm. . 46

103

,, ,, ,, Arm. but not in Old Syr. . . 49
,, ,, ,, D or Old Lat. but not in ℵ, B or L 85
,, ,, ,, ℵ or B but not in D or Old Lat. . 90

In considering these statistics it should be remembered that many variants in the Greek cannot be represented in Syriac or Armenian, and therefore the proportion of agreements with these versions as contrasted with B, ℵ D or L, etc., is necessarily understated. Nevertheless they show clearly (*a*) that *fam*. 1 (which previous statistics have shown is a typical representation of *fam*. Θ) does not by any means stand to the Old Syriac in the same relation as does D to the Old Latin. (*β*) That its affinities with the Armenian are almost as numerous (95 as against 103) as those with the Old Syriac.

When this chapter was already in slip proof Dr. R. P. Blake, who is working on the text of the Georgian version, showed me a collation of Mk. i. in the Adysh MS. (dated A.D. 897) and in the recently discovered X[cent.] Chanmeti fragments, which appear to represent an older form of that version than that reproduced in the printed editions.[1] The MSS. frequently differ from one another; but the remarkable fact stands out that in the majority of cases in which one or more of these Old Georgian

[1] Of the Adysh Gospels there is a photographic facsimile by E. S. Tagaishoibi (Moscow, 1916). The two Chanmeti fragments are dated respectively A.D. 914 and 995; edited by V. N. Beneševič (Petropoli, 1908–9).

MSS. differs from the T.R., its reading is supported by *fam.* Θ. In Mk. i. in the Georgian there are altogether 83 variants from the T.R. Of these 28 are found nowhere else ; and most of them look as if they were due to a translator's freedom. Of the remaining 55, no less than 38 occur in one or more of the seven main authorities for *fam.* Θ ; and 5 others occur in MSS. classed by von Soden as minor supporters of the I text.[1] If, on further investigation, it should appear that this close relation between *fam.* Θ and the Georgian holds throughout all four Gospels, the Old Georgian version will become an authority of the first importance for the text of the Gospels ; for it will enable us to check and supplement the evidence of Θ and its allies much as the Old Latin does for that of D.

THE TEXT OF ORIGEN AND EUSEBIUS

Seeing that *fam.* Θ includes the main authorities for what von Soden calls the "I text," *with the three all-important exceptions of D, the Old Latin and the Old Syriac*, it seemed worth while to ask whether his theory that this text represents a recension by Pamphilus, the friend of Eusebius, would hold good, provided the authorities for it were restricted to *fam.* Θ. I, therefore, turned to his discussion (vol. i. p. 1494) of the quotations of Eusebius of Caesarea, whom he regards as the leading patristic authority for the I text. He gives a list of Eusebian readings, of which the great majority are found in *fam.* Θ ; but a substantial number are quoted as if they occurred in D only. After my results had been published K. Lake proved that in Mark (*i.e.* where our MS. authority for *fam.* Θ is at its best), Eusebius actually used the *fam.* Θ text ; but from the facts as presented by von Soden I drew the faulty conclusion that the text of Eusebius had much the same relation to that of *fam.* Θ as ℵ C. L. 33 bear to B, *i.e.* that the text of Eusebius represents a somewhat degenerate form of the text found in

---

[1] Old Georgian has the notable readings (p. 87) in Mt. xxvii. 16-17, xxviii. 18 ; Mk. x. 14. Lacking photographs of the MSS. those in John were not checked.

fam. Θ—a degeneration largely due to mixture with a text of the D type.

At this point there flashed across my mind the distinction between the two texts used by Origen which was worked out as long ago as 1811 by Griesbach in his *Commentarius Criticus* [1]— a book to which my attention had been called by Prof. C. H. Turner some months before. Griesbach's thesis was that Origen in his *Commentary on John* used an " Alexandrian " text of Mark for Mk. i.-xi., and a " mixed text " for the remainder of the Gospel, but that he used a " Western " text of Mark in his *Commentary on Matthew* and in his *Exhortation to Martyrdom*, both of which belong entirely to the period when he lived in Caesarea. It occurred to me to review the evidence submitted by Griesbach in the light of MSS. of the Gospels which have only been discovered or properly edited since his time. The results were astonishing.

Two points became clear. (*a*) The difference noticed by Griesbach between the use of an " Alexandrian " and of a " mixed " text of Mark corresponds to the change, not from the earlier to the later chapters of Mark, but from the earlier to the later books of the *Commentary on John*. (*b*) Both this " mixed " text of Mark and the so-called " Western " text used in the *Commentary on Matthew* and in the *Exhortation to Martyrdom* are practically identical with the text of *fam.* Θ. At once we notice the salient fact that the change in the text used corresponds, roughly speaking, to a change of residence. Origen himself tells us that the first five books of the *Commentary on John* were written before he left Alexandria for Caesarea, in 231. The *Exhortation to Martyrdom* was written shortly after the outbreak of the persecution of 235 ; the *Commentary on Matthew* (about 240) is probably one of the works taken down by shorthand from lectures delivered on week-days in the church at Caesarea.

I proceed to submit statistics in support of the above conclusions.

[1] Part II. pp. x-xxxvi.

(1) In books i.-x. of the *Commentary on John*, Origen quotes the greater part of Mk. i. 1-27 and the whole of Mk. xi. 1-12, besides a few odd verses. The number of variants in Mk. i. 1-27 cited by Griesbach is 36. For 2 of these there is no support in MSS. of the Gospels; but in one, and perhaps both, of these cases Origen seems to be paraphrasing rather than quoting his text. In the remaining 34 readings Origen is supported 31 times by one or both of the MSS. B ℵ and once each by the other Alexandrian MSS. C, L, Δ; but in only [1] 17 of the 34 is he supported by *fam.* Θ. From the shorter passages quoted in books i.-x. (*i.e.* Mk. vi. 16; x. 18; xi. 15-17; xii. 26-27; xiv. 60) Griesbach cites 16 variants. Origen is supported in 10 of these by B, and in 1 each by C, Δ; for 3 there is no MS. support, and 1 occurs in the T.R. The continuous passage Mk. xi. 1-12 is specially important, for it is so long that by no possibility can it be a quotation from memory; it must therefore represent the third-century MS. of the Gospel used by Origen. Apart from an accidental omission (I think in some ancestor of our copy of Origen on John) [2] the variants noted by Griesbach number 31; in 29 of these the reading of Origen is supported by one or both of the MSS. B ℵ; in 1 by *fam.* Θ, and in 1 by the T.R., where these texts differ from B ℵ. It may be of interest to note that in the passages examined above, where B and ℵ differ, Origen has 6 agreements with B as against 7 with ℵ.

(2) The number of variants in Mark cited by Griesbach from the later books of the *Commentary on John* is 43. For 5 of these the text of Origen has no MS. support; in 6 cases it agrees with the T.R. We have seen (p. 45 ff.) that when a quotation by an

---

[1] Of these readings 16 occur in B or ℵ and the remaining 1 in D; so there are *none* distinctive of *fam.* Θ. *N.B.*—In two cases, where Griesbach, using the Benedictine text, cites variants of Origen which differ from B ℵ, in Brooke's edition Origen's reading agrees with those MSS.

[2] In Mk. xi. 7-8 Origen omits καὶ ἐκάθισεν . . . ὁδόν, but to make sense adds the last four words after ἀγρῶν. Burkitt (*J.T.S.* xvii. p. 151) thinks this was a defect in Origen's MS. of the Gospel. As, however, there is a similar omission (through homoioteleuton) in the quotation of Mt. xxi. 8 on the same page in Brooke's edition (i. p. 208), it seems to me more likely to be a defect in the MS. of the *Commentary on John*, an ancestor of which was prone to omission

ante-Nicene Father agrees with the T.R. against earlier texts, there is always a possibility that this may be the result of later scribal alteration in the MS. of that Father ; again, whenever a reading in a patristic quotation is not supported by a single MS. of the Gospels, there is a presumption, either that the author is quoting from memory or paraphrasing, or that it is an error in the MSS. of his work. In view of these considerations it is highly significant that of the remaining 32 variants no less than 30 are found in *fam.* Θ (10 occurring only in the MSS. of this family), while Origen is supported only once each by ℵ and D, and never by B, against the family.

(3) From Origen's *Commentary on Matthew*, Griesbach cites 99 variants in Mark ; of these 8 are peculiar to Origen, and 13 occur in the Byzantine text.[1] Of the remaining 78 as many as 74 are found in one or more members of *fam.* Θ ; while Origen has one single agreement with each of the four MSS. B, C, Δ, D, where these differ from *fam.* Θ.

(4) The figures in regard to the passages of Mark quoted in the *Exhortation to Martyrdom* are, if anything, more striking. Of the 15 variants instanced by Griesbach, 11 occur in *fam.* Θ ; 1 goes with the T.R. against *fam.* Θ ; 3 are unsupported by any MS., but of these 1 is practically the reading of *fam.* Θ, and the other 2 spoil the sense and are obviously errors in the MS. (or printer) of Origen. Figures like these amount to demonstration. The text of Mark which Origen used at the time he wrote these works was that of *fam.* Θ.

The next step was to test the character of the text of Matthew

---

[1] The suspicion that some, if not all, of the 13 Byzantine variants do not represent what Origen actually wrote, is partially justified by the fact that one of them (Mk. xiv. 62) is quoted in Origen's *Commentary on John* (bk. xviii.) according to the reading of *fam.* Θ. Of these 13 variants 2, though found in the great majority of Byzantine MSS., do not occur in the printed T.R., which has, besides some very late readings, a few derived from Codex 1. Since this MS. was used by Erasmus, the T.R. occasionally supports *fam.* Θ against the Byzantine text. For the purpose of the above calculations, the only MS., except those mentioned in the table on p. 83, which I have reckoned as evidence for *fam.* Θ is 544.

which was used by Origen. I recollected that books on textual criticism commonly speak of the reading " Jesus Barabbas " in Mt. xxvii. 17 as found " in MSS. known to Origen," as if this characteristic reading of *fam.* Θ was one which, though known to Origen, did not occur in the text he ordinarily used. But on turning to the passage in the *Commentary on Matthew* I found to my surprise that this reading occurs in the text recited and commented on by Origen. It is the *omission* of the name Jesus before Barabbas that should properly be described as a reading " found in MSS. known to Origen." Origen dislikes the reading of the text he is using, and suggests that the name Jesus may be an heretical interpolation ; but it is in his text. He informs his readers that it is absent from MSS. known to him, but, presumably, not equally well known to them.[1]

An investigation of several sections in this *Commentary* (chosen for the exceptional length of the quotations they included) revealed the facts set out in Appendix III. Briefly, the majority of readings in Origen are found in one or more members of *fam.* Θ ; but a minority are not. Further examination, however, showed that, where the text of Origen deserts that of *fam.* Θ, it is almost always in order to agree with the Byzantine text. In Mt. xxii. and xxv., which were selected for minute study, Origen's quotations differ from the T.R. in 45 variants. In 37 of these his reading is supported by one or more members of *fam.* Θ. Clearly we must make a choice. Either Origen used a text which in the main was that of *fam.* Θ, but occasionally went over to the side of the Byzantine text, or the Gospel quotations in the MSS. from which is derived the printed text of Origen have been to a slight extent assimilated to the Byzantine standard. This is obviously the more probable

---

[1] The mystical interpretation, *verum mysterium*, of the contrast of the two prisoners Christ and Barabbas which he proceeds to develop has much more point if regarded as his way of making the best of a text which gave to both the name Jesus ; though the meaning is slightly obscured by the fact that it is introduced by the word *enim*, which I cannot help thinking stands for γοῦν, misread or misrendered as if it were γάρ.

alternative, and affords one more example of that assimilation of biblical quotations to the standard text which is one of the principal causes of corruption in the text of the Fathers (cf. p. 45 ff.). That this assimilation has affected the MS. tradition of Origen's quotations from Matthew more than those from Mark is only what we should expect ; for precisely the same distinction is found in the textual traditions of the Gospels themselves.

The evidence given above as to the assimilation to the Byzantine text of the quotations of Origen in the *Commentary on Matthew* compels us to discount the appearance in other works of Origen of occasional readings of the Byzantine type. In particular we can disregard the Byzantine readings which occur here and there in the Gospel quotations in the *Commentary on John*—more especially as that work depends upon a single MS. of the tenth century. Bearing this in mind I proceeded to test the quotations in the *Commentary on John* of Gospels other than Mark, selecting for the purpose a number of the longer, and therefore presumably more representative, passages. The tests, though by no means exhaustive, all pointed in one direction. Origen, so long as he was at work on the *Commentary on John*, continued to use his Alexandrian MS. for John (and in the main, I think, for Matthew); and where א B differ, Origen's MS. of John more often agreed with B than with א. But at some point or other he seems to have changed his MS. of Luke, as well as that of Mark, for one of the type of *fam.* Θ. Incidentally, we may infer that for some time after he reached Caesarea Origen read the Gospels, not in a Four-Gospel Codex, but on separate rolls.

After reaching these results, it occurred to me to check them by the discussion on " the Bible-text of Origen " by E. Preuschen in the Berlin edition of the *Commentary on John*, 1903. Preuschen shows conclusively that Origen frequently quotes from memory, conflating, for example, the Matthean and Lukan versions of the Parable of the Supper. From this it follows that we cannot indiscriminately take all his quotations as evidence of the text he used ; we must be careful to use only passages where it is evident from the context that he is commenting on a MS. open before him. But Preuschen goes on to argue that, even where it is clear that Origen is using a written copy, the text from which he quotes does not correspond at all closely with that found in any extant family of MSS. To prove this point Preuschen (p. xciv) selects three passages (all from tom. xix.), and gives the variants with the MS. evidence for each. The central column in the tables given below reproduces his statement of the facts. The right-hand column is my own addition, and gives the MS. evidence (much of which, of course, was not available when he wrote) for the readings of *fam.* Θ. It will be seen at once that this fuller statement of the evidence points to a conclusion very different from that which Preuschen draws.

ORIGEN.	SUPPORT QUOTED BY PREUSCHEN.	SUPPORT FROM *FAM.* Θ.
Mk. xii.		
v. 41. καὶ ἑστὼς (for καθίσας)	1, 69, Syr. Sin., Hcl[mg.], Arm.	Θ, 1, 13, 28, 69, 565.
κατέναντι (T.R.) (ἀπέναντι B 33 579)	ℵ A D L al	(T.R.) Θ, 1, 69, 124, 565. κατενώπιον 13 &c. ἀπέναντι 1424 &c., U, 544.
καὶ πᾶς (for πῶς)	*Solus* *	
ἔβαλλεν (for βάλλει)	69[2]	13, 69[1] (ἔβαλε), 124.
v. 42. ἐλθοῦσα δὲ (καὶ . . .)	D, Latt., Boh. Sah.	Θ, 565, 700.
v. 43. εἶπεν (for λέγει)	B ℵ A D L, Δ, 33 K U a. k. verss.	Θ, 565, 700.
ἡ πτωχὴ αὕτη (order)	D, a, b, ff, g[2], i	Θ, 565, 700.
ἔβαλεν (for βέβληκεν)	B A D L, Δ, 33	Θ, 565.

* πῶς mis-spelt πᾶς : καὶ added to restore grammar.

H

LUKE xxi. 1-4

ORIGEN'S TEXT.	SUPPORT AS QUOTED BY PREUSCHEN.	SUPPORT FROM *FAM.* Θ.
Lk. xxi. *v.* 1. εἰς ... εἰς ... (for εἶδε ... εἰς) T.R.	Syr. Cur.	13 and 124 read εἶδε. Was εἶδε a marginal note, correcting the *first* εἰς to εἶδε, which has been applied to *both* occurrences of εἰς ?
v. 1. εἰς τὸ γαζο-φυλάκιον τὰ δῶρα αὐτῶν πλουσίους (order)	B א D L X 1, 33, 69. e, Syr. Pesch.	1, 69.
v. 2. om. δὲ . . om. καί before τινα . (T.R. καί τινα)	S, *a*, Boh., Arm. B א L Q X, 33. K M, Γ, *c*, *ff*, *i*, Syr. Hcl.ᵗᵉˣᵗ, Aeth.	124. 124. (Θ, 1, 700 τινὰ καὶ.)
om. ἐκεῖ . . .	D, Syr. Sin. Cur. Pesch. Aeth.	2193 (of *fam.* 1).
λεπτὰ δύο . . . (order)	B א Q L X, 33. Vulg. Syr. Sin. Cur. Pesch. Boh.	Θ.
v. 3. ἡ πτωχὴ αὕτη (T.R.) (for αὕτη ἡ πτωχὴ א B D, 13 &c.)	A X, 1, E G H *al.* *a*, Syr. Hcl.	(T.R.) Θ, 1, 565, 700.
v. 4. πάντες . . (for ἅπαντες)	B א D Δ	
τὰ δῶρα τοῦ θεοῦ (T.R.) (om. τοῦ θεοῦ B א 1 &c.)	A D Q ? E G H *al.* Latt. verss.	(T.R.) Θ, 13 &c., 700.
πάντα . . . (for ἅπαντα)	B א D Q L X 33, 69	13 &c., 1071

As displayed by Preuschen in the central column, the MS. evidence appears amply to justify his conclusion that the text of Origen does not correspond to any of the recognised families. But the right-hand column tells a different tale. It shows that, so far as these particular passages are concerned, the text used by Origen has the closest resemblance to that of *fam.* Θ —though I suspect that the two readings in which Origen and Θ *both* agree with the T.R. against a few members of *fam.* Θ are not original, but the result of the text of both having been conformed to the Byzantine standard. Now, if the above passages had been selected by myself to substantiate the conclusion for which I have argued above, the remarkable coincidence they exhibit between the text of Origen and *fam.* Θ would have been impressive. But they are passages specially selected by Preuschen in order to prove a thesis precisely opposite to mine, viz. that Origen's quotations correspond to no known form of text. The fact, therefore, that they so exactly bear out my own conclusion is, I venture to think, a strong confirmation of the correctness of this conclusion.

The third passage which Preuschen selects is Jn. vii. 40-46. In this he quotes five variants. In three of these the reading of Origen is supported by B T L; in the fourth, by T. There remains the substitution of the perfect γεγένηται for the aorist ἐγένετο, a reading of Origen found in no extant MS. of the Gospels. Seeing that the text of the *Commentary on John* depends on a single copy of the tenth century, our confidence that this last variant really stood in the passage as originally quoted by Origen must be very small. Since of the four other variants three are found in B T L and the fourth in the Graeco-Sahidic MS. T—the text of which, so far as it survives, is even nearer to B than א—the passage merely serves to corroborate my own observation that the text of the Fourth Gospel used by Origen throughout the *Commentary* was on the whole nearer to B than to א.

I have not found leisure to test the scattered quotations

from Luke or John which occur here and there in the *Commentary on Matthew*—a peculiarly delicate task, since most of them are short passages likely to be quoted from memory. But I have noted one passage where the context makes it clear that he is quoting from a written text, for he contrasts the readings of John with the Synoptics. This occurs in his comment on Mt. xvi. 24 (tom. xii. 24). Origen here (Greek and Latin support one another) quotes John with the addition of the words "and they laid upon him the cross." This addition is one of the most remarkable of the Ferrar readings and is only found elsewhere in Syr. Hier. This in itself is almost enough to prove that, whether he always quoted from it or not, Origen at this time certainly had access to a copy of John with the *fam.* Θ text.

A further question must now be raised. Does *fam.* Θ represent a text which Origen found already in possession in A.D. 231 when he moved to Caesarea ? Or is it a recension which he himself made at a subsequent date ? There can, I think, be no reasonable doubt that *fam.* Θ represents the old text of Caesarea and not a recension by Origen. The following are relevant considerations.

(1) In his *Commentary on Matthew* (tom. xv. 14), Origen, after deploring the number of variants between texts of the Gospels, gives a brief account of the efforts that he had himself made, θεοῦ διδόντος, towards the restoring the true text of the LXX ; but adds that he had not dared to do the same thing for the text of the New Testament. *In exemplaribus autem Novi Testamenti hoc ipsum me posse facere sine periculo non putavi.* This passage would be decisive evidence that, at the time of writing the *Commentary on Matthew*, Origen had produced no recension of the Gospels, but for the fact that the words I have quoted from the old Latin version are not found in the Greek. But the Greek MSS. of the *Commentary on Matthew* ultimately all go back to a single much mutilated, and possibly intentionally abbreviated, archetype ; also the clause in question,

read in its full context, seems essential to the point which Origen is wishing to make. Hence it may be taken as reasonably certain that an equivalent clause originally stood in the Greek. In view, however, of the margin of uncertainty, further considerations may be adduced in support of that conclusion.

(2) Eusebius devotes a large part of the sixth book of his *Ecclesiastical History* to a description of the work of Origen ; but, though he expatiates at length on Origen's critical labours on the text of the Greek Old Testament, he says nothing at all about any such work on the New.

(3) Origen's discussion of the reading Jesus Barabbas, Mt. xxvii. 16, 17, makes it quite clear that he objected strongly on theological grounds to the idea that the sacred name of Jesus should be borne by a robber. He affirms that it was absent from many MSS., and suggests that it was an heretical interpolation in the text on which he is commenting. This surely implies that it was in the text most familiar at Caesarea. Indeed, as he was obviously lecturing with a copy of the Gospel open before him, one would naturally suppose that it was the copy ordinarily used for public worship in the church in which his homiletical lectures were delivered. In a recension made by himself the offending passage would have been omitted, since he had excellent MS. authority for so doing.

(4) Jerome twice alludes to *exemplaria Adamantii*, that is, "the copies of Origen" (Adamantius was another name of Origen). The allusion is obscure. Jerome, however, shows no knowledge of any reading characteristic of *fam.* Θ ; [1] but he frequently appeals to MSS. practically identical with ℵ. Reasons will be given (cf. App. IV.) for the view that if Jerome associated any text with the name of Origen it was that of ℵ.

We conclude that *fam.* Θ represents the text which Origen found already established in the Church of Caesarea in 231.

---

[1] This statement is based on a fairly thorough examination of the lists of non-Byzantine readings, either expressly cited by Jerome or introduced by him into the Vulgate, given in Wordsworth and White's Vulgate, pp. 653-671

This affords another fixed point for the history of the text of the New Testament.

The text of the New Testament is a subject about which so many theories have been spun that it may be well to recapitulate the evidence that this particular conclusion is not a matter of theory but rests on definitely ascertained fact. (*a*) Θ and the group of allied MSS. contain between them an enormous number of readings which deviate from the standard text ; in the great majority of these deviations different members of this group support one another in the readings substituted for those of the standard text. (*b*) The readings in which one or more of this group of MSS. disagree with the Byzantine text are a definite set, to be ascertained by purely objective observation ; it is found that these residual readings correspond to the text of the Gospels of Matthew and Mark used by Origen in his *Commentary on Matthew*, and to the text of Mark and Luke used in the later books of his *Commentary on John*. There is no room here for subjective judgements, the facts either are, or are not, as I have stated.

The MSS. sent to Constantine

Caesarea and its Library had a considerable reputation in the Nicene and early post-Nicene period. Nevertheless, the number of MSS. which show a larger or smaller admixture of the Θ text is larger than we should have antecedently expected if it represented merely the local text of Caesarea. Again, the very different way in which the Caesarean and the Byzantine texts are mixed in the different members or sub-families of the Θ group suggests that these MSS. represent different mixtures current in several different localities. This implies that the Θ text was at one time very widely circulated. Here, I believe, von Soden is on the right track.

When Constantine rebuilt the old city of Byzantium, hoping by magnificent buildings and imported works of art to make it worthy to replace Rome as the capital of the Empire, from policy and conviction he showed himself specially lavish towards the Church. About 331 he wrote to Eusebius—the correspondence is still extant—desiring him to prepare at the Imperial expense fifty copies of the Scriptures on vellum for the use of that number of churches in the new city. von Soden suggested that what he calls the " I text " is descended from a recension made by Eusebius and disseminated through these copies. von Soden's " I text," however, never existed, nor is there any evidence that Eusebius undertook a recension of the Gospels. But the natural thing for Eusebius to do would be to have the copies asked for by Constantine made from the text he used himself, *i.e.* that of MSS. deemed good at Caesarea. This would differ very little from that of the MS. used by Origen a century earlier in the same Church ; and, as K. Lake has recently shown, Eusebius as well as Origen used a text of the type preserved in *fam.* Θ.

Some fifty years later, *c.* 380, Jerome was at Constantinople. He found that the authorities there advocated the text of the martyr Lucian—a text which, as we shall see later, was practically identical with what I have called the Byzantine text. We can readily understand their preference of the Lucianic recension ; it includes the longer conclusion of Mark and so many other interesting passages omitted by the Caesarean text. (Cf. the list, p. 88.) Assuming, then, that the authorities at Constantinople had decided to adopt it, what would become of the fifty copies given by Constantine ? They were not written on perishable papyrus, but on vellum ; and the vellum on which the two contemporary MSS. B ℵ were written is still in excellent preservation after the lapse of nearly 1600 years. They would not be destroyed, they would be corrected—some copies more thoroughly than others, some in one place, some in another. In the course of time the wealthier churches of the city would desire clean new copies, undisfigured by constant correction. They would get these from the best reputed copying establishments, whether secular or monastic, in Constantinople. Such establishments would have been careful to provide them-

selves with copies of the standard text ; so the new copies
would represent the Lucianic text. What would become of the
old ones ? Most probably they would be given away or sold
cheaply to smaller churches or monasteries in the provinces,
who could not afford to buy new and clean copies of the standard
text. Thus many of the fifty copies originally made for Constantinople, more or less corrected to the standard text, would
get into the provinces. Some of them in all probability are
the ancestors of some of the mixed MSS. we now possess.[1]

I venture the suggestion that one of these discarded MSS.
was used by St. Mesrop and St. Sahak to revise the Armenian
version. These two, we are told, translated the Scriptures
into Armenian about A.D. 400 ; but subsequently, receiving
" correct " copies *from Constantinople*, proceeded to revise their
earlier work. Dean Armitage Robinson [2] argues that the
original translation was made from the Old Syriac. This has
been lately disputed by the French scholar Prof. F. Macler—
a summary account and criticism of whose theories is given
by R. P. Blake in the *Harvard Journal of Theology*, July 1922.
Macler holds that the Armenian was derived directly from a
Greek text of the type which von Soden calls the " I text," most
nearly related to Θ, and lacking many of the characteristic readings
of D—a phrase which would serve as a description of *fam.* Θ.
The question is one which hinges largely on linguistic considerations, a judgement on which demands a knowledge of both
Armenian and Syriac, which I unfortunately lack. But it
certainly fits in with statistics given on p. 90, which show
that the Armenian is frequently a supporter of *fam.* Θ, not
only where *fam.* Θ and the Old Syriac agree, but almost as often
where they differ. The hypothesis that the Greek MS. used by
St. Mesrop to revise his first translation had the *fam.* Θ text
might, I think, explain the phenomena noted by Armitage

[1] Since this was written the belief has been growing in my mind that
most of the *mixed* MSS. (*i.e.* the Greek MSS. other than D and W in Mk. i.-v.)
assigned by Soden to his I text are descended from these 50 copies—which thus
had an influence comparable to that of the *recensions* of Lucian and Hesychius.

[2] In " Euthaliana," *Texts and Studies*, iii. 3.

Robinson, and also those brought forward by Macler. Its verification, however, must await the publication of a text of the Armenian version based on a critical study of the oldest MSS. with complete apparatus, which, to the best of my knowledge, does not yet exist. Meanwhile it would seem sufficiently plausible to justify us in *provisionally* regarding the Armenian as a supplementary witness for the text of *fam.* Θ.

Besides this, in Palestine itself, there would necessarily be in circulation many copies of the old text of Caesarea. These also would suffer correction from the standard text ; and these half-corrected copies may be the ancestors of some surviving members of the Θ group. One such copy, very heavily revised, was, I believe, used by the corrector of ℵ, known as ℵ^c, who worked in the library of Caesarea (cf. p. 578). Again, since Jerusalem, until the Council of Chalcedon, 451, was under the jurisdiction of the metropolitan of Caesarea, it is possible that Jerusalem used much the same text as Caesarea. It is at any rate an interesting fact that in 565, at the end of Mark, there is a colophon stating that it was copied from old MSS. from Jerusalem. If Constantinople, Caesarea, and Jerusalem were all centres of distribution, the evidence for a wide circulation of the Θ text is readily accounted for.

But though there is an element of speculation in any theory as to how this Caesarean text came to be propagated, there is none, I submit, in the conclusion that in *fam.* Θ this text is preserved. Superficially the MSS. of this family differ greatly from one another ; but on examination it appears that this is solely due to the different degree to which they have been corrected to the Byzantine standard. Deduct the Byzantine readings, and the differences between these MSS. in regard to the residual text is very small. There are differences, but they differ far less from one another than do ℵ B L. From this fact, and from the very close correspondence of this residual text with the quotations of Origen, we are entitled to infer that (however we may explain its preservation) the readings of this family give the text read at Caesarea about 230 in an extremely pure form.

It would be well worth while for some scholar to prepare a continuous text of *fam.* Θ, after the model of Ferrar and Abbott's edition of **13** &c. It would then, I think, appear that a practically continuous text of this type, at least for Mark, has been preserved. And this text would rank alongside B and D as the third primary authority for the text of the Gospels.

Concluding Survey

If we look at the map we see at once that the Churches whose early texts we have attempted to identify stand in a circle round the Eastern Mediterranean—Alexandria, Caesarea, Antioch, (Ephesus), Italy-Gaul, and Carthage. The remarkable thing is that the texts we have examined form, as it were, a graded series. Each member of the series has many readings peculiar to itself, but each is related to its next-door neighbour far more closely than to remoter members of the series. Thus B (Alexandria) has much in common with *fam.* Θ (Caesarea); *fam.* Θ shares many striking readings with Syr. S. (Antioch); Syr. S. in turn has contacts with D *b a* (Italy-Gaul); and, following round the circle to the point from which we started, *k* (Carthage) is in a sense a half-way house between D *b a* and B (Alexandria again).

Antecedently we should rather expect the text of any particular locality to be, up to a point, intermediate between those of the localities geographically contiguous with it on either side. But the exactness of correspondence between the geographical propinquity and the resemblance of text exceeds anything we should have anticipated. And this fact is, I feel, of some weight in confirming the general thesis propounded in these chapters.

There remains to draw a practical conclusion. In discussions of variants in commentaries and elsewhere it is usual, in quoting the MS. evidence for a particular reading, to cite first the uncials which support it in *alphabetical* order, then cursives in *arithmetical* order. This practice is fundamentally misleading. von Soden's method of quoting authorities in three great groups (K H I) would have been a great improvement had he divided his I group into three, corresponding to Θ, D, Syr. S., and their respective allies. What we want to know in any given case is the reading (*a*) of B ℵ and their allies, (*b*) of D and its allies W^{Mk.} Old Lat., (*c*) of the leading members of *fam.* Θ, (*d*) of the Old Syriac, Armenian, and Old Georgian, and (*e*) of the T.R. In subsequent chapters, therefore, I shall cite MSS. thus. Further, it is not as a rule necessary to cite all the evidence of each group. Thus, if a reading is supported by ℵ B L, nothing is gained by adding C Δ Ψ to the list; if it is supported by *a*, *b*, *e*, *k*, it is superfluous to add further Old Latin evidence. Only where the leading authorities of any of the great texts disagree with one another is it, for ordinary purposes, important to cite their subordinate supporters. The method of citing all uncials, and that in alphabetical order, disturbs the judgement and inevitably gives an undue weight to mere numbers. The fallacy of numbers is insisted on by Hort (ii. p. 43 ff.), as it is only through a chapter of accidents, different in every case, that any MS. not representing the standard text has survived. The first principle of scientific criticism is that MSS. should be not counted but weighed. And the weight of a MS. depends on the extent to which it preserves, more or less, one of the ancient local texts.

P.S.—For a summary account of the confirmation by subsequent research of the main conclusions of this chapter, see above (p. vii.), *Preface to Fourth Impression.* The reconstructed Caesarean text for three chapters of Mark is given in the article by K. Lake, etc., there referred to.

THE MSS. AND THE LOCAL TEXTS

(The student should memorise primary and secondary authorities.)

	ALEXANDRIA.	ANTIOCH.	CAESAREA.	ITALY AND GAUL.	CARTHAGE.
Primary Authority	B	Syr. S.	Θ 565$^{Mk.}$	D	$k^{Mk.\ Mt.}$
Secondary do.	$\aleph$ L Sah. Boh.	Syr. C.	1 &c. 13 &c. 28 700 (W$^{Mk.}$) Old Georgian	b a	(W$^{Mk.}$) e
Tertiary do.	C, 33, W$^{1\,Lk.\ Jn.}$ $\Delta^{Mk.}$ $\Psi^{Mk.}$ *Frags.*: T$^{Lk.\ Jn.}$ Z$^{Mt.}$ $\Xi^{Lk.}$	Syr. Pesh. (Arm.)	1424 &c. 544 N-Σ-O Φ 157	ff^2 $h^{Mt.}$ i r $c^{Mt.\ Jn.}$ *Frag.*: n (cf. a)	$c^{Mk.\ Lk.}$
Supplementary	579$^{Mk.\ Lk.\ Jn.}$ 892 1241 X	Syr. Hcl. Syr. Hier.	U Λ 1071 1604 Old Arm.	ff, g, l, q (?) f	m
Patristic	Origen A.D. 230 Cyril Alex. 430		Origen A.D. 240 Eusebius 325	Tatian 170 Irenaeus 185	Cyprian 250

1 &c. = 1—22—118—131—209—872$^{Mk.}$—1278—1582—2193.   **13 &c.** = 13—69—124—230—346—543—788—826—828—983—1689—1709.
1424 &c. = 28 MSS., including M, cited by Soden as I$^{\Phi}$.   Byzantine Text: S V Ω; E F G H; (A, K Π, Y); (Γ); (W$^{Mt.}$).
Mixed Frags. P Q R$^{Lk.}$ *N.B.*—1 &c. = *fam.* 1 = Sod. I$^{\Phi}$; 13 &c. = *fam.* 13 = Sod. I$^{\Gamma}$, Sod. I$^{\alpha}$ misleadingly includes D with Θ, 28, 544, 565. 700.

V

THE REVISED VERSIONS OF ANTIQUITY

SYNOPSIS

THE BEGINNINGS OF CRITICISM

Alexandria the birthplace of Textual Criticism in its application to the Greek Classics. The Christian scholarship of Alexandria. Origen's Hexapla, an attempt to produce a critical text of the Septuagint or Greek O.T. The recensions of Lucian in Antioch and of Hesychius in Egypt.

THE REVISION BY LUCIAN

Evidence that the Byzantine text is ultimately descended from the recension of Lucian. Although, however, it originated in Antioch, the capital of the Roman province of Syria, it is preferable to call this text " Byzantine " (with Griesbach) rather than (with Hort) " Syrian." It appears to be an eclectic revision based on earlier texts, including, as well as the Alexandrian and Western texts, a text akin to Syr. S.

CHARACTER OF THE RECENSION

Probably Lucian attempted to produce a " catholic " text ; it is nearer to the Alexandrian than to other local texts. The nature and origin of the " Western " element accepted by Lucian. The problem whether the Byzantine text has preserved readings of earlier texts not otherwise known to us.

The earliest MS. with a text approximately that of Lucian is $V^{cent.}$ A ; von Soden, however, thinks the purest form of this text is to be found in S V Ω, and next to them in the group E F G H. He classes A with K II, which, he thinks, give Lucian's text with an appreciable admixture of readings of *fam.* Θ. Safest to take S V Ω as the typical MSS. of the Byzantine text without begging the question as to whether A, E, or S nearest to Lucian.

THE RECENSION OF HESYCHIUS

Bousset finds this in the B ℵ text ; Hort (but tentatively) in that of C L Boh., etc.

There were two schools of textual criticism, one preferring the " inclusive " method followed by Lucian and the scribes (or editor) of C L Ψ, etc., the other following the strict Alexandrian tradition, which is comparable to Hort's. B is the product of the latter school.

To which school did Hesychius belong ? Significance of Jerome's strictures on his recension. Possibly connection of B ℵ text with Pierius.

In any case the B ℵ text goes back in essentials to the time of Origen or earlier, and represents the oldest text of Alexandria.

CHAPTER V

THE REVISED VERSIONS OF ANTIQUITY

THE BEGINNINGS OF CRITICISM

THE science of textual criticism was born in Alexandria when Aristarchus (c. 200 B.C.) made his famous effort to produce a critical text of the poems of Homer. Subsequent scholars followed his lead. Diligent search was made for the oldest and most authentic texts with the support of the royal patrons.[1] Ptolemy Euergetes had already begged of Athens the loan of the official copies of the Greek Tragedians—and afterwards refused to restore the originals. And till its ultimate destruction it was the pride of the Library of Alexandria to possess and reproduce the purest texts of the Greek classics. The name Library disguises the fact that the institution in question corresponded much more closely to what we mean by a University, considered especially as a centre of specialist learning and research. About A.D. 180 the Christian Pantaenus started what is known as the Catechetical School, which, as Dr. Bigg remarked, had very much the same relation to the Royal Library as a denominational Theological College in Oxford or Cambridge has to the University.

It is not, therefore, surprising to find Origen, the third head of this School, very early in his career already at work on a critical edition of the text of the Old Testament. This was known as the *Hexapla* and was finished about 240, some years after his retreat to Caesarea. The *Hexapla* presented in six

[1] Cf. T. W. Allen, *Homer: The Origins and the Transmission* (Oxford, 1924), p. 292 ff.

parallel columns the original Hebrew, a transliteration of it into the Greek alphabet, and four rival Greek translations of it then current. Eusebius (*H.E.* vi. 16) tells us of the diligent search in out-of-the-way places made for the most ancient MSS. of these versions. Fragments of the *Hexapla* survive, but the work as a whole must have been so cumbrous that it is unlikely it was ever copied except in certain books. But the column containing the LXX version was published separately by Eusebius and Pamphilus, and became the standard text of the Greek Old Testament used in Palestine. This text appears to be preserved in a relatively pure state in two MSS. of the Pentateuch and two of the Prophets.[1]

Jerome tells us that the Churches of Antioch and Constantinople preferred a text revised by the martyr Lucian, while at Alexandria the text approved of was that of a certain Hesychius.[2]

Lucian of Antioch died a martyr A.D. 312. The identity of the Hesychius here mentioned is uncertain, but he is generally supposed to be the Egyptian bishop of that name who also, in 307, suffered martyrdom. In the passage just cited, Jerome is speaking of the Old Testament. But in the open letter to Damasus (cf. p. 590), which stands as a preface to the Gospels in the Vulgate, he makes it clear that the recensions of Lucian and Hesychius included the New Testament as well.

THE REVISION BY LUCIAN

It is practically certain that what I have spoken of as "the Byzantine text" of the New Testament goes back to this revision by Lucian of Antioch to which Jerome alludes. Or,

---

[1] Cf. H. B. Swete, *Introduction to the Old Testament in Greek*, p. 76 ff.

[2] "Alexandria et Aegyptus in Septuaginta suis Hesychium laudat auctorem, Constantinopolis usque Antiochiam Luciani Martyrii exemplaria probat, mediae inter has provinciae Palestinae codices legunt, quos ab Origene elaboratos Eusebius et Pamphilus vulgaverunt : totusque orbis hac inter se trifaria varietate compugnat." From Jerome's Preface to the Vulgate version of Chronicles.

to speak strictly, the Byzantine text, as it appears in the Textus Receptus, has the same relation to the text of Lucian as the ordinary printed editions of the Vulgate have to the text of Jerome. It is the same text, but somewhat corrupted during the Middle Ages, partly by the fresh errors of generations of copyists and partly by an infiltration of readings from the older texts it superseded. The evidence for this conclusion may be briefly summarised. It is stated in the Menologies—short accounts of a Saint for reading on his day—that Lucian bequeathed his pupils a copy of the Old and New Testaments written in three columns in his own hand. A famous representative of the school of Lucian is John Chrysostom, who wrote at Antioch from 381 onwards. Towards the end of his life he was for a short time, over the turn of the century A.D. 400, Patriarch of Constantinople. The quotations of the New Testament in his voluminous works are numerous ; and they prove that the text he used was substantially the Byzantine, apart from its mediaeval corruptions. But the Byzantine text, we shall see, when closely examined *looks as if* it was formed as the result of a revision made on the principle of following alternately or, if possible, combining Alexandrian, Western and Eastern texts. Also, a text giving just these particular combinations and alternations of readings is not found in the quotations of any Father earlier than Chrysostom ; but after that it becomes more and more common, beginning with writers connected with either Antioch or Constantinople, until it replaces all others. The conclusion, then, seems obvious that the text of Chrysostom represents a revision made at or near Antioch early in the fourth century, and speedily adopted not only there but in Constantinople. And since Jerome, who had himself studied in both these cities before 380, expressly says that these Churches used the revised text of Lucian, it would seem gratuitous scepticism to suppose that the apparently revised text used by Chrysostom was other than that of Lucian.

But, if it be asked for, there is further evidence. Ulfilas, who converted the Goths, translated the Gospels and parts of the Old Testament into Gothic. As he died about 380, the Gothic version must be earlier than that date. The Gothic is the first of the early versions to show a predominantly Byzantine text ; and in 341 Ulfilas, we know, was consecrated Bishop *at Antioch.* It may be added that the great LXX scholars, Field and Lagarde, starting from certain readings definitely marked as Lucianic in the *Syro-Hexapla,* produced convincing reasons for supposing that in some books certain MSS. of the Old Testament give the text of Lucian.[1] The text of these MSS. agrees with the Old Testament quotations of Chrysostom, and also with such fragments of the Gothic version of the Old Testament as survive. It is also remarkable that the Lucianic recension of the Old Testament appears, like the Lucianic text of the New Testament, to be a revision which aims at combining earlier texts.

The contention that the Byzantine text is an essentially revised text—following sometimes one, sometimes another of the earlier texts—made in or near Antioch about 300, was the foundation - stone of Westcott and Hort's theory of the textual criticism of the New Testament. To appreciate its full force, the student must read the relevant parts of Hort's Introduction. And nothing that has been discovered since appears to me to have weakened their case, so far as the main issue is concerned. Hort himself believed that this revision was most probably the work of Lucian ; but, to avoid committing himself on this point without further evidence, he gave this text the name " Syrian " to indicate that it originated in the Greek-speaking province of Syria of which Antioch was the capital. The name was unfortunately chosen. It is very confusing to the uninitiated, who naturally suppose it implies some special connection with the " Syriac " versions—which belong, as a matter of fact, not to " Syria," but to the Syriac-speaking Church, whose centre was Edessa in Mesopotamia. Moreover, the term " Syrian," though applicable to the original recension

---

[1] H. B. Swete, *An Introduction to the Old Testament in Greek,* p. 82 ff.

of Lucian, is not appropriate to the standard text of the Byzantine Empire if, as Hort himself thought, this is the result of a later revision. Whether the Byzantine text of the IX$^{cent.}$ is identical with the text of Lucian or a slightly revised form of it is a question not easy to answer. But, paradoxical as it sounds, it is this IX$^{cent.}$ text that really concerns us most ; for it was by the Byzantine standard, not by that of the actual text of Lucian—supposing these to be different—that MSS. of mixed texts, which are of such importance to the critic, have been corrected. It is, therefore, by deducting actual Byzantine, not hypothetical Lucianic, readings that we get back to the older element in their text. For these reasons I have reverted to Griesbach's nomenclature, and speak of this text, not as " Syrian," but as " Byzantine."

But there are some important respects in which Hort's view of the constituent elements in the Lucianic revision must be modified in the light of subsequent discovery. As Burkitt points out, in the Additional Notes contributed by him to the second edition of Westcott and Hort's Greek Testament (p. 330), " a text like Syr. S. stands in places against ℵ B D united, entering not infrequently as an independent constituent element into the Antiochian (Syrian) text." A notable instance is the famous " On earth peace, goodwill towards men." Here the reading of Syr. S. has passed into the Textus Receptus, against the united testimony of ℵ B D Latt., which read " peace among men in whom he is well pleased." So again the Byzantine text reads ἄριστον, with Syr. S. and C., Arm., against the ἄρτον of ℵ B D Latt. in Lk. xiv. 15.

Conflate readings, in which the Lucianic text puts side by side a variant found in ℵ B with the alternative given in D Lat., formed one of the most striking pieces of evidence adduced by Hort to prove that the Lucianic text was a revision based on texts of the other types. Hence a " conflate reading," in which Syr. S. supplies one member and ℵ B and D Lat. combined provide the other, is striking evidence, not only of the independence of the Syr. S. type of text, but of the importance attached to it by the revisers.

Of the instances quoted by Burkitt, Mk. i. 13 may be cited. The Byzantine text reads ἐκεῖ ἐν τῇ ἐρήμῳ. One member of this phrase, ἐκεῖ, is found in Syr. S., supported in this instance by some representatives of *fam.* Θ ; the other member, ἐν τῇ ἐρήμῳ, is in ℵ B D Latt. Another very pretty example is noted by Prof. Lake.[1] The Byzantine μὴ προμεριμνᾶτε μηδὲ μελετᾶτε (or προμελετᾶτε) (Mk. xiii. 11) is a conflation of μὴ προμεριμνᾶτε B D Latt., etc., with μὴ προμελετᾶτε Ψ 047 Syr. S. Another example is the reading of the T.R. in Lk. ii. 5, τῇ μεμνηστευμένῃ αὐτοῦ γυναικί " his betrothed wife." Here ἐμνηστευμένῃ without γυναικί is read by ℵ B ; but Syr. S., supported by *a, b, c, ff*[2], reads " wife," omitting the word for " betrothed." Curiously enough, D and *e* in this case support B against the combined Latin and Syriac.

CHARACTER OF THE RECENSION

If the Lucianic revision originated in Antioch, the revisers (we should expect) would start with a bias in favour of the traditional text of that Church. Nevertheless, the Byzantine text is fundamentally nearer to the Alexandrian than to the " Western " type. There was an ancient rivalry between Antioch and Alexandria, and antecedently we should not have expected an Antiochian revision to start off, as it were, from the Alexandrian text. Burkitt suggests that the fall of Paul of Samosata, 270, may have had something to do with it. Certainly this meant the triumph of the " catholic " as opposed to the " nationalist " tendency in theology ; and it is possible that Lucian definitely set out to produce a " catholic " recension of the Scriptures. That is, he may have sent for MSS. from Alexandria, Ephesus, and, perhaps, even Rome, and endeavoured, with the aid of these as well as the local text of Antioch, to

[1] *J.T.S.*, Jan. 1900, p. 291.

produce a text representing the combined traditions of the Great Churches. Whether because of the special prestige enjoyed by Alexandrian scholarship in regard to textual criticism in general, or from the accident that of the MSS. he used the Alexandrian happened to be the oldest, he seems to have taken that text as the basis for his revision. Strange, then, as it sounds, it really does look as if Lucian and his fellow-revisers were in very much the same position as the English and American revisers after another fifteen hundred years. All desired to restore the true original text of the Gospels, all desired to retain the traditional text of their own Church, except in so far as the latest researches in textual criticism made this impossible, and all accepted MSS. of the B ℵ type as the best.

It would, however, seem a fair presumption that the majority of readings in which the earliest form of the Lucianic text differs from that of ℵ B L is likely to represent a text traditional at Antioch. This leads us to take a slightly different view of the so-called "Western" element in the Lucianic text. Most of the "Western" readings adopted by Lucian might have been derived from *either* Syr. S. *or* D, since there is so much in common between these two. But if, on other grounds, we regard Syr. S. as descended from the old text of Antioch, then we should suppose that Lucian did, as a matter of fact, adopt these readings because they occurred in the current text of Antioch, and did not go abroad, as it were, to derive them from MSS. of the type of D.

What, then, are we to say of the readings in the Lucianic text which occur in D but not in Syr. S. ? They may, as suggested above, have been derived from MSS. brought from Ephesus or Rome for the use of the revisers. But the phenomenon cannot be considered apart from the occurrence in Syr. C. of D readings not found in Syr. S. and of the occurrence in the text of Eusebius [1] of D readings not found in *fam.* Θ. The text of Syr. C., it is generally agreed, is later than that of Syr. S. ;

[1] My argument is weakened by the discovery that Eusebius used the *fam.* Θ **text.**

Eusebius is later than Origen, who in Eusebius' own city seems
to have used the *fam.* Θ text ; and Lucian of Antioch is later
than the translator of Syr. S., who may be presumed to have
used the old text of Antioch. In each case we have evidence
that the D element is later. We have already seen that the
later text of Alexandria suffered considerably through infiltration of Western readings. It would look as if the same thing
happened everywhere. Indeed, if Italy and Asia both used a
text of the D type, it would be inevitable that copies of the
Gospels brought by Christians from these provinces should
everywhere be a source of mixture. We conclude, then, that
the old text of Antioch had suffered a degeneration similar
to that we find in the later Alexandrian MSS., and that the
Antiochene MSS. used by Lucian had much the same relation
to the Greek text underlying Syr. S. as C L 33 579 have to B.
That is, he used a form of the old text of Antioch corrupted
by stylistic amendment, assimilation of parallels, and an infiltration of readings from texts of the D type.

The importance of this point is largely indirect. It bears
on the question, whence did Lucian get the readings known to
us only from their occurrence in the Byzantine text. Most of
the readings of the Byzantine text, which do not also occur
in one or other of the earlier texts, are of the nature either of
minor stylistic improvements or of assimilation of the text of
one Gospel to a parallel passage in another. Very few look
original ; but Lucian must have found them somewhere.

Hort held that the Lucianic revision was based solely on
texts of the three types of early text which he distinguished
—the "Neutral," represented by B א ; the "Alexandrian," C L ;
and the "Western," D Old Lat. He concluded that any
readings of the Lucianic text not to be found in our existing
authorities for these earlier texts were either very late or due
to the editorial efforts of the revisers. The discovery of Syr. S.
has shown that some readings of the Lucianic text were older
than Hort supposed. But two incomplete MSS. of the Old

Syriac form but slender evidence for the old Greek text of Antioch, and it is probable that some of the readings of the Lucianic text which do not appear in the Syriac were derived from the old text of Antioch. It is even possible that some of the agreements with the Byzantine text found in Origen's *Commentary on Matthew* may be original. Most of these are no doubt due to scribes and translators who have modified what he actually wrote to conform with their own Biblical text. But some may well be readings common to the texts of Antioch and Caesarea. Unfortunately we cannot detect such readings in Θ and its allies, supposing any occur there, simply because we have no means of distinguishing them from the admixture of Byzantine readings due to later revisers. Thus we have really no means of identifying those readings of the old text of Antioch, which survive in the Byzantine text, but which do not happen to occur in the Old Syriac, except internal probability. That criterion is, as a matter of fact, unfavourable to most characteristically Byzantine readings ; but there are some few which I think are deserving of more serious consideration than was accorded them by Hort. For the old Alexandrian text we have MS. evidence not substantially inferior to that possessed by Lucian, and we know how to use it better ; but for the various types of Eastern text Lucian must have had MSS. of a greater variety and better quality than any we possess. Hence, though the principles on which he made use of them may have been the reverse of critical, to say offhand that he has never preserved an ancient reading for which we have no other authority seems over-bold.

The fifth-century Codex A is the earliest Greek MS. giving a text which is approximately that of Lucian, though it seems to have a small proportion of readings belonging to earlier texts. The name Alexandrinus which it bears (it was given to Charles I. by an ex-Patriarch of Alexandria) is thus another pitfall for the innocent student, who naturally supposes that the text it represents is Alexandrian ; and, curiously enough, outside the

Gospels its text is Alexandrian ; for the rest of the New Testament A is a most constant ally of B ℵ.[1]

In von Soden's opinion, the purest form of Lucian's text is to be found in the group S V Ω, which he calls the K^1 text. In this judgement he may be right ; but it is safer to regard this text as that received at Constantinople in the $VI^{cent.}$, and thus as the purest type of the " Byzantine " text. The group E F G H he regards as the K^1 text, with a small infusion of " Ferrar " readings. Another group, headed by K Π, preserves, he thinks, the text used by Chrysostom in his Homilies on John and has a small mixture of " I " readings ; he regards A as a member of this group with a few intrusive readings.

But once it is conceded that Lucian's revision was based on the eclectic principle of choosing, now an Alexandrian, now a " Western " reading, it ceases to be of any great importance to know, in the case of any particular reading, whether as a matter of fact it is the one which Lucian happened to prefer. All that really matters is the broad fact that the Byzantine text is ultimately descended from his revision. Whether the oldest form of it is to be found in A or E or S is a comparatively small matter. The difference between the text of A and that of most

---

[1] The evidence for the ordinary view that it was written in Alexandria has been seriously shaken by Burkitt (*J.T.S.*, 1910, pp. 603 ff.), who suggests that it came, *via* Mt. Athos, from Constantinople. Personally, I should rather assign it to some place like Caesarea or Berytus (Beyrout) half-way between Antioch and Alexandria—for three reasons. (1) It contains, immediately after the New Testament, the two Epistles of Clement. An attempt to assign to these canonical or quasi-canonical authority is made in the *Apostolic Constitutions*, a late fourth-century work which undoubtedly emanated from that part of the world. (2) The combination of an Antiochian text of the Gospels with an Alexandrian text of the Acts and Epistles suggests some place where the influence of Antioch and of Alexandria met. (3) Its text of the Old Testament appears to be a non-Alexandrian text heavily revised by the *Hexapla* which we know was the dominant text of Palestine. The quotations of the LXX in New Testament writers and Josephus more often than not agree with A against B, which MS. seems to represent a pre-Origenic Alexandrian text (H. B. Swete, *op. cit.* p. 395). But the Gentile mission started from Antioch, not Alexandria ; and the New Testament writers and Josephus wrote in Antioch, Asia Minor, or Rome ; and would be likely to have used the Antiochian rather than the Alexandrian recension of the Jewish Bible.

of the uncials in the long list headed by E and ending with S V
(Ω was unknown to Tischendorf, and von Soden does not give its
readings [1]) in an ordinary Apparatus Criticus is really very small.
In fact, the group A E S would be found supporting one another
far more often than the leading members of the Egyptian group
א B L. The one really important reading which was certainly
absent from the text of Lucian, although it is found, sometimes
with, sometimes without, asterisks or obeli, in a majority of the
Byzantine MSS., is the Pericope Adulterae (Jn. vii. 53-viii. 11).

THE RECENSION OF HESYCHIUS

Is it possible to identify that recension of Hesychius which
Jerome tells us was preferred in Alexandria in his day ? Hort,
very tentatively, suggested that it is to be found in what he
called the " Alexandrian " text, i.e. in that later form of the
B text whose characteristic readings appear most abundantly
in C L and in the Bohairic version. Bousset, in his *Textkritische
Studien*, argued that B represents this recension. In that case,
since B was probably written in Alexandria within twenty years
or so of the death of Hesychius and was copied by an exceptionally careful scribe, it will represent an almost exact transcript
of what Hesychius wrote. On the other hand, the early date of
B makes it equally possible that it was produced, before the
Hesychian revision had had time to become the standard text of
Alexandria, by some scholar who dissented from his critical
methods.

It is not sufficiently realised that the difference of temperament and method which divided Hort and Scrivener in the
nineteenth century, existed also in the fourth. Eusebius, in
whose lifetime B, and possibly א also, were written, virtually
formulates two contrary principles, upon either of which an

---

[1] Von Soden assigns Ω to VIII[cent.], but Dr. Blake (having photographed the
original on Mt. Athos) tells me he feels certain it is late IX[cent.] or X[cent.]. If
so, no MS. earlier than IX[cent.] gives the K[1] text; but von Soden holds that it is
found in the VI[cent.] Purple MSS. (apart from their I mixture).

acceptable text of the Gospels could be framed. In various passages where he writes as a textual scholar, he says that the last twelve verses of Mark are absent from " almost all " or from " the more accurate " copies. But in his letter to Marinus,[1] after discussing the possibility of rejecting this passage altogether, he proceeds, " While another, not daring to reject anything whatever that is in any way current in the Scripture of the Gospels, will say that the reading is double, as in many other cases, and that each reading must be received ; on the ground that this reading finds no more acceptance than that, nor that than this, with faithful and discreet persons." Now this " inclusive " principle, that no reading can safely be rejected which has behind it a considerable weight of authority, is precisely that upon which the Lucianic revision was based.[2]

But the tradition of Alexandrian scholarship in regard to the text of Homer and the Greek classics was in favour of the opposite principle, that, namely, of basing a text on the oldest MS. The Ptolemies, we have seen, made great efforts to procure the oldest possible copies, and the emphasis laid by Eusebius on the efforts of Origen to do the same for the Greek Old Testament, shows that Christian scholarship inherited this tradition. A typical Alexandrian editor would have diligently sought out the oldest copy attainable and followed that. And, if it omitted passages found in later MSS., he would have regarded these as interpolations. Hort speaks of " the almost universal tendency of transcribers to make their text as full as possible, and to eschew omissions " ;[3] and infers that copyists would tend to prefer an interpolated to an uninterpolated text. This

[1] Quoted by Westcott and Hort, vol. ii. Appendix, p. 31.
[2] But Lucian also had a critic's conscience and the " inclusiveness " of his method may easily be exaggerated. He omits, for example, two notable interpolations in Matthew. The section "Seek ye to rise," etc., Mt. xx. 28, found in D Φ Syr. C. Hcl^mg. Old Lat., is shown by the MS. evidence to have been widely current, both in East and West. He also omits the spear-thrust, Mt. xxvii. 49, found in ℵ B C L U Γ, etc. ; but a reading so supported and also known to Chrysostom can hardly have been unknown to Lucian.
[3] W.H. ii. p. 175.

may be true of some of the local texts of the second century ;
it is the very opposite of the truth where scribes or editors
trained in the tradition of Alexandrian textual criticism are
concerned. The Alexandrian editors of Homer were as eagle-
eyed to detect and obelise "interpolations " in Homer as a
modern critic. That they actually excised such passages without MS. authority is improbable, for most of the passages they
suspect are found in existing MSS. On the other hand, many
lines occur in papyri and in quotations of Homer by earlier
writers, like Plato, which are not in our MSS. ; so it would seem
as if, wherever there was MS. authority for omission, they
inclined to *prefer the shorter reading.*

That Christian scholars and scribes were capable of the
same critical attitude we have irrefragable evidence. The
obelus, invented by Aristarchus to mark suspected passages in
Homer, is frequent in MSS. of the Gospel to mark just those
sections, like the Pericope in John, which modern editors reject.
The first corrector of א, probably the contemporary διορθωτής,
was at pains to enclose in brackets and mark with dots for
deletion two famous passages in Luke written by the original
scribe which, being absent from B W 579 and the Egyptian
versions, we infer were not accepted in the text at that time
dominant in Alexandria, viz. the incident of the " Bloody
Sweat " in Gethsemane (Lk. xxii. 43 f.) and the saying "Father
forgive them " (Lk. xxiii. 34). This is conclusive evidence, either
that the passages in question were disliked on dogmatic grounds,
or that the Christian scholars of Alexandria were as much alert
as Hort to rid the text of interpolations. In either case the
notion is completely refuted that the regular tendency of scribes
was to choose the longer reading, and that therefore the modern
editor is quite safe so long as he steadily rejects. And that
there were Christian scholars outside Egypt who adopted the
Alexandrian principle we have abundant evidence. Take two
of the critical notes in 565. The words " Blessed art thou among
women " are omitted in the text of Lk. i. 28 ; they are added

in the margin with the note " not found in the ancient copies "
οὐ κεῖται ἐν τοῖς ἀρχαίοις. Similarly in John there is the even
more remarkable note . . . ὡς ἐν τοῖς νῦν ἀντιγράφοις μὴ
κείμενον παρέλειψα, " (The section about the Adulteress) . . .
I have omitted as not read in the copies now current." Thus
two passages, both in themselves attractive and dogmatically
unobjectionable, are rejected, the one because it was omitted
by the ancient, and the other by the modern, copies. Surely
we have evidence of a resolution to purify the text from all
possible interpolation equal to that of Hort, who omitted one
set of passages because absent from the pure " Neutral " text,
and another set because absent from the " aberrant " " Western"
text. In codices 1 and 1582 the note on the Pericope points
out that it is not mentioned in the Commentaries of Chrysostom,
Cyril, and Theodore of Mopsuestia. 1582, besides having the
foregoing note on the Pericope, also, as we have seen, gives
Mk. xvi. 9-20 as a sort of Appendix ; but in the margin it has
at v. 19 the note, " Irenaeus, who was near to the apostles
(ὁ τῶν ἀποστόλων πλησίον), in the third book against heresies
quotes this saying as found in Mark." This is criticism of a
high scientific order.

Now, whoever was responsible for it, the B text has been
edited on the Alexandrian principle. Indeed the difference
between B and the Lucianic recension would be comparable
to that between the text of Westcott and Hort and the text
of the Revised Version. The Revisers definitely reject no reading
for which there is respectable authority, W.H. follow the oldest
MS. and suspect interpolation even in that. Now, Hesychius
may have gone on this principle. His recension may, like
Jerome's Vulgate, have been made at the invitation of the
Patriarch. And if the Patriarch deemed an official revision
desirable, diligent search would be made throughout Egypt for
the oldest copies. The climate of Egypt is exceptionally
favourable for the preservation of papyri, as the discovery in a
jar the other day (cf. p. 56) of a copy in the Coptic of the Gospel

of John 1500 years old reminds us. It would be remarkable
if Hesychius could not procure copies well over a century old.
Certainly, whoever edited it, the text of B looks as if it had been
based on copies old enough to have escaped serious corruption ;
and there is no conceivable reason why copies may not have
been used as old as the middle of the second century.

If B represents the recension of Hesychius—as, on the whole,
I am inclined to believe—then the later Alexandrian text
C L Δ Ψ 33, 579 must bear the same relation to it as the later
Byzantine text does to Lucian's revision, or the mediaeval
Vulgate to Jerome's authentic text—that is, it must represent
the inevitable degeneration which frequent copying entails, along
with a certain amount of re-infiltration into the revised text of
readings from older unrevised texts.

But there is another possibility. Hesychius may have had
more concern for the practical needs of the plain man than for
the demands of strict scholarship. Like Lucian he may have
preferred a text which included such " Western " readings as
were well known and long established, in which harsh grammar
and inelegancies of style had been emended, and in which
Mark's Gospel did not break off short in the middle of a sentence
but had a reasonable ending. Now this is precisely the kind
of text which we find in C L Ψ 33, 579 and the Bohairic version,
which Hort describes as a " partially degenerate form of the
B text." Three of these, L Ψ 579, besides some fragments
which belong to the same family, have the Shorter Conclusion
of Mark. Some of the " Alexandrian " grammatical improvements can be traced back as far as Clement and Origen ; the
Shorter Conclusion of Mark occurs in the third century Sahidic.[1]
Thus there is no convincing reason for dating the " Alexandrian "
text later than Hesychius.

The main objection to identifying B with the Hesychian
recension is Jerome's emphatic denunciation of the text of

---

[1] As the Shorter Conclusion occurs in the African Latin k, it may be part
of the " Western " mixture in the Sahidic.

Hesychius, along with that of Lucian, as an interpolated and corrupt revision. His attack on the Lucianic text is not difficult to explain ; after all, what Jerome says about the Lucianic text is practically what Hort, judging by the B ℵ standard, said of it fifteen hundred years later. But if B represents the Hesychian text, it is hard to see how Jerome can speak of it as "inter- polated." For the reasons given in Appendix IV.—where his words are quoted in the original—I am personally not disposed to attach much weight to his statement.

On the other hand, if L Ψ 579 represent the text of Hesychius, another explanation is possible. Jerome had studied in Antioch and Constantinople and must have been familiar with the Lucianic text, but at the date when he wrote the Preface to the Vulgate Gospels he had not yet been to Alexandria. Hence his knowledge of the Hesychian text may have been at second-hand, and may have been derived from some Alexandrian scholar of the school of Origen who, like Hort, regarded the "Alexandrian" corrections of L Ψ 579 as corruptions and the Shorter Conclusion of Mark as an interpolation, and had expressed his views with vigour. Now there was a certain Pierius, known as "the younger Origen," a disciple of Origen and head of the Catechetical School c. 265 ; from Jerome's notice of him (*De vir. illustr.* 76) he would seem to have survived by some years the persecution in which Hesychius was martyred, and to have lived the last part of his life at Rome. We know that Jerome had read and admired some of his writings, and he once appeals to the authority of "the MSS. of Origen and Pierius."[1] Is it possible that Jerome derived from some statement of Pierius the unfavourable verdict which he expresses on the text of Hesychius ? In that case the B ℵ text represents the text of the Catechetical School which prided itself on keeping alive the traditions of Origen.[2]

[1] Jerome's *Commentary on Matthew*, ad ch. xxiv.
[2] Burkitt, *J.T.S.*, Jan. 1916, p. 149, suggests that Origen himself may have discovered some old MS. which escaped corruptions which were already wide spread, and so was responsible for the revival of a purer text.

The question, however, whether we owe the B ℵ text to the action of Hesychius, Pierius, or some unknown scholar, is quite of minor importance. The essential point is that these MSS. appear to represent, more nearly than any others, the text used by Origen before A.D. 230 ; and Origen, especially when engaged on such an important work as his *Commentary on John*, would certainly have used the oldest text he could procure. We may, then, affirm with confidence that any reading of B which is supported by ℵ, L, or any other MS. of the Egyptian family almost certainly belongs to the Alexandrian text in its earliest form.

INTERPOLATION AND ASSIMILATION

SYNOPSIS

THE FALLACY OF THE SHORTER TEXT

Prof. Clark's criticism of the maxim *brevior lectio potior*; in classical authors accidental omission is more common than interpolation, hence the presumption is in favour of the genuineness of the *longer* reading. This principle cannot be applied without reservation to the text of the Gospels. But it has an important bearing on the general discredit attached to the Western text, as interpolated and as at times paraphrasing the true text.

The number of omissions in ℵ through homoioteleuton illustrates the possibility of accidental omissions having occurred in the earliest copy which reached Alexandria. The very conscientiousness of Alexandrian scribes would prevent the restoration at a later date of the omitted passages.

SOME NOTABLE READINGS

Accidental omission would be soon repaired in the place where a book was originally published, more slowly elsewhere ; but an insertion found in a local text remote from the place of writing may be suspected as an interpolation. Consideration of some famous readings in the light of this principle.

" Neither the Son," Mt. xxiv. 36 ; Jesus Barabbas, Mt. xxvii. 17 ; the spear thrust, Mt. xxvii. 49 ; " Seek to rise," etc., Mt. xx. 28 ; " The Light at the Baptism," Mt. iii. 16 ; " The Bloody Sweat," Lk. xxii. 43 f. ; " Father, forgive them," Lk. xxiv. 34.

ASSIMILATION OF PARALLELS

The tendency of scribes to make small verbal alterations in the direction of bringing passages where the Gospels already resemble one another into a still closer resemblance. This assimilation of parallels the main cause of textual corruption and has affected all lines of transmission. The B text has suffered less in this way than any other but is by no means immune.

" Western non-interpolations," the name given by Hort to some nine conspicuous readings, found in B, but absent from D or the Old Lat. He regarded these as harmonistic interpolations ; but he unduly isolated these nine from a large number of additions in the B text which, though less striking, are much more obviously due to assimilation to parallel passages.

Nevertheless it is fallacious to suppose that every omission by the Western text is right ; thus the omission of the words " He was taken up into heaven," Lk. xxiv. 51, is quite possibly an attempt to harmonise the Gospel with the Acts, and not *vice versa*.

The Voice at the Baptism, Lk. iii. 22, is another case where the Western text is probably original. B and its allies (here followed by T.R.) assimilate the text in Luke to the parallel version in Mark and Matthew. In the main, however, the Western text has suffered most, and the Alexandrian least, from assimilation.

Conclusion

A notable set of variants illustrating three principles : (1) the operation of assimilation on different lines of text tradition ; (2) the " conflate " character of the Byzantine text ; (3) the relative immunity of texts of Mark from later revision.

Although we may think that Hort relied too exclusively upon the B text, and that an " eclectic " text following now one, now another, of the old local texts is theoretically a sounder basis, it in no way follows either (*a*) that we return to Lucian's text, much less to its degenerate descendant the T.R., or (*b*) that we deny the Alexandrian text, preserved in B ℵ, to be the best of the local texts, and therefore the one which, in the main, a critical modern editor must follow.

For most practical purposes Westcott and Hort's edition is satisfactory ; but there is a real need for a new thesaurus of variants to take the place of Tischendorf's great edition.

In conclusion, the delimitation of local texts shows that our evidence for the substantial integrity of the text of the Gospels as a whole rests on a wide and multiple basis. When, however, fine points of scholarship or the niceties of evidence bearing on the Synoptic problem are at issue, we may have at times to go behind the text found in the best modern printed editions of Greek Testament.

CHAPTER VI

INTERPOLATION AND ASSIMILATION

THE FALLACY OF THE SHORTER TEXT

THE whole question of interpolations in ancient MSS. has been set in an entirely new light by the researches of Mr. A. C. Clark, Corpus Professor of Latin at Oxford, *quem honoris causa nomino.* In *The Descent of Manuscripts,*[1] an investigation of the manuscript tradition of the Greek and Latin Classics, he proves conclusively that the error to which scribes were most prone was not interpolation but accidental omission. It is not too much to say that this conclusion entails a revolution in accepted critical methods. Hitherto the maxim *brevior lectio potior,* that is, that the shorter reading of two readings is probably the original, has been assumed as a postulate of scientific criticism. Clark has shown that, so far as classical texts are concerned, the facts point entirely the other way. " A text," as he puts it, " is like a traveller who loses a portion of his luggage every time he changes trains." Once this is stated, its truth is self-evident ; any one who has ever sent his own MS. to a typist knows that the accidental omission of words, lines, or sentences is a constant occurrence, while interpolation is not. Of course marginal notes, various readings, etc., do constantly creep into the text of ancient MSS. But while intentional interpolation is quite exceptional, omission—commonly accidental, but some-times, it would seem, intentional—is a constant phenomenon.

---

[1] Oxford, 1918.

In a smaller work,[1] Clark applies to the Gospels and Acts
the principles which he had worked out in the sphere of classical
studies. So far as the Acts are concerned, he goes a long way
towards proving his case. But, if I may take it upon me to
pronounce upon the work of so eminent an authority, I would
say that he underestimates the difference between the textual
traditions of the Gospels and of classical literature in two
important respects. First, it so happens that the omission of
passages found in other texts is specially characteristic of B, and
next to B of ℵ, *fam.* Θ, Syr. S., and *k, i.e.* of the authorities which
in other respects preserve good and ancient texts. Secondly, the
antecedent probability that some traditions as to the sayings
or deeds of Christ, not included in any of the Gospels, would
have been in circulation in the early Church is high ; and it
would be very natural to record them in the margin of a Gospel,
from whence they might easily slip into the text. For these
two reasons the principle that " the longer text is probably the
more original " cannot be applied without considerable reservation to the particular case of the Four Gospels.

This principle, however, has an indirect bearing on the
" bad name " given to " Western " readings as such. It was not
merely on account of its alleged abundance of interpolation
that a general discredit was attached by Hort to the " Western "
text. It was even more on account of a supposed tendency
to " paraphrase." The text of B ℵ, being held innocent of this
free treatment of the original, acquired the credit which always
attaches to a respectable witness as against one known to be
in some respects disreputable.[2] But to speak of a passage in
one MS. as being a " paraphrase " of the text found in another
implies that we know already the answer to the prior question,

---

[1] *The Primitive Text of the Gospels and Acts,* Oxford, 1914. The main
argument of this book is very conveniently summarised and in some ways
strengthened in an article in *J.T.S.,* Jan. 1915.

[2] So far was this preference carried that, even in cases where the
" Western " reading, on the face of it, appears more probable, Hort rejects it.
Perhaps the clearest example is the preference of the reading Ἑλληνιστὰς
which makes nonsense, to Ἕλληνας Acts xi. 20.

which of the two represents the original. In the case of the B and D texts this was supposed to be settled in principle by the phenomena of Acts. Here the D text is almost invariably the longer, and, if we accept as a self-evident principle *brevior lectio potior*, it follows that it is a paraphrastic expansion of the shorter text. But ever since Prof. Ramsay wrote his *St. Paul the Traveller*, scholars *on purely historical grounds* have been emphasising the claims of quite a number of the Bezan additions to be authentic. Clark shows in a large number of these cases, that, if we accept the longer text of D as original,[1] we can explain the origin of the shorter B text. All we need suppose is that one or more ancestors of B had suffered considerably from what is, after all, the commonest of all mistakes of careless scribes, the accidental omission of lines. Wherever the grammar of a sentence was destroyed by the omission, some conjectural emendation of the injured text was made to restore sense. The result of this process would inevitably be the production of a shorter text, by the side of which the original would look like a paraphrastic expansion.

But, if the riot of " paraphrase " supposed to be characteristic of the Western text of Acts is otherwise explained, the accusation of paraphrase in regard to the text of the Gospels must be given a rehearing. In the Gospels the difference between the text of B and D is much less striking. Except occasionally in Luke, there are very few readings to which, without exaggeration, the name paraphrase can be applied. There are variations in the order of words, in the use of tenses, prepositions, conjunctions, there is an occasional substitution of synonyms. But, as we shall see later (p. 328 f.), differences of this sort are to be found even between MSS. as closely related as ℵ B L. The differences between D and any one of these MSS. are far more numerous and more conspicuous than their differences from one another ; but they are not such as to entitle us to assert that the D text

---

[1] Cf. *J.T.S.*, Jan. 1915, p. 226 ff. Intentional omission of details thought unimportant is also likely.

is a paraphrase of the B, while the text of L is not. And if we once admit an element of corruption in B, then both B and D might, though in a very different degree, be described as " paraphrasing " the original text.

But the question whether *in other respects* the B or the D text is the purer has really very little to do with the value of their evidence for insertions or omissions. Take a MS. like ℵ. In this, in the Gospels alone, there are no less than 46 instances of accidental omission, which probably formed one or more complete lines of the exemplar from which it was copied, due to homoioteleuton. There are other omissions, presumably of lines in the exemplar, where homoioteleuton cannot be invoked in extenuation of the error. And there are innumerable omissions of single words. Almost all the longer and many of the shorter omissions have been added in the margin, by the first corrector or sometimes by the original scribe. If one glances through the photographic facsimile of ℵ, there is hardly a page without such correction. But ℵ is a handsome expensive copy produced in a regular scriptorium, written by a professional scribe and corrected by a careful διορθωτής. Now let us suppose that the original text of Acts was something like D, and that the first copy which reached Alexandria was separated from the autograph by half a dozen ancestors. And suppose that two or three of these ancestors had been copied by scribes neither better nor worse than the scribe of ℵ, but had not been gone over by a διορθωτής. At each stage where the omission made nonsense or bad grammar the owner would make the minimum of conjectural emendation that would make the construction grammatical or restore what from the context appeared to be the sense intended. This process of omission and correction repeated two or three times would result in a copy of the Acts with a text like that of B.[1] If this was the first copy of the book

[1] The hypothesis that accidental omission was supplemented by intentional omission of what seemed unimportant detail is not to be entirely excluded. Probably a longer period elapsed before the Acts was regarded as inspired scripture than was the case with the Gospels.

to reach Alexandria, the original, being on papyrus, would soon be worn out; but all the earliest copies known in Alexandria would be derived from it. It follows that the more scrupulously subsequent scribes copied these, and the more anxious Alexandrian scholars were to go back to the earliest copies, the less chance would there be of the original omissions being repaired from MSS. brought in from outside. Even if a copy of the more complete text was brought from Rome, the Alexandrian scholar, like Hort, would condemn it as a corrupt and paraphrastic text.

Some Notable Readings

This leads me to suggest a principle of criticism which, so far as I am aware, has not hitherto been formulated. Accidental omissions are most likely to be made good in the place where a book was first given to the world ; for there more than one copy made from the autograph will be in circulation. On the other hand, in a city far removed from the place of publication the higher the local standard of textual purity, the greater the likelihood that an accidental omission in the earliest copy which had arrived there would remain unrepaired. The principle, of course, must not be pressed too far. Indeed it only applies to omissions which contained something of a more or less interesting character. Omissions of words that added little to the sense, or which people would prefer to think spurious, would be as likely to remain unrepaired in the Church where a Gospel was first published as in any other. The omission, for example, by Syr. S. of the words οὐδὲ ὁ υἱὸς Mt. xxiv. 36, cannot be defended, even if proof positive was produced that this was the old text of Antioch and that Matthew was written there. But the principle does give a new importance to the identification of local texts. If, as I think probable, Luke and Acts were written either at Rome or Corinth, omissions in B אּ will carry less weight than those which occur in the Western text. In that case, we shall be inclined to follow Hort in suspecting what he calls the

" Western non-interpolations " of Luke, on the ground that they are absent from the Roman text of Luke ; but we shall hesitate to agree with him in rejecting passages for which Western evidence is good, simply because they are absent from B. Again, if Matthew, as I believe, was written in Antioch, passages found only in Alexandrian or geographically Western authorities will be regarded with suspicion, but we shall look with special favour on any insertion attested by Syr. S. ; and so far as this Gospel is concerned we shall not be in too great a hurry to reject readings which are only attested by the Lucianic text.

This principle works out well in practice. The most interesting addition in Syr. S. is in Mt. xxvii. 17. Pilate says to the Jews, " Whom will ye that I release unto you ? Jesus Barabbas, or Jesus whom they call Christ ? " Thus phrased the alternative offer made by Pilate has an extraordinarily original look. The omission of the name " Jesus " before Barabbas might easily be accidental. ὑμῖν Ἰησοῦν in Θ is written YMIN̄IN̄—the omission of the second IN would be an instance of an error so common in ancient MSS. that a technical term " haplography " has been invented to describe it. Once omitted, motives of reverence would come into play ; and the dislike of the idea that a brigand bore the sacred name, would lead to the preference of the shorter text. This is not mere conjecture ; Origen, we have seen, found it in the text of Caesarea, but tries to reject it on the ground that the name Jesus could not have belonged to one who was a sinner.[1] And the weight of his opinion would lead to its wholesale excision in other texts.

On the other hand there are three striking additions in Matthew found in the non-Antiochene types of text represented by B and D Old Latin respectively, which do not commend themselves as genuine. The spear-thrust at the Crucifixion (Mt. xxvii. 49) in B א, etc., is easily explicable as an attempt at harmonising Matthew and John. The saying " Seek to rise, etc.," found in D Φ Syr. C. after Mt. xx. 28 is a feebler and, I

---

[1] Cf. the discussion by Burkitt, *Evangelion da Mepharreshê*, vol. ii. p. 277.

would add, less Christian way, of putting the maxim "take the lowest place" as found in Lk. xiv. 8 f. The Light at the Baptism, inserted by the Old Lat. MSS. *a g* (Mt. iii. 16), which was known to Justin and Tatian (and therefore may be early Roman), is obviously legendary embellishment.

Similar results appear when we compare and contrast the additions made to Luke in the Western and Alexandrian texts respectively. We have already noted that a study of the Acts tends *on the whole*—there are exceptions in all statements with regard to MSS.—to confirm the originality of the longer Western text. Of the additions to the Gospel, the longest and the best attested outside is the incident of the Bloody Sweat and the comforting angel in Gethsemane, Lk. xxii. 43-44 : Justin Martyr, *c.* 153, alludes to this and expressly says that it occurs "in the memoirs," his term for the Gospels. It was in the text known to Irenaeus, Tatian, and Hippolytus. Thus it must have stood in the Roman text at a very early date. The fact that it was known to Dionysius of Alexandria, *c.* 250, and occurs in ℵ L suggests that it may have belonged to that very early state of the Western text which had invaded Alexandria at the time of Clement *c.* 200. True it is omitted by Syr. S., but it occurs in Syr. C., and in the oldest MS. of the Armenian there is a note saying that it occurred in the "first translations" but was omitted in the "newly issued translations." Since the oldest Armenian seems to have been made from the Syriac, it is not impossible that it has been "revised out" in Syr. S. Linguistically, as I think Harnack was the first to point out, the passage, short as it is, betrays several characteristically Lucan expressions. Lastly, we gather from Epiphanius, who defends the reading on account of its antiquity, that it caused serious perplexity to some orthodox persons as seemingly derogatory to the full Divinity of our Lord. Presumably it seemed beneath the dignity of the Uncreated Word Incarnate to evince such a degree of πάθος ; and still more to require a created angel as a comforter. Hence there was every reason, if not for excising it

from the text, at least for regarding MSS. in which it had
been accidentally omitted as original. We conclude then that
B W 579, etc., which omit the words, though they may possibly
give the earliest Alexandrian text, do not preserve the original
words of Luke.

Another famous omission attested not only by B W 579 but
also by *fam*. Θ and Syr. S. is the cry from the Cross, "Father
forgive them, for they know not what they do," Lk. xxiii. 34.
Here we cannot be quite sure that the reading stood in the earliest
form of the Roman text; for, though found in *c e* and known
to Irenaeus and Tatian, it is omitted by D *a b*. But *c e*, though
mixed MSS., probably represent the African Latin, which on
the whole seems nearer than *a b* to the oldest Roman text. And
the reading is found in Origen (Lat. trans.) as well as א L Syr. C.
Arm. Some years ago the suggestion was made, I think by
Dr. Rendel Harris, that the passage had been deleted because
some Christian in the second century found it hard to believe
that God could or ought to forgive the Jews, since they were the
chief instigators in all the persecutions, and, unlike the Gentiles,
had no excuse for their villainous conduct—being originally
called to be the chosen people and the possessors of the scriptures
that spoke of Christ. One might add, it would have appeared
to a second-century Christian that, as a mere matter of fact,
God had not forgiven the Jews. Twice within seventy years
Jerusalem had been destroyed and hundreds of thousands of
Jews massacred and enslaved. It followed that, if Christ had
prayed that prayer, God had declined to grant it. How much
simpler to surmise the words to be an interpolation ? And, if
even a single copy could be found lacking the words, the surmise
would become a certainty. From the MS. evidence we must
infer that the omission, if it be an omission, must have been
made at an earlier date than that of the Bloody Sweat. The
words, of course, may well have been handed down in a genuine
tradition, even if they were not recorded by Luke. But their
claim to be an authentic part of the text of the Third Gospel

deserves serious consideration ; and, whatever may be the final verdict, it will be worth while to have stated the case, if only to illustrate the fact that absence from certain MSS. is not necessarily evidence of interpolation.

ASSIMILATION OF PARALLELS

Jerome in his preface to the Vulgate Gospels mentions assimilation of the texts of the Gospels to one another in parallel passages as one of the chief sources of corruption of the text. The remark was an acute one, and a study of the existing MSS. shows that it is the commonest of all forms of error. The best known example is the Lord's prayer, which in the oldest MSS. occurs in a shorter form in Luke ; in the Byzantine text it is assimilated to Matthew. As a textual phenomenon assimilation is not peculiar to the Gospels. It occurs to a small extent in Homer, where it is found that recurrent phrases tend to resemble one another more closely in the inferior than they do in the better MSS. It has also operated as a corrupting influence on the text of the Epistles to the Ephesians and Colossians. But the Gospels are a special case, since such a large proportion of their total contents, expressed in language often all but identical, occurs in more than one of them, so that the opportunity they afford for assimilation of parallel passages is quite unique. The danger of this particular form of corruption would be still further increased by the fact that, not only would most scribes know the Gospels almost by heart, but a scribe who was copying Mark or Luke was usually one who had just refreshed his memory by copying out the text as it stands in Matthew. With the words of one Gospel running in his head it would be exceedingly difficult to copy accurately passages in another Gospel which were almost but not quite the same.

But assimilation is not only the commonest source of corruption of the text of the Gospels, it is also the one most difficult to check. Other forms of corruption would result in each separate local text having its own special set of wrong readings ; these can be detected by comparison with other texts. But assimilation of parallels, being a process which must have gone on independently in all local texts, might easily result in identical errors along different lines of transmission. Hence, though each text will have its own special set of assimilations, there is no security that occasionally, especially in certain striking passages, all texts may not have coincided upon the same assimilation. This is a possibility that neither textual critics nor students of the Synoptic Problem have ever really faced.

Now the strongest argument for the general purity of the B text is that it is free from so many of the assimilations that are found in the Later Alexandrian, the " Western." or the Byzantine texts. But, though far freer from assimilation of parallels than any other text, B is not entirely immune. And there are quite a number of cases where the Western text—though on the whole it has suffered far more than any other in this way—is free from particular assimilations which have infected B. Detailed evidence on this point I shall reserve for the chapter on the Minor Agreements of Matthew and Luke against Mark. In this place I propose merely to call attention to the importance in regard to this particular issue of the set of readings called by Hort " Western non-interpolations," and to connect it with the previous discussion of the Roman and Alexandrian texts of Luke.

Eight of the nine readings to which Hort gave the name " Western non-interpolations " occur towards the end of Luke, no less than seven being in the last chapter (the ninth is the spear thrust, Mt. xxvii. 49). These are omitted by D and the Old Latin, but, with two exceptions, by no other MS. Hort coined the complicated title " Western non-interpolation," in order to avoid smirching the fair name of the " Neutral " text by speaking of these readings as " Neutral interpolations " ; but, assuming them not to be genuine, that is what they really are. All the same I believe he was right in rejecting at any rate the majority

of them. Firstly, if Luke was written in the West, it is hard to
suppose that the omission of so many passages, all of an interesting
character and all crowded into the same context, would have
escaped notice at Rome, where presumably other copies from
which the gaps could be refilled would be available. Secondly,
as Hort saw, most of these additions are of the nature of har-
monisations between Luke and other parts of the New Testament.
But Hort was, I think, mistaken in his emphasis on these nine
out of a large number of omissions by the same Western
authorities.

Besides the eight striking readings in the last three chapters
of Luke and the one in Matthew to which Hort gives the special
title " Western non-interpolations," there are a large number of
smaller omissions in the Old Latin, sometimes supported by D,
of words or sentences found in the B text. To some of these
Hort himself calls attention (ii. p. 176), and he puts them in
single brackets in his text—whereas the selected nine are distinguished by double brackets.[1] But there are other omissions
consisting only of a word or two which he ignores. But, if Hort
was right in definitely rejecting as assimilations the major
" non-interpolations " in Matthew and Luke (which merely reproduce the *general sense* of something found in another Gospel),
he ought to have rejected more than twenty other passages in
most of which the insertion reproduces in one Gospel the
actual words of a parallel passage in another. To the student of
the Synoptic Problem these minor omissions in the Western
text are all important, though it would be unsafe to assume that
the omission is in every case original ; D is no more infallible

---

[1] The " Western non-interpolations " in double brackets are in Lk. xxii.
19-20, xxiv. 3, 6, 12, 36, 40, 51, 52 ; also the mention of the spear thrust not
found in the T.R., Mt. xxvii. 49.   Those in single brackets, sometimes consisting of only a few words, occur in Mt. vi. 15, 25, ix. 34, xiii. 33, xxi. 44,
xxiii. 26 ; Mk. ii. 22, x. 2, xiv. 39 ; Lk. v. 39, x. 41 f., xii. 19, 21, 39, xxii. 62,
xxiv. 9 ; Jn. iii. 32, iv. 9 (cf. W.H. ii. p. 176).   Among those not noted in
Hort's text are Mt. xxi. 23 διδάσκοντι (om. *a b c e* Syr. S. C.) ; Mk. ix. 35 (om.
D *k*) ; Mk. xiv. 65 καὶ περικαλύπτειν (om. D *a f*) ; Lk. viii. 44 τοῦ κρασπέδου
(om. D Lat.) ; Jn. xii. 8 (om. D Syr. S.) ; others are discussed below, Chap. XI.

when it omits than when it inserts. I emphasise this point because Hort's isolation of these nine passages very much obscures the extent to which the B text has suffered from assimilation, not only as between Matthew and Luke, but also between the Synoptics and John.

Nevertheless it is worth while to protest against a too ready inference that, in regard to genuineness, the whole series, whether of major or minor " non-interpolations," must stand or fall together. This is a fallacy. What the MS. evidence proves is that these passages were, as a matter of fact, absent from the ancestor of D and the Old Latin, but present in an ultimate ancestor of all other texts. The tacit assumption that either the one or the other of these ancestors was in *every* case correct is quite unwarranted. No MS. or group of MSS. is even approximately infallible ; and all have suffered from some accidental omissions. It is more probable that in some cases B is correct in retaining the words, even if in the majority D is right in omitting them. The real case against the genuineness of these readings rests, I must repeat, not on their omission in one line of the MS. tradition, but in the fact that they look like attempts at harmonisation, especially between the Synoptics and John.

But there is one of Hort's nine passages where the argument from assimilation seems to me to cut the other way. Can the sentence, " and he was taken up into heaven," Lk. xxiv. 51, really be regarded as due to " assimilation " from the story of the Ascension in the Acts ? If so, it is an assimilation of an incredibly unskilful kind ; for it makes the Ascension take place on Easter Day instead of forty days later as the Acts relates. Besides, the words " he was taken up into heaven " seem required to explain the back reference in Acts i. 2, which implies that the Gospel contained an account of what Jesus began to do and to teach " until the day when he was taken up." This is rather pointless unless the Gospel contained an account of the Ascension. On linguistic grounds it is probable [1] that a con·

Cf. Hawkins' *Hor. Syn.* p. 177 ff.

siderable interval elapsed between the writing of the Gospel and
Acts. In the interval the author may have come across a fresh
cycle of tradition. If so, Acts i. 2 should be read as an attempt
by the author to recall his former statement with the object of
correcting it in favour of the account of the Ascension forty days
later which immediately follows. In that case the omission
of the words in Lk. xxiv. 51 is an attempt to remove a contradiction between the Gospel and the Acts ; it is the text which
omits, not that which inserts, that has suffered harmonistic
correction.

Another clear example of the avoidance by the Roman text
of Luke of an assimilation found in the Alexandrian is the
Voice at the Baptism, Lk. iii. 22. In B א, etc., the words are
practically identical with those in Mark and Matthew, *i.e.*
" Thou art my beloved Son, in thee I am well pleased." But
D *a b c ff*[2], etc., with the notable support of Clement of Alexandria, read " Thou art my [beloved] Son, this day have I begotten
thee." Now this reading is quite definitely that cited by
Justin and was therefore current in Rome *c.* 155. Again, on
grounds of internal probability it is clearly to be preferred for
two reasons. (*a*) The tendency of scribal alterations would be
to make the text of Luke agree with Matthew and Mark, as
in B ; with this reading, on the contrary, there is a discrepancy
between the Gospels. (*b*) The Lucan reading could readily be
quoted in favour of the view, afterwards regarded as heretical,
that Christ only became the Son of God at his Baptism. Once,
therefore, the assimilation with the other Gospels had been
made in any MS., it would be preferred as more orthodox, and
would rapidly be taken up into other texts.

I would not, however, leave the reader with the impression
that the D text has suffered less from assimilation than that
of B. Quite the contrary. In D assimilation is, not only more
frequent, but more thoroughgoing. Take, for example, μὴ
φοβοῦ· ἀπὸ τοῦ νῦν ἀνθρώπους ἔσῃ ζωγρῶν, Lk. v. 10. Here
D, with the partial support of *e*, reads δεῦτε καὶ μὴ γένεσθε

ἁλιεῖς ἰχθύων· ποιήσω γὰρ ὑμᾶς ἁλιεῖς ἀνθρώπων, which is very
much closer to the language of Matthew. But it is unnecessary
to labour this point, since everybody admits that, not only the
" Western " and the Byzantine texts as a whole, but each
different sub-group of MSS. of these texts, have in different
ways and in different places suffered assimilation. The text
of B alone has been placed by critics on a pedestal by itself,
and, because it has undoubtedly suffered less than any other
MS., has been supposed to be immune. And this unfounded
supposition has played havoc with the scientific study of the
Synoptic Problem.

CONCLUSION

The history of the text of the Gospels is, as it were, concentrated into a single passage in the set of variants in the lists of
the Twelve Apostles (Mt. x. 2-4, Mk. iii. 16-19, Lk. vi. 14-16).
It would appear that in the first century local traditions varied
as to the twelfth name ; and each of the Synoptics embodies a
different tradition. Origen remarks,[1] " The same man whom
Matthew calls Lebbaeus and Mark Thaddaeus, Luke writes as
Judas of James." It appears, then, that in the text he used.
obviously in this instance the correct one, each Gospel gave a
different name. In Syr. S. Judas, in *a b h* (but not in D *k*)
Judas Zelotes is substituted for Lebbaeus in Matthew, though
not in Mark. For this part of Matthew *e* is missing, but in this
MS. the name Judas is substituted in Mark also. If we remember that Judas, not Iscariot, is mentioned as one of the
Twelve by John, we understand why the list which contained
his name should be supposed the more authentic. Clearly the
discrepancy troubled scribes. We turn to the Greek uncials
and what do we find ? There is no variant in Luke ; but B ℵ
read Thaddaeus in both Matthew and Mark ; [2] D reads Lebbaeus

[1] *Com. in Rom.* praef.
[2] **124** (probably also the Ferrar ancestor) supports B ℵ. Other members
of *fam.* Θ have the Byzantine conflation.

in both Gospels ; while the Byzantine text reads " Lebbaeus who is called Thaddaeus " in Matthew, but is content to follow B א in Mark. We notice three points. (1) The tendency to assimilation is seen at work everywhere—in א B, in D, and in the Old Latin and Old Syriac—but in each case operates somewhat differently. (2) The Byzantine text is " conflate " ; it ingeniously combines the readings of two ancient traditions each of which had good support. (3) Editors and scribes are less concerned to correct the text of Mark.

Hort, we have argued, was right in regarding the Textus Receptus as a descendant of the revision made by Lucian of Antioch about A.D. 300. And he was right in his contention that in the main this revision was based on earlier texts which we can still identify. We group these earlier texts into an Egyptian, admirably preserved in א B L ; an Italian and Gallic, represented, with many corruptions, in D $a\,b\,ff^2$; an African (perhaps = earlier Roman), found in $k, e,$ (W$^{Mk.}$); an Antiochene, less adequately known to us through the Old Syriac; a Caesarean, fairly well preserved in the non-Byzantine readings of *fam.* Θ (W$^{Mk.}$). This grouping of the older texts differs radically from Hort's, but not in a way that seriously affects his view of the methods of Lucian's revision, though we may feel a little less confident than he that Lucian possessed no MS. containing ancient and possibly correct readings not found in our surviving authorities. But then comes the really fundamental question : was Hort right in reprinting almost in its entirety the oldest Egyptian text ? Or was Lucian right in the principle, if not in its detailed application, of framing an eclectic text, adopting readings now from one text, now from another, presumably on the combined grounds of extent and antiquity of attestation and of " internal probability " ?

To this question one must, I think, answer that the eclectic principle of deciding in each separate case on grounds of " internal probability " what appears to be the best reading is, in spite of its subjectivity, *theoretically* sounder than the almost slavish following of a single text which Hort preferred.

L

But this in no way means that we return to the Textus Receptus. Lucian's canons of " internal probability " differed fundamentally from ours. For example, his eye would be inclined to look with most favour on that one of two readings which attributed to an evangelist a more smooth, graceful, and stately style. To us, roughness, within limits, is a sign of originality. Again, to him it would seem more likely that a reading, supposing it was found in MSS. sufficiently numerous and ancient, which brought two evangelists into closer agreement with one another was more likely to be original than one which enhanced the difference between them. We should judge otherwise. Hence, even if we accept the necessity of an eclectic text, the selection of readings admitted to it would differ very considerably from that made by Lucian. On the other hand, while realising that B has more wrong readings than Hort was ready to admit, due weight must be given to Hort's principle that the authority of a MS., which in a majority of cases supports what is clearly the right reading, counts for more than that of others in cases where decision is more difficult. Hence a critical text of the Gospels (though not, I think, of Acts) will, like that of Hort, be based mainly on the text of Alexandria as preserved in our two oldest MSS. B ℵ. But a future editor will be on the look out for evidence that will enable him to detect instances where these, like all other MSS., have been corrupted by assimilation of parallels or grammatical touching up, and he will be ready to accept a far larger number of readings from authorities which represent the local texts of other churches. In particular he will give special weight to the readings of *fam.* Θ.

The rejection, however, of a theory which enabled Hort to attribute supreme authority to the B text complicates *in practice* the task of the textual critic. Textual criticism is not the only department of life where an infallible guide, if such existed, would save us trouble and uncertainty. No purely external mechanical test of the genuineness of readings has yet been devised. Where important variants exist, and can be shown to have existed as

early as the third century, we can in the last resort only fall back
on the exercise of insight and common sense to make our choice.
Those qualities being rare, or, at any rate, hard to recognise by
any objective test in a matter of this kind, there will always
remain a difference of opinion on many points. It follows that,
if by a " scientific " text is meant one reached by some mechanical
and objective principles which completely rule out the subjective
vagaries of the individual editor, such cannot be attained. In this
department of knowledge the appeal is in the last resort to the
insight, judgement, and common sense of the individual scholar,
which are necessarily " subjective."

What, however, is most wanted at the present moment is
not a new critical text—for most purposes Westcott and Hort
is good enough. The real need is for an edition of an entirely
different character—a thesaurus of various readings to bring up
to date Tischendorf's large edition of 1869. von Soden attempted
this and failed ; his edition is not only full of inaccuracies, it is
often actually unintelligible. But, I would insist, in such an
edition, it is of quite fundamental importance that the text
printed above the Apparatus Criticus should be, not an eclectic
text constructed by the editor himself, but the Byzantine text.[1]
The reason is obvious. The number of MSS. which have
altogether escaped revision from the Byzantine standard is
extremely small, yet the readings which the critic most wants
to know are those of older texts which *differ* from the
Byzantine text ; if, then, the Byzantine text is printed above
the Apparatus Criticus, the readings the critic first wants are
those which first strike the eye. Again the Apparatus itself would
be enormously simplified ; for it need only contain readings which
differ from that text. Any MS. not cited in the Apparatus would
be understood, either to agree with the text printed at the top of
the page, or not to be extant for that passage ; and accordingly

---

[1] For this purpose the Byzantine text should be determined by some
purely objective criterion, such as the agreement of two out of the three
MSS. S V Ω, or, perhaps better, E S V.

the extent of hiatus in important MSS. should be noted on each page. MSS. should be cited in separate groups, according as they habitually agree with the Alexandrian, Eastern or Western type of text. Lastly, since textual criticism under the most favourable circumstances involves great strain on the eyesight, small print and small numbers and letters above the line, such as von Soden delights in, should be resolutely eschewed.

In conclusion it is worth while to note that those same investigations which have compelled us to reject Hort's theory have shown that the authorities available for determining the text are more numerous and more independent of one another than that theory would allow. It follows, therefore, that, though on minor points of reading absolute certainty may often be unobtainable, a text of the Gospels can be reached, the freedom of which from serious modification or interpolation is guaranteed by the concurrence of different lines of ancient and independent evidence. For the historian, as well as for the ordinary Christian reader, a text like that of Hort or Tischendorf, or that used in preparing the Revised Version, may be taken as reliable for all ordinary purposes. But for fine points of scholarship, or when dealing with the Synoptic Problem, where the settlement of a question of great import may depend on the minutest verbal resemblances or differences between the Gospels, it is vital to realise that in our search for the original reading we must, on occasion, go behind the printed texts.

PART II

THE SYNOPTIC PROBLEM

DIAGRAM: THE SYNOPTICS AND THEIR SOURCES

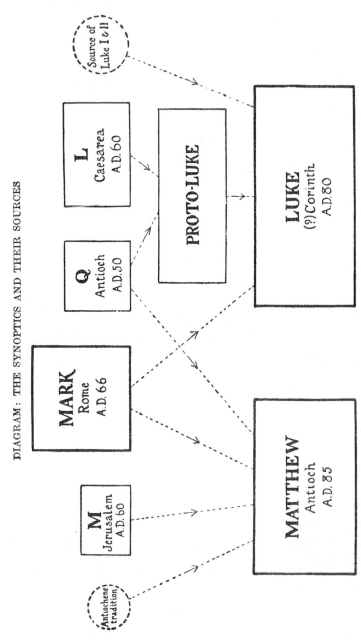

Mark has 661 verses; Matthew 1068; Luke 1149; Proto-Luke c. 700; Q (Hawkins) 200, (B.H.S.) 270 +; M 230 +; L 400 +.

VII

THE FUNDAMENTAL SOLUTION

SYNOPSIS

HISTORIANS AND THEIR SOURCES

The conception of " copyright "—a consequence of the invention of printing—has entirely changed the conditions under which it is legitimate for authors to make use of previous writers. Ancient historians frequently reproduce almost verbatim considerable portions of the work of their predecessors.

THE PRIORITY OF MARK

The accepted view that Mark (so far from being, as Augustine thought, an abridgement of Matthew) was a source used by Matthew and Luke requires slightly restating. Matthew may be regarded as an enlarged edition of Mark ; Luke is an independent work incorporating considerable portions of Mark.

Five reasons for accepting the priority of Mark.

(1) Matthew reproduces 90 % of the subject matter of Mark in language very largely identical with that of Mark ; Luke does the same for rather more than half of Mark.

(2) In any average section, which occurs in the three Gospels, the majority of the actual words used by Mark are reproduced by Matthew and Luke, either alternately or both together.

(3) The relative order of incidents and sections in Mark is in general supported by both Matthew and Luke ; where either of them deserts Mark, the other is usually found supporting him.

This conjunction and alternation of Matthew and Luke in their agreement with Mark as regards (a) content, (b) wording, (c) order, is only explicable if they are incorporating a source identical, or all but identical, with Mark.

(4) The primitive character of Mark is further shown by (a) the use of phrases likely to cause offence, which are omitted or toned

down in the other Gospels, (b) roughness of style and grammar, and the preservation of Aramaic words.

(5) The way in which Marcan and non-Marcan material is distributed in Matthew and Luke respectively looks as if each had before him the Marcan material *in a single document*, and was faced with the problem of combining this with material from other sources.

Matthew's solution was to make Mark's story the framework into which non-Marcan material is fitted, on the principle of joining like to like. Luke follows the simpler method of giving Marcan and non-Marcan material in alternate blocks; except in the Passion story, where, from the nature of the case, some interweaving of sources was inevitable.

Two objections to the view that the document used by Matthew and Luke was *exactly* identical with Mark. (1) Why did they omit certain sections of Mark? (2) How explain certain minute verbal agreements of the other two against Mark? To meet these, the theory of an Ur-Marcus, or earlier edition of Mark, has been proposed. Its merits will be determined by the study of the facts that follow—subject to the general consideration that they were authors not scribes, and its implications.

MATTHEW'S OMISSIONS

At first sight, these seem to number 55 verses (of which 25 are found in Luke), but under examination even this small amount rapidly shrinks.

Matthew appears to omit three miracles recorded by Mark; but details from the omitted sections appear elsewhere in Matthew as amplifications or modifications of similar stories which he has embodied from Mark. Matthew, then, was not omitting, but rather conflating, incidents which stood in Mark.

Three other items omitted by Matthew are guaranteed as Marcan by internal evidence. Matthew therefore used our Mark.

LUKE'S GREAT OMISSION

The case for an Ur-Marcus rests mainly on the fact that Luke omits the long section Mk. vi. 45-viii. 26.

The theory is plausible that Luke's copy of Mark lacked vi. 53-viii. 21, *i.e.* all but the first and last paragraphs of this section. Formidable objections, however, arise from (a) linguistic evidence for genuineness of the section adduced by Hawkins, (b) the need of postulating *two* editions of Mark, *both* of which were without a conclusion; for the text of Mark used by Matthew and Luke seems, like that of our oldest MSS., to have ended at xvi. 8.

It is possible that Luke *intentionally* omitted this section. As an alternative, a case is stated for the view that, in the copy of Mark used by him, the section was absent through accidental mutilation of the papyrus roll.

MINOR AGREEMENTS OF MATTHEW AND LUKE

These are discussed at length, with reference to the original Greek, in Chapter XI. They appear to be due to three causes. (1) In a few passages there is evidence for the existence of a version of a saying or incident in Q parallel to that of Mark. (2) Matthew and Luke consistently improve Mark's style and grammar ; inevitably, therefore, they will sometimes coincide in the more obvious corrections. (3) A larger number are explicable as corrupt readings of the great MSS., due to assimilation of parallels as between Matthew and Luke or to minute errors in the text of Mark.

In the majority of cases the reading found in Matthew and Luke is, from the standpoint cf grammar or style, an *improvement* on Mark. It follows that if the agreements of Matthew and Luke against Mark cannot be entirely explained by the causes above mentioned, the only alternative is the hypothesis of Dr. Sanday that the text of Mark used by the other evangelists had been subjected to a slight stylistic revision. But this, be it noted, is the exact reverse of any Ur-Marcus theory ; for it implies that our text of Mark is *more primitive* than the text used by Matthew and Luke.

THE DOCUMENT Q

Matthew and Luke have in common material, which is not found in Mark, amounting to about 200 verses, mostly discourse. The hypothesis that this was derived from a document now lost— commonly alluded to by the symbol Q—is more probable than the view (*a*) that Luke copied Matthew (or *vice versa*), or (*b*) that the common source was oral tradition.

The Q hypothesis, however, can be pressed too far. (1) Where the versions of sayings in Matthew and Luke differ considerably, the probability is high that one (or both) of the two versions did *not* come from Q. (2) Matthew probably omitted some sayings of Q which Luke retained, and *vice versa*. (3) Short epigrammatic sayings would be likely to circulate *separately* by word of mouth. Hence all attempts at a reconstruction of Q must be tentative.

THE OVERLAPPING OF Q AND MARK

Certain items, in all about 50 verses, occur in *both* Mark *and* Q. Each had a version of John's preaching, the Baptism and Temptation, the Beelzebub Controversy, the parables of the Mustard Seed and Leaven and of some shorter sayings.

Some critics hold that Mark's version of the above items was derived from Q. More probably Mark and Q represent independent traditions. This is shown by detailed examination of the passages in question.

A Modern Illustration

An illustration from contemporary literature of the necessity on occasion, and of the working out in practice, of editorial processes like " conflation," " agglomeration," etc.

The representation of Christ's life and teaching in Matthew and Luke comparable, not to the exactness of photographic reproduction, but rather to the creative interpretation in a great portrait.

Additional Notes

(A) *Omissions from Mark*

List of passages of Mark which are absent (*a*) from both Matthew and Luke, (*b*) from Matthew only, (*c*) from Luke only ; (*d*) list of passages of Mark which are absent from Luke but for which Luke *in another context* substitutes a version from a different source.

(B) *The non-Marcan parallels in Matthew and Luke*

(C) *Passages peculiar to Matthew*

(D) *Passages peculiar to Luke*

CHAPTER VII

THE FUNDAMENTAL SOLUTION

HISTORIANS AND THEIR SOURCES

THE mechanical invention of printing has reacted on the methods and conventions of authorship itself in more ways than we are apt to imagine. When books were copied by hand, copyright had no commercial value ; no kind of injury could be done either to author or publisher by any one who made and sold copies. But in the setting up of a printed book capital is sunk ; work has been done and a risk has been incurred, in return for which it is reasonable that the publisher should enjoy such legal protection against unauthorised reproductions as will enable him to derive a fair profit. Again, in antiquity an author, unless, as most commonly happened, he was a man of inherited wealth, lived on the bounty of some noble patron of letters. Printing has enabled a modern Horace to live, not by flattering a Maecenas, but on the profits of his books. For both these reasons the conception of property in literature has arisen.

Hence there has gradually grown up an entirely different convention as to the manner and conditions under which it is legitimate to make use of what others have written. The change is one which affects historical more than any other kind of writing. Whenever a historian is not an actual eye-witness of the events he records, or the first to write down a living tradition, he is bound to depend to a large extent on the works of previous historians. The modern convention requires that when this happens he shall either quote the exact words of his authority or entirely re-write the whole story with some general indication of the source from which it comes. Here again the printing press has made a difference. It has facilitated the development of inverted commas, footnotes for reference, and other such devices unknown to the scribes of Classical Antiquity, which make it easy for an author to indicate without clumsy circumlocutions the exact extent of his debt to predecessors. The conventions of every art are determined by what is mechanically possible; it is not, therefore, surprising that these inventions have reacted on actual methods of composition employed by the modern author in so far as these entail a use of previous writers. In antiquity, however, and in the Middle Ages, only the writings of a few outstanding men like Thucydides are wholly original; more commonly the historian pursued what we should call a method of " scissors and paste." Without any acknowledgement, he will copy page after page from his source, omitting passages that for his purpose seem irrelevant, adding here and there material from some other authority. What he copies he frequently gives almost word for word, but he will often abridge, and occasionally paraphrase, in order to elucidate some difficulty or to preclude what he would regard as a false impression which the language of the original might convey.

This kind of editorial adaptation of earlier sources can be traced in all the historical books of the Old Testament, and in many classical and mediaeval writers. I would call attention to one example in each of these fields where the survival of the original sources, the nature of the subject matter, and the accessibility to the ordinary reader of the relevant literature, combine to make a study of ancient methods and their bearing on our present investigation both exceptionally profitable and relatively easy. Turn to the books of Chronicles in a reference Bible. It is clear that, from 1 Chron. x. on, almost everything is an abridgement, with trifling modifications, of the narrative

in the books of Samuel and Kings.[1] Consult the appendices
dealing with the earliest accounts of St. Francis of Assisi, either
in the Life by Sabatier or in that by Father Cuthbert, and you
will see a " synoptic problem," explicable on these lines. Lastly,
compare the fragment of the Greek historian Ephorus lately
discovered at Oxyrhynchus with the account of the same events
in Diodorus,[2] and you will find an illustration in a Greek writer
practically contemporary with the authors of the Gospels of
Matthew and Luke. You will notice, and the analogy is
important, that the Greek writer, in contrast to the Hebrew,
makes many more little alterations of phrase so as to leave
upon all that he has incorporated the impress of his own style.

The Priority of Mark

Such being the almost universal method of ancient historians,
whether Jewish or Greek, it is natural to ask whether the
remarkable resemblance between the first three Gospels, which
has caused the name Synoptic to be applied to them, would not
be most easily explained on the hypothesis that they incorporate
earlier documents. A century of discussion has resulted in a
consensus of scholars that this is the case, and that the authors
of the First and Third Gospels made use either of our Mark, or
of a document all but identical with Mark. The former and the
simpler of these alternatives, viz. that they used our Mark, is
the one which I hope in the course of this and the following
chapters to establish beyond reasonable doubt.

The attempt has recently been made to revive the solution,
first put forward by Augustine (cf. p. 10), who styles Mark a
kind of abridger and lackey of Matthew, " Tanquam breviator
et pedisequus ejus." But Augustine did not possess a Synopsis
of the Greek text conveniently printed in parallel columns.

---

[1] These and other O.T. analogies may most conveniently be studied in
Deuterographs by R. B. Girdlestone (Oxford, 1894), where the relevant passages
are printed in parallel columns with the differences indicated by italics.

[2] Cf. *Oxyrhynchus Papyri*, xiii. p. 102 ff.

Otherwise a person of his intelligence could not have failed to perceive that, where the two Gospels are parallel, it is usually Matthew, and not Mark, who does the abbreviation. For example, the number of words employed by Mark to tell the stories of the Gadarene Demoniac, Jairus' Daughter, and the Feeding of the Five Thousand are respectively 325, 374 and 235 ; Matthew contrives to tell them in 136, 135 and 157 words.[1] Now there is nothing antecedently improbable in the idea that for certain purposes an abbreviated version of the Gospel might be desired ; but only a lunatic would leave out Matthew's account of the Infancy, the Sermon on the Mount, and practically all the parables, in order to get room for purely verbal expansion of what was retained. On the other hand, if we suppose Mark to be the older document, the verbal compression and omission of minor detail seen in the parallels in Matthew has an obvious purpose, in that it gives more room for the introduction of a mass of highly important teaching material not found in Mark.

Further advance, however, towards a satisfactory solution of the Synoptic Problem has been, in my opinion, retarded by the tacit assumption of scholars that, if Matthew and Luke both used Mark, they must have used it in the same way. To Professor Burkitt, I believe, belongs the credit of first protesting against this assumption : " Matthew is *a fresh edition* of Mark, revised, rearranged, and enriched with new material ; . . . Luke is a new historical work made by combining parts of Mark with parts of other documents." [2] The distinction thus stated by Burkitt I shall endeavour to justify and to elaborate in a new direction in Chap. VIII. I conceive it to be one of fundamental importance in any attempt to estimate the value of the Third Gospel as an historical authority for the life of Christ.

Partly in order to clear the way for a more thorough investigation of this point, partly because this book is written for others

[1] Cf. J. C. Hawkins, *Horae Synopticae*[2], p. 159 (Oxford, 1909).
[2] *The Earliest Sources for the Life of Jesus* (Constable, 1922).

besides students of theology, I will now present a summary statement of the main facts and considerations which show the dependence of Matthew and Luke upon Mark. Familiar as these are to scholars, they are frequently conceived of in a way which tends to obscure some of the remoter issues dependent on them. They can most conveniently be presented under five main heads.

I. The authentic text of Mark contains 661 verses. Matthew reproduces the substance of over 600 of these. Mark's style is diffuse, Matthew's succinct ; so that in adapting Mark's language Matthew compresses so much that the 600 odd verses taken from Mark supply rather less than half the material contained in the 1068 verses of the longer Gospel. Yet, in spite of this abbreviation, it is found that Matthew employs 51 % of the actual words used by Mark.[1]

The relation between Luke and Mark cannot be stated in this precise statistical way—for two reasons. First, in his account of the Last Supper and Passion, Luke appears to be " conflating "—to use the convenient technical term for the mixing of two sources—the Marcan story with a parallel version derived from another source, and he does this in a way which often makes it very hard to decide in regard to certain verses whether Luke's version is a paraphrase of Mark or is derived from his other source. Indeed there are only some 24 verses (cf. p. 216 f.) in this part of Luke's Gospel which can be identified with practical certainty as derived from Mark, though it would be hazardous to limit Luke's debt to Mark to these 24. Secondly, there are also, outside the Passion story, a number of cases where Luke appears deliberately to substitute a non-Marcan for the Marcan version of a story or piece of teaching. Thus the Rejection at Nazareth, the Call of Peter, the parable of the Mustard Seed, the Beelzebub Controversy, the Great Commandment, the Anointing, and several less important items are given by Luke in a version substantially different from that in Mark, and always, it is

[1] *Oxford Studies in the Synoptic Problem*, ed. W. Sanday, pp. 85 ff. (Clarendon Press, 1911).

important to notice, in a context quite other from that in which
they appear in Mark.

Another striking feature in Luke's relation to Mark is his
" Great Omission," so called, of a continuous section of 74
verses, Mk. vi. 45-viii. 26. Besides this he omits several shorter
sections, which added together amount to 56 verses. If we
leave out of account all passages where there is reason to suspect
that Luke has used a non-Marcan source, it appears on an approximate estimate that about 350 verses (*i.e.* just over one half of
Mark) have been reproduced by Luke. When following Mark,
Luke alters the wording of his original a trifle more than
Matthew does ; on the other hand he retains many details which
Matthew omits, and he does not compress the language quite so
much. The result is that on an average Luke retains 53 %
of the actual words of Mark, that is, a very slightly higher
proportion than does Matthew.

From these various figures it appears that, while Matthew
omits less than 10 % of the subject matter of Mark, Luke omits
more than 45 %, but for much of this he substitutes similar
matter from another source. Each of them omits numerous
points of detail and several complete sections of Mark which
the other reproduces ; but sometimes they both concur in
making the same omission. The student who desires to get
a clear grasp of the phenomena would do well to prepare for
himself, by the aid of the lists in the Additional Note (A) at the
end of this chapter, a marked copy of the second Gospel, indicating by brackets of four different shapes or colours—(*a*) passages
peculiar to Mark ; (*b*) those reproduced by Luke, but not by
Matthew ; (*c*) those reproduced by Matthew, but not by Luke ;
(*d*) those which Luke omits, but for which *in another context* he
substitutes a parallel version.

II. Let the student take a few typical incidents which occur
in all three Synoptists—I would suggest Mk. ii. 13-17 and
xi. 27-33 to begin with—and, having procured a Synopsis of the
Gospels, underline in red words found in all three, in blue words

found in Mark and Matthew, in yellow words found in Mark and Luke. If this is done throughout the Gospels it will appear that a proportion varying from 30 % to over 60 % of the words in Mark are underlined in red, while a large number of the remainder are marked *either* blue *or* yellow.[1] What is still more significant, if the collocation of words and the structure of sentences in Matthew and Luke be examined, it will be found that, while one or both of them are constantly in close agreement with Mark, they never (except as stated p. 179 ff.) support one another against Mark. This is clear evidence of the greater originality of the Marcan version, and is exactly what we should expect to find if Matthew and Luke were *independently* reproducing Mark, adapting his language to their own individual style.

III. The order of incidents in Mark is clearly the more original ; for wherever Matthew departs from Mark's order Luke supports Mark, and whenever Luke departs from Mark, Matthew agrees with Mark. The section Mk. iii. 31-35 alone occurs in a different context in each gospel ; and there is no case where Matthew and Luke agree together against Mark in a point of arrangement.

A curious fact, of which an explanation is suggested later, p. 274, is that, while in the latter half of his Gospel (chap. xiv. to the end) Matthew adheres strictly to the order of Mark (Mk. vi. 14 to end), he makes considerable rearrangements in the first half.[2] Luke, however, though he omits far more of Mark than

---

[1] The happy possessor of W. G. Rushbrooke's magnificent *Synopticon* will find the work done for him by the use of different types and colours. Of Greek Synopses on a smaller scale, the most conveniently arranged are A. Huck's *Synopse* (Mohr, Tübingen) and Burton and Goodspeed's *Harmony of the Synoptic Gospels* (Universities of Chicago and Cambridge). For those who have little or no knowledge of Greek an admirably arranged Synopsis based on the English of the Revised Version is *The Synoptic Gospels* by J. M. Thompson (Clarendon Press).

[2] A convenient chart showing Matthew's rearrangements of Mark's order is given in the *Commentary on Matthew* by W. C. Allen in the " International Critical " series (T. & T. Clark, 1907), p. xiv. The discussion of the relation of Matthew and Mark in this work, pp. i-xl, is the most valuable known to me ; I cannot, however, accept the theory of Matthew's second main source, p. xli ff

M

does Matthew, hardly ever departs from Mark's order, and only in trifling ways.[1] On the other hand, wherever Luke substitutes for an item in Mark a parallel version from another source, he always gives it *in a different context* from the item in Mark which it replaces. This, as we shall see later, is a fact of very great significance for the determination of the source of Luke's non-Marcan material.

We note, then, that in regard to (a) items of subject matter, (b) actual words used, (c) relative order of sections, Mark is in general supported by *both* Matthew and Luke, and in most cases where they do not both support him they do so alternately, and they practically never agree together against Mark. This is only explicable if they followed an authority which in content, in wording, and in arrangement was all but identical with Mark.

IV. A close study of the actual language of parallel passages in the Gospels shows that there is a constant tendency in Matthew and Luke—showing itself in minute alterations, sometimes by one, sometimes by the other, and often by both—to improve upon and refine Mark's version. This confirms the conclusion, to which the facts already mentioned point, that the Marcan form is the more primitive. Of these small alterations many have a reverential motive. Thus in Mark, Jesus is only once addressed as " Lord " (κύριε), and that by one not a Jew (the Syrophoenician). He is regularly saluted as Rabbi, or by its Greek equivalent διδάσκαλε (Teacher). In Matthew κύριε occurs 19 times ; in Luke κύριε occurs 16, ἐπιστάτα (Master) 6 times. In the same spirit certain phrases which might cause offence or suggest difficulties are toned down or excised. Thus Mark's " he *could* do there *no* mighty work" (vi. 5) becomes in Matthew (xiii. 58) " he *did not many* mighty works"; while Luke omits the limitation altogether. " Why callest thou me good ? " (Mk. x. 18) reads in Matthew (xix. 17) " Why askest thou me concerning the good ? " Much more frequently, however, the

---

[1] These are enumerated and discussed in *Oxford Studies*, p. 88 ff.

changes merely result in stylistic or grammatical improvements, without altering the sense.

But the difference between the style of Mark and of the other two is not merely that they both write better Greek. It is the difference which always exists between the spoken and the written language. Mark reads like a shorthand account of a story by an impromptu speaker—with all the repetitions, redundancies, and digressions which are characteristic of living speech. And it seems to me most probable that his Gospel, like Paul's Epistles, was taken down from rapid dictation by word of mouth. The Mark to whom tradition ascribes the composition of the Gospel was a Jerusalem Jew, of the middle class ;[1] he could speak Greek fluently, but writing in an acquired language is another matter. Matthew and Luke use the more succinct and carefully chosen language of one who writes and then revises an article for publication. This partly explains the tendency to abbreviate already spoken of, which is especially noticeable in Matthew. Sometimes this leads to the omission by one or both of the later writers of interesting and picturesque details, such as " in the stern . . . on a cushion " (Mk. iv. 38), or " they had not in the boat with them more than one loaf " (Mk. viii. 14). Usually, however, it is only the repetitions and redundancies so characteristic of Mark's style that are jettisoned. Sir John Hawkins [2] collects over 100 instances of "enlargements of the narrative, which add nothing to the information conveyed by it, because they are expressed again, or are directly involved in the context," which he calls " context-supplements." The majority of these are omitted by Matthew, a large number by Luke also ; though Luke sometimes omits where Matthew retains, as well as vice versa. Again, Mark is very fond of " duplicate expressions " such as " Evening having come, when the sun set " (i. 32).[3] In these cases one or

[1] His mother had a house large enough to be a meeting-place for the church, and kept at least one slave girl (Acts xii. 12 f.), and his cousin Barnabas had some property.   [2] Hor. Syn.[2] p. 125.
[3] Cf. Hor. Syn.[2] p. 139 ff., where 39 instances are given.

other of the later Evangelists usually abbreviates by leaving out one member of the pair ; and not infrequently it happens that Matthew retains one and Luke the other. Thus in the above example Matthew writes " evening having come," Luke "the sun having set."

Matthew and Luke regularly emend awkward or ungrammatical sentences ; sometimes they substitute the usual Greek word for a Latinism ; and there are two cases where they give the literary equivalent of Greek words, which Phrynichus the grammarian expressly tells us belonged to vulgar speech. Lastly, there are eight instances in which Mark preserves the original Aramaic words used by our Lord. Of these Luke has none, while Matthew retains only one, the name Golgotha (xxvii. 33) ; though he substitutes for the Marcan wording of the cry from the Cross, " Eloi, Eloi . . ." the Hebrew equivalent " Eli, Eli . . ." as it reads in the Psalm (Mk. xv. 34 = Mt. xxvii. 46 = Ps. xxii. 1).

The examples adduced above are merely a sample given to illustrate the general character of the argument. But it is an argument essentially cumulative in character. Its full force can only be realised by one who will take the trouble to go carefully through the immense mass of details which Sir John Hawkins has collected, analysed and tabulated, pp. 114-153 of his classic *Horae Synopticae.* How any one who has worked through those pages with a Synopsis of the Greek text can retain the slightest doubt of the original and primitive character ✓ of Mark I am unable to comprehend. But since there are, from time to time, ingenious persons who rush into print with theories to the contrary, I can only suppose, either that they have not been at the pains to do this, or else that—like some of the highly cultivated people who think Bacon wrote Shakespeare, or that the British are the Lost Ten Tribes—they have eccentric views of what constitutes evidence.

V. An examination of the way in which the Marcan and non-Marcan material is distributed throughout the Gospels of Matthew and Luke respectively is illuminating. The facts seem only explicable on the theory that each author had before him the Marcan material already embodied in one single document; and that, faced with the problem how to combine this with material from other sources, each solved it in his own way —the plan adopted by each of them being simple and straightforward, but quite different from that chosen by the other.

Certain elements in the non-Marcan matter clearly owe their position in the Gospels to the nature of their contents. For example, the two first chapters of Luke, with their account of the Birth and Infancy of Christ, differ so much in style and character from the rest of the Gospel that they are almost certainly to be referred to a separate source, whether written or oral we need not now discuss; and the same remark applies to the first two chapters of Matthew. Obviously, however, these stories, whencesoever derived, could only stand at the beginning of a Gospel. Similarly the additional details, which Matthew and Luke give in their accounts of the Temptation and the Passion, could only have been inserted at the beginning and at the end of their Gospels. But the greater part of the non-Marcan matter consists of parables or sayings which do not obviously date themselves as belonging to any particular time in the public ministry. It would appear that the Evangelists had very little to guide them as to the exact historical occasion to which any particular item should be assigned. That, at any rate, seems to be the only explanation of the curious fact (to which my attention was drawn by Sir John Hawkins) that, subsequent to the Temptation story, there is not a single case in which Matthew and Luke agree in inserting a piece of Q material (the meaning of the symbol Q will appear later) into the same context of Mark. The way, then, in which materials derived from the Marcan and from non-Marcan sources are combined must have been determined mainly by literary considerations, and very little, if at all, by extrinsic historical information.

The student who wishes to get a thorough grasp of the facts is advised to mark off in blue brackets—in a New Testament, *not* in a Synopsis of the Gospels—all passages of Matthew and Luke which appear to be derived from Mark. For this purpose the list of parallels in Additional Note B will be of assistance. He will then see clearly the difference in the methods adopted by Matthew and by Luke.

Matthew's method is to make Mark the framework into which non-Marcan matter is to be fitted, on the principle of joining like to like. That is to say, whenever he finds in a non-Marcan source teaching which would elaborate or illustrate a saying or incident in Mark, he inserts that particular piece of non-Marcan matter into that particular context in the Marcan story. Sometimes he will insert a single non-Marcan verse so as most appropriately to illustrate a context of Mark, *e.g.* the saying about faith (Mt. xvii. 20), or about the Apostles sitting on twelve thrones (Mt. xix. 28). Sometimes he expands a piece of teaching in Mark by the addition of a few verses from another source on the same subject; *e.g.* the non-Marcan saying on divorce, Mt. xix. 10-12, is appropriately fitted on to Marcan discussions of the same theme. So the Marcan saying, repeated in Mt. xix. 30, " The first shall be last and the last first," suggests to him the addition in that particular context of the parable of the Labourers in the Vineyard which points the same moral. Similarly the moral of the Marcan parable of the Wicked Husbandmen, Mt. xxi. 33 ff. (which is directed against the Jewish authorities), is reinforced by the addition immediately before and after it of the anti-Pharisaic parables of the Two Sons and the Marriage Feast.

Examples of this kind of adaptation of non-Marcan matter to a Marcan context could be indefinitely multiplied. But it is worth while to call special attention to the bearing of this process on the longer discourses in Matthew. All of them are clear cases of " agglomeration," that is, of the building up of sayings originally dispersed so as to form great blocks. Four times, starting with a short discourse in Mark as a nucleus, Matthew expands it by means of non-Marcan additions into a long sermon. Thus the 7 verses of Mark's sending out of the Twelve (Mk. vi. 7 ff.) become the 42 verses of Mt. x. The three parables of Mk. iv.—with one omission—are made the basis of the seven parable chapter, Mt. xiii. The 12 verses, Mk. ix. 33-37, 42-48, are elaborated into a discourse of 35 verses in Mt. xviii. The " Little Apocalypse " (Mk. xiii.) is expanded, not only by the addition of a number of apocalyptic sayings (apparently from Q), but also by having appended to it three parables of Judgement, Mt. xxv. To some extent analogous is the way in which the Sermon on the Mount, far the longest and most important block of non-Marcan matter, is connected with the Marcan framework. It is inserted in such a way as to lead up, and thus give point, to the Marcan saying, "And they were astonished at his teaching : for he taught them as one having authority, and not as the scribes." Cf. Mk. i. 22 ; Mt. vii. 29. That the Sermon on the Mount is itself an agglomeration of materials originally separate will be shown later (p. 249 ff.).

Luke's method is quite different and much simpler. There are half-a-dozen or so odd verses scattered up and down the Gospel in regard to which it is disputable whether or not they are derived from Mark. Apart from these, we find that, until we reach the Last Supper (Lk. xxii. 14), Marcan and non-Marcan material alternates in great blocks. The sections, Lk. i. 1-iv. 30 (in the main) ; vi. 20-viii. 3 ; ix. 51-xviii. 14, and xix. 1-27 are non-Marcan. The intervening sections, iv. 31-vi. 19 ; viii. 4-ix. 50 ; xviii. 15-43 ; xix. 28-xxii. 13, are from Mark, with three short interpolations from a non-Marcan source. From xxii. 14 onwards the sources, as is inevitable if two parallel accounts of the Passion were to be combined, are more closely interwoven. This alternation suggests the inference that the non-Marcan materials, though probably ultimately derived from more than one source, had already been combined into a single written document before they were used by the author of the Third Gospel. The further inference that *this combined non-Marcan document* was regarded by Luke as his main source and supplied *the framework into which he fitted extracts of Mark* is worked out in Chap. VIII. of this volume.

The net result of the facts and considerations briefly summarised under the foregoing five heads is to set it beyond dispute that Matthew and Luke made use of a source which in content, in order, and in actual wording must have been *practically identical* with Mark. Can we go a step farther and say simply that their source *was* Mark ?

To the view that their common source was *exactly* identical with our Mark there are two objections.

(1) If the common source used by Matthew and Luke was identical with our Mark, why did they omit some whole sections of their source ?

(2) How are we to account for certain minute agreements of Matthew and Luke against Mark in passages which, but for these, we should certainly suppose were derived from Mark ?

It has been suggested (*a*) that the omissions of material found in Mark would be explicable on the theory that the document used by Matthew and Luke did not contain the omitted items — that it was an earlier form of Mark, or " Ur-Marcus," of which our present Gospel is an expanded version ; (*b*) that if the text of Ur-Marcus differed slightly from that of Mark, the same theory would account for the minute agreements of Matthew and Luke.

Clearly a decision as to the merits of an Ur-Marcus hypo-thesis can only be made after a study of the actual passages omitted by Matthew and Luke respectively, and a careful scrutiny of the so-called " Minor Agreements." But there is one preliminary consideration which ought not to be overlooked.
In estimating the probability of Matthew or Luke pur-posely omitting any whole section of their source, we should remember that they did not regard themselves merely as scribes (professedly reproducing exactly the MS. in front of them), but as independent authors making use, like all historians, of earlier authorities, and selecting from these what seemed to them to

be most important. Moreover, for practical reasons they probably did not wish their work to exceed the compass of a single papyrus roll. If so, space would be an object. As it is, both Matthew and Luke would have needed rolls of fully thirty feet long ; and about twenty-five feet seems to have been regarded as the convenient length.[1] And, when compression of some kind is necessary, slight reasons may decide in favour of rejection. Very often we can surmise reasons of an apologetic nature why the Evangelists may have thought some things less worth while reporting. But, even when we can detect no particular motive, we cannot assume that there was none ; for we cannot possibly know, either all the circumstances of churches, or all the personal idiosyncrasies of writers so far removed from our own time.

MATTHEW'S OMISSIONS

Matthew's supposed omissions from Mark shrink on examination to very small dimensions. Matthew reproduces the substance of all but 55 verses of Mark : of these 24 occur in Luke, a fact which creates a strong presumption that these at any rate were in the original source. But Mk. iv. 21-24, and xiii. 33-37, which account for 9 of the 55 verses, are really cases, not of omission, but of substitution ; for in other contexts Matthew has sayings equivalent to, and usually more elaborate than, those which he here omits.[2] It is usually said that Matthew's omissions include three miracles of healing—a Demoniac (Mk. i. 23 ff.), a Dumb man (vii. 32 ff.), and a Blind (viii. 22 ff.). In the first of these the demon, as if by way of protest, "rent" the patient before coming out, and in the other two the cure is a gradual process with the use of a medicament like spittle instead of by a mere fiat. Such details obviously would make these three healings less miraculous, less "evidential" of supernatural power, and, therefore, from an apologetic point of view, less worth recording, than others.

[1] Cf. *Oxford Studies*, p. 25 ff.   [2] See footnote, p. 196.

But is it correct to say that Matthew has " omitted " these three incidents ? In his account of the Gadarene Demoniacs (viii. 29) he modifies the words of the demoniac so as to combine the cry, as given in his immediate source (Mk. v. 7), with that of the demoniac as given in the apparently omitted section (Mk. i. 24). This proves that Mk. i. 24 stood in the copy of Mark he used. Moreover, Matthew makes the demoniacs two in number, instead of one as in Mark. Taken together, these phenomena suggest that Matthew considers himself to be, not omitting one, but, as it were, telescoping two healings of demoniacs which he found in Mark. Again, Mark's cure of the dumb man is not " omitted," for Matthew substitutes *in the same context as Mark* a general statement that Jesus healed various sick persons, including dumb and blind, and calls attention to the impression produced on the multitude in words that appear to be suggested by the omitted section in Mark (cf. Mt. xv. 31 = Mk. vii. 37). Also he inserts in another context (Mt. ix. 32-33) a healing of a dumb man. Here we have an example of the importance of textual criticism for the Synoptic Problem ; verse 34, which says that Jesus was accused of healing by the prince of devils, is omitted by D, *a*, *k*, Syr. S., and is a textual assimilation to the almost verbally identical passage in Lk. xi. 15 ; it is a " Western non-interpolation " with more than ordinarily good MS. support. Read without this verse, the story in Mt. ix. 32-33 looks like an abbreviated version of Mk. vii. 32 ff. (with the " offending " details excised), transferred after Matthew's manner to another context. In that case one would be inclined to think that Matthew originally intended the healing of two blind men—which he inserts immediately before this (Mt. ix. 27-31)—as another telescoping of two Marcan miracles into one (*i.e.* Mk. viii. 22 ff. and Mk. x. 46 ff.), for the detail " touched their eyes," ix. 29, may well have come from Mk. viii. 23, the other apparently omitted miracle. When, however, in copying Mark he actually reached the story of Bartimaeus, Mk. x. 46 ff., he preferred to retell it in its original context, but forgot to delete it in the earlier part of the Gospel.

The rebuke of John for forbidding those who cast out devils in Christ's name but do not follow with the disciples (Mk. ix. 38 ff.) is a passage which would so readily lend itself to being quoted in favour of the Gnostics who were already, when Matthew wrote, beginning to demoralise the Church,[1] that its omission can occasion no surprise. Again, the attempt of our Lord's relatives to arrest Him (Mk. iii. 21) and the incident of the young man with a linen cloth in Gethsemane (xiv. 51 f.) are both cases where it is harder to explain why Mark thought it worth while to record than why Matthew (and Luke also) omitted. The parable of the Seed growing secretly is also omitted by both Matthew and Luke. In favour of its originality in the text of Mark is the fact that, with the Mustard Seed, it forms one of those pairs of twin parables illustrating different aspects of the same idea which are a notable feature of the tradition of our Lord's teaching (cf. p. 189 f.). I think one must seriously consider the possibility that this had accidentally dropped out of the copy of Mark used by one or both of the other Evangelists owing to " homoioteleuton." The eye of the scribe might very easily pass from the first to the third of the three successive paragraphs, each of which open with the words καὶ ἔλεγεν (Mk. iv. 21, 26, 30). If there are 48 examples in the Gospels of omission through homoioteleuton in א alone,[2] it would be odd if there were none in the first copy of Mark which went to Antioch. Or again, either Matthew or Luke may have omitted it because he preferred to reproduce the Mustard Seed along with the Leaven (its twin parable in Q), and having already a pair to illustrate the idea of the Kingdom as a gradual growth, thought a third

---

[1] Cf. Matthew's significant addition to Mark, "By reason of the spread of antinomianism (ἀνομία) the love of the many shall wax cold," xxiv. 12. N.B. also Matthew elsewhere records a condemnation of some who profess to cast out devils in Christ's name, Mt. vii. 22.

[2] For the whole N.T. the number is 115. Cf. Scrivener's collation of א, p. xv.

with the same moral superfluous. Since Matthew's personal predilections are all on the side of the more catastrophic apocalyptic conception of the Kingdom ; and since Luke, as we shall see, inclines to prefer his non-Marcan source (which gives the pair in another context), this may seem to some a more probable explanation. But it is quite possible that the omission of the parable by Matthew may be due to one of these causes, and its omission by Luke to the other ; both, at any rate, are causes which we can verify as operating elsewhere. In fact the only omission by Matthew for which it is hard to find a satisfactory explanation is the story of the Widow's Mite, Mk. xii. 41-44. But here considerations of style almost guarantee the section as original in Mark. In four verses we find no less than four examples of the most characteristic features of Mark's style—a " context supplement," [1] a " duplicate expression," the idiom ὅ ἐστι, and the Latinism κοδράντης—all of which we may note Luke is careful to revise away.

Luke's Great Omission

It would seem, then, that there is no sufficient reason for supposing that any substantial passage in our present text of Mark was lacking in that known to Matthew. When, however, we turn to Luke, the case is more debateable. Luke frequently omits a section of Mark, but *substitutes* for it in a different context another version of the same saying or incident—apparently derived from the source which, as will appear in Chap. VIII., he on the whole preferred to Mark. Obviously where this has occurred, though we cannot prove that the omitted passages stood in his copy of Mark, there is not a shadow of a reason for supposing that they did not. The real problem arises from Luke's one " great omission " totalling some 74 consecutive verses (Mk. vi. 45-viii. 26).[2] Apart from this, his omissions are

---

[1] On the significance of this and the following expression the student is referred to Hawkins' *Hor. Syn.* pp. 125, 139 ; cf. also pp. 34, 132.

[2] If vii. 16 is genuine (om. B ℵ L 28) the number is 75.

few, short, and easily accounted for. But the absence from
Luke of the equivalent of Mk. vi. 45-viii. 26 is, *prima facie*,
evidence that at any rate the greater part of this section was
absent from his copy of Mark, although it was indubitably
present in that used by Matthew.

Internal evidence also is, up to a point, favourable to the
theory that the section is a later insertion into the text of Mark,
provided we suppose the opening and concluding paragraphs of
it to be original. In Mk. vi. 45 Jesus sends the disciples on
ahead by boat to Bethsaida, while He Himself stays behind to
dismiss the crowd. He rejoins them, walking on the water
during the storm, vi. 51 ; but the arrival at Bethsaida, the
destination for which they set out, is not mentioned till viii. 22.
That is to say, the omission, not of the whole section omitted
by Luke, but of vi. 53-viii. 21, viz. all of it except the first and
last paragraphs, would make, superficially at any rate, a more
coherent story. Curiously enough, some critics who wish thus
to connect the start for and arrival at Bethsaida have failed to
notice that the Walking on the Water, which tells how Jesus
rejoined the disciples, is needed to make the narrative cohere.

On the hypothesis that the original Mark omitted, not the
whole section, but vi. 53-viii. 21, it could be argued that there
are three paragraphs in the inserted section which might very
plausibly be regarded as parallel versions or " doublets " of
matter occurring in the uninterpolated edition. These are (*a*)
the Feeding of the Four Thousand, viii. 1 ff., cf. Feeding of the
Five Thousand, vi. 30 ff. ; (*b*) the gradual cure of a deaf man
by means of spittle, vii. 31 ff., cf. the similar use of spittle to
cure a blind man, viii. 22 ff. ; (*c*) a voyage across the lake,
immediately following a feeding of a multitude, in which the
failure of the disciples to understand about the loaves is
specially emphasised, Mk. viii. 17, cf. vi. 52.

Further, if only the Walking on the Water and the gradual
Cure of the Blind Man, which are the first and last paragraphs of
the " great omission," had stood in Luke's copy of Mark, it

would not be hard to explain his electing not to reproduce them. The gradual cure by means of spittle may have seemed to him a miracle lacking in impressiveness, while the story of the Walking on the Water might appear to play into the hands of the Docetae, who asserted that Christ's human body was a phantom, and were already beginning to cause trouble in the Church before the end of the first century.

Lastly, the retirement of Jesus into a mountain alone after the Feeding of the Five Thousand (Jn. vi. 15, Mk. vi. 46-47) and the Walking on the Water must have stood in the copy of Mark used by John. For John's version of this has (p. 410) conspicuous agreements with Mark against Matthew. Again, if, as many think, the healing of a blind man with spittle, Jn. ix. 6-7, implies a knowledge of the similar story, Mk. viii. 22-26, this too must have stood in John's copy of Mark. Thus, though John's copy cannot have lacked the whole of Luke's " great omission," it may have omitted all but the first and last paragraphs.

Nevertheless, to the attractive hypothesis that the original Mark lacked the section vi. 53-viii. 21, there are two very formidable objections.

(1) There are some remarkable facts to which attention was first drawn by Sir John Hawkins.[1] By a careful tabulation of minute linguistic peculiarities he has shown that in style and vocabulary the section Mk. vi. 45-viii. 26 resembles Mark in no less than eleven striking points in which Mark's usage differs conspicuously from that of Matthew and Luke, and, indeed, from all other New Testament writers. In fact, the style and vocabulary of this section are, if anything, more Marcan than Mark. Sir John's argument, being cumulative in character and dependent on a statistical comparison of minute details, cannot be summarised without weakening its force ; but to my mind it is all but unanswerable.

(2) The difficulty in the way of supposing that the passage was absent from the original text of Mark is enormously enhanced

[1] *Oxford Studies*, p. 64 ff.

by the fact that it was present in that used by Matthew. For, once postulate two editions of Mark—a shorter edition known to Luke and a later longer edition known to Matthew—and the question of the lost end of the Gospel cannot be excluded from consideration. It is incredible that the editor of a second edition, whether it was Mark himself or some other, who was prepared to take upon himself to add as much as a couple of chapters in the middle, should have left the Gospel without an end—supposing the first edition had already lost it. But if the first edition had *not* already lost its end, how explain Luke's desertion of Mark's narrative at Mk. xvi. 8, viz. at the *exact point* at which later on an accidental injury was to cause a mutilation ? There are, moreover, further reasons (cf. p. 338 ff.) for supposing that Matthew and Luke both used a text of Mark which, like ours, ended at xvi. 8. It is very remarkable that *any* edition should have circulated which broke off short without giving an account of the Resurrection Appearances ; but that a second and greatly enlarged edition should have been published without an ending is quite incredible.

The precise weight to be attached to these two objections will be estimated differently by different people. But at least they are serious enough to compel us to ask whether Luke's " great omission " can be explained by any other hypothesis than the absence of this material from his source. Now it is a fact that plausible reasons can be produced why most of the contents of this particular section of Mark would not have appealed to Luke. Motives which might have induced him to omit each separate item are put forward by Sir John Hawkins ; [1] moreover, if, as I argue in Chap. VIII., Luke regarded Mark, not as his main authority, but as a supplementary source, the hypothesis of intentional omission cannot be ruled out.

My own mind has of late been attracted by a third alternative, that Luke used a mutilated copy of Mark. The case for this I state, but merely as a tentative suggestion.

[1] *Oxford Studies*, p. 67 ff.

There are four features in Luke's narrative which cry out for an explanation. (1) Why does he place the Feeding of the Five Thousand at a " village [1] called Bethsaida," ix. 10, when Mark, his source, expressly says that it was in a " desert place " ? (2) Why does he omit the place-name Caesarea Philippi as the scene of Peter's Confession (ix. 18) ? (3) Why does he say that Jesus was " praying alone " on that occasion, while Mark distinctly says that the incident occurred " in the way " ? (4) How is the reading of B in Lk. ix. 18, which on transcriptional grounds looks the more original, to be accounted for ? B is supported by 157 f. Goth. and three other cursives in reading συνήντησαν (f, occurrerunt) for συνῆσαν—"they met" for "they were with."

All these questions receive a completely satisfactory answer if we suppose that Luke's copy of Mark included merely the beginning of the "great omission," as far as the words αὐτὸς μόνος in vi. 47, and then went straight on to καὶ ἐν τῇ ὁδῷ ἐπηρώτα, viii. 27. Now, if a piece is torn out of the middle of a roll the mutilation is not likely to begin and end exactly with a paragraph which opens a new section ; an accidental loss is far more likely to cut across the middle of a sentence at both ends. Let us for the moment assume just such a mutilation. Luke's MS. of Mark would have run as follows (words in italics are specially significant ; asterisks indicate where the break in the papyrus occurred) : " And straightway he constrained his disciples to enter into the boat, and to go before him [unto the other side] [2] unto *Bethsaida*, while he himself sendeth the multitude away. And after he had taken leave of them, he departed into the *mountain to pray*. And when even was come, the boat was in the midst of the sea, and *he alone* * * * * and *in the way* he asked his disciples, saying unto them, Who do men say that I am ? " (Mk. vi. 45-47 . . . viii. 27b).

Granted such a text, what would Luke make of the story ? What he actually does (in the B text) is to write, immediately

---

[1] Reading κώμην for πόλιν with D Θ, discussed p. 569.   [2] Om. W Θ 1&c. Syr. S. q.

after the account of the Feeding of the Multitude, " And it came
to pass, as he was *praying alone*, the disciples *met* him : and he
asked them, saying, Who do the multitudes say that I am ? "
And he inserts the place-name *Bethsaida* into the opening
sentence of the Feeding of the Multitude, though in other
respects he closely follows Mark's version of the story. A study
of the passage shows that this procedure is of the most natural
and reasonable kind.

(1) From the mutilated text before him he might infer that
Bethsaida was only a short way off, so that the disciples would
be able to land and come back to meet our Lord by road, after
He had dismissed the multitude. It would follow that both
the Feeding of the Five Thousand and Peter's Confession took
place near Bethsaida. That being so, if the story is to be clear
to the reader, the proper place to insert the name is obviously
before the Feeding of the Five Thousand, not in between the
two incidents. Luke, therefore, inserts the name Bethsaida in
the most appropriate place, ix. 10.

(2) Luke's omission of the name Caesarea Philippi has been
quoted as evidence of his indifference to geographical detail.
But the whole case for this indifference rests on his supposed
omission of the geographical details contained in this section of
Mark. And if the mutilation in his MS. of Mark included the
half of verse viii. 27, then Bethsaida was the only place-name
he had in his source ; and he does the best he can with that.

(3) The incident of Jesus " praying " and being " alone " is
not an " editorial addition " directly contradicting Mark, but a
reproduction of what in Luke's text of Mark was the immediate
introduction to Peter's Confession.

(4) The reading of B (συνήντησαν [1] =*occurrerunt* =" go to

---

[1] Probably the original reading was ἤντησαν =" met." συνῆσαν =" were
with," the reading of most MSS., is a very early scribe's emendation. Someone
then tried to correct an ancestor of B by this text and wrote συν over the ἤν.
but the next copyist combined the two. A similar reading of B has been
pointed out by Prof. Burkitt. In Lk. xix. 37 D has πάντων (neut.), ℵ πασῶν
δυναμέων ; B (supported curiously enough by 579) has πάντων δυναμέων, a false
concord explicable if πάντων was original, δυναμέων an addition from the margin.

N

meet ") is, as so often, shown to be original. It translates Mark's
ἐν τῇ ὁδῷ in the only meaning that could be given to it, if it
followed just after Mk. vi. 47.

If Luke wrote at some distance from Rome, no difficulty is
presented by the hypothesis that the only copy of Mark which
had reached him was a mutilated one. Speculation, however,
as to how the mutilation occurred is not very profitable. A
papyrus roll was a very fragile thing, and the number of
accidents that could happen to it was very large. All I submit
is that, in view of such a possibility and of the difficulties of
supposing the section was not in the original copy of Mark, its
absence from Luke constitutes quite insufficient ground for
postulating an Ur-Marcus.

But if the theory of an older and shorter edition of Mark
is not needed to explain Luke's Great Omission, it is certainly
not called for to explain his shorter omissions. Several of them
only amount to one or two verses, and there are obvious
reasons why Luke should have left out the others. Three
passages, for instance (ix. 28-29, x. 35-41, xiv. 26-28), reflect
some discredit on the Apostles, and Luke always " spares the
Twelve "—omitting the rebuke " Retro Satanas " (Mk. viii. 33), and
excusing the slumber in Gethsemane as due to sorrow (Lk. xxii.
45), and only recording one of the three lapses. The dancing of
Salome (Mk. vi. 17-29) has little value for edification. The pith
of the long discussion on Divorce (x. 1-12) is given in the last
two verses, for which Luke has an equivalent in another context (Lk. xvi. 18). The Cursing of the Fig Tree (xi. 12-14,
20-22) might seem a harsh act for the Great Healer ; besides,
Luke has the parable of the Fig Tree (Lk. xiii. 6 ff.), which
may be the origin of the story, and at any rate contains all the
moral that can be drawn from it. Mark ix. 43-47 may already,
for all we know, have been seized upon by certain over-zealous
believers as an exhortation to self-mutilation of the kind which
others justified from Mt. xix. 12. Finally, some of the omitted
passages must have stood in Luke's copy of Mark, for Luke

reproduces some verses which *in Mark* are intimately connected with others which he omits. Thus Lk. ix. 36 is an abbreviation of Mk. ix. 9, but in Mark this verse forms the introduction to the four verses that follow.

These facts must be considered in the light of the evidence to be submitted in the next chapter that Luke regarded his non-Marcan source as primary, and conceived himself as producing a new and enlarged edition of that work, incorporating what seemed most important in Mark. In that case passages of Mark not included in Luke must be regarded, not so much as " omissions " as " non-insertions," and the absence of any particular passage from Luke creates no presumption that it was absent from the copy of Mark which he used.

Minor Agreements of Matthew and Luke

Accordingly it is clear that the only real difficulty in accepting out of hand the conclusion that the document used by Matthew and Luke was identical with Mark lies in the occurrence of agreements between Matthew and Luke against Mark consisting either in minor omissions or in some minute alterations in a turn of expression. A full discussion of this subject is attempted in Chap. XI. But for the benefit of the reader who is not conversant with the Greek language, I will briefly sum up the conclusions there reached. (1) Such agreements are only significant in contexts where there is no reason to suppose that the passage also stood in Q. (2) Most commonly these agreements result from Matthew and Luke changing a historic present in Mark into an imperfect or aorist tense, in their substituting a participle for a finite verb with " and," or in using a different conjunction or preposition from Mark. In every instance the change is, from the stylistic or grammatical point of view, an improvement. And as both Matthew and Luke continually make this kind of improvement *independently*, it is not surprising that both sometimes concur in doing so in the same place. (3) If the agreement consists in an omission it is almost invariably of the unnecessary or unimportant words which are characteristic of Mark's somewhat verbose style. Matthew and Luke both compress Mark ; it would be hard to find three consecutive verses in the whole of his Gospel of which either Matthew or Luke have not omitted some words, apparently with this object. Since, then, both Matthew and Luke *independently* compress Mark by the omission of unnecessary words or sentences, and since in any sentence only certain words can be spared, they could not avoid frequently concurring in the selection of words to be dispensed with. *Under such circumstances, coincidence in omission calls for no explanation.*

There are, however, three instances where the agreement of Matthew and Luke against Mark amounts to five consecutive words ; and there are perhaps thirty of an agreement in one or two words. These agreements are all of a kind which, if there were fewer of them, could easily be attributed to accidental coincidence. But there are just too many of them to make this at all a plausible explanation.

But though some explanation is required, a study of the phenomena reveals the fact that the hypothesis of an Ur-Marcus is of no service to us whatever for that purpose. The essential point that emerges is that in the great majority of cases where Matthew and Luke agree against Mark, the *existing text of Mark seems the more primitive* and original. If, then, the document used by Matthew and Luke was not identical with our Mark, so far from being an earlier form of Mark, it must have been a later and more polished recension, all copies of which have since disappeared. This is the explanation of the phenomena which was adopted by Dr. Sanday in the *Oxford Studies* (pp. 21 ff.) and is, I believe, accepted by the majority of authorities as the most probable. It involves no *a priori* difficulties. There would have been several copies of Mark at Rome at a very early date ; and it is quite likely that one copyist would have felt free to emend the style a little. From this copy those used by Matthew and Luke may have been made, while the unrevised copies, being in the majority, may yet have determined the text that has come down to us.

Personally, however, I am inclined to seek a different explanation of that residue of the agreements between Matthew and Luke which cannot naturally be ascribed to occasional coincidence in the type of improvement in Mark which they constantly make independently. The Synopses of the Gospels in Greek most widely used by scholars give the text either of Tischendorf or of Westcott and Hort which are based on the text of Alexandria as preserved in B א. But in nearly every case where a minute agreement of Matthew and Luke against Mark is found in B א it is absent in one or more of the other early local texts; though, on the other hand, these other texts frequently show such agreements in passages where they do not occur in B, while quite a different set of agreements is found in MSS. which give the Byzantine text. Indeed, even as between א and B there is a difference in this respect ; there are agreements of Matthew and Luke against Mark in the text of B which are not in א, and *vice versa*. A careful study of the MS. evidence distinctly favours the view that all those minute agreements of Matthew and Luke against Mark, which cannot be attributed to coincidence, were absent from the original text of the Gospels, but have crept in later as a result of " assimilation " between the texts of the different Gospels. Detailed evidence for this conclusion is submitted in Chapter XI. ; and, if it is correct, the one objection to the view that the document used by Matthew and Luke was identically our Mark completely disappears. If, however, that evidence be deemed inconclusive, then Dr. Sanday's hypothesis best explains the facts. But in any case, as I have already urged, they offer no support to the hypothesis of an Ur-Marcus.

The Document Q

Although Matthew embodies about eleven-twelfths of Mark he compresses so much that the Marcan material only amounts to about half of the total contents of his Gospel. It is remarkable that the additional matter consists preponderantly of parable and discourse.[1] Of Luke rather less than one-third appears to be derived from Mark, though owing to the greater length of his Gospel—1149 verses as compared with 661—and to some compression of Mark's style, this one-third of Luke includes the substance of slightly more than half of Mark. Luke's additional matter includes both more narrative and more parables than Matthew's, but not quite as much discourse. The discourse occurs in shorter sections, and is not to the same extent as in Matthew collected into large blocks.

We notice that, of this large mass of material which must have been derived from elsewhere than Mark, a certain amount, approximately 200 verses, appears in *both* Matthew and Luke. This matter, which they have in common, includes most of John the Baptist's Preaching, the details of the Temptation, the Sermon on the Mount, the Healing of the Centurion's Servant, John's Message, " Art thou he that should come," " Be not anxious for the morrow," and many more of the most notable sayings in the Gospels. But there are two facts of a puzzling nature. (1) The common material occurs in quite different contexts and is arranged (cf. p. 273 ff.) in a different order in the two Gospels. (2) The degree of resemblance between the parallel passages varies considerably. For example, the two versions of John the Baptist's denunciation, " Generation of vipers . . ."

---

[1] Narratives peculiar to Matthew, apart from generalised statements of healing like xv. 30 and xxi. 14, are as follows : the Infancy, i.-ii. ; Peter walking on the water, xiv. 28 ff. ; the coin in the fish's mouth, xvii. 24 ff. ; various small additions to Mark's story of the Passion (*i.e.* xxvi. 52-54; xxvii. 3-10, 19, 24-25, 51b-53, 62-66) ; the Resurrection Appearances. The two miracles, ix. 27-34, are possibly intended to be the same as two recorded by Mark, which otherwise Matthew has omitted. Cf. p. 170.

(Mt. iii. 7-10 = Lk. iii. 7-9), agree in 97 % of the words used ; but the two versions of the Beatitudes present contrasts as striking as their resemblances.

How are we to account for this common matter ? The obvious suggestion that Luke knew Matthew's Gospel (or *vice versa*) and derived from it some of his materials breaks down for two reasons.

(1) Sir John Hawkins once showed me a Greek Testament in which he had indicated on the left-hand margin of Mark the exact point in the Marcan outline at which Matthew has inserted each of the sayings in question, with, of course, the reference to chapter and verse, to identify it ; on the right-hand margin he had similarly indicated the point where Luke inserts matter also found in Matthew. It then appeared that, subsequent to the Temptation story, there is not a single case in which Matthew and Luke agree in inserting the same saying at the same point in the Marcan outline. If then Luke derived this material from Matthew, he must have gone through both Matthew and Mark so as to discriminate with meticulous precision between Marcan and non-Marcan material ; he must then have proceeded with the utmost care to tear every little piece of non-Marcan material he desired to use from the context of Mark in which it appeared in Matthew—in spite of the fact that contexts in Matthew are always exceedingly appropriate —in order to re-insert it into a different context of Mark having no special appropriateness. A theory which would make an author capable of such a proceeding would only be tenable if, on other grounds, we had reason to believe he was a crank.

(2) Sometimes it is Matthew, sometimes it is Luke, who gives a saying in what is clearly the more original form. This is explicable if both are drawing from the same source, each making slight modifications of his own ; it is not so if either is dependent on the other.

A second explanation of the phenomena that has been suggested is that Matthew and Luke had access (in addition to the written Gospel of Mark) to different cycles of oral tradition, or to documents embodying such, and that these cycles, though in the main independent, overlapped to some extent. For those cases where the degree of verbal resemblance between the parallel passages is small I myself believe that some such explanation is a true one. For the more numerous examples where the verbal resemblances are close and striking it is far from convincing.

Accordingly a third hypothesis, that Matthew and Luke made use of a single common document that has since disappeared, has secured, if not quite universal, at any rate an all but universal, assent from New Testament scholars. This hypothetical source is now by general consent referred to as "Q," though in older books it is spoken of as "the Logia" or "the Double Tradition." Seeing that Q, if such a document ever existed, has disappeared, the hypothesis that it was used by Matthew and Luke cannot be checked and verified as can the hypothesis that they used Mark. But it explains facts for which some explanation is necessary, and it has commended itself to most of those, who have studied the subject minutely in all its bearings, as explaining them in a simpler and more satisfactory way than any alternative suggestion which has so far been put forward. We are justified, then, in assuming the existence of Q, so long as we remember that the assumption is one which, though highly probable, falls just short of certainty.

But it does not follow, because we accept the view that Q existed, that we can discover exactly which passages in Matthew and Luke were, and which were not, derived from it. Nearly all writers on the Synoptic Problem have attempted to do this. I have done so myself.[1] But, for reasons which will be developed in Chap. IX., I now feel that most of these attempts to reconstruct Q have set out from false premises. (1) Critics have under-

[1] *Oxford Studies*, Essay VI. On the hazards of reconstructing Q there are some valuable warnings in Burkitt's review of Harnack's attempt, *J.T.S.*, Ap. 1907, p. 454 ff. I cannot, however, accept his own suggestion that Q contained an account of the Passion.

estimated the probability that in many cases slightly differing versions of the same sayings or parables would be in circulation. They have therefore been unduly anxious to extend the boundaries of Q by including passages, like the Lord's Prayer and the parable of the Lost Sheep, where the parallelism between Matthew and Luke is not exact enough to make derivation from a common written source its most likely explanation. Even if items like these stood in Q, it is probable that one or other of the Evangelists also had before him another version as well. Further study of the facts convinces me that a substantial proportion of the 200 verses in question were probably derived from some other source than Q. (2) On the other hand, since Matthew and Luke would presumably have treated Q much in the same way as they treated Mark, it is fairly certain that some passages which are preserved by Matthew only or by Luke only are from Q ; but I feel less confidence than heretofore in the validity of some of the principles by which it has been sought to identify them. (3) Not enough allowance has been made for the extent to which sayings of a proverbial form circulate in any community. One such, " It is more blessed to give than to receive," which does not appear in any of the Gospels, is quoted by Paul (Acts xx. 35). At the present day, at the Bar, in the Medical Profession, in every College in Oxford or Cambridge, professional maxims, or anecdotes and epigrams connected with names well known in the particular society, are handed down by word of mouth. The same thing must have happened in the early Church ; and it does not at all follow that a saying of this character, even if it occurs in almost identically the same form in two Gospels, was derived from a written source. Where, however, a number of consecutive sayings occur in two Gospels with approximately the same wording, or where a detached saying is not of a quasi-proverbial character, a documentary source is more probable. Hence, while the phenomena make the hypothesis of the existence of a written source Q practically certain, its exact delimitation is a matter of a far more speculative character. A tentative reconstruction is essayed in Chap. X.

THE OVERLAPPING OF Q AND MARK

But although it is impossible to determine exactly what was and what was not contained in Q, one fact cannot be disputed—there is a certain amount of overlapping between Q and Mark. This observation holds good in principle even if we think (with Prof. E. de W. Burton [1]) that the "Q material" was derived, not from a single document, but from two, or (like the late Dr. A. Wright) that it represents a cycle of tradition and was not derived from a document at all. In other words, whatever the theory we accept as to the character of the source or sources of the non-Marcan matter common to Matthew and Luke, it is clear that certain items were known to Matthew and Luke both in Mark's version and also in another decidedly different. In fact, to put it paradoxically, the overlapping of Mark and Q is more certain than is the existence of Q.

The student will find convincing proof of this, if, in his Synopsis of the Gospels, he will underline in red words found in all three Gospels, in blue those found in Mark and Matthew, in purple those in Mark and Luke, and, say, in yellow words found only in Matthew and Luke, in the accounts of John the Baptist's Preaching, the Baptism and Temptation, the Beelzebub Controversy, the parables of the Mustard Seed and Leaven, and the Mission Charge (Mk. vi. 7-11, cf. Mt. x. 1-16a = Lk. x. 1-12). The phenomena revealed are only explicable on the theory that Matthew and Luke had before them a version of these items considerably longer than that of Mark. And it will be noticed that, while Matthew carefully combines the two versions, Luke prefers the non-Marcan, introducing at most a few touches from that of Mark.

[1] *Principles of Literary Criticism and the Synoptic Problem,* p. 41 ff. (Chicago, 1904).

This overlapping of Mark and Q, found in the above sections
and in a few other short sayings, covers about 50 verses of Mark.[1]
And, wherever it occurs, we find that Luke tends to preserve
the Q version unmixed, while Matthew combines it with that
of Mark. This, indeed, only means that Matthew and Luke
differ in their treatment of Q in precisely the same way as in
their treatment of Mark—in both cases Matthew conflates his
sources, Luke alternates them. This difference, of which we
shall see many examples, affords a valuable principle for
distinguishing the Marcan and the Q versions in doubtful
cases.

Many critics explain this overlapping of Q and Mark on
the theory that Mark knew and made extracts from Q. In
favour of this view there is the fact that in many cases where
Mark and Q overlap the Q version is longer and also looks the
more original. In fact, as I put it in an Essay in the *Oxford
Studies*, the Marcan often looks like a "mutilated excerpt"
from the Q version.[2] In that case the first difficulty would be
to explain the very small amount of matter (not more than
50 verses) which Mark derives from Q. The suggestion I then
made was that Mark wrote for a Church in which Q was already
in circulation, and intended to supplement rather than to supersede Q, and he therefore only drew from it some brief allusions
to certain outstanding points which could not be altogether
passed over in a life of Christ. But the net result of the
discussion of the question among scholars during the last thirteen
years has been to add weight to, rather than to detract from,
the difficulty I even then expressed of supposing that Q lay
before Mark in a *written* form.

In Mark's account of the Temptation there is no mention
of the fast. Indeed, if we did not unwittingly read into Mark's

[1] Most of the relevant passages are printed in parallel columns and discussed in my essay in *Oxford Studies*, p. 167 ff. There is a valuable discussion
in *Sources of the Synoptic Gospels*, p. 234 ff. (C. S. Patton, Macmillan Co., New
York, 1915).

[2] *Oxford Studies*, p. 171.

account what is so familiar to us from the other two Gospels, we should naturally interpret the imperfect tense of the verb in the phrase " the angels ministered to him " as meaning that Jesus was continuously fed by angels, as once Elijah was by ravens. Again, while in Matthew and Luke the emphasis is on the internal content of the various temptations of our Lord to a misuse of His lately realised Messianic powers, in Mark it is on the external fact that " he was with the wild beasts," which is not even mentioned in the other accounts. Mark's representation of this incident is so wholly different from that in Q that, if we were compelled to assume that he could have derived it from no other source, we must say that he had read Q long enough ago to have had time to forget it.

John's Preaching, the Baptism, and the Temptation obviously form a single section, and a source which contains the first and third must have contained the second, which not only connects the other two but is the point round which they hinge. Q, therefore, must have contained an account of the Baptism. But whereas in Mark's version the voice from heaven is " Thou art my beloved Son, in thee I am well pleased," in Q it more probably read as, " Thou art my Son, this day have I begotten thee " ; which is the reading of the Western text of Luke, and is undoubtedly right. As has been already pointed out (p. 143), it can be traced back to Justin Martyr ; and since it is a reading which not only introduces a discrepancy between the Gospels but also seems to favour what was later regarded as the dangerous heresy that Jesus only became Son of God at His Baptism, its " correction " in the Alexandrian MSS. is easy to explain. But if Luke wrote this, and that with Mark in front of him, it must have been because it stood in his other source.

Again, the picturesque details which Mark (i. 6) gives as to John's dress and food look authentic, but there is no reason to suppose they stood in Q. Here, and indeed wherever Mark and Q overlap, Matthew conflates the two versions ; Luke prefers that of Q. But if we take Luke as on the whole representing Q,

and consider the section John's Preaching, Baptism and Temptation as a whole, the differences between his version and Mark
are far more striking than the resemblances. It is only the fact
that Matthew combines the two versions, and most people read
Matthew first, that has concealed the extent of the contrast so
long even from students.

The case for regarding Mark's version of the Beelzebub
Controversy as an extract from Q is stronger. But, again, if we
realise that Matthew's version is partly derived from Mark, and
therefore take Luke's version as on the whole nearer to Q, the
verbal resemblances between the two accounts are no more than
would be inevitable if they represent two quite independent
traditions of the same original incident and discourse. In this
case, however, part of the argument that Mark derives from Q
depends on the suggestion that the way in which the section
appears in Mark is such that it looks as if it were an interpolation.
But this contention disappears on closer investigation. The
removal of Mk. iii. 22-30 does not leave the smooth connection
we should expect if it was really an interpolation. On the
other hand, if the words " they said " in Mk. iii. 21 are interpreted as meaning " people were saying," *on disait*, the section
reads, not like an interpolation, but as a digression intended
to explain their action. " They did so, for report said He was
mad, and the scribes had gone so far as to say He was Beelzebub,
but He made short work of them." Mark's phrase is ambiguous
and not very good Greek, and, as usually happens with imperfectly
educated writers, the digression is clumsily introduced. But it
is more likely that our Lord's relatives should have come to
apprehend Him, because they had heard a report that He was
beside Himself, than that they should have arrived at such a
conclusion for themselves. And it is by no means likely that
Mark would have told the story at all, if he had meant what
he is usually understood to mean.

In all our sources we find the phenomenon of twin-parables [1]

---

[1] *Oxford Studies*, p. 173.

illustrating different aspects of the same idea—the Hidden Treasure and the Pearl of Great Price (Mt. xiii. 44-46), the Tower Builder and King making War (Lk. xiv. 28-32), the New Patch and the New Wine (Mk. ii. 21-22), the Lost Sheep and the Lost Coin (Lk. xv. 3-10). In the *Oxford Studies* I argued that the Mustard Seed in Mark was the mutilated half of the Mustard Seed and Leaven, which since they stand together in both Matthew and Luke must have formed such a twin pair in Q. But Mr. E. R. Buckley [1] acutely points out that in Mark the Mustard Seed does not stand alone ; it is paired with the parable of the Seed growing secretly, which is quite as appropriate a twin as the Leaven to illustrate the idea of the gradual growth of the Kingdom. It would seem, then, that the twin-parable argument really cuts the other way, and suggests that in Mark and Q we have two pairs which have descended along quite independent lines of tradition.

Mt. x. 5-16 is clearly a conflation of the Q discourse, given by Luke as the Charge to the Seventy (Lk. x. 1-12), with Mark's discourse on the Mission of the Twelve (Mk. vi. 7-11). Matthew has additional matter both at the beginning and the end which may possibly come from a third source (cf. p. 255), but in the central part of his version of the discourse (Mt. x. 9-16a) there is hardly a word which is not to be found either in Mk. vi. 7-11 or in Lk. x. 1-12. The five words, on the other hand, common to Mk. vi. 7-11 and Lk. x. 1-12 (I do not count καί, ἄν and μή, the definite article and personal pronouns, which for this purpose are not significant), " wallet," " enter," " house," " remain," " feet," are such as must occur in *any* version of this discourse. Assuming, then, that Luke x. 1-12 (not being conflate with Mark) represents Q, the differences between Mark and Luke are so great and the resemblances so few that they favour the view that Mark's version is independent, not derived from Q. If Mark did use Q, he must have trusted entirely to memory and never once referred to the written source.

---

[1] *Introduction to the Synoptic Problem*, p. 147 (Arnold, 1912).

There remain no other considerable passages where Mark and Q are parallel ; for only portions of Mk. iv. 21-25 and Mk. ix. 42-50 have their equivalents in Q, and that in scattered contexts. The rest are all quite short, consisting of one or two verses. Mostly they belong to the class of proverb-like saying which, as has been argued above (p. 185), would be likely to be circulated in different forms by word of mouth. To the critic perhaps the most interesting examples are Mk. viii. 34, cf. Mt. x. 38 = Lk. xiv. 27, " take up the cross," and Mk. viii. 38, cf. Mt. x. 33 = Lk. xii. 9, " denies me on earth." A glance at the Synopsis will show that Matthew and Luke give these sayings twice over—once in the context parallel to Mark and in a version very close to Mark's, and again in the quite different contexts to which the references are given above, but in a version much less close to Mark's. This shows beyond doubt that Matthew and Luke had versions of the sayings in two distinct sources. The two versions differ to an extent which makes it improbable that Mark's was derived from Q, unless his dependence on Q is held to be already securely established on other grounds.[1]

On the whole, then, the evidence is decidedly against the view that Mark used Q. In that case the general, though not invariable, superiority of the Q version remains to be accounted for. This can only be done if we suppose that Q was a document of very early date and represents a peculiarly authentic tradition.

A MODERN ILLUSTRATION

Small things that fall within our own experience may often illuminate great things known to us only through books. Says Gibbon, speaking of the insight into military system which he

[1] Prof. C. H. Dodd points out to me that in three cases (Mk. iii. 28, iv. 22, vi. 8) the variations between the Marcan and the Q versions might be explained as divergent translations of Aramaic : iii. 28 בְּרִי נִשָּׁא singular or collective; iv. 22 ד = ἵνα or δ; vi. 8, where לֹא for אֶלָּא would give μὴ ῥαβδόν instead of εἰ μὴ ῥαβδόν.

gained from the peaceful manœuvres of his county militia :
" The captain of the Hampshire grenadiers (the reader may
smile) has not been useless to the historian of the Roman
Empire." In a similar spirit it may be worth while to quote
an experience of my own, which shows the psychological working
out in practice of " conflation," " agglomeration," and other
kinds of " editorial modification." A prolonged study of ancient
documents compels the professional critic to assume such
processes, but to the plain man the hypothesis often seems
over-ingenious, unverifiable, and unreal.

In 1920 I undertook, in collaboration with a friend, to
prepare for publication a sketch of the personality and teaching
of Sadhu Sundar Singh,[1] commonly known as " the Indian
St. Francis." The Sadhu had left England, and any extensive
correspondence with him seemed impracticable. Hence we had
to rely upon a collection of printed and manuscript material,
and on the recollections of our own personal intercourse with
him and that of some other friends. That is to say, we were
dependent on written documents supplemented by a certain
amount of " oral tradition."

Our materials included two brief " lives " written in India,
which to some extent overlapped. We had also three different
collections of addresses, given by him in India, Ceylon, and
Great Britain respectively, and various newspaper reports.
Seeing that the Sadhu is in the habit of freely repeating the
same story or parable on different occasions, the phenomenon
of parallel versions of the same material frequently occurred.
Thus the problem we had to solve was essentially that of combining into a single whole materials derived from a number of
disconnected, independent, but to a large extent overlapping,
sources. It was not, however, till the book was in proof that
I realised that circumstances had forced us to devise ways of
dealing with our materials having the closest analogy to those

[1] *The Sadhu : A Study in Mysticism and Practical Religion*, by B. H.
Streeter and A. J. Appasamy (Macmillan, 1921).

which criticism suggests were habitually employed by editors in antiquity.

(1) Our first step was to single out the central ideas and leading topics to which the Sadhu most frequently recurred ; our next, to sort out roughly the materials from various sources under headings corresponding to these main ideas. Then we carefully rearranged and fitted together the sayings and parables collected under each several head in such a way as to present, in the Sadhu's own words, a coherent, connected, and as far as possible complete, account of his teaching on that particular topic. Thus almost every discourse in the book is an " agglomeration," containing material drawn from two or three different sources.

(2) The frequent occurrence in our sources of two and sometimes three versions of the same story or saying presented us with a problem we could not avoid facing. The solution that seemed obvious was to select what seemed the freshest and most original version. But wherever an otherwise inferior version contained a detail or a phrase which, from our knowledge of Indian conditions or our interpretation of the character and philosophy of the man, seemed to us specially interesting or authentic, we worked this detail or phrase into the substance of the selected version. In other words, we " conflated " two, and occasionally even three, parallel accounts.

(3) For a variety of reasons, one of which was the desire not to swell the size of the book in view of the high cost of production, we decided not to reproduce the whole of our materials. Inevitably, in considering what to jettison, we were guided by our own feeling, or by the opinion of friends, as to which sections were the less interesting, valuable, or characteristic, and decided to omit these.

(4) Since the Sadhu's knowledge of English was limited, we considered ourselves free to amend the grammar and style wherever it seemed desirable, so long as we did not alter the sense.

Modern devices like an introduction, footnotes, and inverted commas enabled us to take our readers into our confidence as to our method, and to give references to original sources where anything depended on it. An ancient author was not expected to do this, and for purely mechanical reasons it would have been impossibly cumbrous with the ancient form of book. But the point I wish to bring out is how a personal experience has caused me to realise that—given a multiplicity of sources—some such editorial methods are forced upon an author who wishes to present the reader with a biographical portrait rather than a chaotic mass of disconnected *obiter dicta*.

To hint at a comparison, though it be only in regard to the mere mechanism of editing, between a work of one's own and a book of the Bible will seem, I fear, to some readers, to border on indecency. I conceive, however, that it is worth while to incur the risk of such a criticism in order to be able more firmly to substantiate a proposition on which I laid some stress in the *Oxford Studies*. It is really important for the ordinary man to realise that the use by the authors of our Gospels of editorial methods like " conflation " and " agglomeration " of sources does not necessarily impair, indeed under the circumstances it may well have been the best way to secure, an effective presentation of the total impression of our Lord's teaching. On this subject I venture to repeat some words I wrote thirteen years ago.[1]

" Insomuch as the loss of a single syllable which might throw a ray of light on any act or word of our Lord is to be regretted, we must regret that Q, and possibly some other early writings used by Matthew and Luke, have not been preserved unaltered and entire. Yet perhaps the loss is less than we may think. Who does not feel that St. Mark, the oldest of the Gospels we still have, is the one we could best spare ? Without him we should miss the exacter details of a scene or two, a touch or two of human limitations in the Master, or of human infirmity in the Twelve, but it is not from him that we get the portrait of the Master which has been the inspiration of Christendom. A mechanical snapshot is for the realist a more reliable and

---

[1] *Oxford Studies*, p. 226.

correct copy of the original than a portrait by Rembrandt, but it cannot give the same impression of the personality behind. The presence of a great man, the magic of his voice, the march of his argument, have a mesmeric influence on those who hear, which is lost in the bare transcript of fragmentary sayings and isolated acts such as we find in Mark or Q. Later on, two great, though perhaps unconscious, artists, trained in the movement begun by the Master and saturated by His Spirit, retell the tale, idealise—if you will—the picture, but in so doing make us to realise something of the majesty and tenderness which men knew in Galilee.

"An instance will make this clear. The realist may object that the Sermon on the Mount is not the sermon there delivered, but a mosaic of the more striking fragments of perhaps twenty discourses, and may approve rather of St. Mark or Q because there we have the fragments frankly as fragments. But on the hill or by the lake they were not listened to as scattered fragments but in the illuminating context, and behind the words was ever the speaker's presence. 'The multitude marvelled as they heard,' says Mark in passages where *his* story leaves us cold. We turn to the arresting cadence of the Sermon on the Mount and it is no longer the multitude but *we* that marvel."

ADDITIONAL NOTES

(A) Omissions from Mark

(*N.B.*—These lists do not include odd verses which add nothing material to the sense.[1])

(*a*) The passages of Mark which are absent from both Matthew and Luke are :—i. 1 ; ii. 27 ; iii. 20-21 ; iv. 26-29 ; vii. 3-4 ; vii. 32-37; viii. 22-26 ; ix. 29 ; ix. 39 *b* ; ix. 48-49 ; xi. 11 *a* ; xiii. 33-37 [2] ; xiv. 51-52 ; total, 32 verses.

---

[1] The lists of passages here given differ occasionally from the similar lists in my article on the Synoptic Problem in Peake's *Commentary on the Bible*.

[2] But Matthew has similar matter, Mt. xxiv. 42, xxv. 13-15; cf. also xii. 38-40, xix. 12.

(b) The passages of Mark which are absent from Matthew but present in Luke are :—i. 23-28 ; i. 35-38 ; iv. 21-24[1] ; vi. 30 ; ix. 38-40 ; xii. 40-44 ; total, 23 verses.

(c) The passages of Mark which, though present in Matthew, have no equivalent in Luke are :—i. 5-6 ; iv. 33-34 ; vi. 17-29 ; ix. 10-13 ; ix. 28 ; ix. 41 ; ix. 43-47 ; x. 1-10 ; x. 35-41 ; xi. 12-14, 20-22 ; xi. 24 ; xiii. 10, 18, 27, 32 ; xiv. 26-28[2] ; xv. 3-5 ; total, 62 verses. To which must be added the long continuous passage of 74 verses, vi. 45-viii. 26, commonly spoken of as Luke's "great omission." As, however, the two miracles of gradual healing (vii. 32-37 and viii. 22-26) which Matthew also omits occur in this section of Mark, we must beware of counting these 11 verses twice over in estimating the total omissions by Luke from Mark. Thus the total of Luke's *complete* omissions will then amount to 155 verses.

(d) The passages of Mark—*excluding* the Passion story (*i.e.* Mk. xiv. 17 ff. = Lk. xxii. 14 ff.)—which do not appear in Luke in the same context as in Mark, but for which there is substituted a different version in another context, are :—Mk. i. 16-20, cf. Lk. v. 1-11 ; iii. 22-27, cf. Lk. xi. 14-23 ; iii. 28-30, cf. Lk. xii. 10 ; iv. 30-32, cf. Lk. xiii. 18-19 ; vi. 1-6, cf. Lk. iv. 16-30 ; viii. 15, cf. Lk. xii. 1 ; ix. 42, cf. Lk. xvii. 2 ; ix. 50, cf. Lk. xiv. 34 ; x. 11-12, cf. Lk. xvi. 18 ; x. 31, cf. Lk. xiii. 30 ; x. 42-45, cf. Lk. xxii. 25-27 ; xi. 23, cf. Lk. xvii. 6 ; xi. 25, cf. Lk. xi. 4 ; xii. 28-34, cf. Lk. x. 25-28 ; xiii. 15-16, cf. Lk. xvii. 31 ; xiii. 21-23, cf. Lk. xvii. 23 ; xiv. 3-9, cf. Lk. vii. 36-50 ; [xv. 16-20, cf. Lk. xxiii. 11] ; total, 58 verses. The Passion story in Mk. xiv. 17-xvi. 8 contains 100 verses ; *at least* 20 (perhaps over 30) of these appear in Luke, cf. p. 222. In the main Luke follows a non-Marcan source, but in many passages it is not possible to differentiate the two.

[1] But Matthew has matter similar to Mk. iv. 21, 22, 24 elsewhere, *i.e.* Mt. v. 15, x. 26, vii. 2, and has already (Mt. xiii. 9) given Mk. iv. 23, but in the form in which it occurs in Mk. iv. 9. Mk. iv. 25 is placed by Matthew a little earlier, Mt. xiii. 12.

[2] But for xiv. 30 Luke in another context has an equivalent, Lk. xxii. 34.

(*B*) *The non-Marcan Parallels in Matthew and Luke*

N.B.—Where Mark and Q overlap the reference to Mark is given within round brackets. Where the version in Matthew is probably in the main not derived from Q the reference is within square brackets.

LUKE	MATTHEW	LUKE	MATTHEW
iii. 7-9, 16-17	=iii. 7-10, 11-12 (cf. Mk. i. 7-8).	xii. 10	=xii. 32 (nearer than Mk. iii. 28-29).
iv. 1-13	=iv. 1-11 (cf. Mk. i. 12-13).	xii. 22-32	=vi. 25-33.
		xii. 33-34	=vi. 19-21.
vi. 20-23	=v. [3-4, 6], 11-12.	xii. 39-46	=xxiv. 43-51.
vi. 27-33, 35-36	=[v. 44, 39-40, 42 ; vii. 12 ; v. 46-47, 45, 48].	xii. 51-53	=x. 34-36.
		xii. 54-56	=xvi. 2-3 (om. B ℵ 13 &c. Orig.).
vi. 37-38, 39-40, 41-42	=vii. 1-2, [xv. 14 ; x. 24-25] ; vii. 3-5.	xii. 58-59	=[v. 25-26].
		xiii. 18-19	=xiii. 31-32 (cf. Mk. iv. 30-32).
vi. 43-45	=vii. 16-18, 20 ; xii. 33-35.	xiii. 20-21	=xiii. 33.
vi. 46	=[vii. 21].	xiii. 23-24	=[vii. 13-14].
vi. 47-49	=vii. 24-27.	xiii. 26-27	=vii. 22-23.
vii. 1-10	=viii. 5-10, 13.	xiii. 28-29	=viii. 11-12.
vii. 18-20, 22-28, 31-35	=xi. 2-11, 16-19.	xiii. 34-35	=xxiii. 37-39.
ix. 57-60	=viii. 19-22.	xiv. 11 = Lk. xviii. 14b	=xxiii. 12.
x. 2	=ix. 37-38.		
x. 3-12	=x. 16, 9, 10a, 11-13, 10b, 7-8, 14-15 (cf. Mk. vi. 6-11).	xiv. 26-27	=x. 37-38 (cf. Mk. viii. 34).
		xiv. 34-35	=v. 13 (cf. Mk. ix. 50).
x. 13-15	=xi. 21-24.	xv. 4-7	=[xviii. 12-14].
x. 21-22	=xi. 25-27.	xvi. 13	=vi. 24.
x. 23-24	=xiii. 16-17.	xvi. 16	=xi. 12-13.
xi. 2-4	=[vi. 9-13].	xvi. 17	=v. 18.
xi. 9-13	=vii. 7-11.	xvi. 18	=v. 32 (cf. Mk. x. 11-12).
xi. 14-23	=xii. 22-27 (cf. Mk. iii. 22-27).	xvii. 1-2	=xviii. 6-7 (cf. Mk. ix. 42).
xi. 24-26	=xii. 43-45.	xvii. 3-4	=[xviii. 15, 21-22].
xi. 29-32	=xii. 38-42 (cf. Mk. viii. 12).	xvii. 6	=xvii. 20 (cf. Mk. xi. 22-23).
xi. 33	=v. 15 (cf. Mk. iv. 21).	xvii. 23-24	=xxiv. 26-27 (cf. Mk. xiii. 21).
xi. 34-35	=vi. 22-23.	xvii. 26-27	=xxiv. 37-39.
xi. 39-44, 46-48	=xxiii. [25-26], 23, 6-7a, [27], 4, 29-31 (cf. Mk. xii. 38-40).	xvii. 34-35	=xxiv. 40-41.
		xvii. 37	=xxiv. 28.
		xxii. 30b	=[xix. 28b].
xi. 49-52	=xxiii. 34-36, 13.		
xii. 2-9	=x. 26-33 (cf. Mk. iv. 22, *hidden*, and Mk. viii. 38, *ashamed*).		

To this list may be added the parables:

LUKE	MATTHEW
xix. 11-27 (Pounds)	=[xxv. 14-30](cf.Mk. xiii. 34) (Talents).

And the still more diverse

LUKE	MATTHEW
xiv. 15-24 (Great Supper)	=[xxii. 1-10] (Marriage Feast)

(C) Passages peculiar to Matthew

i.-ii. ; iii. 14-15 ; iv. 13-16, 23-25 ; v. 1-2, 4-5, 7-10, 13a, 14, 16-17, 19-24, 27-28, 31-39a, 41, 43 ; vi. 1-8, 10b, 13b, 16-18, 34 ; vii. 6, 12b, 15, 19-20, 28a ; viii. 1, 5a, 17 ; ix. 13a, 26-36 ; x. 2a, 5b-8, 16b, 23, 25b, 36, 41 ; xi. 1, 14, 20, 23b, 28-30 ; xii. 5-7, 11-12a (cf. Lk. xiv. 5), 17-23, 36-37, 40 ; xiii. 14-15, 18, 24-30, 35-53 ; xiv. 28-31, 33 ; xv. 12-13, 23-25, 30-31 ; xvi. 2b-3, 11b-12, 17-19, 22b ; xvii. 6-7, 13, 24-27 ; xviii. 3-4, 10, 14, 16-20, 23-35 ; xix. 1a, 9-12, 28a ; xx. 1-16 ; xxi. 4-5, 10-11, 14, 15b-16, 28-32 (cf. Lk. vii. 29-30), 43 ; xxii. 1-14, 33-34, 40 ; xxiii. 1-3, 5, 7b-10, 15-22, 24, 28, 32-33 ; xxiv. 10-12, 20, 30a ; xxv. 1-13, 31-46 ; xxvi. 1, 44, 50, 52-54 ; xxvii. 3-10, 19, 24-25, 36, 43, 51b-53, 62-66 ; xxviii. 2-4, 9-10, 11-20.

(D) Passages peculiar to Luke [1]

i.-ii. ; iii. 1-2, 5-6, 10-14, 23-38 (cf. Mt. i. 1-17) ; iv. 13, 15 ; v. 39 ; vi. 24-26, 34 ; vii. 3-6a, 11-17, 21, 29-30, 40-50 ; viii. 1-3 ; ix. 31-32, 43, 51-56, 61-62 ; x. 1, 16 (cf. Mt. x. 40), 17-20, 29-42 ; xi. 1, 5-8, 12, 16, 27-28, 36-38, 40-41, 45, 53-54 ; xii. 13-21, 32-33a, 35-38 (cf. Mt. xxv. 1-13), 41, 47-50, 52, 54-57 (cf. Mt. xvi. 2-3) ; xiii. 1-5, 6-9 (cf. Mk. xi. 12-14), 10-17, 22-23, 25-27 (cf. Mt. xxv. 11-12), 31-33 ; xiv. 1-14, 15-24 (cf. Mt. xxii. 2-10), 28-33 ; xv. 1-2, 7-32 ; xvi. 1-12, 14-15, 19-31 ; xvii. 7-22, 25-29, 32 ; xviii. 1-13a, 34 ; xix. 1-10, 11-27 (cf. Mt. xxv. 14-30), 39-44 ; xx. 34-35a, 36b, 38b ; xxi. 19-20, 22, 24, 26a, 28, 34-38 ; xxii. 15-18, 28-30a, 31-32, 35-38, 43-44, 48-49, 51, 53b, 61a, 68, 70 ; xxiii. 2, 4-12, 13-19 (cf. Mk. xv. 6-9), 27-32, 34a, 36, 39-43, 46b, 48, 51a, 53b-54, 56b ; xxiv. 10-53.

[1] This list may be supplemented, for the very small Lucan additions, by that in Hawkins' *Hor. Syn.*², p. 194 ff.

VIII

PROTO-LUKE

SYNOPSIS

LUKE'S DISUSE OF MARK

Hawkins showed that in the great Central Section of Luke, ix. 51-xviii. 14, and also in the section vi. 20-viii. 3, which he called respectively the " Great " and the " Lesser " Interpolations, Luke deserts Mark. The material in these blocks is derived either from Q or from a source peculiar to Luke which may be styled L. The section xix. 1-27 is a third block of similar character.

Once, however, we grasp the full implication of the fact that Q as well as Mark contained an account of John's Preaching, the Baptism and the Temptation, it becomes evident that the section Lk. iii. 1-iv. 30 constitutes yet another example of Luke's " disuse " of Mark. Again, Luke's account of the Resurrection Appearances is wholly, his account of the Passion mainly, derived from a non-Marcan source. But, if the Gospel began and ended with non-Marcan material, is not " interpolation " the wrong word to use of the other non-Marcan passages mentioned above ? The distribution of Marcan and non-Marcan sections suggests rather the hypothesis that the non-Marcan material formed the framework into which extracts from Mark were " interpolated " by the editor of the Gospel.

THE COMPOSITE DOCUMENT (Q + L)

Our hypothesis implies that the editor of the Gospel found Q, not in its original form, but embodied in a much larger document (Q + L), which was in fact a complete Gospel, somewhat longer than Mark. Summary statement of facts which tell in favour of this hypothesis. It would appear that, though Luke valued Mark highly, he regarded the document Q + L as his primary authority ; when this and Mark contained alternative versions of the same incident or saying, he usually preferred that of Q + L. This document Q + L may be styled " Proto-Luke."

The Reconstruction of Proto-Luke

Certain passages in Luke, besides the five considerable sections discussed above, were probably derived from Proto-Luke. Some of these can be identified with practical certainty, others are more doubtful.

Authorship and Tendency

The existence of Proto-Luke a scientific hypothesis which, up to a point, is capable of verification ; its authorship a matter of conjecture.

The " tendency " of Proto-Luke seems to be identical with that of the author of the third Gospel and of the Acts, and that whether we consider the first or the second part of the Acts. This suggests the view that Luke himself may have been the person who originally combined Q and L, and then, at some subsequent date, produced an enlarged edition of his earlier work by incorporating large extracts from Mark and prefixing an account of the Infancy.

Whatever view be held as to authorship, Proto-Luke appears to be a document independent of Mark and approximately of the same date—a conclusion of considerable moment to the historian.

CHAPTER VIII

PROTO-LUKE [1]

LUKE'S DISUSE OF MARK

IN the study of the Synoptic Problem, next in importance to the fundamental discovery of the use of Mark by Matthew and Luke, I would place the conclusion that Q and Mark overlapped. This conclusion, we have seen, is in no way dependent on the exact content we give to the symbol Q. The essential fact stands that the source (or sources) of the non-Marcan material common to Matthew and Luke—whatever its (or their) exact nature or extent, or in whatever form or forms it lay before them respectively—contained certain items which also appear in Mark but in a different version.

Closely related to this is a further conclusion, partly anticipated by previous writers, but most completely demonstrated by Sir John Hawkins, in an essay in the *Oxford Studies*, "Three Limitations to St. Luke's Use of St. Mark's Gospel." Sir John there pointed out that, whereas over a large part of his Gospel Luke is clearly reproducing the story of Mark, not only in substance and in order but with the closest verbal agreements, there are two large tracts, viz. Lk. vi. 20 - viii. 3 and Lk. ix. 51-xviii. 14, in which he makes no use of Mark at all, or, at most, derives from him a few odd verses. He further shows that in yet another great tract of the Gospel,

---

[1] The main argument of this chapter appeared in an article in the *Hibbert Journal* for October 1921, certain extracts from which (with the kind permission of the Editor) are reprinted here along with much fresh material.

the section beginning with the Last Supper (Lk. xxii. 14) and
ending with the discovery of the Empty Tomb (Lk. xxiv. 12),
the relation of the Lucan to the Marcan story in regard to
substance, order, and verbal parallelism is entirely different
from that in the other sections where Luke appears to be using
Mark.

I propose in this chapter to take up the investigation at the
point at which Sir John laid it down, and I hope to establish
a conclusion which may not only advance one step further the
solution of the interesting critical problem of the literary relations
of the first three Gospels, but which has also, if I mistake not,
an important bearing on the question of the historical evidence
for the Life of Christ.

In the Passion narrative Luke recounts several important
incidents not mentioned at all by Mark ; but there are, on the
reckoning of Sir J. Hawkins, some 123 verses of Luke which in
substance have a parallel in Mark.   But whereas elsewhere in
the Gospel where such parallelism exists 53 % of Luke's words
are found in Mark, in this section the percentage falls to 27.
And since in some 20 out of the 123 verses in question the
resemblance of Luke to Mark, both in the structure of sentences
and in verbal similarities, is very close, the average for the
remainder is much less than this 27 %.   Besides this there are
no less than twelve variations in the order in which incidents
are recorded by Mark and Luke.   Lastly, whereas the additions
which Matthew makes to Mark are clearly detachable from the
context, those made by Luke are not ; they are woven into
the structure of the narrative [1] in such a way that they cannot
be removed without reducing the story to confusion.   The
conclusion to which these facts point Sir John himself hesitates
to draw.   It is that Luke is in the main reproducing an account
of the Passion parallel to, but independent of, Mark, and enriching
it with occasional insertions from Mark.   But the conclusion has
been drawn by various other authorities.   The most elaborate

---

[1] Cf. *Oxford Studies*, pp. 78-80.

attempt to work it out in detail is perhaps that of the American scholar, Mr. A. M. Perry.[1]

The section Lk. vi. 20-viii. 3 contains the Sermon on the Plain, the Centurion's Servant, the Widow of Nain, John's Message, the Anointing, the parable in the house of the Pharisee, and a brief mention of a preaching tour with the names of the ministering women. Clearly Luke is not indebted to Mark for any of this ; on the contrary, it is fairly clear that the reason why in the account of the last week at Jerusalem he omits the Anointing at Bethany recorded by Mark is that he has previously related this somewhat different story of an Anointing in Galilee.

The section Lk. ix. 51-xviii. 14 is the centre and core of the Third Gospel. It occupies 25 out of the 80 pages of Luke in the Greek Testament before me, and it contains most of the parables and narrative peculiar to Luke as well as about half of the material in Luke which can plausibly be assigned to Q. It is often spoken of as " The Peraean section." This is a misnomer. Mark represents our Lord's last journey to Jerusalem as having been through Peraea on the east of Jordan, but there is absolutely no hint of this in Luke. On the contrary, the way in which allusions to Samaria and Samaritans are introduced in this section suggests that he conceived of the journey as being through Samaria.[2] But the geographical notices are of the vaguest. Some scholars have spoken of this section of the Gospel as " the travel document." This is, from the critical standpoint, an even more dangerously misleading title, as it implies that this section once existed as a separate document. The only safe name by which one can call it is the " Central Section " —a title which states a fact but begs no questions.

[1] A. M. Perry, *The Sources of Luke's Passion-Narrative* (University of Chicago), 1920. As long ago as 1891 P. Feine, *Eine vorkanonische Ueberlieferung des Lukas,* elaborated a theory which implied something of the sort.

[2] Of course the most direct route from Galilee to Jerusalem would be through Samaria. The roundabout route on the east of Jordan was preferred by Galilean pilgrims on account of the religious hostility of the Samaritans. If, as the Fourth Gospel represents, our Lord visited Jerusalem more than once, He may, at different times, have used both routes.

Sir John Hawkins shows that in this Central Section Luke makes no use, or practically no use, of Mark. It includes versions of the Beelzebub Controversy and the parable of the Mustard Seed, but these are from Q. It includes the Great Commandment in a version which has some few points of agreement with Matthew against Mark and may therefore be from Q, but which is at any rate strikingly different from Mark's—in particular in placing the Great Commandment itself in the mouth of the scribe and not of our Lord. It includes also seven short sayings which form " doublets " with sayings found elsewhere in Luke in contexts derived from Mark.[1]

In at least five of these the version of the saying found in the context of Luke derived from Mark is very much closer to the Marcan form than is the version found in Luke's Central Section. An author may always think one or two particular sayings so important as to be worth repeating, but where such repetition occurs several times the " doublets " are presumptive evidence of the use of parallel sources. There are also nine sayings of one verse each having a general resemblance to sayings also found in Mark and in Matthew. In several of these the versions in Matthew and Luke agree together against Mark in a way which suggests that Luke's version is really derived from Q ; in all there are notable divergences between the Lucan and Marcan versions. The conclusion to be drawn from these facts is that, while there is no reason to believe that Luke would have religiously avoided introducing an odd saying or a word or two from Mark in his Central Section, yet as a matter of fact he has done so, if at all, to an extent that is practically negligible.

Sir John named the two sections (Lk. vi. 20-viii. 3 and ix. 51-xviii. 14), in regard to which he proved Luke's " disuse of Mark," respectively " the lesser interpolation " and " the great interpolation." Each of them, as we have seen, contains material which, as it occurs also in Matthew, we may assign to Q, mixed up with material peculiar to Luke. This latter

---

[1] For details and full discussion cf. *Oxford Studies*, pp. 35-41.

material it will be convenient to speak of as L. But there
is a third section (Lk. xix. 1-27), differing from these only in
the matter of length, to which by parity of nomenclature there
might be given the name " the third interpolation." It contains
the story of Zacchaeus, which is L, and the parable of the
Pounds. Harnack and others, from the close resemblance of
this last to Matthew's parable of the Talents, are inclined to
assign this parable to Q. In that case " the third interpolation "
is also a mixture of Q and L material, though that is not a point
to which much significance attaches.

But, and here I come to a point fundamental to my argument,
there is yet another considerable section in Luke (Lk. iii. 1-iv. 30),
compiled like these out of Q and L material. It comprises an
account of John's Preaching, the Baptism, the Genealogy, the
Temptation, and the Rejection at Nazareth. In this section,
just as in the " great interpolation," there are indeed a few
points of contact with Mark ; but closer examination makes
it evident that the majority of these passages are not likely
to have been actually derived from Mark. For it is certain
that Q, as well as Mark, had an account of John's Preaching, the Baptism and the Temptation (cf. p. 186 ff.), and that
Luke is in the main reproducing that of Q ; also it is clear that
Luke's account of the Rejection of Nazareth is quite different
from Mark's. Once these facts are grasped, we must ask
whether the " disuse of the Marcan source," which was demonstrated by Hawkins in regard to the " interpolations," may not be
a principle which is equally applicable to the section iii. 1-iv. 30.

The number of verses in this section of Luke which contain
anything at all closely resembling Mark are very few (Lk. iii. 3-4 ;
iii. 16, 21-22 ; iv. 1-2). The first is the most striking ; for Luke
agrees with Mark against Matthew (who therefore possibly
here represents Q) in reading " the baptism of repentance for
the remission of sins " (Lk. iii. 3) instead of " repent ye, for
the kingdom of heaven is at hand " (Mt. iii. 2). Mark's phrase
(it occurs also in Acts ii. 38) may well have seemed to Luke an

improvement. But Mt. iii. 2 *may* be, not Q, but an assimilation
of John's words to Jesus' (cf. Mt. iv. 17, x. 7). The application to
John) Lk. iii. 4) of the prophecy in Isaiah, "The voice of one crying
in the wilderness," was probably a piece of primitive Christian
apologetic antecedent to all written documents, and therefore probably stood in Q as well as in Mark. The probability is *slightly* enhanced by the fact that Matthew and Luke *concur* in giving this
quotation alone, without that from Malachi which Mark prefixes.

If the other passages (Lk. iii. 16, 21-22, iv. 1-2) are examined
two things will be found. (1) The rest of the Q material which
appears in both Matthew and Luke is not self-explanatory
without these words ; and Q must have included either them
or something more or less equivalent. (2) In every case there
are notable verbal agreements between Matthew and Luke
against Mark, which show that they derived the words which
stand in Mark, as well as those which do not, partly, if not wholly,
from Q. The saying "he shall baptize you with the Holy Spirit
and with fire " is the only one in Luke where it is likely that he
is influenced by Mark. In this case it is possible that the
contrast, as the saying stood in Q, was between baptism by
water and by fire. In Mark it is between baptism by water
and by the Spirit. If so, it would appear that neither Matthew
nor Luke liked to dispense with either expression, and conflated
the two versions. The conflation is such an obvious one that
it would be quite likely they should both make it independently.

It is remarkable that, whereas Mk. i. 14 says that Jesus
after the Temptation went into *Galilee*, Matthew and Luke
agree in mentioning that He went first of all to *Nazareth*
(Mt. iv. 13, Lk. iv. 16). Still more remarkable, they both agree
in using the form Nazara—which occurs nowhere else in the
New Testament. It would look as if Q, which clearly had a
word or two of narrative introduction to John's Preaching and
the Temptation, had a brief notice of the change of scene in
which the name Nazara occurred. This would also explain
why in the Lucan version the story of the Rejection at Nazareth

is inserted in this context—or rather it would justify the insertion, placing as the opening incident of the ministry a story which the author evidently regards as symbolising in little the whole course of Israel's rejection of Christ and His religion. We infer, then, that Lk. iv. 14-15, which has hardly any points of verbal agreement with Mark, except in the unavoidable proper names Jesus and Galilee, was derived from Q, not Mark.

Lastly, it is hardly likely that Luke would have ignored Mk. i. 6 (camel's hair, locusts and wild honey), and i. 13b, " and the angels ministered unto him," if he had been following Mark as his principal source. Accordingly, we conclude that the indebtedness of Luke to Mark in the section iii. 1-iv. 30 is so small that, for practical purposes, the section may fairly be classed with the three previously mentioned as an example of Luke's " disuse " of Mark.

Connect this with another observation. The account of the Resurrection Appearances which forms the conclusion of Luke's Gospel must have come from a non-Marcan source. It cannot have been taken from the lost ending of Mark, for it only records Appearances in Jerusalem, instead of the Appearance in Galilee which Mark's original conclusion evidently recorded. Also it is led up to by an account of the Last Supper and Passion, which, as we have seen, differs so considerably from the Marcan in substance and in the relative order of events, and which resembles Mark so much less than usual in its actual wording, that it looks as if it were derived in the main from an independent source.

At once there leaps to the mind the suggestion, surely " interpolation " was quite the wrong title to give to any of these non-Marcan blocks. Taken all together they are much larger in extent than the sections derived from Mark. From them comes the beginning, and from them also comes the end, of the Gospel. Suppose, then, they stood all together in a single document—this would form something very like a complete Gospel, opening with the Preaching of John and ending with the Resurrection Appearances. But, if so, it is not the non-Marcan sections, it is those derived from Mark, that should be styled the " interpolations." We are on the verge of a conclusion of the first importance. At least we are compelled to test the hypothesis that *the non-Marcan sections represent a single document, and to Luke this was the framework into which he inserted, at convenient places, extracts from Mark.* If so, there is an essential difference in the way in which Mark is used by the authors of the First and of the Third Gospels. To Matthew, Mark is the primary source and provides the framework into which matter from other sources is inserted. To Luke the non-Marcan source is the more primary authority. To it he prefixes chaps. i. and ii. as an introduction, and into the framework which it provides he fits materials derived from Mark.

The Composite Document (Q + L)

The hypothesis I propose in no way conflicts with the generally accepted view that Matthew and Luke are ultimately dependent not only on Mark but on Q—meaning by Q a single written source. Most, if not all, of the agreements of Matthew and Luke, where Mark is absent, are, I think, to be referred to Q ; but I desire to interpolate a stage between Q and the editor of the Third Gospel. I conceive that what this editor had before him was, not Q in its original form—which, I hold, included hardly any narrative and no account of the Passion—but Q + L, that is, Q embodied in a larger document, a kind of " Gospel " in fact, which I will call Proto-Luke. This Proto-Luke would have been slightly longer than Mark, and about one-third of its total contents consisted of materials derived from Q.

The hypothesis of a Proto-Luke was suggested in the first instance by the observation that in the Third Gospel Marcan and non-Marcan materials are distributed, as it were, in alternate stripes, and that both the beginning and the end of the Gospel belong, not to the Marcan, but to the non-Marcan strain. It is fortified by a consideration of the comparative extent of the material derived from the two sources. If we leave out of account the story of the Passion from the Last Supper onwards, since from this point it is often difficult to be sure what comes from Mark and what from elsewhere, we find that the non-Marcan material between iii. 1 and xxii. 14 amounts to at least 671 verses, while the extracts from Mark total only 346, even if we assign all doubtful cases to the Marcan source. In the Passion and Resurrection story (from xxii. 14) the non-Marcan elements may be roughly estimated as 135 verses, those probably derived from Mark at perhaps not more than 30.

Luke iii. 1 opens with an elaborate chronological statement : " In the fifteenth year of the reign of Tiberius, when Pontius Pilate was . . . the word of the Lord came to John the son of Zacharias in the wilderness." This surely reads—I owe the observation to a conversation with Sir J. Hawkins—as if it was originally written as the opening section of a book. The impression is strengthened by the curious position of the genealogy of our Lord (iii. 23). If this had been inserted by the last editor of the Gospel, we should have expected to find it, like the genealogy in Matthew, somewhere in chaps. i. or ii. in connection with the account of the Birth and Infancy. If, however, it was originally inserted in a book which only began with Lk. iii. 1, its position is explained ; for it occurs immediately after the *first* mention of the name Jesus.

A further reason for supposing that Luke found the Q and the L elements in the non-Marcan sections already combined into a single written source is to be derived from a consideration of the way in which he deals with incidents or sayings in Mark, which he rejects in favour of other versions contained either in the Q or in the L elements of that source.

Of the most conspicuous of these, two, the Beelzebub Controversy (Mk. iii. 22 ff., cf. Lk. xi. 14-23) and the Mustard Seed (Mk. iv. 30 ff., cf. Lk. xiii. 18-19), must be assigned to Q ; two, the Rejection at Nazareth (Mk. vi. 1 ff., cf. Lk. iv. 16-30) and the

P

Anointing (Mk. xiv. 3 ff., cf. Lk. vii. 36 ff.), belong to L ; and one, the Great Commandment (Mk. xii. 28 ff., cf. Lk. x. 25-28), may be from either Q or L. If we look up these passages in Mark in a Synopsis of the Gospels and notice the incidents which immediately precede and follow them, we shall see that Luke reproduces everything else in the neighbourhood from Mark in the original order, but that he simply omits Mark's account of these incidents. The alternative versions which he gives are *always* given in a *completely different context*—presumably, then, their context in the source from which he took them. Of special significance in this regard is the context in which he places the story of the Anointing. Mark gives an Anointing at Bethany the day before the Last Supper ; Luke omits this, but gives an Anointing by a woman that was a sinner in Galilee. That Luke, with his special interest in repentant sinners, should have preferred the version he gives is quite explicable ; but his desertion of the Marcan context is unintelligible if the version he substitutes was a floating tradition attached to no particular occasion. His proceeding is quite explicable if the version substituted stood along with the other matter with which Luke connects it in a written document which Luke on the whole preferred to Mark.

In the instances just quoted the non-Marcan version is a fuller and more interesting version. But there are other cases where the contrary seems true. If we compare the saying in Luke about Salt (Lk. xiv. 34) with that in Mark (ix. 49-50) ; or Mark's long discussion of Divorce (Mk. x. 2-12) with the single verse in Luke (Lk. xvi. 18) ; or the two versions of the saying contrasting the Rulers of the Gentiles and the Son of Man (Mk. x. 42-45, Lk. xxii. 25-27), we shall see that every time Mark's version is the more vigorous and interesting. It would look, then, as if Luke's *preference is for the non-Marcan source as a whole*, not merely for particular items in it on account of their intrinsic merit.

Luke's preference of his non-Marcan source to Mark. so **far**

at least as the Q element in that source is concerned, may be
further shown by a comparison with Matthew. We have already
seen that when Mark and Q overlap, Matthew carefully conflates
the two; e.g. in the account of John the Baptist, of the Temptation, and of the Beelzebub Controversy, he gives, not only the Q
account, but certain details which occur only in Mark (Mt. iii. 4 =
Mk. i. 6 ; Mt. iv. 11b = Mk. i. 13b ; Mt. xii. 31 = Mk. iii. 28).
Luke, on the other hand, appears either to discard the Marcan
version altogether, or to take over only a few words. Again,
when Q and Mark overlap, Matthew is in sharp contrast to
Luke in preferring the context in which the saying occurs in
Mark ; the Beelzebub Controversy and the Mustard Seed may
be instanced. But perhaps the best illustration of the difference
in their method is the conflation by Matthew (x. 1 ff.) of the
Charge to the Seventy (Lk. x. 1-10) with Mark's Charge to the
Twelve (Mk. vi. 7 ff.), as contrasted with Luke's presentation
of the same material as two distinct episodes.

But a similar preference by Luke of the non-Marcan source
may be detected in regard to the L as well as the Q element in
that source. In the Passion story Luke not only rearranges
the Marcan order some twelve times, he also three times
substitutes the non-Marcan for the Marcan representation on
important points of fact. He speaks of a mocking by Herod,
not by the soldiers of Pilate ; he makes the trial take place
in the morning instead of at night ; and, most conspicuous of
all, makes Jerusalem rather than Galilee the scene of the
Resurrection Appearances.

It would look, then, as if Luke tends to prefer the non-
Marcan to the Marcan version, and this whether it be the longer
or the shorter, and whether it belongs to that element in the
source which we can further analyse as being ultimately derived
from Q or from the element which we call L. But such a preference, especially where it is a preference in regard to the order
of events, is much more explicable if Q and L were already
combined into a single document. For the two in combination

would make a book distinctly longer than Mark, and would form a complete Gospel. Such a work might well seem to Luke a more important and valuable authority than Mark. But this would not be true of either Q or L in separation. The conclusion, then, that Q + L lay before the author of the Third Gospel as a single document and that he regarded this as his principal source appears to be inevitable.

This last argument has been impugned on the ground that, while we can observe all cases where Luke has preferred his other source to Mark, we do not know, since Luke's other source or sources are lost, that he may not as often have discarded their version in favour of Mark's. It is, I concede, quite possible that in some cases Luke thought Mark's version superior, and therefore omitted the non-Marcan version. I am not concerned to prove that Luke thought meanly of Mark as an authority— had he done that he would not have incorporated two-thirds of it—nor yet that he *always* preferred the non-Marcan version. My point is, firstly, that the frequency of his preference, and especially the fact that it extends to matters of order, is explicable only if the non-Marcan material formed a complete Gospel so considerable as to seem worthy not only of being compared with, but even of being preferred to, Mark. Secondly, for the verifiable reason that Luke derives about twice as much from Proto-Luke as he does from Mark, I beg leave to think that Luke regards this as his principal source ; in which case it is probable that he would prefer it to Mark more frequently than *vice versa.*

Collateral evidence that the Q and L material had been combined before they were used by the editor of the Third Gospel can be found in the use of the style ὁ Κύριος, "the Lord," instead of the simple name Jesus in *narrative.* This usage is not found at all in Matthew [1] and Mark ; though it is found twice in the spurious conclusion of Mark (xvi. 19, 20). It occurs

---

[1] In Mt. xxviii. 6 it is found in the T.R., but is omitted by B ℵ 33, Θ, Syr. S., e.

5 times in John. In Luke it occurs 14 times, or, if we accept the, probably here correct, reading of the T.R. (om. B L T) in xxii. 31, 15 times. But the striking fact is that while it *never* appears in passages clearly derived by Luke from Mark, the 15 instances are divided between sections derived from Q and from L in numbers roughly proportionate to the extent of matter derived from each of these sources. Seven occurrences are in material clearly from L (vii. 13 ; x. 39, 41 ; xiii. 15 ; xviii. 6 ; xix. 8 ; xxii. 31) ; 4 are connected with matter certainly from Q (vii. 19 ; x. 1 ; xi. 39 ; xii. 42) ; 2 (xvii. 5, 6) are connected with a saying which may be either L or Q. The remaining 2 occur in one verse (xxii. 61), " The Lord turned and looked upon Peter. And Peter remembered the word of the Lord, how he said unto him . . ." The first half of the verse is peculiar to Luke, the second half *may* be from Mark. In that case it is the one exception to the rule that the phrase does not occur where Luke is copying Mark, but it is one readily explained by assimilation of the " Jesus " that stood in Mark to " the Lord " in the previous sentence—ancient taste rather avoided the practice, dear to the modern reporter, of alluding to the same person in the same context by two different names or descriptions.

A similar but no less significant phenomenon is the use of the title in the Vocative in personal address to Jesus. κύριε, " Lord," though common in Matthew (19 times), only occurs once in Mark, and that on the lips of the Syrophenician. ἐπιστάτα is peculiar to Luke. Luke has κύριε 16 times ; 14 of these are in the sections assigned to Proto-Luke, only 2 in those derived from Mark. And there is something notable about each of these two exceptional cases. In the first (Lk. v. 12) the addition of κύριε may be suspected as a textual assimilation to Matthew, since it makes a minor agreement of Matthew and Luke against Mark. In the second (Lk. xviii. 41) it is substituted for ῥαββουνεί, a more impressive form of ῥαββεί which is only used once in Mark and once in John. Luke, it may be noted, avoids all Hebrew words ; he never uses ῥαββεί. Of the

14 cases of κύριε in non-Marcan passages, 8 are L, 6 are in the midst of, or in the (possibly editorial) introductions to, Q sayings. That is to say, this use of κύριε, if not conspicuously characteristic of *both* elements of the sources of Proto-Luke, must be due to a hand that combined them *before* they were further combined with matter derived from Mark.[1]

Finally, the hypothesis that Proto-Luke was Luke's main source explains why Luke omits so much more of the contents of Mark's Gospel than Matthew does; in particular—if the view (cf. p. 176 ff.) that Luke used a mutilated copy of Mark be rejected—it would account for the so-called "great omission," Mk. vi. 45-viii. 26, which linguistic statistics[2] show clearly was an original part of Mark. To Luke Mark was a supplementary source, from which, if pressed for space, he would refrain from extracting material which seemed to him of subordinate interest.[3]

THE RECONSTRUCTION OF PROTO-LUKE

Granted the existence of Proto-Luke—a kind of half-way house between Collections of Sayings, like Q, and the biographical type of Gospel of which Mark was the originator—it is probable that Luke derived from it some other sections of his Gospel besides the four large blocks iii. 1-iv. 30, vi. 20-viii. 3, ix. 51-xviii. 14, xix. 1-27, and the greater part of the Passion and Resurrection story. We must almost certainly assign to it the clearly non-Marcan Call of Peter and the sons of Zebedee (v. 1-11),

---

[1] I have to thank Miss M. J. M'Nab of Edinburgh for kind assistance in collecting some further statistics of linguistic usage. The results obtained, though in general confirmatory of the Proto-Luke hypothesis, were not sufficiently striking to be worth quoting as evidence. This, so far as it goes, favours the view maintained below that Q and L were originally combined by the same editor as the one who subsequently united Q + L with Mark to form our present Gospel.

[2] *Oxford Studies*, pp. 61 ff.

[3] Various reasons why most of the matter in this section of Mark would be likely to appeal to Luke as of inferior interest are suggested in *Oxford Studies*, pp. 67-74 and p. 223.

and also the list of the Apostles (vi. 14-16), since the names
given are not quite the same as in Mark. In that case the brief
summary, Lk. iv. 14-15, the Rejection of Nazareth, the Call
of the Three, the names of the Twelve, no doubt with a word
or two of connection, would have formed in Proto-Luke the
transition, a very natural and appropriate one, between the
Temptation story and the Sermon on the Plain. Unless Luke
has omitted something to make room for Marcan material the
account of the Galilean ministry in Proto-Luke must have
concluded with the residue of the " lesser interpolation," ending
Lk. viii. 3. The Central Section, though vague in its geographical
setting, seems, as already noted, to be conceived of as a slow
progress towards Jerusalem, apparently through Samaria. The
shorter passage (xix. 1-27), dated at Jericho, would follow on
naturally.[1] A little later, in a section otherwise derived from
Mark, Luke inserts the Lament over Jerusalem (xix. 41-44). But
the mention of the Mount of Olives, a note of place with other
details not found in Mark, in Lk. xix. 37-40 suggests that Proto-
Luke may have contained a version of the Triumphal Entry
of which these verses are a fragment. The last four verses of
the Apocalyptic discourse, xxi. 5-36, and possibly some others
(*e.g.* 18) which do not occur in the parallel in Mk. xiii., may be
from this same source.

Some scholars have argued the influence of a source parallel
to Mark in some of the minor variants of Luke in other places
where his narrative is clearly in the main derived from Mark,
as for instance in the additions made in Luke's version of the
Transfiguration, ix. 28-30, and of the reply to the Sadducees
about the Resurrection, xx. 34-38, or in details such as the
mention of Satan (xxii. 3) or of the names Peter and John (xxii. 8).
But additions of this kind, as well as, at any rate, the majority
of Luke's divergences from Mk. xiii. in his Apocalyptic chap. xxi.,
are well within the limits of editorial conjecture or inference
from the context. They are not enough to justify the assertion

---

[1] I think it possible xix. 28 may have stood in Proto-Luke.

that Proto-Luke contained a parallel version of these sections
of Mark, though it is not impossible that this was the case.

The disentanglement of the elements derived from Mark and
from Proto-Luke respectively in the section xxii. 14 to the end
of the Gospel is in points of detail highly speculative. Luke
writes in a literary style, he is not a mere " scissors and paste "
compiler of sources. Besides, two independent accounts of a
story of which the outstanding episodes are a farewell Supper,
a Trial, and a Crucifixion, could not but each contain certain
sections in which precisely the same incident was described, and
where the words employed, " accuse," " scourge," " crucify,"
would be determined as much by the necessary vocabulary of
the subject matter as by the taste of a writer. But, if the
general position that Luke preferred Proto-Luke to Mark is
correct, we are entitled to approach the question with the
preliminary assumption that everything after Lk. xxii. 14 is
derived from Proto-Luke, except those verses which there are
special reasons for assigning to Mark on account of their close
verbal resemblance to Mark and the possibility of their being
detached from the context without spoiling the general sense.
This assumption is fortified by the observation of the remarkable variations in order between Mark and Luke which
suggest that Luke is in the main following his non-Marcan
source.

Hawkins [1] selects the following passages as closest to Mark in
the smaller structure of the sentence as well as in actual wording :
Lk. xxii. 18, 22, 42, 46, 47, 52 f., 54b, 61, 71 ; Lk. xxiii. 22,
26, 34b, 44 f., 46, 52 f. ; Lk. xxiv. 6a. Others which may
possibly be derived from Mark are Lk. xxii. 33-34a, 55 f., 59 f.,
69 ; xxiii. 3, 25, 33, 35, 38, 49, 51 ; also xxiv. 6b, clearly an
adaptation of Mk. xvi. 7. But even of the passages in Hawkins'
list two (Lk. xxii. 61 ; xxiii. 46) are conflated with material
from some other source. But, taking Hawkins' list as representing the minimum of what Luke derived from Mark, we

[1] *Oxford Studies*, p. 77.

note that it includes nearly all the passages which deal with
Peter's Denial and the incident of Simon of Cyrene carrying
the Cross. I incline to think Luke's non-Marcan source did not
contain these incidents. Its account of the actual Crucifixion,
and probably also of the Entombment, seems to have been
quite brief—possibly little more than a bare statement of the
facts—so that from xxiii. 33 to xxiv. 10a Luke reverses his
ordinary procedure and makes Mark his main source.[1]

In framing our mental picture of Proto-Luke as practically a
Gospel, giving a story parallel with Mark's, from the Preaching
of John to the Passion and Resurrection, we have noted
numerous cases where the two writings give divergent versions
of what is clearly the same event, parable, or saying. To complete the picture we must note parallels which should probably
be viewed, not so much as different versions of the same incident,
but as similar incidents recounted in order to bring out the same
moral. Such are the two examples of our Lord's "breaking the
Sabbath" by works of healing (Lk. xiii. 10-17, xiv. 1-6), to be
compared to the two slightly different stories told for a similar
purpose by Mark (ii. 23-iii. 6)—cf. also John (v. 1-18). So, too, the
command "show yourself to the priest" is an illustration, in
the contrary sense, of our Lord's attitude to the Law, but is
connected with two quite different stories of Cleansing Lepers in
Mark and in Luke (Mk. i. 44, Lk. xvii. 14); cf. the two occasions
on which His claim to forgive sins is challenged (Lk. vii. 48-49,
cf. Mk. ii. 7 = Lk. v. 21). Lastly, may not the Mission of the
Seventy (Lk. x. 1 ff.) and the parable of the Barren Fig Tree
(Lk. xiii. 6-9) be parallel versions of Mark's Mission of the
Twelve and Cursing of the Fig Tree?

AUTHORSHIP AND TENDENCY

We proceed to ask the question, Can we in any way determine
the date and authorship of Proto-Luke?

---

[1] The most thorough attempt I know to unravel Luke's sources is *The
Sources of Luke's Passion-Narrative*, A. M. Perry (Chicago, 1920).

I think we can. But before putting forward a suggestion on this point I must emphasise that it is put forward only as a suggestion. The *existence* of Proto-Luke is, I claim, a scientific hypothesis which is, to a considerable extent, capable of verification ; and since it was put forward in my article in the *Hibbert Journal*, it has received the adhesion of not a few New Testament scholars. But the suggestion I make as to its authorship is one which, from the nature of the case, does not admit either of verification or refutation to anything like the same extent.

I suggest that the author of Proto-Luke — the person, I mean, who combined together in one document Q and the bulk of the material peculiar to the Third Gospel—was no other than Luke the companion of Paul. And I suggest that this same Luke some years afterwards expanded his own early work by prefixing the stories of the Infancy and by inserting extracts from Mark—no doubt at the same time making certain minor alterations and additions. For reasons summarised in the last chapter of this volume, I hold that the author of the Third Gospel and the Acts was Luke the companion of Paul, who kept the diary which forms the basis of the so-called "we sections" or "travel document" in the latter part of Acts. But if Luke wrote the Acts twenty years or so later than the events with which it ends—and I cannot personally accept an earlier date—there were at least two periods of literary activity in his life. There was the period when, while in attendance on Paul, he wrote the "travel document," and a later period when, years after the Apostle's death, he embodied this early sketch into a larger and maturer history. The suggestion I make is that what is true of the Acts is also true of the Gospel. Luke during the two years he was at Caesarea in the company of Paul made good use of his opportunities of collecting information and made copious notes.[1]

---

[1] For evidence that in certain respects Luke's account of the Trial of our Lord is superior to Mark's, see H. Danby, *J.T.S.*, Oct. 1919, p. 61 ff. On the Trial before Herod, cf. *Oxford Studies*, p. 229 ff.

Later on, probably not till after the death of Paul, a copy of Q
came his way, and on the basis of this and his own notes he
composed Proto-Luke as a Gospel for the use of the Church in the
place where he was then living. Still later a copy of Mark
came his way, and he then produced the second and enlarged
edition of his Gospel that has come down to us.

The main reason for supposing the author of the Third
Gospel and the Acts to be the same person as the author of
Proto-Luke is that the "tendency," that is, the interest and
point of view evinced in the selection of incidents, the emphasis
laid on them, and the general presentation of Christianity and
its history which we find in the two works, is exactly the same
throughout. The special tastes, sympathies, and characteristics
of the author are equally conspicuous in the parts of the Gospel
derived from Proto-Luke, in those which we must attribute to
the editor of the whole, in the first part of Acts, in the "we
sections," and in the final editor of Acts.

Thus the author of the "we sections" tells us that he stayed
two years in Caesarea, which had once been the capital of the
Herod dynasty; a special knowledge of, and interest in, the
Herods is found both in Proto-Luke and in the *first* part of Acts.
He stayed in the house of Philip, the evangelist of Samaria; an
interest in Samaria and Samaritans—a notable feature of Proto-
Luke—appears in the selection of materials (whoever made it)
in the first part of Acts, and in the final editor by whom, of
course, the Preface to the Acts was written.

The desire to represent Christ as the Saviour of the world,
accepted by Gentiles but rejected by His own people, is the
main theme of the Acts,—witness the Preface, the whole development of the history as related with special emphasis on each
stage in opening the Gospel to a wider field—to a eunuch,
to Samaritans, to Cornelius a proselyte, to pagans—and the fact
that it ends on the last words of Paul, "We go to the Gentiles,
they will hear." Similarly the editor of Luke (or Proto-Luke)
carries on some lines further the quotation from Isaiah which

he found in Mark or Q in order to reach the words " all flesh shall see the salvation of God " ; he traces the genealogy of Christ, not (like Matthew) to Abraham the father of Israel, but to Adam the father of all men ; he records as the Master's final commission (xxiv. 47) the command to go to the Gentiles ; most significant of all, he narrates, as if it were the first act of our Lord's ministry, the Rejection of Nazareth (though he knew it was *not* the first, since he alludes to previous miracles in Capernaum), because it seemed to him to sum up the history of the Christian message—the prophet has honour, but not in his own country ; and just as Elijah and Elisha had been sent, not to the widows or the lepers of Israel, but to her of Zarepta and to Naaman the Syrian, so it had been with the Christ Himself.

Again, what to the historian is one of the weak points of Luke, his preferring the more to the less miraculous of the two versions of a story laid before him, is characteristic both of the editor and his sources. Thus Luke or Proto-Luke adds to the account of the descent at the Baptism of the Spirit as a dove the words " in bodily form," ruling out the possibility of its being a vision. Proto-Luke contains, and Luke prefers to Mark's version of the Call of Peter, another which includes a miraculous draught of fishes. The last editor of Acts never seems to have reflected that the story of speaking with other tongues at Pentecost might have been only a magnified account of that ecstatic " speaking with tongues " which was quite common in the early Church. The author of the " we sections " sees a resurrection in the recovery of Eutychus, even while he records Paul's own remark to the effect that he was not dead, and apparently never asked whether the serpent which clung to Paul at Malta was really poisonous, or, if so, had actually bitten him.

Again, there is throughout the Lucan writing an atmosphere of extraordinary tenderness, somehow made quite compatible with the sternest call to righteousness, sacrifice, and effort— an atmosphere which can be felt rather than demonstrated—

and finding expression in a unique sympathy for the poor, for women, for sinners, and for all whom men despise. But this attitude can be felt equally in the Infancy stories, in Proto-Luke, and in the Acts; it is also what determines many of those omissions from Mark [1] which can only be due to the final editor of the Gospel. Now, of course, it can be argued that this " tendency " may be explained as that of a particular church or school of thought rather than of an individual. It may. But for myself, I cannot resist the impression that the " atmosphere " I have vainly tried to recall has a subtle individuality which reflects, not a Church tradition, but a personality of a very exceptional kind.

Dr. Headlam,[2] in reference to my article in the *Hibbert Journal*, demurs to the idea of two editions of the Gospel, but suggests two stages in its composition before it was put into circulation. I have no particular objection to this modification of the Proto-Luke hypothesis. It is extremely difficult to define what would have constituted " publication " in an illicit society like the early Church. If Proto-Luke was composed in some provincial town, very few copies would get abroad. But if after it had been enlarged by the author a copy came to Rome and was approved by that Church, this edition would very rapidly get known elsewhere. All I am concerned to argue is that Proto-Luke was, and was originally intended as, a complete Gospel; but it is quite likely that it was only meant for what in modern phrase would be called " private circulation."

But whether the compiler of Proto-Luke was Luke or not, the historical importance of the identification of a source of the Third Gospel entirely independent of Mark is obvious. All recent discussion of the historical evidence for the Life of Christ has been based on the assumption that we have only two primary

---

[1] *E.g.* the Cursing of the Fig Tree. The Syrophenician Woman, with its reference to Gentiles as dogs and the implication that the Lord hesitated to heal such, is in Luke's "great omission." On Luke's "tendency" see *Oxford Studies*, p. 222 ff.

[2] *The Life and Teaching of Jesus Christ*, p. 20 f. (Murray, 1923).

authorities, Mark and Q; and, since Q is all but confined to discourse, Mark alone is left as a primary authority for the Life. If, however, the conclusions of this chapter are sound we must recognise in Proto-Luke the existence of another authority comparable to Mark. It is true that Proto-Luke is of later date than Q, but in all probability so is Mark. The essential point is that Proto-Luke is independent of Mark. Where the two are parallel it would seem that Proto-Luke is sometimes inferior in historical value (*e.g.* in the details of the Call of Peter), sometimes superior (*e.g.* the addition of an account of the trial before Herod). Neither Mark nor Proto-Luke is infallible; but as historical authorities they should probably be regarded as on the whole of approximately equal value. But, if so, this means that far more weight will have to be given by the historian in the future to the Third Gospel, and in particular to those portions of it which are peculiar to itself.

ADDITIONAL NOTE

Appended is a list of the passages most probably to be assigned to Proto-Luke : Lk. iii. 1-iv. 30 ; v. 1-11 ; vi. 14-16 ; vi. 20-viii. 3 ; ix. 51-xviii. 14 ; xix. 1-27 ; xix. 37-44 ; xxi. 18, 34-36 ; xxii. 14 to end of the Gospel, except for the verses derived from Mark the identification of which is very problematical.

The following are probably from Mark : xxii. 18, 22, 42, 46 f., 52-62,[1] 71 ; xxiii. 3, 22, 25 f., 33-34b, 38, 44-46, 52 f. ; xxiv. 6.

The following may be derived from Mark, or represent Proto-Luke partially assimilated to the Marcan parallel : xxii. 69 ; xxiii. 35, 49, 51 ; xxiv. 1-3, 9 f.

---

[1] But xxii. 62 is probably not genuine, being an assimilation to Matthew, om. Old Lat. Similarly xxiv. 6a, and the words ἀπὸ τοῦ μνημείου xxiv. 9, are omitted by D Old Lat. It is notable that all three omissions reduce the extent of Luke's debt to Mark.

IX

A FOUR DOCUMENT HYPOTHESIS

SYNOPSIS

Unconscious Assumptions

Three unconscious assumptions which have led to a misinterpretation of the available evidence.

(1) The name "Two Document Hypothesis" suggests that no other sources used by Matthew and Luke are comparable to the "Big Two." Hence an undue importance has been assigned to Q as compared with the sources used by Matthew or Luke only.

(2) It is assumed that a hypothesis which reduces the number of sources to a minimum is more scientific.

(3) It is taken for granted that the same saying is not likely to have been reported by more than one independent authority.

But a plurality of sources is historically more probable. In particular, if Mark is the old Roman Gospel, it is antecedently to be expected that the other Gospels conserve the specific traditions of Jerusalem, Caesarea, and Antioch.

Jerusalem, Caesarea, and Antioch

A priori probabilities in regard to the traditions of these Churches.

The non-Marcan matter in Luke has been analysed further into at least two sources, Q and L ; similarly we may expect to find that Matthew used a peculiar source, which we may style M, as well as Q.

The Judaistic character of much of the material in M suggests a Jerusalem origin. L has already been assigned to Caesarea. Q may be connected with Antioch. Most probably Q is an Antiochene translation of a document originally composed in Aramaic—perhaps by the Apostle Matthew for Galilean Christians.

On this view our first Gospel is a combination of the traditions of

Jerusalem, Antioch, and Rome, while the third Gospel represents Caesarea, Antioch, and Rome. The fact that the Antiochene and Roman sources are reproduced by both Matthew and Luke is due to the importance of the Churches; it is no evidence that the other sources are less authentic.

Although, however, historical considerations favour a Four Document Hypothesis, the verification of the hypothesis must depend entirely on the results of a critical study of the documents apart from any theory as to the geographical affiliation of any particular source.

The Theory of two Recensions of Q

It has already been recognised by critics that the Two Document Hypothesis in its simplest form has broken down. The theory of two recensions of Q, designated as $Q^{Mt.}$ and $Q^{Lk.}$, has been put forward to meet the difficulty. But on examination this theory is seen, not to solve, but to disguise, the problem by an ambiguity latent in the symbols used.

Parallel Versions

General considerations as to the extent and ways in which collections of sayings or parables, though made independently, would nevertheless inevitably overlap.

Evidence from non-Canonical sources as to the existence of independent parallel versions of sayings of Christ.

The Overlapping of Sources

Three clear cases of this in the Gospels. (1) Mark and Q. (2) Mark and L. (3) The collections of Parables in Matthew and Luke.

Evidence that the versions of the Lost Sheep found in Matthew and Luke were drawn from two different sources; *a fortiori* this holds good of the Marriage Feast and the Talents.

All analogies, then, suggest that Q and M would overlap.

Matthew's Method of Conflation

The meticulous way in which Matthew conflates his sources illustrated by a study of two examples where he is combining Mark and Q.

This compels us to formulate a new principle of Synoptic criticism: " Wherever parallel passages of Matthew and Luke show substantial divergence, editorial modification is a less probable explanation than conflation by Matthew of the language of Q with that of some other version."

The Sermon on the Mount

In view of the evidence as to overlapping of sources and Matthew's method of conflation set out in the two preceding sections, we may now test the hypothesis that Q and M overlapped.

The Sermon on the Mount is a conflation of a discourse in Q (approximately represented by Luke's Sermon on the Plain) and a discourse from M which happened to begin with a series of Beatitudes —very different in detail from those in Q—and to contain a divergent version of " Love your Enemies " and a few other sayings. Into this conflated discourse Matthew has introduced some additional fragments of Q which Luke gives in his Central Section, presumably in their original context.

The Woes to the Pharisees, Mt. xxiii., is probably another case of conflation by Matthew of discourses in Q and M which had certain points of contact—Luke's version again being nearer to Q.

Judaistic Tendency of M

The question must be faced, did the Judaistic sayings in Matthew stand originally in Q, being omitted by Luke owing to his pro-Gentile proclivities, or are they to be assigned to M? Reasons for choosing the latter alternative.

Overlapping of Mark and M

Three passages in Matthew, in the main clearly derived from Mark, contain certain added details of a specially interesting character. Possibility that these were derived from a parallel version in M.

The Great Discourses of Matthew

Evidence that the five great discourses of Matthew are agglomerations by the editor of the Gospel, and do not correspond to collocations of the material in an older source.

The Infancy Narratives

The first two chapters of Matthew are probably derived from oral sources, but the corresponding section in Luke is more likely to have been found by him in a written document, possibly Hebrew.

Some points of textual criticism bearing on the evidence for the Virgin Birth.

Q

CONCLUSION

The Four Document Hypothesis, besides explaining a number of facts which are not accounted for by the Two Document Hypothesis, materially broadens the basis of evidence for the authentic teaching of Christ.

N.B.—The Diagram : The Synoptics and their Sources (p. 150 above) should be referred to in connection with this chapter.

CHAPTER IX

A FOUR DOCUMENT HYPOTHESIS

UNCONSCIOUS ASSUMPTIONS

THE psychologists are all warning us of the peril of the " uncon‧ scious motive." It is against " unconscious assumptions " that critics of the Gospels most need to be on their guard.

(1) It is unfortunate that the name " Two Document Hypothesis " should have been given to the theory that the authors of the First and Third Gospels made use of Mark and Q, for it conceals the unconscious assumption that they used no other documents, or, at least, none of anything like the same value as the " Big Two." Hence a quite illusory pre-eminence has been ascribed to the document Q in comparison with the sources for our Lord's teaching made use of by Matthew or by Luke alone. To this illusion I must confess that I have been myself for many years a victim. The idea has grown up that it is just a little discreditable to any saying of our Lord if it cannot be traced to Q. Immense efforts are accordingly made to extend the boundaries of Q as much as possible—as if a sentence of exclusion from this document meant branding the excluded saying with a reputation of doubtful historicity. Much of what is clearly authentic teaching of Christ—quite half of the Sermon on the Mount, for instance—is found in only one Gospel. An effort, then, must be made to get all this material somehow or other assigned to Q ; and ingenious motives must be discovered to explain why the other evangelists omitted it. Once, however,

the "unconscious assumption" of some special superiority of Q is brought up into the daylight of clear consciousness, a moment's consideration will show that it is wholly baseless. One has only to mention the fact that hardly any of the parables are found in Q to realise that a large part of the most obviously genuine, original, and characteristic teaching of our Lord is derived, not from Q, but from sources peculiar to Matthew or Luke. The Good Samaritan, the Prodigal Son, the Pharisee and the Publican, are peculiar to Luke; the Labourers in the Vineyard, the Pearl of Great Price, are given by Matthew alone. There cannot be the slightest presumption that a source which lacked such material as this is a more reliable authority than those which contained it.

Some scholars, indeed, have been so far hypnotised by the prestige of Q that, from the possible absence from Q of the longer narrative parables, they have drawn the conclusion that such parables formed no part of the original teaching of our Lord but are developments in later tradition, though probably in some cases being expansions of shorter authentic sayings. Nothing could be more absurd. Our Lord was above all a popular teacher; it was the common people who heard Him gladly. But everybody knows that a story told vividly and in detail is the one thing most likely to attract the attention and to remain in the memory of a popular audience. A friend once said to me, "You can preach the same sermon as often as you like, provided you don't repeat your illustrations; but tell the same story twice, and, even if the rest of your sermon is on a totally different topic, people will say that you repeat yourself." If one considers the teaching of Christ from the standpoint of the psychology of everyday life and not of academic theory, it is obvious that the parables, and that in their most graphic and least curtailed form, such as we find in Luke, are just the element most likely to belong to the earliest stratum of tradition. Why the author of Q included so few (or, possibly, none at all) of them, we cannot say, any more than we can say for certain why he did not include an account of the Passion. Probably the reason for both omissions was the same. He wrote to supplement, not to supersede, a living oral tradition. Both the longer parables and the Passion story were easy to remember, and every one knew them ; and what he was most concerned to write down was something which was either less well known or easier to forget.

(2) Another equally misleading assumption, again more or less unconscious, has been the idea that antecedent probability is in favour of a hypothesis which so far as possible reduces the number of sources used by Matthew and Luke, and minimises the extent and importance of the sources of material peculiar to one Gospel. This is due to a confusion of thought. Since Matthew and Luke appear to have written in churches in every way far removed from one another, that hypothesis is the most plausible which postulates the smallest number of sources used by them *in common*. But that same removedness only increases the likelihood that each had access to sources not known to the other, outside the two (Mark and Q) which they *concur* in using.

(3) There is yet a third false assumption current—that it is improbable that the same or similar incidents or sayings should have been recorded in more than one source, and that, therefore, if the versions given by Matthew and Luke respectively of any item differ considerably, this is to be attributed to editorial modification. On the contrary, given the existence of independent reports of the sayings of a great teacher, these would inevitably overlap and would sometimes give almost identical, at other times widely different, versions of the same saying. The overlooking of this consideration has had fatal effects on Synoptic criticism.

One reason why these erroneous assumptions have held sway so long is that the Synoptic Problem has been studied merely as a problem of literary criticism apart from a consideration of the historical conditions under which the Gospels were

produced. A factor of cardinal importance has been ignored—
the preponderating influence of the great Churches in the determination of the thought and literature of primitive Christianity.
Mark, says an ancient and probably authentic tradition, was
written in Rome—a long way from Palestine. But Jerusalem
and Caesarea, the two great Palestinian Churches, and Antioch,
the original headquarters of the Gentile Mission, must each have
had a cycle of tradition of its own. It is in the last degree
improbable that the characteristic traditions of any of these
three Churches have completely disappeared. It is far more
likely that, in one form or another, they are incorporated in
the Gospels which were ultimately accepted as exclusively
canonical by the Church at large. Thus traces of at least
three different cycles of tradition, besides the material derived
from Mark, are what antecedently we should expect a critical
examination of Matthew and Luke to reveal.

JERUSALEM, CAESAREA, AND ANTIOCH

Accordingly, before entering upon a critical examination
of actual documents, it will be worth while to consider the
historical probabilities in regard to the collection and transmission of sayings of our Lord by Christians of the first
generation.

In Jerusalem it is on the whole likely that the sayings would
for some considerable time be handed down in oral tradition
after the manner of the sayings of the Rabbis, and that in
the original Aramaic. But in the Greek-speaking Churches a
beginning would be made at writing them down almost at once.
Collections of sayings regarded as specially valuable for the
instruction of converts would very soon be formed in various
Churches. But the Churches of Antioch and Caesarea are those
where we should expect to find not only the earliest, but also
the most considerable and the most valuable, collections written

in the Greek language.   For these were the first Gentile Churches to be founded, and also, from their geographical position, were peculiarly well situated for procuring authentic material.   Indeed both these Churches had been visited by Peter himself at a very early date.   But sooner or later—possibly not till the flight of Christians to Pella just before the final siege—the Jerusalem collection also would be committed to writing.   Once that was done, it would sooner or later reach Antioch or Caesarea, and a Greek translation of it would be made and so become available to the Gentile Churches.   The antecedent probabilities, then, are that there would be at least three considerable collections of the teaching of Christ, associated with the Churches of Jerusalem, Antioch, and Caesarea.   The Church of Jerusalem was for a time "knocked out" by the Jewish War.   But Antioch and Caesarea were sufficiently influential to secure that the traditions which they specially valued did not completely disappear.   They were also Churches to which those who wished for authentic information about our Lord could readily resort.

Supporters of the Two Document Hypothesis usually assign to Q the bulk of the discourse material in Matthew, apart from the longer parables.   This involves as a corollary *either* that Luke has made very drastic omissions from Q *or else* that Matthew used an expanded edition $Q^{Mt.}$—a hypothesis to which I adduce objections below, p. 235 ff.   But in view of the *a priori* probability of there being three cycles of tradition available, besides that of Mark, I would suggest the simple hypothesis that, just as Luke ultimately goes back to at least two sources besides Mark, viz. Q and L, so it is with Matthew.   Provisionally I will assign to Matthew's third source all discourse peculiar to Matthew, and also that part of the material usually assigned to Q which differs so much from its Lucan parallels as to have suggested the need for the $Q^{Mt.}$ hypothesis ; retaining Q as the name of the source of the close parallels only.   This third source of Matthew it will be convenient to call M.

The material peculiar to Matthew, in sharp contrast to Luke's, is characterised by a conspicuously Jewish atmosphere; and, though rich in anti-Pharisaic polemic, it asserts the obligation of obeying not only the Law but " the tradition of the scribes," and it has a distinctly anti-Gentile bias. It reflects the spirit and outlook with which in the New Testament the name of James is associated; though James himself, like most leaders, was doubtless far less extreme than his professed followers. The source M will naturally be connected with Jerusalem, the head-quarters of the James party.

The Caesarean tradition, we naturally surmise, has survived by its incorporation in the Third Gospel. The reasons for connecting Luke's special source L with Caesarea have been given above (p. 218 f.) and need not be repeated.

Antioch, then, remains as a possible place for the origin of Q. In the *Oxford Studies* I suggested a Palestinian origin, with the probability that the Apostle Matthew was its author.[1] The two suggestions are not in the slightest degree incompatible. The source Q, with which the student of the Synoptic Problem is concerned, is a *Greek* document which the authors of the First and Third Gospels had in common, and the fact that this Greek document was known to the authors of both these Gospels means that it probably came to them with the backing of the Church of some important Greek city. But that is no reason why it may not have been a translation of an Aramaic work by Matthew—possibly with some amplification from local tradition. What became of the Twelve Apostles is one of the mysteries of history. The resident head of the Jerusalem Church was, not one of the Twelve, but James the brother of the Lord. From Galatians and Acts we should gather that to

---

[1] I also suggested that Mark was written for a Church that already possessed a collection of Christ's sayings and desired a biography to supplement it. The suggestion, I still think, is worth consideration, although the conclusion there drawn that this collection must have been Q was too hasty. Why should it not have been the local Roman collection of sayings from which Clement seems to quote ? Cf. p. 240 *n.*

Peter and the sons of Zebedee Jerusalem was for a time a kind
of headquarters. But in regard to the rest there is no tradition
which, either from its early date or its intrinsic probability,
deserves credence. But we know from the Rabbis that for
many centuries Capernaum was a great centre for " Minim "
or Christians, so that it is probable that others of the Twelve
made that city their headquarters. Geographically Capernaum
is between Antioch and Jerusalem, and some Christian trader
from Antioch having business at Capernaum, or in some city of
Decapolis, may well have come across a collection of sayings
made by Matthew and brought it home.

The hypothesis that Q emanated from the (perhaps, freer)
atmosphere of Galilee and became the primitive " gospel " of a
Gentile Church, like Antioch, accounts for its inclusion of the
saying (Lk. xvi. 16, Mt. xi. 13), " The law and the prophets
were until John." It also explains at once the puzzling fact
that in a document, otherwise apparently entirely confined to
discourse, there should have stood the one single narrative of
the Centurion's Servant. That story leads up to, and gives
the facts that called forth from Christ, the saying, " I have not
found so great faith, no, not in Israel." At a time when the
Judaising section of the Church wished to give the uncircumcised
an inferior status, that story was in itself a charter of Gentile
liberty.

The Greek translation of Q, at any rate, must have been
made for the use of a Greek Church, and since, if we regard
the material peculiar to Luke as representing the tradition of
Caesarea, that city is ruled out, Antioch, the first capital of
Gentile Christianity, is the most likely place of origin. In
Ch. XVII. I shall give reasons for supposing that our Gospel
of Matthew was written in Antioch. There is also, for what
it is worth, a tradition, found in Eusebius and in the Latin
Prologues to the Gospels, which has some support in the
occurrence in D, etc., of a " we section," Acts xi. 27, that
Luke was by descent a Syrian of Antioch. I should not care

to lay much weight on either of these considerations as evidence
for connecting Q with Antioch, but so far as they go they are
in favour of the connection.

If the suggestions put forward above be accepted, it would
follow that Matthew's Gospel represents a combination of the
primitive " gospels " of Jerusalem, Antioch, and Rome ; while
Luke's is ultimately based on those of Caesarea, Antioch, and
Rome. Either of these combinations would be eminently
reasonable from the point of view of the authors of the Gospels,
who would naturally set the highest value on sources so weightily
authenticated. The hypothesis would also explain both why
these Gospels seem never to have any serious competitors in
the Church, and why so little of authentic tradition survives
outside the canonical Four. Since the specifically Ephesian
tradition may be supposed to be reproduced in John, there
did not exist anywhere any considerable body of tradition
authenticated by any important Church which was not represented in one of the Four Gospels.

But if this view is correct it means that the Roman and the
Antiochene sources are *made use of twice over.* In view of the
prestige and wide influence of these two Churches this is not
surprising. But the historian must realise that the fact that
Mark and Q were used by the editors of two later Gospels does
not create any presumption that, because a thing occurs in Mark
or in Q, the historical evidence for it is twice as strong as if it
occurred once only either in the Jerusalem or in the Caesarean
tradition. And this last consideration, I would observe, is not
substantially affected, supposing that the scheme of connection
between the several sources and particular churches which I
have suggested is not exactly correct. All that I wish to press
is the broad principle that a plurality of sources is antecedently
probable, and the fact that the relative historical value of a
source is not increased by the number of times it is copied.

I suggest, then, that we should, provisionally at any rate,
abandon, not the theory that Matthew and Luke made use

of Mark and Q, but the conception of a "Two Document Hypothesis"; and explore the possibilities of substituting for it that "Four Document Hypothesis" which from the standpoint of historical probability seems to have far more to recommend it.

A Four Document Hypothesis has claims to investigation quite apart from the theory as to the geographical affiliations of particular sources suggested above. To avoid, therefore, complicating critical with geographical questions, I shall for the rest of this chapter use the symbol M for the source of the discourse and parables peculiar to Matthew; but, for reasons which will be obvious to any student of the Synoptic Problem, I shall not use it to include any *narrative* peculiar to Matthew. M and Q will be of much the same length. There are eight parables (= 59 verses) peculiar to Matthew—not including the Lost Sheep, the Marriage Feast, and the Talents (= 34 verses) —to which must be added approximately 140 verses of discourse of the same character as the bulk of Q. The passages which Hawkins reckons as probably belonging to Q (he includes the parables of the Lost Sheep and Talents but not the Marriage Feast) total a little less than 200 verses. Thus, if we assign the bulk of the discourse and parables peculiar to Matthew to M, we have a document quite as considerable in extent as Q. This, however, is merely a matter of arithmetic; the points on which our argument will turn are : (1) the evidence that M and Q to some extent overlapped ; (2) the Judaistic character of the source M.

THE THEORY OF TWO RECENSIONS OF Q

The "Two Document Hypothesis," so far as it concerns the non-Marcan element in Matthew and Luke, has broken down. But the breakdown has been concealed by the hypothesis that Matthew and Luke made use of two different recensions of Q which have been styled respectively $Q^{Mt.}$ and $Q^{Lk.}$. The most thoroughgoing and scientific attempt to work out this distinction in detail which has come into my hands is by an American scholar, Mr. C. S. Patton.[1] The idea of two recensions of Q is at first sight attractive ; but the moment one attempts to visualise to one's mind's eye the exact kind of documents implied by the symbols $Q^{Mt.}$ and $Q^{Lk.}$, its attractiveness begins to wane. The symbol Q, by itself, stands for a perfectly definite concept —a written document from which both Matthew and Luke made copious extracts with some slight amount of editorial change. Also—since Matthew and Luke each omit some passages from Mark which the other retains, and may be presumed to have treated Q in the same way—it is legitimate to suppose that Q contained certain passages that occur only in one Gospel, so long as we recollect that the identification of these can never be more than a " skilful guess." But to what definite concept do the symbols $Q^{Mt.}$ or $Q^{Lk.}$ correspond ?

These symbols are intended to imply two things : (1) That the document Q did not reach the authors of the First and Third Gospels in its original form, but with extensive interpolations —the interpolations in Matthew's copy being quite different from those in Luke's. We note, however, that each of these sets of interpolations is as considerable in extent as the original Q to which they are supposed to have been added. And since the additions in Matthew's copy are quite different from those in Luke's, their respective additions must have been derived from two totally different cycles of tradition. It follows that at least one, and probably both, of these cycles must have emanated from a locality or informant different from that of the cycle embodied in the original Q. We are forced, then, to assume the existence of at least one, and probably two, cycles of tradition besides Q. But, if so, what presumption is there that the material preserved in these other cycles reached Matthew and Luke attached to Q and not in independent sources ? (2) The symbols $Q^{Mt.}$ and $Q^{Lk.}$ are mainly intended to meet the difficulty

[1] *Sources of the Synoptic Gospels*, The Macmillan Company, New York, 1915.

that some of the parallels between Matthew and Luke—the two versions of the Beatitudes, for instance—are so inexact that it is not possible to suppose that Matthew and Luke derived them from the same written source.   Now if the symbols $Q^{Mt.}$ and $Q^{Lk.}$ were meant to stand for two related but divergent versions of *an oral tradition still in a fluid state*, they would be illuminating. But they do not mean this ; they stand for *documents*.   The fallacy is obvious.   Q itself is held to be a written document, because the verbal resemblances between the majority of the parallels between Matthew and Luke are so close as to demand for their explanation the fixity of writing in the common source. But if there are certain passages found in both Matthew and Luke (the Beatitudes or the Lord's Prayer, for example) where the verbal differences between the two versions are so great that they cannot reasonably be supposed to be copied from the same written source, then the only legitimate inference is that one, or possibly both, of these items were *not* derived from the same written source to which we have referred the closer parallels.   But, if they were not derived from the *same* document, they must either have come from oral tradition or from a *different* document.   A saying which occurs *only* in Matthew *may* possibly have stood in Q and have been omitted by Luke ; but where a saying occurs in both Matthew and Luke, but Matthew's version is so different from Luke's that the difference cannot be explained as merely editorial, we have clear proof that at least one of the two versions did *not* stand in the common source.

The fact we have to explain is the occurrence in Matthew and Luke of two sets of parallelism, one set in which the verbal resemblances are so close as to favour, if not actually compel, the conclusion that they were derived from a common *written* source, and another set in which the divergences are so great that they cannot be explained in that way.   And this distinction is not affected by the existence of border-line cases which would be susceptible of either explanation.   This two-sided fact is precisely what constitutes the problem we have to solve : and the symbols $Q^{Mt.}$ and $Q^{Lk.}$ are discovered on analysis to be merely a means of covering up the phenomena to be explained. Scholars like Mr. Patton have done very valuable service in proving that a number of the parallels cannot be referred to Q. But Q is Q, a document which can be clearly conceived. $Q^{Mt.}$ is " Q with a difference "; and it may turn out on examination that the difference is just the thing that matters. It may be hard to decide in certain cases whether editorial modification of a saying in Q will or will not account for the differences between the form in which it occurs in Matthew and Luke ; but in the last resort we must choose between Q and not-Q. We cannot fall back on $Q^{Mt.}$ and $Q^{Lk.}$ as a kind of Limbo for innocent sayings unfortunately disqualified from entering Q.

PARALLEL VERSIONS

Wherever the sayings and doings of a remarkable person are preserved in the memory of his followers, different versions of what is substantially the same matter soon become current. If at a later date different individuals in different places conceive the idea of setting down in writing the most interesting or important of the incidents and sayings which they either remember or can collect from others, four things will inevitably follow. (1) With each writer the total range of incidents and sayings available will be different; but so also will be the principle in accordance with which each selects from the available material what seems to him of special interest. (2) Each selection will, therefore, be to a large extent a different one ; on the other hand, it would be nothing short of a miracle if the difference were so great that in no case did the same incident or discourse occur in more than one selection. (3) Where the same item occurs in more than one selection, sometimes it will occur in both in substantially the same form ; sometimes two versions will develop which, in the vagaries of oral tradition, will become considerably differentiated. (4) The sayings having the most universal appeal will be likely to appear in more than one source, and also in the most divergent versions. This last phenomenon is a notable feature of the Gospels. A comparatively unimportant discourse, like John the Baptist's denunciation of the Pharisees, occurs word for word the same in both Matthew and in Luke, and presumably, therefore, stood in Q, but probably in no other source. But things of outstanding interest like the Beatitudes, the Lord's Prayer, the Lost Sheep, the teaching about Loving Enemies, Forgiveness, or the Strait Gate, are given in strikingly different forms. These then, we infer, stood in at least two sources, and circulated widely in more than one version.

From this it follows that we start out on our investigation with the *a priori* assumption that we are likely to find numerous cases where the same or similar material stood in more than one source. The assumption is one which justifies itself at once. We cannot move a step without running up against evidence for a considerable amount of *overlapping of sources*. Indeed, blindness to the evidence for the phenomenon of overlapping sources—a blindness artificially induced by the " unconscious assumptions " implied in the " Two Document " nomenclature—has, more than anything else, retarded a satisfactory solution to the Synoptic Problem.

The existence of parallel traditions is conspicuous the moment we study the evidence of the non-canonical sources of parables or sayings of our Lord.

(a) I print in a footnote the passage from the Epistle of Clement (xiii. 1 f.), to which I have already referred, with the nearest parallels in Matthew's Sermon on the Mount and Luke's Sermon on the Plain. In view of the express formula of quotation with which Clement introduces the words, it is difficult to believe that it is merely a free rendering of the general substance of mingled reminiscences of Matthew and Luke combined. But, if they are a quotation, they are evidence of the existence in the Church of Rome of a discourse document to some extent parallel to the Great Sermon in Matthew and Luke.[1]

(b) The relation of the Gospel according to the Hebrews to that of Matthew is a question that has been much disputed. But we know that it contained a version of the parable of the Talents (with details not unlike parts of the Prodigal Son) and of the injunction " Forgive seven times " (cf. p. 282). It also gave variant versions of the Healing of the Withered Hand and of the story of the Rich Young Man. The resemblances and differences between these and the Synoptic versions can only be explained by the theory of overlapping between the sources of this Gospel and those of the Synoptics. Even if we accept the theory that the document quoted by Jerome was a translation into Aramaic of the Greek Matthew, we must still assume that the text has been influenced by interpolation of parallel versions of these particular sayings current in oral tradition.[2]

[1] Clem xiii. 1 f.

μάλιστα μεμνημένοι τῶν λόγων τοῦ κυρίου Ἰησοῦ οὓς ἐλάλησεν διδάσκων ἐπιείκειαν καὶ μακροθυμίαν. οὕτως γὰρ εἶπεν.

Ἐλεᾶτε ἵνα ἐλεηθῆτε, ἀφίετε ἵνα ἀφεθῇ ὑμῖν· ὡς ποιεῖτε, οὕτω ποιηθήσεται ὑμῖν· ὡς δίδοτε, οὕτως δοθήσεται ὑμῖν· ὡς κρίνετε, οὕτως κριθήσεσθε· ὡς χρηστεύεσθε, οὕτως χρηστευθήσεται ὑμῖν· ᾧ μέτρῳ μετρεῖτε, ἐν αὐτῷ μετρηθήσεται ὑμῖν.

Matt. v. 7, etc.

v. 7. μακάριοι οἱ ἐλεήμονες· ὅτι αὐτοὶ ἐλεηθήσονται.

vi. 14. ἐὰν γὰρ ἀφῆτε τοῖς ἀνθρώποις τὰ παραπτώματα αὐτῶν, ἀφήσει καὶ ὑμῖν ὁ πατὴρ ὑμῶν ὁ οὐράνιος· ἐὰν δὲ μὴ ἀφῆτε τοῖς ἀνθρώποις τὰ παραπτώματα αὐτῶν, οὐδὲ ὁ πατὴρ ὑμῶν ἀφήσει τὰ παραπτώματα ὑμῶν.

vii. 1. μὴ κρίνετε, ἵνα μὴ κριθῆτε· ἐν ᾧ γὰρ κρίματι κρίνετε, κριθήσεσθε· καὶ ἐν ᾧ μέτρῳ μετρεῖτε μετρηθήσεται ὑμῖν.

vii. 12. πάντα οὖν ὅσα ἂν θέλητε ἵνα ποιῶσιν ὑμῖν οἱ ἄνθρωποι, οὕτω καὶ ὑμεῖς ποιεῖτε αὐτοῖς· οὗτος γάρ ἐστιν ὁ νόμος καὶ οἱ προφῆται.

Luke vi. 31, 36-38.

vi. 36-38. γίνεσθε οἰκτίρμονες, καθὼς ὁ πατὴρ ὑμῶν οἰκτίρμων ἐστί. καὶ μὴ κρίνετε καὶ οὐ μὴ κριθῆτε; καὶ μὴ καταδικάζετε, καὶ οὐ μὴ καταδικασθῆτε. ἀπολύετε, καὶ ἀπολυθήσεσθε· δίδοτε, καὶ δοθήσεται ὑμῖν· μέτρον καλόν, πεπιεσμένον, σεσαλευμένον ὑπερεκχυνόμενον, δώσουσιν εἰς τὸν κόλπον ὑμῶν. ᾧ γὰρ μέτρῳ μετρεῖτε, ἀντιμετρηθήσεται ὑμῖν. vi. 31. καὶ καθὼς θέλετε ἵνα ποιῶσιν ὑμῖν οἱ ἄνθρωποι, καὶ ὑμεῖς ποιεῖτε αὐτοῖς ὁμοίως.

[2] The relevant passages from the Gospel according to the Hebrews, from

(c) The same kind of evidence is afforded by two very ancient interpolations in the text of Matthew. In the Western text, after Mt. xx. 28, is inserted a parallel version of the saying about taking the best seats at banquets which is recorded in Lk. xiv. 8 f. An exactly similar " Western " insertion is the saying " Signs of the times," Mt. xvi. 2-3. This, though found in most later MSS. and included in the Textus Receptus, stands, so far as the early authorities for the text are concerned, on practically the same footing. Both passages are found in D Old Lat. ; while the support for " Signs of the times " by C L and the Eusebian canons is of no more weight than that of Φ Syr. (C and Hcl^mg·) for the addition to Mt. xx. 28. Both seem to have been lacking in the oldest Alexandrian, Caesarean, and Antiochene text, being absent from fam. Θ, Syr. S., and Origen's *Commentary on Matthew*, as well as from B ℵ. But the point I wish to make is that these passages are not harmonistic insertions derived from the text of Luke. For if a later scribe, who had Luke before him, had desired to insert equivalent sayings in Matthew, he would have adhered far more closely to Luke's version. The passages are printed below in a footnote.[1] One

---

2 Clement, and, with one exception, from the Oxyrhynchus Logia, are printed at length in the article " Agrapha " in the supplementary volume of Hastings' *Dictionary of the Bible.*

[1] Matt. xvi. 2-3.
Om. B ℵ Syr. S. and C. Arm. Orig.^Mt.

Ὀψίας γενομένης λέγετε Εὐδία, πυρράζει γὰρ ὁ οὐρανός· καὶ πρωΐ Σήμερον χειμών, πυρράζει γὰρ στυγνάζων ὁ οὐρανός. τὸ μὲν πρόσωπον τοῦ οὐρανοῦ γινώσκετε διακρίνειν, τὰ δὲ σημεῖα τῶν καιρῶν οὐ δύνασθε.

Luke xii. 54-57.

Ὀταν ἴδητε νεφέλην ἀνατέλλουσαν ἐπὶ δυσμῶν, εὐθέως λέγετε ὅτι Ὄμβρος ἔρχεται, καὶ γίνεται οὕτως· καὶ ὅταν νότον πνέοντα, λέγετε ὅτι Καύσων ἔσται, καὶ γίνεται. ὑποκριταί, τὸ πρόσωπον τῆς γῆς καὶ τοῦ οὐρανοῦ οἴδατε δοκιμάζειν, τὸν καιρὸν δὲ τοῦτον πῶς οὐκ οἴδατε δοκιμάζειν ; Τί δὲ καὶ ἀφ' ἑαυτῶν οὐ κρίνετε τὸ δίκαιον ;

Matt. xx. 28.
Add. D Φ Old Lat. Syr. C. Hcl^mg

ὑμεῖς δὲ ζητεῖτε ἐκ μικροῦ αὐξῆσαι καὶ εκ μείζονος ἔλαττον εἶναι. εἰσερχόμενοι δὲ καὶ παρακληθέντες δειπνῆσαι μὴ ἀνα-

Luke xiv. 8-10.

Ὄταν κληθῇς ὑπό τινος εἰς γάμους, μὴ κατακλιθῇς εἰς τὴν πρωτοκλισίαν, μή ποτε ἐντιμότερός σου ᾖ κεκλημένος ὑπ' αὐτοῦ,

R

has only to read them through side by side to see that the verbal
agreements between the two versions are almost nil, and can
only be accounted for on the hypothesis that the interpolations
are drawn from a tradition independent of Luke. Probably they
are excerpts from the primitive discourse document of the local
Church in which the interpolator worked. The MS. evidence
would favour the view that both readings originated in Rome.
In that case they may well be fragments of the same document
or catechetical tradition from which Clement quotes.

(d) The Oxyrhynchus Logia contain some sayings of our
Lord which have a close resemblance to sayings found in the
Gospels, and others which exhibit a remarkable combination of
resemblance and divergence. The definite citations of words
of Christ in the second century homily known as II. Clement
exhibit the same phenomena of versions of sayings more or less
parallel to those contained in the Canonical Gospels. Some
scholars think the sayings preserved in the Oxyrhynchus Logia
and by 2 Clement are all from the same lost Gospel—" according
to the Egyptians " or " according to the Hebrews." If so, they
prove that the sources of that Gospel to a considerable extent
overlapped with those of the Synoptics. If, on the other hand,
the sayings in question come from more than one lost document,
the evidence for parallel traditions is further multiplied.

THE OVERLAPPING OF SOURCES

Let us now, from the standpoint of this evidence, re-examine
certain phenomena in the Canonical Gospels.

(1) It has long been recognised that Q and Mark to some

κλίνεσθε εἰς τοὺς ἐξέχοντας τόπους, μήποτε
ἐνδοξότερός σου ἐπέλθῃ καὶ προσελθὼν ὁ
δειπνοκλήτωρ εἴπῃ σοι, Ἔτι κάτω χώρει,
καὶ καταισχυνθήσῃ. ἐὰν δὲ ἀναπέσῃς εἰς
τὸν ἥττονα τόπον καὶ ἐπέλθῃ σου ἥττων,
ἐρεῖ σοι ὁ δειπνοκλήτωρ, Σύναγε ἔτι ἄνω,
καὶ ἔσται σοι τοῦτο χρήσιμον.

καὶ ἐλθὼν ὁ σὲ καὶ αὐτὸν καλέσας ἐρεῖ σοι
Δὸς τούτῳ τόπον, καὶ τότε ἄρξῃ μετὰ
αἰσχύνης τὸν ἔσχατον τόπον κατέχειν.
ἀλλ' ὅταν κληθῇς πορευθεὶς ἀνάπεσε εἰς
τὸν ἔσχατον τόπον, ἵνα ὅταν ἔλθῃ ὁ κε-
κληκώς σε ἐρεῖ σοι Φίλε, προσανάβηθι
ἀνώτερον· τότε ἔσται σοι δόξα ἐνώπιον
πάντων τῶν συνανακειμένων σοι.

extent overlap. The question whether in these passages Mark is directly or indirectly dependent on Q has been discussed above (p. 187 ff.), and the conclusion was reached that it is more probable that Mark and Q represent two independent traditions.

(2) We have also seen that there is similar overlapping between Mark and *the narrative* material in the source L, since Luke evidently had before him versions of the Rejection at Nazareth, the Call of Peter, the Anointing, and of the whole story of the Passion, which on the whole he preferred to the accounts which he found in Mark.

(3) A third clear case of overlapping is seen in the parables of Matthew and Luke. It is sometimes doubtful whether we ought to call a particular saying a short parable or an extended illustration, but taking the list on p. 332 plus those named here we count fifteen parables in Matthew and twenty-three in Luke. Two of these, the Sower and the Wicked Husbandmen, are derived from Mark;[1] two more, the Mustard Seed and Leaven, certainly stood in Q. There remain to be accounted for two collections of parables—though, of course, in speaking of them as " collections " I do not wish to imply that they were derived from different sources from the rest of the peculiar matter in the Gospels where they occur. These collections number respectively eleven and nineteen. But they overlap to the extent of three parables, since each collection includes a version of the Lost Sheep, the Marriage Feast (= the Great Supper),[2] and the Talents (= Pounds). But though these three parables occur in both Matthew and Luke, they do so in such very different forms that the supposition that they were derived

---

[1] The Mustard Seed, of course, stands in Mark as well as Q.

[2] Matthew's Marriage Feast (the King's Son) (xxii. 1 ff.) is really two parables. Verse 2, or words to that effect, has evidently been omitted before verse 11. Repeat verse 2 here, and verses 11-14 are seen to form the second half of one of those pairs of "twin parables" enforcing a different aspect of the same general moral, so characteristic of our Lord's teaching. Without such emendation the second half is pointless. How could the man, just swept in from the highways, be expected to have on a wedding garment ?

from Q postulates too large an amount of editorial manipulation of that source.

But the ingenuity that attempts to derive them from a single written source is wholly misdirected. Given that two different persons set about collecting parables of our Lord, and that one of them succeeded in finding eleven and the other as many as nineteen. Would it not be an astounding circumstance if the two collectors never happened to light upon the same parable ? The remarkable thing is, not that the two collections have three parables in common, but that they have *only* three.

Thirteen years ago I myself, under the malign influence of the " unconscious assumptions " of the Two Document Hypothesis, argued that these three parables occurred in Q.[1] But one day, while I was meditating on the curious fact that the moral which Matthew draws from the parable of the Lost Sheep is quite different from that drawn by Luke, it occurred to me that this is precisely what one would expect if the two versions had been handed down in two different traditions. People so often remember a story or an illustration, but forget the point it was told to illustrate. Then I turned to Harnack's famous reconstruction of Q.[2] I found that, in order to derive both versions from Q, he had to maintain that the saying " There shall be joy in heaven over one sinner that repenteth more than over ninety and nine just persons which need no repentance " was an editorial addition. The scales fell from my eyes. No saying attributed to Jesus can have struck those who first heard it as so utterly daring as this. I reflected that, if a man of Harnack's insight can be driven by the logic of his premises to the conclusion that such a saying is an editorial addition, there must be something wrong about the premises. Then it dawned on me that the assumption on which he—and I too—had been working was fundamentally false. Even if the differences

---

[1] *Oxford Studies*, p. 197 ff.
[2] A. Harnack, *The Sayings of Jesus*, p. 93 (Williams and Norgate, 1908).

between the versions did not demonstrate, antecedent probability would lead us to expect, that two different collections of
parables would certainly overlap.

I proceeded at once to re-examine the parable in a Synopsis,
and I saw at once that if, instead of mechanically counting
the number of Greek words common to the two versions, one
asked which of the really significant words were found in both
versions and which in only one, the conclusion that the versions
were independent was confirmed. The words which are found
in both versions are the words without which the story could
not be told at all—" man," " sheep," " go," " find," " rejoice,"
the " I say unto you " (which is the regular formula for pointing
the moral in our Lord's teaching), and the three numerals, 100,
99, and 1, which since $100 - 1 = 99$ would be inevitable in any
version. But where the versions can differ, they do so. For
Matthew's " if it happen to a man," Luke has " what man of
you ? "; for " be gone astray " (passive), " having lost "
(active); for " into the mountains," " in the wilderness "; for
" seek," " go after "; for " layeth it on his shoulder rejoicing,"
" rejoiceth over it." Luke adds the calling together of friends
and neighbours, about which Matthew is silent, and the saying
about the joy in heaven over the sinner repentant; while
Matthew, instead of this, points the moral, " Even so it is
not the will of your Father that one of these little ones should
perish."

The differences between the two versions of the parable
of the Lost Sheep are as nothing compared to the differences
between the other two pairs, the Marriage Feast = the Great
Supper, and the Talents = Pounds. But since Matthew has
eleven and Luke nineteen parables, and twenty-seven of these
thirty must have been derived from two quite different cycles
of tradition, the probability that the two cycles overlapped
to the extent of including divergent versions of at least three
parables is a high one.

It appears, then, that the occurrence in overlapping sources of parallel versions of the same saying is characteristic alike of canonical and extra-canonical reports of the teaching of Christ. All analogies, therefore, are in favour of the hypothesis that Q and M also would at some points overlap.

Matthew's Method of Conflation

When an editor combines sources which cover the same ground along some part of their extent, he has a choice of two methods. He can either accept the version given by one source and ignore the other, or he can make a careful mosaic by " conflating " the two. We noticed in a previous chapter (p. 187 ff.) that, when the same saying occurs in both Mark and Q, Luke commonly accepts the Q version and ignores Mark's; Matthew, on the other hand, usually conflates Mark and Q, though with a tendency to abbreviate. Now, if it was Luke himself who first combined Q and L, and *if* on this occasion he followed his *later* practice of choosing one of two versions rather than combining them, all traces of any overlapping there may have been between Q and L will have been eliminated. On the other hand, if Matthew pursued as between M and Q the same method of conflation which he used where Q and Mark overlap, some traces of the double version will still remain. The detection of these is the immediate goal of our inquiry.

In order, however, to do this we must first study the way in which Matthew conflates. It will appear that he not only pieces together the substance of sayings that occur in two different sources, but he combines minute points of difference in their expression of the same thought.

The way in which the wording of Matthew's parable of the Mustard Seed conflates the versions of Mark and Luke is particularly instructive. In the parallels printed below, words found in both Matthew and Mark, but not in Luke, are printed in heavy type ; words found in Matthew and Luke, but not in Mark, are underlined. Words found in all three are in extra small type.

Mark iv. 30-32.	Matthew xiii. 31-32.	Luke xiii. 18-19.
Καὶ ἔλεγεν	Ἄλλην παραβολὴν παρέθηκεν αὐτοῖς λέγων	Ελεγεν οὖν
Πῶς ὁμοιώσωμεν τὴν βασιλείαν τοῦ θεοῦ, ἢ ἐν τίνι αὐτὴν παραβολῇ θῶμεν ;	Ὁμοία ἐστὶν ἡ βασιλεία τῶν οὐρανῶν	Τίνι ὁμοία ἐστὶν ἡ βασιλεία τοῦ θεοῦ, καὶ τίνι ὁμοιώσω αὐτήν ;
		19. ὁμοία ἐστὶν
31. ὡς κόκκῳ σινάπεως, ὃς ὅταν σπαρῇ ἐπὶ τῆς γῆς, μικρότερον ὂν	κόκκῳ σινάπεως, ὃν λαβὼν ἄνθρωπος ἔσπειρεν ἐν τῷ ἀγρῷ αὐτοῦ· 32. ὃ μικρότερον μέν ἐστιν	κόκκῳ σινάπεως, ὃν λαβὼν ἄνθρωπος ἔβαλεν εἰς κῆπον ἑαυτοῦ,
πάντων τῶν σπερμάτων τῶν ἐπὶ τῆς γῆς—	πάντων τῶν σπερμάτων	
32. καὶ ὅταν σπαρῇ ἀναβαίνει καὶ γίνεται μείζων πάντων τῶν λαχάνων καὶ ποιεῖ κλάδους μεγάλους, ὥστε δύνασθαι ὑπὸ τὴν σκιὰν αὐτοῦ τὰ πετεινὰ τοῦ οὐρανοῦ κατασκηνοῖν.	ὅταν δὲ αὐξηθῇ μεῖζον τῶν λαχάνων ἐστὶν καὶ γίνεται δένδρον ὥστε ἐλθεῖν τὰ πετεινὰ τοῦ οὐρανοῦ καὶ κατασκηνοῦν ἐν τοῖς κλάδοις αὐτοῦ.	καὶ ηὔξησεν καὶ ἐγένετο εἰς δένδρον καὶ τὰ πετεινὰ τοῦ οὐρανοῦ κατεσκήνωσεν ἐν τοῖς κλάδοις αὐτοῦ.

In the above parallels we must ignore as irrelevant for such comparisons all occurrences of the word "and," the verb "to be," the definite article, and all pronouns; there remain 31 words in Matthew's version. Of these only 7 are his own; 7 occur also in Mark and Luke; 10 in Mark; 7 occur in Luke but not in Mark, and so presumably stood in Q. Now if Mark had been lost, every one would have explained the verbal differences between Matthew and Luke as due either to editorial amplification by Matthew or to abbreviation by Luke. As it is, we see that practically every word in Matthew is drawn from one or other of his two sources. But the differences between the Marcan and the Lucan (i.e. the Q) version of the parable are entirely unimportant. They in no way affect the general sense, and no one antecedently would have expected that Matthew would take the trouble to combine the two versions. The fact that he has done so where so little was to be gained is thus a very important revelation of the care he would be likely to take when combining sources containing differences of real interest.

Another example, hardly less illuminating, of the almost meticulous care with which Matthew conflates Mark and Q is the discourse Mt. x. 9-15. This example is somewhat complicated by the existence of a fourth version, Lk. ix. 3-5. This is mainly from Mark, but its differences from Mark seem to arise from conflation with the same Q discourse as that best preserved in Lk. x. 4 ff.; Lk. ix. 3-5, however, seems to retain a word or two from Q which has been modified in Lk. x. 4 ff. This complication, and the fact that Matthew repeats the words " entering," " house," " peace," and " worthy " more than once, would make a merely statistical statement misleading. The notable thing is that the only real additions he has to make are the words " gold " (verse 9) and " Gomorrha " (verse 15), both of which are due to verbal association—" Gomorrha " is suggested by Sodom, and " gold " by silver. Gold is hardly original; it was not a commodity which those for whom the words were first intended needed exhortation not to carry, though copper or silver might be. Apart from these two, obviously editorial, additions, there is not a word in any way significant which is not to be found either in the Marcan or one of the Lucan parallels.

There is another point to notice. The necessity of conflating the Marcan and the Q versions has led Matthew entirely to rearrange the order of the sentences in Q, which we may presume to be preserved in Lk. x. 4 ff. There are only two other possible Q passages where such a redistribution of sentences *within a single section* occurs (I do not speak of diversity in the order of complete sections dealing with separate topics, which is quite another matter). These are Mt. v. 38-48 =Lk. vi. 27-36, " Love your enemies " and the Denunciation of the Pharisees, Mt. xxiii. 1-36 =Lk. xi. 39-52. We shall see later (p. 252 f.) that here also Matthew may have rearranged the order of Q, preserved by Luke, in order to conflate with a parallel version from another source.

A study of these and other cases, similar though not quite so striking, shows that, wherever we have reason to suspect that Q and M overlap, we must insist on the probability that the divergence between the two versions was originally greater than that between the parallels as they now stand in Matthew and Luke. Indeed, Matthew's habit of conflating the actual language of parallel sources compels us to formulate a new principle of Synoptic criticism. Wherever parallel passages of Matthew and Luke exhibit marked divergence, *editorial modification of Q is a less probable explanation than conflation of Q by Matthew with the language of a parallel version*. I need not pause to point out the havoc wrought by the formulation of this principle in various critical reconstructions of Q—my own included—which are based on exactly the opposite assumption.[1]

The Sermon on the Mount

In view of the evidence that the overlapping of sources is a *vera causa*, and of the principle deduced above from a study of Matthew's method of conflation, let us explore the hypothesis that there is overlapping between Q and M. This, unless I am altogether mistaken, will lead to results of a highly illuminating character. In particular it will explain those well-known difficulties concerning the composition of the Sermon on the Mount to which the Two Document Hypothesis has never been able to give a really satisfactory answer.

The Sermon on the Mount (Mt. v.-vii.) is four times as long as Luke's Sermon on the Plain (Lk. vi. 20-49) ; but there are two considerable sections of it which, though absent from the Sermon on the Plain, occur in Luke scattered in *different contexts*. These show such close verbal parallelism to Matthew that they must certainly be referred to Q (Mt. vi. 22-33 = Lk. xi. 34-36, xvi. 13, xii. 22-31 and Mt. vii. 7-11 = Lk. xi. 9-13). These create no difficulty ; they have obviously been inserted in

---

[1] For similar "conflation" in Mediaeval documents see C. Plummer, *Expositor*, July 1889.

their present context by Matthew in accordance with his practice of " agglomerating," *i.e.* of collecting into large discourses all the available material dealing with the same or related topics.[1]

Both sermons begin with Beatitudes, both end with the parable of the House built upon the Sand, and to all but six of the intervening verses in Luke's Sermon there are parallels, more or less exact, in the Sermon on the Mount ; and both are followed by the story of the Centurion's Servant. The natural inference is that Q contained a Great Sermon followed by the story of the Centurion's Servant. But on closer study it appears that the Sermons in Matthew and Luke can be derived from a single written source only if we postulate an almost incredible amount of editorial freedom in rewriting portions of the original. Thus Matthew has nine (originally, perhaps, eight)[2] Beatitudes, all but one in the *third* person ; Luke has four Beatitudes balanced by four corresponding Woes, all in the *second* person. Only the final Beatitude in Mt. v. 11-12 (= Lk. vi. 22-23), unlike the rest, which are in the third person, is in the second person like all the Beatitudes of Luke, and is almost verbally identical with the Lucan parallel. This divergence would not be unnatural if they followed two independent oral traditions of the same discourse ; it is not plausibly explained as the result of editorial modification of a written source, for we can check the editorial methods of the authors by studying their handling of the sayings of our Lord which they derive from Mark. Besides the Beatitudes there are in the two Sermons other parallels

---

[1] Curiously enough, apart from the final Beatitude, and the House on the Sand, all the material in the Sermon on the Mount, which is *certainly* from Q, comes in the block vi. 22-vii. 12 ; and all but two verses in this block are Q.

[2] Verses 4 ("they that mourn") and 5 ("the meek") are transposed by 33 D a c k *fam.* Θ Syr. C. Orig.Mt.. Transposition results when a sentence written in the margin is inserted in the wrong place by the next copyist. But, though a passage thus inserted may replace an accidental omission, it *may* be an interpolation. I incline to agree with Harnack that Mt. v. 5 is an interpolation from Ps. xxxvii. 11, against Dr. Charles, who, in his *The Decalogue* (T. & T. Clark, 1923), argues that verse 4 is the interpolated verse, through assimilation from Luke.

where the degree of verbal resemblance is really not much greater, for example the two very different versions of the saying " Lord, Lord," Mt. vii. 21 = Lk. vi. 46. Again, in the striking section " Resist not evil. . . . Love your enemies " (Mt. v. 38-48 = Lk. vi. 27-36), not only are there considerable diversities of language, but the order in which the component sayings are arranged is entirely different, which, as the example of Mt. x. 9 ff. showed, suggest conflation of two sources. Indeed, there are only two *considerable* passages which occur in both sermons, *i.e.* " Judge not " (Mt. vii. 1-5 = Lk. vi. 37-38, 41-42) and the House on the Sand (Mt. vii. 24-27 = Lk. vi. 47-49), which can, without postulating a good deal of editorial modification, be explained as being entirely derived from a single common written source.

Let us now try the simple experiment of deducting from the Sermon on the Mount just these passages which, on account of their close resemblance to parallels in Luke, can with the maximum of probability be assigned to Q. What remains— more than two-thirds of the whole—reads like a continuous and coherent discourse. Most of it is peculiar to Matthew ; but some passages, for example " Love your enemies " and the Lord's Prayer, have parallels in Luke—sometimes within, sometimes outside, the Sermon on the Plain. But these parallels have no more than that general resemblance which one would expect in divergent traditions of the same original saying. All the phenomena, however, can be satisfactorily explained by the hypothesis that Matthew is conflating two separate discourses, one from Q practically identical with Luke's Sermon on the Plain, the other from M containing a much longer Sermon.

Both Sermons opened with four Beatitudes. The Sermon in Q contained the four Blessings in the second person, as in Luke ; that in M gave four in the third person, corresponding to Mt. v. 7-10. The Q Beatitude, " Blessed are ye when men shall . . . reproach you . . . and evil for (my) sake " (Mt. v. 11-12), is a doublet of that in Mt. v. 10, " Blessed are they which are

persecuted for righteousness' sake," which stood in M; otherwise the two sets of four do not overlap. Matthew has simply
added the two sets together, changing the person and slightly
modifying the wording in three of those he takes from Q.[1]
Mt. v. 5, "the meek," is, as the transposition in the MSS.
suggests, an early interpolation from Ps. xxxvii. 11. The four
Woes in Luke vi. 24 ff. may have stood in Q and been omitted
by Matthew. His explanatory additions to the Blessings,
on the Poor (+ in spirit), and on those that hunger (+ after
righteousness), show that he might well have thought the
denunciations of the "rich," and the "full" (Lk. vi. 24-25),
open to misunderstanding; poverty and hunger *as such* have
no ethical value.

The Sermons in Q and M occasionally overlapped, *e.g.* in the
section on Loving Enemies,[2] Mt. v. 38-48; the variation in
order between the parallels in Matthew and Luke is here very
marked, and wherever this happens (cf. p. 248), judging from
the way in which the editor of Matthew deals with overlapping
of Mark and Q, we suspect that there has been a certain
amount of conflation. Hence the Q and M versions of any saying
which occurred in both Sermons would in the original sources
have shown greater divergence than do the present texts of
Matthew and Luke. Having thus conflated the two Sermons
from Q and M, Matthew proceeded to add to them certain
other passages of Q, which Luke gives later in his Gospel in
what is more likely to be their original context in that source.

The hypothesis of a summary of Christian teaching intended
for catechetical instruction, current in oral tradition in more
than one form, has often been invoked to account for the combined phenomena of resemblance and difference between the
versions of the Great Sermon in Matthew and in Luke. But
as usually presented it goes shipwreck on the fact that, in the

[1] I owe several points in this analysis to suggestions by Prof. Dodd.
[2] Rom. xii. 14, "Bless them that persecute you," etc., suggests that various
summaries of this part of our Lord's teaching were current.

source used by both Matthew and Luke, the story of the
Centurion's Servant follows immediately after the Great Sermon.
That difficulty disappears if, instead of supposing that Matthew
and Luke had each a different version of the *same* Sermon, we
suppose that Matthew had before him *two* documents, Q which
contained *both* the Sermon on the Plain *and* the Centurion's
Servant, and M which gave a substantially different version
of the Sermon, but did *not* include the Centurion's Servant.
The idea of conflating the two would be inevitably suggested
to Matthew by the fact that both Sermons began with Beatitudes
and also that they overlapped at certain other points.

We proceed to consider the long discourse Mt. xxiii., the
Woes to the Pharisees. This is, next to the Sermon on the Mount,
the longest connected discourse of which both the Matthean and
the Lucan versions (Mt. xxiii. 1-36 = Lk. xi. 37-52) cannot be referred to a single written source without raising great difficulties.
Matthew's is much the longer version, and it reads like an early
Jewish Christian polemical pamphlet against their oppressors
the Pharisees. No doubt it is largely based upon a tradition
of genuine sayings of Christ, but we cannot but suspect that it
considerably accentuates the manner, if not also the matter,
of His criticism of them. Indeed it is the one discourse of our
Lord which, from its complete ignoring of the better elements
in a movement like Pharisaism, it is not easy to defend from the
accusation made by students of Jewish religion of being un-
sympathetic and unfair. Now it is quite commonly assumed
as almost self-evident that Matthew's version stood in Q and
that Luke's is an abbreviated reproduction of the same source.
But there are three considerations which give us pause. (1) The
divergence between the parallels is well above the average in
wording and it is accompanied by a great variety in the order—a
signpost for conflation (p. 248). (2) There is a fundamental difference in structure between the two discourses. The core of the
discourse in Matthew is the *seven* times repeated " Woe unto
you, Scribes and Pharisees." But in Luke what we have is

three Woes against Pharisees followed by *three* against Lawyers.
(3) It is to be noted that quite the most striking of the very
few cases in the Gospels where the diversity between Matthew
and Luke can be plausibly accounted for by independent translation from Aramaic occur in this discourse.[1]

The fact that Luke's version of the discourse, xi. 37-52,
comes in the middle of a section of which the rest is certainly
derived from Q, makes it probable that his version stood in that
document and that Matthew has again conflated a discourse
of Q with one on the same topic which came to him in M. But
here, again, the very fact that Matthew's version is a conflation
of Q and M means that Mt. xxiii. as it now stands bears a much
closer resemblance to Lk. xi. 37-52 than did the original discourse that stood in M. Yet again, Matthew, besides placing
the discourse in a Marcan context, adds to it a few words
from Mark, *e.g.* πρωτοκλισίας, κτλ., Mt. xxiii. 6 = Mk. xii. 39.
Finally, we must notice that Matthew has completed his
structure by appending xxiii. 37-39, the Q saying, " Jerusalem,
Jerusalem," which occurs in what to me looks a far more
original context in Lk. xiii. 34-35.

JUDAISTIC TENDENCY OF M

Mt. x. 9-16 is, as we have already seen, a most careful combination of the Charge to the Twelve (Mk. vi. 7-11) and the
Charge to the Seventy (Lk. x. 3-12) which we assign to Q.
Besides this, the chapter contains other sections derived from
either Mark or Q. Mt. x. 17-22 seems to have been transferred
by the editor from Mk. xiii. 9-13. Mt. x. 26-38 (? 39) seems to be
from Q, while x. 40, 42 are from Mark. Only about half a dozen
verses remain which are without close parallels in either Mark
or Luke. We ask whence were these derived. Much the most
striking are the words which precede the conflated discourse :

---

[1] Wellhausen suggests that רכי (cleanse) misread as וכי (give alms) would
account for Luke's τὰ ἐνόντα δότε ἐλεημοσύνην as compared with Matthew's
καθάρισον πρῶτον τὸ ἐντός.

" Go not into any way of the Gentiles, and enter not into any city of the Samaritans : but go rather to the lost sheep of the house of Israel " (Mt. x. 5-6). There is, I think, a close connection of thought between this opening and the words which conclude the first half of the discourse, " Ye shall not have gone through the cities of Israel, till the Son of man be come " (x. 23). This verse appears to be intended to give a reason for the previous prohibition to preach to Gentiles or Samaritans. It is not that Gentiles cannot or ought not to be saved, but the time will not be long enough to preach to all, and Israel has the first right to hear. But if I am correct in this interpretation, the two passages must originally have stood much closer together. They look like the beginning and end of a Judaistic version of the Charge to the Twelve, the wording of which has taken the precise form it now bears under the influence of the controversy about the Gentile Mission which almost split the early Church.[1] The question then arises, Did these words stand in Q and form the original beginning and end of the discourse which Luke gives as that to the Seventy ? Or does Mt. x. 5-8, 23, with the possible additions of x. 24, 25, 41, represent a short Judaistic charge, which Matthew has conflated with the versions given by Mark and Q ? If we elect for the former alternative, we must say that Luke, convinced that a command of the Lord not to go to Gentile or Samaritan could not be genuine, has intentionally left out the words. We should also have to say that Q in its original form was a document emanating from the Judaistic section of the Church.

Against the view that Q was a Judaistic document two considerations may be urged :

[1] Schweitzer argued, from Mt. x. 23, that Christ expected the Parousia before the return of the Twelve from their preaching tour ; but the words clearly reflect a situation which did not come into existence till the Missionary Journeys of Paul. Incidentally, I may remark that Schweitzer's whole argument depends on the assumption that Mt. x. is word for word an exact report of what was said at the time. The demonstration I have given above, that Mt. x. 5-23 is a late conflation of at least two sources, Mark and Q, would alone be a sufficient refutation of his argument.

(1) The occurrence in it of the pro-Gentile incident of the
Centurion's Servant, and the saying about the Law and the
Prophets being until John, which, whatever its original meaning,
certainly lends itself to the view that the Old Law was in a
sense superseded by the Gospel. To this it may be objected
that since in Matthew these and similar sayings occur side by
side with ones of a Judaistic tenor, the same thing may have
happened in Q. But to this I would reply that it is not very
likely that the author of a primitive document would put side
by side sayings implying contrary rulings on what at the time
he wrote was a highly controversial issue ; it is quite another
matter for a later writer, very conservative as Matthew is in
his use of his sources, to include contrary sayings found in two
different ancient documents, especially as the controversy in
question had by that time largely died down.

(2) Judaistic sayings in Matthew only occur in contexts
which on other grounds we should refer to M, or where there
is evidence of conflation between Q and another source. In
all these Judaistic passages it is difficult not to suspect the
influence of the desire of the followers of James to find a
justification for their disapprobation of the attitude of Paul,
by inventing sayings of Christ, or misquoting sayings which,
even if authentic, must originally have been spoken in view of
entirely different circumstances. The sayings of every great
leader have always been quoted by his followers in the next
generation to justify their own attitude in circumstances quite
different from his ; and where there exists no written or printed
record to check their original form it is easy for the actual
wording, as well as the application, of the sayings to become
changed.

The first of these passages is Mt. v. 17-20, which defines
the relation of Christianity to the Law. The saying, "Whosoever
therefore shall break one of these least commandments, *and
shall teach men so*, shall be called *least* in the Kingdom of
Heaven," is sharply contrasted with " Whosoever shall *do and*

teach men so, he shall be called *great* in the Kingdom." This reflects the attitude of the Jewish Christians who, while barely tolerating the proceedings of Paul, regarded as the pattern Christian, James, surnamed the Just, because his righteousness, even according to the Law, *did* exceed that of the Scribes and Pharisees.[1] It is to be remarked that this passage does not come in that part of the Sermon on the Mount which we have referred to Q.

The same idea is still more clearly enforced in Mt. xxiii. 2-3, "The Scribes and Pharisees sit in Moses' seat: all things therefore whatsoever they bid you, these do and observe." Here we have attributed to our Lord an emphatic commandment to obey, not only the Law, but the scribal interpretation of it. That is to say, He is represented as inculcating scrupulous obedience to that very "tradition of the elders" which He specifically denounces in Mk. vii. 13. But here again we have already, on other grounds, seen reason to suppose that Matthew's version of this discourse was derived largely from M.

The section (Mt. xviii. 15-22) "If thy brother sin against thee . . . till seventy times seven" differs in wording from Lk. xvii. 3-4 so much that it is not likely that both passages were taken from Q ; especially as we know of another version of this particular saying—in some ways intermediate between those of Matthew and Luke—preserved in the Gospel according to the Hebrews (cf. p. 282). It must therefore be assigned to M. Now an important little point, affording confirmatory evidence that the sayings of a Judaistic type are connected with M rather than with Q, is the fact that on examination it appears that this saying, as it occurred in M, was set in a Judaistic context. Only here, and in the passage "Thou art Peter," does the word "Church" occur in the Gospels ; and the word "Church" in this context clearly means the little

[1] It is possible that the passionate protest, "I am the least of the apostles . . but I laboured more abundantly than they all," 1 Cor. xv. 9 ff., has a reference to a description of him and his work by the Judaisers in words not dissimilar to those in the text.

S

community of Jewish Christians. In a Gentile community
tradition would surely have modified the form of the injunction
" If he refuse to hear the Church, let him be unto thee as the
Gentile and the publican." [1]

It might be argued that a similar " tendency " appears in
the famous " Thou art Peter " (Mt. xvi. 18 ff.). In the Jewish
idiom, " I will give unto thee the keys of the Kingdom of
Heaven " means " I appoint thee my Grand Vizier " ; and
" to loose " and " to bind " are technical terms for declaring
permissible or the reverse particular lines of conduct in the
light of the obligations of the Law. The passage, in the form
in which we have it, is an emphatic declaration that Peter is
the Apostle who on these points could speak with the authority
of Christ. What our Lord really said to Peter, and what at
the time of speaking He meant by it, is an entirely different
question ; and it is not one to which we are likely to find an
answer with which everybody will be convinced. But whatever
the words meant as originally spoken, it is hard not to suspect
that they have since been modified by some controversy between
the followers of different leaders in the early Church. But to
my mind it is less likely to have been the controversy between
the party who said " I am of Peter " and the admirers of Paul,
than that between the extreme Judaisers who exalted James to
the supreme position and the intermediate party who followed
Peter.[2] In that case " Thou art Peter " will have been derived,

---

[1] As early as Hermas, ecclesiastical writers use the term " Gentiles " as
equivalent to pagans ; but this usage implies a time when the controversy
whether Gentiles could be admitted to the Church on equal terms with Jews
had long ago been settled. τὰ ἔθνη occurred in Q (Mt. vi. 32 = Lk. xii. 30), but
not in such an invidious sense as the ἐθνικός of Mt. xviii. 17 and Mt. v. 47.
Luke, however, tones it down in xii. 30 by adding τοῦ κόσμου.

[2] The Clementine Homilies open with a letter from Peter to James beginning, " Peter to James, the lord and bishop of the holy Church, under the
Father of all, through Jesus Christ." This is followed by one from Clement,
"Clement to James, the lord (or lord's brother) and the bishop of bishops, who
rules Jerusalem . . . and the churches everywhere." The Homilies probably
date ± 225, but in this particular regard must represent a party feeling of an
earlier period.

not from M, but from the local traditions of Antioch—the headquarters of this intermediate party.[1]   But we shall refer to M the doublet of this saying, Mt. xviii. 18, which confers the power " to bind and loose " upon the Ecclesia, that is, on the righteous remnant of the People of God, of which the Jerusalem Church was the natural headquarters and shepherd.

OVERLAPPING OF MARK AND M

Seeing there is evidence of the existence of a source evidently emanating from a Judaistic circle, we must not overlook the possibility that there would be overlapping between it and Mark as well as between it and Q.   And it is the fact that the occurrence of parallel versions of the same incident in Mark and M would explain three cases where Matthew's account appears to be in some ways more original than Mark's.

(1) Matthew's section on Divorce (Mt. xix. 3-12) is both more naturally told and more closely related to Jewish usage than the parallel in Mark (Mk. x. 2-12).[2]   The words " for every cause " in the question put by the Pharisees look more original, since thus expressed the point submitted to the reputed Prophet in regard to the grounds of divorce was one actually debated at the time between the schools of Hillel and Shammai. So does our Lord's reply, referring them for an answer to the fundamental principle stated in Genesis, " They two shall be one flesh."   The reference to the law of divorce in Deuteronomy comes more appropriately, as in Matthew, in *their* reply to Him than, as in Mark, as our Lord's original answer.   And, finally, Matthew's arrangement makes His final rejoinder, that this was merely permissive, more effective.

(2) In the story Mt. xii. 9-13—told, not for the sake of the healing miracle, but to illustrate our Lord's attitude to the Sabbath—Matthew adds to Mark the detail " a sheep in a pit."

[1] Cf. p. 504 and p. 511 ff. ; Foakes-Jackson and Lake, *op. cit.* i. p. 328 ff.

[2] Cf. R. H. Charles, *The Teaching of the New Testament on Divorce*, p. 85 ff. (Williams and Norgate, 1921).

If we compare with this the addition "ox in a pit" in the similar story in Luke (xiv. 1-6), we shall be inclined to attribute it to conflation with another version rather than to editorial expansion.

(3) The account of the Syrophenician woman, as given by Matthew, is made, by an addition of the two and a half verses (Mt. xv. 22b-24) (which suggest very great reluctance on the part of our Lord to heal a Gentile), very much more Judaistic than the version given by Mark (vii. 24-30).[1]

But Divorce, the Sabbath, and the position of Gentiles were all burning questions, especially among Jewish Christians. Hence we should expect that sayings or stories which could be quoted as defining Christ's attitude towards them would be current at a very early time in nearly every Church—and most certainly in the Church of Jerusalem. It seems likely, then, that in these three instances Matthew had before him a parallel version in M. But in each case he tells the story in the context in which it occurs in Mark. Probably, then, he takes Mark's version as his basis, adding only a few notable details from that of M. Thus only fragments of the M version are likely to have been preserved, and its original form may have differed considerably from Mark. Hence here, as so often, we cannot reconstruct the M version.

In view of the evidence submitted in this and the two preceding sections, it is, I think, clear that Matthew made use of a cycle of tradition of a distinctly Judaistic bias which to some extent ran parallel to the cycles preserved in Mark, in Q, and in L. If we suppose that the whole of the Parable and Discourse material peculiar to Matthew, plus the sections commented on above, came from a single source, it would be of much the same length as Q; and the proportion of this source paralleled in other sources would not be greater than the proportion of Q that is paralleled by Mark. For the view that the whole of this material came from a single source the amount of evidence

---

[1] The reading of Syr. S. is even more Judaistic: "I have not been sent save after the flock, which hath strayed from the House of Israel."

that can be produced is small. All that we can say is that, while only a few passages are Judaistic in the party sense, the whole of it is redolent of the soil of Judaea ; that it is the kind of collection we should expect to emanate from Jerusalem ; and, lastly, that it is hard to account for the fact that so very little tradition of any value has survived outside the Four Gospels, unless we suppose that the tradition of the Church of Jerusalem, which we should expect to be quite exceptionally rich, is incorporated in one or other of those Gospels. That Matthew made use of a source or sources which were in some respects parallel to Q and L, I regard as proved ; that this material, along with, at any rate, the bulk of his peculiar matter, was the cycle of tradition of the Church of Jerusalem, is in no sense proved ; but it seems more probable than any alternative suggestion.

The Great Discourses of Matthew

In past times more than one critic has put forward the hypothesis that five great discourses of Mt. v.-vii., x., xiii., xviii., xxiv.-xxv.[1] were taken over by him practically unaltered from an earlier source. One great objection to this theory is that the four lesser ones seem largely built up of material derived from Mark. But, of course, if there is reason to believe that M contained material closely parallel to parts of Mark, that objection is shaken. Accordingly I have felt it incumbent on me to reinvestigate this hypothesis. The result of such reinvestigation is distinctly unfavourable to its acceptance. But as the conclusion come to on this point has an important bearing on any reconstruction of Q we may attempt, I will briefly lay the facts before the reader.

The chief attraction of this hypothesis is that it would explain

[1] Some think that chap. xxiii. should be regarded as part of the same discourse as xxiv.-xxv., the saying, "Thy house is left unto thee desolate" (xxiii. 38), being interpreted of the Temple, whose destruction is the theme of chap. xxiv.

the occurrence five times, after each of these great discourses, of
the formula, " It came to pass when Jesus had finished these
sayings that. . . ." It has been pointed out that the number
five is a standard number in literary usage, both Jewish and early
Christian. There are five books of the Law and of the Psalms,
five *Megilloth*, and five original divisions in the Rabbinic work
the *Pirqe Aboth*; so also Papias wrote " Interpretations of the
Sayings of the Lord," divided into five books. It has been
suggested [1] that the above formula is the remains of a colophon,
comparable to " The prayers of David the Son of Jesse arc
ended " which appears to have once marked the conclusion of an
earlier collection included in the Psalms (cf. Ps. lxxii. 20). To
this I would reply that a colophon, though appropriate at the
end of a volume, would seem a trifle ridiculous at the end of
collections of sayings not longer than Mt. x., xiii., or xviii. Again,
the formula has really no resemblance to a colophon ; its
emphasis is not on the " Here endeth " but on " Here begin-
neth " ; it is a formula of *transition from discourse to narrative.*
Nor does its occurrence five times in Matthew constitute evidence
that it occurred just that number of times in his source ; for
" repetition of formulae " is one of the notable characteristics
of his Gospel.[2] It is just possible that Matthew may have
found the formula in Q, for a phrase rather like it occurs after
Luke's Sermon on the Plain in a context parallel to the occurrence of the formula in Matthew after the Sermon on the
Mount (Lk. vii. 1 = Mt. vii. 28). But, if it stood in Luke's copy
of Q, there also it would have done so as a formula of transition
from *discourse to narrative*; for in Luke it occurs between the
Great Sermon and the story of the Centurion's Servant. It
would seem likely, then, that Matthew found the formula in Q,
and thought it a convenient one to repeat whenever he had
occasion to mark a similar transition from a long discourse to
narrative.

But, whatever may be the origin of this formula, there are

---

[1] Hawkins' *Hor. Syn.*[2] p. 163 ff.   [2] Cf. *ibid.* p. 168.

insuperable difficulties in the way of supposing that these five great discourses stood in M in anything like their present form. I. The Sermon on the Mount we have already discussed. We have seen that perhaps two-thirds of it did stand in M as a continuous discourse, but that it was by no means the equivalent of Mt. v.-vii., for Matthew has inserted into it large sections of Q.[1] An examination of the other discourses yields even clearer results. II. The discourse part of Mt. x. opens, as we have seen above (p. 254 f.), by conflating a Mission Charge from the three sources, Mark, Q, and M (Mt. x. 5-16, 23). Verses 24-25 and 41, being peculiar to Matthew, are probably M. Everything in 26-39 has parallels in Luke in different contexts, but as these are not all equally close, we may leave it an open question how much of this section is from Q and how much from M. But there are three other passages which have close parallels in Mark (Mt. x. 17-20, 40, 42). In the first and third we may be pretty certain that Matthew is dependent on Mark. Thus the saying " Stand before governors . . . as a testimony unto them. And the gospel must *first* be preached to the Gentiles," in its Marcan form and context (Mk. xiii. 10), gives a reason for that delay of the Parousia which it is one of the main themes of the " Little Apocalypse " to account for, cf. " The End is not yet " (xiii. 7). In Mark's view the End is postponed in order to allow time for the conversion of the Gentiles, which this persecution and its resultant " testimony " will help forward. But Matthew's abbreviation of Mark " As a witness to them and to the Gentiles " (Mt. x. 18) misses this point. Again Matthew's " Whosoever shall give to drink *one of these little ones* a cup of cold water " (Mt. x. 42) is clearly secondary to Mk. ix. 41, " Whosoever shall give *you* a cup of cold water " ; for Matthew's addition " one of these little ones " is derived from *another* saying of Mark which occurs in the immediate context (Mk. ix.

---

[1] There are a few short sayings in it which have parallels in Mark, but whether these have been inserted by Matthew from Mark, or whether in these instances there were sayings in Q or M similar to Mark it is not possible to determine.

42), so that Matthew is (unconsciously) conflating two passages in Mark. On the other hand, the saying " He that receiveth you receiveth me, and he that receiveth me receiveth him that sent me " (Mt. x. 40, cf. Mk. ix. 37) is quite possibly a case where Mark and M overlap. At any rate it is worth while noticing that this saying occurs in four slightly different forms in the Gospels, and is one of those cases (cf. p. 185) where the incorporation by different authors of different versions of a widely circulated quasi-proverbial saying is quite as probable as dependence on a written source.

ὁ δεχόμενος ὑμᾶς ἐμὲ δέχεται· καὶ ὁ ἐμὲ δεχόμενος δέχεται τὸν ἀποστείλαντά με, Mt. x. 40.

ὃς ἐὰν ἓν τῶν τοιούτων παιδίων δέξηται ἐπὶ τῷ ὀνόματί μου, ἐμὲ δέχεται· καὶ ὃς ἐὰν ἐμὲ δέξηται, οὐκ ἐμὲ δέχεται, ἀλλὰ τὸν ἀποστείλαντά με, Mk. ix. 37.

ὁ ἀκούων ὑμῶν ἐμοῦ ἀκούει· καὶ ὁ ἀθετῶν ὑμᾶς ἐμὲ ἀθετεῖ· ὁ δὲ ἐμὲ ἀθετῶν ἀθετεῖ τὸν ἀποστείλαντά με, Lk. x. 16.

ἀμὴν ἀμὴν λέγω ὑμῖν, ὁ λαμβάνων ἐάν τινα πέμψω, ἐμὲ λαμβάνει· ὁ δὲ ἐμὲ λαμβάνων, λαμβάνει τὸν πέμψαντά με, Jn. xiii. 20.

III. Chap. xiii., the Parable chapter, is obviously an agglomeration *compiled by the editor of the Gospel.* The parable of the Sower, with the narrative introduction and the explanation appended, must be from Mk. iv. 1-20. The Mustard and Leaven stood together as a pair in Q. The other four parables are from M or some other source. Thus the evidence of compilation from at least three different sources is conclusive.

IV. The Apocalyptic chapter, Mt. xxiv., is simply Mk. xiii. ingeniously expanded with material from Q.[1] It is worth while for the student, if only on account of the light it throws on Matthew's editorial method of agglomeration, to look up the passages, and see how neatly this is done. Mt. xxiv. 26-28 and 37-39 are from the Q Apocalypse (Lk. xvii. 22-37). Two

This conclusion is not affected if we suppose, with some critics, that Matthew had before him, in addition to Mark's version, a copy of the Little Apocalypse with some slight textual variations. xxiv. 11-12, 30a are editorial

fragments of this, in an order the reverse of the original, are inserted in such a way that the warning against false Christs amplifies Mark's similar warning, while the Noah illustration reinforces Mark's words on the suddenness of the Parousia. This again is further emphasised (43-51) by a Q passage, which Luke (xii. 42-46) gives elsewhere.

V. Matthew xviii. consists very largely of material peculiar to the First Gospel. It contains two items, the Lost Sheep and the saying on Forgiveness (Mt. xviii. 12-14, 15, 21-22), which in Luke's version differ so much that it is improbable that both can be derived from Q. Both of these may be provisionally assigned to M. But the context in which Matthew places the discourse, as well as the structure of the first half of it, are determined for him by the context and structure of the discourse in Mark (Mk. ix. 33-50). Matthew habitually abbreviates Mark, and xviii. 8-9 is clearly a contracted version of Mk. ix. 43-48. The offending hand and foot have a verse each in Mark, but Matthew combines it into one sentence, " if thy hand or thy foot offend." Again, in Matthew the two words " eternal fire " (v. 8) and the addition " of fire " (v. 9) are a brief substitute for Mark's quotation from Is. lxvi. 24, " where the worm dieth not and the fire is not quenched." A comparison of Mk. ix. 42 with both Mt. xviii. 6-7 and Lk. xvii. 1-2 makes it fairly certain that both Mark and Q must have contained the saying about " offending little ones," but that Q contained it with the addition which appears in Lk. xvii. 1 = Mt. xviii. 7. But Luke, and therefore probably Q, connected the saying on Offences with that on Forgiveness. It does not, however, follow that the saying on Forgiveness, Mt. xviii., is derived from Q. Matthew knew Q as well as M ; he may well have put the *similar* saying on Forgiveness from M in the same discourse as that which contains the Q saying on Offences.

We conclude that an analysis of every one of the Great Discourses yields evidence that it is an agglomeration put together by the editor of the Gospel.

The Infancy Narratives

The phrase "Four Document Hypothesis," I need hardly say, is no more intended than was the older term, "Two Document Hypothesis," to rule out the view that the first two chapters in either Matthew or Luke may have been derived from written sources. That is a subject not strictly relevant to the present chapter ; nor is it one on which I feel I have anything of much value to contribute. Lest, however, I should seem to ignore altogether so interesting a section of the Gospels, I will take this opportunity briefly, and without going elaborately into reasons, to state my own conclusions.

For the first two chapters of Matthew I see no reason to postulate a written source. For them, as for the *narrative* additions of the First Gospel, the local tradition of the Church— probably Antioch—where that Gospel was written seems an adequate source. With Luke the case is otherwise. Professor C. C. Torrey [1] argues on linguistic grounds that Lk. i.-ii. must have been translated, not merely from a Semitic language, but from Hebrew as distinct from Aramaic.[2] The point is one on which I have not the linguistic qualifications needed to pronounce a judgement. But on one point I feel fairly clear. The Magnificat and the Benedictus were not originally written in Greek. No one who thought in Greek could have produced, either ἐποίησε κράτος ἐν βραχίονι αὐτοῦ i. 51, or ἤγειρε κέρας σωτηρίας ἡμῖν ἐν τῷ οἴκῳ Δαβίδ i. 69.

The question whether the narrative as a whole, as distinct from the hymns it embodies, was written in Hebrew is more difficult. Linguistically it has been pointed out that Lk. i. and ii. are replete both with words and expressions characteristic of Luke's style and also with reminiscences of the LXX. These two

[1] *The Translations made from the Original Aramaic Gospels*, The Macmillan Company, New York, 1912, pp. 290 ff.

[2] The point is worked out still further in the article, "The Ten Lucan Hymns of the Nativity in their Original Language," by R. A. Aytoun, *J.T.S.*, July 1917.

observations, however, to some extent cover the same ground ; one of the things by which Luke's style is distinguished from that of the other Gospels is his fondness for Septuagintal language. Luke knew his Greek Bible very well, and may have thought a kind of " biblical Greek " appropriate for a Gospel.

A similar consideration would apply, if we supposed that Luke derived these chapters from a Hebrew source. Whoever wrote them was familiar with, and had modelled his style on, the accounts of the birth and infancy of Samson and Samuel in the Old Testament. But, just as modern archaeologists translate Babylonian documents into a style modelled on that of the Authorised Version of the English Bible, so it would be natural to the translator of a Hebrew Protevangelium to adopt the familiar wording of the LXX. Again, Luke himself, if he had a Greek translation of the document in question, would deal with it in the same way as he does with his other sources ; he would slightly abbreviate and polish up the Greek, but in this case his very considerable literary instinct would lead him to do the re-writing in Septuagintal Greek.

Taken all in all, the probabilities point to a written source. A question, then, of special interest arises : Did the document as it came to Luke include any indication of a Virgin Birth ? In Matthew the virginity of Mary pervades the whole story ; for, as we have seen above (p. 87) the reading, " Joseph . . . begat Jesus," Mt. i. 16, in Syr. S. has small claim to be regarded as the true text. But in Luke extraordinarily little emphasis is laid on it. Indeed, if, with Syr. S. *a b c ff*², we read γυναικί instead of μεμνηστευμένη in ii. 5, the idea of virginity is only clearly brought out in i. 34, " And Mary said unto the angel, How shall this be, seeing that I know not a man ? " It is notable that the Old Latin MS. *b* omits this verse, substituting for it " And Mary said, Behold, the handmaid of the Lord ; be it unto me according to thy word." In the ordinary text these words occur later on, as the first half of verse 38 ; but *b* omits them in 38, and in this omission it has the support of *e*. This partial support of *b* by *e* *may* be accidental, but it makes it harder to brush aside the reading of *b* as an idiosyncrasy of the scribe of that MS.[1] And as the reading of *b* makes excellent sense, the possibility must be considered that it represents the text as Luke wrote it, the ordinary text being a piece of harmonistic editing intended to make it clear that Luke as well as Matthew attached importance to the Virginity. But the question whether the reading of *b* should be regarded as original is not one which anyone is likely to decide purely on grounds of textual criticism. Those who believe that Christ was born of a Virgin will think it improbable that Luke should have neglected to make this clear, and will scoff at the idea of rejecting the evidence of all the Greek MSS. and all the versions in favour of that of a single Latin MS. of the fifth century. On the other hand, those who regard the Virgin Birth as improbable, but are aware of the immense importance attached to the belief by the Fathers at least as early as Ignatius of Antioch, A.D. 115, will think it remarkable that a reading which ignores it should have survived till so late a date even in a single MS.

Conclusion

By making it possible to connect the sources of our Gospels with the great Churches, a Four Document Hypothesis explains a wider range of phenomena than the Two Document Hypothesis at present current.

(1) It gives a fuller meaning to the reference in the Preface of Luke to the " many " who had written previously and to the plan and purpose of his own work. Luke knew that several little Churches had their own collection, larger or smaller, of sayings of Christ and stories about Him ; but nobody could be sure where they came from or how far they could be trusted.

---

[1] By a curious coincidence this same MS. is the only one which preserves the reading in Jn. i. 13, quoted by various Western fathers (cf. p. 70 above), which makes John assert the Virgin Birth.

Luke therefore brushes them all aside. He will use only the materials collected by himself in Caesarea or those of which the authenticity is attested by their reception in the great Churches of Antioch and Rome. The " accuracy " of these materials he can guarantee to Theophilus by reason of his own connection, and the connection of the tradition of these Churches, with the names of those who had been from the beginning " eye-witnesses " like Peter or " ministers of the word " like Philip or like Mark.

(2) It also explains the curious mixture in Matthew of Judaistic with Universalistic sayings, and the concurrence of conspicuously ancient along with some highly doubtful matter. Luke's Gospel bears the impress of an individuality, Matthew has more of an official quality ; there is less literary freedom, more careful conflation of written sources. This, too, is explained if we think of Matthew as a studiedly conservative combination of the " gospels " of the three Churches whose traditions would seem to carry the greatest weight, Jerusalem, Antioch, and Rome, expanded with an account of the Infancy and some details of the Passion derived from oral tradition current in the author's own Church—most probably the Church of Antioch.

(3) The connection of these Gospels with the traditions of the great Churches explains the authoritative position which, as against all rivals, they so soon achieved, and thus their ultimate selection as the nucleus of the Canon. It was because the Synoptic Gospels included what each of the great Churches most valued in its own local traditions, and much more also, that the records of these local traditions were allowed to perish.

Thus a Four Document Hypothesis not only offers an extremely simple explanation of *all* the difficulties which the Two Document Hypothesis cannot satisfactorily meet, but also reflects far better the historical situation in the primitive Church. But there is one thing it does not do. It does not enable us to make a " tidy " scheme showing us *exactly* which sayings or incidents belong to M, which to L, and which to Q. If Matthew and Luke used four sources, every one of which to a certain extent overlapped with every other, the problem of disentangling them, beyond a certain point, is one which no amount of ingenuity can solve.

But so far as the historian is concerned, this is a matter of very little importance. Only if Q is regarded as the earliest and most authentic of all sources, is it of any special interest to know whether or not it included a particular saying. There was a time when a special authority was attributed to anything which occurred " in all Four Gospels " ; again, " the triple tradition " sounded impressive till it was pointed out that a statement of Mark did not become more certain because it happened to be copied by both Matthew and Luke ; it is now seen that even the " double tradition " has no special sanctity. So far as historical detail is concerned, Mark and Luke are more to be relied on than Matthew ; and where Mark and Luke conflict, Mark is more often to be followed. But as regards the teaching of Christ, much that occurs in a single Gospel is as likely to be genuine as what occurs in two or in all three.

But there is still a value in a " double attestation." If a saying occurs in Q we know for certain that it was written down at a date considerably earlier than that at which the existing Gospels of Matthew and Luke were composed—probably also earlier than Mark. Of a saying that is not in Q, all we can say is that this *may* have been the case. Whenever, however, we find a saying or parable occurring in two different versions —whether it be in Q and Mark, Q and M, Q and L, M and L, or M and Mark—we have evidence that the saying in question has come down by two different lines of tradition, which probably bifurcated at a date earlier even than that at which Q was written down.

Thus the final result of the critical analysis which has led to our formulating the Four Document Hypothesis is very materially to broaden the basis of evidence for the authentic teaching of Christ.

THE RECONSTRUCTION OF Q

SYNOPSIS

THE ORIGINAL ORDER OF Q

If attention is concentrated on the larger groups of sayings, to the exclusion of scattered fragments, there is considerable agreement between Matthew and Luke in the relative order in which they arrange material from Q.

The diversity in order results chiefly from the incorporation by Matthew into the three great discourses, v-vii., x., xxiii-xxv., of material disposed of by Luke in different parts of his " Central Section."

Generally speaking, Luke seems to preserve the original order of Q.

TEXTUAL ASSIMILATION AND THE LORD'S PRAYER

The Synoptic critic must be on the look-out for the possibility that even the best MSS. have been corrupted by assimilation from parallel passages in another gospel.

Evidence that the true text of Luke xi. 2 read, " Thy Holy Spirit come upon us and cleanse us," which has been replaced by the words " Thy Kingdom come " from Matthew. If so, the Lord's Prayer was not found in Q ; but two different versions of it were found by Matthew and Luke in M and L respectively.

FIVE BLOCKS OF Q

In Luke's " Central Section " Q and L material is arranged, roughly speaking, in alternate blocks. A study of some shorter passages, *within* the blocks derived from Q, which are *not* found in Matthew, suggests that these passages may have stood in Matthew's copy of Q, but that he preferred and substituted for them the parallel versions of the same item which he found in Mark or M.

Overlapping of Q and M

Five passages considered, in which Luke appears to have preserved the version of Q with but little modification, while Matthew has conflated Q with similar sayings from M.

Scattered Fragments

Though Luke normally gives Q material in its original context, he occasionally allows himself to depart from this usage in order to secure appropriateness of connection of subject matter.

The saying " Ye shall sit on thrones . . ." and some editorial formulae.

Omissions from Q

The probability that neither Matthew nor Luke made any considerable omissions from Q.

The Reconstructed Q

List of passages from Luke probably derived from Q.

The document so reconstructed is one whose purpose and character is intelligible, in spite of its not having contained an account of the Passion.

CHAPTER X

THE RECONSTRUCTION OF Q

THE ORIGINAL ORDER OF Q

THE critic who wishes to reconstruct Q can start off at a run. It having already been decided (p. 188) that Q contained an account of the Baptism and Temptation, we find at once five items which occur in the same order in both Matthew and Luke —John's Preaching, the Baptism, the Temptation, the Great Sermon, and the Centurion's Servant. Those portions of the Sermon on the Mount which, though not contained in the Sermon on the Plain, are yet from closeness of parallelism obviously derived from Q, must, we have already seen, have occurred in that document in some later context. In Luke the next Q item after the Centurion's Servant is John's Message, "Art thou he that should come?" This occurs somewhat later in Matthew; but the motive for postponement is obvious. Jesus refers John's disciples to the evidence afforded by certain miracles (Mt. xi. 5); Matthew postpones the incident until he has had time to give an example, taken from Mark, of each of the miracles mentioned. Luke solves the same problem in another way, by inserting (vii. 21) a statement, " In that hour healed he many, etc.," which he doubtless supposed was implied in the context. We infer that Luke's order is original. Both Matthew and Luke then concur again in the relative order in which they introduce " Foxes have holes," " The harvest is plenteous," and the Mission Charge (which Luke gives as the Address to the Seventy, but which Matthew conflates with

Mark's Charge to the Twelve); but it is noticeable that Matthew places the Charge much earlier than does Mark, a rearrangement of Mark which is probably due to the influence of the order in Q. Matthew also expands the discourse with Q material found elsewhere in Luke, as well as with material from other sources.

If we ignore the Q matter added to the Mission Charge, and also the section Lk. xi. 9-13, which Matthew has given already in the Sermon on the Mount, the coincidence in order is interrupted by the occurrence in Luke of two verses (Lk. x. 23-24) which Matthew postpones to a later context. But of the next five items, Woes to the Cities, " I thank thee, Father," Beelzebub Controversy, Parable of Unclean Spirit, and Sign of Jonah, the relative order (except that the last two are transposed) is the same in both Gospels. The next item in both is the pair of parables, the Mustard Seed and Leaven. This brings us into Mt. xiii. Now we have observed (p. 161) that up to this point Matthew seems to have rearranged the materials he took from Mark with the greatest freedom; but that from chap. xiv. onward he never departs from Mark's order. We seem to have lighted on the explanation. Matthew's rearrangement of Mark has been, at any rate partly,[1] determined by the necessity of combining Mark with Q. Thus the order of Q has evidently suggested to him to anticipate the place of the Mission Charge in Mark; and the late occurrence of the Mustard Seed and Leaven in Q has led him to postpone Mark's collection of parables of the Kingdom, among which he desired to include this pair from Q and others from M.

Most of the remaining Q material Matthew disposes of by working it into one of his great blocks of discourse, the Sermon on the Mount, v.-vii., the Mission Charge, x., or the Denunciation of Judgement, xxiii.-xxv. The problem, then, of the original

---

[1] The endeavour to group together representative miracles seems to have been another motive for rearrangement. Cf. W. C. Allen, *Commentary on Matthew*, p. xiv ff.

order of Q resolves itself into the question, Are the additions
in Matthew's versions of the Great Sermon and Mission Charge,
the half-dozen or so scattered sayings and the Q matter in
Mt. xxiii.-xxv., in a more original context in Luke or in
Matthew ?   If, however, we consider (1) Matthew's proved habit
of piling up discourses compacted from Mark, Q and M ; (2) the
fact that sayings like " Blessed are your eyes," Mt. xiii. 16-17,
concerning Offences, Mt. xviii. 7—being embedded in extracts
from Mark—cannot possibly be in their original context as they
occur in Matthew, the presumption is plainly in favour of the
view that *Luke's order is the more original.*

This conclusion is important for the light it throws on the
problem of the original *extent* of Q, for this, it will appear, is
more closely bound up than one would suppose with the
question of the original *order.*   Luke in his use of Mark and
Proto-Luke differs from Matthew in three ways.   (1) He *as a
rule* avoids conflating his sources.   (2) He usually gives them
in approximately their original order.   (3) He has a tendency
to follow one source at a time.   It looks as if the person who
combined Q and L so as to form Proto-Luke, whether that
person was (as I believe) Luke himself or some one else, adhered
to the same methods.

TEXTUAL ASSIMILATION AND THE LORD'S PRAYER

At this point Textual Criticism must be summoned to the
rescue of the puzzled Synoptic critic.   The evidence accumulated
in Chap. XI. shows that assimilation between the texts of the
Gospels in parallel passages has operated along every line of
textual transmission, and that, though B has suffered less in
this way than any other MS., it has not entirely escaped.   That
chapter being a study of minor agreements of Matthew and Luke
against Mark, the passages examined are necessarily ones in
which three Gospels were involved ; but obviously assimilation
would not be less likely to operate in passages contained only in

Matthew and Luke. If an example is required of the avoidance
by B of an assimilation found elsewhere, I would instance the
omission by B Syr. S. of the words " bread, will he give him a
stone, or," Lk. xi. 11—an interpolation from the parallel Mt. vii. 9.
As an example of an assimilation which has infected B א but not
the mass of MSS. we may quote τασσόμενος, Mt. viii. 9—an
intrusion from Lk. vii. 8.[1]

But there are two cases where assimilation has affected
B א etc. which are of real importance in the attempt to reconstruct Q. The first is the version of the Voice from Heaven at
the Baptism, " this day have I begotten thee," Lk. iii. 22, which
has already been fully discussed, pp. 143, 188. All I need do
is to recall the fact that the acceptance of the Western reading
(in preference to the reading of B א, which has been assimilated
to the other Gospels) proved that Luke derived his account
of the Baptism, not from Mark, but from Q. The second occurs
in the Lord's Prayer. The liturgical use of the Lord's Prayer in
the form in which it is given by Matthew would make assimilation of the shorter form in Luke to that of Matthew more
inevitable than in any other passage in the Gospels. And
the great MSS. and early versions show it at work in a very
varied way.

In A D and the T.R. the assimilation of Lk. xi. 2 ff. to
Mt. vi. 9 ff. is almost complete. Syr. C. has effected it, but for
the clause " Thy will be done, etc." which it omits. א curiously
enough inserts this clause, but leaves out " Deliver us from
evil " which Syr. C. contains ; א also joins B L Syr. S. etc. in
omitting " our, which art in heaven " after " Father " in the
opening address. B L Syr. S., and apparently the ancestor of
fam. Θ, agree in all the omissions.

Here we find that B, as usual, has been less affected by assimilation than most other MSS. ; but here also there is evidence

[1] " After these things," Mt. viii. 5, Syr. S. k, instead of " He having entered
into Capernaum " (= Lk. vii. 1), and the omission by the same authorities of
καὶ πτωχοὶ εὐαγγελίζονται, Mt. xi. 5 (= Lk. vii. 22), are probably original readings which have been altered through assimilation in all other MSS.

that B has not entirely escaped. For **700, 162**, instead of " Thy kingdom come," read " Thy holy spirit come upon us and cleanse us " (ἐλθέτω τὸ πνεῦμα . . . ἐφ' ἡμᾶς). And D has ἐφ' ἡμᾶς ἐλθέτω σου ἡ βασιλεία, where, as Rendel Harris pointed out, ἐφ' ἡμᾶς is only explicable as a remainder of the other reading which a corrector of some ancestor of D omitted to strike out. And this reading was in the text of Luke used by Gregory of Nyssa in Cappadocia in 395 ; he says so plainly twice, and moreover gives no hint that he had even heard of any other reading. It is also quoted by Maximus of Turin, *c.* 450. So the reading was current both in the East and in the West to quite a late period. But it also stood in the text of Marcion (A.D. 140), and from Tertullian's comment on this it is not at all clear that his own text was in this respect different from Marcion's. Now in view of the immense pressure of the tendency to assimilate the two versions of this specially familiar prayer, and of the improbability that various orthodox Fathers should have adopted (without know- ing it) the text of Marcion, the probability is high that the reading of **700, 162**, which makes the Gospels differ most, is what Luke wrote. Matthew's version is here more original.

Now, even if we accept the reading of B, the difference between the two versions of the Lord's Prayer, Lk. xi. 1-4 and Mt. vi. 9-13, is so great as to put a considerable strain on the theory that they were both derived from the same written source. But, if we accept the reading of **700** and its supporters, that theory becomes quite impossible.[1] We next notice that in neither Matthew nor Luke are the sayings in the immediate context derived from Q ; the Lord's Prayer in Matthew is in the middle of a block of M, in Luke in the middle of a section of L, material. The natural inference is that the respective versions belong to these two sources. I am aware that to some who have fallen into the habit of regarding Q as the sole citadel of authenticity it will be some-

---

[1] The rare word ἐπιούσιος remains as a remarkable point of contact between the two versions. I think it not impossible that its presence in Luke is due to an assimilation to Matthew which has infected all our authorities.

thing of a shock to realise that the document did not include the Lord's Prayer. I would suggest, however, that the real effect of the discovery is to enhance our conception of the value of the special sources of Matthew and Luke.

FIVE BLOCKS OF Q

We now turn to the text of Luke and discover that the assignment of the Lord's Prayer to L, instead of to Q, makes x. 25-xi. 8 a single block of L. Then we perceive that in Luke's " Central Section " the Q and the L material tends to sort itself out into alternate blocks—the five blocks ix. 57-x. 24, xi. 9-xii. 12, xii. 22-xii. 59, xiii. 18-xiii. 35, and xvii. 22-37, being in the main derived from Q, while the intervening blocks are mainly L. There are never more than four, and rarely more than two, consecutive verses in any of the Q sections which do not also occur in Matthew. We may conjecture, then, that they are really solid blocks of Q, from which Matthew, in the course of rearranging to fit into his great discourses, has omitted a few odd verses. This gives us a working hypothesis with which to start our quest.

The provisional hypothesis that the five passages just indicated are solid blocks of Q receives a good deal of confirmation from a closer scrutiny of a number of the short passages within these blocks, which Matthew omits, but for which he *substitutes* something derived either from Mark or M which might well be regarded as an equivalent. These are as follows :

(*a*) Lk. x. 16 ὁ ἀκούων ὑμῶν . . . For this Mt. x. 40 substitutes ὁ δεχόμενος ὑμᾶς . . . from Mk. ix. 37.

(*b*) Lk. xi. 27-28. An unknown woman cries, " Blessed is the womb that bare thee . . ." Our Lord replies, " Nay, blessed are they that hear the word of God . . ." In Luke this follows immediately after the parable of the Unclean Spirit. Matthew immediately after this same parable (Mt. xii. 46-50) inserts our Lord's reply to the announcement, " Thy mother and brethren

without seek thee," from Mk. iii. 31, a different incident but one of
which the moral is the same, " whoso will do the will of my Father
. . . the same is my brother and sister and mother." As there is
no connection of thought between this and the preceding parable,
the position of Matt. xii. 46-50 can only be due to a deliberate
substitution of the Marcan for the Q version of the saying as to
what constitutes true relationship to Christ.

(c) Lk. xi. 37-38, on not washing before meat. Matthew
omits this, but in xv. 2 ff. has a much longer discussion of this
point derived from Mk. vii. 1 ff. which Luke omits.

(d) The same thing probably applies to the " Leaven of the
Pharisees" (Lk. xii. 1b). The phrase stood both in Q and Mark.
Matthew omits it where it occurs in Q, because he has it in a more
meaningful context, xvi. 6, from Mk. viii. 15.[1]

(e) Lk. xii. 35-38, " loins girded, lights burning." Matthew
leaves this out; but immediately after the (Q) paragraph which
follows in Luke (Lk. xii. 39-46 = Mt. xxiv. 43-51) he inserts
the parable of the Wise and Foolish Virgins, which contains the
same point as Lk. xii. 35-38, but considerably amplified. Accordingly " substitution " rather than " omission " again seems the
proper description of his procedure.

(f) Lk. xiii. 25-27. The main ideas, and even the more striking
phrases " open," " I know you not," " depart from me," occur
in the Apocalyptic parables of Matthew ; cf. Mt. xxv. 11-12, 41.

(g) Lk. xiii. 30, " the last shall be first." There are two
reasons—in addition to the fact that it occurs in Luke in
connection with Q sayings—for referring this saying to Q. Mark
x. 31, followed by Matthew in the same context, Mt. xix. 30, has
the saying, but in the reverse order, " the first shall be last."
But Matthew repeats the saying in another context, xx. 16, but
this time he gives the words *in the same order as Luke.* This then
will be the Q order. Luke has it in a Q context (xiii. 30) ; but

[1] The Marcan equivalent of both (c) and (d) occur in Luke's " great omission " of Mark which I have argued (p. 175 ff.) did not stand in the copy of
Mark which Luke used.

note that, when he is copying the context in which it occurs in Mark (Lk. xviii. 30), he leaves out just this one sentence—evidently because he has already recorded the saying in its Q form.

(h) Lk. xii. 11-12.	Mk. xiii. 11.	Mt. x. 19-20.
And when they bring you before the synagogues, and the rulers, and the authorities, be not anxious how or what ye shall answer, or what ye shall say: for the Holy Spirit shall teach you in that very hour what ye ought to say.	And when they lead you to judgement, and deliver you up, be not anxious beforehand what ye shall speak: but whatsoever shall be given you in that hour, that speak ye: for it is not ye that speak, but the Holy Ghost.	But when they deliver you up, be not anxious how or what ye shall speak: for it shall be given you in that hour what ye shall speak. For it is not ye that speak, but the Spirit of your Father that speaketh in you.

We note Mark and Luke are furthest apart. Matthew is almost verbally identical with Mark.[1] The only verbal agreement of Matthew and Luke against Mark is "how or what"—probably a textual assimilation, since $\pi\hat{\omega}\varsigma$ $\mathring{\eta}$ is omitted in Matthew by *a b k* Syr. S. Cypr. and $\mathring{\eta}$ $\tau\acute{\iota}$ in Luke by D **1 157** Old Lat. Syr. S. and C. It is, however, noticeable that in both Matthew and Luke the saying occurs in the same discourse as, though separated by a few verses from, " there is nothing hidden which shall not be revealed," etc. (Mt. x. 26 ff. = Lk. xii. 2 ff.). As there is no obvious connection of thought to suggest bringing the two together, the view that Lk. xii. 11-12 stood in Q and formed part of the block of Q material, xii. 2-10, would explain the collocation in both Gospels. The saying will then be one of those which in a slightly different form occurred in both Mark and Q.

The reader who has followed the above with a Synopsis and a

---

[1] In Lk. xxi. 14-15, which is the actual parallel to Mk. xiii. 11, there is a kind of paraphrase, " Settle it therefore in your own hearts, not to meditate beforehand how to answer: for I will give you a mouth and wisdom, which all your adversaries shall not be able to withstand or to gainsay." I suggest that Luke, recollecting that he had already copied from Proto-Luke a sentence practically identical with that in Mk. xiii. 11, paraphrased Mark's wording here to avoid tautologous repetition. In the parallel context Mt. omits Mk. xiii. 11.

marked copy of the Gospels will see that the facts noted all tend
to justify our provisional assignment to Q of the five specified
blocks.   I proceed to show that, if we invoke the principle of
parallel versions worked out in the previous chapters, we discover
phenomena which not only add further confirmation to the above
hypothesis, but also help to identify as Q certain passages of
Luke which are outside these blocks.

OVERLAPPING OF Q AND M

There are certain cases where the parallels between Matthew
and Luke are not close enough to make derivation from the same
written source probable, but where the hypothesis which most
easily explains the phenomena is that the saying stood in both
Q and M—Luke reproducing the version of Q, Matthew conflating Q and M.

(a) The saying about Forgiveness is perhaps the clearest
example.   In Lk. xvii. 1-4 this saying follows immediately after
one about Offences, a version of which seems to have stood in both
Q and Mark.[1]   In Mt. xviii. 15 ff. also the saying about Forgiveness follows that about Offences in the same discourse—only with
half-a-dozen verses (from Mark and M) intervening.   Seeing there
is no very obvious connection of thought between the two topics,
the connection (Offences—Forgiveness) must have been made
in the common source Q.   How, then, are we to explain the fact
that, while the Offences saying is virtually identical in Matthew
and Luke, that on Forgiveness appears in versions exceptionally
diverse ?   I suggest that M also contained a version of the latter
saying, which Matthew on the whole prefers ; and this is not pure
conjecture, for in the fragments of the Gospel according to the
Hebrews we have evidence that this saying was in circulation in
more than one version.   It will be instructive to set the three
versions side by side.

[1] Mk. ix. 42 has only one member of the double antithetical saying which
occurs Lk. xvii. 1-2, Mt. xviii. 6-7.

Mt. xviii. 15-16, 21-22.	Lk. xvii. 3-4.	Ev. Heb. (quoted by Jerome).
And if thy brother sin against thee, go, shew him his fault between thee and him alone : if he hear thee, thou hast gained thy brother. But if he hear thee not, take with thee one or two more, that at the mouth of two witnesses . . . Then came Peter, and said to him, Lord, how oft shall my brother sin against me, and I forgive him ? until seven times ? Jesus saith unto him, I say not unto thee, Until seven times ; but, Until seventy times seven.	Take heed to yourselves : if thy brother sin, rebuke him ; and if he repent, forgive him. And if he sin against thee seven times in the day, and seven times turn again to thee, saying, I repent ; thou shalt forgive him.	If thy brother shall have sinned in word and given thee satisfaction, seven times in a day receive him. His disciple Simon said unto him, Seven times in a day ? The Lord answered and said unto him, Yea, I say unto thee until seventy times seven ; for even in the prophets after they had been anointed by the Holy Spirit, there was found *sermo peccati* (probably an Aramaism = " matter of sin," not merely = " sinful speech ").

(*b*) The Parable of the Pounds = Talents. A glance at a Synopsis shows that in the latter part of this parable the verbal agreements between the two versions are such as to favour, though not actually to compel, the assumption of a common written source. But the divergences between the versions in the first half are so great as to make this assumption highly improbable. Here again the Gospel according to the Hebrews may help us. Eusebius tells us that the Parable of the Talents stood in this Gospel but " told of three servants, one who devoured his Lord's substance with harlots and flute girls, one who gained profit manifold, and one who hid his talent ; and then how one was accepted, one merely blamed, and one shut up in prison." Is it not possible that M had a version something like this and that Matthew has conflated Q and M, following M more closely at the beginning and Q at the end ? Luke, then, preserves approximately the Q form. Only the very daring, nowadays, venture on

speculations in regard to the Gospel according to the Hebrews.[1]
Nevertheless, I would *in parenthesi* throw out the suggestion that
the same Jerusalem tradition which we have postulated as the
source M used by Matthew was incorporated in, or in some
other way affected the text of, that lost Gospel. At any rate
we have here evidence, outside the Synoptic Gospels, for the
contention of the previous chapter that there were in circulation
divergent versions of exactly those of our Lord's sayings in which
the versions in Matthew and Luke differ too widely to be referred
to a common written source.

(c) The two versions of the saying about " the strait gate,"
Lk. xiii. 23-24, cf. Mt. vii. 13-14, cannot reasonably be referred
to a common source.

Lk. xiii. 23-24.	Mt. vii. 13-14.
And one said unto him, Lord, are they few that be saved ? And he said unto them, Strive to enter in by the narrow door : for many, I say unto you, shall seek to enter in, and shall not be able.	Enter ye in by the narrow gate : for wide [is the gate], and broad is the way, that leadeth to destruction, and many there be that enter in thereby. For narrow [is the gate], and straitened the way, that leadeth unto life, and few there be that find it.

But Luke's version comes in the middle of a section of which the
beginning (Mustard Seed and Leaven), xiii. 18-21, the middle,
xiii. 28-29, and the end, xiii. 34-35 (" Jerusalem, Jerusalem "),
are certainly Q, and of which, as we shall see later, much of
the rest is probably Q ; the probability, then, is that Luke here
also follows Q.   But the words ἡ πύλη (" *is* the gate ")
are omitted in Matthew on their second (א Old Lat.) and
third (544 Old Lat.) occurrence.   If this reading is original,
Q had the Lucan saying about " the narrow *gate*," M had one
quite different—the antithesis between the " broad and the

---

[1] The theory that the Gospel written in Chaldee characters here quoted
by Eusebius was not the same as that quoted by Jerome seems to me un-
proved ; but in any case the evidence for the existence of divergent traditions
of our Lord's sayings is in no way impaired.

narrow *ways*." (The contrast of the Two Ways occurs in the
Didache and elsewhere.) Matthew has conflated Q and M.[1]

(*d*) A fourth example of the same kind may be Lk. xii.
32-34, " Fear not, little flock . . ." cf. Mt. vi. 19-21, " Lay not
up for yourselves treasures on earth. . . ." In the first two
verses the differences between Matthew and Luke are considerable, but the third verse in each is practically identical,
" Where your treasure is there will your heart be also." Matthew
has disconnected this verse from the discourse, " Be not anxious "
(Mt. vi. 25-34), of which it forms the concluding sentence in Luke.
Here the combination of variation in order with diversity of
wording suggests that Matthew is conflating Q and M—in which
case Luke may be presumed to follow Q.

(*e*) Mk. xi. 22-23.	Mt. xvii. 19-20.	Lk. xvii. 5-6.
And Jesus answering saith unto them, Have faith in God. Verily I say unto you, Whosoever shall say unto this mountain, Be thou taken up and cast into the sea ; and shall not doubt in his heart, but shall believe that what he saith cometh to pass ; he shall have it.	Then came the disciples to Jesus apart, and said, Why could not we cast it out ? And he saith unto them, Because of your little faith : for verily I say unto you, If ye have faith as a grain of mustard seed, ye shall say unto this mountain, Remove hence to yonder place ; and it shall remove ; and nothing shall be impossible unto you.	And the apostles said unto the Lord, Increase our faith. And the Lord said, If ye have faith as a grain of mustard seed, ye would say unto this sycamine tree, Be thou rooted up, and be thou planted in the sea ; and it would have obeyed you.

Here Matthew agrees with Mark in speaking of the " mountain,"
with Luke in " the grain of mustard seed." The most natural
conclusion would be that Luke gives the saying as it stood in Q,
while Matthew, as usual where Mark and Q overlap, conflates
the two. In further confirmation of this we note that in Luke
the saying occurs immediately after xvii. 1-4, which we decided

[1] The relevance of the textual variants was pointed out to me by
Prof. Dodd.

above was from Q ; also that Matthew inserts it in a context, derived indeed from Mark, but occurring much earlier (Mk. ix. 28), which is the first occasion appropriate for the insertion, from another source, of a saying on faith.

SCATTERED FRAGMENTS

The observation that Luke in general seems to follow one source at a time and to reproduce it in its original order has proved a valuable clue. But a generalisation of this kind must not be made a fetish. There is always an incalculable element in the working of the human mind ; and there is no reason to suppose that in following one source at a time Luke was adhering to a consciously formulated principle. It was merely that he refrained from rearranging or conflating sources where there was no special reason for doing so. But to any rule of average human behaviour there are always some exceptions ; and there are several sayings in Luke which there is good reason to assign to Q, although they are not found embedded in a mass of other material from that source.

(a) " No man can serve two masters," Lk. xvi. 13. This is very close in wording to Mt. vi. 24, and is therefore to be referred to Q ; but its context in Luke, immediately following the parable of the Unjust Steward, is obviously suggested by the accidental occurrence of the rare word Mammon both in this saying of Q and in the parable.

(b) The saying " Whoso exalteth himself shall be humbled . . ." occurs twice in Luke, xiv. 11, xviii. 14. As it occurs in Mt. xxiii. 12, it probably stood in Q ; although, for a short proverbial saying of this kind, there is really no need to postulate a written source at all.

(c) The pair of sayings, Lk. xiv. 26-27, " If any one cometh unto me and hateth not his father, etc." and " Whoso beareth not his cross," occur together and in the same order in Mt. x. 37-38. Hence, though the wording differs to a certain extent, they are probably to be referred to Q. Here again their present position in Luke seems to be due to their eminent fitness as an introduction to two parables—the Tower Builder and the King making War——which emphasise the same idea of counting the cost. I would remark that, if they are Q, Luke's harsh-sounding " hateth his father " obviously preserves the wording of the original more closely than Matthew, "He that loveth father, etc., more than me." The saying about carrying the cross occurs also in Mark (viii. 34) in a slightly different version—which is copied by both Matthew and Luke in the same context (Mt. xvi. 24, Lk. ix. 23)—in spite of the fact that they give another (? from Q) version elsewhere, Mt. x. 38 = Lk. xiv. 27.[1]

(d) The saying about Salt, Lk. xiv. 34-35, shows several agreements between Luke's version and that in Mt. v. 13 against the version of Mk. ix. 50, and also Matthew and Luke agree in omitting it in the context parallel to Mark's, which looks as if both had already extracted it from Q. It is separated in Luke from the saying about carrying the cross by the Tower Builder and its twin parable. But if, as it stood in Q, it followed immediately after Lk. xiv. 27, its meaning would be quite clear. In that connection, " Salt is good, but if the salt have lost its savour . . ." would naturally mean, " Disciples are good, but if they have lost the power to carry the cross they cease to be a leaven to the lump of humanity." It would seem to follow that the words " Salt is good," καλὸν τὸ ἅλα, stood in Q as well as in Mark; but that Matthew in the Sermon on the Mount has altered them to " Ye are the salt of the earth " in order to make the interpretation quite clear, the wording of the alteration being suggested to him by that of the M saying " Ye are the light . . ." to which he has prefixed it.

(e) The three sayings, Lk. xvi. 16-18, are perhaps from Q. Q, so far as one can make out, was a collection of the " Wise Sayings " of Christ, comparable to a book like Proverbs or the *Pirqe Aboth*, with very little attempt at arrangement. And what we have in the passage of Luke is three separate aphorisms (the Law and the Prophets until John, the passing of the Law, Divorce), the only connection between which is that they are

[1] The passages are printed in parallel columns in Hawkins, *Hor. Syn.*[2] p. 86.

epigrammatic rulings on disputed points connected with the Law. In Matthew they appear in a somewhat modified form and in three quite different contexts, worked into connected discourses. The Lucan version looks *on the whole* [1] more primitive ; but the modifications of it in Matthew do not go beyond what an editor, who, like Matthew, evidently felt that he was also to some extent an interpreter, might consider legitimate.

(*f*) Where Matthew has fitted an isolated saying into a new context—whether in Mark or in a larger block of Q—some modification of its wording might be required to make it harmonise with its new context.   In such cases, therefore, we must recognise that a greater divergence than elsewhere between the parallels in Matthew and Luke is compatible with derivation from Q.   In the light of this reflection we may consider certain sayings found in Mt. xxiv. 25-28, 37-41, ingeniously fitted into the " Little Apocalypse " of Mk. xiii. in such a way as to amplify certain ideas taken over from Mark.   All these sayings occur in the discourse Lk. xvii. 22-37, but somewhat differently worded.   Can we, in spite of the considerable verbal differences, hold that the whole section, Lk. xvii. 22-37, which has been described as " the Apocalypse of Q " has been legitimately so named ?   I think so. For if Q had contained an Apocalypse, Matthew would certainly have conflated it with the Apocalypse of Mark.   If it stood in Q at all, Lk. xvii. 22-37 must have stood at, or very near, the end. That is an additional reason for supposing the passage stood in Q; for, in view of the absorbing interest of the early Church in the subject of the Parousia, we should naturally expect to discover a quantity of Apocalyptic matter at the end of any primitive " Gospel."   For that same reason I am inclined to think that Q not only contained, but actually ended with, the Parable of the Pounds, the moral of which—" Occupy till I come "—would be so extraordinarily appropriate to the hopes and circumstances of the time.   This presumption is distinctly strengthened by the

---

[1] Not always, *e.g.* Lk. xvi. 16 ἡ βασιλεία τοῦ θεοῦ εὐαγγελίζεται is a Lucan phrase—an attempt to explain an extremely obscure saying.

fact that the *Didache*, a first-century manual of Christian instruction, ends with an Apocalyptic passage.

There remains to be considered one other saying which occurs
in both Matthew and Luke.

Mt. xix. 28.	Lk. xxii. 29-30.
And Jesus said unto them, Verily I say unto you, that ye which have followed me, in the regeneration when the Son of man shall sit on the throne of his glory, *ye* also *shall sit upon* twelve *thrones, judging the twelve tribes of Israel.*	And I appoint unto you a kingdom, even as my Father appointed unto me, that ye may eat and drink at my table in my kingdom; *and ye shall sit on thrones judging the twelve tribes of Israel.*

Observe that, apart from the words in italics, there are no
points of contact between these parallels. No doubt the words
found in both are the most striking, but to assume that these
alone stood in Q and that all the rest in both Matthew and Luke
is " editorial " is a *reductio ad absurdum* of the theory of a written
source, only possible under the distorting influence of an *a priori*
Two Document Hypothesis. Rather, this is a good example
of the currency of widely different versions of the same saying;
and since neither in Matthew nor Luke is it found in a Q
context, we naturally assign the two versions to M and to L.

In the above survey no notice has been taken of short
passages, evidently inserted in order to break the monotony of
discourses following one another with no obvious connection.
Phrases like " He said to the disciples," " He said to the multitude," are evidently merely inferences from the context of the
sayings, made explicit in words to improve the literary form.
Probably the same thing applies to some longer phrases like
Lk. xiv. 25, "There were journeying with him great crowds; and
he turned and said unto them," or the triple " He said to the
guests," " He said to the host," " One sitting at meat said to him,"
Lk. xiv. 7, 12, 15. The occurrence of stylistic improvements of this
kind has prejudiced many critics against Luke's version of Q as
compared with that of Matthew. But these are obvious and
superficial adornments easily separable from the actual saying.

And when one studies the actual Logia of Christ, the advantage in respect of accuracy of preservation of the original form is, I believe, more often with Luke. " Blessed are ye poor, ye that hunger " is surely more original than " poor in spirit " or " hunger after righteousness " ; " hateth father and mother " is more original than " loveth father and mother more than me."

OMISSIONS FROM Q

The question must now be raised, Have any sections of Q which have been completely ignored by Matthew been preserved in Luke and *vice versa* ? To this I am inclined to answer, Very few. Before I had disentangled myself from the Two Document Hypothesis I used to suppose that the more Judaistic sayings in Matthew were probably in Q, but omitted by Luke. But reasons have been given above for assigning these to M. Of his other source, Mark, Matthew omits very little, so the probability is that he would omit very little of Q, unless to substitute for what was omitted something which he regarded as a superior version of the same thing. Nevertheless, as he seems completely to omit a few items in Mark which Luke retains, the same thing has probably happened in regard to Q. To identify these, we return to the examination of those passages in Luke's great blocks of Q which have no sort of equivalent in Matthew. But we cannot assume that all of them stood in Q. We have seen above that Lk. xiv. 26-27 probably stood in Q followed immediately by xiv. 34-35. If so, then we have evidence that Luke (or the compiler of Proto-Luke) sometimes allowed himself to interpolate into a Q section highly appropriate matter (*e.g.* xiv. 28-33) from L. That shows that, on occasion, he would break away from his general rule of following one source at a time. Accordingly we cannot be sure that Lk. ix. 61-62, " No man putting his hand to the plough," and x. 18-20, "I saw Satan fall," xii. 47-50, xii. 54-57, have not similarly been interpolated from L into what looked like highly appropriate contexts of Q. In the *Oxford Studies* I endeavoured

U

to find reasons why, even if they should be in Q, Matthew should
have omitted them. I now feel less confidence in their validity.
To feel confidently that any at all notable saying in Q was
omitted by Matthew one must see clearly that the saying would
lend itself to an interpretation by the faithful which he definitely
disliked. Two such passages there are—Lk. ix. 51-56, the
Samaritan village, and xvii. 20-21, "The Kingdom of God cometh
not with observation . . . the Kingdom of God is within you."
Both of these stand at the head of a block of Q material, and
both are passages which Matthew would have had good reason to
omit. The one involves a rebuke to the Apostles, and Matthew
elsewhere tends to tone down or omit such.[1] The other suggested
a view of the Kingdom which Matthew, who more than any other
evangelist emphasises the objective catastrophic side of the
Apocalyptic hope, believed to be incorrect.

My view on the question of whether Luke omitted any substantial amount of Q has been modified by three new considerations. (a) The evidence submitted previously (cf. p. 175 ff.) that
the long section Mk. vi. 48-viii. 26 did not stand in the copy of
Mark used by Luke. If one supposed that Luke was capable of
leaving out over 70 continuous verses in one source, he would be
capable of making drastic excision in another. Apart, however,
from this one passage, Luke's omissions—as distinct from substitution of parallel versions—of material found in Mark are on
a very small scale. (b) If I am right in supposing that Q and L
were combined into one document by Luke himself before he
came across Mark, he would not at that earlier date be em-
barrassed by the problem of getting all his material into a
roll of manageable size, as probably was the case at the later
stage. Hence he had a motive for omission at this later stage,
when he expanded Proto-Luke with extracts from Mark (which,
moreover, he seems to have regarded as a source of subordinate
authority) which would have been inoperative at the time when
he combined Q and L. (c) If there is a shadow of ground for the

[1] Hawkins, *Hor. Syn.*[2] p. 121.

guess that Q was the old Gospel of the pro-Gentile church of
Antioch, it would not have contained Judaistic passages which
Luke would have wanted to excise.[1] Accordingly the probability is high that the passages of Luke that we can identify
as Q represent that document, not only approximately in its
original order, but very nearly in its original extent. And seeing
that Matthew's method of rearranging sources led necessarily
to considerable verbal modification, it is probable that, allowance
being made for a slight polishing of the Greek, the form in which
the sayings appear in Luke is also on the whole more original.

THE RECONSTRUCTED Q

For the convenience of the reader I append a list of the passages I should assign to Q. Brackets signify considerable doubt :
Lk. iii. 2a-9, (10-14), 16-17, 21-22 ; iv. 1-16a ; vi. 20-vii. 10 ;
vii. 18-35 ; ix. (51-56), 57-60, (61-62) ; x. 2-16, (17-20), 21-24 ;
xi. 9-52 ; xii. 1b-12, 22-59 ; xiii. 18-35; xiv. 11, 26-27, 34-35 ;
xvi. 13, 16-18 ; xvii. 1-6, 20-37 ; xix. 11-27. Unbracketed
verses = 272.

As thus reconstructed, Q is a document the purpose and
character of which are perfectly intelligible. It is comparable
to an Old Testament prophetic book like Jeremiah, consisting
principally of discourse, but with an occasional narrative to explain some piece of teaching. The Baptism and Temptation are
described because the author regarded these as virtually the "call"
to the Messianic office. The author would regard them, like the
"call" of the Prophet so often given in the Old Testament, as of
great apologetic value as evidence of the Divine authorisation of
our Lord's mission. The relatively large amount of space given to
John the Baptist, and the emphasis on his relations with our Lord,
suggest that Q was composed at a time and place where the

[1] This argument might appear to prove too much, for the passages do
occur in the probably Antiochene Gospel of Matthew. But their presence in
Matthew may well be due to their occurrence in a document already too
ancient to be ignored. Matthew prefers to counteract, e.g. the prohibition to
preach to Gentiles and Samaritans, x. 5, is revoked by the command to preach
to all nations, xxviii. 19.

prestige of John was very considerable. There is here a contrast between Mark and Q.[1] In Q John's testimony to Christ is appealed to, because among those for whom it was written " all held John to be a prophet." In Mark the apologetic motive for mentioning John is that he fulfilled the prophecy of the fore-runner ; that is to say, it is not John's personal prestige which is appealed to, but the fact that his coming at all was part of that " programme," so to speak, of events, anciently foretold and in the career of our Lord recently fulfilled, which was the main plank of early Christian apologetic. It is the difference between the point of view of Rome c. A.D. 65 and Syria (where John's name and following were great) fifteen or twenty years earlier.

The absence in the Passion story of any substantial agree-ments of Matthew and Luke against Mark, in the view of most scholars, compels us to conclude that Q contained no account of the Passion. We must ask, Why ? I think the answer must be sought in two directions.

(1) The Passion and its redemptive significance could readily be taught in oral tradition. But ethical teaching implies detailed instruction which sooner or later necessitates a written document. Such a document is found in the Didache, which obviously presupposes a general knowledge of the central facts of the Christian story. Similarly Q was probably written to *supplement* an oral tradition.

(2) Of less weight is the consideration that, while to Paul the centre of the Gospel was the Cross of Christ, to the other Apostles it was His Second Coming. Peter's speeches in the Acts show that to them, as to other Jews, the Crucifixion was a difficulty. It had been cancelled, so to speak, by the Resurrec-tion. It had been foretold by the Prophets, and this showed that it was somehow part of the Divine Plan; but it was still one of those calamities which darken men's understanding of His Purpose, rather than the one act that has unveiled the mystery.

---

[1] The point is elaborated in my Essay on " The Literary Evolution of the Gospels " in *Oxford Studies*, p. 210 ff.

THE MINOR AGREEMENTS OF MATTHEW AND LUKE AGAINST MARK

SYNOPSIS

IRRELEVANT AGREEMENTS

Since both Matthew and Luke consistently compress Mark, the occurrence not infrequently of coincident omissions is only to be expected. Mark's Greek is colloquial, Matthew and Luke revise throughout in the direction of the literary idiom. The results of independent correction of style and grammar must, in a long document, occasionally coincide if the revision is sufficiently thorough.

DECEPTIVE AGREEMENTS

Certain agreements, which, at first sight, are too striking to be attributed to coincidence, are shown, on closer inspection, to be alterations which would naturally occur to independent editors. But, on any view, none of the agreements so far studied, being of the nature of editorial improvements, can be explained by the hypothesis of an Ur-Marcus, though they might be explained by Sanday's hypothesis that the text of Mark used by Matthew and Luke had undergone a slight stylistic revision.

INFLUENCE OF Q

In passages where, *on other grounds,* we have reason to believe that Mark and Q overlapped, agreements of Matthew and Luke against Mark may be explained by the influence of Q; but it is unscientific to invoke this explanation in other contexts.

TEXTUAL CORRUPTION

The most probable explanation of the remaining agreements is to be sought in the domain of Textual Criticism.

(1) Any corruption of the original text of Mark would leave Matthew and Luke in agreement against Mark in any passage where they had happened both to copy the text of Mark in its original form.

(2) Assimilation of parallel passages, wherever it occurred between Matthew and Luke, would be likely to create an Agreement against Mark.

(3) Since assimilation is the one form of corruption which is likely to occur independently in more than one line of manuscript tradition, the grouping of MSS. evidence in accordance with local texts is specially important. It is not the number of MSS. which support a given reading, but of the local texts they represent, that matters.

The MS. Evidence

A survey of all the significant Minor Agreements not previously discussed, reveals the fact that there is usually MS. evidence in favour of the view that the agreement of Matthew and Luke against Mark did not occur in the original text of the Gospels, but is the result of scribal alteration, from which a few MSS. here and there have escaped.

Some Residual Cases

Special discussion of the reading " Who is he that struck thee ? " Mt. xxvi. 68 = Lk. xxii. 64.

The significance of agreements more minute than those examined above cannot be considered apart from the general fact of the abundance of such minutiæ of variation in all MSS., even between B and ℵ.

Conclusion

The bearing of the above examples on the theory and practice of textual criticism. The dependence of Matthew and Luke on Mark may be taken as an assured result, which in doubtful cases may enable us to decide between rival variants in different MSS. ; and is thus of material assistance in the determination of the true text of the Gospels.

CHAPTER XI

THE MINOR AGREEMENTS OF MATTHEW AND LUKE AGAINST MARK

MANY years ago Dr. Sanday expressed the opinion that the solution of this problem would be found in the sphere of Textual Criticism; and from time to time Professors Burkitt and Turner have called attention to facts pointing in this direction. But, so far as I am aware, no consistent attempt has been made to explore the question thoroughly in the light of the latest researches into the grouping of MSS. and the history of the text.

IRRELEVANT AGREEMENTS

Before, however, attempting to do this, I must elaborate the point made in Chap. VII. that the majority of these agreements do not require any explanation at all. Matthew and Luke, it must be realised, were not mere scribes commissioned to produce an accurate copy of a particular MS. ; they were historians combining and freely rewriting their authorities, and, what for our immediate quest is even more important, consistently *condensing* them. From this certain consequences follow.

(1) Compression can only be effected by the omission of details regarded as unimportant or of words and phrases deemed to be superfluous. Hence it would have been quite impossible for two persons to *abbreviate* practically every paragraph in the whole of Mark without concurring in a very large number of their omissions. In a diffuse style like that of Mark certain passages are so obviously redundant that they would be dispensed with

by any one desiring to be concise. Coincidence in omission
proves nothing as to the source used.

(2) Mark's native tongue was Aramaic and his Greek is quite the
most colloquial[1] in the New Testament. The style and vocabulary
of Matthew and Luke, by reason of the subject treated and the
sources used, is naturally coloured to some extent by Semitic
idiom ; but in the main they write the κοινή, *i.e.* the ordinary
Greek of the educated man of the period who was not of set
purpose trying to revive the Greek of the classical age. What
would happen if two such writers were working over the narrative
of Mark ? I may illustrate from a personal experience. The late
Professor Troeltsch sent me a literal translation, made in Berlin,
of an article of his in order that I might correct it for publication
in an English magazine. Wherever I noticed a grammatical
construction possible, but unusual ; a phrase, passable but not
idiomatic; a word understandable, but not the most appropriate—
I substituted what seemed the natural English expression. Now
in any language there are certain constructions and turns of
expression which come naturally to all educated men ; there are
certain words which are the only appropriate ones in certain
contexts. Suppose that the article in question had been corrected, not by me, but by the editor of the magazine, the passages
that would have struck him as needing correction would not
have been exactly the same as those which struck my notice,
but they must have coincided to a considerable extent ; for it
would be precisely the words or sentences which were most
glaringly unidiomatic which would be likely to attract the
attention of us both. The way in which he would have corrected
them would in most cases have differed slightly from mine, but
in a minority of cases it would have been identical, for the simple
reason that there are certain standard differences between the
turns of expression naturally used in German and English sentences which would cause any two Englishmen, aiming at making
a translation more idiomatic, to make precisely the same alteration.

[1] The Greek of the Apocalypse is not so much colloquial as Semitic.

Now Mark's Greek is that of a person who had been brought up to think in Aramaic ; and I conceive that Matthew and Luke would have been on the look-out to correct his unidiomatic style much in the way I have described. Hence, where the process of correction is carried on with a document of the length of Mark's Gospel, it is impossible that two correctors should not frequently concur in making the same or substantially the same alteration. In Aramaic the verb is conjugated on a radically different principle from the Greek; it is peculiarly poor in the variety of particles, conjunctions, prepositions, for the number and variety of which Greek is so conspicuous, and the construction of sentences is far looser. Hence changes intended to make the Semitic style of Mark more idiomatically Greek would all be in the same general direction. The " historic present," for example, a fairly common idiom in Latin, is comparatively rare in Greek, as it is in English ; but Mark uses it, apparently as the equivalent of the Aramaic " participle," 151 times.[1] Matthew cuts these down to 78, Luke to 4. Obviously, then, Matthew and Luke *cannot but* concur in the alteration of tense upwards of 60 times, though as they often change the word as well as the tense the resultant agreements do not always strike the eye. But the historic present most often used by Mark is λέγει ; the natural change of tense to the aorist results in εἶπεν appearing some 20 times in both Matthew and Luke—thus creating to the eye of the English reader an appearance of agreement against Mark which is quite illusory. Another stylistic improvement made innumerable times by Matthew and Luke is the substitution of δέ for καί ; what wonder if about 20 times they both do so in the same place ?[2] Yet another of their most frequently recurring alterations is the substitution of the favourite Greek construction of a participle with a finite verb for the Semitic usage of two finite verbs connected with the conjunction καί.

[1] Hawkins, *Hor. Syn.*[2] p. 143 ff.

[2] *The Principles of Literary Criticism and the Synoptic Problem*, p. 17, E. de Witt Burton, Chicago, 1904.

Is it surprising that 5 times they happen to do so in the same context ?

Mark, like the Old Testament writers, leaves the subject of the sentence to be inferred from the context more frequently than would be quite natural in Greek or in English. Thus Matthew and Luke often make " he " or " they " clearer by introducing a name or title. And, as they do this often, it is inevitable that sometimes they should do it in the same place ; for the places where they would wish to make the insertion would naturally be those where the sense seemed specially to require the addition, and these places would be fixed, not by their arbitrary selection, but by the degree of obscurity in a particular context. We need not, then, suspect collusion, if we occasionally find that Matthew and Luke agree in inserting ὁ Ἰησοῦς, οἱ μαθηταί, οἱ ὄχλοι, οἱ ἀρχιερεῖς, in passages where these subjects can all be inferred from the context.

Yet another example of what I may call an "irrelevant agreement " of Matthew and Luke against Mark arises from the use of the word ἰδού. Mark, for some reason or other, never uses this word in narrative ; Matthew uses it 33 times, Luke 16. No explanation, then, is required for the fact that 5 times they concur in introducing it in the same context—for obviously the number of contexts is limited where its use would be at all appropriate.

DECEPTIVE AGREEMENTS

The above constitute considerably more than half the total number of the Minor Agreements we are discussing, and it goes without saying that they have no significance whatever. But there remain quite a number of cases where the coincidence of Matthew and Luke does at first sight appear significant, but where further scrutiny shows this to be a mistake. Thus frequently, when Mark uses a word which is linguistically inadmissible, the right word is so obvious that, if half-a-dozen independent correctors were at work, they would all be likely to light upon it.

For example, Mark 4 times uses the verb φέρειν of animals or persons, and every time Matthew and Luke concur in altering this to ἄγειν or some compound of ἄγειν. φέρειν, like its English equivalent " carry," is properly used of inanimate objects which one has to lift ; when speaking of a person or an animal that walks on its own legs the natural word to use is ἄγειν, the equivalent of the English verb " to lead." Equally inevitable are corrections like κλίνη, θυγάτηρ, and ἑκατοντάρχης for the apparent vulgarisms κράββατον, θυγάτριον, and κεντυρίων ; or the substitution of τετράρχης, the correct title of the petty princelet Herod, for βασιλεύς, which was the style ordinarily used of historical characters or of the reigning emperor. Hardly less inevitable is the explanatory substitution by Matthew and Luke of " Son of God " for " Son of the Blessed " in the high priest's question to our Lord (Mk. xiv. 61).

Even more necessary is the alteration twice made of μετὰ τρεῖς ἡμέρας to τῇ τρίτῃ ἡμέρα in speaking of the Resurrection, since in strict Greek the former phrase might seem to imply an extra day. Lastly, seeing that the first four disciples were constituted of two pairs of brothers, it is far more natural to mention Andrew next to Simon, as do Matthew and Luke, than to name the sons of Zebedee, as Mark does, in between those two. But granted that this obvious improvement in the order occurred to Matthew and Luke independently, then the addition by both of the words " his brother " is almost inevitable.

I proceed to consider some further Agreements of a more striking character, which nevertheless I believe are really deceptive.

Mark.	Matthew.	Luke.
ii. 12.	ix. 7.	v. 25.
ἐξῆλθεν ἔμπροσθεν πάν-των.	ἀπῆλθεν εἰς τὸν οἶκον αὐτοῦ.	ἀπῆλθεν εἰς τὸν οἶκον αὐτοῦ.

A coincidence like this in five consecutive words seems at first sight to belong to a different category from the single word agreements so far discussed. But it is instructive as illustrating the

fallacy of merely counting words or considering extracts without
a study of the context. The only *real* coincidence between
Matthew and Luke is that both of them are at pains to bring out
more clearly than Mark that the man did *exactly* what our Lord
commanded him. In Mark this command runs, " Arise, take up
thy bed and go to thy house." Matthew proceeds, " And having
arisen, he went away to his house." Luke even more precisely :
" Having stood up before them, and having taken up what he
lay on, he went away to his house." εἰς τὸν οἶκον αὐτοῦ is simply
the echo of Mark's εἰς τὸν οἶκον σοῦ. The change from Mark's
ἐξῆλθεν to ἀπῆλθεν is even more inevitable. Mark describes the
scene from the spectator's point of view, the man went *out*, and
that was the last they saw of him, ἐξῆλθεν. But if, with Matthew
and Luke, you wish to say in Greek that a person left one place
for another with the emphasis on the destination, ἀπῆλθεν is the
appropriate word. Very similar is the way they deal with the
concluding words of Mark's Gospel.

Mark.	Matthew.	Luke.
xvi. 8	xxviii. 8.	xxiv. 9.
οὐδενὶ οὐδὲν εἶπον, ἐφο-βοῦντο γάρ	μετὰ φόβου καὶ χαρᾶς ἔδραμον ἀπαγγεῖλαι τοῖς μαθηταῖς αὐτοῦ.	ἀπήγγειλαν πάντα ταῦτα τοῖς ἔνδεκα καὶ πᾶσιν τοῖς λοιποῖς.

If, as I believe, the text of Mark known to Matthew and Luke
ended at this point, as it does in א B Syr. S., they would be
obliged to *guess* at the further proceedings of the women. The
women had just been *expressly* commanded by an angel to
give an important message to the disciples; it would never have
occurred to Matthew or Luke that the women could have failed
to carry out the instructions. Mark's words " they told no man "
would certainly have been interpreted to mean " they did not
spread the news abroad," not " they did not deliver the message
of the angel." But if Matthew and Luke took it for granted that
the lost ending of Mark told how the women carried out their
orders, it was natural, by way of concluding their account of
the incident, to say as briefly as possible that they gave the

message. But the words in which they do this coincide only in the verb ἀπαγγέλλειν—the natural word for any one to use.

Another still more illusory Agreement is the insertion (Mt. xxvi. 50, Lk. xxii. 48) of a word of Christ to Judas on receipt of the kiss of treachery. In Matthew He says, "Friend, do that for which thou art come " ; in Luke, " Judas, betrayest thou the Son of Man with a kiss ? " Surely the insertion at a moment like this of words of a tenor so totally different is a *disagreement* striking enough to outweigh many small agreements.

Among the twenty Agreements picked out by Sir J. Hawkins[1] as most remarkable is the verb αὐλίζεσθαι (to lodge) (Mt. xxi. 17, Lk. xxi. 37). The word is found nowhere else in the Gospels ; but this also seems to me to constitute a Deceptive Agreement for two reasons. (*a*) The word occurs in passages inserted by Matthew and Luke into the Marcan outline, but the insertions are made in quite different contexts—Matthew's after the Cleansing of the Temple (= Mk. xi. 15-19), Luke's after the Apocalyptic discourse which corresponds to Mk. xiii. (*b*) Matthew says our Lord lodged at Bethany, Luke that he lodged on the Mount of Olives. The *disagreement* in substance is so much more obvious than the concurrence in a single by no means out-of-the-way word that it clearly points to independent editing.

Mark.	Matthew.	Luke.
iii. 1.	xii. 9-10.	vi. 6.
εἰσῆλθεν πάλιν εἰς συναγωγήν, καὶ ἦν ἐκεῖ ἄνθρωπος ἐξηραμμένην ἔχων τὴν χεῖρα.	ἦλθεν εἰς τὴν συναγωγὴν αὐτῶν· καὶ ἰδοὺ ἄνθρωπος χεῖρα ἔχων ξηράν.	ἐγένετο δὲ ἐν ἑτέρῳ σαββάτῳ εἰσελθεῖν αὐτὸν εἰς τὴν συναγωγὴν καὶ ἦν ἄνθρωπος ἐκεῖ καὶ ἡ χεὶρ αὐτοῦ ἡ δεξιὰ ἦν ξηρά.

I should hardly have thought this instance worth quoting but for the fact that it is included by Prof. Burton[2] as one of the 15 Minor Agreements which appreciably affect the sense.

The text is not beyond dispute. All Greek MSS. except B א and one cursive insert τήν in Mark as well ; also ξηράν is read

---

[1] *Hor. Syn.*[2] p. 210 ff.   [2] *Op. cit.* p. 17.

in place of ἐξηραμμένην in Mark by D W. But as the readings
of the other MSS. are of the nature of assimilations, the text
of B ℵ is to be preferred. On the assumption, however, that
the B text is correct the insertion of τὴν by both Matthew and
Luke requires no special explanation. The natural—though
possibly not the correct—interpretation of πάλιν in Mark is
that He returned to a place previously mentioned, in which
case the article is grammatically indispensable. The difference
between ξηράν and ἐξηραμμένην corresponds to the difference
in English between the words " dry " and " dried " ; and the
question, which would be the more natural word to use in this
particular context is one that depends on those subtleties of
linguistic usage which only contemporaries can appreciate.

Mark.	Matthew.	Luke.
iv. 10.	xiii. 10.	viii. 9.
οἱ περὶ αὐτὸν σὺν τοῖς δώδεκα	οἱ μαθηταὶ	οἱ μαθηταὶ αὐτοῦ

Mark's phrase is quite strikingly cumbrous, and " disciples " is
the obvious simplification.

Mark.	Matthew.	Luke.
iv. 36.	viii. 23.	viii. 22.
ἀφέντες τὸν ὄχλον παραλαμβάνουσιν αὐτὸν ὡς ἦν ἐν τῷ πλοίῳ.	ἐμβάντι αὐτῷ εἰς πλοῖον, ἠκολούθησαν αὐτῷ οἱ μα θηταὶ αὐτοῦ.	αὐτὸς ἐνέβη εἰς πλοῖον καὶ οἱ μαθηταὶ αὐτοῦ.

The *prima facie* implication of the language of Mark would be
that the disciples took charge of the situation, so to speak, and
almost hustled our Lord into the boat. I do not suppose Mark
intended to convey that impression ; but Matthew and Luke
obviously go out of their way to emphasise the contrary. Intentional correction to avoid possible misapprehension is plain,
but they correct in such different ways that they are clearly
acting independently. The example is important as illustrating
the futility of counting verbal coincidences without scrutinising
the actual words. οἱ μαθηταὶ αὐτοῦ is the *inevitable* subject,
and ἐμβαίνω is as obvious as " go on board " would be in English.

Mark.	Matthew.	Luke.
xiii. 19.	xxiv. 21.	xxi. 23.
ἔσονται γὰρ αἱ ἡμέραι ἐκεῖναι θλίψις.	ἔσται γὰρ τότε θλῖψις.	ἔσται γὰρ ἀνάγκη.

This is another of Professor Burton's 15 instances. But Mark's phrase is stylistically intolerable in Greek. Note, however, that though they agree in changing the verb to the singular, Matthew and Luke differ in the substantive which they make its subject, *i.e.* in the actual alteration made, they differ more conspicuously than they agree.

Mark.	Matthew.	Luke.
viii. 29.	xvi. 16.	ix. 20.
ἀποκριθεὶς ὁ Πέτρος λέγει αὐτῷ, Σὺ εἶ ὁ Χριστός.	ἀποκριθεὶς δὲ Σίμων Πέτρος εἶπεν, Σὺ εἶ ὁ Χριστός, ὁ υἱὸς τοῦ θεοῦ τοῦ ζῶντος.	Πέτρος δὲ ἀποκριθεὶς εἶπεν, Τὸν Χριστὸν τοῦ θεοῦ.
xv. 30-32.	xxvii. 40.	xxiii. 35-37.
σῶσον σεαυτὸν καταβὰς ἀπὸ τοῦ σταυροῦ . . . ὁ Χριστὸς ὁ βασιλεὺς Ἰσραήλ.	σῶσον σεαυτόν· εἰ υἱὸς εἶ τοῦ θεοῦ, κατάβηθι ἀπὸ τοῦ σταυροῦ.	σωσάτω ἑαυτόν, εἰ οὗτός ἐστιν ὁ Χριστὸς τοῦ θεοῦ ὁ ἐκλεκτός· . . . εἰ σὺ εἶ ὁ βασιλεὺς τῶν Ἰουδαίων σῶσον σεαυτόν.

Note that in two different contexts Matthew and Luke each alter Mark's simple title " the Christ." In both cases Matthew alters to " the Son of God," Luke to " the Christ of God," *i.e.* each prefers a *different* title. This example is most instructive; for, if either of these parallels had stood alone, we might have supposed the addition of τοῦ θεοῦ to be the result of a coincident agreement of Matthew and Luke in an alteration of Mark. Whereas, having both sets of parallels, we see that, while Matthew and Luke agree in altering Mark, each alters in a way characteristic of himself. That is to say, the passages are, so far as they go, evidence of *independent* alteration.

Mark.	Matthew.	Luke.
xiv. 47.	xxvi. 51.	xxii. 49-50.
εἷς δέ [τις] τῶν παρεστη-κότων σπασάμενος τὴν μά-χαιραν ἔπαισεν.	καὶ ἰδοὺ εἷς . . . ἀπ-έσπασεν τὴν μάχαιραν αὐτοῦ, καὶ πατάξας.	. . . εἰ πατάξομεν ἐν μαχαίρῃ; καὶ ἐπάταξεν εἰς τις ἐξ αὐτῶν . . .

There is a tendency in Greek authors to use παίω of striking

with the hand or stick, πατάσσω of striking with a cutting instru-
ment. The usage is not at all rigid, but is sufficiently pronounced
to make it likely that both Matthew and Luke would independently make these substitutions.

Mark.	Matthew.	Luke.
xv. 43.	xxvii. 57.	xxiii. 50.
ἐλθὼν Ἰωσὴφ ἀπὸ Ἀ.,	ἦλθεν ἄνθρωπος πλού-	ἀνὴρ ὀνόματι Ἰωσήφ,
εὐσχήμων βουλευτής	σιος ἀπὸ Ἀ., τοὔνομα	βουλευτὴς ὑπάρχων
	Ἰωσήφ . . .	

From a literary point of view Mark's construction could only be
justified if Joseph had been previously mentioned. A new
character requires a phrase like " by name " or " named " to
introduce him. N.B. also Matthew and Luke use *different*
phrases for the purpose.

   If all the agreements so far discussed occurred in the course
of two or three chapters, the suggestion that they are " deceptive,"
i.e. that they are explicable as the result of independent editing,
would be precarious. But they are spread over the whole of a
lengthy document. Moreover, we must remember that every
verse of Mark incorporated by Matthew and Luke has been so
drastically rewritten that upwards of 45 % of the words he
uses have been changed by each of them. That is to say, the
alterations are many times as numerous as any modern editor
would make in a translated article which he wished to turn into
idiomatic English. Thus, although the number of coincident
alterations may seem large, the proportion of them to the total
number of alterations is extraordinarily small. On a rough
estimate the number of words in Mark is about 12,000—I do
not profess to have counted—the words altered by each will
be over 5000, while the coincidences so far discussed would not
amount to 100. Hence the coincident alterations would be less
than 2 % of the whole number of alterations. And considering
the natural and obvious character of every one of these, this does
not seem a large proportion.

   If, however, any one thinks the proportion too large to be

accidental, it is open to him to accept Dr. Sanday's hypothesis
that the text of Mark used by Matthew and Luke had undergone
a slight stylistic revision.   But, I would submit, it is not open
to him to account for the phenomena reviewed above by the
hypothesis of an " Ur-Marcus," that is, a more primitive edition
of Mark.   For *in every case* the coincident language used by
Matthew and Luke has been shown to be more polished and in
every way less primitive than the existing text of Mark.   If,
therefore, the coincident agreements of Matthew and Luke can
only be explained on the theory that they used a different edition
of Mark from the one we have, then it is the earlier of the two
editions, the Ur-Marcus in fact, that has survived.

INFLUENCE OF Q

In the " Complete Table " of Agreements, very conveniently
printed in parallel columns in the Appendix of E. A. Abbott's
Corrections of Mark,[1] the eye lights at once on a number of passages
which cannot reasonably be explained on the hypothesis of
coincident alteration by independent editors.   But, of these,
most of the more striking disappear if we reflect that, when
Abbott wrote, the overlapping of Q and Mark had not yet been
clearly grasped by students of the Synoptic Problem.

It is now realised that Q, as well as Mark, contained versions of John's Preaching, the Baptism, Temptation, Beelzebub
Controversy, Mission Charge, parable of Mustard Seed, and that
Matthew regularly, Luke occasionally, conflates Mark and Q.
Hence agreements of Matthew and Luke against Mark in *these*
contexts can be explained by the influence of Q.   This covers
phrases like $\pi\epsilon\rho\acute{\iota}\chi\omega\rho\sigma\varsigma$ $\tauo\hat{v}$ $\check{}I\omicron\rho\delta\acute{a}\nu\omicron\upsilon$ (Mt. iii. 5 = Lk. iii. 3),
$\dot{a}\nu\epsilon\acute{\omega}\chi\theta\eta\sigma\alpha\nu$ (-$\eta\nu\alpha\iota$) (Mt. iii. 16 = Lk. iii. 21), $\dot{a}\nu\acute{\eta}\chi\theta\eta$ ($\mathring{\eta}\gamma\epsilon\tauo$)
(Mt. iv. 1 = Lk. iv. 1), which occur in *introductions* to Q sayings,
since the Q sayings must have had some word or two of
introduction.

---

[1] *The Corrections of Mark adopted by Matthew and Luke* (A. & C. Black),
1901.

Some scholars, however, have laid far too much stress on the bearing of the overlapping of Mark and Q on the problem of the minor agreements. We have no right to call in the hypothesis of the influence of Q for this ulterior purpose except in places where the existence of obviously different versions, or of doublets very distinctly defined, provides us with objective evidence of the presence of Q. Apart from the list of passages just enumerated, there are only three in Abbott's list where it seems to me that an agreement of Matthew and Luke against Mark ought to be explained by conflation from Q. In Mk. iv. 21 =Mt. v. 15 =Lk. viii. 16 =Lk. xi. 33 ; Mk. iv. 22 =Mt. x. 26 =Lk. viii. 17 =Lk. xii. 2. In both of these the doublet in Luke is evidence that the saying stood in Q. Again, in Mt. xvi. 4 the addition of the word πονηρά and the mention of the Sign of Jonah—which are absent from the parallel in Mk. viii. 12—are due to the influence of the long Q passage Mt. xii. 39 ff. =Lk. xi. 29 ff. Abbott here prints Lk. xi. 29 side by side with Mk. viii. 12, but it comes from an entirely different context. I mention this fact in order to emphasise the point that looking at selected lists of parallels may be misleading unless one also turns up the context in a good Synopsis of the Gospels.

TEXTUAL CORRUPTION

I proceed to explore the hypothesis that a large number of the Agreements are due, not to the original authors, but to later scribes, being, in fact, examples of the phenomena of accidental omission, or of assimilation between the texts of parallel passages, which we have seen to be the main source of textual corruption.

Our examination, however, of passages in detail will be far more illuminating if we give due weight to three preliminary considerations.

(1) The Gospel of Mark could not compete in popularity with the fuller and richer Gospels of Matthew and Luke, and although I cannot agree with Burkitt's theory (cf. p. 339) that it went

completely out of use for some time in the second century, it is probable that it was very much less frequently copied than the other Gospels. At a later date, when the practice of having each Gospel on a separate roll was discontinued, and the Codex containing all Four Gospels came into fashion, Mark, though much less read, was necessarily copied as often as the others.

Now, most ancient MSS. teem with accidental omissions of single words, of lines, and occasionally of paragraphs. There are MSS. of Homer where as many as 60 lines at a time are omitted. Where many copies of a work were in circulation, omissions would be soon repaired ; but where there were only a few copies, omissions which did not attract attention, either from spoiling the sense or leaving out some familiar saying or incident, would easily escape notice. It is, therefore, antecedently probable that some lines or words which stood in the copies of Mark known to Matthew and Luke have dropped out of the text of all our oldest MSS. It may, then, not infrequently be the case that a verbal agreement of Matthew and Luke preserves a word or a line which once stood in Mark. I do not think this has happened very often, but it would be rather surprising if it had never happened at all.

(2) Assimilation of parallel passages in the Gospels is the commonest form of textual corruption. Accordingly, a reading which makes the wording of parallels differ is in general to be preferred to one that makes them agree, even if the MS. evidence is comparatively slight. But this principle is sometimes pushed too far. In any average Synoptic parallel, perhaps 35 % of the words used by Matthew and Luke are identical, being taken over from Mark. It follows that an accidental corruption of the text of Mark which affected an alteration in any of the words which both of them had happened to take over would leave an agreement of Matthew and Luke against Mark. But the number of variants in the text of Mark in existing MSS. is very large, so that the chance that some of the readings found in the printed texts are the result of textual corruption is quite high.

(3) The classification of the MSS. along the line of local texts attempted in Chaps. III. and IV. is of such fundamental importance for our present investigation that, at the risk of repetition, I venture to recall certain considerations there laid down.

(*a*) If the Byzantine text goes back in essentials to the revision of Lucian about A.D. 300, the evidence of all MSS. which present this text (and of all mixed MSS., in so far as they present it) may be treated as a single witness, and that not one of the most important. Hence, in citing MS. evidence for a particular reading it will considerably clarify the issue to use for all these authorities the single symbol Byz. (*b*) Again, the whole importance of the identification of local texts lies in the fact that these represent relatively independent lines of transmission of the text. Hence, instead of quoting MSS. in alphabetical order, as in the ordinary Apparatus Criticus, I shall cite them, so far as possible, by their grouping. (*c*) If the MS. evidence for a reading belongs to the oldest recoverable form of a local text, nothing is gained by citing subordinate authorities. Thus where B ℵ agree in a particular reading, the evidence for it is not much increased by the fact that C L 33 may be cited in support. The important question to ask is, Is the reading supported by B ℵ, by D, by *a b*, by *k e*, or by *fam*. Θ or by Syr. S., since these represent *independent* traditions ? Hence the common practice of citing *all* the MS. evidence is actually misleading. I propose, therefore, only to quote the evidence of subordinate MSS. where the evidence of the leading authorities is divided or obscure. (*d*) What carries most weight—apart from considerations of the intrinsic probability of a given reading—is not the number of MSS. which support it, but the number of local texts which the MSS. supporting it represent, or the age to which by patristic quotations it can be pushed back. A reading, for instance, supported by *k*, Syr. S. and **69**, or one supported by only one of these MSS. and a quotation of Marcion or Justin, deserves most serious consideration, even if every other MS. is against it.

The MS. Evidence

The passages which follow include all the minor agreements not already discussed in this chapter which seem to me at all significant. They include those mentioned by Hawkins and by Burton; also all those in Abbott's exhaustive list which are in the slightest degree remarkable, along with certain others I have myself noticed.

Mark.	Matthew.	Luke.
i. 40-42.	viii. 2-3.	v. 12-13.
καὶ ἔρχεται πρὸς αὐτὸν λεπρὸς . . . λέγων αὐτῷ ὅτι Ἐὰν θέλῃς δύνασαί με καθαρίσαι, καὶ σπλαγχνι- σθεὶς ἐκτείνας τὴν χεῖρα αὐτοῦ ἥψατο [αὐτοῦ] καὶ λέγει . . . καὶ εὐθὺς	καὶ ἰδοὺ λεπρὸς προσ- ελθὼν προσεκύνει αὐτῷ λέγων Κύριε, ἐὰν θέλῃς δύνασαί με καθαρίσαι. καὶ ἐκτείνας τὴν χεῖρα [αὐτοῦ] ἥψατο αὐτοῦ λέγων . . . καὶ εὐθέως	καὶ ἰδοὺ ἀνὴρ πλήρης λέπρας . . . ἐδεήθη αὐτοῦ λέγων Κύριε, ἐὰν θέλῃς, δύνασαί με καθαρίσαι. καὶ ἐκτείνας τὴν χεῖρα ἥψατο αὐτοῦ εἰπών . . . καὶ εὐθέως

(a) ἰδού is never used by Mark in narration, but is found 33 times in Matthew and 16 in Luke; it is not, therefore, surprising that they concur occasionally in a stylistic alteration of Mark which they are always making independently.

(b) Κύριε. But the word occurs in Mark also in B C L 579 Sah., W c e ff², Θ 700. It is omitted by ℵ D b, Syr. S. Boh. Byz. Hort for once deserts B, thinking B here assimilates (κύριε only once in Mk.). But the combination of the three distinct traditions, Egyptian B C L Sah., " African " W c e, and Caesarean Θ 700, is a very strong one. Either, then, B is right and there is no agreement of Matthew and Luke against Mark ; or we have, not only a clear case of B L convicted of assimilation, but evidence of such an orgy of assimilation in these small details that no text can be relied on, and it is just as likely that the presence of Κύριε in either Matthew or Luke may be due to the same cause.

(c) The order of Matthew and Luke is ἥψατο αὐτοῦ against Mark's αὐτοῦ ἥψατο; but in Θ 565 Mark also has ἥψατο αὐτοῦ. But D e a ff² have αὐτοῦ ἥψατο αὐτοῦ in Mark, and in Matthew ℵ 124 (D hiat.) Syr. Sah. Boh. attest the double αὐτοῦ, a reading hard to explain unless this was the original reading in Mark and was adopted by Matthew from him. If we accept the reading of D as original all is explained. Mark's Aramaic idiom is full of pronouns unidiomatic in Greek ; the MS. tradition represented by Θ 565 drops the first αὐτοῦ ; that represented by B, which is here followed by Byz., drops the second instead. Luke preferred the former course, which is really the more obvious, since it is the first αὐτοῦ that is redundant with χεῖρα, and, only if the second is dropped, can it be construed as object of ἥψατο.

(d) ἥψατο λέγων (or εἰπών) for ἥψατο καὶ λέγει. Mark's historic present, unidiomatic in this use, is regularly altered by both Matthew and Luke, and in this instance the only natural thing was to put a participle ; but though an identical construction was practically forced on them, they differ in the choice of the verb meaning " to say."

(e) εὐθέως against εὐθύς. The fact is that εὐθέως is the form preferred in all the Gospels in the majority of MSS. and is found here in Mark also in all MSS. except in ℵ B L 33 and Θ, 164. But throughout Mark, B (usually supported by ℵ L and sometimes by C) prefers εὐθύς ; the same MSS. often read εὐθύς in other Gospels against εὐθέως in the other MSS. It looks as if Mark preferred the form εὐθύς, while the other evangelists (and scribes as a rule, except in Alexandria) preferred εὐθέως. But if by both authors and scribes εὐθέως was the form preferred, an agreement of Matthew and Luke against Mark is inevitable wherever the word is used by all three.

Mark.	Matthew.	Luke.
ii. 21-22.	ix. 16-17.	v. 36-37.
ἐπίβλημα ... ἐπιρράπτει	ἐπιβάλλει ἐπίβλημα ...	ἐπίβλημα ἐπιβάλλει ...
... εἰ δὲ μή	εἰ δὲ μήγε	εἰ δὲ μήγε

But (a) B 301 read μὴ in Matthew. Was Hort right in deserting B ? (b) The noun ἐπίβλημα almost shouts out to an editor to alter the verb to ἐπιβάλλει.

Mark.	Matthew.	Luke.
ii. 22.	ix. 17.	v. 37.
καὶ ὁ οἶνος ἀπόλλυται καὶ οἱ ἀσκοί. [ἀλλὰ οἶνον νέον εἰς ἀσχοὺς καινούς.]	ὁ οἶνος [ἐκχεῖται] καὶ οἱ ἀσκοὶ ἀπόλλυνται· ἀλλὰ βάλλουσιν οἶνον νέον εἰς ἀσκοὺς καινούς.	καὶ αὐτὸς ἐκχυθήσεται καὶ οἱ ἀσκοὶ ἀπολοῦνται ἀλλὰ οἶνον νέον εἰς ἀσκοὺς καινοὺς βλητέον.

In Matthew D *a k* omit ἐκχεῖται (and otherwise alter), a
" Western non-interpolation."

Curiously enough, however, while the acceptance of this as an
interpolation gets rid of this, the first of the twenty agreements
picked out by Hawkins as being specially conspicuous, acceptance of the Western reading produces an agreement later in the
same verse, for D Old Lat. omit ἀλλὰ οἶνον νέον εἰς ἀσκοὺς
καινούς. Synopses based on Hort's text ignore this omission;
Huck accepts it. But both ignore the former instance. The
line divisions in D (which Rendel Harris[1] has shown to be much
older than the actual MS.) are such that, if the omitted line had
stood in D, the words οἶνος ἀσκός, separated by only a few letters,
would have occurred in each of three successive lines. This is a
formation which invites accidental omission : the scribe copies the
second line, and then glancing back to the model mistakes the
third line for the one he has written and goes on with the line
that follows. I hold, therefore, that א B Byz. are right in retaining the bracketed words in Mark, but that ἐκχεῖται in Matthew
is due to assimilation from Luke.

Mark.	Matthew.	Luke.
ii. 23.	xii. 1.	vi. 1.
ἤρξαντο ὁδὸν ποιεῖν τίλλοντες	ἤρξαντο τίλλειν . . . καὶ ἐσθίειν	ἔτιλλον . . . καὶ ἤσθιον

Scribes could make no satisfactory sense of ὁδὸν ποιεῖν, as the
following variants show.

> ὁδὸν ποιεῖν א C L Byz.
> ὁδοποιεῖν B G H.
> ὁδοιπορούντες 13 etc. *a q f* Arm. Goth.
> Omit D W *c e, b ff*[2], Syr. S.

[1] *Texts and Studies*, II. i. p. 241 ff. (Cambridge, 1891).

If the phrase were an easy one, we should accept the combination D Afr. and Eur. Lat. Syr. S. as final for *an omission*. But the meaning of ποιεῖν—in place of ποιεῖσθαι—in literary Greek is "make a road through the corn"[1] (a proceeding which, even if morally justifiable, is a curious way of satisfying hunger); hence the omission of the difficult words is probably intentional.

Now Matthew and Luke must have felt the same difficulty as later scribes, and would, therefore, be compelled to rewrite the sentence. But anyone who began to rewrite a sentence about rubbing ears of corn for a meal would find the verb " to eat " come into his mind.

Mark.	Matthew.	Luke.
ii. 24	xii. 2	vi. 2.
ἔξεστιν	ἔξεστιν ποιεῖν	ἔξεστιν [ποιεῖν]

In Luke ποιεῖν occurs in the Synopses of Huck and Rushbrooke, but it is omitted by Westcott and Hort, with B R, D Old Lat., 69, 700, Arm. (hiat. Syr. S.).

Mark.	Matthew.	Luke.
ii. 26.	xii. 4.	vi. 4.
εἰ μὴ τοὺς ἱερεῖς	εἰ μὴ τοῖς ἱερεῦσιν [μόνοις]	εἰ μὴ μόνους τοὺς ἱερεῖς

It is worth noting that in Mark μόνοις ἱερεῦσι is read by 33 (579) Sah. Boh., or ἱερεῦσι μόνοις by D, most Old Lat., 13 &c., Φ Arm. The variation in position suggests interpolation; but the reading is instructive as illustrating the possibility of assimilating along three independent lines of MS. tradition— Egyptian, Western, and Eastern.

μόνοις in Matthew is omitted by 1 &c., and *a*, while L Δ and *k* read μόνον. Variants of this sort are most easily accounted for if the word was absent from an ancestor of the MS. in which they occur, and have been supplied later by conjecture from recollection of the parallel gospel; so that L Δ *k* really support the omission.

---

[1] But F. Field quotes a parallel from LXX (Judg. xvii. 8) for the use of τοῦ ποιῆσαι τὴν ὁδὸν αὐτοῦ = "as he journeyed," *Notes on the Translation of the New Testament*, p. 25 (Cambridge, 1899).

Mark.	Matthew.	Luke.
iv. 11.	xiii. 11.	viii. 10.
καὶ ἔλεγεν αὐτοῖς, Ὑμῖν τὸ μυστήριον δέδοται τῆς βασιλείας τοῦ θεοῦ.	ὁ δὲ ἀποκριθεὶς εἶπεν ὅτι Ὑμῖν δέδοται γνῶναι τὰ μυστήρια τῆς βασιλείας τῶν οὐρανῶν.	ὁ δὲ εἶπεν, Ὑμῖν δέδοται γνῶναι τὰ μυστήρια τῆς βασιλείας τοῦ θεοῦ.

The phrase " the mystery is given to you " is obscure ; the verb γνῶναι (to understand) is the most natural one for two independent interpreters to supply.   But note the singular μυστήριον is read in Matthew by k c, a ff², Syr. S. and C., Clem. Iren.

Mark.	Matthew.	Luke.
v. 27.	ix. 20.	viii. 44.
ἐλθοῦσα ἐν τῷ ὄχλῳ . . . ἥψατο τοῦ ἱματίου αὐτοῦ.	προσελθοῦσα . . . ἥψατο τοῦ κρασπέδου τοῦ ἱματίου αὐτοῦ.	προσελθοῦσα . . . ἥψατο [τοῦ κρασπέδου] τοῦ ἱματίου αὐτοῦ.

τοῦ κρασπέδου in Luke, om. D a ff² rl, a " Western non-inter-polation."

Mark.	Matthew.	Luke.
vi. 32-34.	xiv. 13, 14.	ix. 10, 11
καὶ ἀπῆλθον ἐν τῷ πλοίῳ εἰς ἔρημον τόπον κατ᾽ ἰδίαν. καὶ εἶδον αὐτοὺς ὑπάγοντας καὶ ἔγνωσαν πολλοί, καὶ πεζῇ ἀπὸ πασῶν τῶν πόλεων συνέδραμον ἐκεῖ καὶ προ-ῆλθον αὐτούς . . . εἶδεν πολὺν ὄχλον καὶ ἐσπλαγ-χνίσθη ἐπ᾽ αὐτούς . . . καὶ ἤρξατο διδάσκειν αὐτοὺς πολλά.	ἀκούσας δὲ ὁ Ἰ. ἀνεχώ-ρησεν ἐκεῖθεν ἐν πλοίῳ εἰς ἔρημον τόπον κατ᾽ ἰδίαν· καὶ ἀκούσαντες οἱ ὄχλοι ἠκολούθησαν αὐτῷ πεζοὶ ἀπὸ τῶν πόλεων . . . καὶ ἐθεράπευσεν τοὺς ἀρρώ-στους αὐτῶν.	καὶ παραλαβὼν αὐτοὺς ὑπεχώρησεν κατ᾽ ἰδίαν εἰς πόλιν καλουμένην Βηθ-σαϊδά. οἱ δὲ ὄχλοι γνόντες ἠκολούθησαν αὐτῷ, . . . καὶ τοὺς χρείαν ἔχοντας θεραπείας ἰᾶτο.

The Feeding of the Five Thousand is a section in which there are more minor agreements than in any other of the same length. They include, besides the parallels printed above, those to Mk. vi. 43 and the words βρώματα (Mt. xiv. 15, Lk. ix. 13) and ὡσεί (Mt. xiv. 21, Lk. ix. 14) discussed below.   Hence it is of particular importance to notice that the majority of them are distinctly of the nature of stylistic improvements on Mark, and therefore point away from an Ur-Marcus hypothesis.

The T.R. with 13 &c., and some late MSS., adds ὄχλοι in Mk. vi. 33. This, however, is probably due to assimilation; but since the subject of εἶδον (Mk. vi. 33) is different from that of the previous verb ἀπῆλθον, grammar and sense in Greek, as in English, demand that the subject of εἶδον be expressed. As the unexpressed subject is the people, described in the next sentence of Mark as πολὺν ὄχλον, Matthew and Luke naturally supply οἱ ὄχλοι. Again, the word ἀκολουθέω in Greek, like "follow" in English, is the only natural one to employ, if Matthew and Luke both wished to cut short Mark's more elaborate, but obviously more primitive, "ran together there and arrived before them." It may be added that the phrase ἠκολούθει αὐτῷ ὄχλος πολύς occurs in Mk. v. 24, where curiously enough it is not reproduced exactly by either Matthew or Luke; the trick of memory which leads Matthew or Luke to introduce a collocation of words from one context in Mark into quite another in their own Gospels is very frequent. Hawkins [1] collects the instances under the heading "Transference of Formulae."

A more striking coincidence between Matthew and Luke is their addition of the statement that our Lord healed the sick. But the words in which they express this are as different as they well could be. Probably, therefore, this statement is an interpretative inference, made by both independently, of Mark's phrase ἐσπλαγχνίσθη ἐπ' αὐτούς—it being taken for granted that the pity expressed itself in action of this kind. There are other passages where one or other of the later evangelists adds to Mark a generalised statement of our Lord's healing, e.g. Mt. xv. 30, Lk. vii. 21. The actual words ἀρρώστους ἐθεράπευον occur Mk. vi. 13, and it is quite in Matthew's habit to transfer such a formula. An alternative possibility is that καὶ ἐθεράπευσεν ἀρρώστους πολλούς, or something like it, originally stood in the text of Mark after διδάσκειν αὐτούς, if καὶ ... ἀρρώστους was omitted through homoioteleuton with αὐτούς, the surviving πολλούς would inevitably be altered to πολλά to make sense.

[1] *Hor. Syn.*[2] p. 168 ff.

Mark.	Matthew.	Luke.
vi. 43.	xiv. 20.	ix. 17.
καὶ ἦραν κλάσματα δώ-δεκα κοφίνων πληρώματα. Huck and T.R. read κλασμάτων.	καὶ ἦραν τὸ περισσεῦον τῶν κλασμάτων δώδεκα κοφίνους πλήρεις.	καὶ ἤρθη τὸ περισσεῦσαν αὐτοῖς κλασμάτων κόφινοι δώδεκα.

Mark's use of πληρώματα is not really Greek ; and if one is to express the idea of surplus or residue in Greek neatly it can only be done by some derivative of the word περισσόν, and this word is used in Mark in the parallel sentence of the account of the Feeding of the Four Thousand, which, of course, Matthew (and, perhaps, Luke) had read. W D e 13 &c. have the noun form περίσσευμα in Luke, while ℵ D 13 &c. om. αὐτοῖς (W. αὐτῶν), which is perhaps right.

There are two other agreements in this same section. βρώματα = " food," Mt. xiv. 15, Lk. ix. 13, is such an obvious word to use in this context that, seeing that it does not occur in verses in other respects verbally parallel, it is of no real significance. ὡσεί (Mt. xiv. 21, Lk. ix. 14) ; but this is omitted in Matthew by W, the uncial fragment 0106, Old Lat. Syr. C. (hiat. S.) Orig.^Mt. ; and ὡς is substituted in Δ 33, D, Θ 1.

Mark.	Matthew.	Luke.
ix. 2-3.	xvii. 2.	ix. 29.
καὶ μετεμορφώθη ἔμ-προσθεν αὐτῶν, καὶ τὰ ἱμάτια αὐτοῦ στίλβοντα λευκὰ λίαν . . . Huck and T.R. ἐγένετο after αὐτοῦ.	καὶ μεταμορφώθη ἔμ-προσθεν αὐτῶν, καὶ ἔλαμ-ψεν τὸ πρόσωπον αὐτοῦ ὡς ὁ ἥλιος, τὰ δὲ ἱμάτια αὐτοῦ ἐγένετο λευκὰ ὡς τὸ φῶς.	καὶ ἐγένετο ἐν τῷ προσ-εύχεσθαι αὐτὸν τὸ εἶδος τοῦ προσώπου αὐτοῦ ἕτερον καὶ ὁ ἱματισμὸς αὐτοῦ λευκὸς ἐξαστράπτων.

In a Greek Synopsis the underlined πρόσωπον strikes the eye of an English reader ; but in real life, if we speak of a change in a person's appearance, the first thing we think of and mention is the *face*. If, then, there is anything that requires to be explained in this agreement—which I am inclined to doubt—it is not why both Matthew and Luke use the word πρόσωπον, but how Mark managed to avoid doing so. It reads a little strangely to say a

person was transfigured, and then to go on to speak of the difference
in his clothes without mentioning the face. Of course, the point
in itself would be too small to be significant ; but it is never safe
to ignore the readings of *fam.* Θ, Syr. S. and *k*, when they agree
in departing from the ordinary text. 1 &c. 346, Syr. S. *k*[1]
concur in omitting στίλβοντα (Θ 565 transpose λευκὰ and
στίλβοντα, a sign that one of these words was absent from their
ancestor) ; but Syr. S., after "transfigured before them," adds
the words " and he became gleaming," which may imply a Greek
reading καὶ ἐγένετο στίλβων. Is it possible that the original
text of Mark was καὶ ἐγένετο στίλβον τὸ πρόσωπον, καὶ τὰ ἱμάτια
αὐτοῦ λευκὰ λίαν ? If πρόσωπον was accidentally omitted,
στιλβοντο—written of course as one word and without accents—
would be left " in the air." Sense had to be made somehow.
The ancestor of *fam.* Θ *k* solved the difficulty by leaving out the
words altogether; that of Syr. S. by changing them to στίλβων,
which could then refer to Jesus ; that of B by emending to
στίλβοντα and transferring the words ἐγένετο στίλβοντα to
another place in the sentence so as to construe with ἱμάτια.

Mark.	Matthew.	Luke.
ix. 6-7.	xvii. 5.	ix. 34.
(No corresponding words.)	ἔτι αὐτοῦ λαλοῦντος	ταῦτα δὲ αὐτοῦ λέγοντος

Matthew and Luke have no word in common except αὐτοῦ,
which of course proves nothing, and the insertion of some such
words to mark the transition is a literary improvement. Still it
is perhaps a little odd—though by no means impossible—that two
independent writers should hit so nearly upon the same phrase
by way of addition. An obvious hypothesis would be that
ἔτι λαλοῦντος αὐτοῦ—the phrase is Marcan, cf. Mk. xiv. 43—
represents a line in the original text of Mark which has
dropped out.

[1] *k* reads *candida aba*. The *aba* is erased, and is probably an incorrect
anticipation of the *alba* which occurs two lines later. It cannot have been
meant as a translation of στίλβοντα.

Mark.	Matthew.	Luke.
ix. 19.	xvii. 17.	ix. 41.
ὁ δὲ ἀποκριθεὶς αὐτοῖς λέγει, Ὦ γενεὰ ἄπιστος, . . . φέρετε αὐτὸν πρός με.	ἀποκριθεὶς δὲ ὁ Ἰησοῦς εἶπεν, Ὦ γενεὰ ἄπιστος καὶ διεστραμμένη . . . φέρετέ μοι αὐτὸν ὧδε.	ἀποκριθεὶς δὲ ὁ Ἰησοῦς εἶπεν, Ὦ γενεὰ ἄπιστος [καὶ διεστραμμένη] προσάγαγε ὧδε τὸν υἱόν σου.

In Luke καὶ διεστραμμένη om. e Marcion (as quoted by both Tert. and Epiph.), i.e. by African [1] and old Roman text. Syr. S. and C. (also in Mt.) transpose with ἄπιστος, perhaps for the sake of rhythm; but transposition always suggests an insertion.

In Luke ὧδε om. D r; T.R. transposes.

The aorist εἶπεν is the usual substitution by Matthew and Luke for the unidiomatic historic present in Mark.

Mark.	Matthew.	Luke.
x. 25.	xix. 24.	xviii. 25.
διὰ τρυμαλιᾶς ῥαφίδος διελθεῖν ἢ πλούσιον . . . εἰσελθεῖν	διὰ τρήματος ῥαφίδος εἰσελθεῖν ἢ πλούσιον . . .	. . . διὰ τρήματος βελόνης εἰσελθεῖν ἢ πλούσιον . . . εἰσελθεῖν
Huck and T.R. read διὰ τῆς . . . τῆς.		

(a) But D L and the majority of MSS. read τρυπήματος in Matthew, and the reading is quoted (without specifying from which Gospel) by Clem. Orig.[Cels.]. But C, Θ 124 565 700, etc., with Orig.[Mt.], read τρυμαλιᾶς in Matthew as in Mark; and there is respectable MS. authority for both τρυμαλιᾶς and τρυπήματος in Luke. In other words assimilation has run riot. But the reading of D τρυμαλιᾶς Mark, τρυπήματος Matthew, τρήματος Luke, which is supported by ℵ B in Matthew and Luke, and by the majority of other MSS. (but not ℵ B) in Mark, makes all three Gospels different. As therefore it cannot be suspected of harmonisation, and also accounts for all the other variants, it is almost certainly correct—in which case the agreement disappears.

(b) In Matthew B Sah.[codd.], D Lat., Θ, Syr. S. and C. Orig.[Mt.] read διελθεῖν. Why Hort should have deserted B, when so well supported, I cannot imagine.

---

[1] Tischendorf in his Apparatus overlooks the omission by e, but it is in his edition of that MS., *Evangelium Palatinum ineditum* (Leipzig, 1847).

Mark.	Matthew.	Luke.
x. 30.	xix. 29.	xviii. 30.
ἑκατονταπλασίονα	πολλαπλασίονα	πολλαπλασίονα

D Old Lat. read ἑπταπλασίονα in Luke. This reading, which makes all three Gospels differ, is surely right.

Mark.	Matthew.	Luke.
xi. 1.	xxi. 1.	xix. 28, 29.
ὅτε ἐγγίζουσιν εἰς Ἱερο- σόλυμα καὶ εἰς [Βηθφαγὴ καὶ] Βηθανίαν	ὅτε ἤγγισαν εἰς Ἱερο- σόλυμα καὶ ἦλθον εἰς Βηθφαγὴ	... ἀναβαίνων εἰς Ἱερο- σόλυμα ... ὡς ἤγγισεν εἰς Βηθφαγὴ καὶ Βηθανίαν

In the text of W.H. and in the T.R. (which is supported by א B L and the mass of MSS.) there is no agreement of Matthew and Luke against Mark. But D, Old Lat. 700, omit [1] Bethphage in Mark—and this "Western non-interpolation" is accepted by Tischendorf. Thus in Huck's Synopsis an agreement is shown. But, if the original text of Mark omitted the name Bethphage, where did Luke get it from? It is not mentioned elsewhere in the Gospels. Moreover, as Burkitt points out,[2] the way in which Mark mentions the three names is confusing. Both Matthew and Luke simplify in different ways by rearranging the sentences. The Western text does it by the easier method of omitting Bethphage. This is the second case which has already come under our notice of omission by D, Old Lat. to meet a difficulty. The lesson is a valuable one. Western omissions are not always "non-interpolations."

Mark.	Matthew.	Luke.
xi. 27.	xxi. 23.	xx. 1.
καὶ ἐν τῷ ἱερῷ περι- πατοῦντος αὐτοῦ ἔρχονται ... οἱ ἀρχιερεῖς ...	καὶ ἐλθόντος αὐτοῦ εἰς τὸ ἱερὸν προσῆλθον αὐτῷ [διδάσκοντι] οἱ ἀρχιερεῖς ...	καὶ ἐγένετο ... διδά- σκοντος αὐτοῦ τὸν λαὸν ἐν τῷ ἱερῷ ... ἐπέστησαν οἱ ἀρχιερεῖς

[1] The readings of Origen (iii. 743, iv. 182) are especially interesting. In his *Commentary on John* (tom. x.) he quotes Mk. xi. 1-12 in close accord with the B א text including Bethphage; but in the *Commentary on Matthew* he expressly contrasts the reading of Mark (Bethany only) with that of Matthew and Luke. Our previous observation that he had by that time changed his text from B א to that of *fam.* Θ, is confirmed by the absence of Βεθφαγὴ καὶ from 700.

[2] *J.T.S.* Jan. 1916, p. 148.

In Matthew διδάσκοντι omitted by Old Latin (a b c e ff¹ g² h l), Old Syr. (S. and C.).

Mark.	Matthew.	Luke.
xi. 29.	xxi. 24.	xx. 3.
ὁ δὲ . . . εἶπεν . . . Ἐπ-ερωτήσω ὑμᾶς ἕνα λόγον, καὶ ἀποκρίθητέ μοι.	ἀποκριθεὶς δὲ . . . εἶπεν . . . ἐρωτήσω ὑμᾶς κἀγὼ λόγον ἕνα, ὃν ἐὰν εἴπητέ μοι	ἀποκριθεὶς εἶπεν . . . ἐρωτήσω κἀγὼ λόγον, καὶ εἴπατέ μοι.

ἀποκριθείς is found in Mark also, in D, Old Lat., Syr. S., and Byz. This may be the right reading ; but, other things being equal, a text which makes the Gospels differ is to be preferred. But no one who has glanced at the verb ἀποκρίνομαι in a concordance to the New Testament will attach any significance to a concurrent use of the constantly recurring phrase ἀποκριθεὶς εἶπεν. But it is obvious that, having chosen this conventional opening for the sentence, Matthew and Luke were bound to substitute another verb of saying for the ἀποκρίθητε of Mark a few words later.

κἀγὼ occurs in Mark in ℵ, D, Old Lat., Old Syr., Byz.—a strong combination ; but, as the word is not elsewhere used by Mark, it is probably rightly rejected. But the sense requires the emphasis ; perhaps the ἐπερωτήσω was Mark's way of getting this ; the others substitute the natural Greek expression, which is one they frequently use elsewhere.

Mark.	Matthew.	Luke.
xii. 11, 12.	xxi. 44.	xx. 18.
(Omits.)	[καὶ ὁ πεσὼν ἐπὶ τὸν λίθον . . .] W.H. bracket.	πᾶς ὁ πεσὼν etc.

The verse is omitted in Matthew by 33, D, Old Lat., Syr. S. ; Orig.^Mt. Euseb.

Mark.	Matthew.	Luke.
xii. 12.	xxi. 45.	xx. 19.
(Simply 3rd pers. pl. "they".)	οἱ ἀρχιερεῖς καὶ οἱ Φαρισαῖοι	οἱ γραμματεῖς καὶ οἱ ἀρχιερεῖς

Marcion omitted the words in Luke, and this may represent the

earliest Roman text. But Mark had last named the opponents
of Jesus in xi. 27 = Mt. xxi. 23 = Lk. xx. 1; stylistically speaking,
it was time to repeat the subject of the verb ; and this was more
necessary for Matthew than Luke since he had interpolated a
series of parables since the last mention of the chief priests. The
subject in Mark xi. 27 is οἱ ἀρχιερεῖς καὶ οἱ γραμματεῖς καὶ οἱ
πρεσβύτεροι ; Luke repeats the first two ; Matthew, whose
Gospel often elsewhere reflects anti-Pharisaic polemic, substitutes
Pharisees. So far, therefore, from agreeing against Mark, they
differ *as far as was possible* (granted each wished to name a subject
to the verb), since the high priests were so obviously the leading
characters that they *could* not be omitted.

Mark.	Matthew.	Luke.
xii. 22.	xxii. 27.	xx. 32.
ἔσχατον πάντων	ὕστερον δὲ πάντων	[ὕστερον] καὶ . . .

Luke ὕστερον om. Syr. S. and C. Old Lat. *a c i*; *e* om. whole
verse from " hour."

Mark.	Matthew.	Luke.
xii. 28.	xxii. 35, 36.	x. 25, 26
εἷς ᾿τῶν γραμματέων . . . ἐπηρώτησεν αὐτόν, Ποία ἐστὶν ἐντολὴ πρώτη πάντων ;	ἐπηρώτησεν εἷς ἐξ αὐτῶν [νομικὸς] πειράζων αὐτόν, Διδάσκαλε, ποία ἐντολὴ μεγάλη ἐν τῷ νόμῳ ;	ἰδοὺ νομικός τις ἀνέστη ἐκπειράζων αὐτόν, λέγων, [Διδάσκαλε,] τί ποιήσας ζωὴν αἰώνιον κληρονομήσω ; ὁ δὲ εἶπεν πρὸς αὐτόν, Ἐν τῷ νόμῳ τί γέγραπται ;

(a) Apart from this passage the word νομικός is found in the
Gospels only in Luke. This fact practically compels us to accept
as original its omission in Matthew by 1 &c., *e*, Syr. S., Arm.,
Orig.[Mt.] (b) διδάσκαλε in Luke is omitted by D and by Marcion
as quoted by Tertullian. It may further be remarked that, in
this passage, while Matthew is mainly following Mark, Luke seems
to derive the incident from another source. Hawkins [1] suggests
the incident might have stood in Q.

---

[1] *Oxford Studies*, p. 41 ff.

Mark.	Matthew.	Luke.
xiv. 62.	xxvi. 64.	xxii. 69-70.
ἐγώ εἰμι καὶ ὄψεσθε τὸν	σὺ εἶπας· πλὴν λέγω	ἀπὸ τοῦ νῦν ἔσται ὁ
υἱὸν . . . καθήμενον	ὑμῖν, ἀπ᾽ ἄρτι ὄψεσθε τὸν	υἱὸς . . . καθήμενος . . .
	υἱὸν . . . καθήμενον	ὑμεῖς λέγετε, ὅτι ἐγώ εἰμι.

This is our Lord's reply to the question of the high priest, "Art thou the Christ?" In the actual words used there are no *verbal* agreements against Mark; but it is remarkable that Matthew and Luke should agree in adding two points so alike in *sense* as ἀπ᾽ ἄρτι = ἀπὸ τοῦ νῦν and σὺ εἶπας = ὑμεῖς λέγετε. The latter especially is an obscure phrase which apparently means " it is your statement, not mine." What is still more remarkable is that both these additions introduce difficulties which are not in the text of Mark—an apparent disclaimer of the title Christ and (in Matthew's form) a statement which history falsified that the high priests would immediately see our Lord's Parousia.

(a) In Syr. S. the equivalent of ἀπ᾽ ἄρτι stands in Mark; and this reading cannot be dismissed forthwith as an assimilation, for in both Matthew and Luke the Syriac reading is the equivalent of ἀπὸ τοῦ νῦν, *i.e.* in Syriac assimilation has worked in the reverse direction. If the words had accidentally dropped out of some MSS. at a very early date, the fact that they seemed to imply a prophecy which history had falsified would tend to prevent their reinsertion. Nevertheless I am inclined to think the words are independent editorial insertions by Matthew and Luke for four reasons : (a) Precisely the same addition (ἀπ᾽ ἄρτι Mt. = ἀπὸ τοῦ νῦν Lk.) is made in the parallel Mk. xiv. 25 = Mt. xxvi. 29 = Lk. xxii. 18. (β) The word ἄρτι is used 7 times by Matthew (ἀπ᾽ ἄρτι 3 times), never by Mark or Luke. (γ) The phrase ἀπὸ τοῦ νῦν is used 5 times in Luke and once in Acts, never by Mark or Matthew. (δ) Orig.[Mt.] (iii. 911) explicitly contrasts the absence of the words from Mark with their presence in Matthew. This shows that the words were absent from the old Caesarean text as well as from the Alexandrian and Western texts.

Y

(b) Θ, 13 &c., 565, 700, 1071, Arm., Orig. read σὺ εἶπας ὅτι ἐγώ εἰμι in Mark. Now ordinarily one would suspect this reading as due to assimilation from Matthew. But here again the obscurity of the expression, or the apparent hesitancy it might seem to imply in our Lord's acceptance of the title Christ, would favour its omission. Moreover, the view that the words originally stood in Mark explains the language of Matthew and Luke. Mark wrote σὺ εἶπας ὅτι ἐγώ εἰμι, an answer intended to preclude the acceptance of the title Messiah in the sense that the High Priest might mean, which looks like a genuine utterance of our Lord. Matthew leaves out the last three words and inserts πλὴν κτλ., i.e. he interprets the words "You have said it in scorn, but very soon, I tell you, you shall see with your eyes." Luke preserves Mark's sense and phrase, but he makes it plural, perhaps influenced by his other source. Hence it is probable that *fam.* Θ here preserves the true reading. If, however, the ordinary text be preferred, I would suggest that the σὺ εἶπας of Matthew and the ὑμεῖς λέγετε of Luke are independent adaptations of the σὺ λέγεις of Mk. xv. 2, intended to assimilate our Lord's reply to the High Priest to His reply to Pilate.

Mark.	Matthew.	Luke.
xiv. 70.	xxvi. 73.	xxii. 58.
. . . Ἀληθῶς ἐξ αὐτῶν εἶ	. . . Ἀληθῶς [καὶ σὺ] ἐξ αὐτῶν εἶ	. . . καὶ σὺ ἐξ αὐτῶν εἶ

In Matthew καὶ σὺ om. D, Θ 1 &c., Syr. S. *b c h l* Orig.

Mark.	Matthew.	Luke.
xiv. 72.	xxvi. 75.	xxii. 61.
ἀνεμνήσθη . . . τὸ ῥῆμα	ἐμνήσθη . . . τοῦ ῥήματος	ὑπεμνήσθη τοῦ ῥήματος (Huck, λόγου)

Verbs of remembering in Greek normally take the genitive; the case alteration is then one that would inevitably occur to two editors independently. But λόγου, the reading of D and T.R. in Luke (since it makes Matthew and Luke differ), is probably correct.

Mark.	Matthew.	Luke
xiv. 72.	xxvi. 75.	xxii. 62.
ἐπιβαλὼν ἔκλαιεν	ἐξελθὼν ἔξω ἔκλαυσεν πικρῶς	[ἐξελθὼν ἔξω ἔκλαυσεν πικρῶς]

In Luke the verse is omitted by *a b e ff*² *i l*, *i.e.* by both African and European Latin.

Mark.	Matthew.	Luke.
xv. 39.	xxvii. 54.	xxiii. 47.
(Nothing corresponding.)	τὰ γινόμενα	τὸ γενόμενον

This is one of Hawkins's twenty selected cases. I should not myself regard this coincidence as a real one, as the "what had happened" referred to by Matthew and Luke respectively are, in the one case an event, in the other a saying, neither of which are found in Mark. It is, however, curious that D omits the words in Luke and substitutes φωνήσας.

Mark.	Matthew.	Luke.
xv. 43.	xxvii. 58.	xxiii. 52.
εἰσῆλθεν πρὸς τὸν Πειλᾶτον καὶ ᾐτήσατο	οὗτος προσελθὼν τῷ Πιλάτῳ ᾐτήσατο	[οὗτος] προσελθὼν τῳ Πιλάτῳ ᾐτήσατο

In Matthew προσῆλθε καὶ is read by D, Old Lat., (Syr. S.), (Sah.). In Luke οὗτος om. D, Sah. Since οὗτος has been already used once by Luke in this sentence, its insertion here is awkward, so D is probably correct. 69 reads αὐτός.

Mark.	Matthew.	Luke.
xv. 46.	xxvii. 59-60.	xxiii. 53.
. . . καθελὼν αὐτὸν ἐνείλησεν τῇ σινδόνι καὶ κατέθηκεν αὐτὸν	λαβὼν τὸ σῶμα . . . ἐνετύλιξεν αὐτὸ σινδόνι καθαρᾷ καὶ ἔθηκεν αὐτὸ	καὶ καθελὼν ἐνετύλιξεν αὐτὸ σινδόνι καὶ ἔθηκεν αὐτὸν

The agreement against Mark in three consecutive words ἐνετύλιξεν αὐτὸ σινδόνι followed by agreement in the uncompounded ἔθηκεν against κατέθηκεν is striking. But observe the MS. evidence.

(*a*) Mark, ἔθηκεν ℵ B L, D, Θ W 1 &c. 13 &c. 565. Mark is fond of compounds, so κατέθηκεν *may* be original; but if original, the fact of scribal correction along several independent

lines of transmission shows that independent correction by
Matthew and Luke would be inevitable. (*b*) Matthew ἐν σινδόνι
B D, Latt. Θ, Sah., Boh., Orig. With this reading another
small agreement vanishes. αὐτὸ for αὐτὸν is a "deceptive"
agreement. Matthew and Luke have rewritten Mark's
sentence in different ways, but in both αὐτὸ refers back to
σῶμα. (*c*) There remains the striking agreement ἐνετύλιξεν
against ἐνείλησεν. But 13 &c. read ἐνείλησεν in Matthew, as
in Mark. This is almost certainly right; for it is very unlikely
that the text of Matthew would be assimilated to that of Mark,
the least read Gospel, whereas assimilation to Luke, as we have
seen, is not infrequent. I suspect that ἐντυλίσσω was the more
dignified word and was the one conventionally appropriate to
this funeral operation ; as in English, when speaking of a shroud,
three writers out of four would instinctively prefer the word
" wind " to " wrap."

Mark.	Matthew.	Luke.
xvi. i.	xxviii. 1.	xxiv. 1.
καὶ διαγενομένου τοῦ σαββάτου	ὀψὲ δὲ σαββάτων τῇ ἐπιφωσκούσῃ εἰς μίαν σαββάτων	τῇ δὲ μιᾷ τῶν σαββάτων ὄρθρου βαθέως
		xxiii. 54.
		καὶ ἡμέρα ἦν παρασκευῆς καὶ σάββατον ἐπέφωσκεν

For the whole verse in Luke D *substitutes* ἦν δὲ ἡ ἡμέρα πρὸ
σαββάτου ; and for καὶ σαβ. ἐπέφ. c has *cenae purae ante
sabbatum*. The πρὸ σαββάτου of D could be accounted for as
a paraphrase of παρασκευῆς in an original text which omitted
the words καὶ σαβ. ἐπέφ. The reading of *c* might be a conflation of this text with another in which παρασκευῆς was
rendered *cenae purae*. If the omission was original, καὶ σαβ.
ἐπέφ. is an assimilation from Matthew.

In any case we note (*a*) that ἐπέφωσκε in Luke can only be
translated " begin," not " dawn " ; for he goes on to say that
they rested during the Sabbath ; while in Matthew it can only
have its natural meaning " dawn." (*b*) The passage in Luke

is not strictly parallel to those in Mark and Matthew printed above.

Mark.	Matthew.	Luke.
xvi. 5.	xxviii. 3.	xxiv. 4.
νεανίσκον . . . περι-βεβλημένον στολὴν λευκήν	ἦν δὲ ἡ εἰδέα αὐτοῦ ὡς ἀστραπὴ καὶ τὸ ἔνδυμα αὐτοῦ λευκὸν ὡς χιών.	ἄνδρες δύο . . . ἐν ἐσθῆτι ἀστραπτούσῃ

Luke has used the participle ἐξαστράπτων of garments in his account of the Transfiguration (ix. 29), and what Matthew compares to lightning is not the garments but the face ; so coincidence may be the explanation. But Marcion read λαμπρᾷ in Luke, and the author of the Gospel of Peter, who was familiar with all three Synoptics, reads βεβλημένον στολὴν λαμπροτάτην, which looks like a conflation of Mark with Marcion's (based on the Old Roman) text of Luke. Byz. reads ἐν ἐσθήσεσιν ἀστραπτούσαις, but L Syr. Hier. have λευκαῖς ; so that the B ℵ reading has not universal support.

SOME RESIDUAL CASES

I have purposely kept to the last the most remarkable of all the minor agreements, as it illustrates in a peculiarly interesting way the extent to which the problem we are considering belongs to the sphere, not of documentary, but of textual criticism.

Mark.	Matthew.	Luke.
xiv. 65.	xxvi. 67-68.	xxii. 64.
. . . καὶ ἤρξαντό τινες ἐμπτύειν αὐτῷ [καὶ περι-καλύπτειν αὐτοῦ τὸ πρό-σωπον] καὶ κολαφίζειν αὐτὸν . . . καὶ λέγειν αὐτῷ Προφήτευσον.	Τότε ἐνέπτυσαν εἰς τὸ πρόσωπον αὐτοῦ καὶ ἐκολά-φισαν αὐτόν, οἱ δὲ ἐράπισαν λέγοντες, Προφήτευσον ἡμῖν, χριστέ, τίς ἐστιν ὁ παίσας σε ;	καὶ περικαλύψαντες αὐ-τὸν ἐπηρώτων λέγοντες, Προφήτευσον, τίς ἐστιν ὁ παίσας σε ;

The words χριστέ, τίς ἐστιν ὁ παίσας σε ; occur in Mark also in some MSS. ; but, if one merely looks up the authorities in Tischendorf, the list is not imposing. But it takes on quite a different complexion when one discovers that the addition is found also in W, Θ, 13 &c., 579, 700. It then becomes apparent that the addition in Mark is influentially supported in each of three main streams of textual tradition: by the later Egyptian Δ, X, 33, 579, Sah.$^{cod.}$, Boh.; c. A.D. 400 by the African father Augustine (expressly, in a discussion of "The Agreements of the Evangelists"); by the Caesarean Θ, W, 13 &c., 565, 700, N, U, also by Arm., Syr. H$^{cl.}$. In the face of this evidence only two conclusions are open to us. *Either* the reading is correct and the words have accidentally dropped out of the text of Mark both in ℵ B L and in D *k*, *or* the passage is one which has specially invited assimilation, and this to such an extent that it has taken place independently along three different lines of transmission. The second alternative I believe to be correct. But the MS. evidence suggests that at any rate a certain measure of assimilation has infected the ℵ B L text also in this particular context. For the words describing the veiling, which I have bracketed in Mark, are omitted by D *a f*, with the substitution of τῷ προσώπῳ for αὐτῷ. Further, Θ, 565, Arm. have this substitution *in addition* to the ordinary reading—a conflation of two types of text which shows clearly that originally they agreed with D *a f*, the conflation being due to a reviser. Syr. S. agrees with D in the omissions, but makes the guards slap " his cheeks " instead of " him." This looks as if in the text from which the Syriac was translated the words τῷ προσώπῳ had been slightly displaced—a hypothesis confirmed by the reading "slapped his face" in some MSS. of the Sahidic. Further, it is to be noticed that the omitted clause does not occur in Matthew ; but he would have been unlikely to omit such a striking point, if it had occurred in his source, more especially as the whole point of the taunt " *Prophesy* who it is that struck thee " depends upon the fact that He was prevented by the veil from *seeing* who did it. Indeed this last consideration leads up to what I believe is the true solution—that the original text of Matthew and of Mark omitted *both* the veiling and the words " Who is it, etc." These two stand or fall together. In Luke they are both original ; and from Luke the first has got into the Alexandrian (but not into the earliest Antiochene and Western) text of Mark; the second has got into all the texts of Matthew.

The view that τίς ἐστιν κτλ. is an interpolation into Matthew from Luke was originally suggested to me by Prof. C. H. Turner, and at first I demurred to the view. But a consideration of the evidence that in Mark assimilation has been at work both in B ℵ and *fam.* Θ has removed my previous hesitation to believe that these MSS. have suffered interpolation in Matthew also. Further, the view argued in Chapter VIII., that Luke had an account of the Passion which was quite independent of, and in certain ways very different from, that of Mark, affects our judgement on this issue. Luke inserts the incident of the Mocking *before* the Trial by the high priest, instead of *after* the Trial, as in Mark and Matthew. This alteration of order in itself suggests he was following a different source. If, then, we accept the shorter text in Mark and reject τίς ἐστιν κτλ. in Matthew, we shall find that Matthew as usual is substantially reproducing Mark, but that Luke has an entirely different representation. In Mark the mockers spit on His face and slap Him and cry, "Play the prophet now!" In Luke they veil His eyes and then, striking Him, say, "Use your prophetic gift of second sight to tell the striker's name." Each version paints a consistent picture; but, if one half of Luke's picture is pieced on to Mark and the other half to Matthew (as in the ℵ B text), both are blurred, with the result that in the accepted text Matthew's version dulls the edge of the taunt in Mark, but does not succeed in substituting the quite differently pointed taunt in Luke.

Assimilation of parallels is a form of corruption which can result, and, as I have shown, has often actually resulted, in producing an *identical* corruption along more than one *independent* line of transmission. I suggest that for once this has happened along all lines. I should say, rather, all lines for which evidence is extant, for *k*, *e*, and Syr. C. are not here extant for Matthew. I will conclude with a quotation from Hort (vol. i. p. 150)—the italics are mine. "It must not of course be assumed to follow that B has remained unaffected by *sporadic* corruption . . . in the *Gospel of Matthew*, for instance, it has occasionally admitted widely spread readings of very doubtful genuineness." I suggest that the insertion of τίς ἐστιν ὁ παίσας σε is one of these.

The minor agreements which I have examined above include all that are sufficiently striking to be worth discussing in detail. The residue are agreements still more minute. Of these textual assimilation is the probable explanation. Indeed, it would perhaps be a better explanation of some of those which in the earlier part of this chapter I have attributed to the coincident editorial activity of Matthew and Luke. Very few of the scholars who have treated of this aspect of the Synoptic Problem appear to me to have an adequate appreciation of the immense amount of variation that exists, even between MSS. of the same family, in regard to just the kind of small points that are here involved, such as the order of words, interchange of prepositions especially in composition, substitution of one conjunction for another, the use of the article with proper names, and the like. Burton, using the printed text of Huck's Synopsis, has counted the agreements—apart from mere variation in order—and finds 275 words distributed over 175 separate phrases, of which all that are in any degree significant have been discussed above.[1] Other scholars have produced similar calculations.[2] But when the question at issue depends on minutiae of this kind, any figures whatsoever based on the printed text are wholly fallacious. The Byzantine MSS. present a fairly uniform text ; not so the earliest copies. We have 6 MSS. earlier than the year A.D. 500 ; of these B ℵ are very much closer to one another than any other two. So far as those readings are concerned which make any appreciable difference to the sense, the differences between these MSS. are not numerous. In the *Appendices ad Novum Testa-*

---

[1] *Principles of Literary Criticism of the Synoptic Problem*, p. 17.

[2] Hawkins (*Hor. Syn.*[2] p. 208 ff.), using the text of W.H., gives $20 + 118 + $ " about 100 " $= 238$, excluding cases which are obviously due to the influence of Q.

mentum (Oxford, 1889) Dr. Sanday gave a comprehensive selection of the important variants in the Gospels ; and so far as B ℵ are concerned, recent discovery has nothing to add to this list.   In the 166 variants here selected B ℵ differ 44 times, *i.e.* there are in all four Gospels only 44 differences between these MSS. sufficient to affect the sense to any appreciable extent.   Nevertheless, Mr. Hoskier[1] has found it possible to collect 3036 instances of divergence between B and ℵ.   The majority of these, I take it, are slips of the pen by the individual scribes; but the rest are made up of exactly the sort of minute points in regard to which Matthew and Luke agree against Mark.   But, if there are as many as 500 differences of this order between those two of our oldest MSS. which in general are the most closely agreed with one another, what is the use of calculations based on a printed text ?

CONCLUSION

In conclusion, I would offer certain general reflections suggested by the detailed evidence discussed above.   I apprehend that a reader who has read this chapter hastily, without having previously perused the chapters on the Manuscript Tradition, might possibly be inclined to say that I have taken the liberty of deserting the accepted text to pick and choose from any out-of-the-way MS. any reading that happens to fit in with my argument.   Quite the contrary ; I have purposely limited my citations to a very few MSS., selected because on other grounds they can be proved to represent local texts current at the beginning of the third century.   And the principles on which I have used their evidence are, in the main, those formulated by Hort, modified in their application by the discovery of fresh evidence since his time.   It may be worth while to elaborate this point.

[1] *Codex B and its Allies*, vol. ii., Quaritch, 1914.   I have to thank the learned author for a presentation copy of this work, which I have found useful, especially in drawing up Appendix I.   I am, however, unable to assent to the main conclusions which he draws from the phenomena.

(*a*) The great step forward made by Hort in restoring the original text of the Gospels was his inflexible resolution, first, to go behind the printed text to the original MSS. ; secondly, to go behind the evidence of the mass of MSS. to the small minority which could be proved to represent texts current in the earliest period. When Hort wrote, several of our most important authorities were unknown. This new knowledge has not altered Hort's principles, but it has considerably extended the field of early texts which the critic must consider.

(*b*) Hort recognised assimilation as a principal cause of corruption, and made freedom from assimilation one of his principal criteria of a pure text. He found the text of B the one that best satisfied this criterion, as well as certain others ; but in a few cases he judged that B also had suffered from assimilation in the form of interpolations of a harmonistic character from which D and the Old Latin had escaped. These he designated " Western non-interpolations." He also noticed and put in brackets as doubtful a number of minor " non-interpolations " of the same kind—though he hesitated definitely to reject them. I suggest that, in view of the evidence submitted above, this hesitation is shown in many cases to be unnecessary. Again, the determination of " Eastern " texts as well as " Western " has been made possible by recent discoveries ; surely Hort would have attached equal weight to the " non-interpolations " of this group of " Eastern " authorities.

(*c*) The reader may have noticed that, in the list of passages discussed above, there are four instances in which Hort deserted B—and the result was to create a minor agreement. Elsewhere, if he had deserted B, a minor agreement would have vanished If the instances are examined, it will be seen that in each of these cases Hort was faced by a conflict between two of the principles of criticism on which he worked. On the one hand, there was the principle that a reading which makes the Gospels differ is more likely to be original than one that makes them agree ; on the other was the principle that a MS. which approves itself as correct in five cases out of six is, other things being equal, entitled to be very seriously considered in the sixth. Now when, in their practical application, two critical principles conflict, the choice of reading necessarily becomes a matter of entirely subjective preference—unless we can find some objective criterion.

The moral I would draw is, that, if we will only use it, the objective criterion we desiderate is in our hands. The investigation summarised in this chapter has shown, I claim, that the only valid objection to the theory that the document used by Matthew and Luke was our Mark—that, namely, based on the existence of the minor agreements of these Gospels against Mark—is completely baseless. But if so, it follows that we are entitled—I would rather say we are *bound*—whenever the balance of MS. evidence is at all even, to make the determining factor in our decision the compatibility of a particular reading with the demonstrated fact of the dependence of Matthew and Luke on Mark. Renounce once and for all the chase of the phantom Ur-Marcus, and the study of the minor agreements becomes the highway to the recovery of the purest text of the Gospels.

LIST OF PARABLES

A

In Matthew only

The Tares (xiii. 24 ff.).
The Hid Treasure (xiii. 44).
The Pearl of Great Price (xiii. 45 f.).
The Drag-net (xiii. 47 ff.).

The Unmerciful Servant (xviii. 23 ff.).
The Labourers in the Vineyard (xx. 1 ff.)
The Two Sons (xxi. 28 ff.).
The Virgins (xxv. 1 ff.).

B

In Mark only

The Seed growing secretly (iv. 26 ff.).

C

In Luke only

The Two Debtors (vii. 41 ff.).
The Good Samaritan (x. 30 ff.).
The Importunate Friend (xi. 5 ff.).
The Rich Fool (xii. 16 ff.).
The Watching Servants (xii. 35 ff.).
The Barren Fig-tree (xiii. 6 ff.).
The Lowest Seat (xiv. 7 ff.).
The Tower Builder (xiv. 28 ff.).

The Rash King (xiv. 31 ff.).
The Lost Coin (xv. 8 ff.).
The Prodigal Son (xv. 11 ff.).
The Unrighteous Steward (xvi. 1 ff.).
Dives and Lazarus (xvi. 19 ff.).
Unprofitable Servants (xvii. 7 ff.).
The Unjust Judge (xviii. 1 ff.).
Pharisee and Publican (xviii. 9 ff.).

D

The parables occurring in more than one Gospel are given on p. 243.

Conventional usage seems to include " The Watching Servants " and " The Lowest Seat " in the category parable; but, curiously enough, it excludes " The Houses on Sand and Rock," Mt. vii. 24 ff. = Lk. vi. 47 ff., and " The Children in the Market Place," Mt. xi. 16 ff. = Lk. vii. 31 ff.

XII

THE LOST END OF MARK

SYNOPSIS

THE MS. EVIDENCE

Greek, Syriac, Armenian and Old Georgian evidence for complete omission of Mk. xvi. 9-16.

Significance of the Shorter Conclusion and of the epithet κολοβο-δάκτυλος.

Early evidence for the Longer Conclusion. The " Freer logion " —an addition found in W.

THE LOSS A PRIMITIVE ONE

There is no difficulty in supposing either (*a*) that the Gospel was never finished, or (*b*) that the earliest copy was accidentally mutilated.

The view that Mark went out of circulation for a time so that only one damaged copy survived is incompatible with the evidence for its wide use in the first half of the second century.

There are also fatal objections to the theory that the original ending was deliberately suppressed.

The copies of Mark used by Matthew and Luke seem to have ended abruptly at the same point as our oldest MSS. If so, the loss must be primitive.

THE LONGER CONCLUSION

The note in a X^cent. Armenian codex attributing the Longer Conclusion to the Presbyter Ariston probably represents, not a genuine tradition, but an ingenious conjecture by some reader of Eusebius.

Considerations of textual criticism suggest a Roman origin for the Longer Conclusion.

The addition found in W favours the hypothesis that it was

originally composed as a catechetical summary of Resurrection Appearances, not as a conclusion to the Gospel.

The Lost Ending—A Speculation

Tentative suggestion that the Appearance to Mary Magdalene and that to Peter by the lake in the Fourth Gospel represent, directly or indirectly, the lost ending of Mark.

Two objections from the standpoint of textual criticism considered.

The possibility that the conclusion of the Apocryphal Gospel of Peter was derived from the Lost End of Mark.

Considerations which suggest that John xxi. represents a portion of the Lost Ending.

Considerations in support of the view that an Appearance to Mary Magdalene was also found in Mark.

The evidence available quite insufficient to establish an assured result. But the improbability that the earliest tradition of the Resurrection Appearances should have left no trace at all in the Gospels is so great that even a tentative hypothesis is worth consideration.

CHAPTER XII

THE LOST END OF MARK

The MS. Evidence

Eusebius, *c.* 325, the most widely read scholar of Christian antiquity, states that in the oldest and best MSS. known to him the Gospel of Mark ended with the words " for they were afraid," xvi. 8 ; and he did not include the succeeding twelve verses in his canons or tables of parallel passages.[1] The Gospel ends at this point in B א, the two oldest and best MSS. known to us ; and as, in view of the statement of Eusebius, we should expect, there is good evidence (cf. p. 88) that it was absent from the old text of Caesarea represented by *fam.* Θ. The Gospel ends at the same point in Syr. S. ; also in nine of the ten oldest MSS. of the Armenian, which is additional evidence for the omission either in *fam.* Θ or in the Old Syriac. One early Armenian MS.—dated 989 (*sic*)—has the last twelve verses, but separated from the rest of the Gospel with a note " Of the presbyter Ariston." In the oldest MS. of the Georgian version, which is dated 897, the Gospel ends at xvi. 8. But the " Longer Conclusion " (as the last twelve verses are usually styled) is added as a sort of Appendix to the Four Gospels after the end of John, having apparently been copied from another text.[2]

What is known as the " Shorter Conclusion " is found in

---

[1] The fact that the verses were ignored in the Eusebian canons is noted at the end of Codex 1, 1582, and other MSS.

[2] *The Adysh Gospels* (Phototypic edition), Moscow, 1916. I owe this information to my friend Dr. R. P. Blake.

L Ψ 579 and two uncial fragments, in the Sahidic and Aethiopic versions, and in the African Latin k ; also in the margin in one Greek cursive, in the Harclean Syriac, and in the oldest MS. of the Bohairic. It reads as follows : " And all that had been commanded them they briefly reported to Peter and his company ; and after these things Jesus himself appeared, and from the East to the West sent through them the sacred and incorruptible proclamation of eternal salvation." In these Greek MSS. and most of the versions, but not in k, the Longer Conclusion (Mk. xvi. 9-20) follows the Shorter, being usually introduced by the words, " This also is current," ἐστὶ καὶ ταῦτα φερόμενα.

As the Shorter Conclusion is obviously an attempt by some early editor to heal the gaping wound, the MSS. and versions which contain it really afford additional evidence for a text that ended with ἐφοβοῦντο γάρ.

The distribution of the MSS. and versions, taken in connection with the statement of Eusebius, compels us to assume that the Gospel ended here in the first copies that reached Africa, Alexandria, Caesarea, and Antioch. Since in all probability the African text originally came from Rome, the burden of proof lies on the person who would argue that it was not also missing from the most ancient Roman text. And this would explain the epithet κολοβοδάκτυλος (as if in English one were to say " docked ") applied to Mark by the Roman theologian, Hippolytus, c. 200. Hippolytus himself used a text of Mark which contained the last twelve verses and understands the epithet of its author ; but its origin is more easily explained as originally applied to the book. Originally κολοβοδάκτυλος was used of a man who cut off a thumb in order to escape military service. Wordsworth and White suggest it may have come to mean " shirker," and that Hippolytus found the term applied to Mark by Marcion in order to discredit his Gospel, in allusion to the withdrawal from the work in Pamphylia which St. Paul so much resented, Acts xv. 38. But even so, Marcion's attack would have been twice as effective if the epithet carried a *double entendre*,

the author a *shirker*, his Gospel a *torso*. At any rate the author
of the Gospel cannot have originally meant to end it without the
account of the Appearance to the Apostles in Galilee which is
twice prophesied in the text (Mk. xiv. 28, xvi. 7). Indeed, the
words ἐφοβοῦντο γάρ in Greek may not even be the end of a
sentence; they lead us to expect a clause beginning with μή,
" They were afraid, lest they should be thought mad," or something to that effect.

The Longer Conclusion, found in the majority of MSS. and
in our printed texts, is not at all in the style of Mark ; and, as
will appear later, a close study of its contents makes it in the
last degree improbable that it was written by Mark himself.
But it must have been added at a very early date. Irenaeus,
c. 185,[1] quotes xvi. 19 expressly as from " the end of Mark " ;
and the Longer Conclusion already stood in the text used by
Tatian when compiling his Diatessaron c. 170 ; and there are
possible, though not quite certain, reminiscences of it in Justin
and in Hermas.   Since B ℵ were written in the fourth century,
both the Longer and the Shorter Conclusions were already of
great antiquity, and can hardly have been unknown to the scribes
who wrote these MSS. and, for that matter, to a fairly long
succession of MSS. from which they were copied.   Incidentally
I may be permitted to remark that an asceticism which could
decline to accept either of these endings argues a fidelity to a
text believed to be more ancient and more authentic, which
materially increases our general confidence in the textual tradition which these MSS. represent.

The discovery of W has added yet another to the previously
known endings of the Gospel. After xvi. 14 occurs the section
(part of which is quoted by Jerome, as occurring in some
MSS.), " And they replied saying, This age of lawlessness and
unbelief is under Satan, who does not allow what is under the
unclean spirits (emending two words of the Greek to correspond
with Jerome's Latin) to comprehend the true power of God;

---

[1] " In fine autem evangelii ait Marcus," *Adv. Haer.* iii. 10. 6.

therefore reveal thy righteousness. Already they were speaking
to Christ ; and Christ went on to say to them, The limit of the
years of the authority of Satan has been fulfilled, but other
terrible things are at hand, even for the sinners on whose behalf
I was delivered up to death, that they might turn to the truth
and sin no more, in order that they may inherit the heavenly
spiritual incorruptible glory of righteousness."

The Loss a Primitive One

But how are we to account for the Gospel thus breaking off
short ? It is, of course, possible that Mark did not live to finish
it. But, if he did, it would seem probable that the end of the
roll on which it was written must have been torn off before any
copies of it had got into circulation. Otherwise such a loss
would have been repaired at once from another copy.

There is no difficulty in supposing that the original copy of
Mark, especially if the Gospel was written for the Church of
Rome about A.D. 65, almost immediately lost its conclusion.
The two ends of a roll would always be the most exposed to
damage ; the beginning ran the greater risk, but, in a book
rolled from both ends, the conclusion was not safe. How in the
case of Mark the damage occurred it is useless to speculate. At
Rome in Nero's days a variety of " accidents " were by way of
occurring to Christians and their possessions. The author of
Hebrews, writing to the Roman Church,[1] alludes to the patient
endurance of " spoiling of their goods." That the little library
of the Church, kept in the house of some prominent adherent,
should have suffered in some " pogrom " is highly credible.
Curiously enough, there is evidence that copies of Romans were
in circulation which lacked the last two chapters, which looks

[1] This is not undisputed, but it is the simplest explanation of the fact that
while Hebrews profoundly influenced the theology of the Roman Church as early
as 1 Clement (c. A.D. 96), it was only quite late, on the authority of the East,
that it was accepted at Rome as by Paul. Probably for many years the Roman
tradition preserved the name of the real author.

as if one of the earliest copies of that Epistle, the one other document of which we can be quite sure that the Roman Church had a copy at this time, was similarly mutilated.

Professor Burkitt accounts for the disappearance of the original conclusion of Mark on a different hypothesis.[1] Mark, he argues, contained nothing that interested the Early Church which was not included in either Matthew or Luke ; hence for a generation or two, after those Gospels had been composed, it ceased to be copied. Later on, when, in face of the struggle with Gnosticism, a formal canon of accepted Gospels was under discussion, the Roman Church remembered that among its archives was an old copy of Mark, and insisted on this being included. But the end of the roll had been torn off, and there was no other copy in existence from which to repair the loss. To this theory there are formidable objections.

(1) A world-wide circulation of Mark in the first century is implied by the use made of it by the authors of Matthew, Luke, and John, who must have written in Churches at a wide remove from one another in theological outlook, and probably also in geographical situation. In view of this, the total disappearance in the course of the next fifty years of all copies but one is not very likely.

(2) Since Mark was made use of in the Diatessaron of Tatian, c. 170, the supposed rediscovery of the Gospel must have taken place before this date. And it must have been some considerable time before, for two reasons. First, the only point of compiling a Harmony of the Gospels at all was to meet the inconvenience, for purposes of practical teaching, of having four parallel, and in some points apparently conflicting, Lives of Christ. But the difficulty arising from there being four standard Lives must have been in existence long enough to be felt as a difficulty, before the remedy was looked for. Secondly, Tatian's copy of Mark contained the Longer Conclusion. But since the earliest copies of the rediscovered Gospel which reached Africa,

[1] F. C. Burkitt, *Two Lectures on the Gospels*, p. 33 ff. (Macmillan, 1901).

Alexandria, and Syria did not contain this, there must, on Burkitt's theory, have been an interval of time after the rediscovery of Mark during which the Gospel circulated without this addition to its text. The supposed rediscovery, then, must have been some time before 170, at the latest 165. Hence the period of complete disuse (during which all copies but one had time to disappear) must have been the fifty years or so previous to this. But for this period we have evidence of a widespread interest in and use of the Gospel.

(a) I regard it as practically certain that Mark was known to Justin c. 155 ; also to Hermas either c. 140, or, as I think more likely, c. 100. Both these are evidence for use in Rome.

(b) For Asia we have the evidence of Papias. He wrote rather late in life at a date which Harnack fixes as between 145–160 ; other scholars prefer an earlier date, 130–145.[1] His quotation of the famous statement about Mark made by John the Elder has already been discussed (p. 17 f.), so I will only stay to point out that, whatever else it proves, it is convincing evidence of three facts. First, at the time when Papias wrote, Mark was regarded in Asia as a standard work about whose origin Christians in general were interested. Secondly, the same thing held good in Papias' youth; or why, when he was collecting what seemed to him the most valuable of the teachings of the elders, did he trouble to note what they said about this Gospel ? Thirdly, if we accept the view maintained by some scholars that

---

[1] Irenaeus, A.D. 185, styles Papias "a hearer of John, a companion of Polycarp, and an ancient worthy " (ἀρχαῖος ἀνήρ). This distinctly favours the earlier date. But the De Boor fragment (printed Lightfoot and Harmer, *Apostolic Fathers*, p. 518 f.) seems to imply that he looked back on the time of Hadrian, who died A.D. 138. As, however, the statement containing the reference to Hadrian is attributed by Eusebius, iv. 3, to Quadratus, who, he expressly says, lived in the reign of Hadrian, it is probable that the fragmentist (who is undoubtedly indebted to Eusebius elsewhere) is really quoting, not Papias, but Eusebius—especially as the statement that a contemporary of Christ lived till the time of Hadrian is absurd, while it is by no means unlikely that one should have lived till the time (*i.e.* till the birth) of Quadratus, who may have been an old man in Hadrian's reign. See the discussion by Prof. J. V. Bartlet in Hastings' *Dict. of Christ and the Gospels,* ii. p. 311, col. 2.

Papias had not actually met the Elder John, Papias was not the first to elicit the statement from the Elder, in which case the date at which the Gospel of Mark, and the degree of authority to be attached to it, was a matter of public interest is pushed back earlier than Papias' youth.

(c) Irenaeus [1] says that Mark was the Gospel quoted as their authority by those heretics " who separate Jesus from Christ and say that Christ remained impassive while Jesus suffered." This statement is borne out by the fact that the apocryphal Gospel of Peter, which was evidently written in order to promulgate views of that kind, exhibits a special preference for Mark. The date assigned to " Apocryphal Peter " by most scholars is 130–140. Personally I think that too early ; but, on any hypothesis, the above statement of Irenaeus and the preference shown by " Peter " for Mark are evidence of the vogue of that Gospel in yet another circle in the middle of the second century.

The only conclusion that can be drawn from the facts is that the comparative neglect of Mark, of which there is plenty of evidence in later times, began *after*, not before, the universal acceptance of the Four Gospel Canon.

There is still less to be said for a hypothesis, at one time popular on the Continent, that the original end of Mark was deliberately suppressed and the Longer Conclusion substituted for it. This is supposed to have been done in Asia as part of the process of forming an official Four Gospel Canon in the latter part of the second century, the object of the suppression being to get rid of the discrepancy between Mark's account, in which the first Resurrection Appearance is in Galilee, and the Jerusalem tradition, followed by Luke and John.

The main objections to this theory are four.

(1) The idea that the Four Gospel Canon arose in Asia, or, indeed, that it came into existence as a result of any one official act at all, is one for which, so it seems to me, the evidence is non-existent.

[1] *Adv. Haer.* iii. 11. 7.

(2) While the revisers were about it, why did they not suppress the end of Matthew as well, since, in the matter of the first Appearance being in Galilee, his account equally conflicts with that of Luke and John ?   Again, if they were out to remove discrepancies between the Gospels, why did they not begin the " cut " a verse earlier, so as to remove the contradiction between Mark's statement that the women " told no man," and the statement by Matthew and Luke that they at once went and told the disciples ?

(3) How was it that revisers succeeded in getting the Churches of Africa, Alexandria, and Syria to accept at once the excision of the original ending, which spoils the Gospel, without accepting the substitute which is said to harmonise it with the others ?

(4) The use made of Mark by the authors of the other three Gospels proves, I must repeat, that Mark was universally read at the end of the first century ; and it continued to be so throughout the second.   Hence the suppression of the ending of a Gospel so widely circulated—and that at such an inappropriate point, ἐφοβοῦντο γάρ—would only have been possible if there had existed, as in the modern Roman communion, a highly centralised organisation able to enforce world-wide uniformity.   All our evidence as to the history of the Church during the first two centuries points to the lack of any such thing.   Least of all was it exercised to secure uniformity in the text of the Gospels.   We have actual MSS. written in the fifth century to show that even then there were still current three different endings of Mark (not counting the absence of an ending found in ℵ B), viz. the Longer Conclusion A C D, the augmented Longer Conclusion W, the Shorter Conclusion k (L Ψ).   If this variety was possible in the fifth century, after a hundred years of oecumenical conference, the notion is absurd that a machine existed in the second century capable of securing a world-wide excision in the text.

Let us now ask whether the end of Mark may not have been

already missing in the copies of the Gospel used by Matthew and Luke.

(1) The message of the Angel, " Go tell his disciples and Peter he goeth before you into Galilee : there shall ye see him as he said unto you " (Mk. xvi. 7), is clearly intended to refer back to the previously recorded prophecy of Christ, " Howbeit after I am raised up I will go before you into Galilee " (Mk. xiv. 28). Thus we are bound to infer that the lost conclusion of Mark contained an account of an Appearance to the Apostles in Galilee. Further, this must either have come after an Appearance to Peter separately, or it must have been an Appearance in which Peter was in some way especially singled out for notice, as he is in Jn. xxi.

Now Matthew follows the text of Mark all through the Passion story with great fidelity ; if, then, the copy of Mark used by him had contained a conclusion of this sort we should expect to find it reproduced by Matthew. But Matthew, though he records an Appearance to the Eleven in Galilee, does not especially mention the name of Peter in connection with it. Again, the most striking thing about the Gospel of Mark is the author's gift for telling a story in a vivid, picturesque, and realistic way. Elsewhere, wherever Matthew is following Mark, he abbreviates slightly and occasionally omits a picturesque detail ; nevertheless the account he gives is always a vividly realised and well-told story—full of detail, though not quite so full as the Marcan original. But Matthew's account of the Resurrection Appearances—to the two Maries (Mt. xxviii. 9-10) and subsequently to the Eleven (xxviii. 16-20)—is extremely meagre and is conspicuously lacking in these usual character-istics. Both, then, because Matthew does not mention Peter and because his narrative becomes exceptionally vague at the exact point where the authentic text of Mark now ends, we infer that his copy of Mark ended at that point.

(2) Luke, we have seen, based his account of the Passion and Resurrection mainly on his non-Marcan source ; but he has

omitted nothing of interest in the Passion story as found in Mark. He prefers his own source wherever it gives an equally elaborate or interesting version of any incident, but, where Mark contained something not occurring in his other source, he has added it in an appropriate context. If, then, Mark contained a detailed description of an Appearance to Peter and to the Apostles in Galilee, it would have been, to say the least of it, a " strong " procedure to ignore completely this well-established tradition and represent all the Appearances as having taken place in or near Jerusalem. But if in his copy of Mark, as in ours, there was no account of Appearances to ignore, that difficulty disappears. There is a more important consideration. At the end of the Emmaus incident Luke has a reference to the Appearance to Peter. The disciples are made to say, " The Lord is risen indeed and hath appeared to Simon " (Lk. xxiv. 34). That the first Appearance was to Peter is stated by Paul (1 Cor. xv. 5) and is implied in Mark. Luke's allusion makes it clear that he wished to bring out this fact. He accepted the tradition ; but it would seem as if he knew no more details about it than can be inferred from 1 Cor. and the existing text of Mark. If he had found a detailed account of the Appearance to Peter in his copy of Mark he would surely have made some effort to adapt it to his story, even if he was puzzled by the Galilean tradition.

We conclude, then, *either* that Mark did not live to finish his Gospel—at Rome in Nero's reign this might easily happen—*or* that the end of the Gospel was already lost when it was used by Matthew and Luke.

The Longer Conclusion

The note by an unknown scribe of an Armenian MS. of the tenth century which suggests that the Longer Conclusion was the work of the " Presbyter Ariston " has been taken rather too seriously in some quarters. It is, of course, always possible that a genuine tradition may survive in some late MS. in an out-of-the-way district. But the principles of historical criticism, as ordinarily accepted, do not encourage us to begin by taking for granted that a statement is good evidence when it appears for the first time in a writer who, on the face of it, is far removed both in time and place from the facts he attests.

That the evidence in this case is completely worthless will appear from the three following considerations.

(1) In nine of the ten oldest Armenian MSS. (dated from 887 to 1099 A.D.) the Gospel of Mark ends as in B ℵ. This is a piece of evidence for the history of the text of some importance ; for it shows that MSS., either Greek or Syriac, which lacked the Longer Conclusion were used by the original translators c. 400, or else by those who revised it at a slightly later date. Thus in any case it is evidence of the circulation or superior repute of the shorter text in the Far East. The fourth MS., which (after a break, indicating that the scribe regarded what follows as a sort of Appendix) adds the Longer Conclusion, does so with the words " of the Presbyter Ariston " in the margin of the first line.[1] This again is an important piece of evidence ; it is *prima facie* evidence that the Longer Conclusion was a late introduction in Armenia, and that when first introduced it was not regarded as being by the pen of Mark himself.

The possibility is theoretically open that the Longer Ending, plus the note attributing it to Ariston, was in the earliest form of the Armenian, but that later scribes—feeling that, if it was not by Mark himself, it was not canonical—dropped it out. But against this are the facts—(*a*) that from the fifth century onward the Longer Conclusion stood in the texts received in both the Greek and the Syriac Churches, both of which had considerable influence on Armenian Christianity. (*b*) In other respects the Armenian text is closely related to that of *fam.* Θ and Syr. S., which omit the Longer Conclusion. (*c*) Later Armenian MSS. included the Longer Conclusion without any note of doubt.

[1] Etchmiadzen MS. 229 ; phototypic reproduction, F. Macler (Paris, 1920).

It appears, then, that all the influences known to have operated
were in the direction, not of excluding, but of accepting this
particular reading. In that case the words " of the Presbyter
Ariston " must either have come in at the same time as the
Longer Conclusion, or else must represent a conjecture made
at a still later date to account for the fact that the addition
was not contained in the older text. Hence, whatever the
origin of the tradition, it has no claim to be regarded as specially
ancient ; for if the oldest Armenian did not contain the Longer
Conclusion it could not have contained a note about its authorship.

(2) The end of Mark was a problem much discussed. Eusebius
alludes to it several times, Jerome more than once. It is treated
in the Commentary attributed to Victor of Antioch found in
many MSS. ; and numerous MSS. have scholia dealing with it.
It is thus extremely improbable that any authentic tradition
as to the authorship of the Longer Conclusion which survived
would have entirely escaped the notice of all these, to turn up
in Armenia in the tenth century.

(3) The occurrence in a tenth-century Armenian MS. of
interesting information about the authorship of the disputed
ending of Mark is a phenomenon which cannot be estimated
apart from the appearance in the Greek-speaking world a century
earlier of much information of the same sort, quite obviously
based on mere conjecture or on tradition of no value at all.
From the IX[cent.] MS. K, for example, we learn that the Gospel
of Matthew was published by him in Jerusalem eight years after
the Ascension. From Y, of the same date, we gather that it was
written by Matthew in Hebrew, but translated by John ; later
MSS. have a similar note, but substitute for the name John that
of James, the brother of the Lord, or Bartholomew. A Vulgate
Latin MS. of the same century tells us that the fourth Gospel
was written by Papias at the dictation of the Apostle John.[1]
Surely, when we find a whole crop of this sort of thing springing
up in Greek and Latin MSS., the burden of proof lies with

[1] Quoted in Tischendorf, i. p. 967 *ad fin.*

anyone who wishes us to take seriously a piece of information
of a precisely similar character which turns up in an isolated
Armenian MS. a century later.

If anyone asks, why should conjecture light on the name of
Ariston in particular—or Aristion, which seems to have been an
interchangeable form of it—one may hazard a guess. What was
wanted was a name which would give to the Longer Conclusion
the authority of an eye-witness. But all names of Apostles
were excluded, since an Apostle would be hardly likely to add
an appendix to a Gospel written by one not an Apostle. The
Church history of Eusebius was everywhere read, and no passage would be more familiar than the one (cf. p. 18 above) on
the origin of the Gospels in which he tells how Papias reports
that he diligently sought for authentic traditions from Apostles
and from Aristion and the elder John, disciples of the Lord.
Here we have all the materials for a " brilliant conjecture." Is
not the Longer Conclusion of Mark one of the traditions derived
by Papias from an eye-witness, Aristion, the disciple of the
Lord ? Eusebius in the very same context alludes to the theory
(of Dionysius of Alexandria) that the Apocalypse was the work
of John the Elder. In the Eastern Church in the third and
fourth centuries there was a strong tendency to regard the
Apocalypse as, at best, of sub-canonical authority, and it was
not in the canon of the Syriac-speaking church on which the
Armenian largely depended for its literature. The Longer
Conclusion of Mark was another such sub-canonical writing—
what more natural than to surmise that it was the work of the
second of the two " disciples of the Lord " mentioned by Papias.
The conjecture is such a brilliant one that we might be tempted
to accept it and believe that Papias had actually said so, did we
not know how puzzled were Eusebius and others, who must have
read Papias, about the authenticity of the Longer Conclusion.

But if the Longer Conclusion has really nothing to do with
Papias' Aristion, where did it come from ? At any rate we have
two facts to start from.

(1) It was in the text of Mark used at Rome before Tatian, 170 ; *possibly* [1] in that used in Ephesus by the author of *Epistula Apostolorum, c.* 180, and certainly in the text of Irenaeus, 185, who was connected with both Rome and Ephesus.

(2) It was *not* in the text used in Africa, Alexandria, Caesarea, and Antioch half a century later ; and, to judge from the MS. evidence, did not establish itself there before the end of the fourth century.

It is thus a fair presumption that it originated either in Rome or in " Asia." The case for Asia depends, so far as I can see, on four pieces of evidence. (*a*) The idea that the Longer Conclusion is connected with the Aristion mentioned by Papias. On that no more need be said. (*b*) The theory that the original Conclusion was suppressed and this substituted for it at the time of forming of the Gospel Canon. The baselessness of this theory I have, I hope, sufficiently demonstrated above. (*c*) Mk. xvi. 18 reads, " if they shall drink any deadly thing, it shall in no wise hurt them." Papias, according to Eusebius,[2] gave, perhaps on the authority of the daughters of Philip who lived at Hierapolis, a " wonderful story about Justus who was sur-named Barsabas, how that he drank a deadly poison, and yet, by the grace of God, suffered no inconvenience." It is inferred that a document which apparently alludes to this incident must have been written in Asia where the story was known. The inference is precarious. It is not suggested Justus ever left Palestine ; but " all roads led to Rome," and if a story of a wonderful escape of an eminent Christian from poisoning was current it would probably be told in Rome before long. (*d*) The Longer Conclusion is supposed to be dependent upon the Fourth Gospel, and, therefore, to have been written in the Church where

---

[1] Even in view of the other passages (cf. p. 70) which suggest that the *Epistula* used a Western text, the inference that its author knew the Longer Conclusion is highly precarious. The women go to the tomb " weeping and mourning," *Epist.* 9 ; Mary goes to the Apostles " as they mourned and wept," Mk. xvi. 10.

[2] Euseb. *H.E.* iii. 39.

that Gospel was earliest in circulation. But, if the author of the Longer Conclusion knew John, why did he ignore the Appearance to Thomas? Presumably he compiled his list of Appearances with an apologetic purpose; why then leave out the most "evidential" of them all? There is only one point of contact between John and the Longer Conclusion, and that is the mention of Mary Magdalene as the witness of the first Appearance. But Matthew also records the first Appearance as being to Mary Magdalene and Mary the mother of James and Joses. This second Mary is otherwise an absolutely unknown figure.

It is a law of the evolution of tradition that names to which no incident of dramatic interest is attached tend, either to gather incidents round themselves, or else to drop out. Consider this series. Mark mentions three women at the tomb, Matthew mentions two, the Longer Conclusion only one. That one was not only their leader, but also the only one about whom a fact of interest was known, "that seven devils were cast out of her." Besides this tendency in tradition, the author of the Longer Conclusion was evidently influenced by the desire to be brief. If he summarises in two verses the Emmaus story, which takes twenty-three verses in Luke, he obviously does not want to fill up space with mere names. Obviously a knowledge of John is not required to explain the dropping of the other names. The Appearance to Mary may be derived *either from Matthew or else from oral tradition,* for it is the kind of thing in which oral tradition would be interested. Again, if we look more closely at the parallels we note that in the Longer Conclusion the disciples, when they heard from Mary that "he was alive and had been seen by her, disbelieved." There is not the slightest hint of this in John; Thomas, who does doubt, is not *then* present; but it *is* emphatically asserted in Luke in regard to the reception by the Apostles of the news of the three women that they had seen the angels who said He was risen. Thus, while the mention of Mary, the one supposed point of contact with John, can equally well be interpreted as a point of contact with Matthew, there is

a notable absence of allusion to the Thomas story—for the
author's purpose the most useful story in John.   But, since John
was the characteristically Ephesian Gospel, we should expect to
find quite a number of rather marked points of contact with it
in a document of this sort emanating from Asia.

If, however, the case for Asia collapses, we may be content
to accept the alternative view to which the textual evidence
very decidedly points, and affirm that the Longer Conclusion
was added in Rome.

With this in mind let us examine the document a little more
closely.   Everything in it, except the mention of the Appearance
to Mary and the drinking poison, appears to be derived either
from the Gospel of Luke or from the Acts.   There are summary
allusions to the disbelief by the Apostles in the women's message
(Mk. xvi. 11, cf. Lk. xxiv. 11); to the walk from Emmaus ; to
the Appearance to the Eleven, with their hesitation to believe the
reality of the thing they saw and the command to preach to all
nations ; to the Apostolic signs—casting out devils, speaking
with tongues, the viper which clung to St. Paul in Malta but
did not hurt him.   Even the Appearance to Mary Magdalene,
though not derived from Luke, identifies her by a formula
taken from Lk. viii. 2, "from whom he had cast out seven devils."

The natural inference that we should draw is that the Longer
Conclusion was written in a Church where Luke and Acts had
been long established, but where Matthew, if known at all, had
only recently been accepted; and Harnack produces some reasons
for the belief that Matthew was not accepted at Rome till
about A.D. 120.[1]   The Longer Conclusion opens in a way which
suggests that it was not originally intended, like the Shorter
Conclusion, to heal a wound in the text of Mark.   It reads as if
it was originally a summary intended for catechetical purposes ;
later on the bright idea occurred to some one of adding it as a
sort of appendix to his copy of Mark.   In the first instance an

---

[1] Cf. p. 525 below; also *The Date of the Acts and the Synoptists*, E.T., p. 134 n.
Williams and Norgate, 1911).

interval of a blank line might be left to mark that it was not part of the authentic text, but in subsequent copies this blank line would soon disappear. The hypothesis that Mk. xvi. 9-20 was originally a separate document has the additional advantage of making it somewhat easier to account for the supplement in the text of W (cf. p. 337 f.) known as the " Freer logion." A catechetical summary is a document which lends itself to expansion ; the fact that a copy of it had been added to Mark would not at once put out of existence all other copies or prevent them suffering expansion. No doubt as soon as the addition became thoroughly established in the Roman text of Mark, it would cease to be copied as a separate document. But supposing that a hundred years later an old copy of it in the expanded version turned up. It would then be mistaken for a fragment of a very ancient MS. of Mark, and the fortunate discoverer would hasten to add to his copy of Mark—which, of course, he would suppose to be defective—the addition preserved in this ancient witness.

THE LOST ENDING—A SPECULATION

If I venture a suggestion on this subject, it is with the distinct proviso that what I write is intended to be read, not as "criticism," but merely as "scientific guessing." No harm is done by guessing of this sort, it may even have a certain interest, provided always that no one mistakes the speculations so reached for " assured results of criticism," and then proceeds to use them as premises from which further deductions may be drawn. The " scientific guess " in which I venture to indulge is that the lost end of Mark contained an Appearance to Mary Magdalene, followed by one to Peter and others when fishing on the Lake of Galilee, and that John derived his version of these incidents from the lost conclusion of Mark. I do not, of course, suggest that we have either of these stories exactly as they stood in Mark. Wherever John adopts a story from Mark, he does so with a considerably greater freedom in regard to language and details than do Matthew or Luke. Nevertheless, except where he is conflating material from Mark with another source, John does not seem substantially to alter the main facts and the general impression. This hypothesis I believe is worth working out in detail. But before doing this, two *prima facie* objections must be met.

(1) At first sight it may seem unlikely that the original ending of Mark should be preserved in Ephesus but lost in Rome. But we know that during Paul's imprisonment at Rome, Mark was contemplating a visit to Asia (Col. iv. 10), and a little later (2 Tim. iv. 11) Paul summons him to return to Rome, "for he is useful to me for ministering." The words occur in that portion of 2 Timothy which is most universally recognised as a fragment of a genuine letter, probably preserved at Ephesus. If so, Mark had been working in or near Ephesus ; and, as the context implies, was regarded by Paul as a useful and effective worker very shortly before the date at which he wrote the Gospel. What, then, could be a more natural thing for Mark to do, the moment he has finished writing a Gospel for the Church of Rome, than to send a copy to the Church of Ephesus by the next Christian who was travelling that way on any kind of business ? In that case the Ephesian copy would be the first ever made, and would have been made before the original was mutilated.

We may surmise that Mark's "usefulness for ministering" lay in some part in his command of anecdotes about the life and teaching of Christ. But he would have told these stories in Ephesus also. Hence the fact that Mark had worked in Asia makes it possible to suggest an alternative hypothesis that John is dependent, not on the lost written end of Mark, but upon Mark's account of the Resurrection Appearances, which survived in Asia in the form of oral tradition. This hypothesis, however, is for practical purposes so nearly equivalent to the one I have propounded above that it may, so far as arguments for or against it are concerned, be treated as a minor variation of the same hypothesis.

(2) If the original conclusion survived at Ephesus, how came that which now stands in our New Testament to take its place ? The answer to this question may well be that the present ending was added so soon that it had time to become part of the text accepted at Rome before the date—some time in the latter half of the second century—when (as seems likely) the Churches of Rome and Ephesus exchanged notes on the Canon. At any rate we have already seen that it must have been added at a very early date. If the Longer Conclusion was composed as a separate document about 100–110, and had become firmly established in the text of Mark as read in Rome, say by A.D. 140, the original ending, even if preserved at Ephesus, would never be restored. Mark being the Roman Gospel, the Roman text of Mark would everywhere be regarded as the more authentic—except perhaps in Alexandria, which also claimed a special connection with its author. But the oldest Alexandrian text lacked an ending. Supposing the early Ephesian and the Roman text showed two different endings, this, if known to a scholar like Origen, would only confirm him, brought up as he was in the traditions of textual criticism current in Alexandria, in the belief that the mutilated text was the original. Moreover, as we have already seen (p. 69), the Textus Receptus was the text adopted in the great sees of Antioch and Constantinople, so that the old text of Ephesus was swamped at an early date and has left no trace on the MS. tradition. This would the more easily happen since, on our hypothesis, the same story, but told in a form more attractive to the Christian public, was contained in John. There would be no strong motive to keep alive what would seem a less interesting version of the same story.

The suggestion that the story of the Appearance and final charge to Peter on the Lake of Galilee in Jn. xxi. was derived, with some modification, from the lost ending of Mark has been commended by Harnack and others, on the ground mainly that the Apocryphal Gospel of Peter contained a version of the incident. The surviving fragment of the Apocryphal Gospel

2 A

of Peter ends : " But we the twelve disciples of the Lord wept and were grieved : and each one grieving for that which was come to pass departed to his home. But I, Simon Peter, and Andrew my brother took our nets and went away to the sea ; and there was with us Levi, the son of Alphaeus whom the Lord. . . ." Here, unfortunately, the text of the fragment breaks off ; but evidently the words constitute the beginning of an account of an Appearance of the Lord by the Sea of Galilee. From the fragment of it that remains it is evident that the Gospel of Peter can in no way be regarded as an independent historical authority. It is written in the interest of the theory—already combated in the Asian document 1 John[1] —that the Divine Christ departed from the human Jesus and was taken up into Heaven before the latter died on the Cross.

Professor C. H. Turner[2] in a brilliant, and on the whole convincing, article argues that the author of the Gospel of Peter was familiar with our Gospel of John. It does not, however, necessarily follow that he derived this particular incident from Jn. xxi. If so, why does he put first an Appearance which John distinctly affirms to be the third ? Also, why are the names of disciples mentioned as present so different—Andrew and Levi as against Thomas, Nathaniel, the sons of Zebedee, and two others ? The mixture of resemblance and difference is accounted for more easily if John and Peter are divergent versions of a third source than if either is dependent on the other. But it is clear that the main source used by the author of Apocryphal Peter was Mark. And since " Peter " claims to be written by Mark's master, we should expect it to concur with Mark, except where the author desired to supplement the traditional narrative with doctrinal modifications or legendary embellishments of his own. It is noticeable that Levi the son of Alphaeus is mentioned in " Peter " : the description of him, " son

[1] 1 Jn. v. 6, " not with water only, but with the water and the blood " (*i.e* a real death)—a reply to the position of Cerinthus, or some predecessor.
[2] *J.T.S.*, Jan. 1913.

of Alphaeus," only occurs in Mark. Also the account of the visit of the women to the tomb follows Mark rather closely. In particular the author preserves the detail " Then the women feared and fled," which corresponds to the last words of the true text of Mark, but are directly contradictory to the statements of both Matthew and Luke. Hence the hypothesis that in the paragraph which immediately follows he is also dependent on Mark cannot be called improbable.

In support of the view that John xxi. represents either the lost end of Mark or an oral tradition more or less its equivalent, five considerations may be alleged.

(1) The lost ending of Mark must have contained an Appearance to Apostles in Galilee which either followed an Appearance to Peter, or was itself one in which Peter figured in some conspicuous way (cf. p. 343).

(2) If the story in Jn. xxi. had stood alone in a separate document, without the note (xxi. 14) stating that this was the third Appearance, we should have inferred that the Appearance described was meant to be understood as the first. We seem to see (xxi. 2-3) a group of disciples sitting dejected and inert after their disillusioned flight to Galilee, and Peter, always the one with the most initiative, rousing himself to the resolution to go back to the old and ordinary life, " I go a-fishing." The others follow. Jesus is seen on the bank. They do not know Him. They seem to be taken by surprise, which is strange if previous Appearances had already convinced them He was alive. An incident and conversation follow of which the general significance is a second call of Peter to be a fisher of men. His late denial of his Master is wiped out by a reaffirmation of devotion, and he is given the commission " Feed my sheep " and so made the leader in the Christian mission.

(3) The addition of a miraculous draught of fishes in the story of the original call of Peter in Luke v. 4-7, and the addition, in Matthew xiv. 29-31, to the story of the Walking on the Water of the incident of Peter leaving the boat to meet the

Lord, are best explained as fragments of a story like that of Jn. xxi. current in oral tradition. If so, they are independent evidence that the story was in circulation at a very early date.

(4) Like everything else in the Fourth Gospel this story has been remoulded in the light of the experience and outlook of the author and the present needs of the Church, but it is certainly the kind of ending one would have expected Mark to give his Gospel. In particular, I much doubt whether Peter's denial would have been so emphasised in the Gospel unless as a foil to a subsequent story, the point of which lay in its cancelling a former weakness of the Apostle. Again, the fact that Peter, with whatever hesitation, did ultimately come out definitely on the side of the Gentile mission, and that in doing so he felt that he was carrying out his Master's real intention, must, I think, have somehow been adumbrated in a Gospel written for the Church of Rome.

(5) A critical analysis (cf. Chap. XIV.) of the Fourth Gospel suggests that the two main sources which John elsewhere combines are the written documents Mark and Luke (or Proto-Luke). It is, therefore, likely that in this passage also the traditions which he is combining are derived from the same two sources. Since, then, the Appearance to the Apostles in Jerusalem belongs to the Lucan tradition, those to Mary Magdalene and to Peter while fishing by the Sea of Galilee, with the final commission of Christ " Feed my sheep," may well have stood in the conclusion of Mark's Gospel as it was read in Ephesus about A.D. 90. Indeed we may surmise that one reason why the last chapter of John (which is obviously a kind of Appendix) was added was to harmonise that Gospel with the Marcan tradition of the Resurrection Appearances, while affirming that the Appearance by the Lake was the third, not, as previously related in Mark, the first, of the Appearances to any of the Twelve.

The suggestion that the Appearance by the Sea of Galilee was preceded by an Appearance to Mary Magdalene, something like that recorded by John, has not, so far as I am aware, been put forward before. In its behalf I advance the following considerations.

(1) We shall see (p. 408 ff.) that, apart from the Appearance to Mary, John shows no trace of dependence on Matthew. The hypothesis that the Appearance to Mary originally stood in Mark enables us to explain the occurrence in both Mt. xxviii. 10 and Jn. xx. 17 of an Appearance to Mary with the description of the disciples as " my brethren " which is not paralleled elsewhere.

(2) Again, the Appearance to Mary as described by John is entirely in the manner of the vivid and dramatic story-telling for which Mark is famed. Mark is one of those people who simply cannot tell a story badly—witness the tale of the daughter of Herodias and John the Baptist, the appeal of which to the artistic imagination every picture gallery in Europe proves. If ever he finished his Gospel, the Resurrection scenes would have been visualised in every detail. And there is no scene in the Fourth Gospel—again I call the painters in as evidence —more vividly pictured than that of Mary Magdalene in the Garden.

(3) John, as already observed, seems to follow alternately, or to conflate, two main sources, Mark and Luke (or a source of Luke). Since the Appearance to Mary is not found in Luke, it was probably absent from his non-Marcan source—and Luke's copy of Mark, we have seen, ended at xvi. 8. John, then, could not have derived the story either from Luke's source or from our Third Gospel. Whence, then, did John derive it ? Of course he might have got it from Matthew ; but, apart from this incident, John shows no definite knowledge of Matthew, still less any inclination to follow him. Much the simplest hypothesis is that John derived the Appearance to Mary from Mark (or an oral tradition representing what Mark would have contained), especially as an incident which turned the " fear " of the woman into joy would have formed a most appropriate continuation of what remains of his broken text.

(4) Consider the situation at Rome if, after some police raid or riot, the end of the Church copy of Mark was found to have been torn off. Its general purport would have been known; many would remember roughly what it had contained, and the loss might have been replaced from memory. But this would have been inaccurate, and hopes may have been entertained that another copy might turn up. In the meantime there would remain a tradition, growing more vague in course of time, that the lost ending had contained an Appearance to Mary in Jerusalem, followed by an Appearance to the Apostles in Galilee. Now this is what we find in Matthew. The end of Matthew is exactly the kind of conclusion we should expect if the first man who took a copy of the mutilated Gospel to Antioch had written down on the back of the last sheet his recollections of the substance of what he had been told at Rome the lost conclusion had once contained.

(5) The view that oral tradition at Rome, ultimately dependent on the lost end of Mark, represented the first Appearance as being to Mary, would (equally with dependence on Matthew) account for the opening of the Longer Conclusion of Mark, "He appeared first to Mary Magdalene, from whom he had cast out seven devils." The seven devils are derived from Luke (viii. 2); and as we have already noted, apart from the Appearance to Mary, all other details in the Longer Conclusion which occur in the New Testament at all are to be found in Luke and Acts. For though there is a point of contact with Matthew in the command to preach and baptize—Luke also, it should be noted, has the command to preach to all nations—there is in the actual language used nothing in common in the parallel Mk. xvi. 15-16 =Mt. xxviii. 19-20 but the single and inevitable word "baptism."

(6) From Paul's account of the Resurrection Appearance (1 Cor. xv. 5) one would naturally infer that the first Appearance was to Peter. Luke's narrative confirms this impression. How, then, are we to explain the emphatic statement in the Longer

Conclusion that the *first* Appearance was to Mary ? I suggest
that there was ancient tradition at Rome to this effect so firmly
established that it could hold its own against the *prima facie*
evidence of Paul. In that case the Longer Conclusion of Mark
is best understood as the attempt to harmonise the old Roman
tradition of a first Appearance to Mary Magdalene with the
newly authenticated information which the Lucan writings
had brought to the Church. Its addition to the text of Mark
would not only help to preserve this tradition, but would be
almost necessary, if the old Roman Gospel of Mark was to
maintain its existence side by side with the longer and more
interesting, but more recent, Gospel of Luke.

At any rate the preference in three of our Gospels, as we
have them, of a tradition apparently contradicting a written
statement of Paul does require an explanation. We have definite
evidence that 1 Corinthians was the epistle which was most
widely read in Christendom in the Sub-Apostolic Age. The critic
is bound to produce a hypothesis to explain why, in despite
of this evidence that the first Appearance was to Peter, a
tradition prevailed in three different Gospels, representing
presumably three different Churches, which assigns the supreme
privilege of being the first to see the risen Lord, not to the
Prince of the Apostles, but to a woman, of whom nothing is
known save that seven devils were cast out of her. A tradition
established so early in different Churches (most probably in
Antioch, Ephesus, and Rome) must have gone back to great
antiquity and have been regarded as authenticated by irrefutable
authority. But if it originally stood in Mark, which in a point
like this may be supposed to rest on Peter's own reminiscences,
then there was the authority of Peter himself that he had in
this matter been forestalled by a woman.

But why, it may be objected, if the Appearance to Mary
originally stood in Mark, is it omitted in the Apocryphal
Gospel of Peter, which we have assumed is here dependent on
Mark ? Apocryphal Peter, in order to vindicate its doctrinal

curiosities, is particularly concerned to emphasise the fiction of Apostolic authorship. This is shown by the intrusion of the words " I, Simon Peter," which would be wholly unnecessary in a Gospel known to be written by an Apostle, and is, at any rate in this particular context, a most inappropriate repetition of a claim to authorship which must have been stated before. But clearly an author who feels it so necessary to emphasise the ego of Simon at this point cannot afford to let the first Appearance of Christ be to anybody else. There is a further reason. Apocryphal Peter is a second-century work. Celsus, the great second-century opponent of Christianity, pours much scorn on the belief in the Resurrection on the ground that it originated in the fancy of a neurotic woman. There was an apologetic reason for the omission.

Such cogency as the foregoing arguments possess is largely dependent on the correctness of the analysis of the sources of John essayed in a later chapter. And, even if the correctness of that analysis be assumed, they fall far short of proof. Yet the view that the earliest account of the Resurrection Appearances has disappeared without leaving a trace is in itself so improbable that I have thought it worth while to outline a hypothesis which makes it possible to affirm the contrary, even though from the nature of the evidence it can be no more than an interesting speculation.

PART III

THE FOURTH GOSPEL AND ITS SOURCES

I see His blood upon the rose,
   And in the stars the glory of His eyes;
His body gleams amid eternal snows,
   His tears fall from the skies.

I see His face in every flower;
   The thunder and the singing of the birds
Are but His voice—and carven by His power
   Rocks are His written words.

All pathways by His feet are worn,
   His strong heart stirs the ever-beating sea;
His crown of thorns is twined with every thorn,
   His cross is every tree.

From
"The Complete Poetical Works of J. M. Plunkett."
By permission of The Talbot Press, Dublin.

XIII

JOHN, MYSTIC AND PROPHET

SYNOPSIS

Mysticism, Greek and Hebrew

The Fourth Gospel should not be classed among works definitely historical in intention ; it belongs rather to the Library of Devotion. The author is a Christocentric mystic conscious of prophetic inspiration. In him are combined the religious experience of the Hebrew prophet and the philosophic mysticism of the school of Plato.

The Discourses of John

The contrast between the Jewish practice of preserving the *ipsissima verba* of Wise Men and Rabbis and the Greek literary tradition by which an author put into the mouths of historical characters speeches of his own composition.

The Synoptics reflect the Jewish practice ; John's method is akin to the Greek, but with the significant difference that the author regarded himself as a prophet inspired by the Spirit of Jesus, and therefore considered the discourses as the utterances of that Spirit and not as his own individual composition.

The Logos

Probably both the Philonic conception of the Logos and also the paraphrastic expression " the Memra," found in the later Aramaic Targums, were known to the author ; but, since his purpose was to interpret Christianity to the Greek world, his conception is more nearly related to that of Philo.

The Quest for Sources

The ordinary methods of source-criticism cannot be applied to

363

this Gospel; so much so that most of the " Partition Theories " recently propounded may be ruled out at once.

(1) Analogies drawn from Old Testament criticism are not applicable, nor even those supported by the critical study of the Synoptics. Illustration of this.

(2) A further caution suggested by the psychology of authorship.

(3) Certain cases of lack of connection between paragraphs, which might seem evidence of a fusion of written sources, are better explained by the theory of accidental disarrangements in an early MS.

CREATIVE MEMORY

The creative activity of the subconscious mind has always a dramatic quality; this especially true of the mystic or the artistic temperament. In such cases memory tends to enhance detail along the line of the special interest of the individual.

In antiquity this tendency was not checked by the training in accuracy emphasised in modern education, with its stress on the scientific value of correctness of observation. Illustrations of this.

FACT AND SYMBOL

The effort to discover an eternal meaning behind the veil of historic fact might well lead to modifications of detail in John's description of events; but the free invention of incidents would be quite another matter.

The Church in Asia was fighting a battle on two fronts—against the Gnostics, who tended to dissolve the historical into symbol and myth, and against the Judaisers, who could not rise beyond an Adoptionist Christology conceived of in terms of apocalyptic picture-thinking. The *via media* which John champions centres round the conception of the Word made flesh. From this conception it seems to follow (1) that fact as fact is of value, but (2) that it is as an " acted parable " bodying forth some lesson of eternal moment.

Hence it is probable that stories like the raising of Lazarus came to the author in some document or oral tradition which, rightly or wrongly, he believed to be historical.

THE MYSTIC VISION

The possibility that certain of the scenes described had been *seen* by the author in the mystic trance. If so, the allegorical element in them is perhaps to be accounted for by the psychology of dream symbolism. A suggestion of Evelyn Underhill, based on analogies from Mediaeval Mystics.

CHAPTER XIII

JOHN, MYSTIC AND PROPHET

MYSTICISM, GREEK AND HEBREW

THE Gospels were written in the great age of Classical Biography ; Luke, the most cultivated of the Synoptics, differs hardly at all, either in his conception of the purpose of biography as predominantly didactic or in his literary methods, from his famous contemporaries,[1] Plutarch and Tacitus. The difference lies in the subject treated, not in the historical ideal of the several writers. The other two Synoptists—Mark in his unstudied style, Matthew in his more overt expression of an apologetic and practical intention—depart a little, but not strikingly, from the literary model of the day. But the Fourth Gospel stands apart. It does not purport to be a Life of Christ. Avowedly it is a selection, for a special purpose. " Many other signs therefore did Jesus . . . which are not written in this book : but these are written, that ye may believe . . . and that believing ye may have life in his name " (Jn. xx. 30 f.).

If, then, we are asked to what class of literature the Fourth Gospel should be referred, we reply that it belongs neither to History nor Biography, but to the Library of Devotion. It will be misunderstood unless it is approached in a spirit comparable to that in which we approach the *Confessions* of Augustine or the *Imitation* of à Kempis. We must read it, as we read the book of Job, with our attention fixed less on the events recorded or

---

[1] These actually wrote slightly later than Luke; but biography became popular with Hermippus at Alexandria 200 B.C.

on the characters of the dialogue than on the profundities of
thought which through them are dramatically bodied forth.
This Gospel is a meditation, an inspired meditation, on the Life
of Christ. It is the work of one whom one cannot call philosopher,
because he is a mystic who feels that he has got beyond philosophy
—like Plotinus when he had seen the beatific vision, or like
Aquinas, who, when nearing the end of his *Summa*, hung up his
inkhorn and pen, saying, " What I have seen so transcends what
I have written I will write no more."

The starting-point for any profitable study of the Fourth
Gospel is the recognition of the author as a mystic—perhaps the
greatest of all mystics. To him the temporal is the veil of the
eternal, and he is ever, to use von Hügel's phrase, " striving to
contemplate history *sub specie aeternitatis* and to englobe the
successiveness of man in the simultaneity of God." [1] But, if
this is so, it follows that any inquiry into the sources of the
Fourth Gospel will be futile which does not approach the subject
from the standpoint of the psychology of the mystic temper.

The title " mystic " has dubious associations ; it has been used
to cover a very large variety of experiences. It is often employed
to give an imposing sound to childish speculations, or to practices
which in the last resort are merely tricks of narcotic self-bemuse-
ment. In a nobler sense the word is used of the religious side of
the philosophic tradition dominant in Hellenic thought, seen at
its highest in Plato and Plotinus. The mysticism of John is
nearer akin to this, but it is not the same. His mysticism, like
that of Paul, is a mysticism centred, not on Absolute Being, but
on the Divine Christ. The character of the mystic aspiration
is necessarily affected by the conception entertained of the nature
of the object towards which it is directed. The passion for
union with the One becomes qualitatively different if that One
is conceived of in the likeness of the historic Jesus. And just

---

[1] Cf. *Encyclopaedia Britannica*, art. " John, Gospel of "—one of the most
important discussions of the problem of the Fourth Gospel to be found in
English.

in so far as the object is visualised by John as concretely personal,
the religious experience which is its correlate is continuous with
the Old Testament, rather than with the Platonic, apprehension
of the reaction of the soul to the Divine.

The author of the Fourth Gospel stands between two worlds,
the Hebrew and the Greek, at the confluence of the two greatest
spiritual and intellectual traditions of our race.   In him Plato
and Isaiah meet.   To call John a mystic is only correct so long
as one remembers that in the Hebrew tradition the prophet is
the counterpart of him whom elsewhere we style the mystic.   The
religious experience of the prophet is not quite the same as that
of the mystic, though closely allied.   We shall misapprehend
both the psychology and the message of John if we forget that
he is a Jew first, and never quite a Greek, and unless we relate
the experience of which his Gospel is the record with that revival
of prophecy which is the conspicuous feature of the Early Church.

The higher religion of the Old Testament was, humanly
speaking, due to a long line of outstanding prophets.   After the
Captivity, the Law—which, as modern studies of the Old Testament have shown, was in its present form the work of priests and
scribes building on the basis of the ethical monotheism of the
great prophets—came more and more into prominence.   The idea
grew up that the succession of prophets had come to an end and
that no new revelation of God was to be expected.   The claim
of John the Baptist to prophetic inspiration broke a silence
which had lasted for more than three hundred years.   But once
the tradition that direct revelation had ceased was broken,
prophecy as a living contemporary institution resumed its ancient
importance and prestige, within—not outside—the Christian
community.   Prophets are ranked by Paul with Apostles as the
foremost spiritual leaders of the Church,[1] and we have frequent
allusion to them elsewhere in the New Testament.   The essence
of prophecy was the claim to direct inspiration.   The prophet
regarded himself, and was regarded by others, as the mouth-

[1] Cf. 1 Cor. xii. 28.

piece of a Divine communication sent through him to the community. Sometimes this took the form of a premonition of some future event; more frequently it consisted in some message of moral or religious exhortation. Modern historical and psychological investigation would suggest that both the language and thought of the prophet were modified, not only by his individual personal idiosyncrasy, but by the system of ideas prevalent in the community of his time and by the extent to which he had meditated on the problems with which he deals. But the prophet himself was unaware of these conditions. All he felt was that, whereas on ordinary occasions he was on the same level as common men, there were special times when he became the vehicle of a direct communication from God. But there was this difference between prophecy in Old and New Testament times. The Old Testament prophet said, " Thus saith the Lord " ; he believed that his message was from the ancient God of Israel. The New Testament prophet felt that he was in contact with the " Spirit," which he seems to have thought of more often as the " Spirit of Jesus " than as the " Spirit of God."

Paul lays claim to such direct inspiration, though not, be it noted, for all his utterances (cf. 1 Cor. vii. 10) ; so, even more emphatically, does the author of the Apocalypse,[1] c. A.D. 95. The warnings against false prophets in the First Epistle of John and in the Didache are additional evidence of the immense prestige enjoyed by a true prophet ; while the way in which Ignatius of Antioch, c. A.D. 115, appeals to utterances made by himself when inspired by the Spirit,[2] shows that the belief that the age of direct revelation was not yet over was still powerful in the most orthodox circles. To ignore the phenomenon of prophecy is to study the Fourth Gospel apart from its environment. And, for myself, I must say that the more often I read the discourses of the Fourth Gospel the more it is borne in upon me that its author was regarded, by himself, and by the Church for which he wrote, as an inspired prophet.

[1] Cf. Rev. i. 1; xxii. 18-19   [2] *Trall.* 5; *Philad.* 7.

THE DISCOURSES OF JOHN

With this provisional assumption in mind, I proceed to raise the question, In what sense are the discourses ascribed to Jesus in the Fourth Gospel intended to be taken as historical ? I venture to think that the answers given to this question both by the old-fashioned traditionalist and by most modern critical scholars are alike on certain points unsatisfactory.

In the ancient world there were two entirely different traditions in regard to the reporting of the discourses of historical personages or accepted teachers—the Jewish and the Greek.

The Jewish tradition had developed as a result of the existence of a class of " wise men " in the ancient Hebrew community. Epigrammatic sayings of these worthies were carefully preserved, as nearly as possible in their original form. In books like Proverbs, Ecclesiastes, and Wisdom we trace a new type of literature gradually developing out of the practice of making collections of such proverbial sayings. Originally most of the sayings seem to have been preserved without the name of the author. The Book of Ecclesiasticus breaks this tradition of anonymity ; although, even in this case, the innovation was not made by the author of the sayings himself, Jesus the son of Sirach, but by his grandson, who published the collection somewhere about 130 B.C. From this period onwards, more and more of the epigrammatic sayings of Jewish Rabbis came to be preserved with the author's name attached. It is to the continuance, in the preponderantly Jewish communities in the Early Church, of this Jewish practice of preserving as far as possible the exact words of the teacher that we owe the different collections of sayings of Christ which are preserved to us in the Synoptic Gospels.

The Greek tradition was quite different, not only in regard to the public speeches attributed to historical personages, but also as to the private teaching of the philosophers, who occupied in the Greek social and educational system a position not at all unlike

2 B

that of the " wise men " or later Rabbis in the Jewish. Thucydides, the most conscientious of all Greek historians, explains in a famous passage that he has been at the greatest pains carefully to ascertain and accurately to record all matters of fact, but that where he professes to give a speech delivered on any historical occasion, he has as a rule put into the mouths of the characters the sentiments which seemed to him to be proper to the occasion.[1] Similarly Plato, who felt that he owed everything to the teaching of Socrates, never, so far as we are aware, made any attempt to hand down to posterity the *ipsissima verba* of his master. But throughout his life, and it was a long one, he wrote a series of philosophical dialogues in which Socrates is represented as carrying on philosophical discussions either with ordinary citizens inquiring after knowledge or with the defenders of philosophical systems of which Plato disapproved. In most of the series the views which Socrates is represented as expounding are those which Plato himself, at the date of writing a particular dialogue, had come to entertain. Plato attributed his whole philosophical system to the original inspiration of Socrates ; and it is probable that in the earlier dialogues the speeches of Socrates, though written in the style and language of Plato, do not inadequately represent opinions entertained by Socrates. But in the later dialogues Plato had developed his system far beyond anything which is at all likely to have been in the mind of the historic Socrates ; and he seems then to have modified his practice.

John was writing in the Greek city of Ephesus, and for a Church of which the more cultivated, if not the majority, of the members had been educated in Greek schools and on Greek literature. Even Jewish Christians there would be familiar with the Greek tradition in these matters. Realising this, we perceive that the original readers of the Fourth Gospel would never have supposed that the author intended the speeches put into the mouth of Christ to be taken as a verbatim report, or even as a précis, of the actual words spoken by Him on the particular occasions on

[1] Cf. Thucydides i. 22.

which they are represented as having been delivered. They would not have supposed that the author meant that the doctrine propounded in these discourses was verbally identical with what was actually taught by Christ in Palestine, but rather that it was organically related to what Christ taught in such a way as to be the doctrine which Christ would have taught had he been explicitly dealing with the problems confronting the Church at the time the Gospel was written.

In a sense the Discourses of John are an attempt to supply a systematic summary of Christian teaching. We must never forget that the Ephesian Church about A.D. 90 was not in possession of our New Testament. Mark had been in existence perhaps five-and-twenty years, and by the time John wrote would have been firmly established in the Church of Ephesus. Luke was a more recent arrival, and it is possible that Matthew had not yet reached Ephesus (p. 416). The portion of the New Testament upon which the older members of that Church had been brought up was Mark and the Epistles of Paul, their founder. But Mark is conspicuously lacking on the side of teaching. Thus, while to us the Four Gospels, to them the ten Epistles of the Apostle, must have been the main authority for the " essence of Christianity." The discourses of the Fourth Gospel are intended, in combination with the selected narrative, to present the " essence of Christianity." Naturally they present the thinking of Jesus as organically related to the thought of Paul. Paul is the first that we know of the mystics whose mysticism is centred on Christ.[1] John, too, is a Christocentric mystic. But he had lived longer and meditated more than Paul, and is thus able to give a simpler, clearer, and in a sense a calmer, expression to his creed.

Are we, then, to say that the Discourses in the Fourth Gospel are to be conceived of as on exactly the same level as the Melian Dialogue of Thucydides, or the speeches in the *Republic* of Plato ? Far from it. In this, as in other ways, John stands at the

[1] Cf. A. Deissmann, *St. Paul*, E.T. p. 132 f. (Hodder and Stoughton, 1912).

meeting-point of Greek and Hebrew tradition. The analogies
with Greek literary methods are valuable mainly in enabling us
to understand how an author who valued historical accuracy,
even though his purpose was not mainly historical, could, in all
good faith and without any risk of being misunderstood by his
readers, set down as spoken on definite particular occasions
speeches which he knew quite well were not so delivered. But
beyond that the analogy breaks down. First of all, a man of the
temperament of the author of the Gospel must have meditated
year after year, not only on the Epistles of Paul, but on certain
Logia of Christ which had come home to him as being of special
and profound significance. He appears to have a tradition of
events independent of the Synoptics ; it would be strange if
this did not include some sayings as well. But what he gives us
is not the saying as it came to him, but the saying along with an
attempt to bring out all the fullness of meaning which years of
meditation had found in it. It is not difficult, for example, to
detect in the Johannine allegories of the Door, the Good Shepherd,
and the Vine, interpretative transformations of what were originally parables of the Synoptic type. Epigrammatic Logia will
have been modified in a similar way. But behind and beyond
this, we must, I feel, look to that experience of possession by the
Spirit which is the New Testament counterpart of Old Testament
prophecy.

There is no incompatibility between a conscious choice of the
medium of literary expression and the conviction that the thing
expressed has come through some superhuman channel. The
poet Blake in one passage speaks of a poem as given him by an
angel, and then proceeds to give the reason for his choice of a
particular metre. And, viewed as the utterances of a prophet
edited by him in accord with Greek tradition, the discourses
ascribed by John to Jesus take on a significance completely
different from that of the speeches put into the mouths of his
characters by the ordinary Greek historian. John knows that
they are interpretations of the essentials of Christianity rather

than *ipsissima verba* of the historic Jesus ; but they have come to him through direct inspiration from the risen Christ Himself. That is why he insists " The Spirit shall lead you into all truth." John knows quite well that his theology is a development of the original Apostolic teaching, but it is a development directly inspired by the Spirit. It is Christ Himself, speaking " in the Spirit," who says " I have many things to tell you but ye cannot bear them now." It is thus He fulfils the promise, " The Para- clete, when he cometh, he shall take of mine, he shall glorify me." " Glorify me " can only mean " lead you to perceive the truth that I am the Incarnation of the Word." John had reached this conclusion; but he believed that he had reached it, not by his own intellectual efforts, but by direct revelation of the Spirit of Jesus.

The author of the Gospel claims that his interpretation of the Person and Work of Christ is a revelation of the Spirit. That claim must be set side by side with that of the Old Testament prophets that their message was in the same way derived direct from God. At once we are brought up against philosophical and psychological problems of the greatest moment. What is the validity of religious experience ? Does the Divine Personality " communicate " facts and ideas to the human recipient, or does it rather act, like the contact of one inspiring human personality upon others, by stimulating in them insight and capacity beyond their normal selves, yet along the line of their own individuality and within the range of the culture of their age ? What is the relation of conscious thought and purposive endeavour to those subconscious processes of the mind from which an author's "happy thought," or the flash of discovery of the scientist, seems to arise ? What is the connection between phenomena like these and voices or visions of the prophet ? [1] The subject is one to which I hope to return at some future time. To discuss it here would take us beyond the field of the purely historical and critical investigation which is all this book professes to attempt.

[1] Cf. the Essays by C. W. Emmet on " The Psychology of Grace " and " Inspiration " in *The Spirit*, ed. B. H. Streeter (Macmillan, 1921).

In this place, all I desire to emphasise is that the discourses of the Fourth Gospel and the prophetic writings of the Old Testament cannot be considered apart from one another. There is food for reflection in the fact that the original starting-point of the movement towards ethical monotheism in the Old Testament, and also the most complete expression reached in the New of the idea that in Christ God is in man made manifest, both ultimately derive from a conviction of direct inspiration, which to prophet or evangelist himself did not appear to be an open question.

THE LOGOS

The interpretative fusion of Greek philosophic mysticism with the conception of a Personal God reached by the Hebrew Prophets, modified by the religious experience of the Early Church, obtained its classical expression in the Prologue of the Fourth Gospel.

There has been much discussion as to the conception of the Word with which the Gospel opens. Was it derived by the author from the " Logos " of Philo, the philosophic Jew of Alexandria, or from the use of the expression, the " Memra " or " Word " of the Lord, in the popular Aramaic paraphrases of the Old Testament known as Targums ? The controversy has always seemed to me to be a curiously futile one, since it is extremely unlikely that John could have been ignorant of either.

In Philo's system the term God stood, roughly speaking, for the idea of Divine Transcendence, while by the Logos or Word of God he meant something rather like what nowadays would be spoken of as Divine Immanence. His choice of Logos (expressed thought, or word) instead of Nous (reason) or Sophia (wisdom) was no doubt mainly determined by the use of the phrase " God said " in the description of the act of creation in Genesis, and by the way in which in poetical passages in the Old Testament the " word of the Lord " is at times all but personified. The use of the term Memra in the Targums was developed out of these same texts in the Old Testament, and it is quite likely that Philo was familiar with it in the oral paraphrases which later on came to be written down in the Targums. If so, that would be an additional reason for his preferring the word Logos, which was a possible equivalent in Greek.[1]

All the same, the underlying intention of the usage in Philo and the Targums is absolutely different. Philo is working out a philosophical system designed to effect a synthesis between two great monotheisms—the prophetic religion of the Hebrew and the Platonism of the Greek. The Targums are popular renderings of the Old Testament lessons intended for congregations the majority of whom knew neither Hebrew nor Greek, but were sufficiently advanced to find difficulty in the more startlingly anthropomorphic expressions of the Old Testament like " the Lord God walked in the garden." Wherever anything of this kind occurs in the original, the Targum replaces it by some inoffensive substitute ; the " Dwelling of the Lord " (Shekinta = Heb. Shekinah) or the " Word of the Lord " (Memra) are the most common. But as Professor Moore of Harvard [2] has recently shown, these are merely reverential paraphrases ; the expression the " Word," or the " Dwelling," is not meant to be in any sense a metaphysical or theological conception, it is a purely philological subterfuge—a kind of verbal smoke-screen to conceal the difficulty presented by the anthropomorphic language of the original. To Philo, on the other hand, the Logos is the name of a Divine Principle conceived of, along the lines of Greek philosophical thinking, as a connecting link between Transcendent Deity and the material universe.

It is often pointed out that John's conception of the Word is quite different from Philo's. Of course that follows the moment it is said, " the Word was made flesh." It would be equally true to say that Paul's conception of the meaning of Messiah is entirely different from any in the Old Testament or in contemporary

---

[1] ῥῆμα would be a more exact equivalent of Memra, but would be rejected as in no way connoting the idea of " reason."

[2] *Harvard Theological Journal*, January 1922, p. 41 ff.

Jewish thought.   Once you say that the Jesus who died on the Cross is Messiah, that word takes on a meaning radically different from what it bore to the ordinary Jew.   But no one on that score labours to prove that Paul derived the conception " Christ " from some other source than the Old Testament.   Philo wrote fifty years at least before John.   He and his family were famous throughout the Jewish world.   His brother had covered the gate of the Temple with gold; he himself had been chosen to lead a deputation of Jews that waited on the Emperor Caligula, at the most dangerous crisis that had ever yet occurred in the relations between Roman and Jew.   John may not have actually read anything of Philo—there are many to-day who talk, and even write, about Evolution without having read Darwin, or about an *élan vital* or Life-Force without having opened a book of Bergson.   It is not, I believe, quite certain that the Memra usage was earlier than John.   But if it was, John was probably familiar with it, and may even on that account have been the more attracted to Philonic thought.   But the essential consideration is that the Word in John is philosophically conceived; it expresses the idea of the Divine as an indwelling principle in the Universe.   And it was Philo who had popularised the term in that sense in an attempted synthesis of Greek and Hebrew thought. Seeing that the whole of Christian theology is based on the interpretation of the Logos doctrine of John as being a conception of philosophical import, it has always been a matter of no little surprise to me that defenders of orthodoxy, of all people, should be so anxious to find its ancestry, not in a conception of Philo, which (whatever its ultimate value) is at least a noble effort at clear thinking about God and His relation to the world, but in a Rabbinic paraphrase which is at best a rather childish attempt to dodge the necessity of thought.

I am far from asserting—indeed the contrary is probable— that the author of the Gospel was either unfamiliar with, or uninfluenced by, Rabbinic interpretations.   What I do say is that to ignore or minimise the Hellenic element in the Logos doctrine of John is to miss the point of the whole Gospel. For the same reason the suggestion—negligible were it not backed by the great name of Harnack—that the Prologue is a mere accessory or afterthought is one that I cannot entertain for a moment. I cannot but think that Harnack has unconsciously allowed his historical judgement to be warped by his own philosophical proclivities. The neo-Kantian reaction in Germany begot the idea that to seek a metaphysical basis for religion is to plough the sand. This may be true or false—personally I think it false ; but it is beyond dispute that it is the precise opposite of the conviction of the Greek world for whom the author of the Gospel wrote.

THE QUEST FOR SOURCES

Much the larger part of the Fourth Gospel consists in discourse. And many of the incidents—the visit of Nicodemus, for example—are merely a peg on which to hang discourse. This fact alone should have warned critics against the naïve attempt to apply to this Gospel methods of source-criticism which are appropriate to the Synoptics or the historical books of the Old Testament.

Dr. Stanton[1] is at pains to discuss various " partition theories " which aim at getting behind the present text of the Fourth Gospel to earlier documents supposed to have been used by the author. I confess I think he pays them the compliment of a more serious consideration than is properly their due. Some of them are so intricate that merely to state is to refute them. For if the sources have undergone anything like the amount of amplification, excision, rearrangement and adaptation which the theory postulates, then the critic's pretence that he can unravel the process is grotesque. As well hope to start with a string of sausages and reconstruct the pig. But even the more sober seeming of these partition theories appear to me to be based on a method essentially unscientific, for three reasons.

[1] *The Gospels as Historical Documents*, part iii. p. 32 ff. (Cambridge, 1920).

(1) The analogies and methods of Old Testament Criticism cannot be transferred to the New without considerable qualification. In the Pentateuch the main documents are removed from one another by periods centuries in duration, during which the whole social, religious, and political outlook of the people and the very language they used were profoundly changed ; and these changes are clearly reflected in the different sources used by the compiler. Again, the literary aim of each several document is quite different. J E is a national Epic, D a book of state legislation, P is a historically framed manual of Church Law. Yet again, the method of the compiler is what we should style " scissors and paste " ; probably of set purpose, he refrains in general from any attempt at rewriting the original. Thus even when the Synoptic Gospels only are concerned, Old Testament analogies do not hold. In Mark we have extant one of the main sources of both Matthew and Luke. But if we had before us *only* Matthew, or *only* Luke, no critic on earth would have been able to reconstruct a source like Mark. Even where we have two copies of a lost document to help us, we are at times baffled ; witness the fact that no one has yet made a convincing reconstruction of Q.

But John's method is much further removed from that of Matthew or Luke than theirs is from that of the editor of Genesis. An example will make this clear. Mark (xiv. 3 ff.) tells how in the house of *Simon the leper* at *Bethany* a woman *unnamed* anointed our Lord's *head*. Luke mentions an anointing of our Lord's *feet* in the house of *Simon the Pharisee* by a woman *unnamed* in Galilee ; in another context he tells the story of *Martha* cumbered with much serving and her sister *Mary* in a *certain village*. Now in John all these names, places, actions are, so to speak, sorted out and re-combined. The " certain village " is identified as Bethany; the house of the anointing is that of Mary, Martha and Lazarus; the unnamed woman is Mary. Thus the place of the anointing (Bethany) is Mark's, the mode of it (feet not head) is Luke's, while the serving of Martha is alluded to in another context, but in connection with the Lazarus whom John represents to be her brother. Now these facts are susceptible of more than one interpretation. We may either suppose that John knew all about the family of Bethany, and that therefore his account of the Anointing and of the family of Lazarus gives the tradition approximately in its original form, while the stories given by Mark and Luke in different contexts and in diverse versions are, as it were, dislocated fragments of the true account. In that case John did not use a written source at all. Or, on the other hand, we may take the view that the Johannine version has been reached as the result of a fusion of traditions which are preserved separately, and in a more original form, in Mark and Luke. But, supposing Mark or Luke had not been before us, where is the critic with an insight so magical that he would even have suspected that a critical problem of this complexity is involved the moment we ask the source of the simple vivid story of the Anointing as it is told in John ?

(2) Exponents of source criticism, in this and other fields, have not always, I think, sufficiently considered the psychology of authorship. They have an eagle eye for the slightest tendency towards unnecessary repetition, a digression that could be dispensed with, or a qualification of a previous statement, an obscurity of connection between paragraphs, the slightest inconsistency, real or apparent, in thought or expression ; and if they detect anything of the sort in the smallest degree, it is evidence of interpolation, excision, or of a suture with another source. But has anyone ever written anything of which the first draft was not full of this kind of thing ? and how many have published work from which such blemishes have been completely eliminated ? The fact is that the human mind is not naturally tidy. Intellect, at least so Bergson would have us believe, was developed through natural selection, in order to enable man to stone rabbits, not to deploy philosophic arguments. It is only as a result of long training and much effort that most of us can think coherently, still less convey a train

of thought to other minds. Only by the few, and by these as a rule only after a process of careful revision, can a perfect articulation of thought and expression be reached. The author of the Fourth Gospel was a genius. We may presume, then, that he thought more consistently, and could express himself more clearly, than other men. But very likely he dictated his book, and that amidst many interruptions. What is most unlikely is that he would have cared to spend time on that " labour of the file " which is the sole method of perfecting a literary exposition. He did not know that he was writing, he did not aim at writing, a book that would outlast the centuries. He wrote to proclaim a Gospel. His passion was not to produce good literature, but to save souls ; also he was an old man and maybe he wrote in haste.

(3) The only instances in this Gospel where the lack of sequence of thought between one paragraph and another is in the slightest degree remarkable can be explained in a way which is far more satisfactory than the hypothesis of clumsy editing. Everyone who has ever sent manuscript to be copied on a large scale knows that, either through his own inadvertence or that of the copyist, sheets often get transposed, and paragraphs added by way of correction get inserted in the wrong place. The same kind of thing is frequently to be observed in ancient MSS. of classical authors ; [1] and there is not the slightest improbability in its having happened in one of the earliest, or even in the earliest, copy of this Gospel. At any rate there are certain places where the connection is immensely improved if we suppose there has been an accidental transposition of paragraphs or sections. Thus it is difficult to believe that Jn. xiv. 25-31, which reads like a concluding summary,

---

[1] The most remarkable is the series of dislocations in the Commentary of the Pseudo-Asconius, where the original order can be securely reconstructed from the order of the text of Cicero, upon which he comments. These dislocations go far beyond anything that the wildest critic has ever suggested in regard to the Fourth Gospel. Cf. A. C. Clark, *The Descent of Manuscripts*, p. 374 ff.

There is a very interesting discussion by F. W. Lewis, *Disarrangements in the Fourth Gospel*, Cambridge, 1910 ; cf. also Moffatt, *Introd. N.T.* p. 552 ff.

leading up to the words " Arise, let us depart hence," was
intended by the author to be followed by chap. xv.-xvi. But
move these seven verses to the end of chap. xvi., and they make
a magnificent close to the discourse, xiv. 1-24, xv., xvi. Again,
vii. 15-24 would follow excellently on v. 47 ; while vii. 25 would
follow more naturally the thought of vii. 14. Yet again, as
was long ago pointed out, to transpose ch. v. and vi. would
much simplify the sequence of events. Thus from Cana, where He
is at iv. 54, Jesus proceeds (vi. 1) to cross the Sea of Galilee at
a time defined (vi. 4) as shortly before " the Passover, the feast
of the Jews." After feeding the multitude He recrosses the
lake to Capernaum (vi. 17) and discourses in the synagogue
there (vi. 59) ; then (v. 1) He goes to Jerusalem to a feast
unnamed, which has been a standing puzzle to commentators,
but which (the chapters being thus transposed) is seen to be a
reference to the Passover already mentioned (vi. 4) as at hand.
The visit leads to a breach with the Jews of Jerusalem, ending
with His denunciation of them (v. 44-47).[1] This is naturally
followed by vii. 1 : " after this Jesus walked in Galilee : for he
would not walk in Judaea, because the Jews sought to kill him."
If the author of the Gospel wrote on a series of waxed tablets,
or if he dictated to someone using a number of papyrus slips,
such disarrangements could easily occur ; and since the extant
order does make sense, the disarrangement might not be noticed.

There is one rearrangement of the text of John which is
especially interesting as having actual support in an existing
MS. In Syr. S. the order of the verses in Jn. xviii. 12-27 is
modified in a way which much improves the sense.[2] Verse 24
is inserted between 12 and 13, so that there is no trial before
Annas, but merely a halt at his house on the way to that of
Caiaphas. A mystic significance is attached in this Gospel to

---

[1] Or with vii. 15-25, if the additional transposition suggested above be
effected.

[2] On the question whether the lost leaf of e supported Syr S., cf. C. H.
Turner, *J.T.S.*, Oct. 1900, p. 141 f., and F. C. Burkitt, *Ev. Da-Mepharreshe*,
ii. p. 316.

Caiaphas being "high priest that year" (xi. 49-52), and the fact is re-emphasised again in this very context (xviii. 13-14); this makes it very hard to make the high priest in xviii. 19 refer to Annas—whatever claims he may have had, as a matter of usage, to bear the title. But in the text of Syr. S. the difficulty disappears; the high priest who conducts the trial is Caiaphas. Verses 16-18 are also transposed in this MS. so as to follow verse 23 (25a, which is a repetition of 18b, being omitted), so that the whole account of Peter's Denial is given in a single section.

It is possible that the Gospel, like the *Aeneid* of Virgil, was published posthumously. The obscure remark attributed to Papias in a IX^cent. Latin MS.[1] that "the Gospel of John was revealed and given to the Church by John, *adhuc in corpore constituto, i.e.* while still in the body," may be one of those "official denials" which are evidence of a by no means groundless belief in the fact denied. If so, the author may have died, leaving a pile of tablets or a number of loose dictated pieces on sheets of papyrus, and a pupil may have arranged them as best he could for publication. In that case there would be no objection to our supposing a large number of disarrangements, and also a few editorial additions—v. 28-29, for example, which reflects the Apocalyptic conception of an external judgement, thus directly contradicting the tenor of the previous verses. The Appendix, too, ch. xxi., may have been added by the pupil who edited the work. With possibilities of this kind open, considerations drawn from apparent breaks in the flow of argument or narrative, were they twice as many or as striking as they are, would not, to my mind, weigh for a moment against the extraordinary impression of unity of style, temper, and outlook in the Gospel as a whole. It is a book of which every chapter reflects the genius and experience of a tremendous personality —and all through the personality reflected is the same.

---

[1] Printed in Lightfoot and Harmer, *Apostolic Fathers*, p. 524.

CREATIVE MEMORY

And the personality reflected is not that of a man likely to copy painfully other men's writings. Every scene he depicts, every discourse he relates—whencesoever originally derived—is the distilled essence of something that has been pondered upon and lived out in actual life until it has become of the very texture of his soul. But the subconscious depths of the human mind are never inactive, least of all so where thoughts or incidents fraught with passionate interest are concerned. Things disconnected are brought together, things dark become illuminated. Given also a mystic with the creative imagination of the artist—and no one without the artist's mind could have drawn the word pictures of the Fourth Gospel—old scenes will be flashed up into recollection, with new but vivid details embodying the altered emphasis caused by later meditation on the meaning of the original experience.

We must also remember that the stories told by John are avowedly selected to illustrate certain fundamental religious principles. The presumption is a strong one that he has given us the selection which he had found most effective for that purpose, and had already used time after time in discussions with individuals or in addresses to the Church. But whenever any one tells and retells the same story to illustrate some special point—whether the point be a jest, a trait of character of some well-known individual, the magnificence of an exploit, or the enormity of a crime—quite insensibly minor details of the story get modified so as to throw into greater emphasis the main point. The subconscious mind is more primitive than the conscious; it thinks in pictures; it dramatises; thus every time a story is told, it is told more effectively. But that is always at the expense of the minor accuracy which a cross-examining counsel demands of a witness, and which a historical critic ought to be aware cannot often be expected in an ancient document. Indeed, it is only in modern times, and under the influence of the demand for meticulous accuracy which modern science and its methods have made insistent, that people have begun to trouble at all about minutiae of description, so long as these do not seriously affect the general impression. An illustration of this relative indifference to minor details can be found in the Acts. The Conversion of Paul is described no less than three times [1] in that book. The second and third occasions occur in speeches of Paul separated by only three chapters, and the context shows that the difference cannot be explained by the theory that the author is combining two parallel sources. Yet the exact details as to what was seen and heard, and how much of it was experienced by Paul only, and how much by his companions as well, is differently related in each of the three accounts.

That tendency in John, to which attention is so often called, towards an enhancement of detail in the miracle stories he records is to be accounted for in this way. He writes, not with the written document in front of him, but from the vivid reconstruction of the scene as, at the moment of writing, it stood out before his own mind's eye. I may perhaps be pardoned in adducing a modern illustration—the point of which lies precisely in the fact that the person who is the subject of the illustration is notoriously a man of unimpeachable veracity, and was, at the moment of speaking, engaged in emphasising the supreme importance of historical fact and historical evidence. In the peroration of a sermon preached some years ago by a distinguished ecclesiastic on the evidence for the Resurrection, there occurred the words, " And finally He appeared to 500 brethren at once on a mountain in Galilee in broad daylight." As a correspondent of the *Guardian* newspaper, in which the sermon was published, pointed out, this unqualified statement of fact really involved two unconscious inferences : (1) the identification of the appearance to 500 brethren mentioned by Paul in writing to the Corinthians with the appearance to the eleven on a mountain in Galilee recorded in Matthew, which, though not

[1] Acts ix. 3 ff. ; xxii. 6 ff. ; xxvi. 12 ff.

uncommonly made in popular commentaries of the period, is an artificial combination and one of very questionable validity ; (2) the affirmation that the appearance took place in broad daylight. This, though possibly quite correct, is unsupported by any definite statement in the New Testament. The preacher had quite unconsciously described the scene, not from the original authorities, but from the vivid picture, a " composite photograph " as it were, reconstructed by his own imagination on the basis of contemporary apologetic.

FACT AND SYMBOL

To most of the mystics symbolism in one form or another appeals. But from the first century A.D. till well after the Renaissance the peculiar form of symbolism known as Allegory had an attraction for some of the finest minds with which it is difficult for the present age to sympathise. Much has been made by recent scholarship of the idea that the author of the Fourth Gospel was one of them. I quote again from the article in the *Encyclopaedia Britannica* by Baron F. von Hügel :

" Philo had in his life of Moses allegorised the Pentateuchal narratives so as to represent him as mediator, saviour, intercessor of his people, the one great organ of revelation, and the soul's guide from the false lower world into the upper true one. The Fourth Gospel is the noblest instance of this kind of literature, of which the truth depends, not on the factual accuracy of the symbolising appearances, but on the truth of the ideas and experiences thus symbolised."

This reference to Philo is misleading. What Philo allegorises is the legislation. Only rarely does he detect allegory in the Pentateuchal narratives, and he never *invents* stories for their symbolic intention. In the case of John the desire to find in events an allegorical expression of spiritual realities might possibly act as a moulding influence on the imaginative pictures in which the memory of them was stored. Since memory is essentially interpretative, such a desire might

2 c

easily determine the character and direction of the modification
the mental picture of events would undergo. But the suggestion
that John consciously and deliberately composed stories for the
sake of their allegorical meaning seems to me to go too far.
Such a proceeding on his part would, so it seems to me, be
incompatible with the objects which he had in view, so far as
we can estimate these by what we know of the circumstances
and special needs of the Church of his day.

The Church in Ephesus, and indeed the Church throughout
the world at the end of the first century A.D., was fighting a
battle on two fronts. On the one side there was the impinge-
ment of Gnosticism from without, with the even more dangerous
drift towards a gnosticising Christianity within. This threatened
to undermine both the monotheism and the ethical soundness of
the Hebrew and Apostolic religious tradition, and to substitute
a vague mysticism, based upon speculations about complicated
series of graded divinities, along with a belief in the inherent evil
of matter. This tendency was accompanied by an insistence
either that Christ was not really human—the Body which men
saw in Palestine being merely an appearance—or that the Divine
Christ was a separate Being from the man Jesus. On the other
side was the conservative Jewish party, ethically sound and
firmly monotheistic, but conceiving of the Person of Christ and
His relation both to God and man in terms derived from Jewish
eschatology—a naïve form of " picture-thinking " which must
somehow be transcended if Christianity was to mean anything
to the average Greek. The Gospel of Matthew stereotypes this
phase of Christian theology, or rather the more progressive wing
of it, at the stage which it had reached in Antioch about A.D. 85.
The Apocryphal Gospel of Peter, the surviving fragment of which
describes how the Divine Christ went back to Heaven leaving
the human Jesus to die upon the Cross, represents the more
conservative wing of the Gnostic tendency.

John saw clearly that the salvation of the Church lay in a
via media between these two tendencies, in the position which

he summed up in the idea of the Word made flesh. Christ was truly, really, and completely man ; but in Him is incarnate the " Word of God." To John the Word means, roughly speaking, what a modern thinker would speak of as Divinity considered as immanent—that which is really God, not a subordinate emanation from God. But of the two tendencies John is combating, much the more alarming was that which came from the Gnostic ; for the *Zeitgeist* was on that side. Orthodox Christians are so preoccupied nowadays in asserting the Divinity of Christ that it is easy to overlook the fact that in the early Gentile Church, especially in Asia, it was the reality of His Humanity that most needed emphasis. The age was obsessed by the problem of evil, and the Gnostic solution, that evil arose because matter is essentially and eternally bad, necessitated the rejection of the belief that Divinity could possibly have worn a real body of material flesh and blood. That is why, while John dwells far more than the Synoptics on the miraculous power of Christ and the all-seeing intelligence that knows all without needing to ask questions or await information—the evidence of Divinity—he also, to an extent unparalleled in the Synoptics, emphasises the susceptibility of Christ to purely physical and simple human experience. John alone records that Jesus was wearied with a journey (iv. 6), wept for a friend (xi. 35), and in the agony of death could say " I thirst."

Does it not follow that to the mind of a philosophic mystic of that epoch a " mediating theology " would involve a double attitude towards the historical facts of the life of Christ ?

On the one hand, seeing that every action of the historic Jesus is an expression in time of the Universal Divine, it is much more than a mere historical event. The visible fact must necessarily in every case be a symbolic expression of an invisible spiritual principle. If a multitude is fed with loaves and fishes, this is not a mere event which once happened by the Lake of Galilee, it is also symbolically the expression in time of the eternal verity that man attains to the Life Divine by feeding spiritually upon

Christ the Bread of Life. If Lazarus rises from the tomb, this is not merely a wonderful miracle wrought on an individual, it is also an individualised instance of the universal principle that the Immanent Divinity revealed in Christ is eternally the Resurrection and the Life of Man.

On the other hand, from the logic of his position, John is no less bound to emphasise the idea that, because the Word *became flesh*, therefore these things *factually* occurred. To the Gnostic this world of fact was alien to the spiritual ; it was a world in which the Ultimate Divine had no part. John affirms that the Word in becoming flesh demonstrated that this world of concrete fact was the expression of, and was in the control of, the same world-creating Spirit that appeared as a Redeemer in Jesus Christ. It would seem to follow that John could not, consistently with his purpose, have recorded as history any incident which he did not himself believe to have actually occurred.

History to all the ancients, except perhaps Thucydides and Polybius, was a branch, not of science, but of letters. Effective presentation was more valued than accuracy of detail. There is hardly a battle in Livy described in a way which would work out correctly on the actual ground—and yet war was the " leading industry " of Rome. About minor details no one in those days troubled ; what was asked for was the broad facts graphically described. And so far as the broad facts are concerned I think one must affirm that John recorded nothing which he did not believe to be historical. It does not follow that his belief was always justified. He records four stupendous miracles—the Feeding of the Five Thousand, the Walking on the Water, the Changing of Water into Wine, and the Raising of Lazarus. The difficulty to the modern mind of supposing that such events happened exactly and in all particulars as they are described by the Evangelist is a point that needs no elaboration. All I would insist on is that, from the point of view of intrinsic credibility, all four stories stand upon exactly the same level. But two of them could have been derived by John from Mark, a work accepted in the Church at the time he wrote as an unimpeachable historical authority. The obvious presumption, then, is that he derived the other two from an authority which, whether mistakenly or otherwise, he regarded as no less authentic.

Some eminent critics hold that the raising of Lazarus in John has been developed out of the concluding sentence in Luke's parable of Dives and Lazarus. This suggestion is one which has never seemed to me particularly plausible. It will at least be conceded that, on the surface, the two stories and the morals drawn from them are very different. But even if it be granted that a sentence in the parable is the germ out of which the story of the miracle has grown, it is surely psychologically far easier to suppose that the growth had already taken place during an intermediate stage of oral tradition, rather than that the transformation was effected through a conscious manipulation by John of the written text of Luke.

To sum up, John may have been mistaken about his facts, but to him it is as important to emphasise the historical as to see in the historical a symbol of the Eternal. But he was interested in these stories, not so much because they were marvellous, as because they seemed to him to embody eternal truth. To him fact and meaning are related as flesh to spirit—the flesh is a necessary vehicle, but it is spirit which really counts. The familiar observation that in John the miracles are " acted parables " is absolutely correct ; only it does not go far enough. To John the whole of the appearance in history of the Word made Flesh is an acted parable—including the Death and Resurrection. That being so, it is essential surely to his whole theological position, whether against the Docetic Gnostics, who denied the reality of Christ's human body, or against the passionless Christ of Cerinthus, to affirm that the parable *really was acted out* in the plane of material existence in this world of fact.

The Mystic Vision

In reply to this contention it may be urged by some that the symbolism manifest in some of the stories has an allegorical appropriateness not to be accounted for by the normal working on the author's memory of the various unconscious processes I have indicated. The five earlier husbands, for example, of the Woman of Samaria (contrasted with the present husband not her own) are said to symbolise the gods of the five nations planted in that territory by the Assyrians [1] whom the Samaritans worshipped before they accepted the God of the Jews. Again, the number 153 in the miraculous Draught of Fishes is said to represent the inclusion of all nations in the Church, since the ancients believed that this was the total number of species of fish. Personally I am not much attracted by these suggestions; but what I am concerned to argue is that, while the *numbers* and other such details *may* have been modified by the search for allegory, the stories themselves were not invented *ab initio* as allegories. The Draught of Fishes we know was not so invented, since it occurs in Luke: is it not probable that John found also ready to hand a story of a meeting of Christ with a Samaritan woman, which no doubt to some extent he rewrote?

Even if it should be thought that some scenes in the Gospel have no basis either in fact or in tradition, I would submit that the hypothesis of conscious literary invention is still improbable. An alternative explanation can be invoked which is far more consonant with the psychology of the mystic's mind. Evelyn Underhill, quoting analogies from Mediaeval Mystics, hazarded the suggestion that the author of the Fourth Gospel may not only have *heard* (with the prophet's inward ear) the discourses he reports, but may have *seen* some of the events which he depicts—in mystic trance. As this suggestion has not, I think,

---

[1] 2 Kings xvii. 24.

received from scholars the attention it deserves, I venture to quote a significant passage.

Now, as the discourses in which the Divine Nature discloses itself in its relation to man seem to reflect back to " auditive " experiences on the part of the Evangelist, so these incidents—so sharp and realistic in their detail, yet so transfigured by the writer's point of view—suggest to us that another form of automatic activity had its part in the composition of his gospel. As we read them, we are reminded again and again of those visionary scenes, formed from traditional or historical materials, but enriched by the creative imagination, the deep intuition of the seer, in which the fruit of the mystic's meditation takes an artistic or dramatic instead of a rhetorical form. The lives of the later mystics show to us the astonishing air of realism, the bewildering intermixture of history with dream, which may be achieved in visionary experience of this kind ; and which can hardly be understood save by those who realise the creative power of the mystical imagination, the solidarity which exists for the mystic's consciousness between his intensely actual present and the historical past of his faith. In his meditations, he really lives again through the scenes which history has reported to him : since they are ever-present realities in that Mind of God to which his mind aspires. He has a personal interest in doing this, in learning as it were the curve of the life of Christ ; for *vita tua, via nostra* is his motto—" he that saith he abideth in Him ought himself also so to walk even as He walked." [1]

Further, his vivid sense of actuality, the artistic powers which are part of his psychic constitution, help to build up and elaborate the picture of the events upon which he broods. He sees this picture, in that strong light and with that sharp definition which is peculiar to visionary states. He has not produced it by any voluntary process : it surges up from his deeper mind, as do the concepts of the artist, invading that field of consciousness which his state of meditation has kept in a mood of tense yet passive receptivity. So real it is to him, so authoritative, so independent of his deliberate efforts, that the transition is easy from " thus it must have been " to " thus it *was*." [2]

A study of dream psychology and of visions recorded by Mystics affords evidence that the solution of problems, on which the mind has pondered long and deeply, does sometimes come in the form of visions, the symbolism of which is quite as obvious

---

[1] 1 John ii. 6.
[2] *The Mystic Way*, p. 235 ff. (Dent, 1913).

and as elaborate in detail as that of allegories worked out by the conscious mind. And not infrequently these visions have a certain quality which, both at the moment of experiencing them and in subsequent reflection, compels conviction that they are veridical—that is, that they are not dreams or guesses, but revelations of actual fact.[1] I am not, however, concerned to argue that any scene or any detail in a scene came to John in this way. All I would contend is that, *if* any incident in the Gospel is recorded in a form which seems too like allegory to be accounted for by the normal working of interpretative recollection, there is an alternative to the hypothesis of conscious allegory which is, to my mind, psychologically more credible.

From the various considerations I have adduced it would seem clear that the hope that by critical analysis sufficiently refined we can reconstruct sources used by John is chimerical. It is, however, quite another matter to raise the broad question, On what authority does John rely when he takes upon himself to supplement, correct, or contradict the Synoptic story ? Had he some august written source to which he could appeal, or was he in a position to speak from personal knowledge ? If the latter, was his authority that of an eye-witness, or that of one supposed in some other way to have first-hand knowledge of the facts ?

It may be that a critical examination of the documentary relations between John and the Synoptists will place us in possession of materials with the aid of which an answer to this question can be given. At any rate, since such an examination is likely to bring out facts in other ways of interest to the student of the Gospels, it must be essayed.

---

[1] I have put together some evidence bearing on this subject in an article, originally intended as an *excursus* to this volume, which appeared in the *Hibbert Journal* for January 1925 ; also as an appendix in my book *Reality.*

XIV

SYNOPSIS

THE FOURTH GOSPEL AND THE SYNOPTICS

John's Knowledge of the Synoptics

The traditional view that John was familiar with the first three Gospels has recently been challenged. His knowledge of Mark is strongly affirmed by recent critics, but his knowledge of Luke, and still more of Matthew, is questioned. On this view the Fourth Gospel enters the series of relations ordinarily studied under the title Synoptic Problem; but the case is not proved.

John and Mark

A survey of the evidence that John used Mark, and either attributed greater authority to, or was more familiar with, his story than that of either of the others.

This conclusion would seem to preclude the theory that John was written in Aramaic; but it in no way weakens the case for the view that he naturally thought in that language.

John and Luke

The case for John's knowledge of Luke depends mainly on the way in which he introduces, and the details which he connects with, the names of Martha and Mary. But the probability is also high that John knew Luke's Passion story. John's interest in identifying persons and places mentioned by Mark and Luke.

Was the source used by John, Luke, or Proto-Luke?

John and Matthew

The points of contact between John and Matthew are extremely minute, and a closer study suggests that many of them, like the Minor Agreements between Matthew and Luke against Mark, are either (a) deceptive agreements, or (b) due to scribal alterations of text.

From Apocalypse and Papias fragment we infer Matthew had reached Ephesus; but John, whose own theology was largely an endeavour to spiritualise prevalent Apocalyptic ideas, viewed its emphasis on a visible Parousia and its Judaistic element with suspicion.

JERUSALEM TRADITIONS

Dependence on Mark and Luke will not account for all the phenomena of the Fourth Gospel. But neither will the hypothesis of a third written source.

The masterful handling of Synoptic materials, and especially of the Synoptic Chronology, taken in connection with the evidence that the author had a first-hand knowledge of the topography of Jerusalem and of Jewish usage, suggests that the author had a recognised claim to write as one having authority.

THE JOHANNINE CHRONOLOGY

The possibility that the Johannine Chronology is based on an attempt to piece together scattered pieces of information picked up in Jerusalem.

A suggestion to account for the position assigned in the Johannine Chronology to the Cleansing of the Temple and the Raising of Lazarus.

On the whole the Johannine Chronology solves more difficulties than it raises. Illustrations of this thesis.

Fallacy implicit in the comparison of Johannine and Synoptic Chronology. Strictly speaking, a " Synoptic Chronology " does not exist. In the last resort all we have is, Mark *versus* John ; and there is no reason to suppose that Mark's arrangement professes to be in any strict sense chronological. John attempts a chronology, but, in view of the difficulties involved in a pioneer attempt, it may well contain serious inaccuracies. It cannot be simply dismissed.

FINAL RESULTS

Mark, Luke, and John form a series, with a progressive tendency to emphasise the universal element in Christianity and to minimise the Apocalyptic. Matthew represents an independent development, which, as compared with Mark, shows a movement in the reverse direction in regard to both these points.

The dependence of the Fourth Gospel upon Mark and Luke is a fact which militates against the acceptance of Apostolic authorship for the Gospel. But certain other phenomena in the Gospel would be easier to explain on the hypothesis that the author was a personage who had a claim to write with independent authority.

CHAPTER XIV

THE FOURTH GOSPEL AND THE SYNOPTICS

John's Knowledge of the Synoptics

THAT John was familiar with the first three Gospels was taken for granted by the early Fathers, and was until recently assumed as axiomatic by modern critics. Of late that assumption has been questioned, as the following quotations will show. In 1910 Professor B. W. Bacon of Yale, after a careful review of the discussion up to date, pronounced the considered judgement that John is to Mark in a relation of direct literary dependence; that, although Mark is the only Synoptic quoted verbally by him, John's narrative has been largely modified by knowledge of Luke; but that Matthew is "practically ignored" by John.[1] In 1912 Mr. E. R. Buckley[2] wrote: "I have not been able to discover any cases of close resemblance between St. John and passages peculiar to the First Gospel . . . while it seems clear that the author of the Fourth Gospel knew St. Mark and St. Luke's non-Marcan source." Lastly, writing in 1920, Dr. Stanton[3] concludes a careful study of all the relevant passages with the words: "The parallels with St. Mark certainly seem to afford evidence of an amount and kind sufficient to prove that the Fourth Evangelist knew that Gospel fairly well. That he knew either of the others seems more than doubtful."

---

[1] *The Fourth Gospel in Research and Debate* (Moffat, Yard and Co.), pp. 366-368.

[2] *Introduction to the Synoptic Problem*, pp. 271, 275.

[3] *The Gospels as Historical Documents*, pt. iii. pp. 214-220.

Between Matthew and John the points of contact are, on any view, extremely slight. But John has so much in common with Luke that, if he did *not* use our Third Gospel, we must conclude that John and Luke had a common source, either in the form of a written document or of oral tradition. On that assumption an important result follows. The Fourth Gospel enters the series of relations which we ordinarily study under the title of the Synoptic Problem. The relation of John to Luke becomes comparable to that of Luke to Matthew. In both cases there are two sources in common—Mark and another. The difference is that, whereas Matthew and Luke use Mark and Q, Luke and John use Mark and a third source. The common factor is Mark. This leads at once to the conception of Mark as the primitive Gospel, circulated in all the Churches, and of Matthew, Luke, and John as three independent local attempts to enrich and enlarge that gospel by traditions and documents current in the particular region in which they were severally produced. This conception is in itself extremely interesting ; and, if correct, it is one which carries with it consequences historically of the most far-reaching character. The critical conclusion, therefore, formulated by Mr. Buckley and Dr. Stanton demands the most careful examination.

Before reading Dr. Stanton's book I had provisionally arrived at the same conclusion ; and finding the conception of the relation of the primitive Marcan to the three later Gospels which I have outlined above aesthetically and historically attractive, I had worked out it and its implications at some considerable length. To make quite sure of my ground I proceeded to subject the phenomena to a second and more microscopic examination. The result of this I submit to the judgement of the reader. To my own mind it materially strengthens the case for the contention that John did not use Matthew ; but, to my personal regret—since it meant the jettisoning of much that I had written—it decidedly favours the view that John is dependent on Luke as well as on Mark.

JOHN AND MARK

Matthew and Luke, desiring to tell their story faithfully, copied their sources with only such verbal alteration as the exigencies of adaptation, abridgement, and literary embellishment suggested ; and, as we have seen, each of them reproduces over 50 % of the actual words used in Mark. John, the preacher, the thinker, the mystic, aiming avowedly at writing, not a biography, but a message meant to burn—" that believing ye may have life in his name "—was not likely to write, like the other Evangelists, with a copy of Mark or any other document in front of him. The materials he uses have all been fused in the crucible of his creative imagination, and it is from the image in his mind's eye, far more vivid than the written page, that he paints his picture. Accordingly, when he tells a story that occurs in Mark, not 20 % of the words he uses are the same—but that is precisely what makes it specially significant that he often reproduces some of the more out-of-the-way phrases of Mark.

Of these I select six, whose occurrence in both Mark and John can hardly be explained as accidental :

δηναρίων διακοσίων ἄρτους Mk. vi. 37 = δηναρίων διακοσίων ἄρτοι Jn. vi. 7.

μύρου νάρδου πιστικῆς πολυτελοῦς . . . τριακοσίων δηναρίων Mk. xiv. 3 and 5 = μύρου νάρδου πιστικῆς πολυτίμου . . . τριακοσίων δηναρίων Jn. xii. 3 and 5. N.B. πιστική in this sense is not found elsewhere in Greek literature, except in allusions to this passage.

ἐγείρεσθε ἄγωμεν Jn. xiv. 31 recalls Mk. xiv. 42. N.B. If Jn. xv-xvii. is misplaced, Judas' betrayal follows immediately in both Gospels.

ὁ Πέτρος . . . θερμαινόμενος Mk. xiv. 54 = ὁ Πέτρος . . . θερμαινόμενος Jn. xviii. 18.

Pilate's question " θέλετε ἀπολύσω ὑμῖν τὸν βασιλέα τῶν Ἰουδαίων ; " Mk. xv. 9 = " βούλεσθε οὖν ὑμῖν ἀπολύσω τὸν βασιλέα τῶν Ἰουδαίων ; " Jn. xviii. 39.

ἔγειραι ἆρον τὸν κράββατόν σου . . . καὶ ἦρε τὸν κράββατον αὐτοῦ καὶ περιεπάτει Jn. **v.** 8-9 = ἔγειραι . . . ἆρον τὸν
κράββατόν σου . . . καὶ ἄρας τὸν κράββατον ἐξῆλθεν
Mk. ii. 11-12. Notable for two points. Firstly, κράββατον
is condemned by the grammarians as a vulgarism, and it is
altered by both Matthew and Luke wherever it occurs in Mark.
Secondly, in John the phrase occurs in the story of the lame man
at Bethesda, in Mark in that of the paralytic borne of four. But
Christ did not speak in Greek ; the identity, therefore, of the
Greek phrase seems most naturally explained if the vocabulary
of Mark was familiar to John. Analogous instances of this trick
of memory by which a phrase used in one incident by Mark is
transferred to another are specially frequent in Matthew, who
also knew Mark almost by heart.[1] Similarly εἷς ἐκ τῶν δώδεκα
(εἷς ὢν א ϛ) Jn. vi. 71, cf. xx. 24, may be a recollection of the
phrase in Mk. xiv. 10, 20 and 43.

The close agreement of John with Mark in these particular
passages is the more noticeable since the phrases used in the
parallels in both Matthew and Luke happen on all these occasions
to be quite different from Mark's. Besides, agreements of a less
striking character of Mark and John against one or both of the
other two Gospels occur wherever John and the Synoptics run
parallel. To appreciate the full force of this point the student
must be at the pains to work through all the passages in John
which have close parallels to Mark, and to underline all words
which occur in any of the Synoptics, using different colours
according as the words are found in one, two, or three of them.
Or, as an alternative, he may study the parallels carefully in
Rushbrooke's *Synopticon*, where words are differently printed
according as they appear in one, two, three, or four of the
documents.[2]

---

[1] Cf. Hawkins's *Hor. Syn.* p. 168 ff.

[2] The important parallels are as follows : The Baptist (Jn. i. 19-34 =
Mk. i. 7-10) ; the Cleansing of the Temple (Jn. ii. 13-22 = Mk. xi. 15-19) ; the
Feeding of the Five Thousand (Jn. vi. 1-15 = Mk. vi. 31-44) ; the Walking on
the Water (Jn. vi. 15-21 = Mk. vi. 45-52) ; the Anointing at Bethany (Jn. xii.

It will be noticed that John always has a certain number of verbal agreements with Mark ; hence, when either Matthew or Luke has reproduced Mark's wording exactly, John often agrees with them also. But, though he frequently supports Mark where the others have deserted him, he very rarely agrees with either of them when they depart from Mark. To this rule there are a few exceptions, real or apparent, which I shall discuss shortly. Agreements, of course, which are obviously accidental, like the substitution of εἶπεν for λέγει, or the addition of ὁ Ἰησοῦς, or any other name implied in the context, for this purpose may be ignored.

Another point on which Stanton[1] lays special stress is the fact that, whereas both Matthew and Luke (and therefore Q) have much fuller accounts than Mark of the teaching of John the Baptist, the only instance here of verbal resemblance between the Fourth Gospel and the Synoptists is in a sentence where John agrees with Mark *against* the other two. Similarly in regard to the teaching of Christ. There are very few sayings of Christ in John which are verbally at all like sayings found in the Synoptics; all but one (Jn. xiii. 16 = Mt. x. 24 = Lk. vi. 40) occur in Mark, and the wording of John's version is usually a shade nearer to Mark than it is to the others. Seeing that Matthew and Luke are so infinitely richer than Mark in sayings of Christ, the large

1-11 = Mk. xiv. 3-9) ; the Triumphal Entry (Jn. xii. 12-19 = Mk. xi. 1-10) ; certain details in the story of the Last Supper, including the foretelling in sentences verbally identical of Judas' betrayal (Jn. xiii. 21 = Mk. xiv. 18) and of Peter's Denial (Jn. xiii. 38 = Mk. xiv. 30); the Arrest (Jn. xviii. 3-10 = Mk. xiv. 43-50) ; Peter's Denial (Jn. xviii. 15-18, 25-27 = Mk. xiv. 54, 66-72) ; certain details in the Trial, including " Art thou the King of the Jews ? " (Jn. xviii. 33 = Mk. xv. 2), "Thou sayest " (Jn. xviii. 37 = Mk. xv. 2); Barabbas (Jn. xviii. 39-40 = Mk. xv. 6-15) ; the Mocking (Jn. xix. 2-3 = Mk. xv. 16-20) ; the Crucifixion (Jn. xix. 17-24 = Mk. xv. 22-27) ; the Entombment (Jn. xix 38-42 = Mk. xv. 43-46) ; and the Discovery of the Empty Tomb (Jn. xx. 1-2 = Mk. xvi. 1-8). Of these the Walking on the Water and the Anointing at Bethany, though found in Mark and Matthew, are absent from Luke. Besides this, John has a few sayings which occur in the Synoptics in a different context: Jn. iv. 44 = Mk. vi. 4 ; Jn. xii. 25 = Mk. viii. 35 ; Jn. xiii. 20 = Mk. ix. 37 ; Jn. xiii. 16 = Jn. xv. 20 = Mt. x. 24 = Lk. vi. 40.

[1] *Op. cit.* pp. 215, 220.

proportion of sayings derived by John from Mark is remarkable. It seems to prove that Mark was either much better known to John or much more highly valued by him than the others.[1]

Clearly the facts so far stated amount to little short of a demonstration that John knew the Gospel of Mark, and knew it well. But they suggest doubts as to his acquaintance with the other two Synoptics.

I must, however, digress for a moment to point out that this evidence for John's use of Mark cannot easily be fitted in with the hypothesis, recently put forward by Dr. Burney,[2] that the Fourth Gospel is a translation from the Aramaic. The only way it could be done would be to assume that Mark and John are independent translators of the same Aramaic original. Not being an Aramaic scholar myself, I asked a friend who is expert in the language to examine the verbal differences between Mark and John in the accounts of the Feeding of the Five Thousand and the Walking on the Water, which obviously are test passages, in order to ascertain whether or no they were explicable as translation variants. He reported that they were not. There is a further consideration. Mr. G. R. Driver has pointed out that the phenomena, on which Dr. Burney's argument is based,[3] occur most frequently in the discourses and are comparatively rare in the narrative portions of the Gospel. The existence of a linguistic

---

[1] Prof. C. H. Dodd (*Expositor*, Oct. 1921, p. 286 ff.) has an interesting argument depending on the identification of the journey to Jerusalem, Mk. x. 1, with that in Jn. vii. 10 (cf. οὐκ ἤθελεν ἵνα τις γνῷ, Mk. ix. 30, with οὐ φανερῶς, ἀλλ' ὡς ἐν κρυπτῷ, Jn. vii. 10), that the *order of events* in the section Jn. vi. 1-vii. 10 is dependent on that in Mark (vi. 31-x. 1)—in which case we note incidentally John's copy of Mark included Luke's Great Omission. The argument cannot be done justice to if presented briefly, but if, as I am inclined to think, it is sound, it affords strong confirmation of John's use of Mark

[2] *The Aramaic Origin of the Fourth Gospel* (Oxford, 1922). Prof. C. C. Torrey in the *Harvard Theological Review*, p. 326 ff., Oct. 1923, assents to the general position that the Gospel is a translation from Aramaic, but rejects practically all the alleged mistranslations on which Dr. Burney's argument largely rests. He then proceeds to offer another set of "mistranslations" of his own discovering.

[3] Cf. G. R. Driver, "The Original Language of the Fourth Gospel," *Jewish Guardian*, Jan. 5 and 12, 1923.

distinction between the discourses and the narrative is a remark-able fact, and one that calls for an explanation. We may seek it in any one of three directions. (1) We may conjecture that the discourses, though not the narrative, have been translated from an Aramaic document. (2) We may surmise that the discourses are by the author of the Gospel, but embody a larger proportion of authentic sayings of Christ, originally spoken in Aramaic, than is generally supposed. (3) The author of the Gospel belonged to that order of " prophets " which was so conspicuous and influential in the Apostolic age. The discourses came to him " in the Spirit." In that case, it would be psychologically credible that the Greek which he wrote or dictated when under this influence should reflect strongly the idiom of his native Aramaic tongue— just as to-day a Highlander or Welshman, who has lived most of his life in England, may in moments of excitement speak with the accent of earlier years. In view of the arguments adduced in the previous chapter that John was a prophet, I am personally inclined to favour this explanation. But I would point out that the second and third of these hypotheses are not really mutually exclusive. Genuine sayings of Christ, which had sunk down into the depths of memory, might well emerge again amplified and re-orientated by the subconscious workings of the prophet's mind. And the supposition that there was at work a combination of these two influences would give an added meaning to the reiterated emphasis in the Gospel on the work of the Spirit as illuminating and interpreting at some later time the actual teaching of the historic Christ. " I have many things to tell you, but ye cannot bear them now."

JOHN AND LUKE

The case for a literary dependence of John, either on Luke or on a source embodied in Luke, rests in the first instance on the remarkable points of contact between these Gospels in regard to the sisters Martha and Mary. Too much stress ought not to be laid on the fact that the two sisters are suddenly named, xi. 1,

as if they were well-known characters, though that is not without
significance.   But the description in this same verse of Lazarus
as " of Bethany, of the village of Mary and Martha " is very
difficult to explain unless John's readers were familiar with the
story of the two sisters *told in very much the same words* as in
Luke.   For, since Bethany is named four times in Mark in connection with striking incidents, it did not require to be identified.
The point, then, of John's words " of the village of Martha and
Mary " must be, not to identify Bethany by connecting it with
the sisters, but rather to identify the " certain village " unnamed,
where according to Luke (x. 38) the sisters lived, with the well-
known village of Bethany.

Again, in this same passage (xi. 1) John, when introducing
Lazarus for the first time, takes that opportunity, not only of
giving a name to the unnamed village, but also to the unnamed
woman who, according to Mark, anointed our Lord's head in
that place.   She is Mary, the sister of Martha.   And this is what
gives point to the addition later on of the words " and Martha
served " in John's account of the anointing (xii. 2) ; they are
meant to clinch the identification by a further allusion to the
Lucan story.   But this elaborate cross-identification of persons,
places, and incidents as between Mark and Luke is natural if
both these Gospels were standard works read in the Church ;
it is not equally natural if the Martha and Mary story was
merely extant in floating tradition.

What is still more remarkable, John introduces into the story
of this Anointing certain details derived, not from Mark (xiv. 2 ff.)
but from the story of the Anointing by a sinner during the
Galilean ministry (Lk. vii. 36 ff.), which Luke substitutes for the
Marcan Anointing at Bethany in the last week at Jerusalem.
Mark (xiv. 3) says the woman " poured the ointment on his
head," John (xii. 3) agrees with Luke in saying she anointed his
feet and wiped them with her hair.   And this is not an accident,
it is implied in the preparatory allusion to the incident (xi. 2).
The natural explanation of these phenomena is that in John's

mind a combination has been effected between persons and details mentioned in Mark's and Luke's versions of the Anointing and in the anecdote about Martha and Mary related by Luke.

The above examples of the assignment by John to definite persons or places of incidents left vague in Mark and Luke cannot be considered apart from evidence as to the same tendency elsewhere. In Mark and Luke the person who cuts off an ear of the high priest's servant in Gethsemane is unnamed; so is the servant; John gives the names of Peter and Malchus. In Mark (vi. 37) the disciples protest that two hundred pennyworth of bread would not suffice to feed the multitude; in John (vi. 7) it is Philip who says this. Judas is similarly named (xii. 4). The author of the Fourth Gospel, if not himself a Jew of Palestine, at least had a good " pilgrim's knowledge " of the country. Accordingly, some of these identifications, for instance that of Bethany with the village of Martha and Mary, or of Mary with the anointing woman, may possibly rest on a Jerusalem tradition. The possibility, however, that the identifications are made on good authority does not affect our argument. The fact that the identifications required to be made suggests that the public for whom John wrote was already familiar with the persons and incidents in question, and for that reason would be interested in the further details that he adds.

In the light of this conclusion we proceed to examine the resemblances between the accounts of the Passion in Luke and John. And for the sake of brevity I shall for the time being ignore the distinction between Luke and a source embodied in Luke. But we have learnt the lesson that it is unwise to draw wide conclusions in the sphere of higher criticism without being sure of the text we use. Three of the most remarkable points of contact in the Passion Story of Luke and John are Peter's visit to the Empty Tomb (Lk. xxiv. 12), the salutation " Peace be with you " (Lk. xxiv. 36), and the sentence, reminiscent of the Thomas story, " He showed them his hands and his feet " (Lk. xxiv. 40). These constitute three of the eight Lucan major

" Western non-interpolations " definitely rejected by Hort as absent from D and the Old Latin. Whether or not we agree with Hort, it is clear that, the evidence for omission being what it is, they cannot be used to prove a literary connection between the two Gospels. So too βασιλεύς, Lk. xix. 38 (cf. Jn. xii. 13) ; om. WΛ (D Lat.).

The outstanding coincidence between John and Luke is the representation of the first Resurrection Appearance to the Twelve as taking place in Jerusalem, not (as in Mark and Matthew) in Galilee. But agreement on a point of this magnitude, though very natural if John knew and used Luke, cannot in itself, simply because of its magnitude, be quoted as evidence that he did know him. For a fact of this character, divergence between Mark and Luke implies a divergence in the early tradition, and John and Luke *might* be drawing independently on the same tradition. The same thing applies to John's mention of the name Judas, not Iscariot, which otherwise would imply a preference of the Lucan to the Marcan list of the Twelve. To prove literary dependence, we must find examples of the use of language more or less identical, where the resemblance is of a kind not readily explicable by coincidence ; or we must be able to detect in some story additions or modifications of quite minor details of a kind not likely to have been preserved apart from the context in which they are embodied.

Of these there are several : the observation that Judas's offer to the high priests to betray Jesus was a direct suggestion of the devil (Lk. xxii. 3; Jn. xiii. 2); Pilate's *three times* repeated formula, "I find no fault in him " (Lk. xxiii. 4, 14, 22); the detail that it was the *right* ear of the high priest's servant that was cut off (Lk. xxii. 50; Jn. xviii. 10); the point that the tomb was one "in which no one had ever yet been laid " ; the statement that two angels—not one as in Mark and Matthew—were seen by the women at the tomb. Still more evidential is the prophecy by our Lord of Peter's denial (Mk. xiv. 30; Lk. xxii. 34; Jn. xiii. 38).

Mk. xiv 30.	Lk. xxii. 34.	Jn. xiii. 38.
ἀμὴν λέγω σοι ὅτι σὺ σήμερον ταύτῃ τῇ νυκτὶ πρὶν ἢ δὶς ἀλέκτορα φων- ῆσαι τρίς με ἀπαρνήσῃ.	λέγω σοι, Πέτρε, οὐ φωνήσει σήμερον ἀλέκ- τωρ ἕως τρίς με ἀπαρνήσῃ εἰδέναι.	ἀμὴν ἀμὴν λέγω σοι, οὐ μὴ ἀλέκτωρ φωνήσῃ ἕως οὗ ἀρνήσῃ με τρίς.

It will be observed that the Johannine wording is almost identical with the Lucan just where that differs from Mark, but it is pre- fixed by the word *amen* as in Mark. This suggests an unconscious conflation of the Marcan and Lucan versions.

The above passages, added to the impression made by the Martha-Mary incidents, make it difficult to deny some literary connection between Luke and John. That being so, certain infinitesimal points of contact, which if they stood alone would prove nothing, carry weight as confirmatory evidence. With ἆρον ἆρον, Jn. xix. 15, compare αἶρε τοῦτον, Lk. xxiii. 18. The double " crucify him " occurs both in Jn. xix. 6 and Lk. xxiii. 21. The description of the women at the cross opens with ἱστήκεισαν, Jn. xix. 25, cf. Lk. xxiii. 49, as the first word of the sentence.

But once the dependence of John upon Luke (or a source embodied in Luke) is established, certain other features in the Johannine story assume a new significance. They point to the working of a tendency similar to that noted above in the allusions to Martha and Mary. An enhanced definiteness and vividness is given to incidents, recorded separately in Mark or Luke, by bringing them into connection with one another ; and they are further elucidated by modifications and additions derived either from the author's own reflection or from independent tradition.

(1) Mark describes the death of our Lord by the word ἐξ- έπνευσεν. Luke uses the same word, prefaced by the saying, " Father, into thy hands I commend my spirit," παρατίθεμαι τὸ πνεῦμά μου, which (except for the word " Father ") is a quotation from Ps. xxxi. 5. The phrase in which John describes the death παρέδωκε τὸ πνεῦμα is explicable as a conflated recollection of Mark and Luke.

(2) The discrepancy between the Marcan and Lucan accounts

of the Mocking is striking—still more so if we accept the suggestion that Herod gave the robe as a compliment.[1] According
to Luke this was done by Herod *before* Pilate had condemned
Jesus ; Mark places it *after* Pilate's condemnation and makes
it a spontaneous act of Pilate's soldiers. Now Luke represents
Pilate, hoping to placate the Jews, as twice making the offer
" I will chastise him and let him go," as an alternative to the
death penalty. John makes Pilate, with the same hope, actually
chastise Jesus and bring Him out before them clothed with the
purple robe. Thus John agrees with Luke in placing this
incident before Pilate's final condemnation, and in connecting
it with Pilate's effort to induce the Jews to accept less than the
death penalty. But, in the actual details of the incident, John's
version approximates more nearly to Mark's, especially in
assigning the mocking to Pilate's soldiers instead of to Herod.
This again suggests that John is conflating the two accounts.

(3) Assuming that Hort is right in omitting from the text of
Luke (xxiv. 12) the description of a visit of Peter to the tomb,
there remains in Luke (xxiv. 24) the statement by the Apostles
to the two from Emmaus, " Some of them with us went to the
tomb " (after the women had announced their discovery that
it was empty) and found it empty, " but him they saw not."
The visit of Peter and another disciple to the tomb recorded by
John gives detail and precision to this Lucan statement. Our
view on this point will depend on our view of the contents of the
lost ending of Mark. It certainly looks as if this told that the
women, in fear, " told no man " that they had found the tomb
empty, and that the Twelve first saw the Lord in Galilee. If
that is what happened, then the visit of Peter and the other
disciple to the tomb looks like an attempt by conjecture to give
the names of the disciples mentioned as visiting it in the Lucan
story, comparable to the identifications of persons or places left
nameless in Mark and Luke which have been already discussed.

---

[1] Cf. A. W. Verrall in *J.T.S.* x. p. 321 ff. The suggestion does not quite
convince me.

To sum up. The interest shown by John in identifying and connecting persons and places, or in elaborating incidents, mentioned in Luke is more likely if they occurred in some document regarded by his readers as a standard account of the life of Christ rather than in a mere floating tradition.

But we have still to ask whether the source known to John was our Gospel of Luke or the source Proto-Luke, which we have seen reason to believe was incorporated in it. The difficulty of answering this question lies in the rarity of passages which show points of contact between Luke and John (cf. p. 404) where we can be quite sure that Luke is not using the source Proto-Luke. Suppose, for example, that we could be *certain* that Luke's version of Peter's Denial and of the Entombment was dependent on Mark alone, then the fact that John adopts some of Luke's verbal modifications of Mark would prove that he used our Luke. I am inclined to think that Proto-Luke either omitted these incidents or treated them very briefly (cf. p. 217); but the possibility being open that Luke's modifications of Mark *may* be due to a parallel version of the incidents in Proto-Luke, we desiderate further evidence. But from the nature of the case we have only infinitesimals to go upon.

(1) Objectors ask (Jn. vii. 41-42): "What, doth the Christ come out of Galilee? Hath not the scripture said that the Christ cometh of the seed of David, and from Bethlehem, the village where David was?" No reply is given; yet the foundation stone of early Christian apologetic was the exact correspondence of details in the life of Jesus with Old Testament Messianic prophecy. But if every one of John's readers knew that, though His father was a carpenter of Nazareth, He was of the royal seed, and by a seeming accident had been born in Bethlehem, we have a delicate piece of what in Greek tragedy is called εἰρωνεία. That which is alleged as an objection to His Messiahship is really its confirmation. But could John have presumed this knowledge in his readers except in a Church where Luke (or Matthew) was read?

(2) " What then if ye should behold the Son of man ascending where he was before ? " (Jn. vi. 62). This is addressed to murmuring disciples. It gains much in point if we assume that the story of the Ascension was familiar to John's readers. We have seen (p. 142) that the words in Lk. xxiv. 51 which mention the Ascension as taking place *in sight of* the Twelve are probably original. In any case the Acts, by the same author, describes the event.

(3) The Feeding of the Five Thousand is placed by John on the East side of the Lake of Galilee, by Mark (but cf. p. 176 *n.*) and Matthew on the West. It is suggested below that John may have introduced into it details from Mark's Feeding of the Four Thousand which takes place near Decapolis. But the definite statement in Luke that the miracle took place near Bethsaida, which is on the East bank of the entrance of the Jordan into the Lake, would at least be an additional reason for John's supposing it took place on the East side. There is another consideration. John's version of the Feeding of the Five Thousand exhibits two of those Minor Agreements of Matthew and Luke against Mark which we have already discussed (p. 313)—the allusion to the healing immediately before the miracle, and the word $\pi\epsilon\rho\iota\sigma\sigma\epsilon\acute{\upsilon}\sigma\alpha\nu\tau\alpha$ (Jn. vi. 2, 12). The natural explanation of this would be that John had read the story, not only in Mark, but also in either Matthew or Luke. Seeing, however, that his knowledge of Matthew is extremely doubtful, knowledge of Luke is the simplest explanation.

Neither singly nor together do these points amount to demonstrative proof that what John knew was, not Proto-Luke, but our Gospel of Luke ; yet, to my mind, they make the balance of probability incline very decidedly in that direction.

JOHN AND MATTHEW

The points of contact between Matthew and John are extremely few ; fewer still are those which are of a material character. (a) John twice has the saying " The servant is not greater than his master " (Jn. xiii. 16, xv. 20 ; cf. Mt. x. 24 = Lk. vi. 40). John's phrase is slightly nearer to Matthew than to Luke, and the corollary in John, " If they persecuted me they will also persecute you," resembles that in Matthew, " If they have called the master of the house Beelzebub, how much more shall they call those of his household ? " But in view of the great differences of the Lucan, Matthean, and Johannine versions of the saying and also of its epigrammatic character—epigrams easily circulate by word of mouth—there is no need to postulate a written source. The sentiment that Christians could not expect the world to treat them better than their Master must have been replete with practical consolation to the average Christian, and a saying of Christ which put this in a pithy form is likely to have been part of the stock-in-trade of many a Christian preacher. (b) Twice (iii. 35 and xiii. 3) John has the phrase " The Father has given all things into his hands," which has close affinities to " All things have been delivered to me by my Father " (Mt. xi. 27 =Lk. x. 22). But as this saying occurs in Luke it is no evidence that John used Matthew. (c) Again, the healing from a distance of the Nobleman's Son ($\beta \alpha \sigma \iota \lambda \iota \kappa \acute{o}s$ perhaps =king's officer) at Capernaum (iv. 46 ff.) has a general resemblance to the story of the Centurion's Servant (Mt. viii. 5 ff. =Lk. vii. 2 ff.). But, even if John is describing the same incident, his representation of the details is so different that he may well be giving a version of the incident preserved in a different line of tradition, or may, after his manner, be conflating it with another incident. John's verbal agreements with Matthew and Luke are so slight as to be easily explicable by accident—but, such as they are, they are about evenly distributed between the two. In no case is the verbal agreement between John and either Matthew or Luke close enough to prove literary dependence. But, even if this were otherwise, it would not be evidence that John knew *Matthew,* for the incident in question seems to have stood in Q; so that John could have derived it either from Luke or from Q.

There remain to be considered a few minor agreements of Matthew and John against Mark. These are of very much the same order as the Minor Agreements of Matthew and Luke discussed in Chapter XI., and I believe they are to be explained in exactly the same way.

(a) The story of the Walking on the Water does not occur in Luke, but there is one small verbal agreement of John with Matthew against Mark. Mark (vi. 47) says the boat was " in the midst of the sea," John (vi. 19) that it was " about twenty or thirty furlongs from the land," Matthew (xiv. 24) (in the text of W.H.) that it was distant " many furlongs from the land." This reading in Matthew is found in B, the Ferrar Group, and the Old Syriac. But ℵ C L, with the support of D and the Old Latin, read " in the midst of the sea." Clearly assimilation has been at work, either in B or in ℵ and their respective supporters. If B is right, ℵ has assimilated Matthew to Mark; if ℵ is right, B has assimilated Matthew to John. Which is the more probable ? Obviously, since Mark was the least read and John the most valued of the Gospels, assimilation of Matthew to the text of John is more probable than to that of Mark; while, since Matthew indubitably copied Mark, an agreement of Matthew with Mark does not look like assimilation. Accepting, then, the text of ℵ D Old Lat., we discover, on comparing the parallel versions, that the outstanding point is the agreement of Mark and John *against* Matthew in saying nothing whatever about Peter's attempt to walk on the water to meet Jesus, with the notable moral it involves. John's ignoring of this striking addition tells decidedly against his knowledge of the Matthean form of the story.

(b) Jn. xii. 8, " The poor ye have always with you, but me ye have not always." This occurs word for word in Mark, Matthew, and John. But Matthew and John concur in omitting the words " and when ye will ye can benefit them," which

Mark inserts between the two halves of the antithesis. Coincident omission, especially where the construction facilitates it, is not enough to prove literary dependence. But since the whole verse in John is omitted by the strong combination of D with Syr. S., we seem to have evidence that even this slight agreement of Matthew and John is due to textual assimilation.

Matthew and John each add many details not found in Mark's account of the Passion. In particular both are concerned to throw the responsibility of the Crucifixion on to the Jews, and, as far as possible, to exculpate Pilate. Here, then, especially, if there was any literary connection between the two Gospels, we should expect to find agreements in incident or language. But the only points of contact I have noted are insignificant.

(c) Matthew (xxi. 5) and John (xii. 15) agree in connecting with the triumphal entry the passage in Zechariah ix. 9, "Behold, thy king cometh, sitting on the foal of an ass." Seeing that Christians were in the habit of ransacking the Old Testament for Messianic prophecies, concurrence in such an obvious instance proves nothing. What is significant is that the words as quoted by John are so different from Matthew that they must either represent a different translation of the Hebrew or be free quotations from memory.

(d) Matthew (xxvi. 52) and John (xviii. 11) agree in saying that Jesus commanded the person who cut off the ear of the high priest's servant to put up his sword, ἀπόστρεψόν σου τὴν μάχαιραν εἰς τὸν τόπον αὐτῆς (Mt. xxvi. 52), βάλε τὴν μάχαιράν σου εἰς τὴν θήκην (Jn. xviii. 11). But they do not use a single word in common except that for " sword "; while the reason given by our Lord in Matthew, " They that take the sword shall perish by the sword," is quite different from that given in John, " The cup which my Father hath given me, shall I not drink it ? "

(e) In the parallel Mk. xv. 17 = Mt. xxvii. 29 = Jn. xix. 2, speaking of the crown of thorns, Mark says they put it " on him,"

Matthew and John agree in saying " on his head." Since crowns are made to be worn on the head, the coincidence is not remarkable. What *is* remarkable, however, is the difference between Matthew and John in this very same verse. Matthew's account differs from Mark's in adding the detail that the soldiers put the reed (as a mock sceptre) into our Lord's hand. This striking departure from Mark is *not* reproduced by John—which makes it very unlikely that the quite colourless addition of the word " head " was suggested to him by familiarity with this verse of Matthew.

(*f*) Jn. xix. 41, "There was in the place where he was crucified a garden, and in the garden a tomb," $\kappa \alpha \iota \nu \acute{o} \nu$, $\dot{\epsilon} \nu$ $\dot{\phi}$ $o \dot{v} \delta \acute{\epsilon} \pi \omega$ $o \dot{v} \delta \epsilon \dot{\iota} s$ $\dot{\epsilon} \tau \acute{\epsilon} \theta \eta$. In Mt. xxvii. 60, Joseph puts the body $\dot{\epsilon} \nu$ $\tau \hat{\phi}$ $\kappa \alpha \iota \nu \hat{\phi}$ $a \dot{v} \tau o \hat{v}$ $\mu \nu \eta \mu \epsilon \acute{\iota} \phi$. Has the fact that Matthew and John agree in using the common adjective $\kappa \alpha \iota \nu \acute{o} s$ (=new) any significance ? If we examine the passages more closely, we note that the point of Matthew's statement is that the tomb belongs to Joseph, it was *his own* new tomb ; but the language of John implies that he did not know to whom it belonged. This makes decidedly against John having read Matthew. But there is a further point. D$^{supp.}$ 69 and several other MSS. read $\kappa \epsilon \nu \acute{o} \nu$ (=empty) for $\kappa \alpha \iota \nu \acute{o} \nu$ in John. The confusion of $a \iota$ and ϵ is one of the commonest errors in MSS., and even in inscriptions; in late Greek they were, as in Modern Greek, pronounced alike. But if we ask which of the two adjectives is more likely to be the original in this passage, at once it is obvious that a scribe with the phrase of Matthew running in his head would be more likely to alter $\kappa \epsilon \nu \acute{o} \nu$ to $\kappa \alpha \iota \nu \acute{o} \nu$ than *vice versa*. Again, so far as the sense is concerned, $\kappa \epsilon \nu \acute{o} \nu$, " empty," is slightly more appropriate than $\kappa \alpha \iota \nu \acute{o} \nu$, " new " ; for the words which follow, " in which no man had yet been laid," are a mere reiteration if preceded by $\kappa \alpha \iota \nu \acute{o} \nu$, whereas they add a new point if $\kappa \epsilon \nu \acute{o} \nu$ preceded—the tomb was, not only one that happened to be empty, but one that had never yet been used.

(*g*) There is one minor agreement which differs from those

so far discussed, insomuch as the contexts in which the words occur are not exactly parallel, since in John they occur in the introduction to the Feeding of the Five Thousand, while in Matthew they occur immediately before the Feeding of the Four Thousand.

Mt. xv. 29.	Jn. vi. 3.
and going up into the hill country, he sat there.	and Jesus went up into the hill country, and there sat with his disciples.

This passage cannot be discussed apart from the observation that there are several small points in which John seems to combine the accounts of the Four Thousand and Five Thousand. In the account of the Five Thousand in Mark and Matthew, the disciples take the initiative in asking Jesus to deal with the multitude, but with the Four Thousand the initiative is His; also in the Four Thousand εὐχαριστήσας is substituted for εὐλόγησε καὶ. John introduces both these modifications into his version of the Five Thousand. Such modifications are so trifling and obvious that, if they stood alone, they would prove nothing; but, taken in connection with " went up into the hill country, and sat there," they suggest that in John recollection of the details from the one miracle had become confused with the other. But the words " went up into the hill country " stand in Matthew, but not in Mark. At first blush we seem at last to have found definite evidence that John knew Matthew.

Not so, however, if the words in question originally stood in the text of Mark. And the hypothesis that this was the case seems to me much the easiest explanation of the fact that they do occur in Matthew—a thing which, to the student of the Synoptic Problem, really does demand an explanation. Note the last lines of the parallels printed below—each of 26 letters.

Mk. vii. 31.	Mt. xv. 29.
καὶ πάλιν ἐξελθὼν ἐκ τῶν ὁρίων Τύρου	καὶ μεταβὰς ἐκεῖθεν ὁ Ἰησοῦς
ἦλθεν διὰ Σιδῶνος εἰς	ἦλθεν παρὰ
τὴν θάλασσαν τῆς Γαλιλαίας	τὴν θάλασσαν τῆς Γαλιλαίας καὶ
ἀνὰ μέσον τῶν ὁρίων Δεκαπόλεως.	ἀνάβας εἰς τὸ ὄρος ἐκάθητο ἐκεῖ.

Matthew's suppression of the geographical details about Tyre
and Decapolis is quite in accord with his general tendency to
compress Mark. Not so the line that he substitutes. Wherever
Matthew *adds* anything to Mark, it is a saying or an incident
of some special interest, or a turn of phrase which removes a
difficulty. The statement " He went up into the hills, and sat
there " is not at all like the explanatory editorial amplifications
he is in the habit of making ; nor, again, is it a fact of sufficient
moment to be preserved in floating tradition. I suggest that the
words stood in the text of Mark used by Matthew. If a line
beginning ἀνὰ μέσον was followed by one beginning ἀνάβας, an
omission by homoioteleuton would be easy. Or suppose, as in
ℵ, the average line in an early copy of Mark had 13-14 letters.
it might read :

ΑΝΑΜΕΣΟΝΤΩΝΟΡ
ΙΩΝΔΕΚΑΠΟΛΕΩϹ
ΑΝΑΒΑϹΕΙϹΤΟΟΡ
ΟϹΕΚΑΘΗΤΟΕΚΕΙ

Two lines, both beginning with **ANA** and ending with **OP**, form
an attractive invitation to homoioteleuton to a copyist inclined
to that error. Omissions of the *second* " likeness " do occur.

The suggestion that the words in question stood in the
original text of Mark is attractive for another reason. " Transference of formulae," that is, the repetition in more than one
context of phrases found in his source, is a notable characteristic
of Matthew. If the words " going up into the mountain, he
sat there " stood in this place in the copy of Mark used by
Matthew, we have the original of the phrase " He went up into
the mountain, and when he had sat down," which provides the
narrative framework of the Sermon on the Mount. Lastly,
conflation in John's memory of the Five Thousand with the
Four Thousand in Mark's rather than Matthew's version would
help to explain the fact that John places the Five Thousand
on the East of the Sea of Galilee, although Mark appears to place
it on the West shore. The Four Thousand is placed by Mark

on the shore of the lake adjacent to Decapolis, which is on the East side ; but Matthew omits the mention of Decapolis and does not give the slightest hint that the miracle took place on that side of the lake.

(*h*) Matthew and John stand alone in representing the first Appearance after the Resurrection as being to a woman. In Matthew there is a mention of an Appearance to the *two* Maries on their way from the tomb with the angel's message to the Apostles, and our Lord's command, " Go, tell my brethren that they depart into Galilee, and there they shall see me." In John, *after* they have announced the angel's message to the Twelve, and *after* Peter and another disciple have visited the tomb, Jesus appears to Mary Magdalene alone in the garden, and uses the words, " Go unto my brethren, and say unto them, I ascend unto my Father. . . ." Nowhere else does Jesus use the phrase " my brethren " of the Twelve ; but apart from the coincidence in this rare expression, there is little that favours a literary connection, since the first Appearance after the Resurrection is the kind of incident in regard to which parallel versions in oral tradition would be likely to exist.

But this coincidence depends upon the authenticity of the word ἀδελφοῖς in Matthew ; and μαθηταῖς is substituted for this in 157, 1555, and a citation by Cyril of Alexandria. The possibility must be faced that ἀδελφοῖς in the accepted text of Matthew is an assimilation to John ; and, but for the fact that μαθηταῖς might also be explained by assimilation to Mt. xxviii. 7, I should use a stronger word than " possibility." If, however, the suggestion tentatively put forward above (p. 357 ff.) be accepted, that the lost end of Mark contained an account of an Appearance to Mary, Matthew and John will both be dependent, either on the lost conclusion of Mark, or on an oral tradition which represented what people could remember of its contents.

To sum up, the evidence that can be adduced to prove John's knowledge of Matthew is quite inconclusive.

Professor Bacon, taking it for granted that the Gospel of

Matthew cannot have been unknown to John, suggests that he
" ignored it " as being " the most anti-Pauline of the Gospels."
I am inclined to agree with this verdict in substance, but would
express it differently.   Matthew cannot, I think, as a whole
be described as " anti-Pauline "—only the source M.   But the
author of the Fourth Gospel, who had lived through the later
stages of the Judaistic controversy, would have been acutely
sensitive to the implications of commands—emphatic from their
position as the opening words of Great Discourses—like " Go
not into any way of the Gentiles " (Mt. x. 5), " The Scribes and
Pharisees sit in Moses' seat : all things therefore whatsoever
they bid you, these do and observe " (Mt. xxiii. 2 f.).   Again,
since in John's own interpretation of Christ's teaching the
spiritual Presence of the Paraclete is practically substituted for
the visible Return of Christ, there is another element conspicuous
in the Discourses of Matthew which he could not possibly accept
as authentic.   But if (as on the whole I think probable) Matthew
was known to his contemporary, the author of the Apocalypse
(cf. p. 469 n.), it must have been already read in Asia.   I recall
the interpretation (p. 19 f. above) of the Papias fragment on
Matthew : the discourses (τὰ λόγια) in the Greek Gospel are
characterised as being " only a translation, and that unauthorised," of whatever it was that the Apostle Matthew wrote.   If this
is correct, the Gospel of Matthew has just reached Ephesus, but
John the Elder, a personage of great weight in that Church,
declines to accept it as having apostolic authority.   Now if
John the Elder was himself the author of the Fourth Gospel he
could adopt no other attitude.   Himself convinced that Christ
came to supersede the Law and that the Parousia is to be understood spiritually, he could not accept as Apostolic a Gospel
conspicuous for Apocalyptic and Judaistic sayings.

JERUSALEM TRADITIONS

The above comparison of John and the Synoptics leaves on
the mind the impression that besides Mark and Luke (or con-

ceivably Proto-Luke instead of Luke) John used no other documentary source. Deduct from John what seems to be derived
from Mark and Luke and only a few odd incidents remain. Accordingly the departures from the Synoptic order and chronology,
which are such a notable feature of the Fourth Gospel, cannot
plausibly be explained by the influence of a third written source ;
for, if so, that source should have accounted for a larger proportion of his total narrative matter. It is in the direction, then, of
the personality of the author that we must look for an explanation
of the major divergences of the Fourth Gospel from the Synoptics.

A standing difficulty of New Testament scholarship has
always been to explain why the author of the Fourth Gospel goes
out of his way, as it were, to differ from the Synoptics on points
having no theological significance. First and foremost there is
his adoption of a chronological scheme glaringly at variance
with the other Gospels. To a large matter like this, or like the
day of the Last Supper, he may have attached special importance. But he also contradicts them on what seem quite trivial
points ; affirming, for instance, that Bethsaida (not Capernaum)
was the city of Andrew and Peter, or that the Anointing at
Bethany took place four days earlier than the other Gospels put
it, and that Jesus departed and hid Himself (Jn. xii. 36) between
Palm Sunday and the Passion. But John's main purpose in
writing was clearly not historical but doctrinal. He is anxious
to commend to the Church a particular religious and theological
attitude. Now people who wish to gain a hearing for an unfamiliar, and possibly controverted, doctrinal position are usually
particularly careful to emphasise when possible their agreement
with what is already familiar to, and accepted by, their hearers ;
they only dispute the accepted where it is necessary for their
purpose. Scholars who hold that John freely altered or invented
narratives for dogmatic ends have been curiously blind to the
consideration that the more the difference between the theological standpoint of John and the Synoptics is stressed, the
more inexplicable becomes John's policy of contradicting them

2 E

on details of history on which doctrinally nothing turns. But from any point of view the historical discrepancies between John and the Synoptics constitute a difficult problem.

The difficulty is considerably reduced in magnitude by the result, to which a critical comparison of the documents seems to point, that the only Synoptics used by John were Mark and Luke. Where John throws over the Synoptic chronology, or modifies their story in smaller details, he is not flying in the face of a universal Church tradition embodied in three separate Gospels, one of them ascribed to an Apostle ; he is only correcting Mark and Luke, neither of which was reputed to be the work of an eye-witness. But if the author of the Fourth Gospel had himself visited Jerusalem—which would naturally be regarded in the Church at large as the fountain-head of authentic tradition— he might consider himself to be in a position to correct or explain, as one having authority, the story as told in these two Gospels. While the difficulty of explaining his boldness in so drastically correcting the lives of Christ hitherto known in the Church for which he wrote would disappear completely, if we could suppose that he could claim in any sense to be himself an eye-witness— even if that meant no more than that, as a boy of twelve, taken by his father to the Passover, he had been one of the multitude who beheld the Crucifixion. At any rate the hypothesis that the author of the Gospel had a personal acquaintance with Jerusalem tradition would considerably ease the critical difficulties arising from a documentary comparison of this Gospel with the Synoptics.

There can be no reasonable doubt that the author of the Fourth Gospel had a first-hand knowledge of the topography of Palestine, and especially of the city of Jerusalem. He was, moreover, a Jew versed in Rabbinic tradition and the usages of the Temple system. This has of recent years been generally admitted by scholars;[1] but if any doubt on that point remained, it has been removed by the linguistic evidence adduced by Dr.

[1] Cf. B. W. Bacon, *Fourth Gospel in Research and Debate*, 1910, p. 385 ff.

Burney in the book to which allusion has already been made.
That evidence does not, in my opinion, justify Dr. Burney's own
conclusion that our Gospel is a translation from the Aramaic;
but it puts it beyond reasonable doubt that the author was a
man whose thoughts naturally fell into the idiom of that language.
It does not, however, necessarily follow that he was a Jew of
Palestinian origin. Every Jew of the Dispersion endeavoured to
visit Jerusalem at one of the great Feasts to offer the sacrifice—
once at least in his life, oftener if possible. The career of Paul
shows that in the first generation conversion to Christianity in
no way lessened the inborn passion of the Jew to see Jerusalem.
The question whether the author of the Gospel had more than a
pilgrim's knowledge of the city is one that cannot be answered
apart from a consideration of the date of writing and the
personality of the writer, but that he had at least a pilgrim's
acquaintance with Jerusalem may be taken as established.

The Johannine Chronology

A pilgrim who visits sites hallowed by sacred association
always takes the opportunity of asking questions on the spot in
regard to persons or events connected with them. The answers
he gets are not always correct, but they are accepted as authoritative. A Jewish Christian pilgrim any time during the first
century would be able to gather much information of value; but
it would not all be equally authentic. The identity of the village
of Martha and Mary, the name Malchus, the day of the Last
Supper, the fact of previous visits to Jerusalem, are the kind of
details that such an one would learn. Exact chronology is not
a matter in regard to which popular local tradition is apt to be
concerned; nevertheless the Johannine chronology may be
based on a conscientious attempt by the author to piece together
scattered bits of information picked up in Jerusalem. If the
visits of our Lord to Jerusalem were connected in the minds of
his informants with His appearances at feasts, the imperfect

recollections of two different persons might easily connect the same visit with two different feasts ; one visit might then be counted twice in John's chronology.   Again, if John started with the idea that the Cleansing of the Temple occurred at our Lord's *first* public appearance at the Passover, and subsequently learnt that He had been present at more than one Passover, he might infer that the incident had been wrongly placed by Mark.   The greatest difficulty in his chronology would then be explained.

And is it not possible that John had information that Jesus the very first time He came to Jerusalem, after having at the Baptism felt the call to Messiahship, vehemently denounced the Temple traffic ?   We should certainly expect Him to make some protest, although on the first occasion He may not have followed His words by action.   Assuming that he had information to this effect, John would at once relate it with the prophecy in Malachi iii. 1-3, " The Lord whom ye seek shall suddenly come to his temple . . . he shall purify the sons of Levi . . ."; he would then be quite sure that Mark had misplaced the incident.   The *a priori* principle that a particular action of the Messiah is more likely than not to show close conformity to some Old Testament prophecy is certainly not one by which a modern critic would be swayed in determining the choice between two apparently con-flicting traditions.   But to admit that an author's estimate of probabilities is influenced by *a priori* principles does not prove that he is indifferent to fact or to evidence.   At least, we do not usually say this of the Tübingen School because they undertook to correct the traditional dates of documents or events in the light of the no less *a priori* principle that history advances by " thesis, antithesis, and synthesis."   A mistaken conclusion as to what actually happened on a particular occasion by no means argues a general indifference to fact.   Again, if we suppose that the source from which John derived the story of Lazarus was without precise indication of date, but contained a remark that the priests took alarm at the consequent reputation of our Lord and His growing influence with the people, it would be very natural for John to infer that the story was connected with the Passion, especially as, with the removal of the Cleansing of the Temple, some other incident adequate to account for the alarm of the authorities seems required to explain the course of events.

A minor difficulty is solved if we accept the suggestion (p. 381) that chaps. v. and vi. have got accidentally transposed, which removes the allusion to an unknown Feast of the Jews (John v. 1) which has always puzzled commentators, by making it refer to the Passover mentioned vi. 4; this would shorten the total period of the ministry by some months.[1]

Apart from these instances the Johannine chronology solves more difficulties than it raises.

(1) According to the tradition embodied in Matthew, Christ was born under Herod, who died 4 B.C. According to Luke he was "about thirty years old when he began to preach." According both to patristic tradition and most modern calculation He was crucified A.D. 29 or 30. Simple arithmetic shows that these three data can be reconciled with the $2\frac{1}{2}$ years' ministry implied in John, but not with the one year which the Synoptics—though they never actually name a period—are supposed to imply.

(2) In Mark, Jesus is consistently represented as going to Jerusalem, expecting to be rejected. Similarly Luke's peculiar source has "It cannot be that a prophet perish out of Jerusalem," and again, "If only thou hadst known even in this thy day." Q has "How often would I have gathered thy children . . ." [2] That is to say, three independent Synoptic sources agree in representing our Lord as approaching Jerusalem anticipating rejection. But this surely is not the attitude one would expect of Jesus, who was wont to hope the best of every man—unless, indeed, it was based on the experience of failure on one or more previous visits.

(3) Mark explicitly says that the preaching in Galilee which he records began *after* John the Baptist had been imprisoned

---

[1] It is possible that other accidental transpositions have caused an actual multiplication of the number of visits to Jerusalem in the original text.

[2] Lk. xiii. 33; xix. 42; Lk. xiii. 34 = Mt. xxiii. 37.

(Mk. i. 14). The author of the Fourth Gospel represents John
as still baptizing as late as the events in John iii. 23. Seeing that
he wrote for a Church which regarded Mark as an authority, this
can hardly be accidental. He intends to indicate that his story
opens at an earlier date than that of Mark. Calculations about
the season of the year implied in " the green grass " in Mark's
account of the Feeding of the Five Thousand (Mk. vi. 39) show
that, unless the event underlying this story is misplaced in Mark,
there must have been another Passover between it and the Last
Passover, as John says was the case. The story of the Mission of
the Twelve implies that the whole group of twelve was not always
with Jesus. It is indeed improbable that He ever went to Jerusalem accompanied by the whole band before the last visit ; but
that is no reason why He may not have gone there with one or
two.[1] If Peter was not one of these, Mark's silence on the subject
is explicable. It is at any rate a remarkable coincidence—if it is
mere coincidence—that John never mentions Peter in connection
with Jerusalem until the last week. The incident of the apparently prearranged signs by which the disciples would recognise
the man who would take them to the upper chamber (Mk. xiv. 13)[2]
is slightly more intelligible if Jesus had in Jerusalem friends,
gained on previous visits, to whom the Twelve were unknown.

(4) The majority of scholars have for a long while been agreed
that, on grounds of intrinsic probability, the representation of
John, that the Crucifixion took place on the morning of the day
when the Passover was killed, is to be preferred to that of the
Synoptics, which identify the Last Supper with the Passover. It
is unnecessary to repeat the familiar arguments as to the improbability of secular business like the Arrest, the Trials, the buying
of spices, etc., being possible during the most solemn twenty-
four hours of the Festival. The language of Paul, " Christ our
Passover is sacrificed for us . . .," has been regarded as having

[1] Cf. C. A. Briggs, *New Light on the Life of Jesus*, p. 40 ff. (T. & T. Clark,
1904).

[2] Matthew's πρὸς τὸν δεῖνα, xxvi. 18, makes still more clear the point that
it was a specified person.

supplied John with a dogmatic motive for correcting the Synoptic date.   But if, on other grounds, we accept John's date as correct, then Paul's language becomes collateral evidence for the Johannine story.   Again, the words in Luke, " With desire I desired to eat this Passover, but I shall not eat it . . .," suggest, though they do not quite compel, the view that *in his source* the Last Supper was conceived as taking place on the day before the Passover.   If so, Luke, in conflating his special source with the Marcan tradition, has misunderstood and obscured its original purport.   In that case John and Proto-Luke were in agreement, but John preserves the original tradition in a clearer form. Personally I incline to think that the Johannine incident of the Washing of the Disciples' Feet by Jesus at the Last Supper is similarly authentic.   The saying, " I am among you as one that serves," Lk. xxii. 27, is an echo of it which has attracted to this context the saying about the kings of the Gentiles which Mk. x. 42 gives in its true historical setting.

But to talk at all of comparing the Johannine and Synoptic chronology is really unmeaning.   There is no " Synoptic chronology."   Matthew, in the second half of his Gospel, follows the order of Mark ; in the first half, while copying the narrative of Mark closely, he rearranges the order of events in a way which shows, either that he was completely indifferent to chronology, or that he did not regard the order of incidents in Mark as chronological. Luke takes Proto-Luke as his base, and—apparently without appreciably altering the relative order of events in either of his sources—fits extracts of Mark into the scheme of that document. But there is no reason for supposing that Luke possessed, or thought that he possessed, any key to the original order of the sayings and events he records.   The " order " which he speaks of in his preface does not mean chronological order so much as literary form, or, as we should say, " construction." [1]   The resultant scheme is a threefold division of the Gospel into a Galilean, a

[1] Cf. Foakes-Jackson and Lake, *op. cit.* ii. p. 505; also F. H. Colson, *J.T.S.* xiv. p. 62 ff.

Samaritan, and a Judaean section. The long non-Marcan section, Lk. ix. 51-xviii. 14, is somewhat vaguely represented by Luke as a series of wanderings through Samaria in the general direction of Jerusalem. The notion that Luke thinks of it as the journey through Peraea which Mark records is a misconception.[1]

To speak, then, of a Synoptic chronology, as though there were a three-to-one agreement against John, is quite misleading. The chronology of the Life of Christ is simply a question of Mark against John. Now of the last journey to Jerusalem, and the events of Passion Week, Mark presents a clear, detailed, and coherent account; and this, dealing with the events of, at the outside, three weeks, occupies about one-third of the whole Gospel. The rest of the Gospel is clearly a collection of detached stories— as indeed tradition affirms it to be ; and the total number of incidents recorded is so small that the gaps in the story must be the more considerable part of it. Mark probably had information which enabled him roughly to fix the position of certain outstanding incidents like Peter's confession at Caesarea Philippi, but the term chronology is really a misnomer in connection with a work of this character.

John is the first and the only one of the Evangelists who attempts a chronology. It may be that his chronology is not a very good one—but it is the only one we have. Chronology is a very difficult art. Success in it depends, not only on the existence of abundant evidence, but also on complicated calculations, synchronisms, and inferences. In antiquity it was even more difficult than it is now ; and it is only to be expected that John's pioneer attempt at a chronology of our Lord's life contains serious inaccuracies. But to admit that is a very different matter from saying that it is a wholly ideal construction.

FINAL RESULTS

The Gospels of Mark, Luke and John form, it would seem, a series—Luke being dependent on Mark, and John on both the

[1] Cf. p. 203; also J. Moffatt, *Introd. to N.T.* p. 273.

others.   This conclusion of documentary analysis is confirmed by its correspondence with a parallel evolution in the doctrinal emphasis in the several Gospels.   Here also Mark, Luke and John form a progressive series the characteristic direction of which is a tendency to make more and more of the idea of Christianity as the universal religion, free from the limitations of its Jewish origin, and, along with this, to lay less and less stress on the original Apocalyptic expectation of an immediate visible Return of the Master.   The Fourth Gospel is thus the climax reached in the development of theology in the New Testament towards the naturalisation of Christianity in the Hellenic world.

Matthew, on the other hand, though even more indebted to Mark, represents an independent line of development.   In regard both to the universalistic tendency and to the Apocalyptic Hope, Matthew, as compared with Mark, shows a movement in the reverse direction to that shown in Luke and John.   Matthew introduces, doubtless from his Jerusalem source, sayings of a distinctly Judaistic and legalistic character.   At times he even modifies the actual text of Mark in this direction—adding, for example, the demurrer " I was not sent but unto the lost sheep of the House of Israel " to Mark's account of the Syro-Phoenician woman, and the words "neither on a Sabbath" in the little Apocalypse.[1]   Still more noticeably he goes out of his way to elaborate the apocalyptic detail in the same discourse and to emphasise the expectation of a visible Parousia within the lifetime of the Twelve.[2]

The dependence of the Fourth Gospel upon two earlier Lives of Christ, neither of which purports to be the work of eye-witnesses, would make it hard to accept the tradition which ascribes it to an apostle, even if that ascription involved no other difficulties. On the other hand, as we have seen, the masterful way in which

[1] Mt. xv. 24 = Mk. vii. 26, possibly from a parallel source, cf. p. 260 above; Mt. xxiv. 20 = Mk. xiii. 18.

[2] Cp. the additions Mt. xxiv. 30 ; xxiv. 31 (the trumpet) ; other instances are given in *Oxford Studies*, 428 ff.   The immediacy of the Parousia is brought out in three passages in Matthew, of which one is absent from, the others are less emphasised in the nearest parallel in, Mark: Mt. x. 23 ; xxiv. 29 ; xxvi. 64. See the discussion p. 520 ff. below.

the author deals with the narrative of his predecessors—considered in connection with his evident familiarity with the topography of Jerusalem and Rabbinic usage, and also with the fact that in some points his corrections have a look of superior authenticity—is much easier to explain on the hypothesis that he was a personage who possessed, and was recognised as possessing, a claim to write with independent authority.

It is with these conclusions in mind that the study of the purpose and the authorship of the Gospel must be approached.

XV

SYNOPSIS

THE PROBLEM OF AUTHORSHIP

The Beloved Disciple

The verse, xxi. 24, which asserts that the Gospel was written by the Beloved Disciple, is not by the original author; it represents a later, and probably erroneous, identification.

The Beloved Disciple is the Apostle John idealised; the writer of the Gospel a disciple of the Apostle.

John the Elder

The writer of the Epistles 2 and 3 John styles himself " The Elder " : Papias speaks of an " Elder John, a disciple of the Lord." The hypothesis that this John was the author of the Gospel adequately explains the phenomena of the internal evidence; it also accords with (a) evidence that John the Apostle was martyred in Jerusalem; (b) the silence of Ignatius as to his connection with Ephesus; (c) the hesitation in some quarters to accept the Gospel as Apostolic. The tradition that the Apostle lived in Ephesus easily explicable. Not only John the Elder but also John the Seer (who wrote the Apocalypse) lived in Asia; the works of both were regarded as inspired, and by the end of the second century inspiration and apostolicity had become almost convertible terms.

The Hesitation of Rome

Hippolytus, c. 200, wrote a *Defence of the Gospel and Apocalypse of John*. A defence implies an attack. Evidence that the attack came not from heretics outside but from a conservative group within the Church. A scrutiny of the argument of Irenaeus against those who would make the Gospels either more or less than four in number leads to a similar conclusion. Similarly the Muratorian

fragment on the Canon goes out of its way to defend the Fourth
Gospel.

The hesitation of Rome explicable from the popularity of the
Gospel with Gnostics and a suspicion of the Logos doctrine. Probability that Justin Martyr (who was converted in Ephesus) reconciled the Roman Church to the Logos doctrine. Justin quotes the
Fourth Gospel sparingly, as if it was an authority more valued by
himself than by his readers. Possibility that, though he attributed
the Apocalypse to the Apostle, he regarded the Gospel as the work
of the Elder.

IRENAEUS AND POLYCARP

The letter of Irenaeus to Florinus conclusive evidence of a
connection between Polycarp of Smyrna and John " the disciple of
the Lord." Was this John the Apostle or the Elder ? Considerations pointing to the Elder are : (1) Irenaeus heard Polycarp preach
as a boy, but was probably not a personal pupil. (2) Irenaeus
always calls John " the disciple of the Lord," never, except by
implication, " the Apostle." (3) For apologetic reasons he would
wish to ignore the distinction between the two Johns, supposing he
had heard of it. (4) Irenaeus states that Polycarp was consecrated
Bishop by " Apostles " — doubtless meaning John — the Eastern
tradition contradicts this. (5) *The Apostolic Constitutions*, possibly
drawing on the traditional local list of Bishops, names Timothy and
a John, other than the Apostle, as the first two Bishops of Ephesus.

PAPIAS

Conflict between the evidence of Irenaeus and Eusebius (who
quotes Papias against Irenaeus) as to whether Papias was " a hearer "
of the Apostle or of the Elder John. Eusebius is undoubtedly right ;
but how account for Irenaeus' mistake ? Explicable on the hypothesis that Papias quoted the Fourth Gospel, which Irenaeus
accepted as Apostolic, under the title " The Memoirs of the Elder."
Arguments in support of this hypothesis.

POLYCRATES OF EPHESUS

Ambiguities in his evidence. Fragments of a tradition originally
appropriate to the Elder survive in a (probably recent) identification
of him with the Apostle.

ANTIOCH

The Gospel accepted under the name of John and as inspired
Scripture (doubtless, therefore, the Apostle is meant) by 180. Probably known to Ignatius, but by him not accepted as Apostolic.

DATE OF WRITING

John the Elder had " seen the Lord." Supposing he did so as a boy of twelve, he would be 77 years of age in A.D. 95. The Epistle 1 John implies that the writer was a very old man. Works of genius have often been produced at a great age ; no difficulty in dating the Gospel A.D. 90–95.

The Logos theology not inconsistent with this date.

THE AUTHOR'S SIGNATURE

Undoubted genuineness of 3 John—by the Elder (author also of 2 John). If the Gospel and the Epistles are not by the same writer, then we must assume two—one of whom is the pupil of the other. Reasons for rejecting this assumption. The two epistles of the Elder are thus the author's signature to the Gospel and the first epistle.

CHAPTER XV

THE PROBLEM OF AUTHORSHIP

THE BELOVED DISCIPLE

FROM the literary point of view the way in which the Fourth Gospel ends is curious. Elsewhere it is written in the third person, but in the last two verses this suddenly changes to the first person. What is still more strange, while in the last verse but one the person is in the plural, in the last verse of all it is in the singular.

xxi. 24. " This is the disciple which beareth witness of these things, and wrote these things ; and *we* know that his witness is true."

25. " And there are also many other things which Jesus did the which if they should be written every one, *I* suppose that even the world itself would not contain the books that should be written."

We are compelled to ask, Did these verses stand in the Gospel when it left the hands of the original author ?

In the note in his Commentary, Westcott—in matters of criticism the most cautious and conservative of scholars—answers No.

" These two verses appear to be separate notes attached to the Gospel before its publication. The form of verse 24 contrasted with that of xix. 35 shows conclusively that it is not the witness of the Evangelist. The words were probably added by the Ephesian elders, to whom the preceding narrative had been given both orally and in writing. The change of person in verse 25 (*I suppose* compared with *we know*) marks a change of authorship."

It is notable that the second of the two verses is omitted by
the Codex Sinaiticus, and a double change of person in three
successive verses is so remarkable that—especially as the verse
is merely a somewhat magniloquent repetition of the simple and
natural " Many other signs did Jesus . . . which are not written
in this book " of xx. 30—we are perhaps justified in holding
on the evidence of this single MS. that it is an addition by a very
early scribe. But for the omission of verse 24, which is the one
that guarantees the authorship, there is no such MS. evidence.

But why, we ask, *at the time when the Gospel was first published*,
was any guarantee by the Ephesian elders of its authorship and
general credibility required ?   Early Christian writings (cf. p. 221)
were not addressed to a general reading public, but to particular
communities within a secret society frowned upon by the Law.
The Gospels of Matthew and Mark are anonymous ; so are the
three epistles which appear to be by the author of the Fourth ;
these obviously were addressed to a church or churches in which
the prestige and competence of the author were sufficiently well
known. If, then, in the Fourth Gospel we find an addition to
the text, admittedly not by the original writer, which makes a
definite statement as to authorship, is it not more probable that
it was made at some later date, perhaps also in some other
locality, and was intended to assert a view as to the authorship
of the book from which certain persons at that time or place
dissented ?   And that such dissent did exist in the second century
we shall see shortly.   That being so, the addition of the words
" this is the disciple which . . . wrote these things " is to be
interpreted as an attempt to settle a debated question, and is,
therefore, additional evidence of the existence of doubts in regard
to the authorship of the Gospel.

Apart from these last two verses—which, on the admission
of so conservative a scholar as Westcott,[1] cannot be by the
original author—there is not a word in the whole Gospel to suggest
that it is, or claims to be, by the Apostle John. Quite the

---

[1] I note that Bishop Gore accepts Westcott's view, *Belief in Christ*, p. 106 *n*.

contrary. That John should speak of himself, in contra-
distinction from all the rest of the Apostles, as "the disciple whom
Jesus loved," would be, to say the least of it, remarkable. But
it would not be unnatural for a devoted follower and admirer of
one particular Apostle so to speak of his idealised master. If the
Fourth Gospel had come down to us, as originally published,
without the last two verses, every one everywhere would have
taken it for granted that the author intended to distinguish
himself from the Beloved Disciple, and we should have inferred
that its author stood in much the same kind of relation to the
Beloved Disciple as Mark, the author of another of our Gospels,
stood to Peter.

But if the verse (xxi. 24) which identifies the actual author
with the Beloved Disciple is a later insertion, it is open to us to
surmise that it is a mistaken identification—indeed, in face of the
phenomena discussed in the last chapter, it is hard to suppose
that it is correct. We are, then, almost compelled to the conclusion that the Gospel was written, not by the Beloved Disciple
himself, but by some one to whom that disciple was an object of
reverent admiration.

There has been a great battle of the critics as to whether
the Beloved Disciple is intended as a synonym for the Apostle
John, the son of Zebedee, or whether he is meant to be understood
as a purely ideal figure—the perfect disciple who alone really
understood the mind of Christ. Our previous discussion of the
author's conception of the relation of the historical and the
eternal in all things concerning the earthly life of Christ makes it
reasonable to suppose that he intended *both*. It would have seemed
to him that the Revelation of the Word made flesh would not
have been completed unless at least one of the Twelve had understood it. The Beloved Disciple, then, will be an Apostle; but he
is that Apostle transfigured into the ideal disciple. And that the
Apostle the author had in mind was John can hardly, I think,
admit of serious doubt. Peter, James and John in the Marcan
story repeatedly appear as a kind of inner circle of the Twelve—

and the disciple that understood must have been one of these. And since the Beloved Disciple was one whom the Church had expected to tarry till the Lord's coming, James is ruled out by his early death; while Peter's infirmities are too conspicuous a feature in the tradition to make it possible for him to be selected as the ideal: only John is left.

There is indeed no reason why the author of the Gospel should not in his youth have come into personal contact with John, who, even if he was martyred (as some suggest) shortly after the outbreak of the Jewish War in A.D. 66,[1] may well have been the last survivor of the Twelve. If so, one of his temperament might easily come to conceive a mystical veneration for the aged Apostle who had leaned on the Lord's breast at the Last Supper. We need not suppose that he had seen a great deal of John, or that more than a small number of the facts recorded in the Gospel were derived from him; most of them, indeed, we have seen reason to believe came to him by way of Mark or Luke. We need only postulate for him a connection with the Apostle and an attitude to his memory comparable to that of Irenaeus towards Polycarp. A brief and, as it seemed in the halo of later recollection, a wonderful connection with the Apostle—perhaps also a few never-to-be-forgotten words of Christ derived from his lips—would make the attitude towards the Beloved Disciple expressed in the Gospel psychologically explicable.

JOHN THE ELDER

A critical study of the evidence afforded by the Gospel itself has led us to the conclusion that the author, while making no pretence of being an Apostle, did nevertheless claim to write with authority, that he was certainly familiar with Jerusalem and probably with a cycle of tradition current there, and lastly that he may have had some personal connection with the Apostle John.

[1] Cf. B. W. Bacon, *op. cit.* p. 127 ff., and R. H. Charles, *The Revelation of St. John* (T. & T. Clark, 1920), xlv. ff.

2 F

Now we learn from Papias of the existence of a person who seems to fulfil all these conditions—the Elder John. The Elder John he describes, in the passage quoted above (p. 18), as a " disciple of the Lord." Since Aristion and the Elder John are distinguished by this description, both from the Apostles and from the generality of less well-informed Christians, it must at least imply that they had seen the Lord in the flesh. In another passage (quoted p. 17 above) Papias speaks of " the Elder " without the addition of the name John, as if the title—the Elder, *par excellence* —was in some way distinctive.

It is impossible not to connect the evidence of Papias with that afforded by the three Epistles of John, which in style and point of view are so closely connected with one another and with the Fourth Gospel.

Dr. Charles, in his Commentary on *Revelation*, gives an analysis of the language of the Epistles and the Gospel,[1] which materially strengthens the impression made by a first reading that the three Epistles and the Gospel are by the same author. It is thus of extraordinary interest to note that in the second and third Epistles the writer styles himself " the Elder," as though that were a sufficient and a distinctive title, and in the first he writes to the Church as an old man to his " little children," and claims emphatically to have seen with his own eyes the Word incarnate. 1 John iii. 7 ; i. 1-3.

If the only evidence available were that afforded by the Gospel itself and by the fragments of Papias, the hypothesis that it was written by John the Elder would satisfy all the data. But there remains to be considered the ecclesiastical tradition— of which the addition " This is the disciple . . . which wrote these things " (xxi. 24) is perhaps the earliest evidence—that the author was the Apostle John who lived on in Ephesus until (says Irenaeus) the reign of Trajan.

But tradition is not quite unanimous on the point. According to the " De Boor fragment " of Philip of Side, Papias in his

[1] *Op. cit.* i. p. xxxiv. ff.

second book says that John the Divine and James his brother were killed by the Jews;[1] and the Syriac Martyrology states that he was martyred in Jerusalem, which, if a fact, must have happened before A.D. 70. And it would certainly give an added point to the story in Mk. x. 35 ff. of the request made by those two, with the prophecy by our Lord, " The cup that I drink ye shall drink," if, at the time when Mark wrote, the prophecy had been fulfilled. Certain minor pieces of evidence pointing in the same direction are conveniently summarised by Dr. Charles.[2] The amount of evidence that can be summoned in support of the tradition of an early martyrdom of John is not considerable ; but of two alternative traditions the one which would be the more acceptable would be likely to prevail. *Homines facile, id quod volunt, credunt esse,* and the wonder is that any evidence at all should survive of a tradition apologetically so inconvenient as that of John's early death.

This positive evidence is further supported by two pieces of negative evidence of a somewhat striking kind. (*a*) Of the seven letters written by Ignatius of Antioch on his road to martyrdom, two are addressed to the Apostolic Sees of Ephesus and Rome. The letter to Rome contains a possible allusion to the connection of that church with Peter and Paul ; the letter to the Ephesians goes out of the way to emphasise their special claim to be an Apostolic foundation on account of the peculiar affection shown to them by Paul. If Ignatius had ever heard of a long residence and death of the Apostle John at Ephesus, it is very remarkable that he should make no allusion to it in that particular context. (*b*) The hesitation, in some quarters, of which I shall speak

[1] Similarly George Hamartolus, a late chronographer, writes: " Papias, bishop of Hierapolis, who was an eye-witness of this, in the second book of the Oracles of the Lord says that he (John) was killed by the Jews, and thereby evidently fulfilled, with his brother, Christ's prophecy concerning them . . .," and proceeds to quote Mark x. 39. It is probable that George is here dependent on Philip of Side, but may have quoted him more fully than the De Boor fragment, which is possibly an abbreviated excerpt. Both passages are printed in full among the " Fragments of Papias " in Lightfoot and Harmer, 518 f.

[2] *Op. cit.* vol. i. p. xlv. ff.

shortly, to accept the Ephesian Gospel as Apostolic, is hard to explain if all the world knew that the Apostle John was still living there in A.D. 96.

The tradition that the Apostle John lived and wrote in Asia is presupposed in the Gnostic romance known as the Acts of John, which Dr. James thinks may be as early as 150.   It is also implied in the precedence given to John in the *Epistula Apostolorum* (which places him first in the list of the Apostles) which *may* possibly be no later than that date.   But the tradition is one of which the origin is easily explained.   John the Seer, the author of the Apocalypse—as was pointed out as long ago as Dionysius of Alexandria (248–265)—must have been quite a different person from the author of the Gospel, but he wrote from Patmos, and addressed his work to the seven churches of Asia ; and this John is already identified with the Apostle by Justin Martyr.   And if John the Elder also lived in Asia and wrote the Gospel which, already by A.D. 180, was generally regarded as inspired, it would be almost impossible for tradition to keep these two Asian Johns distinct from one another and from the Apostle of the same name ; more especially in an age when the double conflict with Gnosticism and Montanism was forcing the Church to make inspiration and Apostolic authorship more and more nearly identical terms.

The Hesitation of Rome

The view that the Fourth Gospel was the work of the Elder John explains more easily than any other theory the evidence of a certain hesitation in accepting the Gospel as authentic in certain quarters.   This otherwise complicated problem becomes comparatively simple if, pursuing the clue previously found fruitful, we study *separately* the history of the reception of the Gospel in each of the Apostolic Sees—Antioch, Ephesus and Rome.   We may begin with Rome.

The most notable theologian of the Church of Rome during the period A.D. 190 to 235 was Hippolytus.   On his death a statue of him seated was set up, and this was discovered in an old cemetery at Rome in 1551, and is still preserved in the Lateran Museum. On the chair of the statue is inscribed a list of his numerous works. Near the beginning of the list is mentioned a "Defence of the Gospel and Apocalypse of John." [1] No one defends what nobody attacks. We must, then, infer that there were people who rejected both. The only question is, were these heretics or members of the Church ? Hippolytus was a vigorous opponent of the Montanists and the various Gnostic sects. But the Montanists not only accepted but attached special value to the Fourth Gospel, for it was their authority for the doctrine of the Paraclete, whom they believed to be specially manifested in their own prophet. Most of the Gnostics accepted the Fourth Gospel. Heretics who, like Marcion, rejected it, rejected other Gospels also. The Ebionites accepted only Matthew, other heretics only Mark. But, so far as we are aware, there was no heretical sect which in any special way impugned the Fourth Gospel. But in Hippolytus' Defence the Fourth Gospel and Apocalypse are classed together ; there is thus a slight presumption that the attack on both books was made by the same persons. And in regard to the Apocalypse, we have long known of a very vigorous attack made on it inside the Church by an apparently orthodox Roman presbyter named Gaius.

Gaius, in this respect like Hippolytus himself, was a zealous opponent of the Montanist heresy ; and, in a book against the Montanist leader Proclus, he went so far as to say that the Apocalypse was written, not by the Apostle, but by his notorious opponent the heretic Cerinthus. Two late fourth-century writers, Epiphanius and Philaster, both of whom had access to works of Hippolytus now lost, speak of persons who ascribed both the Gospel and the Apocalypse to Cerinthus, and who, among other arguments to discredit the Gospel, stressed the discrepancy in order between it and the Synoptics. Epiphanius names these

[1] ὑπὲρ τοῦ κατὰ Ἰωάνην εὐαγγελίου καὶ ἀποκαλύψεως. Cf. Lightfoot, Clement, ii. p. 325.

persons *Alogi*. In Greek this is a quite tolerable pun—since
ἄλογοι may be translated equally well by " Anti-Logosites " or
" Irrationalists." Obviously they did not call themselves by
such a nickname, and we never hear of them anywhere else either
by that or any other name. This suggests that they were not a
sect at all, but merely a group within the Church who held their
own private opinions on a subject in regard to which no one view
was yet regarded as *de fide*. That the Gospel also was ascribed to
Cerinthus by Gaius himself is now known ; [1] thus the opposition
to it can be definitely localised in orthodox circles in Rome.[1]

The existence within the Church of individuals who rejected
the Fourth Gospel explains the emphasis laid by Irenaeus in the
passage already quoted (p. 8) on his argument for the *a priori* and
eternal necessity that the Gospels could be neither more nor less
than four. The main object of this elaborate construction is to
establish a major premiss from which can be drawn later on the
conclusion that " all those are vain, unlearned and also audacious,
who represent the aspects of the Gospel as being either more in
number than four or fewer." He proceeds to condemn Marcion
who had only one Gospel ; Valentinus who admitted more than
four ; and, along with them, certain others whom he does not
name. These, he complains, " in order to make void the gift
of the Spirit which in the last times at the Father's good pleasure
was poured out on mankind, do not admit that aspect presented
by John's Gospel in which the Lord promised that he would send
the Paraclete ; but set aside at once both the Gospel and the
Prophetic Spirit." Since by the phrase about " the Prophetic
Spirit " he evidently means the Apocalypse, it seems that
Irenaeus, like his pupil Hippolytus, had occasion to defend both
the Gospel and the Apocalypse of John. But Irenaeus makes it
clear that the motive of the opposition to both these works was
hostility to the idea of the outpouring of the Spirit in the latter
days, *i.e.* to the Montanist movement towards which, at any rate

---

[1] From the discovery of two passages in a commentary of Barsalibi. The
evidence is conveniently summarised by H. J. Lawlor, *Eusebius*, vol. ii. p. 208.

in its more moderate form, he himself had considerable sympathy.[1]
Thus, even if Gaius himself had not rejected the Fourth Gospel,
it is fairly clear that others who rejected both it and the
Apocalypse did so because the doctrine of the Paraclete in the
one, and of the Millennium in the other, seemed to give support
to Montanist extravagances. But the objectors are nowhere
accused of being heretics, and it is implied that they recognised
the other three Gospels ; and, as no sect is known which accepted
these and rejected John, we should naturally conclude that they
were a party inside the Church.

We turn now to the Muratorian fragment on the Canon. This
may well, as Lightfoot argues,[2] be from another work of Hippolytus.
In any case it seems to represent the official view of the Roman
Church about A.D. 200.

In this document the Gospel of Luke, about which no one at
Rome had any doubts, is dismissed in seven lines ; but twenty-
five are given to John. Of Luke it is asserted " neither did he
(*ipse*) see the Lord in the flesh and he too (*idem*), as he was able
to ascertain (wrote)." Of what the author said about Mark only
the last line is preserved, which reads, " but at some he was
present, and so he set them down " ; but we must infer from the
emphatic *ipse* and *idem* in his somewhat disparaging remarks
about Luke that they are more or less a repetition of a similar
statement made about Mark, another Gospel accepted at Rome.
But while he goes out of his way to insist that Mark and Luke are
not eye-witnesses, in speaking of John the emphasis is all the
other way : " It was revealed to Andrew, one of the Apostles,
that John was to write all things in his own name, and they
were all to certify. And, therefore, though various elements are
taught in the several books of the Gospel, yet it makes no difference to the faith of believers, since by one guiding Spirit all things
are declared in all of them. . . ." A little later, quoting the
opening words of the first Epistle of John, the writer proceeds :
"For so he declares himself not an eye-witness and a hearer only,

---

[1] Cf. Bacon, *op. cit.* p. 241.   [2] *Clement*, ii. p. 411 f.

but a writer of all the marvels of the Lord in order." Surely all this looks like a reply to arguments that the Fourth Gospel was not by an Apostle on account of its divergences, especially in the matter of order, from the Synoptics, which Epiphanius tells us were put forward by the Alogi. The author says, in effect: there are no real contradictions between the Gospels; and if they differ in the matter of order, John is to be preferred, since he was an eye-witness, while the others were not.

At Rome, then, by the end of the second century, the Fourth Gospel was accepted by the Church; but there had been opposition. Some of the opposition had been unintelligent— the attribution of the Gospel and Apocalypse to Cerinthus is grotesque. It had not denied the antiquity, only the apostolicity, of the works in question; for Cerinthus was a contemporary of John. And the opposition was from a group of orthodox and conservative leanings; for it was not only anti-Montanist in intention, it was equally (since the Gnostic Cerinthus was to these zealots a name of reproach) anti-Gnostic. All the same, the fact that it was possible to attribute the Fourth Gospel to an arch-heretic and yet to regard oneself as championing ortho- doxy is eloquent. It could not yet have been one of the Gospels which the Roman Church accepted as authoritative.

Some hesitation of the Roman Church to accept the Gospel is less remarkable than would at first sight appear. It was partly the result of the cautiously conservative attitude which it habitually adopted in such matters, and of which its attitude towards the Epistle to the Hebrews—which was known at Rome by A.D. 96 but not accepted as Pauline till the fourth century— is the classical example. But it was probably more affected by a general suspicion of the traditions of the Church of Ephesus, due to the fact that the Ephesians were in the habit of quoting Apostolic authority for a date and method of observing Easter which Rome believed to be the reverse of Apostolic. Strange, too, as it seems to us, the doctrine of the Logos would by some be regarded as a hazardous speculation, savouring of that Gnostic theory of Emanations which threatened to destroy belief in the Unity of God, against which the main battle of the Church was directed in the second century. And it cannot be said that the phrase δεύτερος θεός, " a second God," used by Justin Martyr, the great champion of the Logos doctrine at Rome, was altogether reassuring. Yet again, the fact that the Fourth Gospel was highly appreciated by Gnostics would tell against it. Heracleon, the Valentinian, is known to have written a commentary upon it in Rome about A.D. 160. Thus when, a little later, the Gospel and the Apocalypse became the principal authorities quoted by the Montanists in support of their view that their own prophets had a new revelation from the Paraclete which superseded that of the official Church, we can understand the desire of some conservatives to discredit them completely.

There is a good deal to be said for the hypothesis that it was Justin Martyr who first effectively commended both the Fourth Gospel and the Logos doctrine to the acceptance of the Roman Church. Justin had been converted to Christianity at Ephesus, and his whole philosophy is based on the doctrine of the Logos. But, apart from the Logos doctrine, he has only two quite certain, along with half a dozen more doubtful, reminiscences of the Fourth Gospel. But of Matthew and Luke he has over a hundred reminiscences or quotations ; and even to that small part of Mark which has no parallel in either Matthew or Luke he has two allusions. Moreover, there are cases where he quotes to support his argument texts from the Synoptics very badly adapted to prove his point, while forbearing to quote sayings of Christ recorded in the Fourth Gospel which would have been quite conclusive. In fact, he acts like a modern apologetic writer trying to establish the pre-existence of Christ, but, in deference to critical objections, attempting to do so without reference to the Fourth Gospel.

Justin quotes the Apocalypse, and definitely refers to it as the work of the Apostle John, but we may not infer that he

attributed the Gospel to the same author.   In his First Apology
he refers to the " Memoirs of the Apostles which are called
Gospels," and in the Dialogue with Trypho [1] he speaks of the
" Memoirs which were composed by them (the Apostles) and
their followers." This certainly would be an appropriate
description of the four Gospels known by the names of the two
Apostles, Matthew and John, and two followers of Apostles,
Mark and Luke.   But in another context he gives two statements,
both of which are found in Mark and one in Mark only, as being
derived from the " Memoirs of Peter " (cf. p. 447).   If, then,
that was the title by which he referred to the Gospel of Mark,
the phrase " Memoirs of the Apostles and their followers "
would be equally applicable to Gospels attributed to the two
Apostles Matthew and Peter and to the two followers of Apostles,
Luke and John the Elder.   But whatever view we take on this
point we are not entitled to infer from Justin that all four Gospels
were as yet recognised in the Church of Rome.   Justin is writing
a defence of Christianity in general, and is not concerned with
local diversities ; hence his language would be perfectly justified
if, in his time, John was publicly read in Ephesus but not at
Rome.   Moreover, in view of the statement, quoted in the Acts of
his Martyrdom, as to his paucity of following (to which attention
has been already called (p. 71)) and of the fact that he wore the
gown of the professional philosopher, it is not unlikely that
Justin himself, the Logos doctrine, and the Gospel which he
had imported from Ephesus, were all regarded with some suspicion
by the conservative element in the Roman Church.   And it
may have required the glory of martyrdom, as well as a growing
appreciation of the apologetic merits of the Logos doctrine,
completely to dispel this.

IRENAEUS AND POLYCARP

We must now consider the evidence with regard to the
reception of the Gospel in Asia.   For this we possess three

[1] *Apol.* i. 66; *Dial.* 103.

authorities—the fragments of Papias, some statements by Irenaeus, and the letter of Polycrates, Bishop of Ephesus, to Victor of Rome, A.D. 195. Of these much the most important is the letter of Irenaeus written *c.* 190 to his old friend Florinus, then resident in Rome, in which he endeavours to recall him from Gnostic vagaries to the Apostolic faith that he had learned from Polycarp in his youth. I extract the important passage :

> For I saw thee, when I was still a boy, in lower Asia in company with Polycarp, while thou wast faring prosperously in the royal court, and endeavouring to stand well with him. For I distinctly remember the incidents of that time better than events of recent occurrence ; for the lessons received in childhood, growing with the growth of the soul, become identified with it ; so that I can describe the very place in which the blessed Polycarp used to sit when he discoursed, and his goings out and his comings in, and his manner of life, and his personal appearance, and the discourses which he held before the people, and how he would describe his intercourse with John and with the rest who had seen the Lord, and how he would relate their words.[1]

The letter to Florinus would be conclusive evidence of the residence of the Apostle John in Asia, were it not that we know from Papias, who according to Irenaeus was a contemporary and friend of Polycarp, that there was at the time another John who was commonly spoken of as a "disciple of the Lord."[2] That being so, we must be cautious of drawing hasty conclusions. There are a number of considerations which lend plausibility to the suggestion that Irenaeus may have confused the two Johns.

(1) Clearly, Irenaeus is making the most of his connection with Polycarp. Hence, in the absence of any express statement to that effect, we are not entitled to infer that he was in any sense

---

[1] Eus. *H.E.* v. 20.

[2] Prof. Bacon makes two suggestions : (1) that John the Elder never lived in Asia at all, but in Jerusalem ; (2) that the text of Papias should be emended so as to make the Elder the disciple, not of the Lord, but of the Apostles. It is curious that so acute a critic should not perceive how much the acceptance of these, in themselves improbable, hypotheses intensifies for him the difficulty of explaining away the evidence of Irenaeus for the residence in Asia of the Apostle himself. Our text was read by Jerome ; cf. *De vir. illust.* xviii.

a personal pupil of Polycarp. Nor is there any reason to suppose that Irenaeus was born, or long resident, in Asia ; his language would be justified if he had been at Smyrna on a visit for only a few months. While there, a keen and earnest lad, he would have listened, as one of the congregation, to the sermons of the famous Bishop. Since Papias calls John the Elder a " disciple of the Lord," it is probable that Polycarp used the same phrase. In opposition to new-fangled Gnostic theories, he would recur again and again with passionate emphasis to what had been handed down by this " John, the disciple of the Lord," or by " John, and the others who saw the Lord." Polycarp may even have read passages as from a Gospel by this John—in his extant letter there is clear allusion to the first epistle and a possible one to the Gospel. We ask, then, would it ever occur to a lad, perhaps lately come to Smyrna, that this aged Bishop—a boy's chronology is of the vaguest, and every greybeard is a Methuselah —meant any one but the Apostle ? Of course, if Irenaeus had continued to live in Asia, he must sooner or later have corrected such an impression. But if, after a short visit, he left for Gaul, he would have found no one there able to correct his error.

(2) There is a curious fact about Irenaeus, which would be explained by the hypothesis that he confused the Apostle with the Elder John. He speaks of John (the son of Zebedee) some sixteen times as " the disciple of the Lord," but only twice, and that indirectly and by implication, applies to him the title Apostle. It has been suggested that Irenaeus has ringing in his head the description by the author of the Fourth Gospel of himself as " the disciple whom Jesus loved." But surely in this description the distinctive element is not the word " disciple," but the characterisation " whom Jesus loved." A more natural explanation of the usage of Irenaeus would be that the actual words of Polycarp which were printed on his youthful mind were " John, the disciple of the Lord." [1]

---

[1] Dr. Burney, indeed (*op. cit.* p. 138 ff.), argues that Irenaeus recognises a distinction between the Apostle and the Elder, and attributes the Fourth

(3) The argument that the tradition of the great Churches, founded by Apostles, guaranteed the doctrine of the Catholic Church was the very basis of the case against the Gnostics developed in Irenaeus' great book. And the tradition of Asia, guaranteed by Polycarp's connection with John, was, next to that of Rome, the strongest point in it. If in boyhood Irenaeus had taken it for granted that the John whom Polycarp had spoken of was the Apostle, he had the strongest temptation to continue to believe it. Thus his evidence is not that of an impartial, nor, it would appear, of an exceptionally well-informed, witness. But the less weight we lay on the value of the testimony of Irenaeus to Apostolic authorship, the greater becomes its value as evidence for the existence of another John in Asia who had " seen the Lord " ; for only by a confusion in his mind between two such Johns could so gross a misunderstanding of Polycarp be explained.

(4) There is, moreover, a definite reason for suspecting that Irenaeus' connection with, and knowledge of, Polycarp was slight. He states quite definitely that Polycarp " received his appointment in Asia from Apostles as bishop in the Church of Smyrna." [1] Says Lightfoot, " We need not press the plural," and Tertullian—who had read Irenaeus, and is probably dependent on him here—definitely names John. But the Eastern tradition knows nothing of all this. In the Life of Polycarp ascribed to Pionius he is ordained deacon by the Bishop of Smyrna, Bucolus ; and on his death-bed Bucolus, admonished by a vision, indicates him as his successor. And even Bucolus is not the first Bishop of Smyrna ; that distinction belongs to

---

Gospel to the latter. His argument is attractive, but this interpretation does not seem to me quite to satisfy all the passages. But I could readily believe that in the controversies about the Apostolic authorship of the Gospel, which we know were still recent when Irenaeus wrote, some one had called attention to a possible distinction between the Apostle and the disciple, and that Irenaeus, though himself rejecting it, uses language which on either view would be admissible.

[1] *Adv. Haer.* iii. 3, 4 ; Lightfoot, *Apostolic Fathers,* part ii. vol. i. p. 441 ; Tertullian, *De praescr.* 32.

Strateas (a brother of Timothy), and there were others between him and Bucolus.[1]   Not much of the Pionian Life of Polycarp is sober history, but that only makes it the more remarkable that an author concerned to extol and magnify the Saint in every possible way should not breathe a word of his connection with the Apostle.

Another and quite different tradition is embodied in the *Apostolic Constitutions*, a fourth-century document, but largely based on older materials, which appears to belong to Caesarea or Antioch.   In this work [2] are given the names of the bishops of all churches appointed in the lifetime of the Apostles, *i.e.* before A.D. 100, the reputed date of the death of John.[3]   For Smyrna the names given are "Ariston the first, after whom Strateas, the son of Lois, and the third Ariston."   Since the author can hardly have been ignorant of the existence of so famous a saint as Polycarp, we may presume that he supposed Polycarp did not become Bishop until after the death of John.

Pionius and the author of the *Apostolic Constitutions* concur with one another only in the name Strateas; but, if Asiatic tradition had definitely connected the name of Polycarp with that of the Apostle John, it is strange that neither of them had heard of it.   The tendency of later writers is always to enhance, not to minimise, the connections between the Apostles and the early Bishops.

(5) It is remarkable that in the same context the *Apostolic Constitutions* names as the contemporary Bishops of Ephesus—Timothy ordained by Paul, and John ordained by John.   The addition " ordained by John " may be due to the " tendency " of the author; but, as there is a slight presumption that, at any rate for the more famous Churches, the author had recourse to the traditional lists of Bishops (with which the Churches had already before A.D. 200 begun to provide themselves), it may be that the Elder had already attained in Asia a position comparable to that of Ignatius in Syria a little later.   Certainly

---

[1] Lightfoot, *Ignatius and Polycarp*, vol. i. p. 463.
[2] vii. 46, 8.   [3] So Jerome, *De Vir. Illustr.* 9.

2 and 3 John read appropriately as from the Bishop of the
mother, to a daughter, Church.

PAPIAS

As regards Papias there are two standing difficulties : (*a*)
Irenaeus [1] says that Papias was a hearer of John—meaning
apparently the Apostle—and for this Eusebius takes him to task,
quoting against him the opening words of Papias' own Preface,
but suggests that Papias may mean that he was a hearer of the
Elder John.   But how came Irenaeus to make the mistake ?
(*b*) Eusebius expressly tells us that Papias used " testimonies,"
i.e. proof texts, from the First Epistle of John ; if then, as is on
chronological grounds probable, Papias also used the Fourth
Gospel, why does Eusebius say nothing about it ?

Both these difficulties, I believe, can be solved by the simple
hypothesis that Papias used the Fourth Gospel, but quoted it
under the title " Memoirs of the Elder."   Justin Martyr [2] seems
to quote Mark under the title " Memoirs of Peter," but this was
not the ordinary Roman usage ; otherwise (such was the desire
to attach apostolic authority to books accepted as canonical) it
would certainly have prevailed.   But if at Ephesus Mark was
commonly known as the " Memoirs of Peter," then " Memoirs
of the Elder " is just the kind of title by which we should expect
the Fourth Gospel to be then known.

Once assume a confusion in the mind of the youthful Irenaeus
between the Apostle and the Elder John, it follows that, when
in later life he first read Papias, he would take it for granted
that on all points connected with the apostolic tradition of
Asia there could be no essential difference between Papias and
his contemporary and friend Polycarp.   Hence any reference to
John which Irenaeus found in Papias that was in the slightest
degree ambiguous he would invariably interpret on the assumption that Papias, like Polycarp, when speaking of the personality
or the writings of John, the disciple of the Lord, in Asia, could

---

[1] *Adv. Haer.* v. 33, 4.   [2] *Dial.* 106 ἀπομνημονεύματα αὐτοῦ (sc. Πέτρου).

only mean the Apostle and author of the Gospel. Besides, Irenaeus, we know, accepted 2 John as the work of the disciple of the Lord who wrote the Gospel, whom he identified with the Apostle. The author of 2 John styles himself "the Elder." By Irenaeus, then, "the Elder" would naturally be taken as an *alternative title* of the Apostle. If, therefore, he found in Papias a text from the Fourth Gospel quoted as from the "Memoirs of the Elder," even if it was clear from the context that Papias meant the Elder John, it would only strengthen his belief that the Elder John, so often spoken of by Papias, was identical with the Apostle, and would only serve to counterbalance the *prima facie* meaning of the passage quoted by Eusebius from Papias' Preface as evidence that there were two Johns.

That Irenaeus did find in Papias an allusion to the Fourth Gospel by the title "Memoirs of the Elder" is suggested by a remark of Eusebius. He states that Irenaeus, presumably in some work now lost, mentions the "Memoirs of a certain Apostolic Elder,[1] whose name he passes over in silence." Probably the longer phrase "Memoirs of the Apostolic Elder" did not stand in Papias, or Eusebius would hardly have noticed it as characteristic of Irenaeus. But since Irenaeus identified the Elder and the Apostle, he might naturally add the adjective "apostolic" to Papias' phrase the "Memoirs of the Elder" in order to indicate that the reference was to the canonical Gospel written by the Elder who was also an Apostle.

The same hypothesis explains "the Silence of Eusebius."[2] Volumes have been written on this theme. But suppose Papias did quote the Fourth Gospel, but with some such words as "The Elder in his Memoirs says," what would Eusebius have made of it? Long before Eusebius was born the tradition of the Church

[1] ἀπομνημονεύματα ἀποστολικοῦ τινὸς πρεσβυτέρου. *H.E.* v. 8.
[2] In regard to Luke, the silence of Eusebius in regard to any mention by Papias would be easily explained if Papias—whose allusions to the Synoptics I suggest were all in the course of a discussion of the discrepancies between them and John—had alluded to Luke in terms similar to those used in the Muratorian Canon, emphasising his negative qualifications as an evangelist, in a way which would be of no interest to Eusebius or his readers.

had become firmly established that the author of the Fourth Gospel was the Apostle John, and also that that Apostle had lived in Ephesus. Since, then, Eusebius, unlike Irenaeus, distinguishes the Elder from the Apostle, the last thing that would occur to him, if he came across an allusion in Papias to " The Memoirs of the Elder," would be to identify this work with our Fourth Gospel. Eusebius expressly says that Papias " was evidently a man of very mean capacity to judge from his own arguments." If, then, Papias quoted as from the " Memoirs of the Elder " a passage that occurs in the Fourth Gospel, Eusebius would have thought it quite in keeping with Papias' usual stupidity not to recognise a quotation from that Gospel when he saw one.

We must never forget that in the matter of the identification of the Elder with the Apostle John, Irenaeus and Eusebius have precisely opposite interests. Indeed, it is merely in order to confute Irenaeus on this point that Eusebius quoted the passage from Papias' own Preface (printed p. 18). He does this expressly that he may show that Papias distinguished John the Elder from John the Apostle, and to demonstrate that Papias was not " himself a hearer and eye-witness of the Holy Apostles." Eusebius had a double motive for this. First, Papias taught a millenarian doctrine which Eusebius strongly disapproved of ; it was, therefore, worth while to prove that Papias was *not* an actual pupil of the Apostles. Secondly, Eusebius, like most of the Greek Fathers of his time, disliked the Apocalypse, and sympathised with the attempt—which, so far as the Greek Church was concerned, was for a time successful—to exclude it from the Canon of the New Testament. But that was only possible if its apostolic authorship could be impugned ; and this could only be done by accepting the theory of Dionysius of Alexandria that it was the work, not of the Apostle, but of another John, who also lived at Ephesus. But this passage in the Preface of Papias was, by the third century, the only evidence that could be produced for the existence of such a person.

2 G

Irenaeus, on the other hand, revered the Apocalypse and enthusiastically accepted the millenarianism of Papias. He had, therefore, no motive for distinguishing the two Johns. On the contrary, the identification of the John of Asia, of whom Polycarp and Papias had spoken, with the Apostle had become by his time the sheet-anchor of the claim of the Churches of Asia against the Gnostics to be the true depositaries of the apostolic tradition, as well as the main evidence for the apostolic authorship of the Fourth Gospel. Incidentally it left the personality of Polycarp the single link in the chain between himself and the Apostles. By the time of Eusebius Gnosticism had ceased to be formidable, and nobody any longer disputed the apostolic authorship of the Gospel. Thus Eusebius had nothing to lose, and much to gain, by distinguishing the two Johns. Irenaeus, given that other passages of Papias admitted of their being identified, would find some means to explain away his language in the Preface—as has been done in modern times by no less learned apologists than Provost Salmon and Dom Chapman.[1]

The view that Papias regarded the Fourth Gospel as the

---

[1] It would seem probable that Irenaeus was mistaken in inferring from Papias that Papias was himself actually a hearer even of the Elder John. The language of his Preface clearly implies the contrary, though if the present tense " what Aristion and the Elder John *say* " (λέγουσι) is to be pressed, these worthies were still alive when Papias was making his inquiries. And Eusebius, who had read the rest of Papias' book, after remarking that he " says that he was himself a hearer of Aristion and the Elder John," adds significantly, " at all events he mentions them frequently by name, and besides, records their traditions in his writings." Certainly few of the surviving fragments of Papias (including an undefined number preserved by Irenaeus as " Sayings of the Elders "), which are mainly crudely millenarian in character, suggest intimacy with the author of the Fourth Gospel ; but we may probably infer that this material came mainly from Aristion, for it is noticeable that Papias puts his name first. Indeed Eusebius, if we press the strict meaning of the language used, appears to imply a distinction between " words of the Lord " derived from Aristion and " traditions " (? about other matters) derived from John. After alluding to a materialistic millenarian statement attributed by Papias to our Lord, he adds that Papias " gives in his own work *other* accounts of words of the Lord (τῶν τοῦ κυρίου λόγων διηγήσεις) on the authority of the aforementioned Aristion : and traditions (παραδόσεις) of the Elder John." Then he at once gives, as an example of such παραδόσεις from the Elder, the famous statement about the origin of Mark.

work of the Elder John explains another curious fact. Papias
puts the names John and Matthew together at the end of the
list of the Apostles mentioned as those whose teaching he tried
to collect from tradition. Lightfoot argues that this implies
that the names of these two Apostles were connected with
Gospels read in the Church in his day. To my mind it implies
the contrary. " For I did not think," says Papias, " that I
could get so much profit from the contents of books as from
the utterances of a living and abiding voice."   But if Papias
possessed two Gospels, which he *felt sure* had been actually
written by these Apostles, it would have been too incredibly
foolish of him to suppose that such second-hand oral tradition as he could himself collect would be a more accurate
record of their teaching. His attitude would be perfectly
rational if he knew of works attributed to Matthew and John
of which the authenticity was a moot point. I have argued
above (p. 19 ff.) that Papias' allusions to Matthew and Mark
imply that the problem of the divergence between the Gospels
had already within the lifetime of the Elder John given rise
to the question whether the first Gospel, said to be by Matthew,
really gave a reliable account of what Matthew himself taught
about the Parousia, or was only a translation of doubtful accuracy.
If this question was still being discussed when Papias, as a young
man, was collecting traditions, it would be very natural for him
to think that people who had actually met Matthew might settle
the point. But Papias mentions John along with Matthew.
If then we hold that he speaks of Matthew because there was
attributed to that Apostle a Gospel whose complete authenticity
some were inclined to question, must we not say the same thing
of the Gospel of John ?   Not necessarily, for there was another
book bearing the name of John current in Asia about the authorship of which a similar question must have been raised—the
Apocalypse. Its millenarianism was so completely in accordance
with Papias' own views that there is no doubt that he would
have liked to accept it as apostolic ; but he would be aware

that there were people in Asia who took another view. These would allege the tradition, which Irenaeus repeats—and which, since it is almost certainly correct, must ultimately rest on Asian tradition—that "the vision was seen under Domitian," and probably connected this with the other tradition which, according to the De Boor fragment, was also referred to by Papias, that "John and his brother James were killed by the Jews." What solution Papias arrived at we do not know; possibly he may be the ultimate source of the extraordinary suggestion that John's exile to Patmos took place before Paul had written his earliest epistles (*i.e.* about the year A.D. 50), which appears in the Muratorian Canon.[1] Perhaps, however, Papias' reference to the death of John contained no *explicit* reference to the time and place; in that case it would be open to readers of his book, who, like Irenaeus, wished to effect an identification of the author of the Ephesian Gospel with the Apostle John, to suppose that John was killed by Jews in some riot at Ephesus in his old age.

POLYCRATES OF EPHESUS

This stage had certainly been reached in Asia by the time of Polycrates, probably several years earlier. Polycrates, Bishop of Ephesus, in his letter to Victor of Rome A.D. 195, says, "Moreover John, who was both a martyr and a teacher and who leaned upon the bosom of the Lord and became a priest wearing the sacerdotal plate (τὸ πέταλον)—he fell asleep at Ephesus." Polycrates must have read Papias and probably, like Irenaeus, identified the two Johns. He doubtless found there, besides the statement that John and James were put to death by the Jews, references to the great teacher John who wrote "the Memoirs" and died in Ephesus. The description of John as both martyr and teacher is a necessary inference from the identification of the two Johns. Quite possibly in the last part of the sentence

---

[1] "The blessed Apostle Paul himself, following the order of his *predecessor John*, writes only by name to seven churches."

Polycrates is substantially reproducing Papias, only with the substitution of the words " leaned upon the bosom of the Lord " for some phrase of the original like " wrote the Memoirs." But Polycrates is hardly an unbiassed witness. He is writing to Victor of Rome, who had just excommunicated the Churches of Asia for declining to conform to the Roman practice in regard to the keeping of Easter. Victor, presumably, had touched on the possession of the tombs of Peter and Paul—we know these were shown near the Vatican and on the Ostian road before A.D. 200 [1] —as guaranteeing the apostolic priority of the Roman tradition. It was hard lines on the Ephesians that Rome should possess— in repute, if not in fact—the body of their own particular Apostle Paul. But Polycrates will put up a good fight. " Great lights," he replies, " have also fallen asleep in Asia . . ." and he proceeds to claim for Asia the graves of Philip and his daughters, John, Polycarp, and various lesser worthies. He describes Philip as an Apostle ; John has no title but is identified as one " who leaned on the bosom of the Lord." But it is a curious coincidence that both Philip the Apostle and Philip the Evangelist, one of the Seven, should have had daughters who were prophetesses ; and, if we remember that as late as the Didache the title " apostle " was in some parts of the Church applied to many outside the number of the Twelve, the possibility that tradition has effected a con- fusion in the name of Philip as well as John is not remote. We must not forget that Asia and its customs had been on the defen- sive against Rome for many years. The controversy about the date of Easter goes back as far as the time of Xystus, who became Bishop of Rome c. 114. Of one stage in it, the friendly " agree- ment to differ " by Polycarp and Anicetus, 155, we are sufficiently well informed to know that the controversy depended on the antiquity, and therefore apostolic authority, which could be claimed for the custom of the several churches. How could Asia defend its ancient usage against traditions said to derive from Peter and Paul unless it too could quote Apostles among its

[1] Gaius, *ap.* Euseb. *H.E.* ii. 25.

founders ?   And it was historic fact that a disciple of the Lord
named John had ruled the Church of Ephesus till Trajan's days ;
it was indisputable that an apostolic person named Philip had
moved from Palestine to Hierapolis and died there.   Ninety
years had elapsed between the death of this John and the
letter of Polycrates, and for more than threescore of these
the claim of Asia to inherit apostolic custom had been at
stake.   Tradition always errs on the patriotic side, and in
much less time than that would have contrived to identify
both the "Evangelist" with the Apostle Philip, and John of
Asia with the one Apostle who could compare with Peter
in prestige.

But there is a tell-tale point in Polycrates' defence.   Philip
stands first, then his daughters, then John.   Does not this look
like a survival of a traditional order of precedence among the
Saints of Asia which dates from a time when the John in question
was not yet supposed to be an Apostle and was therefore
inferior in years and importance to Philip ?

ANTIOCH

Our evidence for the Church of Antioch in the second century
consists of the Epistles of Ignatius c. 115, and the treatise of
Theophilus, *ad Autolycum, c.* 181.   Theophilus, we have seen
(p. 7), in this, his sole surviving work, quotes the Fourth Gospel
under the name of John as inspired scripture.   Bishops of
Metropolitan Sees are not the kind of men who rush after the
latest thing in doctrine ; and in the second century the preservation of the ancient tradition of the Church against infiltration
from outside was regarded as the supreme function of the Bishop.
We are entitled, then, to infer that at Antioch the Fourth Gospel
had been recognised as an authority, even if not actually attributed
to an Apostle, for a good many years before Theophilus.

This probability is raised almost to certainty when we study
the reminiscences of the language and thought of the Gospel and

First Epistle already occurring in Ignatius. These are discussed in all books on the subject ; but their extent and significance can only be duly weighed if the student has before him, printed in parallel columns, both those where the actual resemblances are close and those where they are less so.[1] The conclusion forced upon my own mind by a survey of the parallels is,that the relation of Ignatius to the Fourth Gospel is exactly the same as that ascribed above to Justin Martyr. His whole outlook and his theology have been profoundly influenced by the study of this Gospel ; but his use of it suggests that it is not yet recognised in his own Church as on the same level of authority as Matthew. And this is just what we should expect if the Gospel had reached Antioch but was not yet attributed to an Apostle. But seeing that, as the use made of it by Ignatius shows, John was already known and valued at Antioch, it is at least probable that Antioch, while still regarding Matthew as the highest authority, would have been inclined to accept John as on the same level as Luke. But once it was accepted and regularly "read" in the Church, in order to distinguish it from the other Gospels, it must be known by the name of John. Even in A.D. 120 there would be very few at Antioch who had ever heard of John the Elder ; in another thirty years there would be none at all. Thus before very long it would be taken for granted that the John who wrote a work of such stupendous merit, so long accepted as authoritative by the Church, was the Apostle. At Rome the Logos doctrine was an obstacle to some, but at Antioch the doctrine had been welcome as early as Ignatius. Its apologetic value dawned slowly on the mind of the prosaic Roman ; but it was obvious at once to the philosophic mystic mind of the Graeco-Oriental East. Thus it is probable that at Antioch, earlier even than in Ephesus, the attribution of apostolic authorship would become, first an accepted belief, then an immemorial tradition.

[1] Cf. the passages set out in *The New Testament in the Apostolic Fathers,* and more fully and conveniently in an appendix to Dr. Burney's *Aramaic Origin of the Fourth Gospel.*

Date of Writing

John the Elder is described by Papias as a " disciple of the Lord," by Polycarp as one " who had seen the Lord." He may have known Him (1 Jn. i. 1) in Jerusalem ; he may have done little more than " see " Him, brought by his father as a boy of twelve years old on pilgrimage to the Passover. And he may have been among the crowd that looked on at the Crucifixion—people in those days were not careful to keep such sights from children. In that case, by A.D. 95 he would have reached the age of seventy-seven. The First Epistle of John was obviously written by a man of advanced years, who can pass quite naturally from " brethren " to " my little children " in the same paragraph (1 Jn. iii. 13 and 18). This last phrase would hardly have been written by a man under seventy. Again, the Fourth Gospel is clearly the summary of a lifetime of thought and mystic communion. It is the sort of book that might indeed have been actually written *currente calamo* in a mood of inspiration—but it embodies the concentrated meditation of a lifetime. Great men sometimes die early, but, when this does not happen, their latter years are often marked by extraordinary vigour. Gladstone at the age of eighty introduced the second Home Rule Bill into the House of Commons in a four hours' speech not inferior to the oratorical triumphs of his middle age. Temple did not become Archbishop of Canterbury till he was seventy-five, and yet had the energy to leave a permanent mark upon the Church of England. Titian, to quote the classic instance, died at the astounding age of ninety-nine, producing masterpieces to the very end. There is, then, no difficulty on this score in supposing that John the Elder wrote the Gospel A.D. 90–95 at the age of seventy or more.

But is it possible that the theological standpoint of the Fourth Gospel could have been reached by A.D. 90 ? At first sight it seems a far cry from the theology of Thessalonians to the Prologue of the Fourth Gospel. But so far as the theological development is concerned, Paul himself has gone almost all the way in the epistles of the captivity. Hebrews is a stage farther on than Paul, or, at least, its Christology is more defined—and Hebrews is fully accepted in Rome, always far slower to move than Asia, before the time of Clement. The difficulty which the Logos doctrine is an attempt to meet is one which must have arisen at a very early date. The ordinary Gentile would find no intellectual difficulty in worshipping Christ as " Kyrios " or " Lord," that is, as a Divine Being other than the Supreme— " Gods many and Lords many " were being worshipped in the various cults of the period. But the Christian was committed to the Old Testament with its central emphasis on the doctrine, " The Lord thy God is One." And the Jew, the bitterest of all the opponents of the Church, was always there to " rub this in " ; he was for ever challenging the Christian to explain why and how to worship Christ did not mean the abandoning of monotheism. What a triumphant reply it was to say, " But did not your own great Philo, the most famous Jew of the age, the man the Jews of Alexandria chose as their spokesman to Caligula in A.D. 40, at a crisis affecting the whole Jewish race, himself distinguish between God and the Divine Word ? Was Philo a polytheist ? And if not, then neither are we, when we worship the Word made flesh." The question we have to ask is, how many years of further theological development must be allowed to a Church which already possessed Colossians, Ephesians and Philippians, to reach the point when it could make this reply ? And the answer is a conditional one—five hundred years in a community that could produce no single mind above the commonplace ; five years, if a man of genius should arise so soon. The category of development, in the slow, patient, biological sense of that term, does not apply in cases of this sort. The Logos doctrine is consistent with almost any date for the Gospel.

THE AUTHOR'S SIGNATURE

There can be no doubt that 3 John is a genuine letter of some one who was regarded by his contemporaries as a person of importance. It cannot possibly be a forgery, for it would be a forgery without motive. It maintains no special doctrine, it enforces no general moral duty, it tells no interesting story. It alludes obscurely to a rebuff received by the author from a certain Diotrephes (who we may infer must have been a local bishop, since he had the power not merely to exclude from the Church brethren travelling with recommendations from other Churches, but also to " cast out " resident members), and it commends a certain Demetrius who appears to be on the side of the writer. But no hint is given of the name of the Church or of the upshot of the affair. That such a document should have been preserved at all is strange ; indeed it is only explicable if it was cherished as a kind of relic of a person regarded by some section of the Church with special reverence and affection.

But the writer of this obviously genuine personal letter calls himself simply " the Elder "—that is its importance, for the three Epistles and the Gospel of John are so closely allied in diction, style, and general outlook that the burden of proof lies with the person who would deny their common authorship. The minute differences in thought or temper which some scholars think they have detected between the Gospel and the first Epistle are far less than those which divide the earlier, middle and captivity epistles of Paul, or the *Dialogues* written by Plato at different periods of his life. It is only a dead mind that shows no change. In regard, however, to the two epistles —2 John is obviously by the same hand as 3 John—which bear the Elder's name, it is clear that, if they are not by the same author as the Gospel, then the relation between the two authors is that of teacher and pupil.

But if they are by two authors, which of the two is the teacher and which the pupil ? and to which of the two are we to assign the First Epistle ?   The opening verses of the First Epistle presuppose the main ideas of the author of the Gospel ; they are the work of the same man or his pupil.   Again, the author of the Gospel is one of the world's creative minds, and if there is dependence, the shorter epistles are secondary.   The Gospel and First Epistle cannot be explained as a development of creative ideas found already in germ in the shorter letters. These two brief notes are *either* by the author of the longer works himself, recurring almost incidentally to ideas which are of the very texture of his mind, *or* they are a mere echo by a docile pupil of that mind.   But a pupil who is dominated, not only by the ideas but by the actual language of his master, to the extent that, on this hypothesis, the Elder who writes 2 and 3 John is dominated by the author of the Gospel and First Epistle, must be a man considerably the junior of his master, or else one lacking sufficient initiative to develop any individual thought and style of his own under the overmastering influence of the older and stronger mind.

But neither is it possible to date the author of the Fourth Gospel a generation *earlier* than John the Elder ; nor do the two shorter letters leave on one the impression of being written by a man dominated by some other master mind.   On the contrary, he is evidently a leader of outstanding prestige and position, for the one is addressed to a Church which he takes it upon him to congratulate on the purity of its doctrine and to warn against false teachers, the other implies the claim to an authority which Diotrephes (apparently the local bishop) has ventured to flout.

It is often said that the similarity in style, in thought, and in general outlook can be explained on the assumption that the authors belong to " the same school."   The word " school " is one of those vague seductive expressions which it is so easy to accept as a substitute for clear thinking.   In the sphere of art in all ages there have been schools; and in antiquity examples can be found in philosophy. But these two Epistles are not treatises in philosophy or theology; they are actual letters called forth by an actual crisis[1]—occasioned by an insult to certain friends of the writer which to his mind constituted, not only a challenge to his own authority, but an attempt to suppress the propagation of true doctrine. That is to say, they are the product of wounded feeling and therefore reveal character. It is a highly individual character, quite as individual as that of Paul, and it is the character of a man who could have written such a Gospel. This is not the kind of thing that is covered by the phrase " a school." Besides this, " a school " in art or philosophy only comes into existence when there is a considerable body of work by the founder which serves as a model and a standard for the pupils. But 2 and 3 John are not long enough to have been the model for the writer of the Gospel and 1 John, nor, as we have seen, can the writer of the shorter letters be the pupil of the other author. Must we then assume that a model—some work greater and nobler than the Gospel—once existed and has since disappeared ? It must have been a marvellous production ! Moreover, a " school " of Johannine literature did as a matter of fact arise, something of which survives in the Acts of John—and this is obviously what artists call " school work," an inferior imitation. We are forced to conclude that all four documents are by the same hand. And few people, I would add, with any feeling for literary style or for the finer *nuance* of character and feeling, would hesitate to affirm this, but for the implications which seem to be involved. For the admission that the second and third Epistles are by the same hand as the Gospel and the first Epistle does lead to very far-reaching consequences. It means that *we do really know*

[1] Dr. Stanton (*op. cit.* p. 107 f.) doubts their being by the same author as the Gospel, since there are several of the great Johannine doctrines to which they make no allusion. But in letters written to announce a visit on urgent business, and respectively 13 and 14 verses in length, one does not expect theology.

who wrote the Fourth Gospel, and therefore, approximately, the date at which it was written.[1]

Sabatier speaks of the Epistle to Philemon, which is so closely interwoven with Colossians (and Ephesians), and which is itself so obviously genuine, in these words : [2] " This short letter to Philemon is so intensely original, so entirely innocent of dogmatic preoccupation, and Paul's mind has left its impress so clearly and indelibly upon it, that it can only be set aside by an act of sheer violence. Linked from the first with the two epistles to which we have just referred, it is virtually Paul's own signature appended as their guarantee, to accompany them through the centuries." When the Elder penned the little notes we speak of as 2 and 3 John, did he not similarly affix to the Gospel and First Epistle the author's signature ?

---

[1] The identification of the author of 2 and 3 John with the Elder John is no modern idea.   Jerome (*De Vir. Illustr.* 18) states it as the official tradition ; and it is authoritatively affirmed in the Decretal of Pope Damasus A.D. 382, which, if genuine (cf. Turner and Howorth, *J.T.S.* i. p. 544 ff., and xiv. p. 321 ff.), is the first official pronouncement on the Canon of the N T. ever made in the Western Church.   *Johannis apostoli epistula una, alterius Johannis presbyteri epistulae duae.*   The apparent separation in the Muratonian Canon between the first epistle, mentioned along with the Gospel, from " the two," is perhaps earlier evidence of the same view—possibly a compromise between those who wanted to identify the Elder with the Apostle, and those who clung to the tradition that he was the author of all four documents.

[2] A. Sabatier, *The Apostle Paul,* p. 227.

XVI

SYNOPSIS

AN OLD MAN'S FAREWELL

The Consolidation of the Church

The Catholic Church conquered the Roman Empire because it achieved an intellectual adaptation to its environment, which saved it from becoming merged in the general welter of syncretistic religion, before the generation brought up in Jewish ethical monotheism had died out. John the Elder the most striking leader in this process. Speculative character of the remainder of this chapter.

The Conservative Opposition

Both the Logos Doctrine and the spiritualising of the expectation of the visible Return of Christ likely to arouse opposition. Evidence of this in the Papias fragments and in 3 John.

The Appendix to the Gospel

(1) The addition spoils the effective climax of ch. xx. It must therefore have been made to meet an acute need.

(2) Partly an attempt to reconcile Galilean and Jerusalem tradition of Resurrection appearances.

(3) It also corrects with great emphasis a current misapprehension that "this disciple should not die." Why was such correction urgent?

The Hope that failed

The revival of Apocalyptic fervour due (a) to persecution of Domitian; (b) to prophecies of John the Seer, author of Apocalypse. This led to popular belief that Christ would return before the death of the Elder John—the last survivor of the generation that had seen

Him in the flesh. The author desires to forestall the dangerous disillusionment which he foresees will inevitably result from the non-fulfilment of this hope.

The Younger Generation

The Logos doctrine is making possible the adhesion to the Church of the educated classes; but there is danger lest the progressive younger clergy may forget the primary command, " Feed my lambs."

XVI

AN OLD MAN'S FAREWELL

(A Reverie on John xxi.)

The Consolidation of the Church

THE Catholic Church could not have become an institution competent to conquer the Roman world unless, in the critical formative period that followed the fall of Jerusalem and the removal of the original Apostles, there had been " raised up " one or more men of genius capable of realising the new situation and responding to it rapidly and effectively—both in the sphere of thought and of organisation. In the sphere of thought the necessity arose for an intellectual basis for a theology which could hold its own in the educated Greek world. To Ionia— that is, to the Greek cities of the coast of what Rome called Asia —we trace the first beginnings of philosophy in Europe. The torch was handed on to Athens, and later on to Alexandria; but the flame was still alight in the old home, and the old Greek search for the immanent Reason behind the Universe had not lost its interest there. Alexandria, behindhand in welcoming Christianity—perhaps for want of such intellectual interpreta- tion—was not yet ready; Athens was too fondly wedded to its immortal past. But Paul had planted a Christianity in Asia sufficiently reasoned to make an appeal to the Greek mind. Hence at Ephesus it first became necessary, and was also possible, for Christians " to give a reason for the hope that was in them." [1]

---

[1] 1 Peter, where that phrase occurs, was written either to, or in, Asia Minor.

Here where the need was earliest felt it was first supplied, by the Logos doctrine of John.

In the sphere of practice the problem was solved by the development of the quasi-military organisation provided by the " monarchical episcopate " in the local churches, subordinated to the patriarchs of the great sees. This made possible a world-wide unity of fellowship, which no persecution could stamp out, and also an effective unity of doctrine and tradition which was proof against the attraction to the half - educated of Gnostic theosophies with their mixture of Persian dualism, Babylonian astrology, Hellenistic speculation, and primitive magic. But the Church, originally Jewish in mentality, and for the first generation mainly inspired by Apocalyptic hopes, had perforce, if it was to survive at all in the Roman Empire, to adapt its theology as well as its organisation to a wholly new and wholly alien environment.

But though without any adaptation Christianity must have remained an unimportant sect, with too ready an adaptation it would have become merged in the welter of syncretistic religions characteristic of the period. This last was the greater danger. The Early Christian Church was a Mission Church, but it had no " home base." The first generation of missionaries were Jews inheriting centuries of ethical monotheism. But in the great centres of Gentile Christianity the breach with the synagogue was very early a complete one ; and after the fall of Jerusalem it is not likely that many Jews became converted. Thus, unlike the Mission Churches of the present day, the early Church lacked the inspiration and the guidance of an old-established community, the continuous influence of which could keep the newly founded churches true to type and check the reinfiltration of pagan ideas from school and club and social custom. It had no collection of sacred books specifically Christian, no coherently thought-out theology, and very little in the way of organisation. Its salvation was that it acquired all these things *before that generation had died out* which had been bred up in the Jewish monotheism, Jewish ethical intensity, and the Jewish conscious-ness of being a separate people.

John the Elder was a Jew; probably the last Jew to be the dominating spirit in a great Gentile Church. His age, his personal gifts, the fact that he had seen the Lord, and the im-portance in Asia of the Church of Ephesus, would give him personally, especially towards the end of his life, an authority all but apostolic. His Gospel is the climax of the development of theology in the New Testament. It gave the Church an expression of its belief intellectually acceptable to the Greek mind, yet true to the Jewish thought of God as personal and as one.

To the theory that John the Elder is the author of the Gospel it is often objected that he is " a very shadowy figure." There are few characters in history who would not become " shadowy " if all their writings were assigned to someone else, and if all the information available about their character and career were supposed to refer to that other person. But the man who wrote the Gospel and First Epistle, who was esteemed as, and acted like, the author of the two minor epistles, and of whom stories such as that told by Clement of Alexandria about John and the robber,[1] even if not actually historical, seemed to a succeeding generation to be " in character," is a man of whose personality and position we get a *very* definite impression. Of course if the Apostle John did live in Ephesus, and if all these things are rightly referred to him, then the other John is a person of whom extremely little can be said. But if the Apostle never was in Ephesus, these things can only belong to the Elder John—and after Peter and Paul, John the Elder is the most striking figure in the early Church.

. . . .

This having been said, I will—for the rest of this chapter—permit myself to stray from the paths of stern historical method, and, in the absence of determinative evidence, allow the

---

[1] *Quis Dives*, xlii., also Eus. *H.E.* iii. 23.

historical imagination to wander freely in the pasture-land of
speculation.

The Fourth Gospel was quite a new departure, and we
must not assume that, even backed as it was by the immense
prestige of the revered Elder who was known to have seen the
Lord Himself, so startling a novelty would be welcomed at once
and by every one, even in Asia. That has never been the fate
of creative ventures in the history of religion.

The doctrine of the Logos, as the author of the Gospel saw,
made it possible to present Christianity to the educated Greek
world in a way that it could accept. It was the boldest " re-
statement " of Christianity in terms of contemporary thought
ever attempted in the history of the Church. True, it did not
in substance go far beyond the later epistles of Paul. But the
word Logos, though possibly familiar in lecture and discussion,
had never been used in anything like an authoritative church
document. Just as the insertion into the Nicene Creed of the
term ὁμοούσιον (of one essence) on the instance of Athanasius
was resisted by the more conservative bishops as unscriptural,
so, we may be sure, the unapostolic term Logos would have been
regarded with suspicion when first the attempt was made to use
it in an official document of the Church by Athanasius' greatest
predecessor.

But a feature in the Fourth Gospel which we may be sure
would have been resented in some circles, far more even than the
doctrine of the Logos, was the attempt to interpret the prophecies
of our Lord about His Second Coming in a spiritual sense. It
is true that John does not absolutely deny an Apocalyptic Judgement ; nevertheless, *for all practical purposes* he substitutes the
Coming of the Comforter for the visible Return of Christ. It
may be argued with some plausibility that in this matter John
was nearer than Matthew to the spirit, if not to the form, of our
Lord's teaching ; but the book of Revelation, produced about

the same time, shows that this was by no means the universal view in Asia. Dr. Charles holds that John the Seer knew the Gospel of Matthew,[1] and it is very likely that by this time copies of Matthew were being circulated in Asia. If so, this Gospel would certainly be appealed to by those who clung to the more literal Apocalyptic view in their attempt to stem the current of the "rationalism" of John. And for Matthew's Gospel the claim of apostolic authorship was made. The fragment of Papias, "Matthew composed the Logia in the Hebrew language, and each one interpreted them as he could," represents, I have argued, the substance of the Elder's reply; asserting that the Discourses in the Greek Matthew—he is thinking mainly of the Apocalyptic sayings—are not a first-hand report of what Christ said, they are only a translation.

The authority of John the Elder would commend the new Gospel to the more advanced circles in the community; in the city of Ephesus itself, where he had lived and taught so long, there would be nothing in it particularly novel. The Epistles to the Colossians and Ephesians contain phrases which, even if they do not imply Paul's own familiarity with some of the ideas which Philo (and no doubt others whose works do not survive) had made current coin in the Judaism of the Dispersion, would be widely interpreted in that sense. The conception of the Divine Logos, as hammered out by Philo to form a synthesis between Jewish and Neo-Platonic thought, was just the concept needed in a place like Ephesus, not only to interpret Christianity to the Greek in terms of Divine Immanence, but also to meet the standing taunt of the Jew that those who worshipped Christ were setting up a second God. Ephesus itself would be familiar with the idea, for John the Elder had of course preached his

---

[1] R. H. Charles, *op. cit.* p. lxxxiv. ff. The difficulty of being quite sure of literary dependence is unusually great where the common matter consists in apocalyptic sayings of a kind which were "in the air," even though it includes a similar combination of two separate O T passages, since this *may* have been derived from a collection of Messianic proof-texts. Nevertheless, in my opinion, the balance of evidence inclines in favour of Charles's view.

Gospel there for many years before he wrote it; but in some of the smaller centres it would probably sound both new and dangerous. In any case, to put it down in black and white as the Preface to a Gospel was a bold step forward.

Progressive movements usually begin in cities; the small towns and villages lag behind. The new Gospel would require commendation in the smaller cities of Asia. That, we may conjecture, was, partly at any rate, the purpose of the First Epistle of John. It is a letter intended to follow up the Gospel and commend its general standpoint and teaching, in the first place to Ephesus, but more especially to the smaller Churches. Its opening words, " That which we have seen with our eyes and our hands have handled," are intended to make it clear from the start that, for all his sympathy with the philosophic intellectuals, the author will have nothing to do with any kind of Gnostic " docetism " which makes the humanity of Christ unreal. Later on, again, the protest that the Christ came both " by water and by blood " (1 John v. 6) brings home the point that he is on the side of the tradition of the Church against innovators like Cerinthus.

A religious community is always conservative in regard to its sacred literature. At the time when the Fourth Gospel was published, Mark had already been *the* Gospel, read aloud at the weekly services, for perhaps five-and-twenty years. It was not as yet regarded as inspired scripture, but already it was looked upon with perhaps the kind of affection and prestige which attaches to the Book of Common Prayer in the Church of England. Here, then, is the most natural explanation of the other Papias fragment about Mark ; it shows us the Elder John put on his defence in regard to the chronology of his own Gospel—though, of course, what reached Papias must be taken as a summary of the general purport of his defence rather than the actual words he used. The Elder replies to his critics with an affirmation of respect for Mark's accuracy in points of fact ; but he puts forth a reason—Mark's dependence on casual utterances of Peter—to

account for its defect in the matter of the order and arrangement
of events.   The introduction of a new Gospel would be regarded
at Ephesus much as that of a new Prayer Book in the Church of
England.   Some would be inclined to welcome, others to resent
it.   But a Gospel so unlike Mark as that of John must have been
regarded even by the moderates without enthusiasm, and by the
conservatives as a highly dangerous concession to that tendency
to philosophising mysticism which, popularised by Gnostics, was
at the moment the greatest peril of the Church.   To old-fashioned
Church members the Logos doctrine would be " the thin end of
the wedge " ; Gnosticism must follow.

It would look as if in 3 John we catch a glimpse of an incident
in this struggle with the conservative party.   I have shown above
that this correspondence implies that Diotrephes, the local Bishop,
had taken upon himself to exercise the right of exclusion—early
conceded to the episcopate as a safeguard against wandering
Gnostic prophets—against the authorised delegates of John the
Elder.   This would be quite explicable if Diotrephes was one of
those who regarded the Johannine theology as dangerously akin
to that of the Gnostics.   It is the first, but not the last, instance
on record when one who has grasped the vital necessity of interpreting the Christian message in terms of the thought of the age
has been accused by certain of the country clergy of " selling the
pass " to the Church's enemies.

THE APPENDIX TO THE GOSPEL

Numberless hypotheses have been put forward concerning
the purpose and authorship of the last chapter of John.   All
those which do not begin by recognising that the chapter is a
work of genius may be dismissed.   Critics who have bemused
their faculties by the study of one another's theories so far as to
think that any purely mechanical editing or any pettifogging
controversial motive has here found expression need not be
listened to.   The style of the added conclusion to Mark is

pedestrian ; the Appendix to John is great literature. Hence no hypothesis need be taken seriously which is not, from a religious and literary point of view, a worthy one. But just for that very reason any hypothesis that we entertain must be recognised as tentative. For of the laws which govern genius we know little. There are, however, three points which seem reasonably clear.

(1) The Gospel was originally intended to end with the concluding verses of chapter xx.—and a magnificent ending it is. " Thomas answered and said unto Him, My Lord and my God. Jesus saith unto him, Because thou hast seen Me, thou hast believed : blessed are they that have not seen and yet have believed." . . . " Many other signs therefore did Jesus in the presence of the disciples which are not written in this book : but these are written that ye may believe that Jesus is the Christ the Son of God; and that believing ye may have life in His name."

But, granted that chapter xxi. is of the nature of an afterthought, was it added by the author himself or by some later hand? The last two verses, we have already seen, by the change from the third person to the first, advertise themselves as by a different author from the Gospel. But the style, the gift of imaginative description, and the spiritual elevation of the rest of the Appendix, suggest the work of the same master mind that conceived and wrote the Gospel. There are, however, certain minutiae of diction [1] which point rather to some other hand, unless indeed it was written by the author of the Gospel after some considerable interval of time. But, if we accept the former alternative, the points of contact in general outlook and in large ideas are so marked that this other hand must have been that of a pupil of the author saturated in his master's spirit—putting in writing, perhaps after that master's death, what he knew to be the substance of his last message to the Church he had loved and served so long. But would such a pupil, any more than the author himself, have been likely to make an addition which so mars the effect of the impressive conclusion of the original

[1] These are conveniently given by Moffatt, *Introduction to the N.T.* p. 572.

work ?   Not unless something had happened in the meanwhile which made what he had to say in the Appendix of vital importance for the Church of the time.   The Appendix then, we may surmise, was added to meet a new need.

(2) Apart from the Appendix, John only records Resurrection Appearances in Jerusalem.   But we have seen some reason to believe that the recension of Mark current in Ephesus represented the first Appearance to any of the Twelve as that to Peter and others by the Sea of Galilee.   Now John frequently corrects, and still more frequently ignores, statements in Mark.   But we may well imagine that on a question like the evidence for the Resurrection a serious discrepancy between two Gospels, both by this time " read " in the Church, might cause disquietude. The Appendix, by its emphatic assertion " This is the *third* time Jesus appeared to His disciples," seems to be insisting that the Fourth Gospel is right in placing the Jerusalem Appearances *first*, while at the same time recognising the substantial historical correctness of Mark in recording an Appearance by the Sea of Galilee.   This, be it observed, is exactly in the spirit of the Elder's comment on Mark preserved by Papias—Mark is correct as to facts, but not as to their order.   But we ought also to explain the immense emphasis thrown, by the way in which the story is told, on the threefold commission to Peter, " Feed my sheep."   It would look as if there were people at Ephesus who, in the author's opinion, would do well to draw a practical moral from the incident.   I shall return to this point later.

(3) The last two verses (Jn. xxi. 24-25), we have seen, are a still later addition ; so the Appendix would originally have ended as follows : " Peter therefore seeing Him, saith to Jesus, Lord, and what shall this man do ?   Jesus said unto him, If I will that he tarry till I come, what is that to thee ? follow thou me.   This saying therefore went forth among the brethren that that disciple should not die : yet Jesus said not unto him that he should not die ; but, If I will that he tarry till I come, what is that to thee ? "

The Gospel is thus made to end on a mere correction of a popular misapprehension of one of our Lord's sayings ; this is the author's last word !   The Greeks, like the French and Italians at the present day, could not tolerate anything rhetorically ineffective.   And we are considering the work of one who was not only a writer of great literary and dramatic sense, but must also have been an experienced preacher.   We can only conclude that the removal of this particular misconception was the *main* reason for adding the Appendix.

We ask, then, what special circumstances, what vital need, of the Church could adequately be met by an Appendix the climax of which deals with a difficulty connected with a supposed prophecy of Christ with regard to the death of the beloved disciple and His own Return.

The Hope that failed

I reiterate that the evidence at our disposal only justifies inferences of a very tentative character.   But as a " provisional hypothesis " the following would, I think, adequately account for the facts to be explained.   The Gospel, I suggest, was originally published without the Appendix shortly before the persecution of Domitian,[1] say about the year A.D. 90.   Next to the Logos doctrine, its most noticeable contribution to contemporary Christian theology was the endeavour to interpret the Apocalyptic expectation of a visible return of Christ in a spiritual sense. This was by no means the ordinary view, but as time went on, and the Lord did not visibly return, Christians became more and

---

[1] The fact of a persecution under Domitian is denied by Prof. E. T. Merrill, *Essays on Early Church History*, ch. vi. (Macmillan, 1924).   He admits, however, that Domitian was " more urgent about enforcing conformity than were his predecessors on the throne and most of his successors," especially in the matter of emperor worship ; since, then, Asia was specially devoted to this cult, the Apocalypse is sufficient evidence of a revival of persecution in that Province.   He admits also that Domitilla, the wife of Flavius Clemens, died a Christian ; if so, it is pure special pleading to say that the " atheism " (*i.e.* non-conformity to the State religion) of which her husband was accused is more likely to have been Jewish than Christian.

more concerned at the apparent non-fulfilment of their hope. John believes that the coming of the Spirit, the Comforter, was, if not the whole, at any rate the only immediate, fulfilment to be expected to the prophecies of Christ in regard to His second coming. To those perplexed by the delay of the Parousia John says, "You are making a mistake, the promise has *already* been fulfilled in the coming of the Paraclete ; both Eternal Life and Judgement have already begun, though neither is completely consummated in this life."

This doctrine would have found a welcome among a very large section of Christians about the year A.D. 90. It provided the answer to the outstanding practical religious difficulty of that age. And it did so on conservative lines, for it was merely a further development, a more definite formulation, and a new application, of the doctrine of the Spirit already to be found in Paul's Epistles.

But the outbreak of persecution under Domitian changed the situation. The whole history of Jewish literature during the three preceding centuries shows that, whenever there was a period of acute persecution, the fact that older writers had foretold a great tribulation as a necessary prelude to a catastrophic intervention of God to deliver His people from their oppressors, led to a revival of Apocalyptic expectation, accompanied by a republication of older Apocalypses and the composition of new ones. The world-wide tribulation of the recent Great War has produced in many circles an immense revival of interest in the doctrine of the Second Advent, Apocalyptically conceived. This gives an analogy which illuminates the psychological conditions of such a revival of Apocalyptic interest in earlier times. That the persecution of Domitian had this effect is not a matter of mere hypothesis. Irenaeus tells us that the Revelation of John, which I need hardly repeat cannot possibly be by the same author as the Gospel, was "seen" toward the end of the reign of Domitian ; and modern critics are practically unanimous, on grounds of internal evidence, in accepting this date. There is, moreover, the fact that the majority of the sayings of the Elders reported by Papias are strongly Apocalyptic in character. Papias himself is evidence how deeply rooted this became in the Christianity of Asia.

The symbolism, and indeed the whole world of thought in which the mind of the author of Revelation moves, is extraordinarily remote to the educated man of the present day. But, in spite of that, no one can read it without feeling the tremendous force and power of conviction that lies behind it. In that age and in those circles it came with a claim to be a direct revelation —a claim taken quite literally when made by a " prophet " recognised as such in the Church—and it came at a moment when the comparative tranquillity of the last twenty years had been brought to an end by Domitian's attempt to promote the worship of the Emperor in the Provinces, and to enforce it by strong methods. We can hardly over-estimate the tremendous impression which such a book, at such a crisis, would produce upon the Churches to which it was addressed. Throughout the province of Asia there would follow a wild revival of Apocalyptic hopes, and of a fanatical conviction that the visible return of Christ was to be expected in the immediate future—doubtless, it would be argued, within the 1290 days spoken of by Daniel (Dan. xii. 11 ; Rev. xi. 2, xiii. 5).

But Domitian was assassinated in A.D. 96, and the persecution died down ; and the 1290 days within which the return of the Lord was expected passed, and the Lord did not return. As usual under such circumstances, perplexed believers sought a new interpretation of the old prophecies, and especially of the words of Christ which stood in the old Ephesian Gospel of Mark, as well as in the new arrival, Matthew. " There be some here of them that stand by, which shall in no wise taste of death, till they see the Kingdom of God come with power " (Mk. ix. 1). The original Apostles had passed away ; but perhaps the Lord had meant that His return would be within the lifetime, not of the Twelve, but merely of some who had been alive at the time and had seen Him in the flesh. There was one man at Ephesus who had seen Christ—the Elder John. Inevitably the idea would get about that the prophecy of the Lord would be fulfilled if this one disciple should tarry till He came, and that this was the true meaning of the original words in Mark.

There are those alive who can remember the feeling of trepidation with which members of the Irvingite Church watched the declining years of the last survivor of those twelve " Apostles " within the lifetime of whom Edward Irving, the founder of the community, had prophesied the visible return of Christ. And when the last of these did die, and the Lord did not return, that community received a grievous shock. A similar situation seemed likely to develop in the Church of Ephesus about the year A.D. 100. The Elder John knew that, if he died before the Lord returned, the faith of many would receive a staggering blow. Long ago he had made up his own mind that Christ's prophecy of an immediate coming bore another interpretation, and that no visible Return was to be looked for. But experience had shown him that it was not possible directly to confute the fanatic hope of an immediate Return, recently revivified by the passionate prophecy of John the Seer. Besides, the Elder was by now an old man with failing powers. All that he could do was to add something to his Gospel which would provide, as it were, a reserve trench against the hour of disillusionment which he saw to be inevitable—to append to it a word of the Master, which would be there when he was gone, as an evidence that it was, not the Lord, but their own misunderstanding that had misled them ; " yet Jesus said not unto him, that he should not die " ; but, " if I will that he tarry . . ."

" There be some which shall not taste of death." Is it fanciful to suggest that it was the death, many years ago, of John the Apostle, the last survivor of the Twelve, that had awakened the Elder himself from Apocalyptic dreams? The last of the Twelve had died, and the Master's words were unfulfilled ; the shock of disillusionment would be intense. To most of that generation the Return of the Lord in glory to inaugurate the new world order *was* " the Gospel "—it constituted the great good news for a despairing world. For a time, perhaps, his belief in Christianity was shattered. Then he had set out on a quest for an alternative interpretation of the Master's words—the quest which led him at last to the doctrine of the Paraclete. Perhaps—for we have seen that he was a " prophet "—while wrestling with the problem he had slipped into a mystic trance, and it was revealed to him [1] that what the Lord had really said to that Apostle was not, " He shall tarry till I come," but, " If I will that he tarry . . . what is that to thee ? "

The doctrine of the spiritual Return—reached in a great religious crisis in his own earlier life—he had in its positive aspect set down in his Gospel. That was all that seemed needed at the time when that was written. But circumstances had changed. Now its negative aspect is of equal importance ; it is vital that the Church should have it authoritatively on record that there was *no foundation* in the words of Christ for the belief that He would return visibly within the lifetime of those who heard Him. The belief, which a generation ago had centred round John the Apostle, the last survivor of the Three, perhaps also of the Twelve, was now attaching itself to John the Elder as the last survivor of the generation who had seen the Lord. But the Elder himself —or an understanding pupil, if the Appendix was written by such an one—knew that it was certain a second time to bring many to disillusionment and perhaps despair. The Appendix to the Gospel is an attempt to forestall this. It is a last message to the Ephesian Church, which, written and made public before the time, might, for some at any rate of his " little children," break the force of the inevitable shock.

---

[1] For an illustration of how a contemporary mystic, in a similar way, finds the solution of difficulties presented by Scripture, especially in regard to Apocalyptic, see *The Sadhu*, Streeter and Appasamy, ch. **v.**

The Younger Generation

The Apocalyptic reaction, of which the book of Revelation and the sayings of Elders which Papias reports are evidence, was, perhaps, not the only element in the religious situation which the Appendix has in view. We may surmise that, in spite of the storm which the publication of the Gospel had aroused in conservative circles, its doctrines had made rapid progress elsewhere. If, in the lack of definite evidence, we may allow ourselves to frame an imaginative reconstruction of the situation, we may conjecture that, since this " modernism " of John had become the fashion, it was noticed that more men of the professional classes were beginning to join the Church. Presbyters who had felt that the Elder was inclined to go a little too far, were reassured by finding that the attitude of educated pagan opinion was beginning to change. Christianity was becoming intellectually respectable; the Church was making headway among the student class, a number of young men from the school of Tyrannus, or rather his successor, had been baptized—a thing hitherto unheard of. All this was to the good; but there was another side. John's doctrine of the Divine Logos and his spiritualising of the Apocalyptic hope had made Christianity a possible religion for an educated Greek; but it had also opened the door to the intellectualism, the passion for eternal argument, to which the Greek mind was all too prone — witness that series of controversies which in the following centuries were the Church's bane. Already some of the younger presbyters, clever argumentative Greeks, were spending half their days in hair-splitting discussion.

That, so the old man may have reflected, was one reason why the obscurantist party was gaining ground—especially with the poorer classes. Hell fire, and the Immediate Coming with exact date given—these the working man could understand. Uncompromising traditionalism inspired by sincere conviction was, no doubt, with its " definite teaching," winning souls.   But what would become of those souls won by that teaching about the Second Coming—definite enough, but definitely untrue—when, as in the course of a very few years or even months was bound to happen, they discovered its untruth ?   What would happen to these then ?

It might avail something to have put on record a saying that would show them that it was not Christ but their teachers who had misled them.   But how many of the poorer sort would ever hear the new ending of the Gospel read, or, if they did, would grasp the point ?   And, their old teachers discredited, to whom would they go for help ?   These young presbyters, who had grasped the new theology, were the only hope—but could they be depended on ?   Would they be ready, as, to do them justice, the reactionaries had been, to meet the poor and simple on their own level, to go out to seek and save, to comfort and befriend ?   Or were "the little children," for whom he had lived and Christ had died, to fall away—between the earnest teachers of beliefs the complete discrediting of which was merely a matter of time, and the bright young progressives interested only in things intellectual ?

The future of the Church depended on the men who would face, frankly and boldly, the intellectual problems of the day—but did the men who saw this see also that, though absolutely vital, this was neither the one nor the first thing necessary ?   And yet everything depended on them.   Perhaps they might listen to him, or rather to a word of the Lord, if he emphatically recalled it to their notice as his own last message to them.   To some of them he was already become something of the old fogey now, but to most he was still the great leader, the founder of a truly scientific theology.   The word he wanted them to ponder may have stood at the end of the Ephesian copies of Mark, but that was the old-fashioned Gospel now.   When originally he wrote his own Gospel it had not seemed worth while to reproduce this —it was so familiar.   But he will do so now.   He will add it to his own Gospel to make it clear that he too thought it worth while to emphasise, as the last will and testament of Christ, the appeal three times repeated : " Simon, son of Jonas, lovest thou me ? " " Yea, Lord, thou knowest that I love thee." " Feed my lambs."

PART IV

SYNOPTIC ORIGINS

XVII

DATE AND LOCAL ORIGIN OF MARK AND MATTHEW

SYNOPSIS

PART I.—MARK

EXTERNAL EVIDENCE

The language of Irenaeus *may* imply that both Mark and Luke were written in Rome—and he was so understood by some of the ancients. Clement's statement that Mark wrote in Rome *may* be derived from Irenaeus. But 2 Timothy and 1 Peter both connect Mark with Rome at about the date of the writing of the Gospel. The evidence of 1 Peter is of value, even if it be held (*a*) that the epistle is not by the Apostle; (*b*) that Peter never came to Rome. The inclusion of this Gospel in the Canon is easier to explain if it was specially connected with Rome.

THE LITTLE APOCALYPSE

The dating of Apocalyptic literature. Mark xiii. is a Little Apocalypse, partially made up of authentic sayings of Christ. The Abomination of Desolation (Mk. xiii. 14), a prophecy that the Anti-Christ (cf. 2 Thess. ii. 3 ff.) will appear in the Temple at Jerusalem. Probability that this " Apocalyptic fly-leaf " was composed some years before A.D. 70, but was slightly modified by Mark when inserting it into the Gospel in the light of the later experiences of Paul, and perhaps also of the Neronian persecution. This fits in with Irenaeus's statement that Mark was written " after the death of Peter and Paul."

THE GOSPEL AND THE APOSTLE

Rome as a distributing centre for the earliest Christian literature. The biographical Gospel an invention of Mark, suggested by Gentile rather than Jewish practice. The expectation of the end of the world unfavourable to historical writing.

An interest in recording the past first awakened after the Neronic persecution and the death of the Apostles.

A new suggestion as to the origin of the title " Gospel."

The Gospel of Mark, with Romans, 1 Corinthians, and, perhaps, Ephesians, became the nucleus of the New Testament in its two main divisions. Historical importance of this body of common literature for preserving the unity of the Church.

PART II.—MATTHEW

THE ANTIOCHENE ORIGIN OF MATTHEW

The tradition that Matthew was written in Palestine a deduction from Papias' statement about the Hebrew λόγια, nevertheless it is evidence that the Gospel came from the East.

The anonymity of the Gospel shows it was written for a definite local Church — the name Matthew a later accretion due to its embodying a document by that Apostle. This Church must have been one of great influence, or the Gospel would not have secured universal acceptance so soon.

Reasons for excluding Rome, Alexandria, Ephesus, Caesarea— and indeed any Church in Palestine. Antioch the only important Church left, and to this there are no objections. Positive considerations favouring Antiochene origin.

EVIDENCE OF IGNATIUS

Antiochene origin confirmed by an examination of certain passages in Ignatius, Bishop of Antioch, which suggest that he not only knew Matthew, but quotes it as " the Gospel."

QUOTATIONS IN THE DIDACHE

The Didache a Syrian document, probably not later than A.D. 100. Its author knew Matthew, and referred to it as " the Gospel."

THE PETRINE COMPROMISE

The hypothesis of Antiochene origin is borne out by internal evidence afforded by the analysis of sources in Chap. IX.

Many Christian refugees from Jerusalem would come to Antioch about A.D. 66, bringing with them the Jerusalem tradition we have styled M, about the same time that the first copy of Mark reached Antioch. These documents represented the moderate liberal (Petrine) and the Judaistic (James) party as against the more liberal (Pauline) tendency. Evidence that the Gospel of Matthew represents a careful compromise, based on the idea of Peter as the supreme interpreter of the New Law (" bind and loose ").

Such a compromise might well have taken twenty years to reach.

ANTIOCH AND THE ANTI-CHRIST

Reasons for placing Matthew after A.D. 70.

The effect on Jews and Christians of the shock of the Destruction of Jerusalem and the Temple.

Three different ways in which John, Luke, and Matthew solve the problem of the non-fulfilment of prophecies about the Parousia and the Anti-Christ.

The Didache correctly interprets the " Abomination " in Matthew as the " World-deceiver," *i.e.* Anti-Christ. The omission by Syr. S. of " standing in the holy place " (Mt. xxiv. 15) probably correct : in that case Matthew disconnects the Anti-Christ prophecy from the Temple, making it possible to connect it (as is done in the Apocalypse, etc.) with the " Nero-redivivus myth."

Enhancement of Apocalyptic interest a conspicuous feature of Matthew. Evidence of this briefly summarised. This partly accounted for by fact that Antioch was the gate of the East and, therefore, peculiarly exposed to the psychological influence of the popular belief that Nero, alive or to be revived, was about to lead the hosts of Parthia across the Euphrates against Rome.

DATE OF WRITING

The use of Matthew in the Didache and the probable knowledge of it by the authors of the Fourth Gospel and of the Apocalypse make a date later than A.D. 85 improbable. Both the relation of Matthew and Mark, and the reconciliation of parties previously discussed, suggest a date twenty years later than Mark. Thus from two sides the year A.D. 85 is fixed as the approximate date of writing.

ACCEPTANCE BY ROME

A.D. 119 the possible date of official recognition.

The four stages in the evolution of the Gospel Canon at Rome paralleled by four stages in the Canon of Pauline Epistles.

ADDITIONAL NOTE

The Date of 1 Clement

CHAPTER XVII

DATE AND LOCAL ORIGIN OF MARK AND MATTHEW

PART I.—MARK

EXTERNAL EVIDENCE

IRENAEUS had read Papias ; but, as his strongest weapon against Gnosticism is his appeal to the open tradition of the Roman Church, and as he had himself resided in Rome, we may reasonably ascribe to that tradition the additional fact (especially as the addition has no apologetic value) which he adds to Papias' account of Mark—namely, that that Gospel was written *after the death of Peter and Paul.* Irenaeus does not actually name the place of writing, but he is arguing in the immediate context (quoted page 8) that Mark and Luke wrote with the idea of carrying on the work of Peter and Paul (" preaching and founding the church in Rome ") presumably in the same part of the world—indeed, the most natural interpretation of his language would be that both Mark and Luke were written in Rome. This would seem to have been the interpretation current at one time in Alexandria ; for in Codex Y, **473,** and other cursives there are " subscriptions "—obviously in the main dependent on Irenaeus —which profess to be derived from Cosmas Indicopleustes, a retired Alexandrian sea captain, who probably gives the view accepted there by the Church authorities in his time, *c.* 522.[1]

---

[1] The " subscriptions " of **473** (Scriv. **512**) are in Scrivener's *Introd. to the Criticism of the N.T.*, 4th ed. i. p. 66, cf. Tischendorf, iii. p. 456; those in Y in W. C. Braithwaite's article, *Expository Times,* Dec. 1901. They assert, among other things, that Mark was dictated by Peter in Rome, and Luke by Paul in Rome.

As regards Mark, we have the statement of Clement of Alexandria, c. 200, who says that Mark wrote in Rome in the absence of, but during the lifetime of, Peter.   But as Clement had undoubtedly read Irenaeus, he is not an entirely independent witness.   But there are two pieces of evidence of a much earlier date.   (1) In an admittedly genuine portion of 2 Timothy (iv. 11), written during Paul's last imprisonment, Mark is summoned by the Apostle to Rome.   (2) The first Epistle of Peter presents us with Peter and Mark as together in Rome.[1]   The authenticity of the Epistle is disputed ; but if the Epistle is not by Peter, then these personal details have been added by its author expressly in order to give an air of verisimilitude to the claim of Apostolic authorship ; but they would not have furthered that object unless the presence of Peter and Mark in Rome together had been already an accepted belief at the time when the Epistle was written.   If the Epistle was not written by the Apostle himself, it may be as late as, but can hardly be later than, A.D. 110, for it is quoted by Polycarp, A.D. 115, more clearly and more often than any other book of the New Testament, so that we may reasonably infer that it was regarded by him as Apostolic.   The belief, then, that Peter and Mark had been together in Rome was current before A.D. 110.

Some critics have rejected the tradition that the Gospel was written in Rome on the ground that it is merely an inference drawn by some early Christian from the connection of Mark with Peter, and the other tradition (which they also reject) that Peter was martyred in Rome.   But, if we suppose that Peter did not

[1] " She that is in Babylon elect together with you " (1 Peter v. 13) can only mean the Church in Rome.   Babylon as a symbolic name of Rome is found in contemporary Jewish writings (cf. *Sibylline Oracles*, v. 143 ; 2 Baruch xi. 1) and occurs six times in the Apocalypse.   If any tradition had existed that Peter visited the Mesopotamian Babylon, the Syriac-speaking Church would have claimed him as a founder.   As a matter of fact they claim Thomas ; while the third-century canon of the New Testament, in the Doctrine of Addai, implicitly denies the personal presence of Peter and implies the Roman tradition : " The Gospel (*i.e.* the Diatessaron) and the Epistles of Paul which Simon Kepha sent you from Rome."   Cf. R. A. Lipsius, *Die apokryphen Apostelgeschichten* (Braunschweig, 1887), ii. 2, p. 193.

die in Rome, how are we to account for the tradition that he did so? Professor Merrill[1]—on the assumption that (a) Babylon in 1 Pet. v. 13 means the Mesopotamian city, (b) the letter is a genuine work of the Apostle—argues that the belief that Peter visited Rome was an inference first made by Hegesippus c. A.D. 160, from the mention of Babylon in 1 Peter. If, however, Babylon in that Epistle *does* mean Rome (cf. p. 489 *n.*), then it follows that, either Peter did visit Rome, or the Epistle is not authentic. But if the Epistle is not authentic, then the belief that Peter came to Rome was well established before the Epistle was written, and we must again ask the question, How (supposing it to be untrue) did such a belief arise?

The only answer I can suggest is to say that it arose as an inference—it is not certain that it is a mistaken one—from the epistle of Clement (v.-vi.), which mentions the deaths of Peter and Paul in close connection with the Neronian persecution, and which had a wide and immediate circulation in the East. But if it is a mistaken inference, the prior belief that a Gospel, representing Peter's reminiscences, had emanated from Rome would obviously be a material factor, both in Rome and elsewhere, in bringing about the acceptance of that interpretation of Clement which affirmed that Peter himself had been in Rome—a view which was held by Dionysius of Corinth by A.D. 170, and possibly even by Ignatius.[2] Thus the hypothesis that Mark was written in Rome is a legitimate inference from the tradition that Peter and Mark were together in Rome, if that is historical; or, if that tradition is not historical, then it helps to explain its origin. At any rate, the evidence of 2 Timothy, that Mark was sent for to Rome, just before the date which internal evidence suggests as probably that of the composition of the Gospel affords sufficient justification—there being not a shadow of

---

[1] *Op. cit.* p. 311 f.

[2] Cf. the letter of Dionysius quoted Eus. *H.E.* ii. 25. Ignatius, *Rom.* iv. 3, "I do not enjoin you like Peter and Paul (ὡς Πέτρος καὶ Παῦλος)," supposing this implies the bodily presence of Peter in Rome. Dionysius certainly, Ignatius probably, had read 1 Clement.

evidence to the contrary—for the acceptance as authentic of the undoubtedly very early belief in the Roman origin of the Gospel. Lastly, the inclusion in the Canon of a Gospel containing hardly anything not found in the more popular Gospels of Matthew and Luke (cf. p. 10 f.) is easier to explain if it had some special connection with the important See of Rome.

THE LITTLE APOCALYPSE

The statement of Irenaeus that the Gospel of Mark was written " after the death of Peter and Paul " fits admirably with what we should infer from a study of the Apocalyptic chapter, Mark xiii.

Apocalyptic is a type of literature which has a long history in Jewish religion. It has certain conventions of its own. One of these is the practice of ascribing the authorship of a writing and the visions and prophecies it contains, not to the real author, but to some great prophet or hero of olden time ; another, almost as persistent, is the incorporation and reaffirmation of previous prophecies, with such modifications as will bring out what the later author believes to have been their original meaning. And he always supposes these to have been written with reference to the events of *his own time*, not that of the original writer, and to foretell the Great Deliverance which he anticipates as near at hand. This fact often makes it possible to determine the date of an Apocalypse by its references (usually symbolic) to well-known historical events.

The first two verses of Mark xiii. probably belong to the same cycle of tradition as the rest of the Gospel. But the remainder of the chapter reads as if it were a " little Apocalypse," attributed (in accordance with the above-mentioned convention of Apocalyptic writers) to some great one of the past—in this case to Jesus himself—and incorporating as usual a certain amount of older material which in this case consisted largely of actual sayings of Christ. Mark xiii. is thus really a mixture of early Christian

Apocalyptic expectations and genuine utterances of our Lord ;
but it was, of course, incorporated by Mark in his Gospel in the
belief that it was wholly authentic.   Until quite recently commentators and critics (myself among them) [1] interpreted the
passage about the Abomination of Desolation (Mk. xiii. 14) as a
reference to the destruction of Jerusalem by the Romans in
A.D. 70, and therefore supposed the Gospel must be subsequent to
that date.   That idea has been exploded by the researches of
Bousset and others into the origin and prevalence of the " Anti-
Christ " legend.   It is now recognised that the Greek text (xiii.
14) which gives a masculine participle ἑστηκότα agreeing with
the neuter noun βδέλυγμα is not, as would appear at first sight,
an atrocious grammatical blunder, but is intentional.   It
is comparable to the use in the Fourth Gospel of the masculine
ἐκεῖνος (Jn. xvi. 13)—or the relative ὅν, אᶜLX Chrys., (Jn. xiv.
26)—when speaking of the Holy Spirit in order to emphasise the
fact that the writer regards the neuter substantive as the name
of a *person*, not a thing.   It is definitely intended to make it
clear that the author interprets the neuter word βδέλυγμα,
" abomination," in the prophecy of Daniel (Dan. xii. 11) as
a title of a personal Anti-Christ.   Modern critics, doubtless
correctly, suppose that the passage in Daniel has reference to
the desecration of the Temple at Jerusalem by Antiochus Epiphanes, which provoked the Maccabean revolt in 167 B.C.   But
neither Mark nor the author of this chapter was versed in the
methods of the Higher Criticism, and the meaning they were
likely to attach to Daniel must be ascertained by studying the
ideas of their age, not ours.   To them Daniel was a prophet and
was supposed to have written centuries before Antiochus ; and
the Abomination of Desolation was a mysterious horror which an
inspired prophet had foretold as destined to appear 1290 days
before the coming of the Messianic Kingdom.   The Apocalyptist
who wrote chapter xiii. was convinced that he had found the
true interpretation of Daniel.   The mysterious horror was no

[1] *Oxford Studies*, p. 182.

other than the Anti-Christ.   And, as in 2 Thess. ii. 3-10, the Anti-
Christ is expected to set himself up as supreme in the Temple of
Jerusalem until the real Christ appears from heaven to destroy
him and all his works.

But if, when Mark wrote, the Anti-Christ was expected to
appear in the Temple at Jerusalem, the presumption is that the
Temple was still standing.   Since the same expectation is to be
found in 2 Thessalonians, written about A.D. 52, we have conclusive evidence that the belief was current among Christians at
least a dozen years before Nero's persecution.   It would seem,
then, that the Apocalypse of Mk. xiii., so far from proving, as
was once thought, that the Gospel was written *after* the destruction of Jerusalem in A.D. 70, is more naturally explicable if it
was written *before* that event.   Indeed, the Little Apocalypse
may well have been composed some years before Mark wrote ;
and I would venture the suggestion that it, or something very
like it, was known to Paul, and was accepted by him too as an
authentic utterance of Jesus.   That at any rate would explain
the teaching about the Man of Sin in 2 Thessalonians.   This expectation of an Anti-Christ is not at all the kind of thing which
a mind like Paul's would have spontaneously introduced into
Christian teaching ; for it was precisely the original and creative
element in Paul's thought which, as time went on, drove him to
make less and less of Apocalyptic.

But even if the Little Apocalypse was already a document of
some age and authority, it would have been contrary to the
editorial methods of the time had Mark incorporated it in his
Gospel without adding some minor touches to emphasise its
appropriateness to the contemporary situation.   The convenient
modern devices of explanatory footnotes, inverted commas,
different forms of type, etc., had not been invented ; and the
ancient historian could not without clumsy circumlocution distinguish between the actual text of an authority and his own
interpretation.   An age which enjoys these facilities properly
demands that they shall be scrupulously used, but it ought not

to condemn the literary conscience of an age in which they were
unknown. But while we have no right to condemn ancient
writers for conforming to the usage of their time, we must always,
in framing historical conclusions, be on the look-out to make
adequate allowance for the difference between their methods and
our own.

Now if we compare Lk. xxi. 20-24 with Mk. xiii. 14-20, we
see how Luke has not scrupled to modify the phraseology of
the Abomination of Desolation passage so as to make quite
clear (what he, of course, with his presuppositions believed to
be the true explanation) that the words were really intended to
be a prophecy of the fall of Jerusalem—an event which must,
then, have taken place in the interval between the publication of
Mark's Gospel and the time at which he was himself writing.

It is probable that Mark, in his turn, had introduced similar
modifications in reproducing the text which stood in the original
Apocalypse, especially in the section xiii. 9-13. Much of this
chapter (*e.g.* 7-8, 24-27) is part of the commonplace of
Apocalyptic tradition. But the phrase " ye shall stand before
governors and kings for my name's sake " is so suggestive of the
experience of Paul; the idea of " witness," resulting from this, so
resembles what Paul himself (2 Tim. iv. 17) regards as having
been the divine intention in overruling the circumstances of his
preliminary trial, and verses 12 and 13 might so well be an allusion
to the Neronian persecution, that one suspects that Mark has
retouched the older source to some extent.[1] If so, the traditional
date, *after* the death of Peter and Paul, is subtly reflected in
the text in the phrases just quoted.

[1] The rebellion of children against their parents appears Micah vii. 6. In
Lk. xii. 53 the emphasis is rather on divisions resulting from some members of
a family accepting, others rejecting, Christ. Mt. x. 34-36 looks like a conflation of Lk. xii. 49-53 (*i.e.* Q) with the passage in Micah. Mk. xiii. 12 f. reads
like a parallel version of the Q saying, slightly modified by a recollection of the
delation by the Christians first arrested of further victims and the accusation
of *odium humani generis*, which Tacitus mentions *Ann.* xv. 14.

THE GOSPEL AND THE APOSTLE

Rome was the most convenient " distributing centre " for the civilised world. The Christian mate of an Alexandrian grain ship, or the confidential freedman of some Antiochene merchant at Rome on his master's business, would hear a reading from the new Gospel at some Sunday gathering. At once he would take steps to acquire a copy of such a treasure to take back to his fellow-Christians at home. But I doubt whether things would have been thus left to chance. The whole Church at this epoch was passionately missionary in character ; and it is very likely that the leaders of the Roman Church themselves took measures, and that without delay, to share their treasures, Epistles as well as Gospel, with the other churches—and that is how Mark came to be a source drawn upon by the authors of the other Gospels.

An interval of something like thirty-five years seems to have elapsed between the Crucifixion and the publication of what, so far as we know, was the earliest Life of Christ. That the Church should have been content to wait so long for a thing which seems to us a *sine qua non* of Christian teaching is a fact that calls for explanation. The question is one to which inadequate attention has been given. Indeed, there are scholars who go out of their way to make it more acute by trying to drag down the date of this Gospel to the latest possible date. These do not perceive that to the historian the real problem is how to explain the lateness of the date to which the Church tradition assigns its official Lives of the Founder ; and not only that, but also to account for the naïve and primitive character of the representation of Christ embodied in Mark, assuming it to have been written after many years of the development of cultus and theological speculation of the kind presupposed in the Epistles of Paul. Ecclesiastically, even if it be assigned to A.D. 65, the Gospel of Mark was already ten years out of date, so to speak, at the time that it was written. Its naïveté and primitive characteristics can only be explained by the dependence of its author on early and unsophisticated tradition.   But there are two reasons which, taken together, are perhaps sufficient to account for the late date of the appearance of the earliest Life of Christ.

(1) The first disciples were brought up in Jewish habits. Jewish religious tradition, while treasuring with the utmost care the words of a great teacher, was strangely indifferent to the biographical interest.   No " Life " of any Prophet or Rabbi has been preserved.   The Greeks and Romans, on the other hand, were intensely interested in biography—particularly so at this period, witness the names of Plutarch, Suetonius, and Tacitus. This striking contrast will partly explain why the earliest Life of Christ was written in a Gentile Church, and also why the writing of it was postponed until the great leaders who were dominated by Jewish tradition had passed away.[1]

(2) The primitive Church lived in daily expectation of that visible return of Christ which would bring the present world order to an end.   They believed that their utmost efforts should be directed towards bringing the knowledge of a few central truths to as many as possible before it was too late and repentance would be fruitless since the Judgement had begun.   At a time when any day might be the last day, it would have seemed absurd to compile history for the benefit of a posterity which would never be born.   But as the years passed by it was inevitable, human nature being what it is, that the past and the remoter future should both reassume their normal importance.   Theoretically Christians still thought the End at hand, practically it interested them less.   But when a change in the focus of interest is taking place in the subconscious mind, it usually needs some kind of shock to bring about such conscious realisation of the change as will lead to definite action.   Such a shock came to the Roman Church with the Neronian persecution.   Catastrophe and tribulation, as a prelude to the supernatural Messianic deliverance, was

[1] Burkitt has called attention to the originality of Mark as the inventor of the biography type of Gospel, *Earliest Sources of the Life of Jesus*,[2] p. 128 (Constable, 1922).   See also my remarks, *Oxford Studies*, p. 216 f.

part of the Apocalyptic expectation which the Church had inherited from Judaism. Catastrophe and tribulation of an unheard-of character had supervened, but the End had not. And the great leaders of the first generation, the only two Apostles whom the Gentile world had ever really known, had passed away. For the first time since the Day of Pentecost a Christian community, instead of concentrating its gaze wholly upon the future, finds it necessary to look backward. The Church of Rome becomes interested in history ; it demands at least a record of the Founder's life.

The Gospel of Mark is the response to that demand. The story told by Clement of Alexandria (ap. Eus. H.E. vi. 14), how the Roman Christians besought Mark, as the disciple of Peter, to produce such an account, may be only a conjecture. But since Mark seems to have been in Rome about this time (2 Tim. iv. 11), it is exactly what we should have expected to occur, though we need not, like Clement, suppose that everything in Mark's Gospel was derived from Peter. Once a Gospel like that of Mark had been composed, its utility and interest—more than that, its indispensability—would have been obvious to all. Christians would have wondered, just as we to-day wonder, how the churches had managed to get along at all without some such work. Everywhere, throughout the Empire, a Life of Christ by a disciple of Peter would have been hailed as the satisfaction of what had been for long a half-conscious need.

The world-wide circulation of Mark affords an easy and natural explanation of what, from the purely linguistic point of view, is the rather curious usage by which the word " Gospel " became the technical name for a biography of Christ. The Greek word *evangelion* means simply " good news," and in the New Testament it is always used in its original sense of the good news of the Christian message. Commentators have tried elaborately to trace a gradual evolution in the meaning of the word until it acquired this new usage. No such gradual evolution is necessary, or even probable. Among the Jews it was a

2 K

regular practice to refer to books, or sections of books, by a
striking word which occurred in the opening sentence. That is
how Genesis and Exodus derived the titles by which they are
known in the Hebrew Bible, *i.e.* " In the Beginning " and " (these
are the) Names." As soon as portions of Mark were read in the
services of the Church—and that would be at once—it would be
necessary to have a name to distinguish this reading from that
of an Old Testament book. Mark opens with the words ἀρχὴ
τοῦ εὐαγγελίου, " The beginning of the Gospel." ἀρχή would be
too like the Hebrew name for Genesis, so εὐαγγέλιον (nom.) would
be an obvious title. When, fifteen or twenty years later, other
Lives of Christ came into existence, this use of "Gospel" as a
title would be an old-established custom (p. 559 *n.*) and would
be applied to them also. Then it would become necessary to
distinguish these " Gospels " from one another—hence the usage
τὸ εὐαγγέλιον κατὰ Μάρκον, κατὰ Λουκᾶν, the Gospel *according
to* Mark, to Luke, etc.

There is a problem in early Church history which few historians
have frankly faced, and which those who have tried to date
the books of the New Testament in an unreal abstraction from
their environment in history have strangely felt themselves
absolved from even raising. How are we to account for that
broad general consensus on the main lines of belief and practice
to be found, amid much local diversity, throughout the loose
federation of communities known as the Catholic Church which
appears all over the Roman Empire by the end of the second
century ?

Consider the weakness of the Christian position, once the
generation contemporary with the Apostles had passed away,
and when Jerusalem, the natural local centre, was destroyed.
What common basis of unity was there ? What was there to
point out some one common guiding and controlling principle
or line of development ? There was the Old Testament. That
was for many purposes of unique value, but it gave little clear
guidance towards the solution of the really burning problems of

the early Church. Was the Law of Moses binding on Christians, and, if not, why not ? Was Christ a merely human Messiah exalted to the right hand of God, or was He the pre-existent Son of God incarnate ? Was the body of Christ real human flesh and blood, or formed of some divine impassible material ? Did Christ really suffer and die upon the Cross, or was this merely semblance ? Does the Church teach the immortality of the soul alone, or the resurrection of the body also, and, if so, in what sense ? These were the questions that agitated the Christian communities scattered over the Roman world ; these were the points on which heresies and schisms arose. For their solution the Churches were compelled to turn, not to the Old Testament, but to Mark, Romans, and 1 Corinthians.[1] Incidentally 1 Corinthians, with its account of the Resurrection Appearances, made up for the most striking lack in Mark. So diverse and conflicting were the influences operating in different parts of the Roman world that, had the Church possessed no other literature than the Old Testament to provide a common standard of practice and belief, no kind of union could have been maintained. It was the acceptance by the leading Churches at an early date of an authoritative Life of Christ, interpreted in the light of the great Epistles of Paul, that made it possible for some kind of unity in the direction of doctrinal development to be preserved.

Thus at once, from sheer necessity, the " Gospel and the Apostle," the legacy of Peter and of Paul, became the rudder of the Church. Later on, the Gospel becomes a fourfold one, and the collection of Apostolic writings expands ; but the nucleus of the New Testament in both its great divisions is there before the catastrophe of A.D. 70.

---

[1] I am inclined to think Ephesians also was included in the earliest *Corpus Paulinum* ; it has probably influenced Clement and Hermas, and certainly the other Apostolic Fathers ; if intended as a " circular letter," a copy would have been kept for use in Rome. There are possible traces of Philippians in Clement. On the development of the Pauline canon see p. 526 f.

PART II.—MATTHEW

THE ANTIOCHENE ORIGIN OF MATTHEW

The Patristic evidence that Matthew was written in Palestine in Hebrew is impressive—until we reflect that all the Fathers had read the statement of Irenaeus, quoted p. 8 (either in the original or as reproduced by Eusebius), and that Irenaeus himself had read Papias' dictum on τὰ λόγια. Thus the tradition can be traced back to a single root ; and, quite apart from the correctness of our interpretation of Papias, it cannot be authentic, for our Gospel of Matthew being based on the Greek Mark cannot be a translation from the Aramaic. At the same time the evidence of Irenaeus and Papias has a negative value. It proves that Matthew was *not* produced either in Rome or in Asia Minor, but was believed to have originally come from the East.

We can be sure, however, that Matthew originated in an important Church for the simple reason that, apart from the title, which, of course, forms no part of the original text, it is anonymous. The significance of this anonymity is apt to be overlooked. The Apocryphal Gospels all try to claim authority by definite and often reiterated assertions of Apostolic authorship in the text itself. The spurious Gospel of Peter (2nd century A.D.), for instance, goes out of its way to introduce " I, Simon Peter," just before the account of the Resurrection. Matthew is anonymous ; it makes no claim to authority, gives no hint of authorship. Now a poem or a pamphlet may lose little by being anonymous—sometimes, indeed, it may gain in effect ; but a record of events, many of them of a marvellous description, purporting to give an authentic account of one whose deeds, words, and divine nature were a matter of acute controversy, would carry no weight at all if by an unknown author. In a work of this kind, therefore, anonymity implies that it was originally compiled for the use of some particular church which accepted it at once as a reliable authority, simply because it knew and had confidence in the person or committee who produced it. It is improbable that in the first instance direct Apostolic authorship was ascribed to the First Gospel. But the substitution of the name Matthew for the Levi of Mark (Mt. ix. 9)—confirmed by the back reference "Matthew the publican" (x. 3)—makes him the one apostle, besides the two pairs of brothers, of whom any incident is recorded. This forcible effort to make Matthew prominent in the story is most naturally explained, if the author of the Gospel knew one of his sources to be the work of that Apostle. If, however, the Gospel incorporated a document which was popularly ascribed to Matthew (I suggest Q), the book as a whole would soon come to be regarded as his in the Church for which it was first written.

But the Gospel would not have been generally accepted as Apostolic unless it had been backed by one of the great Churches ; for the Canon of the Gospels was fixed in the second century for the express purpose of excluding Gnostic Gospels which, like that of Peter, not only were ascribed by certain persons to Apostles, but affirmed the claim in their text. People often talk as if the early Church accepted with avidity any and every book as Apostolic. The evidence points the other way. The Church in the second century had taken fright ; and the primary purpose of the Canon was to exclude. It took centuries for 2 Peter and James, documents of considerable antiquity and un-impeachable orthodoxy, to be generally received, and even the backing of Alexandria could not induce Rome to accept Hebrews as Pauline till the time of Athanasius. That the Church accepted as Apostolic certain writings which in point of fact were not so, is undoubted—the Gospel we are discussing is an instance. But we quite misconceive its attitude unless we recognise that the production by the Gnostics of a quantity of literature claiming Apostolic authorship made the Churches, especially the Church of Rome, almost as suspicious of such a claim as a modern critic—though the test of authenticity applied was not the same

For the determination of Apostolic Doctrine the Church appealed against the Gnostics to the open tradition of the Apostolic Sees; similarly for the determination of the genuineness of writings reputed Apostolic it appealed to the same tradition. The tradition of either Antioch, Ephesus, or Rome would be a sufficient guarantee of Apostolic authorship—but it is doubtful whether anything less than that would have sufficed.

Matthew, then, must have been vouched for as Apostolic by some very important Church. But which Church could this be? Of the greater Churches all but Antioch are excluded. Rome and Ephesus have been already ruled out. Alexandria is an impossible city in which to place the most Judaistic of the Gospels; Barnabas, the only certainly Alexandrian writing we possess of early date, is violently anti-Jewish in feeling; and all we know of the early history of that Church shows that its sympathies were, if anything, in the Gnostic direction. Caesarea has been suggested by some scholars. But we have only to look at the map to see that the official Gospel of a Church which was the port of entry of Samaria was not very likely to have contained the command, "Enter not into any city of the Samaritans," for its author had no scruples in omitting anything likely to cause apologetic difficulty. Besides, as we have seen already, Caesarea is clearly marked out as the home of the specifically Lucan tradition.

There is a further consideration, which seems to me to rule out, not only Caesarea, but any Church in Palestine.[1] The narratives peculiar to Matthew, unlike those peculiar to Luke, so rarely look authentic. Leaving out of account for the moment the Infancy, the only story peculiar to Matthew which stands, so to speak, " on its own legs " is the Stater in the Fish's Mouth. The rest are all, in a way, parasitic; they stand to Mark as the mistletoe to the oak. The story of Peter walking

---

[1] Burkitt points out (*J.T.S.*, July 1913, p. 545) that the use of the verb ἐπιφώσκειν, Mt. xxviii. 1, implies the Gentile mode of reckoning time, and suggests Antioch.

on the water, for example, is an expansion of the Marcan story of Christ walking on the water, and implies the previous existence of the Marcan story. Matthew's additions to the Passion story are similarly of the nature of embellishments of the Marcan account which presuppose Mark as their basis. It is noteworthy that not a single one of them looks like a genuine historical tradition ; while some of them are clearly legendary, *e.g.*[1] the temporary resurrection of saints in Jerusalem at the time of the Rending of the Veil, or Pilate's washing his hands before the multitude—an action as probable in a Roman governor as in a British civil servant in India. The commonest device of the preacher or Sunday School teacher who wishes to bring an incident of Scripture vividly before the minds of his audience is to retell the story with little additions derived from his own imaginative reconstruction of the scene. This kind of thing was familiar to the Rabbis in the popular exposition of the Old Testament, so much so that it has a technical name, "Haggada." The additions which Matthew makes to Mark's story of the Passion are precisely analogous to the Rabbinic Haggada of Old Testament stories. It is improbable that the editor of Matthew made them up himself ; rather they represent the " happy thoughts " of a long series of preachers and teachers. Those which happened to " catch on " would be remembered ; in the course of time their " Haggadic " origins would be forgotten and they would be accepted as authentic traditions. But if this is so, Mark must have been known in the Church where Matthew wrote long enough to have become an established authority—a document which teachers and preachers expounded by methods familiar in the exposition of Scripture. Incidentally I may remark that this compels us to suppose a considerable interval of time between the composition of Mark and Matthew. Ten years seems an absolute minimum, and twenty would be none too many.

But, if the origin of Matthew must be sought in an important Church outside Palestine, Antioch is the only one left. And to

[1] Mt. xxvii. 51-53, 24-25.

the view that Matthew was written there, there are *no* objections. Antioch *must* have had a Gospel, and the guarantee by a Church of that importance is the best explanation of an anonymous work being accepted as indubitably Apostolic by Rome and the other Churches. Again, an Antiochene origin would account for the extraordinary interest shown by its author in the doings and in the primacy of Peter, who is far more prominent in this Gospel than in Mark, although that was written by his own disciple. Antioch follows Peter and stands for the *via media* between the Judaistic intolerance of those who called James master and the all but antinomian liberty claimed by some of the followers of Paul. Lastly, in the Church of Antioch, a city with an enormous Jewish population, we seem to have just the atmosphere of the Gospel of Matthew, which, though frankly recognising that Christianity is for all nations, is yet saturated with Jewish feeling, preserves so many sayings of a particularist Jewish Christian character, and altogether is less touched by the spirit of Paul than any other book in the New Testament. For Matthew Christianity is the " new Law."

One infinitesimal point in favour of an Antiochene origin may be added : the stater varied in weight and value in different districts. The commentators say that only in Antioch and Damascus did the official stater exactly equal two didrachmae, as is implied in Mt. xvii. 24-27. The story itself reads like an adaptation of a popular folk story, of which one version appears as the Ring of Polycrates ;[1] and it solves a problem which the Jew of the Dispersion in a city like Antioch must, when converted to Christianity, face, whether or no he should continue to pay the annual levy of the Temple Tax.

EVIDENCE OF IGNATIUS

The conjecture that Matthew is the Gospel of the Church of Antioch is borne out by the use made of it in the epistles of

[1] Herodotus, bk. iii. 41-42.

Ignatius, Bishop of that city (c. 115). Ignatius has a couple of *possible* allusions to Luke, but they are very uncertain. He has some rather remarkable points of contact with John ; but even if these are quotations, he quotes John rarely, and refrains from doing so in certain doctrinal arguments where we should have expected it if he regarded the Fourth Gospel as an authority. But in his seven short letters there are about fifteen passages which look like reminiscences of Matthew.

Sometimes the language of Ignatius recalls sayings which occur in Mark or Luke as well as Matthew ; but in these cases his wording is usually nearer to Matthew's version.[1] Six of the clearest reminiscences are of passages peculiar to Matthew— two of them being passages which critics unanimously attribute to the editor of Matthew rather than to his sources, *e.g.* " being baptized by John in order that all righteousness might be fulfilled in him " (Ignat. *Smyrn.* i. 1 ; cf. Mt. iii. 15) ; " bear all men as the Lord does thee . . . bear the sicknesses of all " (*Polyc.* i. 2-3 ; cf. Mt. viii. 17). Other passages are significant, less from the fact that they are reminiscences than from the manner of the reminiscence. " Be thou wise in all ways as a serpent, and at all times harmless as a dove " (*Polyc.* ii. 2 ; cf. Mt. x. 16) ; " For if the prayer of one and a second has such avail " (*Eph.* v. 2 = Mt. xviii. 19-20). The point of allusions in this style consists precisely in the fact that, while recalling, they slightly modify, the original wording of a well-known saying to adapt it to the reader's situation. They would have been pointless unless that original wording was to be found in a book already accepted as a classic, a knowledge of which the writer could take for granted in his readers.

Ignatius, again, is the only one of the Apostolic Fathers who refers to the Virgin Birth—and he does so several times and lays stress on its importance (*Eph.* xviii. 2, xix. 1 ; *Smyrn.* i. 1 ;

[1] For complete list of parallels cf. *The New Testament in the Apostolic Fathers*, by a Committee of the Oxford Society of Historical Theology (Clarendon Press, 1905). *N.B.* esp. φυτεία πατρός *Trall.* xi. 1 ; *Philad.* iii. 1 ; cf. Mt. xv. 13.

Trall. ix. 1). Now Matthew has a great deal to say about the virginity of Mary; but in Luke (cf. p. 267 f.) it is extraordinarily little emphasised. Specially significant is the passage in which Ignatius congratulates the Christians of Smyrna on their orthodoxy in that they are " fully persuaded as touching our Lord that He is truly of the race of David according to the flesh, but Son of God of the Divine Will, truly born of a virgin and baptized by John that all righteousness might be fulfilled in him" (*Smyrn.* 1). Here three points characteristic of Matthew come together— Davidic descent, virgin birth, baptism to " fulfil all righteousness," of which the last is only found in Matthew, while Matthew opens his Gospel with the words, " The genealogy of Jesus Christ, the son of David, the son of Abraham." Luke's genealogy lays no special stress on David.

Lastly, Ignatius frequently speaks of " the Gospel " as if this were the name of a book. Certain heretics, he tells us, say ἐὰν μὴ ἐν τοῖς ἀρχείοις [*v.l.* ἀρχαίοις] εὕρω, ἐν τῷ εὐαγγελίῳ οὐ πιστεύω (*Philad.* viii. 2) : " If I find it not in the archives (*v.l.* ancient writings) I believe it not in the Gospel." Evidently " the Gospel " is the title of a book, the authority of which they are not prepared to put on the same level as the ancient Scriptures. Just before this, the triad, " the Gospel," " the apostles," and "the prophets " are put side by side in a way which makes the best sense if these are read as titles of sacred books (*Philad.* v. 1-2). Lightfoot and Harnack, influenced by the *a priori* notion that this use of the word Gospel *must* have been a gradual development and is therefore improbable at this date, say that the usage here is transitional. But this whittling away of the natural meaning of the passages is quite unnecessary. If the use of the term "Gospel" to denote a Life of Christ originated (as suggested p. 497 f.), owing to the occurrence of the word " Gospel " in the opening verse of Mark, out of the Jewish practice of using the first striking word of a book as its title, no period of development is required. At once, from the earliest time, Mark would have been spoken of as " the Gospel." When Matthew was written, the author or committee of authors who produced it aimed at producing a new and enlarged edition of Mark, that is to say, Matthew was intended to supersede Mark ; and in the Church of its origin it no doubt did so for a time, though later on Mark would be reintroduced as part of the Four Gospel Canon accepted by the whole Church. Hence as soon as Matthew was published the title " the Gospel " (see also p. 559 *n.*) would naturally be transferred to it from Mark.

The real significance, then, of the use of the term "the Gospel" in Ignatius is that it probably implies that at Antioch in his day there was as yet only one Gospel recognised as " the Gospel " by the Church—a state of things which still existed among Aramaic-speaking Christians in Jerome's time. And since, whether or no Ignatius had glanced through other Gospels, Matthew is certainly the one he knew best, it is a reasonable inference that when he speaks of *the* Gospel he means Matthew.

QUOTATIONS IN THE DIDACHE

The Didache presents a number of difficult problems, and these have been made more difficult owing to the fact that certain distinguished scholars have allowed themselves the luxury of proposing what I can only call " fancy solutions." [1] For the purposes of what follows I shall assume as reasonably certain (*a*) that it arose somewhere in Syria or Palestine ; (*b*) that, apart from certain (probable) interpolations, it is not later than A.D. 100.

The author of the Didache seems not only to have read Matthew, but also, like Ignatius, to refer to it under the title of " The Gospel." But one passage looks as if, alongside of the official Gospel, there still existed an oral tradition of sayings of our Lord, perhaps derived from recollections of Q.

---

[1] The student will find a fair and well-judged statement of the facts in Hastings' *Dictionary of the Apostolic Church*, art. *Didache*. Prof. Turner dates it A.D. 80–100 (*Studies in Early Church History*, Oxford, 1912, p. 31) ; and (p. 8 *n.*) suggests that Ignatius knew it. To his parallels I would add *Mag.* v. 1 (the Two Ways). Does ἀποστόλοις (*Philad.* v. 1) = Paul's epistles + Didache ?

For the purpose of our study there are certain passages the text of which is not sufficiently certain to bear the weight of an important conclusion. (*a*) The section i. 2-iii. 1 is omitted in the Latin version as well as in the related documents Barnabas and the Apostolic Church Order, and is probably a very early interpolation. (*b*) The same *may* be true of the Matthean saying, " Give not what is holy to the dogs " (Did. ix. 5), since it does not occur in the parallel section of the Apostolic Constitutions which incorporates the Didache almost entire. (*c*) The command to baptize " in the name of the Father, the Son, and the Holy Spirit," which occurs in Matthew only in the New Testament, is a point of contact between the Didache and that Gospel ; but in view of the importance attached in later times to baptism in the name of the Trinity, we may be pretty sure that, even if the original author of the Didache had written something different, later scribes would have substituted the orthodox formula. Obviously, then, the passage cannot be quoted *as evidence* that the author had read Matthew.

There remain, however, certain reminiscences or allusions to texts in Matthew which are so deeply embedded in the argument of their context in the Didache that they cannot be suspected of being later interpolations.

(1) Did. viii. 1 f., " And let not your fastings be with the hypocrites, for they fast on the second and third day of the week ; but do ye keep your fast on the fourth and on the Friday (παρασκευή). Neither pray ye as the hypocrites, but *as the Lord commanded in his Gospel* thus pray ye : Our Father," etc. (the Lord's Prayer practically as in Matthew). The relation of this passage to Mt. vi. 5-16 is clear. It is an interpretation according to the letter, but in flagrant discord with the spirit, of the Sermon on the Mount. Such interpretations only arise where there is a letter to misinterpret, and would compel us to assume that the words stood in some recognised official document, even if the author did not expressly quote them as from " his (*i.e.* the Lord's) Gospel."

(2) Did. xi. 3-4, " But concerning the apostles and prophets,

so do ye according to the ordinances of the Gospel. Let every
apostle, when he cometh to you, be received as the Lord.'
Here "the Gospel" is referred to as containing an ordinance
concerning the reception of touring "apostles." It is difficult
not to see here a direct allusion to the Address to Apostles
about to go on a Mission Tour (Mt. x.), and in the words "Let
every apostle coming to you be received as the Lord" a particular
reference to Mt. x. 40, "He that receiveth you receiveth me,
and he that receiveth me receiveth him that sent me."

(3) Did. xi. 7, "And every prophet speaking in the Spirit ye
shall not try nor judge ; for every sin shall be forgiven, but this
sin shall not be forgiven." The saying referred to occurs in all
three Synoptists; but the application of it in the Didache implies
knowledge of it in a context like that in Matthew or Mark rather
than as in Luke. The wording agrees with Matthew against
Mark ; and this agreement is unusually significant because, as a
glance at a synopsis of the Gospels will show, the wording in
Matthew (xii. 31f.) is determined by the fact that he is conflating
Mark (iii. 28-29) with Q (Lk. xii. 10), so that this precise wording is
individual to Matthew, since no two people would independently
hit upon the same way of conflating two parallel sources.

(4) Did. xiii. 1, "Every true prophet desiring to settle
amongst you is worthy of his food. In like manner a true teacher
is also worthy, like the labourer, of his food." The way in
which the saying "The labourer is worthy of his food" is referred
to implies that it was familiar *in its application* to Christian
missionaries, *i.e. as it appears in* Mt. x. 10. In Luke's version,
though the context is similar, the word "hire" is substituted
for "food" ; and there is the same substitution in 1 Tim. v. 18.

(5) Did. xiv. 2, "Let no man having his dispute with his
fellow join your assembly until they have been reconciled, that
your sacrifice may not be defiled." There is a significant relation
between "that your sacrifice may not be defiled" and "leave
there thy gift before the altar" (Mt. v. 24); the reference in
Matthew to the Jewish sacrifices has been spiritualised to refer

to the Christian Eucharist. But such a reference implies that the
Didache is related to a saying like that in Matthew as commentary
to text ; it must therefore have stood in some document regarded
as authoritative by readers of the Didache.

(6) Did. xv. 3, "And reprove (ἐλέγχετε) one another, not in
anger but in peace, as ye find in the Gospel "—an express
reference to "the Gospel" for further instructions in regard to
procedure, *i.e.* to ἔλεγξον αὐτὸν κτλ. (Mt. xviii. 15 ff.). The
author continues, " But your prayer and your almsgiving
(cf. Mt. vi. 2-15) and all your deeds, so do ye as ye find in the
Gospel of our Lord." With this reiterated reference to "the
Gospel" he concludes his general instructions. It is as if he
said, " The present work is intended merely as an introduction
to Christian practice ; for a full treatment you must refer to the
Gospel, especially the Sermon on the Mount."

(7) Did. xvi. The book ends with an Apocalyptic passage—
obviously based on Matthew :

Be watchful for your life ; *let not your lamps go out* (Mt. xxv. 8) *and
your loins be ungirded* (Lk. xii. 35), *but be ye ready ; for ye know not the
hour in which* our *Lord cometh* (Mt. xxiv. 42, 44). And ye shall gather
yourselves together frequently, seeking what is fitting for your souls ;
for the whole time of your faith shall not profit you, if ye be not
perfected at the last season. For in the last days *the false prophets*
and corrupters shall be *multiplied*, and the sheep shall be turned into
wolves, and *love* shall be turned into hate (Mt. xxiv. 11 f., 24). For as
ἀνομία increaseth, *they shall hate one another* (Mt. xxiv. 10,12) *and shall*
persecute and *deliver up*. *And then* the World-deceiver *shall appear*
as a Son of God, *and shall work signs and wonders* (Mt. xxiv. 30; Mt. xxiv.
24), and the earth shall be delivered into his hands ; and he shall do
unholy things, *which have never been* (Mt. xxiv. 21) since the world
began. Then all created mankind shall come to the fire of testing,
and many shall be offended and perish ; *but they that endure* in their
faith *shall be saved* (Mt. xxiv. 13) by the Curse Himself. *And then
shall the signs* of the Truth *appear* (Mt. xxiv. 30) ; first a sign of a
rift in the heaven, then a sign of a voice *of a trumpet* (Mt. xxiv. 31),
and thirdly a resurrection of the dead ; yet not of all, but as it was
said (Zech. xiv. 5) : "The Lord shall come and all His saints with
Him." *Then shall* the world *see the Lord coming upon the clouds of
heaven* (Mt. xxiv. 30).

Passages in the above quotation of which the reference number is underlined occur *only* in Matthew.

In the foregoing parallels there is one passage, and one only, which is closer to Luke than to Matthew, " and your loins," etc. (cf. Lk. xii. 35). But Lk. xii. 35-38 is a passage which on other grounds we assigned to Q (p. 279), accounting for its omission by Matthew by the fact that its moral, and even some of its language, occurs in a more striking form in the parable of the Virgins. If our hypothesis that Q was the original gospel of the Church of Antioch be correct, and if the Didache was composed in Syria, for some years after Matthew was written certain sayings would still be remembered in their Q form. A work like the Didache would certainly be composed by senior members of the Church in whose recollection turns of phrase in the older document would be likely to be deeply embedded, and all the quotations in the Didache are clearly made from memory.[1]

To sum up. Both Ignatius and the Didache, the earliest Syrian documents we possess, habitually speak of " the Gospel " as if it was the name of a book having a certain authority ; also whenever the same sayings occur in Matthew and in either of these, their versions are always secondary. They stand to Matthew as the preacher to his text.

THE PETRINE COMPROMISE

I proceed now to show that the hypothesis of an Antiochene origin illuminates the facts which were revealed by our critical analysis of the sources of the Gospel, and certain features in the author's presentation of the Apocalyptic hope.

The growing hatred of Rome, which led to the Jewish revolt of 64, was accompanied by a revival of religious fanaticism. Naturally, nationalism and religion were the same thing to the Jew. Hitherto the Palestinian Christians, who zealously observed the Law of Moses and worshipped in the Temple, of whom

[1] The section Did. i. 2-iii. 1 presents close parallels with both Mt. v. 39-47 and Lk. vi. 27-33. If not an interpolation, this also is best explained as a conflation of Matthew and Q, since (p. 249 ff.) Luke is here nearer to Q than Matthew.

James "the Just," the brother of the Lord, was the leader, had
been tolerated. But in the year 62 James was massacred by
the mob. And in obedience, we are told by Eusebius, to an
oracle, most of the Jerusalem Christians fled across the Jordan
to Pella before the Roman armies began the actual siege.   During
the first persecution of Christians in Jerusalem—that which
followed the death of Stephen—some had fled to Antioch ; and it
was they (Acts xi. 19 f.) who founded the Church there.   What
more natural than that some of the refugees from this far worse
persecution should make their escape to the same Church—a
Church which had always (as for instance in the great famine of 46
foretold by Agabus (Acts xi. 28)) shown such practical sympathy
with fellow-Christians in Jerusalem ?

As so often in history, the refugees would bring with them
the books they valued most. If there were already in use in the
Jerusalem Church written summaries of our Lord's teaching,
these would be among them. If, as is not impossible, Jerusalem
had been still content with collections of His sayings learnt by
heart, the retentive memories of the refugees would still have
much which would be of great interest to the brethren at Antioch.
And their tradition, coming as it did with all the prestige of
the parent Church of Christendom, would seem to the elders at
Antioch far too precious not to be rendered into Greek and set
down in writing without more delay.

But this tradition, corresponding to that element in Matthew
which we have styled M, included sayings of a strongly Judaistic
character. The fact is one which has often been misconceived.
It cannot be too emphatically insisted that this element in
Matthew reflects, not primitive Jewish Christianity, but a later
Judaistic reaction against the Petro-Pauline liberalism in the
matter of the Gentile Mission and the observance of the Law.
At Antioch, as elsewhere, there were parties in the Church : the
immediate result of the advent of the Jerusalem refugees would
be to strengthen the hand of the party of the stricter observance
of the Law. It was very hard not to accept as Apostolic a

tradition which came authenticated, as it were, by the recent martyrdom of James.

Mark's Gospel, coming from Rome practically at the same time, would be hailed at once by the more liberal and pro-Gentile party as the Gospel of Antioch's own Apostle.

Q, so far as we can judge, was fairly neutral on the legalistic issue, and, we have seen, Q may well have been the original Gospel-document of the Church of Antioch ; at any rate Q is admittedly older, probably a good deal older, than Mark, and, whatever its original language, the same Greek version was known to " Matthew " as to Luke, so that, even if this Greek translation was not produced in Antioch, the greatest Greek-speaking Church of Syria, it would have reached there at a very early date.

But for some years Mark and M would have existed side by side, and would have been read together with a consciousness of partisanship something like that which in the eighteenth century was attached to the " Whig " and " Tory " collects for the King in the Anglican Communion Service. Religious conservatism has always great capacity of resistance ; but in the Jew—especially as regards the Law for which he and his fathers have bled for centuries—this capacity is raised to the nth power. As late as the fourth century a large section of the vernacular Jewish Christians of Palestine rejected the Epistles of Paul ; but at Antioch in the quarter of a century that followed the Fall of Jerusalem circumstances were unusually favourable to concilia-tion. (1) The living spirit of the Christian mission had not yet lost its original momentum. (2) It was known that Peter, Paul, and James, the revered leaders of the different parties, had in the last resort never repudiated one another ; and within a year or two of one another all three had died for Christ. (3) The destruction of the Temple in 70 meant that at least half the requirements of the Law could no longer be fulfilled. Did this mean that Paul was right then after all, and that Christ had intended to supersede the Law ? (4) It daily appeared that the bitterest of all the enemies of Christianity were the Jews who stood by the old Law.

2 L

All these circumstances were favourable to a *rapprochement*
between the parties in the Church. Neither side could abandon
accepted records of the teaching of Christ; but the possibility
that there had been some misinterpretation of the sayings most
used in controversy could be explored. Perhaps another meaning could be found for those apparently Judaistic words of
Christ which the James party were always quoting.

By the time that Matthew wrote, a new exegesis which could
reconcile the parties had been evolved. It was admitted on the
one hand that the Master had said, " I was not sent but unto the
lost sheep of the house of Israel "; that He regarded the healing
of a Syro-Phoenician as an exception, and that He had not
Himself (as Mark's story would imply), even on that occasion,
stepped outside the sacred soil of Palestine—for the woman had
come across the border to Him (Mt. xv. 22). It was conceded
also by the liberal party that in His first Mission Charge He had
forbidden the Twelve to go into any way of the Gentiles or any
city of the Samaritans (Mt. x. 6); in return, the other side admitted that this limitation was only intended for the time during
which He walked the earth; after His Resurrection He had on
the contrary bade them "go and make disciples of all the
nations" (xxviii. 19). Again, as the context (Mt. viii. 11) in which
the prophecy is placed makes clear (quite a different one from
that which, from its position in Luke (xiii. 28), we may conclude was original in Q), it was now agreed that Christ was
referring to Gentiles, not Jews of the Dispersion, when He said,
" Many shall come from the east and the west, and shall sit down
with Abraham, Isaac, and Jacob in the kingdom of heaven: but
the sons of the kingdom shall be cast forth into outer darkness."
Finally, the fear—a very practical one—of antinomianism is met
by a presentation of Christ's teaching as the New Law: the
Sermon on the Mount is a counterpart to Sinai, and the five Great
Discourses (p. 261 ff.) are, as it were, " the five books " of His
" law of liberty."

Thus complete reconciliation of the two parties of the James and Paul tradition, once hardly even artificially held together by Peter as a middle term, is now effected. That is much the most probable explanation of the famous saying, "Thou art Peter, on this rock I will build my Church" (cf. p. 258). How far the words of this highly controverted saying as preserved in the First Gospel were actually uttered by Christ, and, if so, with what exact significance, it would be profitless to inquire. The form in which we have it is the version as remembered, repeated, and in repetition doubtless not a little modified, by those who disapproved alike of the undue conservatism of James and of Paul's too liberal attitude towards the Law, but were content to accept the *via media* of Peter.[1] At Antioch all could rally round the name of Peter. He is the supreme Rabbi in whom resides the final interpretation (the power " to bind and to loose ") of the New Law given to the New Israel (" my (*i.e.* the Messiah's) Church ") by Christ.

Extremists, of course, on both sides would repudiate the compromise. They always do. They became the forbears on the one side of Ebionites, and on the other of Antinomian Docetae. But if Matthew represents the agreement of the main body of the Church of Antioch, how long a period must be allowed for the settlement to be reached ? When Paul wrote to the Philippians (*c.* 63) the Judaisers were actively, openly, and, from his language, one might infer unscrupulously, attacking him. And in the Church of Antioch the Jewish element was much more powerful than at Rome. Would twenty years have sufficed for the Church of Antioch to reach the degree of peace and unanimity which the Gospel of Matthew implies ? Most

---

[1] I owe to Prof. Burkitt a reference to *Anecdota Oxoniensia* (*Relics of the Palestinian Syriac Literature*), 1896, pp. 85-87, for a homiletic exposition of Mt. xvi. 18, which *denies* that the Rock was Peter. This whole Palestinian Syriac literature was used in the Patriarchate of Jerusalem, which looked to James as its founder, as against Peter, in whose chair sat the Patriarch of the really much more important border See of Antioch. The claim of Rome to be in a special sense the See of Peter is not found in the second century; it is always Peter *and* Paul. If, as is possible (cf. p. 490), the death of Peter in Rome is a mistaken inference from 1 Clem. v., the claim of Rome to have any connection at all with that Apostle must be subsequent to the date of writing of Matthew

probably it would—having in view the favouring circumstances
enumerated above.   But it is a consideration we must bear in
mind in estimating the date of the Gospel.

ANTIOCH AND THE ANTI-CHRIST

That Matthew was written after A.D. 70 may be deduced
from an addition to the parable of the Marriage of the King's
Son, "and the rest laid hold on his servants, and entreated
them shamefully, and killed them.   But the King was wroth; and
he sent his armies, and destroyed those murderers, and burned
their city" (Mt. xxii. 6-7).   There is nothing at all about, either
the persecution of the messengers, or the King's vengeance, in
the parallel parable of the Great Supper in Luke (xiv. 16 ff.).
Besides, the words "their city" do not fit into the rest of the story;
for the invited guests would either be citizens of one or more of
the King's own cities, or, if they were representatives of foreign
powers, would inhabit more than one city.   But the insertion is
intelligible if it is regarded as an attempt to point the moral of
the parable by interpreting it as a prophecy by Christ of the
destruction of the city of Jerusalem, regarded as the judgment
of God—the King in the parable—and in particular as a punish-
ment for the persecution by the Jews of the Christian apostles
and missionaries, who are the messengers sent to them by Him
to invite them to the " wedding feast " of His Son the Messiah.
Such a modification of the parable (which Luke preserves in
what is clearly a more original form) would be very natural after
the Fall of Jerusalem, but not before.   The considerations which
follow suggest that the Gospel was written some time after that
event.

It is impossible for us nowadays to realise the shock of A.D. 70
to a community in which Jewish and Gentile members alike
had been reared in the profoundest veneration of the immemorial sanctity of the Holy City and the Temple.   True, it
was expected that before the Great Deliverance there would be

the Great Tribulation, in the course of which the " Man of Sin,"
the Anti-Christ, would take his stand in the Temple ; and Christ
Himself, it was recorded, had prophesied a destruction of the
Temple as the immediate prelude to His own return.   But the
stupendous fact in the situation was that Jerusalem and the
Temple had been destroyed and neither Anti-Christ nor Christ
had come.   Wars and rumours of wars, world-wide catastrophes,
had taken place.   Huge armies had tramped from the utmost
parts of the Roman world.   Three Caesars had been set up and
three had perished in a single year.   And the accumulation of
horror and desecration connected with the siege of Jerusalem had
seemed to match in actual fact the final " tribulation " which
Apocalyptic expectation had foretold.   These things had come
to pass—and still the Lord did not return.   To such a crisis
different minds would react differently.   To some it would
induce an intensification of Apocalyptic expectation and a more
fanatic conviction of the immediacy of the End.   Others would
slowly awake from Apocalyptic dreams and see the necessity,
before it was too late, of collecting and preserving the surviving
records of the mighty past.   In the Gospel of Matthew both
these tendencies are seen reflected.

That the Fall of Jerusalem did produce an intense revival
of Apocalyptic interest and a new output of Apocalyptic literature, both among Jews and Christians, there is some evidence.
For our present purpose the most important point to note is
that calculations of the exact date of the End, based on the
three and a half years of Daniel xii. 11-12, were actually pre-
occupying Christians about the year 70.   Whatever other views
critics hold about the date and sources of Revelation, there is
practically unanimous agreement that Rev. xi. 1-2 was written
at that date, and that the author expected the End within three
and a half years of the Fall of the City.[1]   Now the prophecy of

---

[1] Daniel gives the figure 1290, Rev. xi. 3-4 has 1260 ; this, the author explains, corresponds to 42 months (= 3½ years) ; he reckons 30 days to a month,
but does not add the " intercalary month," no doubt because he wrote since
the introduction of the Julian Calendar.

which Rev. xi. 1-2 is part must have had a wide circulation, as it, or something very like it, seems to have been known to Luke ; for he adds (Lk. xxi. 24) the words, " Jerusalem shall be trodden under by the Gentiles," which are not contained in the parallel in Mark.   So that we cannot assume that it was unknown at Antioch.

Since, then, Jerusalem fell on 4th September 70, the End of the World would in wide circles be expected to take place early in 74.   But the year 74 closed and the End did not come.   This made a change in the situation.   When Mark wrote (c. 65) it seemed possible that the prophecies of the appearance of the Anti-Christ and the Return of Christ within the lifetime of the first generation might be fulfilled.   But with every year after A.D. 75 the non-fulfilment of these prophecies became a more grievous difficulty to the early Church.   It is interesting to notice that each of the three later Evangelists solved the problem in a different way.   John at Ephesus does so by a spiritual inter-pretation which practically gets rid of the Apocalyptic idea ; the Return of Christ is fulfilled (or for all immediate and practical purposes fulfilled) by the coming of the Paraclete ; while the prophecy of Anti-Christ, instead of being referred to a single half-human, half-demoniac monster, is interpreted as the spirit of the false prophets who deny that Christ has come in the flesh (1 John iv. 2-3) : " This is the spirit of the antichrist, *whereof ye have heard that it cometh*; and now it is in the world already." Luke partly solves the problem by getting rid of the Anti-Christ prophecy altogether, interpreting the Abomination of Desolation as a synonym for the Desolation of Jerusalem by the Roman armies : the Return of Christ he still thinks near, but it is postponed "until the times of the Gentiles be fulfilled" (xxi. 24). Matthew, in the Jewish atmosphere of Antioch, is more con-servative ; he takes both the Anti-Christ and the Parousia in their most literal sense, and he insists that both are overdue. But, as we shall see shortly, he has his own solution of the problem: he disconnects the Anti-Christ from any local con-nection with the Temple.

We have seen that the last chapter of the Didache is, in effect, a hortatory commentary on the Apocalyptic discourse in Mt. xxiv. But what of the sentence (Did. xvi. 3), "and then the World-deceiver ($\kappa o \sigma \mu o \pi \lambda a \nu \acute{\eta} s$) shall appear as a Son of God; and shall work signs and wonders . . . "? In the context, and in the light of the fact that the rest of that context is all dependent on Mt. xxiv., the "World-deceiver" can only be an equivalent, intelligible to the plain man, of the enigmatic "Abomination of Desolation." In fact, the author of the Didache has taken the advice "let him that readeth understand" (xxiv. 15) —he has read, and thinks he has understood. This is evidence that in Syria about A.D. 95 the Abomination was supposed to mean the personal Anti-Christ; the older interpretation of Daniel (that given in Mark) had either been revived or had never been discarded.

Now the author of the Didache is, I feel sure, quite correct in his interpretation of Matthew. To Matthew, as to Mark, the $\beta \delta \acute{\epsilon} \lambda \upsilon \gamma \mu a \ \tau \mathring{\eta} s \ \mathring{\epsilon} \rho \eta \mu \acute{\omega} \sigma \epsilon \omega s$ is, not the Fall of Jerusalem, but the Anti-Christ. In the ordinary text Matthew's alteration of Mark's masculine into the neuter participle ($\mathring{\epsilon} \sigma \tau \eta \kappa \acute{o} \tau a$ into $\mathring{\epsilon} \sigma \tau \acute{o} s$) improves the grammar but does not necessarily imply a desire to change the sense. I believe, however, that the true text of Matthew is that preserved in Syr. S (supported by one cursive of *fam.* 1424) which *omits* "standing in the holy place." Syr. S, representing the old text of Antioch, is an especially good authority for the Antiochene Gospel of Matthew (cf. p. 135 ff.). Against the genuineness of the reading $\mathring{\epsilon} \sigma \tau \grave{o} s \ \mathring{\epsilon} \nu \ \tau \acute{o} \pi \omega \ \mathring{a} \gamma \acute{\iota} \omega$, B ℵ etc., is the absence of any article with $\tau \acute{o} \pi \omega \ \mathring{a} \gamma \acute{\iota} \omega$. But such an omission of the article, though unaccountable in a literary text, would be quite natural in a note scratched in the margin [1] by some one who had looked up (as advised to do in the text) Daniel ix. 27 in the LXX (the English Bible follows the Hebrew, which differs here from the Greek), where the words $\mathring{\epsilon} \pi \grave{\iota} \ \tau \grave{o} \ \mathring{\iota} \epsilon \rho \grave{o} \nu$

[1] If so, $\mathring{\epsilon} \sigma \tau \acute{\omega} s$, D and Byz., is original, since it naturally reads as nominative masculine, though in late Greek it may be neuter also.

βδέλιγμα τῶν ἐρημώσεων occur, and had the parallel passage in Mark in his mind. A marginal gloss, especially if also an assimilation to the parallel in Mark, would be certain to slip into the text. If the true reading is that of Syr. S., Matthew has solved the problem of the non-appearance of the Anti-Christ before the destruction of Jerusalem by the simple expedient of omitting Mark's veiled reference (ὅπου οὐ δεῖ) to the Temple. The Anti-Christ expectation is thus entirely detached from any local connection with Jerusalem, and the possibility is left open of interpreting the Abomination prophecy in the light of the Nero-redivivus myth,[1] which, as we shall see shortly, must for geographical reasons have had a peculiar vitality in Antioch.

No Gospel makes so much as does Matthew of the expectation that the visible Return of Christ will be within the lifetime of those who saw and heard Him. It is often said that this is merely the result of a conservative use of the earlier sources which Matthew reproduces. But Matthew never hesitates to omit from or alter Mark, if thereby he can avoid an apologetic difficulty (p. 162), and he often does this to get rid of quite trifling difficulties; much more, then, would he have toned down the passages implying an immediate Parousia if he had desired. But as a matter of fact he has done the exact opposite. He adds a striking passage, " Ye shall not have gone through the cities of Israel, till the Son of Man be come " (Mt. x. 23), which is not in Mark at all. He twice repeats the saying (conflated from Mark and Q), " Watch, for ye know not the day nor the hour." In reproducing Mark he often enhances the immediacy implied. Thus Mark writes, " There be some of them which stand by which shall not taste of death till they see the Kingdom of God come with power " (ix. 1). Luke avoids the difficulty involved in this saying by omitting the last three words, thus interpreting the " Kingdom of God " as the Church; but, as if to preclude any

---

[1] On the development of the Anti-Christ idea, and the prevalence in Christian circles of an identification of Nero with Anti-Christ, see R. H Charles, op. cit. ii. pp. 76-87.

such interpretation, Matthew substitutes " till they see the Son of Man coming in his kingdom." Again, in two other passages (Mt. xxiv. 29 and Mt. xxvi. 64) he adds words of immediacy (εὐθέως and ἀπ' ἄρτι) to the text of Mark.[1]

Again, quite apart from this underlining of passages which speak of the immediacy of the Parousia, Matthew shows his interest in Apocalyptic in other ways. He frequently makes minor alterations in the form of any sayings of Christ of an Apocalyptic character in his sources which bring them more closely into conformity with the conventional model. In the Appendix to the *Oxford Studies* I argued that Q, Mark, and Matthew show an ascending scale in the tendency to emphasise and conventionalise our Lord's Apocalyptic teaching. The cogency of the argument has been questioned so far as it concerns Q, on the ground that, as we do not possess the original text of Q, we cannot say what it did *not* contain. But at least it holds good in the series, Lk. xii. 9 = Mt. x. 33 (representing Q), Mk. viii. 38, and its parallel Mt. xvi. 27. The saying in Q contains the purely ethical warning, " Whosoever denies me before men, him will I deny"; Mark's "Whosoever shall be ashamed of me, etc.," has the same ethical point, reinforced by an Apocalyptic statement, " when he cometh in the glory of his Father with the holy angels." In Matthew the ethical point is *omitted*, but the Apocalyptic statement is further elaborated. But, whatever may be true of Q, it cannot be denied that as between Mark and Matthew there is a heightening of Apocalyptic interest. Thus in Mt. xxiv. 29-31 = Mk. xiii. 25-27 we find the addition by Matthew of various details, like the trumpet, derived from the conventional scenery of Jewish eschatology. Again, Matthew five times uses the phrase συντέλεια τοῦ αἰῶνος, " the end of the world," which does not occur elsewhere in the Gospels ; he six times speaks of " weeping and gnashing of teeth," a phrase which

---

[1] Burkitt (*J.T.S.* xii. p. 460) argues that, read in the context, Matthew's εὐθέως does not imply an earlier date than Mark's "in those days." Nevertheless that Matthew, *having taken the trouble to alter Mark at all*, should use the word " immediately " is significant.

occurs only once in Luke and nowhere else in the New Testament. Nor is it without significance that in chapter xiii. he refrains from pointing the moral of the parables of the Mustard Seed, Leaven, Hid Treasure, and Pearl of Great Price, to all of which it is difficult to give an Apocalyptic interpretation, but goes out of his way to add an explanation in terms of catastrophic eschatology to the parables of the Tares and the Drag Net.

The enhancement of Apocalyptic interest in Matthew is the more remarkable since in other Christian documents—whether earlier than Matthew, like the later Epistles of Paul, or later, like the Fourth Gospel—the delay in the Second Coming was obviously causing less and less emphasis to be laid on this particular element in early Christian belief.   Even in the Apocalyptic chapter of Mark the emphasis is on " the end is not yet."   Mark, like Paul in 2 Thessalonians, urges Christians *not* to mistake present or recent tribulations for the *immediate* prelude of the Second Coming.   The real prelude will be the appearance of Anti-Christ, and even after *his* appearance there will still be an interval. With Matthew it is otherwise.   Urgency is the note all through his Gospel.   But his Apocalyptic is subservient to a moral purpose.   For him " Repent, for the Kingdom of God is at hand," sums up the teaching of John, of our Lord Himself, and of the Twelve—it is the essence of the Christian message.   " Not every man that sayeth unto me, Lord, Lord ; but he that doeth the will " : the Gospel of Matthew is a call for moral reformation on the basis of the ethic of the Sermon on the Mount, in view of the immediacy of the Great Assize—between which and the date of writing perhaps not more than four short years remained. Indeed, from the occurrence of phrases like " There be some of those standing here who shall not taste of death . . . " it is often argued that the Gospel must have been written while some of the Apostles were still alive.   No doubt that was the meaning given to the words when first written.   But once written, as the whole history of the " interpretation of prophecy " shows, a new meaning would inevitably be read into them when the old one manifestly would no longer work.   And in this case the obvious re-interpretation would be that the prophecy meant that, not the Apostles, but some persons of the generation who were actually alive when Christ spoke would survive till the Parousia.   This would extend the date, if necessary, to the end of the century. All then that we can say is that Matthew must have been written during a period of intense Apocalyptic expectation.

This fervour of expectation has, I suggest, a geographical explanation.   Antioch was the eastern gate of the Roman Empire, and, here more than elsewhere, the popular mind was constantly perturbed by rumours that Nero, at the head of the Parthian hosts, was marching against Rome.   The belief that Nero had not really died but was hidden in Parthia awaiting his revenge, or, as the myth developed, that he had died but would rise again, led to the rise of false Neros across the Euphrates.   Three of these pretenders, in 69, in 80, and in 88, are known to history. The fact of their emergence is strong evidence of the persistence and widespread character of the belief.   Nero was not unpopular with the multitude in the provinces; but the Christians, and for good reason, regarded him as the incarnation of the hostility of Satan to the Church of God.   Very soon (p. 520 n.) they combined the popular Nero-redivivus myth with that conception of the Anti-Christ which they had derived from Jewish Apocalyptic. This fusion is already effected in the Apocalypse, and it is there connected with invasions of the Roman Empire from the Euphrates. Antioch, which was far more Jewish than Asia, and which would be first to feel the brunt if the Euphrates line was broken, would certainly be affected by such fears at an earlier date.

DATE OF WRITING

The use of Matthew in the Didache, with the probability that copies of it had reached Ephesus within the lifetime of John the Elder, and that it was also known to the author of Revelation— who, according to both Irenaeus and modern critics, wrote towards the end of the reign of Domitian, who died A.D. 96—makes it difficult to assign to the Gospel a date much later than the year 85. But the internal evidence—so far as the Apocalyptic atmosphere is concerned—would be consistent with any date between that and 75. If we wish a nearer approximation we must interrogate another aspect of the internal evidence.

I have already argued (p. 502 f.) that the fact that hardly any narrative bearing the hall-mark of authenticity seems to have reached Matthew, apart from what he derived from his written sources, rules out a Palestinian origin for the Gospel. But even in Antioch one would have supposed that some independent traditions, obviously genuine, would have been current for a good many years. The only explanation I can suggest of the absence of such from Matthew is that the written Gospel, Mark, had been in use long enough, not only to become the starting-point of the development of new tradition of a Haggadic origin, but by its superior value and prestige to dry up the stream of genuine independent tradition. Twenty years at least seem to me required for this result to have been reached. Again, twenty years seemed (p. 515 f.) a fair time to allow for that reconciliation of parties which the Gospel appears to imply. On the other hand, if we extend the period beyond this, with every decade Mark's authority would be growing, and it becomes increasingly more difficult to explain the liberties which, at times, Matthew takes with the text. When Matthew wrote, Mark was authoritative, but so far from being Scripture, was, as yet, hardly quite a classic.

Now Mark was probably written about 65, and there is no reason why a copy may not have been sent to Antioch almost at once by the Church of Rome. The year 85, we have seen, is the latest date which can, without strain, be reconciled with the external evidence for the existence of Matthew. It is also the earliest date with which the internal evidence naturally accords. Thus we may assign the Gospel to A.D. 85, not as a date mathematically demonstrated, but as one which satisfies all the evidence and conflicts with none.

ACCEPTANCE BY ROME

Of the reception of Matthew at Ephesus we have the contemporary evidence of John the Elder. It may have been a little, but not much later, that the first copy of Matthew reached Rome ; but it does not follow that it was at once accepted there. Matthew challenged comparison, not only with the old local Gospel of Mark, but with Luke, which, as we shall see in the next chapter, was already established there—the more so because, while no claim of Apostolic authorship was put forward for Mark and Luke, such a claim was by this time (as the attitude of the Elder implies) being made for Matthew. If, therefore, Matthew was accepted at all, it could only be as an authority *superior to* Mark and Luke. But Matthew conflicts with Luke at several points, most conspicuously in the matter of the Genealogy of our Lord and—if we are inclined to regard the omission of Lk. i. 34 in *b* to be original (cf. p. 267)—in its affirmation of a Virgin Birth. Unless, then, the new arrival could substantiate its claim to Apostolic, and therefore to superior, authority, it must have been regarded as a book inaccurate on important points, and only the more to be suspected if without warrant it was ascribed to an Apostle.

There exists in Syriac a treatise, wrongly ascribed to Eusebius, entitled " As to the Star : Showing how and by what Means the Magi knew the Star, and that Joseph did not take Mary as his Wife." [1] This describes a conference at Rome on the subject of its title, which is elaborately dated by four separate synchronisms as occurring during the episcopate of Xystus in A.D. 119. The contents of the document have no claim to be considered historical, but Harnack and others think it probable that the date at least is authentic. I hazard the conjecture that it is the date of a conference at which the Roman Church accepted the

---

[1] First published by W. Wright, *Journal of Sacred Lit.*, Oct. 1866. Harnack translates and discusses the relevant passage in *Date of the Acts and Synoptics*, E.T. p. 134 (Williams & Norgate, 1911).

First Gospel as Apostolic on the testimony of representatives of the Church of Antioch.   The martyrdom of Ignatius, Bishop of Antioch, in the Coliseum was then an event of recent memory. His letter to the Roman Church, which became, as Lightfoot shows, a kind of martyr's handbook, had attracted great attention; his enthusiastic admiration of the Roman Church, his emphasis on ecclesiastical discipline, based on obedience to the Bishop, as a safeguard against heresy, would have specially commended the Church of Antioch and its traditions to the consideration of the authorities of Rome.   Once a favourable hearing was secured for the tradition of Apostolic authorship, the Gospel on its merits would seem worthy of an Apostle.   At any rate, by the time of Justin Martyr, the Gospel of Matthew, alongside that of Mark and Luke, is firmly established as one of the accepted Gospels of the Roman Church.   If such a conference between Rome and Antioch really did take place, Antioch would take as well as give, and the claims of Luke could not be overlooked. Basilides, the great Gnostic, and Cerdo, the master of Marcion, both came from Antioch; and both seem to have known and valued Luke.   From this Prof. Bacon [1] infers that Luke was originally an Antiochene work; it is rather, I would suggest, evidence that, before their time, c. A.D. 130, Luke had been accepted as authoritative by Antioch—very possibly on the guarantee of Rome at the same conference at which Rome accepted Matthew as Apostolic on the guarantee of Antioch.

If our conjecture is correct, four stages can be traced in the evolution of the Gospel Canon at Rome—originally Mark alone; by A.D. 90 Mark and Luke; after A.D. 119 the three Synoptics [2]; from about A.D. 170 the Four.   Curiously enough we can also trace four stages in the growth of the Roman *Corpus Paulinum*— the nucleus (Rom., 1 Cor., Eph., *perhaps* Phil.) known already

---

[1] *Expositor*, Oct. 1920, p. 291.

[2] If, as is possible (cf. p. 349), the Longer Ending of Mark is an attempt to conflate the Matthaean and Lucan endings, it must date from this period.

to Clement, A.D. 96 [1] ; the Ten (Marcion's Canon), c. 140 [2] ; the Thirteen (adding I. and II. Tim., Tit.) before A.D. 200 (Muratorian Canon) ; the Fourteen, including Hebrews, c. A.D. 350. But Hebrews was in the Alexandrian *Corpus Paulinum* at least as early as A.D. 160, for the Alexandrian Clement quotes a "blessed elder" as discussing (on the assumption, be it noted, that it is indubitably by Paul) why Paul did not prefix his name.[3] The hesitations on the ground of its non-Pauline style expressed by Clem. Alex. and Origen are those of the scholar criticising an old and accepted tradition. Similarly, as early as Ignatius, Antioch seems to have accepted the Pastorals.[4] Thus, alike in the matter of Gospels and Epistles, Rome was slower than other Churches to accept a claim to Apostolic origin, and we have one more illustration of the importance of studying the history of the books of the New Testament in the great Churches separately.

ADDITIONAL NOTE

The Date of 1 Clement

The Epistle of the Roman Church to the Corinthian, known as 1 Clement, rapidly gained enormous prestige in the East—doubtless because its emphasis on obedience to ecclesiastical rulers deriving their powers by succession from the Apostles (xxxvii.–xlii.) seemed to the Church authorities a thing on which emphasis was much needed. Most probably it is of this letter of the Roman Church that Ignatius is thinking in his extravagant praises of that Church, in particular

[1] The author of Acts, a Roman document (see p. 531 ff.), can hardly have read Galatians and 2 Corinthians. For an argument that Clement of Rome was ignorant of 2 Corinthians cf. J. H. Kennedy, *The Second and Third Letters of St. Paul to the Corinthians*, p. 148 ff. (Methuen, 1900.)

[2] Marcion freely excised passages he disliked, and I cannot believe he would have rejected the Pastorals altogether, if they had been accepted at Rome, when a very little " Bowdlerising " would have sufficed. Also at a still later date Tatian felt he could reject the epistles to Timothy.

[3] Eus. *H.E.* vi. 14.

[4] Besides some almost certain verbal echoes, there is the fact that Ignatius tells the Ephesians (xii. 2) that Paul mentions them " in every letter." As a matter of fact he mentions them twice in 1 Corinthians, and three times in the Pastorals ; so, if the Pastorals are ruled out, his statement becomes meaningless

when he speaks of the Romans as "the instructors of others" (Rom. iii. 1); to Ignatius exhortation to ecclesiastical discipline was the supreme need of the time. Polycarp, again, must have known 1 Clement by heart. A large literature grew up round the name of Clement, who was regarded as the direct disciple of Peter. The early date of the nucleus of this literature, combined with the definite attribution of the letter to Clement by Irenaeus and Dionysius of Corinth, c. A.D. 170 (Eus. *H.E.* iv. 23, 9), affords good evidence that Clement was the writer of the Epistle. Prof. Merrill (*op. cit.* ch. ix.) maintains that his episcopate, and indeed his existence, is an inference (made by Hegesippus) from the mention in Hermas of a certain "secretary Clement." But the Professor accepts the statement of the Muratorian Canon that Hermas was written by a brother of Pius during his episcopate; and Hegesippus came to Rome when Anicetus, the immediate successor of Pius, was Pope. How then, when Hermas was known in Rome to be by the late Pope's brother, could Hegesippus infer that a contemporary of his was third from the Apostles? The "sudden and repeated misfortunes and hindrances" (Clem. i. 1) which delayed the writing of the letter, taken in connection with the prayer for the release of Christian prisoners (lix. 4), is most naturally referred to Domitian's persecution A.D. 96 —on which see footnote, p. 474. Eusebius dates the death of Clement A.D. 100.

Personally, in view of the arguments of Salmon (in *Dict. Christ. Biogr.*) and Bigg (*Origins of Christianity*, ch. viii.), I incline to date Hermas c. 100, and to regard the statement in the Muratorian Canon (by Hippolytus, cf. Lightfoot, *Clement*, ii. p. 407 ff.) as a by-product of anti-Montanist polemic. For the sake of the principle, "the prophets are complete in number," Hermas must be disparaged; and Hippolytus, as we can see from his biographical remarks on Pope Callistus, was one who as a controversialist prized effectiveness above accuracy. Clement would then be contemporary with Hermas and presiding Elder of the Church. I am attracted by Merrill's interesting suggestion (*op. cit.* p. 305) that Hegesippus was the first to compile a formal list of Roman bishops; if so, as he came to Rome before A.D. 166, it is likely that, at least as far back as Clement, his list is correct.

XVIII

LUKE AND ACTS

SYNOPSIS

The Roman Origin of Acts

Acts is not so much a history of the Apostolic Age as of the march of Christianity from Jerusalem to Rome.

Probably known to Clement of Rome A.D. 96.

Objections to the theory that connects Lucan writings with Antioch.

If Theophilus was a Roman noble the Gospel may have been written and addressed to him when Governor of some province. Possibly, therefore, written in Corinth, the capital of Achaea. In that case it would be brought to Rome by the author himself.

Christianity and the Imperial House in Rome, A.D. c. 90. Acts is " the first of the Apologies," *i.e.* of defences of Christianity addressed to the educated Roman world.

Date of the Gospel

Not later than A.D. 85, more likely about A.D. 80.

Authorship

This important for the indirect light which it throws on the local origin of sources of the Gospels. Authorship of Third Gospel bound up with that of Acts. The Tübingen view of Acts made untenable by subsequent research and discussion. The linguistic, archaeological evidence, and that from " undesigned coincidence," cannot even be summarised here ; but considerations, some of them new, are offered, bearing upon the larger issues involved in the question of the Lucan authorship.

I. Twofold error in the Tübingen view. (*a*) Their formula, " thesis, antithesis, and synthesis," involves an *a priori* dogmatic interpretation of history ; but history is an empiric science. (*b*) The actual evidence shows that Peter occupied a middle position between James and Paul—that is, the middle position was the starting-point, not the result, of the divergence. This shown by a consideration of the Cornelius incident and the dispute at Antioch.

II. The evidence of the " we sections " must be considered in connection with (a) the literary methods of the author, (b) the fact that they break off at Philippi, and recommence at this same city.

III. The antinomian language of Paul was balanced by occasional acts of an extremely conciliatory character. Paul's relation to the " Pillar " Apostles and the Apostolic Decree of Acts xv. The Acts is firstly, " the case for the Christian Church," secondly, an *Apologia pro vita Pauli*; as such it conforms in regard to both emphasis and omission to the traditions of ancient biography.

IV. Reply to the objection that the author of Acts could not be Luke because he shows no appreciation of the specifically Pauline theology. (a) There is no evidence, or even probability, that Luke was converted by Paul or had much to do with him until his own religious outlook was fully matured. (b) Only one brought up a Pharisee could really fathom the inner meaning of Paul's theology, and Luke was a Gentile.

V. The Roman origin of Acts opens up a new possibility in regard to the debated question of the relation of Luke and Josephus.

VI. The Preface to the Gospel implies an intention to improve upon the work of Mark. Since Mark and Luke were read together at Rome, the names of both authors must have been used in order to distinguish the two books. Hence (against H. J. Cadbury) the name Luke could not have been arrived at as the result of conjecture in the second century as to the authorship of a previously anonymous work.

VII. It is a principle of historical criticism, in estimating the value of evidence, to make allowance for any possible bias of the witness. In the second century the bias was very strongly in the direction of attributing Apostolic authorship to documents accepted into the Canon. The burden, then, of proof lies with those who would assert the traditional authorship of Matthew and John, but on those who would deny it in the case of Mark and Luke.

CHAPTER XVIII

LUKE AND ACTS

The Roman Origin of Acts

EVERYTHING points to Rome as the Church for which the Acts was written. Considered as a history of the foundation of Christianity, Acts is entirely out of proportion. Not a word is said of Alexandria, while Antioch, the first centre of the Gentile mission and always the capital of Eastern Christianity, drops out of sight so soon as Paul has begun his great movement of expansion north and west. But the Acts is not intended to be a history of the first thirty years of Christianity. It is rather the story of how that religion travelled from Jerusalem, the capital of Jewry, to Rome, the capital of the world. Its aim is to trace the transition of Christianity from a sect of Judaism into a world religion. The points which the author most emphasises are the crucial stages in this development. The Gospel is preached first to a Eunuch, a Jew by blood, but one who might not be a member of the Jewish congregation; then to the half-Israelitish Samaritans; then to Cornelius, a Gentile proselyte of the synagogue; lastly to the Gentile world at large; and this spiritual expansion, we are led to feel, has reached its consummation when, with the two years' preaching of Paul, the Church has been securely, and by apostolic authority, planted in the capital of the world. Lastly, the book ends with the announcement that the Jewish world has finally rejected Christ, with the unuttered implication that the capital of Christianity has been transferred from Jerusalem to

Rome. In a word, the title of the Acts might well have been
" The Road to Rome."

This inference from internal evidence should be taken in
connection with the probability that the Acts was known to
the writer of the letter of the Roman to the Corinthian Church,
c. A.D. 96, ascribed to Clement. His phrase " more glad to give
than to receive " (Clem. ii. 1) seems to allude to the saying of
Christ recorded Acts xx. 35 but not elsewhere. Again, Acts and
Clement agree in conflating 1 Sam. xiii. 14 with Ps. lxxxviii. 21
(Clem. xviii. 1; cf. Acts xiii. 22). Either, then, Clement quotes
Acts or both draw on the same collection of Messianic proof texts.
If the latter, it must have been a collection used in Rome at this
date. More significant is his allusion to Peter and Paul. Of
Paul, Clement (v. 6-7) says, "seven times in bonds, hurried from
place to place, stoned, a preacher in both the East and the
West . . . having taught the whole world righteousness and
reached the farthest limits of the West, and having borne testimony before the governors . . ." The concluding words depend
for their rhetorical effect on the implication that the Apostle
thus fulfilled the prophecy of our Lord : " Before governors and
kings shall ye stand for my sake for a testimony unto them "
(Mk. xiii. 9). It adds still more point to the whole passage if
what goes before is regarded as being a similar allusion to the
words, "Ye shall be my witnesses in Jerusalem, and in all Judaea
and Samaria, and unto the uttermost parts of the earth " (Acts
i. 8), which states the "programme" of the Acts. True, only four
imprisonments—at Philippi, Jerusalem, Caesarea and Rome—
are expressly mentioned in Acts, but the early tradition embodied in the Latin (Marcionite) Prologues added one more in
Ephesus; and there may have been two periods of imprisonment in
Rome. But Clement's arithmetic must not be pressed; "seven" is
a sacred number into conformity with which Jews and Christians
were always trying to squeeze facts. At any rate Clement's description of Paul's labours and sufferings is very much nearer to
the story in Acts than it is to Paul's own summary in 2 Cor. xi. 24 ff.

There is another feature about this passage. Clement (v. 3-5) is quite obviously trying to suggest a parallelism between the sufferings of " the two good Apostles," Peter and Paul. Peter is mentioned first ; but all Clement has to say about him is that he " endured not one nor two but many labours, and having thus borne testimony [1] went to his appointed place of glory." Why has Clement definite details about Paul's sufferings but only vague generalities about those of Peter ? This would be readily explained if Clement knew Acts—which mentions two imprisonments of Peter, but nothing comparable to the long list of sufferings endured and dangers overcome which it records of Paul— but knew nothing definite about Peter beyond what he found in Acts, except the bare fact (and possibly the time and place) of his death.

Eusebius [2] says that Luke was of Antiochene lineage, and the Monarchian Prologue agrees (*Syrus natione*). This may be an inference from the occurrence of a " we section " in the Western text in Acts xi. 28. But, if so, that only means that the early evidence for the Western reading is much increased; and as the reading is very likely correct, the inference may be so too. But no Church writer and no MS. " subscription " says that Luke wrote at Antioch ; and the fact that the connection of Peter with Antioch—the proudest boast of that Church—is completely ignored is fatal to the theory of some modern scholars that the book was written in and for that Church.[3]

But though the Acts is a sequel to the Gospel, it does not necessarily follow that they were written in the same place, or

---

[1] The οὕτω before μαρτυρήσας implies that the verb refers to the labours— not to martyrdom in the strict sense.

[2] τὸ μὲν γένος ὢν τῶν ἀπ᾽ ʼΑντιοχείας (*H.E.* iii. 4).

[3] A few cursives (incl. 124, 346) and some MSS. of the Peshitta state that Luke wrote in Alexandria. This is perhaps an inference from the statement in the *Apostolic Constitutions* that the second bishop of that Church was consecrated by " Luke, who was also an evangelist." But this is a document of Syrian origin and, as there is no at all early Egyptian tradition that connected Luke with Alexandria, it merely constitutes negative evidence that Syrian tradition did *not* connect the writing of the Gospel with Antioch.

that when Luke wrote the Gospel he already anticipated a sequel.
Linguistic considerations, pointed out by Hawkins,[1] and the discrepancy (assuming the B text to be correct) between the Gospel
and Acts in regard to the day of the Ascension, would favour
an interval of time between the two works ; and this may have
corresponded to a change of residence. And there are four
considerations — though none of them is at all conclusive —
which may be urged in support of the view that the Gospel was
written elsewhere than Rome. (1) The possibility—it is no
more (p. 175 ff.)— that Luke had only a mutilated copy of Mark.
(2) The later Latin tradition, found in the Monarchian Prologue
and accepted by Jerome (though Jerome assigns Acts to Rome),
places the writing of the Gospel in Achaea.[2] In view of this it is
unsafe to press the language of Irenaeus (cf. p. 488) as evidence for
a Roman tradition, c. 170, that Luke wrote in that city : the Roman
Church has never been in the habit of surrendering claims once
made. (3) There is also, for what it is worth, the tradition connecting Luke with Boeotia (Thebes). The tomb shown there as his
must have existed a sufficient number of years to make its legend
respectable before the removal of his bones to Constantinople
in the year 357. (4) The absence of reminiscences of the Gospel
in 1 Clement would be explained if its adoption at Rome was
comparatively recent, so that its phraseology had not yet had
time to become part of the texture of Clement's mind. The
name Theophilus in the Lucan Prefaces looks like a prudential
pseudonym for some Roman of position — κράτιστε might
be translated " your Excellence " ; and if Luke had a
special connection with some personage who, after a provincial

---

[1] *Hor. Syn.*[2] p. 177 ff.

[2] This may be merely an inference from the fact that " the brother whose
praise is in the Gospel " (2 Cor. viii. 18), often identified with Luke, is mentioned
in an epistle addressed to Corinth and " the saints which are in the whole of
Achaea " (2 Cor. i. 1). Luke's connection with Achaea is assumed in an address
by Gregory Nazianzen, *Or.* xxxiii. 11, delivered in Constantinople, so that the
belief was current in the East also. Jerome's phrase (Pref. to Commentary on
Matthew) " in the parts of Achaea and Boeotia " is a rather clumsy conflation of
two traditions ; actually Boeotia was a part of the Roman province " Achaea."

governorship (perhaps of Achaea, resident at Corinth), subsequently returned to Rome, all the conditions would be satisfied. But in that case a copy of the Gospel would have been brought to Rome by Luke himself so soon after it was written that, from the point of view of the history of its circulation in the Church at large, it may practically be reckoned as a second Roman Gospel.

The theory that the Lucan writings were primarily written to present the case for Christianity to certain members of the Roman aristocracy is borne out by a consideration of the internal circumstances of the Church in Rome during the latter part of the first century A.D. Domitian was assassinated in September A.D. 96. Eight months before he had scandalised Rome by putting to death T. Flavius Clemens, his own first cousin, the husband of the only daughter of his only sister. Domitian himself was childless, but Clemens and his wife had two sons. These, by the express order of the Emperor, had been named Domitian and Vespasian respectively, after himself and his father, the founder of the dynasty. This, of course, constituted a public avowal of the Emperor's intention that one or other of these boys should ultimately succeed to the throne. In the year A.D. 95 Domitian had associated Flavius Clemens with himself as joint Consul; gossip would make him heir apparent.[1] But secretly Domitilla, the wife of Flavius Clemens, was, if not actually a baptized member, at any rate an adherent, of the Church; and Clemens himself would seem to have been at least an inquirer. The evidence, archaeological and historical, for this remarkable fact is set out at length by Lightfoot,[2] and more recent excavations at Rome suggest that at this particular date members of more than one aristocratic family were interesting themselves in Christianity. This is not quite so surprising as may appear. Juvenal complains of the " Orontes pouring into the Tiber "[3]; and not infrequently in Roman history did some oriental religion, in a more or less subterranean way, be-

[1] That hypothesis would account for Domitian killing him.
[2] *Clement*, vol. i. p. 29 ff.
[3] " Iam pridem Syrus in Tiberim defluxit Orontes " (iii. 62).

come for a time the vogue in the highest society at Rome. About this date Christianity for a few short years seems to have had its turn—perhaps as a result of the general reaction against the spirit of Nero, and the effort of the Court to promote moral reformation which characterised the reign of Vespasian.

Curiously enough, however, it never seems to have occurred to Church historians to ask what is likely to have been the psychological effect, upon a community situated as was the Christian Church of Rome in the first century, of such a connexion with a possible heir to the throne of Caesar and that at a moment when the reigning Caesar was, not only master of the world, but was claiming and receiving the title *Dominus Deus*. Had Domitian died a year before he did, it might have been, not Constantine, but Flavius Clemens, whose name would have gone down to history as the first Christian Emperor. How different in that case might have been the fate both of the Empire and the Church ? For the Church it was perhaps well that its capture of the Palace was postponed from the first century to the fourth. The conversion of Constantine and the state patronage of Christianity which followed were not an unmixed blessing for a Church which had grown to maturity ; to the infant Church they might have been fatal. But even in the time of Constantine no one foresaw these dangers ; while in the first century the accession of a Christian Emperor would have been regarded by Christians not a few as almost the equivalent of the inauguration of the kingdom of God on earth.

A man in the position of Flavius Clemens could only have been led very gradually, step by step, to contemplate such a complete abandonment of national traditions and intellectual and social prejudice as, at that date, would have been involved in accepting Christianity. It would have been easier in Victorian England for Albert Edward, Prince of Wales, to become an avowed disciple of General Booth than for Flavius Clemens under Domitian to be even a secret sympathiser with the Christian Church. Domitilla, his wife, was sent into exile after her husband's execution, and the Church has always reckoned her as a " confessor " ; but Clemens himself, though actually put to death on a religious charge, was not reckoned as a martyr.   From this we may safely infer that the husband, at least, had never been actually baptized, nor in any way publicly avowed his adhesion to Christianity.   What was noted about him, say secular historians, was a marked abstention from the public duties expected of a man in his position.   This abstention is attributed by Suetonius to laziness ; more probably it was due to the fact that public life at Rome necessarily involved participation in pagan sacrifices and amusements like gladiatorial shows, in which any one who was at all attracted towards Christianity would have found it more and more difficult conscientiously to take part.

But we are not here concerned with the views or feelings of Clemens himself.   What we have to consider is the probable effect on Christians at Rome of the fact that the wife of the heir to the throne was a member of their despised community, and of the hope that her husband might soon become one.   When Paul wrote to the Corinthians, " not many mighty, not many noble " were members of their calling ; and the letters which he writes, though to our taste vigorous and effective in style, would not altogether pass muster according to the conventional rules of writing on which at that period so much stress was laid in educated circles.   Still less would the Gospel of Mark—the only account which the Roman Church possessed of the life of Christ— the Greek style of which is, next to Revelation, easily the worst in the New Testament.   Once Christianity began to reach members of the high aristocracy, there would arise a new and insistent demand for a Life of Christ which would not only jar less on the literary taste of educated circles, but would also make it clearer than does Mark that Christ was, and knew Himself to be, no mere Jewish Messiah, but a World-saviour, the founder of a world-religion.   The Third Gospel is an attempt, and an extraordinarily successful one, to meet this demand.

Again, to the Roman nobility the Church would appear to be
a society of peculiarly sordid origin. The Roman despised the
Jew, and he despised everything new-fangled. Christianity had
the reputation of being both Jewish and new-fangled. Worse
than that, Nero had been able to make scapegoats of the Christians
precisely because there existed a popular belief that they were a
society of secret criminals, who, even if not actually responsible
for the burning of Rome, were at any rate quite capable of desiring
or attempting such an exploit. Lastly, Nero's action had created
a precedent, or at least established a presumption, associating
Christianity and crime ; and a Roman noble, let alone one like
Flavius Clemens who was soon to be responsible for the supreme
administration of the Empire and its laws, had a great respect
for law and precedent. The Acts tells the story of the beginnings
of the Church in a way which unobtrusively presents the answer
to these objections. It shows that Christianity, though it no
doubt began in Palestine, is not really a Jewish but a universal
religion ; nor can it be derided as " new-fangled." Though in one
sense recent, it is the fulfilment of an ancient purpose of the God
of the whole earth—a purpose adumbrated by an age-long series
of prophecies. Precisely because it is essentially a universal
religion, the Jews—who must know best what their own religion
is—have rejected Christ, have persecuted His Apostles, and have
opposed His religion at every stage. Peter had difficulties with
Jewish Christians; Paul was bitterly persecuted by Jews; simply
because those two Apostles had always by word and deed showed
that they regarded Christianity, not as a Jewish, but as a world-
religion. Thus Christianity is neither Jewish nor new-fangled—
indeed, seen in its relation to prophecy, it is of immemorial
antiquity. Nor, again, is it anti-Roman or illegal. Christ was
accused before Pilate of " forbidding to give tribute to Caesar
and saying that he is himself a King " (Lk. xxiii. 2). The Roman
Procurator examines the case and three times declares him
guiltless. Again and again Paul, brought before Roman magis-
trates and accused by the malice of the Jews (Acts xvii. 7)

of fomenting sedition, has been declared guiltless in Roman
law.

It requires very little historical imagination to see that the
Gospel of Luke and the Acts are precisely the kind of literature
which would be needed by the Church in Rome if it was to
make further headway in the circle in which Clemens and
Domitilla were the leading figures.   Indeed, it is not impossible
that Theophilus was the secret name by which Flavius Clemens
was known in the Roman Church.   Theophilus (= devoted to
God) would be a most appropriately chosen name.   It has a
more complimentary sound than $\theta\epsilon\sigma\sigma\epsilon\beta\eta\varsigma$ or " proselyte " ; it
just falls short of definitely asserting quite as much, and at the
same time, being in actual use as a proper name, it had the
advantage of being something of a disguise ; and the title $\kappa\rho\acute{a}\tau\iota\sigma\tau\epsilon$,
" Your Excellence," implies that the person addressed was one
of high position.   Whether, however, " Theophilus " was Clemens
himself, or some other member of the high aristocracy, the Acts
is really *the first of the Apologies*.   It is a forerunner of that series
of " Defences of Christianity," addressed to reigning emperors
and members of the Imperial House, which constitutes the larger
part of the surviving Christian literature of the second century.
On this view its ending, which otherwise seems so flat and pointless, is full of meaning.   It is in a spirit of justifiable exultancy
that its author leads up to the final words of Paul—which, now
that the heir apparent was an inquirer, would seem prophecy
fulfilled—" Behold, we go to the Gentiles, they *will* hear."   And
the calm confidence of the last two verses reflects the high hopes
of what will happen under a Christian Caesar, as Luke records
how, even under Nero, it had been possible for two years at
Rome to proclaim Christianity $\mu\epsilon\tau\grave{a}\ \pi\acute{a}\sigma\eta\varsigma\ \pi\alpha\rho\rho\eta\sigma\acute{\iota}\alpha\varsigma\ \grave{a}\kappa\omega\lambda\acute{\upsilon}\tau\omega\varsigma$,
" with absolute freedom and without restraint." [1]   Thus read,
the end of Acts is a real climax.

---

[1] It is not possible to render in English the strong rolling rhythm of the
Greek.   A Greek tragedy ends thus with words of " good omen " on a note of
calm.

DATE OF THE GOSPEL

The date of the Gospel is determined as not being earlier than A.D. 70 by the alterations which Luke makes in the prophecy of the Abomination of Desolation. And here it is important to think clearly. Harnack and others have urged that there is nothing about the Fall of Jerusalem in Luke xxi. 20 ff. (or in xix. 41 ff.) which could not have been written before A.D. 70. Quite true; but the point to notice is that Luke, who in the context is closely following Mark, suddenly begins to modify the language of his source in an unusually drastic way, with the result that what in Mark xiii. is a prophecy of the appearance of the Anti-Christ in the Temple becomes, in Luke's version, a prophecy of the destruction of Jerusalem and of the enslavement of its population. Now, seeing that in A.D. 70 the appearance of the Anti-Christ did *not* take place, but the things which Luke mentions *did*, the alteration is most reasonably explained as due to the author's knowledge of these facts.

On the other hand, the Gospel of Luke was, we have seen (p. 407 f.), already on the way to becoming a standard work in the Church of Ephesus when the Fourth Gospel was written. If, then, John cannot be dated later than A.D. 95, Luke cannot be much later than A.D. 85. It will appear shortly that a date later than A.D. 90 is not very likely for Acts; hence as the Gospel was written first, we arrive by another route at A.D. 85 as a probable limit. If, however, the Gospel was written some years before the Acts, before Luke returned to Rome and as soon as he came across a copy of Mark, a date like A.D. 80 seems more likely.

AUTHORSHIP

But in the case of the Third Gospel the questions of the date and actual place of writing are of less interest than that of authorship, for two reasons. (1) The author of the Gospel also wrote the Acts, and in large portions—the so-called " we sections "

--of that work he writes in the first person, as if to imply that he was himself present on those occasions. If, then, Luke was the author of the Acts, he lived in Caesarea for two years during Paul's imprisonment there; and this—taken in connection with the nature of the material in question—would make it morally certain that the source we have called L consists largely of information he there collected. (2) If Luke came originally from Antioch, the hypothesis that Q was an Antiochene document is considerably strengthened. For Luke would naturally begin by combining the teaching source of his old Church with his Caesarean material— thus forming Proto-Luke ; and he would inevitably regard Mark, when he came across it later, as a less authoritative source. And this is precisely what a critical analysis of our Third Gospel suggests. Thus the question of the authorship of Luke has in two respects an important bearing on the identification of the locality of origin of the sources embodied in the Third Gospel.

The authorship of Acts, however, cannot be discussed without raising the large issue, whether, and to what extent, inaccuracies and misconceptions of the historical development of the Apostolic Age are to be found in that book, and how far the existence of such is compatible with authorship by a companion of Paul. Such compatibility was vehemently denied by F. C. Baur, and his followers of the " Tübingen School." The first effectively to expose the brilliant fallacies of Tübingen was Renan in his book *The Apostles*, 1866. Renan the sceptic, educated for the priest-hood among the Breton peasants—where miracle is a matter of everyday expectancy—gifted also with a real feeling for style and character, had the requisite combination of freedom from apologetic bias and sympathy with the atmosphere of a believing age to approach the problem from the purely literary and historical point of view. But the Tübingen School were so en-meshed in the Hegelian conception that history moves in accord-ance with the formula " thesis, antithesis, and synthesis "— of which I shall say something shortly—that even to the present day their disciples have never quite succeeded in approaching the question in a purely critical and historical spirit. In the meantime, from the standpoint of linguistic analysis and archaeological research, Hawkins, Ramsay, Harnack and others have been steadily piling up an accumulation of evidence favouring the Lucan authorship. I should have thought the evidence was quite conclusive; it was, therefore, with a good deal of surprise that I read the judgement by the learned editors of *The Beginnings of Christianity* (vol. ii. p. 358) that, though ten years ago they " felt reasonably sure that the Acts was actually written by Luke, the companion of Paul," they had slowly come round to the view that only " the ' we sections ' and probably the narrative adhering to them " are his work.

The evidence from language, archaeology, " undesigned coincidences," etc., for the Lucan authorship is familiar to students; but being of a cumulative character it could not possibly be presented in the space at my disposal. I propose, therefore, to confine myself to some remarks on certain of the larger issues, in particular those which, I gather, weigh most with such of the contributors to the above-mentioned work as reject the Lucan authorship.

I. The discussion is still haunted by the ghost of F. C. Baur; it is time this ghost was laid. Near the beginning of the chapter (vol. ii. p. 299) of *The Beginnings of Christianity* entitled " The Case against the Tradition " occurs the following sentence:

The element of greatness in the Tübingen criticism is to be found in the unity of the fundamental ideas by which it is dominated. We have to deal not with a rationalistic criticism of details, but with a brilliantly chosen point of view from which to examine and interpret the whole of the apostolic and post-apostolic age. In accordance with the Hegelian watchword that all which happens is determined by the sequence, *Thesis, antithesis, synthesis*, the Tübingen School constructed two periods: the first was one of embittered conflict between Paul and the Judaisers, who were at one with the original Apostles; and the second was a period of conciliation, which gradually made itself effective and marked the transition from primitive Christianity to Catholicism.

In the course of the chapter—which I may, perhaps, be allowed to characterise as able, fair-minded, and incredibly learned—Professor Windisch himself refutes one after another the actual conclusions of the Tübingen School ; the one thing he thinks can be saved from the wreck is their denial of Lucan authorship. For myself I have no quarrel either with the date, " the period of the eighties or nineties of the first century," which he suggests, or, except in some points of detail, with his general estimate of its historical value—so far, at least, as the last three-fifths of the book is concerned. It is the very merits of the Professor's discussion of the subject which impelled me to exclaim, However did the sentence I have just quoted come to be written by any-one who had seriously reflected on the principles of criticism or on the nature of historical method ?

History is the endeavour to find out what actually happened, not to force upon the evidence an *a priori* point of view—however " brilliantly chosen." The characteristic singled out by the Professor as constituting " the element of greatness " in the Tübingen criticism is precisely the one which all but deprives it of any right to be styled *historical* criticism at all. History written " in accordance with the Hegelian watchword that all which happens is determined by the sequence ' thesis, antithesis, synthesis,' " is not history at all. It is dogma disguised as history ; it is " tendency-writing " of a far more misleading character than anything produced by the apologetic or theological bias of the writers whose view of history the critic professes to correct. One might as well say that " the element of greatness " in the editor of the books of Kings is " the brilliantly chosen point of view " which interprets the whole of the history of Israel in accordance with the Deuteronomic " watchword " that national prosperity and adversity are determined solely by obedience to the Law of the Central Sanctuary.

The Tübingen criticism was great, not because of, but in spite of, its " unity of fundamental ideas." It created an epoch in New Testament study through its appreciation of two points.

First, the literature of early Christianity must be interpreted in relation to the practical and apologetic needs of the time; secondly, there is a development of theology within the New Testament itself, of which the Fourth Gospel is the crown. Owing, however, to the *a priori* " unity of conception," which Professor Windisch styles its greatness, this school completely misconceived the nature of those practical and apologetic needs; and it was thus led entirely to misrepresent both the causes and the course of that very evolution which it had the merit of being the first to detect.

Karl Marx was a contemporary of F. C. Baur, and he wrote the economic history of Europe on the basis of this same Hegelian triad of thesis, antithesis, synthesis. He, too, made an ideal construction of two periods. The former was a period of embittered conflict between the " thesis " of capitalism and the " antithesis " of proletarian revolt. The latter was to be the " synthesis "—a period of universal brotherhood and goodwill, automatically resultant on the success of the class war. But recent events have shown that, in real life, things do not work out quite that way.

In the science of pure logic this business about thesis and antithesis has some real meaning. As applied to history it is a pedantic way of describing that tendency to react against the fashion last in vogue which politicians call " the swing of the pendulum." But it is worse than pedantic, it is seriously misleading; it ignores the fact that the pendulum only swings because there is a relatively stable pivot upon which to oscillate. In all communities where there is vigorous life three parties are always to be found—the " die-hards," the " moderates," and the " red revolutionaries." If the society manages to hold together, it is usually because the majority hold something resembling the moderate, *i.e.* the " synthetic," view, and in the long run this in the main prevails. But I know no case in history where this has happened—except, perhaps, under the strong hand of an autocratic power—unless the synthetic party, or at least the synthetic spirit, has, though dormant for a time, been there from the beginning. The spirit of conciliation is not a thing that is born of internecine conflict.

The Epistle to the Galatians shows that at the date when it was written there was acute division of opinion with regard to the obligation of the Mosaic Law, especially as it affected the position of Gentiles in the Church. Paul is the leader of the progressives, James of the conservatives, while the leader of the moderates is Peter.

And if the question be asked, which of these is the more primitive ? the answer is contained in the simple observation that Peter was one of those who forsook all to follow Christ ; while James was one of the brethren who in his lifetime did not believe in Him, and even went so far on one occasion as to endeavour to arrest Him on hearing that He was of unsound mind. It would seem, then, that in this case the tendency which Baur would style "synthesis" was earlier in date than both the "thesis" (Judaistic Christianity) and the "antithesis" (Paulinism) which, according to the Hegelian programme, it ought to have succeeded.

But among men of goodwill it is usually the case that the leaders of any party are far less intolerant than the rank and file and far more inclined to stretch a point in order to meet their opponents half-way. It was so in the early Church. James, Peter, and John—observe the order in which they are mentioned (Gal. ii. 9)—gave Paul and Barnabas "the right hands of fellowship," having "perceived the grace that was given" them. They even went so far as to urge them to collect alms from Gentiles for the poor Christians of Jerusalem. We may be pretty sure, then, that those followers of James, who in his name protested against Peter's associating with Gentiles in Antioch, went to the full limit of their instructions. Again, there is no evidence that the persons who visited the Galatian and Corinthian Churches depreciating Paul and denying his Apostleship, did so with the authorisation of the older Apostles. At Corinth there were

2 N

factions who said " I am of Peter " and " I am of Paul " ; but Paul himself is emphatic in declining to recognise the difference as important.

Nothing better illustrates the *a priori* " dogmatic element," as opposed to the empirical historic, in the Tübingen School than their rejection of the story of the conversion of Cornelius at Caesarea as legendary, or to be accepted with the utmost hesitation, on the ground (*a*) that it attributes to Peter an attitude towards Gentiles of which at that date only Paul was capable ; (*b*) that guidance by a Vision is a sign of legend. So far as visions are concerned, the turning points in the lives of half the saints have been accompanied by visions regarded by them as expressions of Divine direction; and in India and Africa to-day the same thing happens. These things are partly a matter of individual psychology, partly of race and training ; and it so happens, as I am arguing elsewhere,[1] that this particular Vision conforms to the laws of dream psychology in a way which guarantees it as a reasonably accurate report of an authentic experience.

As regards the major issue, why, we ask, if Peter was incapable of the attitude implied in the story, is he found at Antioch a few years later ? Why, until pressure is brought upon him by the adherents of James, is he content to be eating and drinking with Gentiles in that city—as though he shared Paul's view of the relative unimportance of the ceremonial law ? Peter's visit to Antioch is not once mentioned in the Acts ; it is attested by the irrefutable evidence of Galatians. But Antioch is a long way from Jerusalem, and Peter's behaviour there in regard to Gentiles is a very big step away from orthodox Jewish legalism. Geographically Caesarea is the half-way house to Antioch ; psychologically the conversion of Cornelius and the need of justifying it to the Pharisaic Christians at Jerusalem is the half-way house to Peter's attitude at Antioch. So far, then, from being historically suspicious, the Cornelius incident is the missing

---

[1] See Appendix, " Dream Psychology and the Mystic Vision," in my book *Reality* (Macmillan, 1926).

link without which the behaviour of Peter, as attested by
Galatians, is psychologically inexplicable.

Under pressure from " certain who came from James," Peter
at Antioch went back on his pro-Gentile liberalism. It was
doubtless represented to him that if he continued thus openly
to break the law he would ruin all possibility of converting " the
circumcision " to Christ. Peter has been much abused for
giving way ; but in all probability those who urged this judged
the situation correctly. Peter was really face to face with the
alternative of, either ceasing to eat and drink with Gentiles, or
wrecking that mission to the circumcised which he felt to be his
primary call (Gal. ii. 9). Is he to be blamed because he declined
that risk ? To Paul, Peter's conduct seemed a disingenuous
abandonment of the principle of the equality of Jew and Gentile
before Christ—a principle which for him was involved in the
religious experience of the sufficiency for salvation of Faith
without the Works of the Law. But Paul's theoretical formulation of the relation between Faith and Works is, as the history
of later theology and exegesis shows, a difficult and a subtle
concept. It is highly improbable that, at any rate in that
abstract form, it had ever entered Peter's head. But to Paul its
courageous assertion seemed vital for the success of the Gentile
mission—and from his point of view he was undoubtedly right.
The fact is that the relations of Jew and Gentile since the persecution of Antiochus Epiphanes and the Maccabean revolt had
brought things to such a pass that to surrender the obligation
of the Law meant the failure of the Jewish mission, while to
retain it was to sacrifice the Gentile. It was one of those tragic
situations that do sometimes occur when the best men for the
best motives feel compelled to differ upon a vital issue.

II. The decisive issue in the determination of the Lucan
authorship is not, primarily, the value to be attached to a
traditional ascription of authorship, however ancient and well
attested. It is, in the first place, the question what is the best
and most natural explanation of the occurrence of the first person

plural in certain of the later chapters of the Acts. The natural
and obvious explanation is that the author wishes, without unduly
obtruding his own personality, to indicate that he is himself the
authority for that part of the story. In view of the emphasis
which he lays upon eye-witness in the preface to the Gospel, it is
explicable that he should attach importance to it also in the
Acts, when it could be indicated without any clumsy quotation
of authorities.

An alternative explanation of the " we sections " is that the
author is incorporating the diary of an eye-witness written in
the first person, and has forgotten to alter the first person to the
third ; or rather, seeing that the " we sections " do not in themselves make a connected and coherent story but are bound
together by those that intervene, it must be supposed that he has
sometimes remembered and sometimes forgotten to make the
necessary alterations. In an ill-educated, clumsy, and careless
compiler, or one, like the editor of the book of Nehemiah, who
pieced together matter from his different sources on a purely
mechanical " scissors and paste " method, this would be conceivable. But the author of the Gospel and Acts, though not,
as has been rashly alleged, " a great historian " in the modern
sense, is a consummate literary artist.[1] One of the sources which
he used for his Gospel was Mark. As this is still preserved, we
are enabled to study his methods of using sources. Nothing
could be further removed from " scissors and paste." The
material derived from Mark is completely re-written in Luke's
own characteristic style. The way in which, by trifling modifications of his original, he removes either faulty grammar or literary
obscurities or passages which might cause disquiet of an apologetic character, shows an acute sense of the subtlest nuances
of language and style. Accordingly, if in another work by the

[1] " A professional writer," " a skilled adapter," are phrases used of him by
Prof. Windisch (*op. cit.* ii. p. 337 f.). But the Professor cannot have it both
ways—if the author is a skilled workman, then the " we sections " are not due to
a careless oversight, they have a meaning.

same author we find the first person occurring in a series of passages where the third might have been expected, we must conclude that it is not there by accident. It is meant to suggest a meaning. It occurs in the brief section (Acts xvi. 10-18) in-cluding the voyage from Troas to Philippi and what happened there; then it completely disappears for four chapters, to reappear again at exactly the same geographical spot when, on his return journey some years afterwards, Paul again passes through Philippi (xx. 5). It then continues, except in scenes and on occasions when Paul might naturally be supposed to have been unattended, until the end of the book. This cannot be accidental. It is done with the express purpose of suggesting that the author was in the company of Paul for the whole of the concluding period covered by the narrative, but was not in his company on any previous occasion, except for the brief voyage from Troas and the visit to Philippi years before. That an actual companion of Paul should have been with him on these occasions, and on these only, is in no way improbable. That a person, who wished to create the impression that he had been a companion of Paul in order to give weight to his story, should limit his claim to be an eye-witness in this extraordinary way is quite incredible.

III. Paul was one of those great men who are a source of anxiety to their friends. His language at times was most " im-politic." Some of the things he said about the Law were enough to make the hair of a pious Jew positively stand on end. Suppose a modern preacher were to say something like this : " The Bible had its function in the Divine economy, but the salvation it offered was always unreal. The Bible is now obsolete ; there is no longer such a thing as a revealed moral code ; henceforth you are free from the bonds of the old religion. Believe, and do what you will—that is the good news I bring you." Such a man would be promptly ejected from the ministry. But if for " Bible " we write " Law," and for " salvation " " justifica-tion "—and to a Jew these are the true equivalents—that is exactly what Paul did say. And to the average Jew the fact that Paul tempered these statements with qualificatory remarks, as that " the Law is just and holy and good," or that he insistently exhorted men to a life of righteousness, did not much affect the issue. If the Law is abrogated, it *is* abrogated, it matters little how politely it is bowed out ; and if in the last resort every man is free to do what is right in his own eyes, it is a small thing that Paul's personal standard happens to be high.

The wonder is, not that the affair caused trouble in the early Church, but that James, Peter, and John, after hearing him explain his position, still felt able to give Paul " the right hands of fellowship " (Gal. ii. 9). Paul must have been exceptionally conciliatory on that occasion. He was conciliatory at times. He was a man of passionate outbursts ; and when conciliation was his mood, he would go to lengths—the circumcising of Timothy is an example—which principle could hardly justify. " To the Jews I became as a Jew, to those that are under the Law as under the Law, if so by any means I might save some." Some pretty big concessions must have been in his mind when he wrote this—perhaps some that he regretted. I do not think Paul ever set his hand to the food-law compromise of the Apostolic Decree (Acts xv. 29), written out in black and white. But it is quite likely that it does represent the agreement reached between him and the Three at Jerusalem, as interpreted and afterwards put in writing and circulated by them. We all know what sometimes happens when " complete agreement " is reached at an " informal conversation," and each party afterwards writes down his own interpretation. That seems to me the point of James's reference to the Decree (Acts xxi. 20-25) ; he delicately insinuates that Paul is reputed to be not quite loyal to the agreement, and exhorts him to do some act which will make it clear to all men that he did not wish to repudiate observance of the Law so far as Jews are concerned. Luke, we note, was present at this interview (Acts xxi. 17 ff.), and it is a natural inference that he derived his conception of events (including the Council of Acts

xv.) from what James then said—re-writing the scene in the
form of a debate, after the manner of ancient historians.   Luke
no doubt is in error; Paul had not set his seal to any compact—
the Decree had been sent out later—but he had, perhaps, in his
private conversations left the Three with the impression that he
had assented to its substance.   And if Luke gathered this from
James's speech, and Paul did not at the time vehemently repudiate
it, his error is a pardonable one.

Luke is also accused of misrepresenting Peter.   But does he ?
In the *Quo vadis* legend is crystallised the popular impression of
Peter—a wobbler, but on the right side in the end.   Peter, with
hesitation it is true, baptizes the Gentile Cornelius.   A little
later he is found at Antioch eating and drinking with Gentile
Christians—and thereby, of course, himself transgressing the Law
of Moses.   This is too much for James.   If Peter is going to
give up keeping the Law, the mission to the Circumcision—
already jeopardised by the antinomianism of Paul—will be
totally wrecked.   He sends a deputation to remonstrate.   Peter
—realising no doubt that what they say is true, and that
if he persists he *will* wreck the Jewish Mission—withdraws,
to the intense indignation of Paul.   About the same time a
mission goes round the Pauline Churches—with the cognisance,
we must suppose, if not at the prompting, of James—to try
and bring them round to a sounder view of the Law ; and
the emissaries roundly deny the claim of Paul to the name of
Apostle at all.

But there is nothing at all about this in Acts !   Why ?
Obviously, replies one school of critics, because its author belonged to a later age when these things were forgotten.   That
answer is possible ; but it strikes me as a little naïve.   The
silence of Luke is susceptible of another interpretation.   In real
life there are things one does not mention because they are
too well known—things of which the proverb holds good, "The
least said, the soonest mended."   The most interesting incidents
in the career of a public character are often those which his

biographer is too discreet to print. And if that is so in our own
age—with its tradition of realism in literature, and its conception
of history as a branch of science—how much more so in an age
in which the idealist tradition in art and letters reigned supreme,
and in which the main purpose of history was supposed to be
moral instruction.[1] The Acts was not written to record the
things which would interest a modern critic, but, in the first place,
to provide a Roman noble with the case for the Christian Church;
and threatened institutions cannot afford to advertise internal
" scandals." Moreover, it looks as if the author had also to
consider the feelings of some difficult brethren inside the Church.
A secondary purpose of the book is quite evidently to be an
Apologia pro vita Pauli.

The hostility of the Judaistic party had pursued Paul to Rome.
They were active during his imprisonment (Phil. i. 15 ff., iii. 2).
If he calls them " dogs "—not a term of endearment in the East
—we may be sure he was driven to it by sore provocation. We
can only guess at some of the things they had said of him—the
least would have been to accuse one who maintained that the
Law was abolished of wishing to abolish morality itself. And
judging by the standard of veracity in what Greek and Latin
orators say of one another, we may be pretty certain that they
accused him of abolishing morality in practice as well as theory.
If the Acts was written when this opposition had not quite
died out, and when the reconciliation of the reconcilable was so
recent that the situation was still delicate, a motive becomes
apparent for the "dragging in" of certain trifling incidents quite
irrelevant to the main course of the story. Why are we told
so carefully that Paul circumcised Timothy, shaved his head
in Cenchreae, was so anxious to attend the Passover, defrayed
the expenses of a ceremonial purification ? Because at the

[1] Livy, *Praef.* 7, " hoc illud est praecipue in cognitione rerum salubre ac
frugiferum, omnis te exempli documenta in illustri posita monumento intueri:
inde tibi tuaeque reipublicae quod imitere capias, inde . . . quod vites."
Tacitus, *Ann.* iii. 65, " quod praecipuum munus annalium reor, ne virtutes
sileantur, utque pravis dictis factisque ex posteritate et infamia metus sit.'

time when Acts was written it was necessary to prove to many excellent folk that Paul was not anything like so black as he was painted ; he was not the antinomian his enemies made out. Not only did he keep the moral law, at times he went out of his way to keep the ceremonial as well.

Peter's position also required explanation. He had committed himself to the Gentile mission ; but later on he had rather gone back on this—and no doubt the Judaisers exaggerated the extent of his withdrawal. Precisely because his later attitude was a shade ambiguous, it was necessary to emphasise the Cornelius incident for all that it was worth in order to show that after all it was Peter who, led by a Divine vision, himself in a sense initiated the Gentile mission.

The Acts reads like a vindication both of Peter and of Paul by one who realises that, up to a point, they had laid themselves open to criticism, but who nevertheless has for them that almost religious veneration which the East still has towards the teacher and the prophet.[1] By the time that 1 Clement was written Peter and Paul are " the good Apostles," almost ranking with the heroes of the Old Testament. We infer that the period when Peter and Paul required defending at Rome was well over by A.D. 96. Acts — known, I suggest, to Clement — had done its work. This would favour a date earlier, rather than later, than A.D. 90.

IV. The Acts shows very little trace, the Third Gospel none at all,[2] of anything that we can call specifically Pauline Christianity. The question, then, arises, can Acts have been written by a pupil of Paul ? But, I submit, to ask the question in this form involves a fallacy ; for there is not the slightest hint in the Acts that the author of the "we sections" was in any sense a " pupil "

[1] It has been argued that the veneration with which the Apostles are regarded implies a late date for Acts. But Gandhi in his lifetime is a Mahatma—i.e. all but an incarnation—and Rabindranath Tagore is saluted by his admirers as *guru deva*, literally " teacher god."

[2] If, that is, with Hort we reject xxii. 19b, 20 as an assimilation from 1 Cor. xi. 24 f. ; om. D Old Lat. and (partly) Old Syr.

of the Apostle. The way in which the " we " suddenly appears would be far more natural if he was already a Christian when he first met Paul. If the Western text of Acts xi. 28 is original—and it is more easy to explain the excision in B א Byz. than the addition in D Lat. of " there was great rejoicing ; and when we were gathered together "—he was a member of the congregation at Antioch to which Agabus prophesied the famine of A.D. 46. Five or six years later he "happens"—I use the word advisedly —to meet Paul at Troas and (Acts xvi. 10 ff.) travels in the same boat as the Apostle to Philippi, where apparently he at that time resided. Of course he would become a member of the Church founded there by the Apostle in his very brief visit. Five or six years later still (Acts xx. 6) he joins Paul on his way through Philippi to Jerusalem, most probably being chosen by that Church to accompany Paul and the delegates from other Churches to Jerusalem, in order to present their contribution toward that collection from the Gentile Churches which Paul had for some time past been organising.

So far there is nothing to suggest any specially close personal connection with the Apostle. But at Jerusalem Paul is arrested —and Paul is the greatest champion of Gentile liberty and the most successful leader in the Gentile mission. Calamity elicits new loyalties. Luke henceforth devotes himself to the service of the Apostle, and is constant to the end—" only Luke is with me " (2 Tim. iv. 11).

But it does not for a moment follow that he accepted Paul's characteristic theology. If Luke had been converted to Christianity fifteen years or so before the time when he became really intimate with Paul, we should not expect him in any fundamental way to change his own religious outlook. There is a further consideration : Luke first met Paul shortly before he wrote 1 Thessalonians, and he was in his company years later when he wrote the Epistles of the Captivity. Now if we only possessed the letters written by Paul at the time Luke knew him best we should never have heard of " justification by faith " and the whole cycle of conceptions linked up with that phrase. Hence, if Paul's letters reflect at all adequately the oral teaching he was giving at the time he wrote them, it would not have been surprising if Luke had said nothing at all about the above-mentioned doctrine. But, as a matter of fact, in the first speech he assigns to Paul, in the synagogue at the lesser Antioch—which, of course, he means to be understood as giving, not the speech actually delivered there, but the line of argument Paul employed when addressing a Jewish audience—he makes this doctrine the climax to which the whole speech leads up. But he does not attempt to elaborate it, for two obvious reasons. (a) If Acts was written at Rome, it was written for a Church where the Epistle to the Romans was already a classic. The mention of "justification by faith" was equivalent to saying "as expounded in Romans." As Luke was compressing thirty years of Church history into a document which occupies that number of pages in a Greek Testament, he had better use for his scanty space than to attempt a " potted version " of the argument of an Epistle with which his audience were already perfectly familiar. (b) It is highly improbable that Luke had any clear appreciation of the real significance of this aspect of Paul's thought—at any rate it is a commonplace of theologians that no other church writer had it before Augustine, and he only in part. This aspect of Paulinism is, of its very nature, a reaction against a religion of Law centring round a sacrificial system related to a deeply ethical sense of guilt. Mediaeval Latin Catholicism was another such religion, and, therefore, Luther understood this side of Paul ; but no Greek ever did, or ever could—so why should Luke ? What Luke and the Gentile Church of his time deduced from Romans was the conclusion that the Mosaic Law was abrogated by Christ ; but the more heartily people welcome a conclusion, the less need they often feel for really comprehending the argument by which it is reached.

A critical historian should, unless the contrary be proved, assume that the speeches in Acts are " Thucydidean," and are to be understood in the same way as the speeches in any contemporary historian—that is to say, though they are written "in character," their real purpose is to afford the historian an opportunity for inculcating ideas which he himself wishes to express. Theologians have often called attention to the primitive Christology of the speeches attributed to Peter—but doctrinally there is no essential difference between them and those attributed to Paul. How could there be? No one in those days had any notion of an "evolution of theology"; to Luke, as to all his contemporaries, that which was true was Apostolic and, therefore, also primitive. The theology underlying the speeches of Acts—and, of course, for this purpose the speeches attributed to Peter must be supplemented by that ascribed to Paul on the Areopagus—should be read as a presentation of Luke's own theology. That is precisely their value to the historian. To the Fathers Luke is the echo of Paul, to the Tübingen School he stands for post-apostolic Christianity; but those early speeches in Acts are too primitive for that—they represent the average Gentile Christianity of Antioch.

What Acts really represents—modified a little by later experience and touched only here and there with a phrase caught up from Paul—is *pre-Pauline Gentile Christianity*. But given the life-history of its author which a natural reading of Acts suggests —that is what we should expect of the Syrian physician Luke.[1]

V. If the Lucan writings were first circulated in Rome it

[1] Since the War we have all become so much accustomed to glaring discrepancies between the accounts of the same event by persons presumably truthful and undoubtedly well-informed, that the sting has been drawn from the pet arguments of the older critics that the existence of discrepancies between Acts and the Epistles proves that Luke could not have been in personal contact with Paul. There is only one such that need concern us—the visits of Paul to Jerusalem and the Apostolic Decree of Acts xv. I mention this because I can neither follow Harnack in accepting the Western text of the Decree (by which it ceases to be a compromise relating to unclean meats), nor would I commit myself unreservedly to the theory of Ramsay—further developed by Emmet—that the visit mentioned in Galatians ii. is the famine visit in Acts. Luke appears to think Paul had assented to the food-law compromise. I have already suggested how we can explain this mistake. There remains, however, the minor discrepancy in the number of visits to Jerusalem. Of this the

becomes unnecessary to decide the vexed question whether or not Luke had read Josephus. The question arises from the fact that Luke's statements violently conflict with those of Josephus in regard to the dates of Lysanias (Lk. iii. 1-2) and Theudas (Acts v. 34 ff.). It has been maintained by distinguished scholars that Luke's statements can be accounted for on the theory that they are the result of a hasty perusal, and a consequently imperfect recollection and misunderstanding, of Josephus. Personally I am quite unconvinced that there is dependence of any kind. Schmiedel, whose statement of the case for dependence is the most elaborate in English,[1] finds it necessary to suppose that Luke was using, not Josephus directly, but some notes that he had made after reading him. But if a gross mistake is to be attributed to imperfect notes, it would surely be more natural to suggest that the notes in question were taken down hurriedly at some lecture, rather than in the course of a perusal of a book, especially as it was not so possible with ancient methods of writing as with modern print to make mistakes through running one's eye rapidly over the page.

Now there is not the slightest improbability in the supposition that Luke had heard Josephus lecture in Rome. Josephus was granted by Vespasian rooms in the Imperial Palace, and remained in favour with subsequent emperors. Luke also, I have suggested, had a connection with the Flavian house. The writings of Josephus were addressed to the Roman world at large, and it would appear that after A.D. 70 he for the most part lived and wrote in Rome. In that case, unless his practice was quite different from that of contemporary writers, it would have been a matter of course for him to recite large portions of his works to public audiences before they were published in written form.

simplest solution has always seemed to me to be that propounded by Renan. The delegates who brought the famine contribution from Antioch (Acts xi. 30) were Barnabas and another; Luke erroneously imagined that other to be Barnabas's (future) colleague Paul. On Luke's representation of the phenomenon of "speaking with tongues" at Pentecost cf. p. 220 above

[1] *Encycl. Bib.*, arts. "Lysanias" and "Theudas."

Pliny and Juvenal constantly refer to this custom—the latter to expatiate on the boredom it induced. Plutarch tells us that while in Rome, at about this date, he was so busy lecturing, and doing minor political business, that he never had time to master the Latin language—an observation which incidentally reveals the extent to which Greek was a second language of the educated native Roman as well as of the immense city population of foreign origin. The *Antiquities* of Josephus was published *c.* A.D. 93. It is a long work and would have taken many years to compose —probably most of the interval since the publication of his earlier work, *The Jewish War*, between 75 and 79. Josephus was extremely conceited, not at all the man to lose any opportunity for publicity, and he would do much to be in the literary and social fashion. Moreover, his writings were largely intended for propaganda purposes ; he wished to do his best to reinstate the credit of the Jewish people. He would certainly have recited parts of the *Antiquities* at intervals during the ten years before its publication. Fashionable Rome felt bound in etiquette to attend the recitations of its noble friends ; but a parvenu like Josephus would have been only too glad to fill up the back seats with unimportant people like Luke.

VI. Inadequate attention has been given to the bearing of the Preface of the Gospel on the question of authorship. The other Gospels are anonymous ; Luke is not. True, his name is not mentioned in the Preface, but that applies to other Roman writers —Livy and Tacitus, for example. The author's name in such cases would be indicated on a title attached to the roll. Luke's Preface would have no point at all if the original readers did not know the author's name. In effect, it is the author's apology for venturing to produce a Gospel at all. It implies that the Church for which he wrote already possessed a work of the kind, but that he claimed to be in a position to improve upon it. But unless his name was well known—one might almost say unless he was known to have had some connection with Apostles— this claim would not have been admitted. Moreover, knowing

the use he made of Mark, we cannot doubt that in his reference to
previous writers, though Q and other such collections may have
been also in his mind, it is of Mark that he is mainly thinking.
With the materials at his disposal he might well consider that he
could improve upon a Gospel which had no account of the
Infancy and the Resurrection Appearances, and very little discourse; but to say this bluntly would have been tactless, for Mark
was the Gospel on which many of his readers had been " brought
up." By the vague and general " Forasmuch as many have
taken in hand . . . " no one's feelings could be hurt.

Luke, unlike Matthew, left a considerable portion of Mark
unincorporated; hence—at any rate at Rome—the new Gospel
did not supersede the older and shorter work. The Roman
Church was conservative ; besides, its claim to possess the most
reliable Apostolic tradition was strengthened by having two
Gospels, one by a disciple of Peter and the other by a follower of
Paul. But the concurrent use in the same Church of two versions
of the story of the Life of Christ demanded a change in current
nomenclature. We are so used to the idea of there being four
Gospels, known always by their authors' names, that we are apt
to forget the earlier period when no Church had more than one
Gospel, and when this was commonly spoken of, not by its
author's name, but simply as " *the* Gospel." [1]   But the moment
two such works began to be current side by side in the same
Church it became necessary to distinguish the Gospel " according
to Mark " from that " according to Luke." Indeed, it is
probably to the fortunate circumstance that Mark and Luke
were so early in circulation side by side that we owe the
preservation of the names of the real authors of these works.

The fact that two books on the same subject cannot be in
circulation together without each bearing some name to mark

[1] This state of things survived till the fifth century or later among the
Aramaic-speaking Christians of Palestine. Burkitt shows from a Rabbinic story of
R. Eliezer that the sacred book of these *Minim* was called *evangelion* (*Christian
Beginnings*, p. 74 f. (London Univ., 1924)). This proves, not only dependence
on a *Greek* Gospel, but the use of " Gospel " as a title of a book before A.D. 100.

their difference disposes of the suggestion of Mr. H. J. Cadbury [1]
that the attribution of the third Gospel to Luke may be merely
an inference from the " we sections " of Acts. He suggests that
some acute critic of the second century, searching for the author
of an anonymous document presumed to be by a companion of
Paul, proceeded by rejecting the names of any whose presence
would not fit the notices in Epistles and Acts combined, and
thus, by a process of elimination, arrived at the name " Luke."
Such a theory overlooks the fact already noted that the Preface
of Luke's Gospel would be meaningless unless its author's name
was known to the original readers ; while if these were members
of a Church which already possessed a Gospel, the necessity of
distinguishing the two would *from the very first* have prevented
the names of either being forgotten. The point, therefore, to
which Mr. Cadbury calls attention really cuts the other way
—for it would be very remarkable that the name which
tradition ascribes to the Gospel should happen to be that of the
only one of Paul's companions who (taking the " we sections "
at their face value) could have written the Acts, unless it were
the name of the actual author.

VII. But it is not only on the merits of the argument that I
personally accept the Lucan authorship of the Gospel and Acts.
Even if the arguments were exactly balanced, the principles of
historical criticism, as I conceive them, would suffice to incline
the scale in that direction. The first duty of the critical historian
is to ask, in regard to every statement made in his authorities,
is there any possible bias for which allowance should be made ?
In the present case we have not far to seek. Wherever the earlier
tradition was vague or doubtful, a Catholic writer of the time of
Irenaeus would be tempted to favour that form of it which gave
the maximum of Apostolic authority to those Four Gospels
which were regarded as the pillars of the Church. Now two of
these are assigned to Apostles ; two are not. This distinction
is, for the critic, of the first importance. The tradition which

[1] Cf. Foakes Jackson and Lake, *Beginnings of Christianity*, vol. ii. p. 261.

assigns two of them to Apostles is one whose credentials will need
most careful cross-examination ; and, if there be found any
features in the Gospels themselves which make it hard to believe
they were the work of Apostles, the tradition will require a proportionately greater amount of evidence to justify its acceptance.
On the other hand, the ascription of the other two Gospels to
persons who were not Apostles appeals at once to the critic as
being almost certainly authentic, just because it runs counter to
the natural bias of the age.

From the point of view both of sentiment and controversial
advantage, it would have been extremely convenient to assign
the Gospel of Mark to Peter and that of Luke to Paul ; and later
writers do their best to effect this. Paul's phrase " according to
my Gospel " (Rom. ii. 16) is interpreted as a direct allusion to
the Gospel of Luke, which is thus assumed to have been written
under his supervision. Again, the Gospel of Mark was written,
according to Irenaeus (185) after the demise of Peter, according
to Clement (200) during Peter's lifetime, but without his approba-
tion, according to Eusebius (324) with his authentication, according to Jerome (397) at his dictation.[1] Indeed it would seem as if
an attempt was made in some circles at a very early date to make

[1] Cf. Iren. I. i. 1 (Gk. in Eus. *H.E.* v. 8); Clem. *ap.* Eus. *H.E.* vi. 14;
Peter neither forbade nor commended ; Eus. *H.E.* ii. 15 (φασί), Peter approves
for reading in Church ; Jerome, *Ad Hedibiam*, xi , " Marcum, cujus evangelium,
Petro narrante, et illo scribente compositum est." But Jerome knew better,
for *De vir. illustr.* viii. he says the same as Eus. *H.E.* ii. 15.

I take this opportunity of suggesting an explanation of the curious " tradition " mentioned by Clement of Alexandria (*ap.* Eus. *H.E.* vi. 14) that " the
Gospels containing genealogies were written first.' This, I think, is not a
tradition of fact but a traditional explanation of the lack of an account of the
Infancy, Resurrection appearances, etc., in Mark, on the hypothesis that, when
Mark wrote, the Roman Church already possessed an account of these things
in Luke. Matthew, it was inferred from Papias, was originally in Hebrew, and
the Greek translation would not yet have reached Rome when Mark wrote.
The Gospel of Mark could conceivably be regarded as a supplement to Luke,
for it contains much that is not in Luke : it could not be intended as a supple-
ment to Matthew *plus* Luke. The idea that Luke wrote before Mark would
naturally be suggested by the common Western order of the Gospels—Matthew,
John, Luke, Mark—(Clement has a Western text), or by the order of Tertullian
(*Contra Marcionem*, iv. 2), a contemporary of Clement—John, Matthew, Luke,
Mark.

the Apostle directly responsible for the Gospel; for Justin Martyr (155) quotes a statement that occurs in Mark as from the "Memoirs of Peter." Irenaeus had read Justin; and he must in any case have known that some people spoke of the second Gospel as Peter's. If, then, he does not accept it as Peter's work, we can only conclude that the tradition assigning the second and third Gospels to Mark and Luke was so definite, so widespread, and, by the time of Irenaeus, already so ancient, that it could not be displaced.

The attribution of one of the four canonical Gospels to Luke is even more remarkable. Mark at least was known to have lived in Jerusalem ; he may have witnessed some of the events he describes, and he had some special connection with Peter, the leader of the Twelve. Luke was not only not himself a witness, he was a follower of an Apostle who was not himself a witness, and he was only that during the last years of that Apostle's life. With a very little "doctoring" of the text— merely changing "we" to "they" in a few passages—the Acts could have been made to read as the *Commentarii* of Paul, writing of himself, like Caesar or Xenophon, in the third person. The Gospel then could have been assigned to Paul himself. But this was not done.

A critic, then, who knows his business—that is, who recognises that his function is analogous to that of the judge ($\kappa\rho\iota\tau\eta\varsigma$) and not of the counsel, whether for the defence or the prosecution— before giving a verdict in favour of a tradition which ascribes a Gospel to an Apostle, will require an attestation stronger than a classical scholar would think necessary for a work attributed to Xenophon or Plato. On the other hand, only if overwhelming evidence is forthcoming that the internal characteristics of Mark and Luke cannot be reconciled with their traditional authorship will he decide that the tradition is open to serious question.

We thus arrive at the quite simple conclusion : the burden of proof is on those who would assert the traditional authorship of Matthew and John and on those who would deny it in the case of Mark and Luke.

APPENDICES

APPENDIX I

THE ORIGIN OF VARIOUS READINGS

It is often forgotten that the ancients did not wear spectacles, and that, therefore, the profession of scribe must have been proportionately more trying to the eyes. Now one of the commonest defects of eyesight is " astigmatism," as a result of which lines drawn in one direction appear much fainter than lines drawn in another. This, obviously, would tend to make it easy to confuse one letter with another ; but a confusion easy to one scribe would not affect another. Again, any weakening of the power of concentration renders it easy to make an error of position—and so to pass from a word in one line to a similar word in a line below. Omissions of lines from this cause are technically described as due to " homoioteleuton "—literally " like end," though as a matter of fact omission from this cause quite as often takes place in the middle of a line as when the identical letters stand at the end of a line. Evidence of this can be found in ancient MSS. It may not be irrelevant to remark that in a type-written copy of one chapter of this book I found no less than three cases of omission, two of one and one of two lines, occurring from the eye of the typist passing about two-thirds from the beginning of a line to similar words in a lower line. Besides this, we must remember that between reading the exemplar and writing there is always a short interval during which the invincible tendency of the human mind to modify anything it apprehends has time to operate, especially if the attention of the scribe wanders or if he has not had special training. At the present day the

difference between the standard of accuracy of one copyist and
another, especially in the matter of omitting or misreading
individual words, varies immensely. But absolute accuracy is
an ideal never attained over a long piece of writing.

It will be worth while to consider briefly how mistakes, other
than intentional additions or corrections, most naturally occur.

(1) Variations in the relative order of the words in a sentence
in different MSS. are very common. Alterations of order would
originate in this way : a scribe accidentally omits a word ; if
he notices it before he has finished writing the next word, he
puts it in himself, sometimes as a marginal or overline correction,
but sometimes, in order to avoid an unsightly mess, at the next
place in the sentence where it makes sense. This latter alternative was specially attractive to a Greek scribe, since in that
language, much more easily than in English, the order of the
words in a sentence can be rearranged without materially
altering the meaning. If the original scribe does not notice an
omission, a corrector puts it in the margin. In that case the
next copyist may easily insert it in the text *in the wrong place*
—this is one of the commonest mistakes in MSS.

(2) Marginal notes, sometimes consisting of various readings
derived from another MS., often led to corruption, through
something being copied into the text by a scribe who supposed
what he saw in the margin to be words accidentally omitted.

(3) Another frequent phenomenon is the substitution of
synonyms. We can see at least four ways in which this might
arise. (a) The attention of the scribe may wander in the
interval between reading and writing and he may reproduce
the sense rather than the actual words of his model. (b) He
may omit a word, or at some subsequent time a drop of water
or a flaw in the papyrus may cause it to be obliterated. The
next copyist will have to make a guess at the missing word.
For example, in Mt. xxvii. 4 the sense requires a word meaning
"innocent" to follow $a\hat{\imath}\mu a$; suppose the original text had $\delta\iota\kappa a\iota o\nu$,
the reading of L, but that in some early copy the word was

omitted; the owner makes a guess at the "missing word," and $\dot{a}\theta\hat{\omega}ov$, the reading of B $\aleph$ etc., is the result.[1] (c) Occasionally we come across cases where it looks as if a literary word has been deliberately substituted for a slang one in order to improve the style.

(4) In the Gospels, the commonest of all corruptions is the result of "assimilation." This occurs when a word or phrase in the original text has been replaced by one which occurs in the parallel passage in another Gospel.

(5) Many variations consist in the substitution of a participle for $\kappa a i$ with a finite verb, or the use of different prepositions, conjunctions, or particles. These may be due to any of the above-mentioned causes—wandering attention between the moment of reading and writing, omission and subsequent correction, influence of the recollection of parallels in another Gospel, or the attempt, unconscious or deliberate, to improve grammar or style.

In the earliest period of all—so the phenomena of the Western text especially suggest—scribes seem occasionally to have attempted quasi-editorial improvements similar to, but much slighter than, those which Matthew and Luke make in reproducing Mark.

In order to illustrate the exact nature of the problem we have to deal with, I set out and discuss briefly the readings of the leading MSS. in three passages in Luke.[2]

Lk. viii. 9, " what this parable might be ? "

$\tau i s$ $a\ddot{v}\tau\eta$ $\epsilon i\eta$ $\pi a\rho a\beta o\lambda\dot{\eta}$;	B 579.
$\tau i s$ $a\ddot{v}\tau\eta$ $\epsilon i\eta$ $\dot{\eta}$ $\pi a\rho a\beta o\lambda\dot{\eta}$;	$\aleph$ W 33 700.
$\tau i s$ $\epsilon i\eta$ $a\ddot{v}\tau\eta$ $\dot{\eta}$ $\pi a\rho a\beta o\lambda\dot{\eta}$;	1 &c.
$\tau i s$ $a\ddot{v}\tau\eta$ $\dot{\eta}$ $\pi a\rho a\beta o\lambda\dot{\eta}$	L Ξ.
$\tau i s$ $\epsilon i\eta$ $\dot{\eta}$ $\pi a\rho a\beta o\lambda\dot{\eta}$ $a\ddot{v}\tau\eta$	A D Θ Ψ.
$\tau i s$ $\dot{\eta}$ $\pi a\rho a\beta o\lambda\dot{\eta}$ $a\ddot{v}\tau\eta$	Γ.
$\pi\epsilon\rho i$ $\tau\hat{\eta}s$ $\pi a\rho a\beta o\lambda\hat{\eta}s$	R.

The seven readings quoted above present an unusually compli-

---

[1] A similar instance is Lk. ix. 35 $\dot{\epsilon}\kappa\lambda\epsilon\lambda\epsilon\gamma\mu\dot{\epsilon}\nu os$ $\aleph$ B L *versus* $\dot{a}\gamma a\pi\eta\tau\dot{o}s$ D Byz.

[2] I have selected these from an immense list drawn up for another purpose by H. C. Hoskier, *Codex B and its Allies*, Quaritch, 1914.

cated instance of diversity in order; they also illustrate two other points. (a) Remembering that all the older MSS. were written in capitals, *with no division between the words and without accents or breathings*, we see that difference between the first two of the list depends on the letter H (=η) being written once or twice before παραβολή. If א is right, the error of B is that technically known as "haplography" (*i.e.* writing only once what should be repeated twice); if B is right, א is guilty of "dittography" or mistaken repetition. (b) The reading of R is particularly instructive. The probable explanation is that τίς αὕτη εἴη ἡ had formed a complete line in an ancestor which had accidentally been omitted in the exemplar copied by R. (MSS. exist with eleven letters to the line). Something had to be done to make grammar and sense of the nominative παραβολή left without a construction. The scribe makes the obvious guess περὶ τῆς παραβολῆς. Note that the differences between the first six variants cannot possibly be reproduced in English.

Lk. xi. 10, " It is (or " shall be ") opened."

ἀνοίγεται	B D.
ἀνοιγήσεται	א C L.
ἀνοιχθήσεται	A E etc.
ἀνηχθήσεται	W.

The first three variants illustrate the tendency towards grammatical improvement; the fourth is probably due to defective eyesight of the scribe of this MS. or its ancestor, or possibly, if the scribe wrote from dictation, to an error of hearing.

Lk. ix. 10.

πόλιν καλουμένην Βηθσαϊδά	B L 33 etc.
κώμην λεγομένην Βηθσαϊδά	D.
κώμην καλουμένην Βηθσαϊδάν· εἰς τόπον ἔρημον	Θ.
τόπον καλούμενον Βηθσαϊδά	Ψ.
τόπον ἔρημον	א 69, 157 Syr. C.
ἔρημον τόπον πόλεως καλουμένης Βηθσαιδάν	A 13, 346.
τόπον πόλεως καλουμένης Βηθσαϊδά	1 &c. 700.
τόπον ἔρημον πόλεως καλουμένης Βηθσαϊδάν	W and Byzantine.

The whole clause καὶ παραλαβὼν . . . Βηθσαϊδά om. 579.

This is an exceptionally complicated, and also an exceptionally instructive, set of variants ; since, in spite of the bewildering diversity of attestation, we can by the application of sound principles of criticism ascertain with practical certainty what Luke originally wrote.   The apparently hopeless confusion begins to disappear the moment we glance at a Synopsis of the Gospels and note that in Matthew (xiv. 13) and Mark (vi. 12) ἔρημον τόπον " a desert place " takes the place of " city called " or " village named, Bethsaida."   We conclude that the reading τόπον ἔρημον may be dismissed as due to " assimilation " of the text of Luke to that of the other Gospels.   It follows that all the readings which contain the word τόπον represent attempts of scribes or editors to combine the readings of two MSS., one containing τόπον ἔρημον, the other a reading mentioning a city or village Bethsaida.   We are thus left to choose between the first three readings which give the name Bethsaida.

$$\pi\acute{o}\lambda\iota\nu \ \kappa\alpha\lambda o\upsilon\mu\acute{\epsilon}\nu\eta\nu \ \mathrm{B}\eta\theta\sigma\alpha\ddot{\iota}\delta\acute{\alpha} \qquad \mathbf{B.}$$
$$\kappa\acute{\omega}\mu\eta\nu \ \kappa\alpha\lambda o\upsilon\mu\acute{\epsilon}\nu\eta\nu \ \mathrm{B}\eta\theta\sigma\alpha\ddot{\iota}\delta\acute{\alpha}\nu \qquad \Theta.$$
$$\kappa\acute{\omega}\mu\eta\nu \ \lambda\epsilon\gamma o\mu\acute{\epsilon}\nu\eta\nu \ \mathrm{B}\eta\theta\sigma\alpha\ddot{\iota}\delta\acute{\alpha} \qquad \mathbf{D.}$$

Here we have a double instance of " substitution of synonyms." It would be most simply explained on the hypothesis that the text presupposed by Θ is original, while κώμην was changed to πόλιν in one local text, and καλουμένην to λεγομένην in another.

This conclusion is shown to be one of high probability by " internal " considerations.   Bethsaida is classed among " cities," Mt. xi. 21 = Lk. x. 13 ; a scribe, therefore, who wished to replace an original κώμην that had fallen out, or to emend the text, would inevitably conjecture πόλιν.   On the other hand, the context makes it extremely unlikely that Luke wrote πόλιν. " He took them and withdrew apart (κατ᾽ ἰδίαν) into a . . . called Bethsaida."   One does not retire for privacy to a " city " ; but one may do so to a country village.   Again, two verses later the disciples say, " Send the multitude away that they may go into the villages and country round about and lodge, and get victuals : for we are here in a desert place." But this would be absurd language to use if they were anywhere near a " city." Again, there can be no reasonable doubt that Luke wrote καλουμένην and not λεγομένην. The word καλούμενος to introduce a name or appellation is used 11 times in his Gospel ; but it does not occur at all in the other Gospels. On the other hand, λεγόμενος, in this usage, while it occurs 13 times in Matthew, is only twice found in Luke (xxii. 1 and 47), and the second of these two cases is doubtful, since D Old Lat. **1 157** support the alternative reading καλούμενος.

There remains to make our choice between the form Βηθσαϊδά B D Old Lat. and Βηθσαϊδάν Θ A and the Byzantine text. Every time the name occurs in the Gospels there is a variation in the MSS. But we note that B, where the name occurs in Matthew and Mark, uses the form with the final ν ; but in Luke, B, both here and in Lk. x. 13, has the form without the ν. But א has the final ν not only in Mark but in Lk. x. 13. Now, since the tendency of scribes is towards " assimilation," a reading which makes the Gospels differ is the one more likely to be original. But Θ has the form with ν here, and in Lk. x. 13 א is supported by **1** &c., **13** &c., **28, 700** etc. This shows that the reading with ν must have arisen long before the date of writing of א. We conclude, then, that Βηθσαϊδά is the true reading, but that Βηθσαϊδάν is a very ancient variant. Not only that ; from the fact that it is preferred elsewhere in Luke by א we may reasonably conjecture that it stood in the text of א in Lk. ix. 10 before the words κώμην (or πόλιν) καλουμένην Βηθσαϊδά were turned out to be replaced by τόπον ἔρημον from the other Gospels. Here, surely, we are on the track of the explanation of this assimilation in א of the text of Luke to Matthew. (κατ᾽) ἰδιαν . . . (Βηθσα)ιδαν is a combination of letters which invited omission by homoioteleuton. The intervening words amounting to 26 letters, i.e. probably two lines, were omitted in a remote ancestor of א ; then, in order to make

sense, the words τόπον ἔρημον were conjecturally inserted from
the parallel passage Mt. xiv. 13.   The fact that 579 has actually
omitted this very passage (only beginning the omission six words
earlier)—apparently through homoioteleuton between (ἐποίησ)αν
and (Βηθσαϊδ)αν—shows the plausibility of this explanation of
the apparently drastic alteration of the text made by ℵ, a MS.
which as a rule is usually exceptionally free from corruption
by assimilation to parallels in other Gospels.

Between them the three passages of Luke above discussed
exhibit the main influences which resulted in the production
of variants in the text.   And since they are influences which
would operate in every locality, but in regard to a different set of
readings in every locality, in the course of time they would inevitably give rise to local texts differing from one another very
little in regard to readings materially affecting the sense, but
very considerably in minute points.

APPENDIX II

THE TEXT OF THE Θ FAMILY

THE TEXTUAL HOMOGENEITY OF THE Θ FAMILY

No early MS. has a text entirely homogeneous. Even B, as Hort insists, has not escaped " sporadic " corruption, while ℵ has a considerable infusion of " Western " readings. In view of the statistics as to the differences of these two Alexandrian MSS., which nevertheless are the most closely related of all MSS. earlier than A.D. 500, given on p. 329, the hypothesis that the various members of *fam.* Θ represent a single local text would not be seriously imperilled unless the number of variants within the family exceeded the number of the differences between ℵ and B. So far, however, as I have been able to test it, they are very few ; from which we may infer that the extent to which the leading MSS. of *fam.* Θ have been crossed by any text, other than the Byzantine, is very small.

Lake's Table[1] of readings in Mk. i. exhibits 102 variants ; but in only 5 of these do members of the family give a reading found in any text other than that of the family or, of course, in the Byzantine text. In regard to the same set of 102 variants ℵ differs from B 16 times. In the Table for Luke ii. 1-25 at the end of this Appendix there appear 44 departures of *fam.* Θ from the T.R. ; out of these 44 variants there are 5 in which members of this family differ from one another, and 6 in which ℵ differs from B. The similar Table for John xii. 1-6

---

[1] *Harvard Journal of Theology*, July 1923, p. 270 ff.

shows 3 differences between א and B, but not a single instance of one member of *fam.* Θ opposing another in any non-Byzantine reading. The Table of variants common to the family and the text used by Origen in his *Commentary on Matthew* tells the same tale. It may, however, be worth while to supplement this evidence by the result of a few preliminary tests which I essayed before drawing up these tables.

(*a*) The lists of classified readings in the Introduction to Lake's *Codex* 1 *and its Allies* afforded another means of testing the relation of Θ to *fam.* 1. List G in the Introduction (p. lxxi) contains readings peculiar to *fam.* 1. In Matthew there are 8 of these. I find that Θ agrees with *fam.* 1 in 3 of these readings, but in the other 5 has been conformed to the Byzantine text. According to von Soden 2 of the 5 not supported by Θ are found in 1424, and 2 more in one of the Purple MSS. List F gives readings " which are supported by a few other MSS., but cannot be identified with any authority generally recognised as primary." I checked this list against Θ for the part of Matthew which is extant in that MS. (much of Matthew i.-v. is lost). Twenty-four readings of *fam.* 1 are concerned. Ten of them appear in Θ ; in all the other instances Θ gives the Byzantine reading. List E gives readings in which *fam.* 1 agrees with B א against D Old Lat., Old Syr., and Byz. In Matthew there are 23 of these ; 12 of them are found in Θ, which otherwise follows the Byzantine text. List B gives the readings found in *fam.* 1, for which the Old Latin is the chief ancient authority. In Matthew there are 11 of these, 4 of which are found in Θ. It appears, then, in whatever direction we look for the readings which are in some special way characteristic of *fam.* 1, we find that a large proportion of them appear in Θ ; and, where that does not happen, the occurrence of the Byzantine reading in Θ shows that in these passages it does *not* represent its own characteristic text.

(*b*) Proceeding to test the relation of Θ and *fam.* 13, I at once noted that Θ exhibits the famous Ferrar reading (found in

346—826—828) ᾧ μνηστευθεῖσα κτλ., Mt. i. 16. Then, by way of a fair test, I opened my copy of Beerman and Gregory's edition of Θ at a venture in that part of the volume which gives a collation of the readings of Θ with the other MSS. The book opened at p. 657, and I worked through the next six pages, which happened to include Mt. xviii. 25 to xxiii. 2. In this short section there are a very large number of readings of Θ in support of which one or more members of the Ferrar group are quoted ; but since the majority of these are also found in at least two of the great uncials B ℵ L D, they afford no evidence of a *special* connection between Θ and *fam.* **13.** There are, however, 9 readings in which Θ is the only uncial (apart from fragments) supporting the reading of *fam.* **13**; 4 readings found in both Θ and *fam.* **13** but supported by B only of uncials ; 4 ditto supported by D only ; 2 ditto supported by D Δ, and 2 ditto supported by inferior uncials. This seems strong evidence of a very close relation between the text of Θ and that of *fam.* **13.**

(c) To test the text of these MSS. in Luke, I turned to the Introduction to Hoskier's collation of **700**, in which he gives the MS. support for all variants of this MS. that are in any sense uncommon. In the first chapter of Luke there are 26 such variants. I found that, if the readings of Θ were added to those of the MSS. cited by Hoskier, every single one of these readings of **700** was supported by at least one other member of the family.

(d) So far as Mark is concerned, **565** would appear to be slightly superior to Θ ; but in the other Gospels it has suffered more from Byzantine revision than any other of the group with which we are concerned. It was for that reason that I selected Luke ii. 1-25, John vi. 55-vii. 3, and John xii. 1-6 for the Tables in the Text and Appendix. A glance through Belsheim's collation had shown me that the proportion of non-Byzantine readings in **565** was above the average in these passages, and therefore their character could be most easily tested here. It so happens, however, that all these are passages in which Θ and **700** have suffered rather heavily from Byzantine correction, so that the Tables somewhat understate the value of these two MSS. as compared with other members of the family,

Theoretically, of course, no proposition as to the homogeneity of the texts of these MSS. can be held to be proved until every reading in all four Gospels in each MS. has been compared. Practically, the chances are very small that the various tests enumerated would have come out as they did unless the fundamental text were unusually homogeneous.

The Purple MSS., *Fam.* 1424, and ℵ^c

There are four MSS. of the sixth century, N—Σ—O and Φ, written on purple parchment in letters of silver—except O, which is in letters of gold. O contains only a fragment of Matthew ; Φ and Σ contain Matthew and Mark almost complete ; N contains portions of all four Gospels. N—Σ—O are so much alike that Mr. H. R. S. Cronin, who has made a special study of the group, believes that they were copied from the same exemplar.[1] In general they present the Byzantine text ; but there is a small proportion of earlier readings. The text of Φ is closely allied to that of N—Σ—O, but with an additional infiltration of D readings.

When I first began testing the homogeneity of *fam.* Θ there happened to be on my table Mr. Cronin's edition of Codex N (*Texts and Studies*, v. 4). Recollecting that the books speak of a connection between this MS. and the Ferrar group, it occurred to me to use some of his lists to test the text of Θ, choosing Luke for the investigation. One list (p. lix) gives the readings in which N agrees with *fam.* **13,** against the T.R. and all the leading uncials. There are 7 such readings in Luke. Of these 3 occur in Θ ; of the remaining 4, 1 occurs in **131** (*fam.* **1**), 1 in **565,** and 1 in M (*fam.* **1424**). Another list (p. lx) gives agreements of N with the texts of the " Better Uncials "—meaning either B or ℵ L combined—against the majority of MSS. In Luke 22

---

[1] *Texts and Studies*, v. 4 (1899), and *J.T.S.*, July 1901, p. 590 ff.

instances are given; Θ supports N in 10 of them. Noticing that for most of the 22 Mr. Cronin quotes the support of *fam.* **1** or *fam.* **13,** I proceeded to test the cases where he does not quote such support by means of von Soden's Apparatus, which of course gives the readings of some new members of the Ferrar group and of **700.** It then appeared that in only 3 of the 22 readings did N lack the support of either Θ or one of the Θ family. That is to say, N hardly ever agrees with ℵ B L except where these support *fam.* Θ.

The early date of the Purple MSS. made it seem specially worth while to explore still further the relation between their pre-Byzantine element and the text of *fam.* Θ. And, as Mark is the Gospel where the characteristic text of both groups of MSS. is best preserved, I proceeded to test the text of N in that Gospel.

Mr. Cronin gives (p. li f.) a list of 48 readings in Mark where N and Σ agree together, and are supported by a very few MSS. against all the leading uncials and also against the Byzantine text; in each he cites the MSS. which support them. From these it appeared that 31 of the 48 readings in N Σ occur in one or more then known members of *fam.* Θ. But, checking the list by the new evidence of Θ **700** and von Soden's revised collations, I found the number rose to 37. This struck me as remarkable. I then noticed that, of the remaining 11 readings, 9 were supported by the group of MSS. which von Soden classes together under the symbol Iᵠ, but which on the analogy of the accepted usage in similar cases I have called *fam.* **1424.** This group he defines as one intimately related to *fam.* **1** and *fam.* **13,** but preserving a few readings which have been eliminated from these MSS.

The next step was to test the combination N Σ by the Table of readings characteristic of *fam.* Θ given in the article by Lake and Blake in the *Harvard Theological Review.* N is not extant for the beginning of Mark, but Σ is. The results of a scrutiny of the 102 variants in Mark i. there tabled, tested against the collation of Σ by Gebhardt and Harnack, may be succinctly presented as follows :

Agreements of Σ with T.R.	84
	—
Agreements of Σ with *fam.* Θ	14
Conflations of text of *fam.* Θ and T.R. . .	2
Agreement of Σ with *fam.* **1424** in a reading not preserved in other members of *fam.* Θ	1
Agreements with other MSS. (A 33) . .	1
	—
	18

These figures materially strengthen the conclusion that the ground text of N Σ was identical with that of *fam.* Θ, only that it has suffered a much larger amount of revision to the Byzantine standard. Obviously, however, they would amount to demonstration if it could be shown that von Soden was right in view of the relation of *fam.* **1424** to *fam.* **1** and *fam.* **13**.

Accordingly I proceeded to test the character of *fam.* **1424** by reference to Lake and Blake's Table for Mark i. Assuming that where von Soden fails to cite the evidence of any of these MSS. it agrees with the Byzantine text, it appears that in 52 of the 102 variants cited *fam.* **1424** represents the T.R., but in 40 it goes with one or other member of the Θ family ; 9 times it has readings differing from the T.R. but not found in any of the six representatives of *fam.* Θ cited in the Table. One of them, however (the omission of εὐθύς i. 43), is found also in 828, a Ferrar MS. quoted by von Soden but not included in Lake's citations ; and one is practically the *fam.* Θ reading (*i.e.* the addition καὶ τεσσαράκοντα νύκτας i. 13, only with a transposition of the last two words) ; and two are found only in one MS. of *fam.* **1424** and look like errors of the individual scribe. In one *fam.* **1424** agrees with D, but all members of *fam.* Θ except Θ itself here go with T.R., and the reading of Θ ἦλθον for ἀπῆλθον, found in no other MS., is probably a slip, so that here *fam.* **1424** may well preserve the original *fam.* Θ reading. In all other variants, so far as one can infer from von Soden's general system of citing (and I know of no collation by which to check him), *fam.* **1424** gives the Byzantine reading.

The Tables of readings in Luke and John, given p. 83 and p. 582 ff., show similar results, and justify us in treating *fam.* 1424 as a genuine and important constituent of *fam.* Θ. I may add that in the course of writing this book I have had to study the MS. evidence given by von Soden in innumerable cases up and down the Gospels, and have found nothing to conflict with the results obtained above. Accordingly, though it may be that a few of the less important of the twenty-eight MSS. which he groups as IΦ ought not to be included, he has discovered a real group ; and *fam.* 1424 must be treated as an important constituent of the Θ family. I have also found reason to accept his view that 544 (ε 337) is a true member of the same family.[1]

It occurred to me to test the readings of the corrector of ℵ whom Tischendorf cites as ℵ\ :c or ℵ\ :ca, and who probably[2] belongs to V or VI\ :cent. The chapters of Matthew which I tested showed a predominantly Byzantine text with a sprinkling of readings definitely of the *fam.* Θ type. This is interesting, as in the O.T. and in the Epistles ℵ\ :c seems to have used a MS. in the hand of Pamphilus.[3] Unless, as is possible, but not probable, Pamphilus in prison copied a MS. of Lucian's recension, this shows the Byzantine text dominant in Caesarea by V or VI\ :cent.

THE K II GROUP

von Soden classes M, which has a very small non-Byzantine mixture, as an inferior member of *fam.* 1424 ; Bousset (*Text-kritische Studien*, chap. iv.) regards M as a poor relation of K II. The lists of the readings in his chapter on "The K II Group" favour von Soden's view that these two uncials (which are supported by a number of cursives) have the same relation as have N Σ to the *fam.* Θ text, except that they are more

---

[1] A partial collation of 544 is given in Scrivener's *Adversaria Critica*, p. l-liv (Cambridge, 1893), under the number 557.

[2] Cf. the facsimile edition of ℵ by K. Lake (Clarendon Press, 1911), p. xvii f.

[3] Bousset, *op. cit.* p. 45 ff.

predominantly Byzantine and have a smaller admixture of the older text. von Soden classes A, the famous Codex Alexandrinus, with K Π; and, so far as I have tested the suggestion, I think he is probably right in supposing that the non-Byzantine element in A represents mainly, if not wholly, the *fam.* Θ text. W. C. Braithwaite (*Expository Times*, xiii. pp. 114 ff.) says that the recently discovered uncial Y has affinities with K Π; and a hurried look at the collation of the MS. given in Gregory's *Textkritik* (pp. 1928 ff.) seemed to show that its non-Byzantine element (perhaps 10 %) is at any rate closely connected with *fam.* Θ. Since, however, all the sub-families of *fam.* Θ overlap one another, it is not of much importance, especially where the non-Byzantine element is small, whether in border-line cases, like A or M or Y, a MS. is included in one sub-family or another, or regarded as forming a class by itself. The same consideration applies to the question (discussed p. 80, note) whether 22 should be included in *fam.* 1 or not. What does matter is to know whether the non-Byzantine element in a mixed MS. belongs mainly or entirely to the Θ family.

The K Π group is regarded by von Soden as a definite recension; he styles it the K^a text, and holds that it was used by Chrysostom in his Homilies on John and in the so-called "Antiochene Commentary" on Mark (by ? Victor of Antioch ±420), and on Luke by Titus of Bosra, 370. I am a little sceptical as to the clear-cut distinctions within the Byzantine text which von Soden believes he can detect; but, if the K^a text was used by these fathers and is that of the V$^{cent.}$ MS. A, may not this be the text of Lucian? The K^1 text in other works of Chrysostom may be due to scribal revision to the VI$^{cent.}$ Byzantine text.

U Λ, ETC.

Two other sub-families of MSS., regarded by von Soden as authorities for his " I text," are headed respectively by U and Λ. The non-Byzantine element in *fam.* U (in which he includes the interesting cursive 1071 [1] (ε 1279)) seems to be about as large as that in the Purple MSS. ; and, so far as I have observed, it represents the *fam.* Θ text. *Fam.* Λ seems to have a smaller non-Byzantine element, and therefore is more difficult to test ; but I do not happen to have noticed any readings which suggest that this element is other than the *fam.* Θ text ; and I would say the same thing of 1604 (ε 1353).

An immense number of MSS. are assigned by von Soden to the I text. Unfortunately, however, his inclusion of DW^Mk, Old Lat., Old Syr. in the I text vitiates his principle of classification ; for it would justify his assigning to that text a MS. containing a considerable mixture of specifically Syriac or Western readings. This consideration precludes one from the simple expedient of classing as authorities for the text of *fam.* Θ all MSS.—merely excepting DW^{Mk i-v}, Old Lat., Old Syr. —cited in von Soden's Apparatus as authorities for the I text. They must be scrutinised again in every case. And this caution is the more necessary as von Soden is over-anxious to enlist MSS. in support of the I text. For example, 157 is reckoned as an I MS., and it undoubtedly has a number of readings characteristic of *fam.* Θ ; but a much more striking feature of this curiously mixed MS. is its support of the Alexandrian text. The fragments P Q and R von Soden classes as authorities for the I text ; Γ also is claimed as a weak supporter of the same text— perhaps rightly, but it also has some striking Alexandrian readings.[2]

One naturally asks if all traces of the old text of Antioch have disappeared. If we are right in surmising that this was the Greek original of the Old Syriac, a predominantly Byzantine MS. in which the remnants of such a text survived as a small

---

[1] Described and collated by K. Lake in *Studia Biblica*, v. p. 132 ff., Oxford, 1903.

[2] My confidence in von Soden's classifications was seriously shaken by testing the VI^cent. fragment 089 (ε 28 = Tischendorf's Θ^e) containing Mt. xxvi. 2-4, 7-9, which he quotes (vol. i. p. 1350) as "a pure I text." Tischendorf gives 8 variants from this fragment, of which 7 occur in B ℵ and the remaining 1 in B Λ.

element of mixture might easily be mistaken for a weak member of *fam.* Θ, since *fam.* Θ and the Old Syriac have so much in common. Again, there must have been early local texts in Asia Minor and Macedonia—the parts of the world in which the majority of our later MSS. were probably produced—and it would be very strange if no readings at all from these texts had crept into the later MSS. The astonishing thing is that, of the sporadic non-Byzantine readings that survive in later MSS., there are so few which are not also found in one or other of the great texts which we can identify. I can only account for this by supposing that, at the time when the transition from papyrus to parchment was made, the smaller churches, instead of copying their local texts, obtained their new parchment copies from the larger centres. This change of material seems to have taken place early in the fourth century, that is to say, just after the revisions by Lucian and Hesychius were accepted at Antioch and Alexandria. And we know that the copies of the text of Caesarea with which Eusebius supplied Constantine (from which we have suggested many representatives of *fam.* Θ are descended) were written on parchment.

In order further to illustrate both the essential homogeneity of *fam.* Θ and the curiously sporadic and unsystematic character of the assimilation of earlier texts to the Byzantine standard, I append two Tables modelled on that drawn up by K. Lake to which reference has been so often made.

[TABLES

Luke ii. 1-25

	#	Family Readings	θ	fam. 1	fam. 13	28	565	700	fam. 1424		Readings of 5
A	1	− δε	s	s	f*	f	s	s	s	ℵBD	+ δε
		+ του (a. απογρ.)	s	s	f	—	s	f	s	ℵBD	− του
ℵBD	2	απογραψασθαι	f	f	s	—	s	f	s	ℵBD	απογραφεσθαι
		− ἡ (a. απογρ.)	s	f	s	—	f	f	f	ℵ	+ ἡ
(ℵ)ℵD	3	απογραψασθαι	s	s	s	—	s	s	s	ℵBD	απογραφεσθαι
D		ἑαυτου	s	s	f*	—	f	f	s		ιδιαν
		πατριδα	f	s	s	—	s	s	s	ℵB	πολιν
ℵD	4	+ ὁ (a. Ἰωσ.)	s	s	s	—	s	s	f	ℵBD	− ὁ
ℵBD	5	απογραφεσθαι	s	f	s	—	f	f	s	B	απογραψασθαι
B		− γυναικι	s	f	f	—	s	s	s		+ γυναικι
ℵD	7	− αυτου 2°	s	s	s	—	s	f	f	ℵD	εγγυω
		εγγυω	s	s	s	—	s	s	s	ℵBD	+ αυτου 2°
	8	τη αυτη χωρα	s	f	f	—	f	s	s	ℵB (D)	τη χωρα τη αυτη
		της ποιμνης	s	s	s	—	s	f	f	ℵBD	την ποιμνην
ℵB	9	− ιδου (p. και)	s	s	s	—	s	s	f	D	+ ιδου
		− κυριου 1°	s	s	s	—	s	f	f	ℵBD	+ κυριου 1°
		εφανη	s	s	s	—	s	s	s	ℵB	επεστη
D		− κυριου 2°	s	s	s	—	s	s	f	ℵB	+ κυριου 2°
	10	+ υμεις (p. φοβ.)	s	s	s	—	s	f	f	ℵBD	− υμεις
	11	ἡμιν	f	f	s	—	s	s	f	ℵBD	− υμιν
		σωτηρ	f	f	s	—	s	s	s	ℵBD	κυριος
ℵBD	12	+ και 2° (a. κειμενον)	f	f	f	f	f	s	s	ℵBD	− και 2°
ℵBD	14	ευδοκιας	f	f	f	f	f	s	s		ευδοκια
D (3rd)	15	οἱ ἀγγελοι (a. εἰς τ. ο.)	f	f	f	f	f	s	f	ℵB	οἱ ἀγγελοι (p. εἰς τ. ο.)
		− εἰς τον ουρανον	s	s	s	s	f	s	s	ℵBD	+ εἰς τον ουρανον

Left MS	Verse / Reading							Reading	Right MS
ℵBD	— και οι ανθρωποι	f	f	f	ꜱ	ꜱ	ꜱ	+ και οι ανθρωποι	D
ℵB	ελαλουν	ꜱ	ꜱ	f	ꜱ	f	ꜱ	ειπον	
	{ εαυτους / αυτους	ꜱ	ꜱ	ꜱ	f	ꜱ	ꜱ	αλληλους }	ℵBD
	+ εις (a. Βηθ.)								
ℵD	16 ευρον							— εις	ℵBD
ℵBD	17 εγνωρισαν	ꜱ	ꜱ	ꜱ	f	ꜱ	f	ανευρον	B
D	— τουτου	ꜱ	ꜱ	ꜱ	f	f	f	διεγνωρισαν	
D	18 εθαυμαζον	ꜱ	ꜱ	ꜱ	ꜱ	f	f	+ τουτου	ℵB
	19 { — παντα	ꜱ	ꜱ	f	ꜱ	ꜱ	f	εθαυμασαν	ℵB
D	συνετηρει παντα	ꜱ	ꜱ	ꜱ	ꜱ	f	f	+ παντα	ℵBD
D	21 { συνετελεσθησαν		f			f		παντα συνετηρει }	ℵB
D	επληρωθησαν		f	f		f		επλησθησαν }	ℵB
D	+ αι (a. ημεραι)	f	ꜱ	f	ꜱ	f	ꜱ	— αι	ℵB
D	21 — και[2]	f	ꜱ	f	f	ꜱ	f	+ και	ℵℵB
ℵℵB	λεχθεν	ꜱ	ꜱ	ꜱ	ꜱ	f	f	κληθεν	BD
ℵℵB	22 επληρωθησαν	f	ꜱ	f	ꜱ	ꜱ	f	επλησθησαν	BD
D	23 — τω (κυριω)	ꜱ	ꜱ	ꜱ	ꜱ	ꜱ	ꜱ	+ τω	ℵB
	25 { — ην	ꜱ	ꜱ	ꜱ	ꜱ	ꜱ	ꜱ	+ ην	ℵBD
ℵB	{ αν θρ. ην	ꜱ	ꜱ	ꜱ	f	f	f	ην ανθρ. }	D
ℵℵ	ευσεβης	f	f	f	f	ꜱ	f	ευλαβης	BD
	τω	f	f	ꜱ	ꜱ	f	ꜱ	του	ℵBD
		—	—		—	ꜱ	—	+ ην	ℵBD
ℵB	{ — ην (p. Πνευμα Αγιον) / Πνευμα ην Αγιον	f		ꜱ	ꜱ		ꜱ	Πνευμα Αγιον ην }	D

Bracketed readings show cases where the family is divided within itself.
* = in one (or two) MSS. only.

John xii. 1-6

	READINGS OF THE FAMILY	Θ	fam. 1	fam. 13	28	565	730	fam. 1424		READINGS OF 𝔖
ℵBD	1 + ὁ (ante Ἰης 1°)	ς	ς	ς	ς	ς	ς	ς	ℵBD	- ὁ
D	+ ὁ Ἰης (p. νεκρων)	ς	ς	f	ς	ς	ς	f		- ὁ Ἰης
	2 και εποιησαν	f	ς	f	ς	f	ς	ς	ℵB	εποιησαν ουν
	- αυτω 1°	ς	ς	f	ς	f	ς	f	ℵBD	+ αυτω 1°
	εκει δειπνον	f	f	f	ς	f	ς	f	ℵBD	δειπνον εκει
ℵBD	Μαρια	ς	ς	ς	ς	ς	ς	ς	ℵBD	Μαρθα
B	- δε (a. Λαζ.)	f	f	f	ς	f	ς	f	ℵBD	+ δε
D	3 Μαριαμ	ς	ς	ς	ς	ς	ς	ς		συνανακειμενων
	- ναρδου	ς	ς	f	ς	f	f	f	ℵD	Μαρια
	πολυτελους	ς	ς	ς	ς	ς	ς	ς	ℵB	+ ναρδου
	ηλειφε	f	f	f	ς	f	ς	f	ℵBD	πολυτιμου
	απεμαξεν	ς	f	f	ς	f	ς	ς	ℵBD	ηλειψεν
	απεμαξ. (p. αυτης)	f	f	f	ς	f	ς	f	ℵBD	εξεμαξεν
	+ ταις 2° (p. θριξεν)	ς	ς	ς	ς	ς	ς	f	ℵBD	εξεμ. a. ταις θρ
	εαυτης	f	f	f	ς	ς	ς	ς	ℵBD	- ταις 2°
	αυτου τους ποδας	f	ς	f	ς	f	ς	ς	ℵBD	αυτης
	om. τ. π. α.	ς	f	f	ς	ς	ς	ς	ℵBD	τους ποδας αυτου
	- αυτου	f	f	f	ς	f	ς	ς	ℵBD	+ τ. π. α.
	+ ολη (p. οικια)	f	f	f	ς	ς	ς	ς	ℵBD	+ αυτου
ℵ	4 - Σιμωνος (p. Ιουδας)	ς	f	ς	ς	f	ς	ς	ℵBD	- ολη
ℵ	+ ὁ (a. Ισκ.)	ς	f	ς	ς	f	f	f	BD	+ Σιμωνος
	5 διακοσιων	f	f	f	ς	f	ς	ς	BD	- ὁ
	δην. τριακοσιων	f	ς	f	f	ς	ς	ς	ℵBD	τριακοσιων
D	+ τους (a. πτωχους)	ς	ς	f	ς	ς	f	f	ℵBD	τριακ. δην.
	6 εμελλεν	f	f	f	f	f	f	f	ℵB	- τους
ℵBD	εχων	ς	f†	ς	f‡	ς	ς	ς	ℵBD	εμελεν
	ετηρει	f	ς	ς	ς	f††	ς	f		ειχεν και
									ℵBD	εβαστασεν

* = in one (or two) MSS. only.

‡ ἐχων και, a conflation.   † ἐχων και

†† Tisch. and von Soden say that 565 supports the family reading ; but this is not to be found in Belsheim's collation of 565.

N.B.—Great care has been bestowed on these Tables : but absolute accuracy is not guaranteed.

APPENDIX III

THE TEXT USED IN
ORIGEN'S "COMMENTARY ON MATTHEW"

OF this work a portion is preserved in Greek, another portion in an old Latin translation ; they overlap to some extent. The Latin and Greek differ in a way which shows that they represent a different line of textual transmission. The quotations from the Gospel of Matthew, which in the earlier part are short fragments, towards the end become almost a continuous text of the Gospel. I therefore select chaps. xxii. (1-36) and xxv., the one extant in Greek, the other only in Latin, as favourable specimens for testing both traditions of this work of Origen. The edition cited is that of Lommatzsch.

The Tables include all variants in which the text as quoted by Origen differs from the Textus Receptus, and show how far his text is supported by either B, ℵ, D, or by any member of *fam.* Θ. Since our object is to test the nature of the non-Byzantine element in *fam.* Θ, readings of individual members of the family are not cited when they agree with the T.R. Readings in which Origen agrees with the T.R. against two or more members of *fam.* Θ are not set out at length in the Tables. It seemed sufficient to state that in chap. xxii. there are 8 such, and 6 in chap. xxv. There are also altogether 11 variants in which Origen agrees with the T.R. against a reading which, since it occurs in only one of the six authorities Θ, 1 &c., 13 &c., 28, 565, 700, may possibly not be a true " family reading." The readings of Θ 1, 13—69—124—346, 565 and 700, also 22, have been derived

direct from the editions or collations of the several MSS. by
Gregory, Lake, Ferrar, Belsheim, Hoskier, and Sanders. For
other MSS. I follow Tischendorf or von Soden. The readings
of Σ, the new members of the Ferrar group (*e.g.* 983), and
fam. 1424 are only given where the better-known members of
fam. Θ give the Byzantine reading.

TABLE I

MSS. supporting.	Text of Origen's *Commentary on Matthew* (xxii.).	MSS. against.
22 33 Latt. 1, 69, 124 אּ B D	1. καὶ ἀποκριθεὶς ὁ Ἰησοῦς εἶπε πάλιν ἐν παραβολαῖς αὐτοῖς.	(πάλιν εἶπεν) אּ B D ς (αὐτοῖς ἐν π.) ς (om. αὐτοῖς) Θ
Θ 1, 22	2. ὡμοιώθη ἡ βασιλεία τῶν οὐρανῶν ἀνθρώπω βασιλεῖ, ὅστις ποιῶν γαμους τω υἱω αὐτοῦ.	(ἐποίησε) אּ B D ς
1	4. ἰδοὺ τὸ ἄριστον (– μου).	(+ μου) אּ B D ς
None	ἡτοίμασα, οἱ ταῦροί μου καὶ τὰ σιτιστὰ τεθυμένα, καὶ (1°) τα παντα [(2°) παντα] ἔτοιμα, δεῦτε εἰς τοὺς γαμους.	(– τα) All known MSS.
Θ 1, 22, 13 &c., 700 אּ B Θ 13 &c. אּ B D	5. οἱ δὲ ἀμελήσαντες ἀπῆλθον, ὃς μὲν ἐπι τον ἴδιον ἀγρόν, ὃς δὲ ἐπι την ἐμπορίαν αὐτοῦ.	(οἱ . . . οἱ) ⎫ (ὁ . . . ὁ) ⎬ D ⎭ ς (εἰς) ς
None	6. οἱ δὲ λοιποὶ κρατησαντες αὐτοῦ τους δούλους ὕβρισαν καὶ ἀπέκτειναν.	(τους δουλους αὐτου) All known MSS.
1, 22 D 1, 22	7. καὶ πεμψας το στρατευμα αὐτοῦ ἀνειλε τους φονεις ἐκεινους, καὶ την πολιν αὐτων ἐνεπρησε.	(τα στρατευματα) אּ B ς (ἀπωλεσεν) אּ B D ς
Σ 983 (=*fam.* 13 D	8. τοτε λεγει τοις δουλοις αὐτου ὁ μεν γαμος ἐτοιμος (– εστιν) οἱ δὲ κεκλημενοι οὐκ ἦσαν ἀξιοι.	(+ εστιν) אּ B ς

TABLE I—(continued)

MSS. supporting.	Text of Origen's *Commentary on Matthew* (xxii.).	MSS. against.	
Θ 1	15. τοτε πορευθεντες οἱ Φαρισαιοι συμβουλιον ἐλαβον κατ' αὐτου ὁπως αὐτον παγιδευσωσιν ἐν λογω.	(– κατ' αὐτου)	ℵ B D ς
	16. διδασκαλε, οἰδαμεν ὁτι ἀληθης ει, και την ὁδον του θεου ἐν ἀληθεια διδασκεις, και οὐ μελει σοι περι οὐδενος· οὐ γαρ βλεπεις εἰς προσωπον		
Θ 1, 28. 565, 700	ἀνθρωπου.	(ἀνθρωπων)	ℵ B D ς
700	18. γνους δε ὁ Ἰησους την πανουργιαν.	(πονηριαν)	ℵ B D ς
253	20. τινος ἡ εἰκων (– αὑτη) και ἡ ἐπιγραφη.	(+ αὑτη)	ℵ B D ς
Θ 565, 700 D	21. ἀποδοτε τα καισαρος τω καισαρι, και τα του θεου τω θεω.	(– τω)	ℵ B ς
1, 13, 28, 700 ℵ B D	23. ἐν ἐκεινη τη ἡμερα προσηλθον αὐτω Σαδδουκαιοι (– οἱ) λεγοντες μη εἰναι ἀναστασιν.	(+ οἱ)	ς
Θ 1, 22, 700 ℵ B	25. ἠσαν δε γαρ ἡμιν ἑπτα ἀδελφοι· και ὁ πρωτος γημας ἐτελευτησε.	(γαμησας)	D ς
22 ℵ B D	30. ἐν τη γαρ ἀναστασει οὐτε γαμουσιν, οὐτε (1⁰, 2⁰) γαμιζονται		
Θ 124, 700	(3⁰, 4⁰) γαμισκονται	(ἐκγαμιζονται)	ς
1	ἀλλ' εἰσιν ὡς	(εισιν after οὐρανω)	ℵ B D ς
		(εισιν before ἐν οὐρανω)	13 etc.
Θ 1, 22	οἱ ἀγγελοι	(– οἱ)	ℵ B D ς
Θ 1, 700 B D	(– του θεου) ἐν	(+ του θεου)	ς
		(+ θεου)	ℵ 13 etc.
1, 13 etc. ℵ B	τω οὐρανω.	(– τω)	D ς

TABLE II

MSS. supporting.	Text of Origen's *Commentary on Matthew* (xxv.) (Old Latin Translation).	MSS. against.
Θ 1, 124 D	1. ... quae ... exierunt obviam sponso et sponsae.	(omit) ℵ B Ϛ
Θ 1, 124, 700 ℵ B D	2. quinque autem ex iis erant	(ἠσαν ἐξ αὐτων) Ϛ
Θ 1 ℵ B D	fatuae, et quinque prudentes.	(φρονιμοι .. μωραι) Ϛ
Θ 1	6. Media autem nocte clamor factus est: ecce sponsus venit, exsurgite obviam ei.	(ἐξερχεσθε) ℵ B D Ϛ
28 ℵ B D	9. Ite (–autem) magis ad venditores.	(+ δε) Ϛ
Θ 1, 565 ℵ B D	13. Vigilate ergo quia nescitis diem et horam.	(+ ἐν ἡ ὁ υἱος του ἀνθρωπου ἐρχεται) Ϛ
M, F[1]	14. Homo quidam peregre proficiscens vocavit servos suos.	(–τις) Ϛ
Θ 1, 69, 124 B D	16 Abiit autem qui quinque talenta acceperat ... et lucratus est alia quinque talenta.	(ἐποιησεν) ℵ Ϛ
Θ ℵ	17. Similiter (–et)	(+ και) B D Ϛ
D	qui duo accepit, lucratus est	(–λαβων) ℵ B Ϛ
ℵ B	(–et ipse)	(+ και αυτος) D Ϛ
Latt.	in iis alia duo.	(–ἐν αὐτοις) ℵ B D Ϛ
Θ 1, 13, 700 ℵ B D	19. Post multum temporis venit dominus servorum illorum.	(χρονον πολυν) Ϛ
1	20. Domine, quinque talenta mihi dedisti, ecce alia quinque superlucratus sum	
Θ 124, 700 ℵ B D	(–ab illis).	(+ ἐπ αὐτοις) Ϛ
Θ 124, 700 ℵ B D	21 Ait (–autem) ei dominus ejus: euge, serve bone et fidelis.	(+ δε) Ϛ

---

[1] M is an inferior member of *fam.* 1424; F is one of Soden's K[1] MSS., *i.e.* Byzantine with a small admixture of readings characteristic of *fam* 13.

TABLE II—(continued)

MSS. supporting.	Text of Origen's Commentary on Matthew (xxv.) (Old Latin Translation).	MSS. against.
Θ 124, 700 ℵ B D	22. Accedens autem et qui duo talenta acceperat, ait : domine, duo talenta mihi dedisti, ecce alia duo lucratus sum. (– ab illis)	(+ ἐπ αὐτοις) ς
Θ D	24. Accedens autem et qui unum talentum acceperat, ait : domine, scio (– te) quia homo durus es.	(+ σε) ℵ B ς
D	25. Et timens abii et abscondi talentum tuum in terra : ecce habes tuum.	(ἀπελθων) ℵ B ς
Θ 1, 565 ℵ B D	31. Cum venerit Filius hominis in gloria sua, et omnes angeli (– sancti) cum eo.	(+ ἁγιοι) ς
D	39. Aut quando te vidimus infirmum aut in carcere ?	(ποτε δε) ℵ B ς
1, 22 D	41. Discedite a me, maledicti, in ignem aeternum, quem praeparavit Pater meus diabolo et angelis ejus.	(το ἡτοιμασμενον) ℵ B ς

The above Tables give all the readings in these two chapters in which Origen differs from the T.R.—45 in number. It will be observed that in 37 of these Origen is supported by one or more members of *fam.* Θ ; while he is supported by D 24 times, by B only 16. Thus in sharp contrast to the steady support by *fam.* Θ is the way in which ℵ B D jump from side to side, now supporting, now opposing, the text of Origen. The conclusion is irresistible : the text upon which Origen was lecturing represented neither an Alexandrian nor a " Western " text, but almost identically that of *fam.* Θ.

APPENDIX IV

JEROME AND THE CODEX SINAITICUS

In the Preface to the Vulgate Gospels, which takes the form of an open letter to Pope Damasus, Jerome defends the principles he has adopted in revising the text of the Old Latin. Of the Latin, he says, no two copies are alike, but we have a standard of authenticity, since for the New Testament, unlike the Old, the Greek was indubitably the original. Hence the discrepancy between the different Latin copies can only be corrected by reference to the Greek original. But the MSS. of the Greek text which are named after Lucian and Hesychius, both in the Old and the New Testament, have been badly edited and interpolated—as may be seen by comparing them with ancient vernacular translations. He has, therefore, used, as a standard by which to correct the Latin, Greek MSS. which are really old.[1]

---

[1] "Si enim Latinis exemplaribus fides est adhibenda, respondeant, quibus; tot enim sunt exemplaria quot pene codices. Sin autem veritas est quaerenda de pluribus, cur non ad Graecam originem revertentes, ea quae vel a vitiosis interpretibus male edita, vel a praesumptoribus imperitis emendata perversius, vel a librariis dormientibus aut addita sunt, aut mutata, corrigimus ? Neque ego de Veteri disputo Testamento. . . . De Novo nunc loquor Testamento: quod Graecum esse non dubium est. . . . Hoc certe quum in nostro sermone discordat, et diversos rivulorum tramites ducit, uno de fonte quaerendum est. Praetermitto eos codices, quos a Luciano et Hesychio nuncupatos, paucorum hominum asserit perversa contentio : quibus utique nec in Veteri Instrumento post septuaginta interpretes emendare quid licuit, nec in novo profuit emendasse : quum multarum gentium linguis Scriptura ante translata, doceat falsa esse quae addita sunt. Igitur haec praesens praefatiuncula pollicetur quattuor tantum evangelia, quorum ordo " (he means the Greek as opposed to the Old Latin order) "est iste, Matthaeus, Marcus, Lucas, Johannes, codicum Graecorum emendata collatione, sed veterum."

Seeing that Jerome is writing a careful and considered Preface to a revised version of the Four Gospels, and that he only mentions the Lucianic and Hesychian versions in order to contrast their inferior text with that of the " ancient codices " he has himself used, I simply cannot understand why some scholars have raised doubts as to whether the Lucianic and Hesychian recensions included the New Testament as well as the Old.

But why, we may ask, was Jerome so contemptuous of the work of Lucian and Hesychius ? I suggest two reasons : (1) Jerome at this date was quite convinced that the true text of the O.T. was only to be found in Origen's Hexapla [1] ; it was only later in his life that he had recourse to the original Hebrew. But the Hexapla had been published a generation before Lucian and Hesychius began their work. What then but native perversity, " a cantankerous wrongheadedness " (*perversa contentio*), could have induced these worthies to insist on producing a text of their own ?   (2) Jerome had just returned to Rome from Constantinople, where, as he tells us, the recension of Lucian was accepted. Now, if we accept the suggestion (cf. p. 102 ff.) that the MSS. with which Constantine had provided his new capital represented the *fam.* Θ text, the Lucianic text must have been a recent importation. Inevitably, then, there would have been some conservatives at Constantinople who grumbled at the innovation ; and these might have very pertinently appealed to the Old Syriac (*multarum gentium linguis scriptura antea translata, doceat falsa esse quae addita sunt*), as evidence that the many striking passages absent from both *fam.* Θ and Syr S. (cf. p. 88) but found in the Lucianic text, were interpolations.   If Jerome had heard from someone at Constantinople some general statement to this effect, it would only confirm his *a priori* suspicion of anyone who dared to think he could improve upon Origen's text of the LXX, and, with his hasty temperament, he would forthwith conclude—without any really careful study—that Lucian's temerity had had equally

---

[1] Cf. passages quoted by Swete, *op. cit.* p. 76 f.

fatal results on the New Testament. Nor would he wait
for further evidence before including Lucian's fellow offender,
Hesychius, in the same sweeping condemnation.

The question, however, in regard to which we should have
liked Jerome to have made a clear statement is the type
of text represented by those ancient MSS. which he himself
so much preferred. Can we identify the Greek text which
Jerome preferred ? The materials on which an answer to this
question must be based are collected in Wordsworth and White's
edition of the Vulgate Gospels and Acts.[1]

(1) In his *Commentary on Matthew* Jerome seven times
discusses various readings in MSS. known to him. Each time
he quotes with approval a reading found in ℵ. In two of the
seven readings ℵ differs from B, and in two of them it differs
from *fam.* Θ. The fact that Jerome had a MS. agreeing with ℵ
seven times out of seven would, even if it stood alone, be a
remarkable coincidence. But it does not stand alone.

(2) When in the Acts Jerome departs from the text of the
Old Latin version, two-thirds of his alterations are in the direction
of agreement with the Alexandrian text which for Acts is represented by B ℵ A C. Where ℵ and B differ he usually goes with
the one which is backed by the other MSS. of the family ; but
six times he agrees with ℵ alone, but only twice (*sic*) with B alone.

(3) For the Gospels Wordsworth and White give (p. 665)
a table showing 39 readings, in which Jerome's Vulgate agrees
with extant Greek MSS. against the Old Latin. Of these 25
are found in one or more of the MSS. ℵ B L Δ[Mk.] ; but the
significance of this figure is altered when we note that only 11
of the 25 seem to be exclusively Alexandrian readings.

Everything, however, depends on their estimate of Codex *f*
(Brixianus), the text of which is a sort of half-way house between
that of Old Latin MSS. of the type of *b* and the Byzantine.
In *f* occur a very large number of readings in which Jerome's

---

[1] Wordsworth and White, *Nov. Test. Lat. sec. ed. S. Hieronymi* (Oxford,
1889–98, 1905).

text and the Byzantine agree against the other Old Latin MSS. Wordsworth and White hold that the Latin MSS. which Jerome started with before he began his revision must have had a text very similar to f; that is to say, that Jerome used a form of the Old Latin version which had already been partially revised by Greek MSS. of the Byzantine type. They conclude that the Greek MSS. which he employed must have been of the אּ B L type, but most closely related to אּ.

On this view most of the agreements of the Vulgate and the Byzantine text were due, not to Jerome, but to the previous revision by an unknown person which is most nearly represented by f. Burkitt, on the other hand (*J.T.S.* i. p. 129), thinks that the Old Latin which Jerome attempted to revise was more like b. The agreements between the Vulgate and f he explains on the hypothesis that f is a text very largely Vulgate which has been copied from the Latin side of a bilingual Gothic-Latin MS., the Latin text of which had been sometimes conformed to that of the Gothic. I cannot pretend to the knowledge of the Old Latin version which would entitle me to express an opinion on this controversy. I believe, however, that the majority of experts incline to Burkitt's view.

But if f is, not the parent of Jerome's version, but its child, and is therefore not to be reckoned as an Old Latin MS. at all, then, so far as the Vulgate Gospels are concerned, the case for Jerome's use of MSS. of the אּ B L type collapses. As Wordsworth and White point out (p. 671), from Luke xvii. to the end of the Gospel, and in a large part of John, Jerome's alterations of the Old Latin are almost entirely into conformity with the later Greek MSS. ; and they cite 27 instances of the same thing for Matthew, Mark, and the earlier part of Luke. It would look then as if the MSS. used by Jerome had a text something like A—mainly Lucianic but with a sprinkling of Alexandrian and other earlier readings. That Jerome, *without knowing it*, should have used a text almost identical with the Lucianic recension, about which he is so scornful, is really funny. I can only suppose that one of the

2 Q

MSS. he possessed looked so old that he imagined it antedated
Lucian.

There still remains, however, the far more impressive evidence
quoted above that, in his *Commentary on Matthew* and in his
revision of the Acts, Jerome used a text akin to ℵ. I suggest that
this is to be explained by his visit to Alexandria, which took place
in 386, that is, between the publication of the Vulgate Gospels and
the work on Matthew.[1] At Alexandria he listened with enthusiasm
to the lectures of the famous Origenist teacher Didymus. What
more likely, then, than that he should seize the opportunity to
acquire a copy of the N.T. in the text which the school of Origen
approved. I would relate this surmise to three facts. (*a*) Our
actual MS. ℵ was, perhaps, forty years old when Jerome was in
Alexandria; (*b*) Jerome died at Bethlehem in 420; (*c*) not
many years later ℵ was in Palestine in the library at Caesarea.
This we learn from a marginal note by a (probably) fifth-
century corrector, who says that he collated some parts of the
Old Testament with the autograph of Pamphilus which was there
preserved. Historically, therefore, there is no difficulty in supposing that ℵ was brought to Palestine by Jerome.

The hypothesis that our ℵ was actually one of the MSS.
used by Jerome would remove a great difficulty. In Jerome's
Commentary on Matthew, in addition to the seven variants
alluded to above, there is a long discussion of the reading
οὐδὲ ὁ υἱος, Mt. xxiv. 36. Jerome asserts that the words were
absent from the approved copies of Origen and Pierius. But
we know that as a matter of fact the words in question did
stand in the text used by Origen. For Origen, in his *Commentary
on Matthew*, discusses at considerable length the theological
difficulty raised by them. He gives two alternative ways of
meeting it; but he never suggests, as he does elsewhere under
similar circumstances, that he knew of any MS. which omitted

---

[1] Whether his revision of the Acts and Epistles took place before or after the
visit to Alexandria is unknown. His text of the Catholic Epistles is closely
allied to that of A.

the offending words. Moreover, we have other evidence that they stood in all the texts likely to have been known to Origen ; for they occur, not only in B ℵ D Old Lat., but also in 13 &c., 28, Φ Arm., from which we may presume their presence in the text of *fam.* Θ. But if Jerome used ℵ, and supposed it to represent the text of Origen and Pierius, his statement is explained ; for although the words οὐδὲ ὁ υἱὸς were written by the original scribe, they *were deleted by a very early corrector.*

The deletion was made—according to the usual practice— by a row of dots above the word. A subsequent corrector has erased the dots. ℵ was corrected by two scribes, who seem to belong to the fifth century and whose corrections can usually be distinguished by minute differences in handwriting and in the colour of the ink they used.   But a row of dots, all but obliterated, cannot by these criteria be assigned to one corrector rather than another. And Tischendorf, in the notes to his four-volume edition of ℵ, in assigning the dots to the corrector ℵ^{ca}, and their erasure to his successor ℵ^{cb}, does so with the qualification *ut videtur.* So far as I can see, there is no reason for identifying the person who deleted οὐδὲ ὁ υἱὸς with the corrector ℵ^{ca}, except that ℵ^{ca} was the first *systematic* reviser who worked on the MS. after the original διορθωτής. But this particular reading was one which might well have stimulated the activity of an earlier owner of the MS. who was not concerned to revise it throughout. Origen had already found the words theologically embarrassing; during the Arian controversy the Son's knowledge of the Father was near the centre of the point at issue : the words are not found in Syr. S. nor in the Byzantine text ; what is even more significant, they are absent from L 33 and from both the Egyptian versions.   That is to say, we have evidence that even in Egypt, the home of the B ℵ text, the words were being discredited as an heretical interpolation.   I suggest, therefore, that the deletion in ℵ was made when the Arian controversy was at its height, and, therefore, before the time of Jerome. Indeed, even if the MS. used by Jerome was not ℵ itself but a sister MS., the probability that the words in question had there also been deleted is by no means low.

On the only other occasion on which Jerome refers to the copies of Origen, the reading quoted (Gal. iii. 1) as Origen's is one supported by B ℵ against the great majority of Greek MSS. This affords some evidence for the view that Jerome regarded the type of text represented by ℵ as that approved by Origen. But if so, we must ask the question : How exactly did he connect his MSS. with those of Origen ? I would hazard the suggestion that Jerome's phrase *exemplaria Adamantii et Pierii* (Adamantius was a second name of Origen) does not mean two different codices, any more than the text of Westcott and Hort means two different editions. Pierius may well have attempted to popularise the text of the Gospels on which Origen lectured, much in the same way as Pamphilus did for the LXX column of the *Hexapla*. In favour of this view two considerations may be advanced. (*a*) Origen stoutly affirms his belief that the Shepherd of Hermas is an inspired work ; Athanasius definitely excludes it from the Canon. Now ℵ contains the Shepherd ; whether B also did we do not know, as the end of the MS. is missing. (*b*) ℵ is written in four columns to the page, B in three, A in two, C in only one—which last became the common type, though two is not unusual. The larger number of columns reproduces the format of the papyrus roll which preceded the codex ; B is transitional ; ℵ represents the most antiquated style of all. Thus, though it is slightly the younger MS., in this respect ℵ reproduces an older tradition than B. This would be accounted for if ℵ was a conservative copy of a MS. of Pierius.

The conjecture that ℵ represents the recension of Pierius is in no way incompatible with the view that B represents that of Hesychius. Hort's arguments,[1] especially if supplemented

---

[1] W.H. ii. p. 213 ff. It is worth noting that K. Lake, in his Introduction to the facsimile reproduction of ℵ, refutes Tischendorf's suggestion (here alluded to by Hort) that a portion of B and ℵ were written by the same scribe.

by a study of the immense list of minute differences between B and ℵ drawn up by Hoskier,[1] makes it difficult to accept von Soden's view that their common ancestor was at all recent. It is more probable that they represent, either two independent traditions of the oldest text of Alexandria, or recensions by two scholars each of whom based his text on the oldest MSS. obtainable in Egypt.

[1] *Codex B and its Allies,* pt. ii. (Quaritch, 1914).

APPENDIX V

W AND THE CAESAREAN TEXT

IN 1926, in time to add this Appendix to the second impression. I discovered that the Washington MS. W—dated c. A.D. 400— is, for two-thirds of St. Mark's Gospel, a member of *fam.* Θ. The evidence submitted below has been amplified by Profs. Lake and Blake and Mrs. New (*Harvard Theological Review*, Oct. 1928). They confirm my conclusion, while finding that W has suffered more from Byzantine revision than I had supposed. It appears that, for Mark, the Greek MSS., as regards relative freedom from Byzantine readings, stand as follows :—565, Θ, 28, 700, W, *fam.* 1, *fam.* 13.

Prof. Sanders in his edition of W shows that for Mk. i. 1-v. 30 the text of W is the Greek equivalent of the Old Latin version, agreeing more particularly with the " African Latin " MS. *e.* He goes on to say : " In the second part of Mark there is still a decidedly close relationship between W and the Old Latin MSS., but the special Latinisms . . . have mostly disappeared. . . . The most interesting feature . . . is the increase in the number of agreements with fam. 13 (Ferrar group) and the other Syriacising MSS. fam. **1, 565,** and **28.**" [1]

A study of his collation led me to suspect that Sanders had underestimated the extent of the change in the type of text ; and it occurred to me to investigate closely the relationship, in Mk. v. 31-xvi. 8, between the text of W and the six chief authorities for the Caesarean text, *i.e.* Θ, 1 &c., 13 &c., 28, 565, and 700.

---

[1] *The Washington Manuscript of the Four Gospels in the Freer Collection* (The Macmillan Co., New York, 1912), p. 73. The MS. was bought in 1906 from an Arab dealer, and seems to have been found in the ruins of a monastery in Egypt.

Selecting for the test the three chapters vi., x., and xv., and ignoring mere mistakes of spelling, I found a total of 260 readings in which W differs from the T.R. In 37 of these the reading of W is supported by no other MS. or version. Most of these seem to be mistakes by the scribe of W or an immediate ancestor ; but on any view " singular readings " can be ignored where the purpose of an investigation is to discover the affinities of a MS. with one or other of the main types of texts found elsewhere. Ignoring these, there remain 223 readings. Of these 189, *i.e.* all but 85%, are, I found, supported by at least one, and usually by several, of the six above-named authorities for *fam.* Θ.

The converse of this relationship—*i.e.* the exact proportion of the non-Byzantine readings in *fam.* Θ which also occur in W—can only be satisfactorily investigated by drawing up Tables similar to those on p. 582 ff.—an extremely laborious process. With the kind assistance of Mrs. J. V. Brook I prepared for my own use such a Table for the whole of Chap. XI. From this I deduce the following statistics.

In this chapter W differs from the T.R. in 67 readings, of which 8 are " singular." Out of the remaining 59, W is supported in 47 by one or more members of the Θ group. There are 17 readings which are not found in W, but in which at least 2 members of *fam.* Θ (reckoning **1** &c. and **13** &c. each as one) agree against the Byzantine text. But in 14 out of these 17 cases W has the Byzantine reading ; in 1 it clumsily mixes *fam.* Θ and Byz., and in 1 it has a singular reading. Thus only in 1 case out of the 17 does W side with any other MS. against both *fam.* Θ and the Byzantine text. Clearly, we have in W a member of the Θ family, the text of which has suffered, but not too greatly, from Byzantine revision.

In Mk. v. 31-xvi. 8, then, W is the oldest, but not quite the purest, authority for this ancient and interesting type of Eastern text ; and it is so ancient that in conjunction with the quotations by Origen and Eusebius it makes the existence of such a text no longer an hypothesis but an ascertained fact.

But how can we account for the sudden change at Mk. v. 30 from a Western to an Eastern text ? An answer is suggested by the following facts. (1) In W, as in D and most Old Latin MSS., the Gospels stand in the Western order (cf. p. 11 *n.*)—Matthew, John, Luke, Mark. (2) The paragraph divisions in Matthew found in W are practically identical with those in D (Sanders, *op. cit.* p. 17). (3) Scattered through the predominantly Byzantine text of Matthew and Lk. viii. 13 to end, and the Alexandrian text of John and Lk. i. 1-viii. 12, occur a large number of distinctively Western readings, best explained as survivals of an earlier text which have escaped the notice of the revisers. We conclude that an ancestor of W came from the West—probably from Rome, the ultimate fount of the " African " Latin text.

Let us suppose that its owner moved to Caesarea. The end of a MS. is frequently damaged ; where the Gospels are arranged in the Western order, this entails the loss of the latter part of Mark. This has actually occurred in MSS. *a, b, e* and *f.* Suppose this happened to the ancestor of W. Its owner would get a Caesarean scribe to replace the lost leaves from a local MS. This would explain the Caesarean text of the latter part of Mark. Marginal correction during a stay at Caesarea would also account for the sprinkling of Caesarean readings found in the other Gospels. Then the MS., or a copy of it, went down into Egypt. The Alexandrian reviser began with John, the favourite Gospel in Alexandria, and went straight on to Luke, which immediately follows John in this MS. ; but he gave over his work at Lk. viii. 12. The next corrector used a Byzantine MS. ; later papyri show that this text did ultimately invade Egypt. But, finding the central part of the MS. already smothered in corrections, he supposed that these had been made from a good text. He therefore only troubled himself to correct Matthew and the uncorrected part of Luke, scamping the revision, as we have seen (p. 63 f.) so often happened, when he came to Mark. Of this much revised MS. our W (except for Jn. i. 1-v. 11, which is a later addition) is a copy.

INDICES

INDEX OF MSS.

With dates and von Soden's notation.

N.B.—The Roman numeral indicates the century to which a MS. is assigned ; the number in brackets represents von Soden's notation.

Only the more important citations of ℵ B C D L Θ and Syr. S. are indexed ; but to other MSS. all references (except those occurring in the Tables pp. 83, 90, 97 f., 108, 582 ff., 586 ff.) are included.

The accepted Latin titles of all uncials are given ; but, as it is rare for any Codex other than ℵ A B C D L (and perhaps *a, b, k, e, f, ff²*) to be so cited, they need not be memorised by the student.

GREEK UNCIALS

F *Boreeli* (є 86) ix . . . 49, 120
G *Wolfii A* (є 87) ix-x . . 120, 311
H *Wolfii B* (є 88) ix-x . . 120, 311
K *Cyprius* (є 71) ix . . . 120, 346, 578 f.
L *Regius* (є 56) viii . . . 42, 48, 54 ff., 59 f., 62 f., 107, 117 f., 121, 126 f., 134, 145, 308, 592 f., and *passim*
M *Campianus* (є 72) ix . . 575, 578 f.
N *Purpureus Petropolitanus* (є 19) vi 81 n., 89, 326, 575 ff.
O *Sinopensis* (є 21) vi (frags. Mt.). . 575 ff.
P *Guelpherbytanus A* (є 33) vi (frags.) 56 n., 580
Q *Guelpherbytanus B* (є 4) v (frags.) . 56 n., 580
R *Nitriensis* (є 22) vi (frags. Lk.) . 56 n., 312, 567 f., 580
S *Vaticanus* 354 (є 1027) x . . 120 f., 147 n.
T *Borgianus* (є 5) v (frags. Lk. Jn.) . 54 f., 56 n., 99, 213
U *Nanianus* (є 90) ix-x . . 122 n., 326, 579 ff.
V *Mosquensis* (є 75) ix . . 120 f., 147 n.
W (Washington, or Freer, MS.) (є 014) v 11, 30, 32, 40, 48, 68 ff., 107, 123, 138, 145, 302, 309, 311, 315, 323, 326, 337, 342, 351, 567 f., 580, 598 ff.
X *Monacensis* (A³) x . . . 56 n., 64, 326, 492
Y *Macedonianus* (є 073) ix . . 346, 488, 579
Z *Dublinensis* (є 26) vi (frags. Mt.) . 56 n.
Γ *Tischendorfianus IV* (є 70) ix-x . 122 n., 567, 580
Δ *Sangallensis* (є 76) ix-x . . 42, 56, 59, 62 f., 68 n., 85, 93 f., 107, 125, 312, 315, 326, 574, 580 n., 592
Θ (Koridethi MS.) (є 050) vii-ix . 32, 42, 48 ff., 79-107, 116 ff., 132, 138, 144 n., 145 f., 308, 316, 318 n., 322 327, 335, 345, 573 ff., 579 ff., 585 589, 591 f., 595, and *passim*
Λ *Tischendorfianus III* (є 77) ix-x . 49, 579 ff.
Ξ *Zacynthius* (A¹) viii (frags. Lk.) . 56 n., 59, 567
Π *Petropolitanus* (є 73) ix . . 120, 578 f.
Σ *Rossanensis* (є 18) vi . . 81 n., 575 ff., 586
Φ *Beratinus* (є 17) vi . . . 122 n., 136, 241, 312, 575 ff., 595
Ψ *Laurensis* (δ 6) viii . . 56, 59, 62 f., 85, 107, 116, 125 f., 336, 342, 567 f.
Ω *Dionysiacus* (є 61) ix-x . . 120 f., 147 n.
047 *Andreensis* (є 95)(formerly ך) x 116
089 (є 28) (= Tisch. Θᵉ) vi (frag.) . 580 n.
0106 (є 40) (= Tisch. Θᵃ) vii (frag.) 315

GREEK MINUSCULES (CURSIVES)

1 (δ 254) xi-xii . . . 46, 50, 75, 80, 81 n., 86 ff., 94 n., 124, 280, 312, 315 f., 320, 322 f., 335 n., 567 f., 570, 573, 576 f., 579, 585
13 (є 368) xiii . . . 46, 49 f., 73, 75, 80, 81 n., 82 n., 86 ff., 100, 106, 120, 144 n., 311 f., 314 f., 322 ff., 326, 410, 570, 573 ff., 585, 595

MSS. of Old Latin Version

a *Vercellensis* **iv** . . . 66, 70, 88 f., 106 f., 116, 138, 141 *n.*, 143 ff., 170, 250 *n.*, 267, 280, 308 f., 311 ff., 319 f., 323, 326

b *Veronensis* **v** . . . 65 f., 70, 89, 106 f., 116, 137 f., 141 *n.*, 143 ff., 267 f., 280, 308 f., 311, 319, 322 f., 525, 592 f.

c *Colbertinus* **xii** . . . 55 *n.*, 65, 116, 138, 141 *n.*, 143, 250 *n.*, 267, 309, 311, 313, 319 f., 322, 324

d = Latin side of **D** . . . 68 *n.*

e *Palatinus* **v** . . . . 65, 66 *n.*, 69, 88, 107, 116, 138, 141 *n.*, 143 ff., 212 *n.*, 268, 308 f., 311, 315, 317, 319 f., 323, 320 f., 381 *n.*

f *Brixianus* **vi** . . . 66, 89, 141 *n.*, 311, 326, 592 f.

ff[1] *Corbeiensis I* **x** . . . 319

ff[2] *Corbeiensis II* **v**-**vi**. . . 66, 116, 143, 145, 267, 309, 311, 313 323

g *Sangermanensis I* **ix** . . 137

g[2] *Sangermanensis II* **x**-**xi** . . 319

h *Claromontanus* **vi** (Vulgate in Mk. Lk. Jn.) 66, 70, 144, 322

i *Vindobonensis* **v**-**vi** . . . 66, 319 f., 323

k *Bobiensis* **iv**-**v** . . . 45 f., 65 f., 69, 71, 88, 106 f., 125 *n.*, 132, 141 *n.*, 144 f., 170, 250 *n.*, 276 *n.* 280, 308, 311 ff., 316, 326 f., **336**, 342

l *Rehdigeranus* **vii** . . . 313, 319, 322 f.

m = *The Speculum* . . . 65

n *Frag. Sangallensia* **iv**-**v** . . 66

q *Monacensis* **vii** . . . 66, 70, 89, 311

r *Usserianus* **vi** . . . 66, 313, 317

ᵭ = Latin of **Δ** . . . 68 *n.*

MSS. of Old Syriac Version

Syr. C. (sy[c]) *Curetonian* **v** . . 73, 76, 87, 89 f., 115, 117 f., 122 *n.*, 136 ff., 141 *n.*, 241, 250 *n.*, 276, 313, 315, 317, 319 f., 327, 568

Syr. S. (sy[s]) *Sinaitic* **iv** . . 32, 71, 73 f., 79, 85-90, 106 f., 115 ff., 132, 135 ff., 308, 335, 345, 519 f., 591 595, and *passim*

The remaining citations (and dates) refer, not to individual MSS., but to Versions

AETHIOPIC

Aeth. ? **v** 336

Armenian

Arm. v . . . . 76, 85 ff., 104 f., 115, 137 f., 241, 311 f.,
320, 322, 326, 335, 344 ff., 595

Egyptian

Boh. (bo) *Bohairic* (=Tisch. *cop*,
   Hort *me*) **vi** . . . 54, 59, 121, 125, 309, 312, 324, 326, 336
Sah. (sa) *Sahidic* (=Hort *the*)? **iii** . 54, 56, 59, 125, 309, 312, 317, 323 f., 326
   336

Gothic

Goth. v . . . . 66 *n.*, 114, **311**

Old Georgian

Georg.? v . . . . 85 ff., 335

Later Syriac

Syr. Hcl. (syʰ) *Harclean* (=Tisch.
   syrᵖ) **vii** . . . . 76, 122 *n.*, 241, 326, **336**
Syr. Hier. (pa) *Jerusalem* **vi** . 55 *n.*, 76, 100, 325, 334
Syr. Pesh. (syᵖ) *Peshitta* (=Tisch.
   syr.ˢᶜʰ) **v** 75, 87

Latin Vulgate

Vulg. (vg) **iv** . . . 43 ff., 590 ff.

INDEX OF SUBJECTS

2 R

INDEX OF PROPER NAMES

INDEX OF SCRIPTURE REFERENCES

N.B.—1. Section A contains all citations made by chapter and verse, also some isolated passages which are quoted without the reference being given in the text. Section B contains passages cited by *name*, where chapter and verse are not given in the text.

2. This Index does *not* include the lists of collected references in the Additional Notes, etc.

SECTION A

SECTION B

THE END